4

STATISTICAL ENCYCLOPEDIA
OF NORTH AMERICAN PROFESSIONAL SPORTS

STATISTICAL ENCYCLOPEDIA OF NORTH AMERICAN PROFESSIONAL SPORTS

All Major League Teams and Major Non-Team Events Year by Year, 1876 through 2006

SECOND EDITION

K. MICHAEL GASCHNITZ

VOLUME 4 • Individual Teams Florida Panthers through Youngstown Bears; Appendices; Bibliography

McFarland & Company, Inc., Publishers
Jefferson, North Carolina, and London

4

LIBRARY OF CONGRESS CATALOGUING-IN-PUBLICATION DATA

Gaschnitz, K. Michael
    Statistical encyclopedia of North American professional sports :
all major league teams and major non-team events year by year,
1876 through 2006 / K. Michael Gaschnitz.—2nd ed.
        p.   cm.
    Includes bibliographical references.

    4 volume set—
    ISBN-13: 978-0-7864-3294-3
    softcover : 50# alkaline paper ∞

    1. Professional sports—North America—History—Statistics.
I. Gaschnitz, K. Michael. Professional sports statistics.   II. Title.
GV581.G37   2008
796.04'4097021—dc22   2007036789

British Library cataloguing data are available

Cover illustrations ©2007 Image 100 Ltd.

Manufactured in the United States of America

McFarland & Company, Inc., Publishers
  Box 611, Jefferson, North Carolina 28640
  www.mcfarlandpub.com

Table of Contents

— VOLUME 1 —

—— **VOLUME 2** ——

— VOLUME 3 —

—— VOLUME 4 ——

FLORIDA PANTHERS

Home City: Miami, Florida (1993-1998)
    Sunrise, Florida (1998-present)
Home Arena: Miami Arena (1993-1998)   Capacity: 14,703 [1998]
    BankAtlantic Center(1998-present)*   Capacity: 19,250 [2005]
Origin of Name: The name was chosen by the team officials in honor of the endangered Panthers which inhabit the Everglades.

Regular Season Record

Season	League	GP	W	L	T	OL	SL	GF	GA	Pts
1993-1994	NHL	84	33	34	17	NA	NA	233	233	83
1994-1995	NHL	48	20	22	6	NA	NA	115	127	46
1995-1996	NHL	82	41	31	10	NA	NA	254	234	92
1996-1997	NHL	82	35	28	19	NA	NA	221	201	89
1997-1998	NHL	82	24	43	15	NA	NA	203	256	63
1998-1999	NHL	82	30	34	18	NA	NA	210	228	78
1999-2000	NHL	82	43	33	6	6	NA	244	209	98
2000-2001	NHL	82	22	38	13	9	NA	200	246	66
2001-2002	NHL	82	22	44	10	6	NA	180	250	60
2002-2003	NHL	82	24	36	13	9	NA	176	237	70
2003-2004	NHL	82	28	35	15	4	NA	188	221	75
2004-2005	NHL	Season cancelled due to lockout.								
2005-2006	NHL	82	37	34	NA	6	5	240	257	85
TOTAL:	12 years	952	359	412	142	40	5	2464	2699	905
AVERAGE:		79	29	34	13	3	202	222	75.4	71

Playoff Record

Season	GP	W	L	GF	GA	Result
1995-1996	22	12	10	61	57	Lost Stanley Cup Final to Colorado.
1996-1997	5	1	4	10	13	Lost Conference Quarterfinal to Rangers.
1999-2000	4	0	4	6	12	Lost Conf. Quarterfinal to New Jersey.
TOTAL:	31	13	18	77	82	
AVERAGE:	10	4	6	26	27	

Regular Season Individual Leaders

Season	Goals		Points		Penalty Minutes	
1993-1994	Scott Mellanby	30	Scott Mellanby	60	Brent Severyn	156
1994-1995	Jesse Belanger	15	Jesse Belanger	29	Paul Laus	138
			Stu Barnes	29		
1995-1996	Scott Mellanby	32	Scott Mellanby	70	Paul Laus	236
1996-1997	Ray Sheppard	29	Ray Sheppard	60	Paul Laus	313
1997-1998	Ray Whitney	32	Ray Whitney	61	Paul Laus	293
1998-1999	Ray Whitney	26	Ray Whitney	64	Peter Worrell	258
1999-2000	Pavel Bure	58	Pavel Bure	94	Todd Simpson	202
2000-2001	Pavel Bure	59	Pavel Bure	92	Peter Worrell	248
2001-2002	Kristian Huselius	23	Pavel Bure	49	Peter Worrell	352
2002-2003	Olli Jokinen	36	Olli Jokinen	65	Peter Worrell	193
2003-2004	Olli Jokinen	26	Olli Jokinen	58	Darcy Hordichuk	158
2004-2005	Season cancelled due to lockout.					
2005-2006	Ollie Jokinen	38	Ollie Jokinen	89	Chris Gratton	104

*-known as National Car Rental Center from 1998-2003 and Office Depot Center in 2004.

COACHING HISTORY: 1993-1995 Roger Neilson 53-56-23-.489; 1995-1998 Doug MacLean 83-71-33-.532; 1997-1998 Bryan Murray 17-31-11-.381; 1998-2001 Terry Murray 79-85-31-5-.485; 2000-2001 Duane Sutter 22-35-8-7-.410; 2001-2004 Mike Keenan 45-73-23-12-.408; 2003-2004 Rick Dudley 13-15-9-3-.475; 2003-2004 John Torchetti 10-12-4-1-.463; 2005-present Jacques Martin

FLORIDIANS
(known also as Miami Floridians)

Home City: Miami, Florida
Home Court: Miami Beach Convention Hall (1968-72)
            Miami-Dade Junior College (1968-1970)
            Dinner Key Auditorium (1969-70)
Origin of Name: The team played it's home games in Florida

Regular Season Record

Season	League	GP	W	L	PPGF	PPGA	Pct	GB
1968-1969	ABA	78	43	35	115.5	115.1	.551	1
1969-1970	ABA	84	23	61	113.2	118.3	.274	36
1970-1971	ABA	84	37	47	114.0	115.6	.440	18
1971-1972	ABA	84	36	48	112.8	114.3	.429	32
TOTAL:	4 years	330	139	191				87
AVERAGE:		83	35	48	113.8	115.8	.421	22

Playoff Record

Season	GP	W	L	PPGF	PPGA	Result
1968-1969	12	5	7	111.3	115.6	Lost 2nd Round series to Indiana.
1970-1971	6	2	4	112.5	114.2	Lost 1st Round series to Kentucky.
1971-1972	4	0	4	106.5	118.0	Lost 1st Round series to Virginia.
TOTAL:	22	7	15			
AVERAGE:	7	2	5	110.8	115.7	

Regular Season Individual Leaders

Season	Field Goal % (min. 70 games)		Points		Points per Game (min. 70 games)	
1968-69	Don Freeman	.484	Don Freeman	1724	Don Freeman	22.1
	Skip Thoren	.484				
1969-70	Don Sidle	.484	Don Freeman	2163	Don Freeman	27.4
1970-71	Larry Jones	.467	Mack Calvin	2201	Mack Calvin	27.2
1971-72	Ron Franz	.485	Warren Jabali	1615	Mack Calvin	21.0

COACHING HISTORY: 1968-1970 Jim Pollard 48-50-.490; 1969-1971 Hal Blitman 36-76-.321; 1970-1972 Bob Bass 55-65-.458

FT. LAUDERDALE STRIKERS
(were Miami Toros)
(became Minnesota Strikers)

Home City: Ft. Lauderdale, Florida
Home Field: Lockhart Stadium   Capacity: 19,600 [1980]
Origin of Name: A striker is a soccer term for a forward player.

Regular Season Record

Season	League	GP	W	L	GF	GA	BP	Pts	Pct
1977	NASL	26	19	7	49	29	47	161	.688

1978	NASL	30	16	14	50	59	47	143	.530
1979	NASL	30	17	13	75	65	63	165	.611
1980	NASL	32	18	14	61	55	55	163	.566
1981	NASL	32	18	14	54	46	44	144	.300
1982	NASL	32	18	14	64	74	57	163	.340
1983	NASL	30	14	16	60	63	54	136	.302
TOTAL:	7 years	212	120	92	413	391	367	1075	
AVERAGE:		30	17	13	59	56	52	154	.435

Playoff Record

Season	GP	W	L	GF	GA	Result
1977	2	0	2	5	11	Lost Division Final to New York.
1978	7	5	2	12	11	Lost Conference Final to Tampa.
1979	2	0	2	0	3	Lost 1st Round series to Chicago.
1980	10	6	4	14	14	Lost Championship series to New York.
1981	6	4	2	15	10	Lost 3rd Round series to New York.
1982	6	3	3	12	9	Lost 2nd Round series to Seattle.
1983	2	0	2	4	7	Lost 1st Round series to Tulsa.
TOTAL:	35	18	17	62	65	
AVERAGE:	5	2	3	9	9	

Regular Season Individual Leaders

Season	Goals		Points		GAA (360 Min)	
1977	Louie Nanchoff	8	Louie Nanchoff	22	Gordon Banks	1.12
1978	David Irving	16	David Irving	37	Ian Turner	1.73
1979	Gerd Mueller	19	Gerd Mueller	55	Arnold Mausser	1.98
1980	Teofilo Cubillas	14	Teofilo Cubillas	42	Jan Van Beveren	1.78
1981	Teofilo Cubillas	17	Teofilo Cubillas	44	Jan Van Beveren	1.29
1982	Brian Kidd	15	Branko Segota	37	Jan Van Beveren	2.31
1983	Brian Kidd	18	Brian Kidd	39	Jan Van Beveren	2.10

COACHING HISTORY: 1977-1979 Ron Newman 52-34; 1980 Cor van der Hart 18-14; 1981-1982 Eckhard Krautzun 36-28;1983 Dave Chadwick 14-16

FT. WAYNE HOOSIERS

Home City: Ft. Wayne, Indiana
Home Court: South Side Gym
Origin of Name: The team was named Hoosiers because Indiana is known as the Hoosier State. Known as the Caseys in 1925-26 because the team was sponsored by the Knights of Columbus (K.C.'s)

Regular Season Record

Season	League	GP	W	L	Pct
1925-1926	ABL	30	13	17	.433
1926-1927	ABL	42	23	19	.548
1927-1928	ABL	51	27	24	.529
1928-1929	ABL	42	29	13	.690
1929-1930	ABL	54	25	29	.463
1930-1931	ABL	38	24	14	.632
TOTAL:	6 years	257	141	116	
AVERAGE:		43	24	19	.549

Playoff Record

Season	GP	W	L	Result
1927-1928	6	3	3	Lost Championship series to New York.
1928-1929	4	0	4	Lost Championship series to Cleveland.
1930-1931	7	3	4	Lost Championship series to Brooklyn.
TOTAL:	17	6	11	
AVERAGE:	6	2	4	

Regular Season Individual Leaders

Season	Points	
1926-27	Benny Borgmann	380
1927-28	Benny Borgmann	391
1928-29	Rusty Saunders	258
1929-30		
1930-31	Frank Shimek	203

COACHING HISTORY: 1925-1927 Not Available; 1927-1928 Frank Morgenweck 27-24-.529; 1928-1931 Not Available

FORT WAYNE ZOLLNER PISTONS
(became Detroit Pistons)

Home City: Fort Wayne, Indiana
Home Court: North Side High School Gym (1948-1952)   Capacity: 3,800
                 Memorial Coliseum (1952-1957)   Capacity: 9,306
Origin of Name: The team was named after team president Fred Zollner, the owner of a large piston manufacturing plant.

Regular Season Record

Season	League	GP	W	L	PPGF	PPGA	Pct	GB
1937-1938	NBL	20	13	7	40.4	31.6	.650	2
1941-1942	NBL	24	15	9	47.0	44.4	.625	5
1942-1943	NBL	23	17	6	51.1	46.4	.739	-
1943-1944	NBL	22	18	4	47.2	41.2	.818	-
1944-1945	NBL	30	25	5	56.9	50.2	.833	-
1945-1946	NBL	34	26	8	58.7	51.0	.765	-
1946-1947	NBL	44	25	19	58.3	55.6	.568	6
1947-1948	NBL	60	40	20	59.9	56.9	.667	4
1948-1949	BAA	60	22	38	74.3	77.5	.367	23
1949-1950	NBA	68	40	28	79.3	77.9	.588	11*
1950-1951	NBA	68	32	36	84.1	86.0	.471	12
1951-1952	NBA	66	29	37	78.0	80.1	.439	12
1952-1953	NBA	69	36	33	81.0	81.1	.522	11.5
1953-1954	NBA	72	40	32	77.0	76.1	.556	6
1954-1955	NBA	72	43	29	92.4	90.0	.597	-
1955-1956	NBA	72	37	35	94.4	93.7	.514	-
1956-1957	NBA	72	34	38	96.4	98.7	.472	-**
TOTAL:	17 years	876	492	384				92.5
AVERAGE:		52	29	23	75.6	74.5	.562	5

*-defeated Chicago 86-69 in a playoff game to determine third place.
**-lost 103 to 115 to St. Louis in a playoff for first place.

Playoff Record

Season	GP	W	L	PPGF	PPGA	Result
1941-1942	6	3	3	49.5	50.0	Lost Championship series to Oshkosh.
1942-1943	6	3	3	42.3	40.7	Lost Championship series to Sheboygan.
1943-1944	5	5	0	49.0	37.0	**Won NBL Championship.**
1944-1945	7	5	2	58.7	50.4	**Won NBL Championship.**
1945-1946	4	1	3	53.0	57.5	Lost 1st Round series to Rochester.
1946-1947	8	4	4	54.3	51.5	Lost 2nd Round series to Rochester.
1947-1948	4	1	3	58.3	66.0	Lost 1st Round series to Rochester.
1949-1950	4	2	2	82.5	86.0	Lost Division Final to Minneapolis.
1950-1951	3	1	2	80.7	95.0	Lost Division Semifinal to Rochester.
1951-1952	2	0	2	82.0	93.5	Lost Division Semifinal to Rochester.
1952-1953	8	4	4	76.4	80.1	Lost Division Final to Minneapolis.
1953-1954	2	0	2	73.0	85.5	Lost Division playoff to Minneapolis.
1954-1955	11	6	5	93.6	91.5	Lost Championship series to Syracuse.
1955-1956	10	4	6	92.8	92.2	Lost Championship series to Philadelphia.
1956-1957	2	0	2	117.5	120.5	Lost Division Semifinal to Minneapolis.
TOTAL:	82	39	43			
AVERAGE:	6	3	3	70.4	70.6	

Regular Season Individual Leaders

Season	Field Goals		Free Throws		Points	
1937-38	Bart Quinn	71	Scotty Armstrong	35	Bart Quinn	170
1941-42	B. McDermott	115	Curly Armstrong	60	Bobby McDermott	277
1942-43	B. McDermott	132	Jake Pelkington	70	Bobby McDermott	316
1943-44	B. McDermott	123	Bobby McDermott	60	Bobby McDermott	306
1944-45	B. McDermott	258	Bobby McDermott	87	Bobby McDermott	603
1945-46	B. McDermott	184	Buddy Jeannette	105	Bobby McDermott	458
1946-47	Chick Reiser	153	Curly Armstrong	134	Chick Reiser	410
1947-48	Jake Pelkington	174	Jake Pelkington	156	Jake Pelkington	504
1948-49	John Mahnken	215	Bruce Hale	172	Charlie Black	567
1949-50	Fred Schaus	351	Fred Schaus	270	Fred Schaus	972
1950-51	Larry Foust	327	Fred Schaus	404	Fred Schaus	1028
1951-52	Larry Foust	390	Frankie Brian	367	Frankie Brian	1051
1952-53	Larry Foust	311	Larry Foust	336	Larry Foust	958
1953-54	Larry Foust	376	Larry Foust	338	Larry Foust	1090
1954-55	Larry Foust	398	Larry Foust	393	Larry Foust	1189
1955-56	George Yardley	434	Larry Foust	432	George Yardley	1233
1956-57	Bob Houbregs	253	George Yardley	1547	George Yardley	1547

COACHING HISTORY: 1937-1938 Byron Evard 13-7-.650; 1941-1949 Carl Bennet 159-70-.694; 1946-1947 Bobby McDermott 7-7-.500; 1948-1949 Curly Armstrong 22-32-.407; 1949-1951 Murray Mendenhall 72-64-.529; 1951-1954 Paul Birch 105-102-.507; 1954-1957 Charlie Eckman 114-102-.528

FRANKFORD YELLOW JACKETS

Home City: Philadelphia, Pennsylvania
Home Stadium: Frankford Stadium
Origin of Name: The team was named after several local football teams that had played in the area since 1913.

Regular Season Record

Season	League	GP	W	L	T	PF	PA	Pct
1924	NFL	14	11	2	1	326	109	.821

1925	NFL	20	13	7	0	190	169	.650
1926	NFL	16	14	1	1	236	49	.906
1927	NFL	18	6	9	3	155	166	.417
1928	NFL	16	11	3	2	175	84	.750
1929	NFL	18	9	4	5	129	128	.639
1930	NFL	18	4	13	1	113	321	.250
1931	NFL	8	1	6	1	13	99	.188
TOTAL:	8 years	128	69	45	14	1337	1125	
AVERAGE:		16	9	6	1	167	141	.594

Regular Season Individual Leaders

Season	Passing Yards		Receiving Yards		Rushing Yards	
1924	Tex Hamer	79	Harvey Haws	59	Harvey Haws	196
1925	Hust Stockton	632	Bob Fitzke	114	Tex Hamer	280
1926	Hust Stockton	245	Charley Moran	111	Tex Hamer	125
1927	Ken Mercer	565			Charley Rogers	508
1928	Hust Stockton	371			Wally Diehl	475
1929	Bill Kelly	482			Wally Diehl	520
1930	Neil Rengel	304			Herb Joesting	376
1931	Mort Kaer	58	Lee Wilson	25	Justin Brumbaugh	155

COACHING HISTORY: 1924 Robert Berryman 11-2-1-.821; 1925-1926 Guy Chamberlin 27-8-1-.764; 1927 Adolph Youngstrom 4-5-2-.455; 1927 Charley Moran 2-4-1-.357; 1928 Ed Weir 11-3-2-.750; 1929-1931 Russell Behman 14-23-7-.398

FRANKFURT GALAXY

Home City: Frankfurt, Germany
Home Stadium: Waldstadion   Capacity: 54,000 [1991]
Origin of Name:

Regular Season Record

Season	League	GP	W	L	T	PF	PA	Pct
1991	WLAF	10	7	3	0	155	139	.700
1992	WFL	10	3	7	0	150	257	.300
TOTAL:	2 years	20	10	10	0	305	396	
AVERAGE:		10	5	5	0	153	198	.500

Regular Season Individual Leaders

Season	Passing Yards		Receiving Yards		Rushing Yards	
1991	Mike Perez	2279	Jason Johnson	635	Tony Baker	648
1992	Mike Perez	985				

COACHING HISTORY: 1991-1992 Jack Elway 10-10-0-.500

GOLDEN BAY EARTHQUAKES

Home City: San Jose, California
Home Field: Spartan Stadium   Capacity: 18,155 [1976]
Origin of Name: The name was picked because of the areas proximity to the San Andreas Fault and chosen by club General Manager Dick Berg. In the last two seasons the team was known as Golden Bay Earthquakes.

Regular Season Record

Season	League	GP	W	L	T	GF	GA	BP	Pts	Pct
1974	NASL	20	9	8	3	43	38	40	103	.572
1975	NASL	22	8	14	-	37	48	35	83	.419
1976	NASL	24	14	10	-	47	30	39	123	.569
1977	NASL	26	14	12	-	37	44	35	119	.509
1978	NASL	30	8	22	-	36	81	35	83	.307
1979	NASL	30	8	22	-	41	74	38	86	.319
1980	NASL	32	9	23	-	45	68	41	95	.330
1981	NASL	32	11	21	-	44	78	42	108	.225
1982	NASL	32	13	19	-	47	62	38	114	.238
1983	NASL	30	20	10	-	71	54	55	169	.376
1984	NASL	24	8	16	-	61	62	49	95	.264
TOTAL:	11 years	302	122	177	3	509	639	447	1178	
AVERAGE:		27	11	16	0	46	58	41	107	.409

Playoff Record

Season	GP	W	L	GF	GA	Result
1974	1	0	1	0	3	Lost Quarterfinal game to Dallas.
1976	2	1	1	3	3	Lost Conference Final to Minnesota.
1977	1	0	1	1	2	Lost 1st Round game to Los Angeles.
1983	5	2	3	11	7	Lost 2nd Round series to Toronto.
TOTAL:	9	3	6	15	15	
AVERAGE:	2	1	1	4	4	

Regular Season Individual Leaders

Season	Goals		Points		GAA (360 Min)	
1974	Paul Child	15	Paul Child	36	Mike Ivanow	1.33
1975	Ilija Mitic	13	Ilija Mitic	29	Mike Ivanow	1.94
1976	Ilija Mitic	14	Ilija Mitic	37	Mike Hewitt	0.92
1977	Paul Child	13	Paul Child	29	Mike Hewitt	1.42
1978	Paul Child	8	Peter Ressel	23	Gerrit Vooys	2.09
	Peter Ressel	8				
1979	Bernie Gersdorff	10	Bernie Gersdorff	25	Chris Turner	2.32
1980	Steve David	16	Steve David	35	Mike Hewitt	1.92
1981	George Best	13	George Best	36		
1982	Godfrey Ingram	17	Godfrey Ingram	37	Mike Hewitt	1.82
1983	Steve Zungul	16	Steve Zungul	47	Bill Irwin	1.66
1984	Steve Zungul	20	Steve Zungul	50		

COACHING HISTORY: 1974-1978 Gabbo Gavric 43-41; 1974-1975 Ivan Toplak 7-14-3; 1978-1979 Terry Fisher 3-19; 1979 Peter Stubbe 8-14; 1980 Bill Foulkes 9-23; 1981 Jim Gabriel 11-21; 1982 Peter Short 13-19; 1983-1984 Don Popovic-28-26

GOLDEN STATE WARRIORS
(were San Francisco Warriors)

Home City: Oakland, California
Home Court: Oakland Coliseum Arena (1971-1996)   Capacity: 15,025 [1995]
          San Jose Arena (1996-1997)   Capacity: 17,190 [1997]
          New Oakland Coliseum (1998-present)   Capacity: 19,596 [2006]
Origin of Name: The team kept the same nickname when it moved from San Francisco.

Regular Season Record

Season	League	GP	W	L	PPGF	PPGA	Pct	GB
1971-1972	NBA	82	51	31	108.2	107.4	.622	18
1972-1973	NBA	82	47	35	108.8	105.7	.573	13
1973-1974	NBA	82	44	38	109.9	107.3	.537	3
1974-1975	NBA	82	48	34	108.5	105.2	.585	-
1975-1976	NBA	82	59	23	109.8	103.1	.720	-
1976-1977	NBA	82	46	36	110.9	107.7	.561	7
1977-1978	NBA	82	43	39	106.1	105.7	.524	15
1978-1979	NBA	82	38	44	105.1	104.8	.463	14
1979-1980	NBA	82	24	58	103.6	108.0	.293	36
1980-1981	NBA	82	39	43	109.8	111.0	.476	18
1981-1982	NBA	82	45	37	110.9	109.8	.549	12
1982-1983	NBA	82	30	52	108.6	112.3	.366	28
1983-1984	NBA	82	37	45	109.9	113.3	.451	17
1984-1985	NBA	82	22	60	110.4	117.7	.268	40
1985-1986	NBA	82	30	52	113.4	116.9	.366	32
1986-1987	NBA	82	42	40	112.0	114.4	.512	23
1987-1988	NBA	82	20	62	107.0	115.3	.244	42
1988-1989	NBA	82	43	39	116.6	116.9	.524	14
1989-1990	NBA	82	37	45	116.3	119.4	.451	26
1990-1991	NBA	82	44	38	116.6	115.0	.537	19
1991-1992	NBA	82	55	27	118.7	114.8	.671	2
1992-1993	NBA	82	34	48	109.9	110.9	.415	28
1993-1994	NBA	82	50	32	107.9	106.1	.610	13
1994-1995	NBA	82	26	56	105.7	111.1	.317	33
1995-1996	NBA	82	36	46	101.6	103.1	.439	28
1996-1997	NBA	82	30	52	99.6	104.4	.366	27
1997-1998	NBA	82	19	63	88.3	97.4	.232	42
1998-1999	NBA	50	21	29	88.3	90.8	.420	14
1999-2000	NBA	82	19	63	95.5	103.8	.232	48
2000-2001	NBA	82	17	65	92.5	101.5	.207	39
2001-2002	NBA	82	21	61	97.7	103.1	.256	40
2002-2003	NBA	82	38	44	102.4	103.6	.463	21
2003-2004	NBA	82	37	45	93.3	94.0	.451	19
2004-2005	NBA	82	34	48	98.7	100.9	.415	28
2005-2006	NBA	82	34	48	98.5	99.8	.415	20
TOTAL:	35 years	2838	1260	1578				779
AVERAGE:		81	36	45	105.9	107.7	.444	22

Playoff Record

Season	GP	W	L	PPGF	PPGA	Result
1971-1972	5	1	4	100.6	112.0	Lost Conf. Semifinal to Milwaukee.
1972-1973	11	5	6	97.9	105.7	Lost Conf. Final to Los Angeles.
1974-1975	17	12	5	100.2	94.9	**Won NBA Championship**.
1975-1976	13	7	6	112.1	106.3	Lost Conf. Final to Phoenix.
1976-1977	10	5	5	105.6	103.7	Lost Conf. Semifinal to Los Angeles.
1986-1987	10	4	6	107.1	111.7	Lost Conf. Semifinal to Lakers.
1988-1989	8	4	4	109.9	116.5	Lost Conf. Semifinal to Phoenix.
1990-1991	9	4	5	114.4	115.9	Lost Conf. Semifinal to Lakers.
1991-1992	4	1	3	117.0	116.5	Lost 1st Round series to Seattle.
1993-1994	3	0	3	116.0	122.7	Lost 1st Round series to Phoenix.
TOTAL:	90	43	47			
AVERAGE:	9	4	5	107.6	109.7	

Regular Season Individual Leaders

Season	Field Goal % (min. 70 games)		Points		Points per Game (min. 70 games)	
1971-72	Nate Thurmond	.532	Jeff Mullins	1720	Jeff Mullins	21.5
1972-73	Jeff Mullins	.493	Rick Barry	1832	Rick Barry	22.3
1973-74	Butch Beard	.512	Rick Barry	2009	Rick Barry	25.1
1974-75	Butch Beard	.528	Rick Barry	2450	Rick Barry	30.6
1975-76	Charles Dudley	.528	Rick Barry	1701	Rick Barry	21.0
1976-77	Clifford Ray	.584	Rick Barry	1723	Rick Barry	21.8
1977-78	Clifford Ray	.571	Rick Barry	1898	Rick Barry	23.1
1978-79	Clifford Ray	.526	John Lucas	1324	Robert Parish	17.2
1979-80	Clifford Ray	.530	Robert Parish	1223	Robert Parish	17.0
1980-81	Bernard King	.588	Bernard King	1771	Bernard King	21.9
1981-82	Bernard King	.566	Bernard King	1833	Bernard King	23.2
1982-83	Sam Williams	.526	J.B. Carroll	1907	J.B. Carroll	24.1
1983-84	Larry Smith	.560	Purvis Short	1803	Purvis Short	22.8
1984-85	Larry Smith	.530	Purvis Short	2186	Purvis Short	28.0
1985-86	Larry Smith	.536	J.B. Carroll	1677	Purvis Short	25.5
1986-87	Larry Smith	.546	J.B. Carroll	1720	J.B. Carroll	21.2
1987-88	J. Whitehead	.483	Chris Mullin	1213	Tellis Frank	8.1
1988-89	Larry Smith	.552	Chris Mullin	2176	Chris Mullin	26.5
1989-90	Chris Mullin	.536	Chris Mullin	1956	Chris Mullin	25.1
1990-91	Chris Mullin	.536	Chris Mullin	2107	Chris Mullin	25.7
1991-92	S. Marciulionis	.538	Chris Mullin	2074	Chris Mullin	25.6
1992-93	Chris Gatling	.539	Tim Hardaway	1419	Latrell Sprewell	15.4
1993-94	Chris Gatling	.588	Latrell Sprewell	1720	Latrell Sprewell	21.0
1994-95	David Wood	.469	Latrell Sprewell	1420	Keith Jennings	7.4
1995-96	B.J. Armstrong	.468	Latrell Sprewell	1473	Latrell Sprewell	18.9
1996-97	Chris Mullin	.553	Latrell Sprewell	1938	Latrell Sprewell	24.2
1997-98	Erik Dampier	.445	Donyell Marshall	1123	Donyell Marshall	15.4
1998-99*	Antawn Jamison	.452	John Starks	690	John Starks	13.8
1999-00	Adonal Foyle	.508	Larry Hughes	1226	Antawn Jamison	19.6
2000-01	Antawn Jamison	.442	Antawn Jamison	2044	Antawn Jamison	24.9
2001-02	Antawn Jamison	.444	Antawn Jamison	1619	Antawn Jamison	19.7
2002-03	Adonal Foyle	.536	Antawn Jamison	1822	Antawn Jamison	22.2
2003-04	Erick Dampier	.535	Jason Richardson	1461	Jason Richardson	18.7
2004-05	Adonal Foyle	.502	Jason Richardson	1559	Jason Richardson	21.7
2005-06	Adonal Foyle	.507	Jason Richardson	1741	Jason Richardson	23.2

COACHING HISTORY: 1971-1983 Al Attles 508-455-.528; 1979-1980 John Bach 6-15-.288; 1983-1986 John Bach 89-157-.362; 1986-1988 George Karl 146-58788-.397; 1987-1988 Ed Gregory 18-4-14-.222; 1988-1995 Don Nelson 277 260 .516; 1994-1995 Bob Lanier 12-25-.324; 1995-1997 Rick Adelman 66-98-.402; 1997-2000 P.J. Carlesimo 46-113-.289; 1999-2000 Garry St. Jean 13-42-.236; 2000-2002 Dave Cowens 26-80-.245; 2001-2002 Brian Winters 12-46-.207; 2002-2004 Eric Musselman 75-89-.457; 2004-present Mike Montgomery

*-minimum 40 games.

GREEN BAY PACKERS

Home City: Milwaukee, Wisconsin
Green Bay, Wisconsin
Home Stadium: County Stadium (1953-1993)   Capacity: 56,051 (Milwaukee) [1993]
               Hagemeister Brewery Park (1922) (Green Bay)
               Bellevue Park (1923-1924) (Green Bay)
               City Stadium I (1925-1956)   Capacity: 24,800 (Green Bay)
               Lambeau Field (1957-present)**   Capacity: 72,515 (Green Bay) [2005]
Origin of Name: The team was first sponsored by the Acme Packing Company of Green Bay.

Regular Season Record

Season	League	GP	W	L	T	PF	PA	Pct
1922	NFL	11	4	4	3	70	54	.550
1923	NFL	10	7	2	1	85	34	.750
1924	NFL	11	7	4	0	108	38	.636
1925	NFL	13	8	5	0	151	110	.615
1926	NFL	13	7	3	3	151	61	.654
1927	NFL	10	7	2	1	113	43	.750
1928	NFL	13	6	4	3	120	92	.577
1929	NFL	13	12	0	1	198	22	.962
1930	NFL	14	10	3	1	234	111	.750
1931	NFL	14	12	2	0	291	87	.857
1932	NFL	14	10	3	1	152	63	.750
1933	NFL	13	5	7	1	170	107	.423
1934	NFL	13	7	6	0	156	112	.538
1935	NFL	12	8	4	0	181	96	.667
1936	NFL	12	10	1	1	248	118	.875
1937	NFL	11	7	4	0	220	122	.636
1938	NFL	11	8	3	0	223	118	.727
1939	NFL	11	9	2	0	233	153	.818
1940	NFL	11	6	4	1	238	155	.591
1941	NFL	11	10	1	0	258	120	.909
1942	NFL	11	8	2	1	300	215	.773
1943	NFL	10	7	2	1	264	172	.750
1944	NFL	10	8	2	0	238	141	.800
1945	NFL	10	6	4	0	258	173	.600
1946	NFL	11	6	5	0	148	158	.545
1947	NFL	12	6	5	1	274	210	.542
1948	NFL	12	3	9	0	154	290	.250
1949	NFL	12	2	10	0	114	329	.167
1950	NFL	12	3	9	0	244	406	.250
1951	NFL	12	3	9	0	254	375	.250
1952	NFL	12	6	6	0	295	312	.500
1953	NFL	12	2	9	1	200	338	.208
1954	NFL	12	4	8	0	234	251	.333
1955	NFL	12	6	6	0	258	276	.500
1956	NFL	12	4	8	0	264	342	.333
1957	NFL	12	3	9	0	218	311	.250

*-The Packers have played some home games in Milwaukee every year from 1933 to 1952
including Borchert Field, State Fair Park and Marquette Stadium, then County Stadium from 1953
to 1994.
**-Lambeau Field was known as City Stadium II from 1957 to 1964.

1958	NFL	12	1	10	1	193	382	.125
1959	NFL	12	7	5	0	248	246	.583
1960	NFL	12	8	4	0	332	209	.667
1961	NFL	14	11	3	0	391	223	.786
1962	NFL	14	13	1	0	415	148	.929
1963	NFL	14	11	2	1	369	206	.821
1964	NFL	14	8	5	1	342	245	.607
1965	NFL	14	10	3	1	316	224	.750
1966	NFL	14	12	2	0	335	163	.857
1967	NFL	14	9	4	1	332	209	.679
1968	NFL	14	6	7	1	281	227	.464
1969	NFL	14	8	6	0	269	221	.571
1970	NFL	14	6	8	0	196	293	.429
1971	NFL	14	4	8	2	274	298	.357
1972	NFL	14	10	4	0	304	226	.714
1973	NFL	14	5	7	2	202	259	.429
1974	NFL	14	6	8	0	210	206	.429
1975	NFL	14	4	10	0	226	285	.286
1976	NFL	14	5	9	0	218	299	.357
1977	NFL	14	4	10	0	134	219	.286
1978	NFL	16	8	7	1	249	269	.531
1979	NFL	16	5	11	0	246	316	.313
1980	NFL	16	5	10	1	231	371	.344
1981	NFL	16	8	8	0	324	361	.500
1982	NFL	9	5	3	1	226	169	.611
1983	NFL	16	8	8	0	429	439	.500
1984	NFL	16	8	8	0	390	309	.500
1985	NFL	16	8	8	0	337	355	.500
1986	NFL	16	4	12	0	254	418	.250
1987	NFL	15	5	9	1	255	300	.367
1988	NFL	16	4	12	0	240	315	.250
1989	NFL	16	10	6	0	362	356	.625
1990	NFL	16	6	10	0	271	347	.375
1991	NFL	16	4	12	0	273	313	.250
1992	NFL	16	9	7	0	276	296	.563
1993	NFL	16	9	7	0	340	282	.563
1994	NFL	16	9	7	0	382	287	.563
1995	NFL	16	11	5	0	404	314	.689
1996	NFL	16	13	3	0	456	210	.813
1997	NFL	16	13	3	0	422	282	.813
1998	NFL	16	11	5	0	408	319	.688
1999	NFL	16	8	8	0	357	341	.500
2000	NFL	16	9	7	0	353	323	.562
2001	NFL	16	12	4	0	390	266	.750
2002	NFL	16	12	4	0	398	328	.750
2003	NFL	16	10	6	0	442	307	.625
2004	NFL	16	10	6	0	424	380	.625
2005	NFL	16	4	12	0	298	344	.250
2006	NFL	16	8	8	0	301	366	.500
TOTAL:	85 years	1155	621	499	35	22642	20186	
AVERAGE:		13	7	6	0	266	237	.553

Playoff Record

Season	GP	W	L	PF	PA	Result
1936	1	1	0	21	6	**Won NFL Championship.**
1938	1	0	1	17	23	Lost NFL Championship to N.Y. Giants.
1939	1	1	0	27	0	**Won NFL Championship.**
1941	1	0	1	14	33	Lost Division playoff to Chicago Bears.
1944	1	1	0	14	7	**Won NFL Championship.**
1960	1	0	1	13	17	Lost NFL Championship to Philadelphia.
1961	1	1	0	37	0	**Won NFL Championship.**
1962	1	1	0	16	7	**Won NFL Championship.**
1965	2	2	0	36	22	**Won NFL Championship.**
1966	2	2	0	69	37	**Won Super Bowl I.**
1967	3	3	0	82	38	**Won Super Bowl II.**
1972	1	0	1	3	16	Lost Divisional playoff to Washington.
1982	2	1	1	67	53	Lost 2nd Round playoff to Dallas.
1993	2	1	1	45	51	Lost Divisional Semifinal to Dallas.
1994	2	1	1	25	47	Lost Divisional Semifinal to Dallas.
1995	3	2	1	91	75	Lost Conference Final to Dallas.
1996	3	3	0	100	48	**Won Super Bowl XXXI.**
1997	3	2	1	68	48	Lost Super Bowl to Denver.
1998	1	0	1	27	30	Lost Wild Card Game to San Francisco.
2001	2	1	1	42	60	Lost Conference Semifinal to St. Louis.
2002	1	0	1	7	27	Lost Wildcard Game to Atlanta.
2003	2	1	1	50	47	Lost Conference Semifinal to Philadelphia.
2004	1	0	1	17	31	Lost Wild Card Game to Minnesota.
TOTAL:	38	24	14	888	723	
AVERAGE:	2	1	1	39	31	

Regular Season Individual Leaders

Season	Passing Yards		Receiving Yards		Rushing Yards	
1922	Curly Lambeau	222	Kyle Wheeler	60	Curly Lambeau	76
1923	Curly Lambeau	752	Charlie Mathys	494	Curly Lambeau	416
1924	Curly Lambeau	1094	Charlie Mathys	579	Curly Lambeau	457
1925	Curly Lambeau	711	Charlie Mathys	180	Myrt Basing	430
1926	Curly Lambeau	504	Verne Lewellen	299	Vern Lewellen	275
1927	Red Dunn	556			Vern Lewellen	305
1928	Red Dunn	700			Vern Lewellen	349
1929	Vern Lewellen	501			Johnny Blood	406
1930	Red Dunn	672			Bo Molenda	458
1931	Red Dunn	399			Bo Molenda	425
1932	Arnie Herber	774	Johnny Blood	168	Clarke Hinkle	451
1933	Arnie Herber	656	Lavie Dilweg	225	Bob Monnett	315
1934	Arnie Herber	799	Milt Gantenbein	165	Clarke Hinkle	384
1935	Arnie Herber	729	Don Hutson	420	Bob Monnett	336
1936	Arnie Herber	1239	Don Hutson	526	Clarke Hinkle	476
1937	Arnie Herber	676	Don Hutson	552	Clarke Hinkle	552
1938	Cecil Isbell	659	Don Hutson	548	Cecil Isbell	445
1939	Arnie Herber	1107	Don Hutson	846	Cecil Isbell	407
1940	Cecil Isbell	1037	Don Hutson	664	Clarke Hinkle	383
1941	Cecil Isbell	1479	Don Hutson	738	Clarke Hinkle	393
1942	Cecil Isbell	2021	Don Hutson	1211	Tony Canadeo	272
1943	Tony Canadeo	875	Don Hutson	776	Tony Canadeo	489
1944	Irv Comp	1159	Don Hutson	866	Ted Fritsch	322
1945	Irv Comp	865	Don Hutson	834	Ted Fritsch	282

Season	Passing Yards		Receiving Yards		Rushing Yards	
1946	Irv Comp	333	Clyde Goodnight	308	Tony Canadeo	476
1947	Jack Jacobs	1615	Nolan Luhn	696	Tony Canadeo	464
1948	Jack Jacobs	848	Clyde Goodnight	448	Tony Canadeo	598
1949	Jug Girard	881	Ted Cook	442	Tony Canadeo	1052
1950	Tobin Rote	1231	Al Baldwin	555	Billy Grimes	480
1951	Tobin Rote	1540	Bob Mann	696	Tobin Rote	523
1952	Babe Parilli	1416	Bill Howton	1231	Tobin Rote	313
1953	Tobin Rote	1005	Bill Howton	463	Breezy Reid	492
1954	Tobin Rote	2311	Bill Howton	768	Breezy Reid	507
1955	Tobin Rote	1977	Bill Howton	697	Howie Ferguson	859
1956	Tobin Rote	2203	Bill Howton	1188	Tobin Rote	398
1957	Bart Starr	1489	Bill Howton	727	Don McIlhenny	384
1958	Babe Parilli	1068	Max McGee	655	Paul Hornung	310
1959	Bart Starr	972	Max McGee	695	Paul Hornung	681
1960	Bart Starr	1358	Max McGee	787	Jim Taylor	1101
1961	Bart Starr	2418	Max McGee	883	Jim Taylor	1307
1962	Bart Starr	2438	Max McGee	820	Jim Taylor	1474
1963	Bart Starr	1855	Boyd Dowler	901	Jim Taylor	1018
1964	Bart Starr	2144	Boyd Dowler	623	Jim Taylor	1169
1965	Bart Starr	2055	Boyd Dowler	610	Jim Taylor	734
1966	Bart Starr	2257	Carroll Dale	876	Jim Taylor	705
1967	Bart Starr	1823	Boyd Dowler	836	Jim Grabowski	466
1968	Bart Starr	1617	Carroll Dale	818	Don Anderson	761
1969	Don Horn	1505	Carroll Dale	879	Travis Williams	536
1970	Bart Starr	1645	Carroll Dale	814	Don Anderson	853
1971	Scott Hunter	1210	Carroll Dale	598	J. Brockington	1105
1972	Scott Hunter	1252	Carroll Dale	317	J. Brockington	1027
1973	Jerry Tagge	720	Jon Staggers	412	J. Brockington	1144
1974	John Hadl	1752	Jon Staggers	450	J. Brockington	883
1975	John Hadl	2095	Ken Payne	766	J. Brockington	434
1976	Lynn Dickey	1465	Ken Payne	467	Will Harrell	435
1977	Lynn Dickey	1346	Steve Odom	549	Barty Smith	554
1978	D. Whitehurst	2093	James Lofton	818	T. Middleton	1116
1979	D. Whitehurst	2247	James Lofton	968	T. Middleton	495
1980	Lynn Dickey	3529	James Lofton	1226	Eddie Lee Ivery	831
1981	Lynn Dickey	2593	James Lofton	1294	Gerry Ellis	860
1982	Lynn Dickey	1790	James Lofton	696	Eddie Lee Ivery	453
1983	Lynn Dickey	4458	James Lofton	1300	Gerry Ellis	696
1984	Lynn Dickey	3195	James Lofton	1361	Gerry Ellis	581
1985	Lynn Dickey	2206	James Lofton	1153	Eddie Lee Ivery	636
1986	Randy Wright	3247	James Lofton	840	Kenneth Davis	519
1987	Randy Wright	1507	Walter Stanley	672	Kenneth Davis	413
1988	Don Majkowski	2119	Sterling Sharpe	791	Brent Fullwood	483
1989	Don Majkowski	4318	Sterling Sharpe	1423	Brent Fullwood	821
1990	Don Majkowski	1925	Sterling Sharpe	1105	Michael Haddix	311
1991	Mike Tomczak	1490	Sterling Sharpe	961	Darrell Thompson	471
1992	Brett Favre	3227	Sterling Sharpe	1461	Vince Workman	631
1993	Brett Favre	3303	Sterling Sharpe	1274	Darrell Thompson	654
1994	Brett Favre	3882	Sterling Sharpe	1119	Edgar Bennett	623
1995	Brett Favre	4413	Robert Brooks	1497	Edgar Bennett	1067
1996	Brett Favre	3899	A. Freeman	933	Edgar Bennett	899
1997	Brett Favre	3867	A. Freeman	1243	Dorsey Levens	1435
1998	Brett Favre	4212	A. Freeman	1424	Darrick Holmes	987

Season	Passing Yards		Receiving Yards		Rushing Yards	
1999	Brett Favre	4091	A. Freeman	1074	Dorsey Levens	1034
2000	Brett Favre	3812	Bill Schroeder	999	Ahman Green	1175
2001	Brett Favre	3921	Bill Schroeder	918	Ahman Green	1387
2002	Brett Favre	3658	Donald Driver	1064	Ahman Green	1240
2003	Brett Favre	3361	Javon Walker	716	Ahman Green	716
2004	Brett Favre	4088	Javon Walker	1382	Ahman Green	1163
2005	Brett Favre	3881	Donald Driver	1221	Samkon Gado	582
2006	Brett Favre	3885	Donald Driver	1295	Ahman Green	1059

COACHING HISTORY: 1922-1949 Earl Lambeau 206-102-20-.658; 1950-1953 Gene Ronzani 14-31-1-.315; 1953 Hugh Devore & Ray McLean 0-2-0-.000; 1954-1957 Lisle Blackbourn 17-31-0-.354; 1958 Ray McLean 1-10-l-.125; 1959-1967 Vince Lombardi 89-29-4-.746; 1968-1970 Phil Bengston 20-21-1-.488; 1971-1974 Dan Devine 25-27-4-.482; 1975-1983 Bart Starr 52-76-3-.408; 1984-1987 Forrest Gregg 25-37-1-.405; 1988-1991 Lindy Infante 24-40-0-.375; 1992-1998 Mike Holmgren 75-37-0-.670; 1999 Ray Rhodes 8-8-0-.500; 2000-2005 Mike Sherman 57-39-0-.594; 2006-present Mike McCarthy

HAILEYBURY COMETS

Home City: Haileybury, Ontario
Home Arena: Plaza Arena
Origin of Name: Probably named after the comet discovered by Edmund Halley.

		Regular Season Record							
Season	League	GP	W	L	T	GF	GA	Pts	Pct
1909-1910	NHA	12	4	8	0	77	83	8	.333

		Regular Season Individual Leaders			
Season	Goals		Points		GAA	
1909-1910	Horace Gaul	22	Horace Gaul	22	Paddy Moran	7.27

COACHING HISTORY: Weldy Young 4-8-0-.333

HAMILTON TIGER-CATS

Home City: Hamilton, Ontario
Home Stadium: Ivor Wynne Stadium   Capacity: 29,220 [2006]
Origin of Name: The team was formed from an amalgamation of the Hamilton Tigers of the IRFU and the Hamilton Wildcats of the ORFU.

				Regular Season Record						
Season	League	GP	W	L	T	OL	PF	PA	Pts	Pct
1950	CRU	12	7	5	0	NA	231	217	14	.583
1951	CRU	12	7	5	0	NA	229	131	14	.583
1952	CRU	12	9	2	1	NA	268	162	19	.792
1953	CRU	14	8	6	0	NA	229	247	16	.571
1954	CRU	14	9	5	0	NA	275	207	18	.643
1955	CRU	12	8	4	0	NA	271	193	16	.667
1956	CFC	14	7	7	0	NA	383	385	14	.500
1957	CFC	14	10	4	0	NA	250	189	20	.714
1958	CFL	14	10	3	1	NA	291	235	21	.750
1959	CFL	14	10	4	0	NA	298	162	20	.714
1960	CFL	14	4	10	0	NA	273	377	8	.286
1961	CFL	14	10	4	0	NA	340	393	20	.714

1962	CFL	14	9	4	1	NA	358	286	19	.679
1963	CFL	14	10	4	0	NA	312	214	20	.714
1964	CFL	14	10	3	1	NA	329	201	21	.750
1965	CFL	14	10	4	0	NA	281	153	20	.714
1966	CFL	14	9	5	0	NA	264	160	18	.643
1967	CFL	14	10	4	0	NA	250	195	20	.714
1968	CFL	14	6	7	1	NA	262	292	13	.464
1969	CFL	14	8	5	1	NA	307	315	17	.607
1970	CFL	14	8	5	1	NA	292	279	17	.607
1971	CFL	14	7	7	0	NA	242	246	14	.500
1972	CFL	14	11	3	0	NA	372	262	22	.786
1973	CFL	14	7	7	0	NA	304	263	14	.500
1974	CFL	16	7	9	0	NA	279	313	14	.438
1975	CFL	16	5	10	1	NA	284	395	11	.344
1976	CFL	16	8	8	0	NA	269	348	16	.500
1977	CFL	16	5	11	0	NA	283	394	10	.313
1978	CFL	16	5	10	1	NA	225	403	11	.344
1979	CFL	16	6	10	0	NA	280	338	12	.375
1980	CFL	16	8	7	1	NA	332	377	17	.531
1981	CFL	16	11	4	1	NA	414	335	23	.719
1982	CFL	16	8	7	1	NA	396	401	17	.531
1983	CFL	16	5	10	1	NA	389	498	11	.344
1984	CFL	16	6	9	1	NA	353	439	13	.406
1985	CFL	16	8	8	0	NA	377	315	16	.500
1986	CFL	18	9	8	1	NA	405	366	19	.528
1987	CFL	18	7	11	0	NA	470	509	14	.389
1988	CFL	18	9	9	0	NA	478	465	18	.500
1989	CFL	18	12	6	0	NA	519	517	24	.667
1990	CFL	18	6	12	0	NA	476	628	12	.333
1991	CFL	18	3	15	0	NA	400	599	6	.167
1992	CFL	18	11	7	0	NA	536	514	22	.611
1993	CFL	18	6	12	0	NA	316	567	12	.333
1994	CFL	18	4	14	0	NA	435	562	8	.222
1995	CFL	18	8	10	0	NA	427	509	16	.444
1996	CFL	18	8	10	0	NA	416	576	16	.444
1997	CFL	18	2	16	0	NA	362	549	4	.111
1998	CFL	18	12	5	1	NA	503	340	25	.694
1999	CFL	18	11	7	0	NA	603	378	22	.611
2000	CFL	18	9	9	0	2	458	446	20	.556
2001	CFL	18	11	7	0	0	440	420	22	.611
2002	CFL	18	7	11	0	1	427	524	15	.417
2003	CFL	18	1	17	0	NA	293	583	2	.056
2004	CFL	18	9	8	1	NA	455	542	19	.528
2005	CFL	18	5	13	0	NA	383	583	10	.278
2006	CFL	18	4	14	0	NA	292	495	8	.222
TOTAL:	57 years	898	440	441	17	3	19886	20992	900	
AVERAGE:		16	8	8	0	0	349	368	16	.501

Playoff Record

Season	GP	W	L	T	PF	PA	Result
1950	2	1	1	0	19	35	Lost Division Final to Toronto.
1951	4	1	3	0	47	56	Lost Division Final to Ottawa.
1952	3	1	2	0	40	45	Lost Division Final to Toronto.
1953	3	3	0	0	71	29	**Won Grey Cup.**

Year							Result
1954	2	0	2	0	28	38	Lost Division Final to Montreal.
1955	1	0	1	0	28	32	Lost Division Semifinal to Toronto.
1956	3	1	2	0	108	99	Lost Division Final to Montreal.
1957	3	3	0	0	88	18	**Won Grey Cup.**
1958	3	2	1	0	82	49	Lost Grey Cup Final to Winnipeg.
1959	3	1	2	0	33	45	Lost Grey Cup Final to Winnipeg.
1961	3	1	2	0	69	48	Lost Grey Cup Final to Winnipeg.
1962	3	2	1	0	85	66	Lost Grey Cup Final to Winnipeg.
1963	3	2	1	0	84	45	**Won Grey Cup.**
1964	3	1	2	0	63	72	Lost Grey Cup Final to B.C.
1965	3	3	0	0	57	36	**Won Grey Cup.**
1966	3	1	2	0	41	86	Lost Division Final to Ottawa.
1967	3	3	0	0	61	4	**Won Grey Cup.**
1968	1	0	1	0	21	33	Lost Division Semifinal to Toronto.
1969	1	0	1	0	9	15	Lost Division Semifinal to Toronto.
1970	2	0	2	0	26	43	Lost Division Final to Montreal.
1971	3	1	1	1	48	44	Lost Division Final to Toronto.
1972	3	2	1	0	43	37	**Won Grey Cup.**
1974	1	0	1	0	19	21	Lost Division Semifinal to Ottawa.
1975	1	0	1	0	12	35	Lost Division Semifinal to Montreal.
1976	2	1	1	0	38	17	Lost Division Final to Ottawa.
1978	1	0	1	0	20	35	Lost Division Semifinal to Montreal.
1979	1	0	1	0	26	29	Lost Division Semifinal to Ottawa.
1980	2	1	1	0	34	61	Lost Grey Cup Final to Edmonton.
1981	1	0	1	0	13	17	Lost Division Final to Ottawa.
1982	1	0	1	0	20	30	Lost Division Semifinal to Ottawa.
1983	2	1	1	0	69	72	Lost Division Final to Toronto.
1984	3	2	1	0	48	71	Lost Grey Cup Final to Winnipeg.
1985	2	1	1	0	74	63	Lost Grey Cup Final to B.C.
1986	3	2	1	0	98	71	**Won Grey Cup.**
1987	1	0	1	0	13	29	Lost Division Semifinal to Toronto.
1988	1	0	1	0	28	35	Lost Division Semifinal to Winnipeg.
1989	2	1	1	0	54	53	Lost Grey Cup Final to Saskatchewan.
1992	2	1	1	0	40	87	Lost Division Final to Winnipeg.
1993	2	1	1	0	40	30	Lost Division Final to Winnipeg.
1995	1	0	1	0	13	30	Lost Division Final to Calgary.
1996	1	0	1	0	11	22	Lost Division Semifinal to Montreal.
1998	2	1	1	0	46	46	Lost Grey Cup Final to Calgary.
1999	3	3	0	0	86	53	**Won Grey Cup.**
2000	1	0	1	0	20	22	Lost Division Semifinal to Winnipeg.
2001	2	1	1	0	37	40	Lost Division Final to Winnipeg.
2004	1	0	1	0	6	24	Lost Division Semifinal to Toronto.
TOTAL:	96	45	50	1	2005	1946	
AVERAGE:	2	1	1	0	44	42	

Regular Season Individual Leaders

Season	Passing Yards		Receiving Yards		Rushing Yards	
1950						
1951						
1952						
1953						
1954	Ed Songin	2433	Ray Ramsey	770	Merle Hapes	581
1955						
1956	Tony Curcillo	1726				

Season	Passing Yards		Receiving Yards		Rushing Yards	
1957					Gerry McDougall	1053
1958	Bernie Faloney	2852	Ron Howell	756	Gerry McDougall	1109
			Tommy Grant	756		
1959					Gerry McDougall	1010
1960	Bernie Faloney	3085	Paul Dekker	790	Gerry McDougall	557
1961	Bernie Faloney	2565	Gerry McDougall	632	Larry Hickman	447
1962	Frank Cosentino	1182	Hal Patterson	881	Bobby Kuntz	813
1963	Bernie Faloney	2318	Hal Patterson	841	Willie Bethea	435
1964	Bernie Faloney	1941	Tommy Grant	1029	Art Baker	726
1965	Frank Cosentino	876	Tommy Grant	558	Willie Bethea	611
1966	Joe Zuger	1251	Tommy Grant	683	Dick Cohee	635
1967	Joe Zuger	2775	T.J. Coffey	683	Willie Bethea	737
1968	Joe Zuger	2616	T.J. Coffey	800	Willie Bethea	607
1969	Joe Zuger	1562	T. J. Coffey	1110	Dave Fleming	641
1970	Joe Zuger	1073	Dave Fleming	692	Dave Fleming	614
1971	Joe Zuger	1632	T.J. Coffey	423	Dick Wesolowski	332
1972	Chuck Ealey	2573	Tony Gabriel	733	Dave Buchanan	1163
1973	Chuck Ealey	2312	Garney Henley	639	Andy Hopkins	1223
1974	Bill Etter	1446	Tony Gabriel	795	Andy Hopkins	943
1975	Jerry Keeling	1933	Terry Evanshen	970	Andy Hopkins	463
1976	Jimmy Jones	1773	Jimmy Edwards	457	Jimmy Edwards	1046
1977	Jimmy Jones	2156	Mike Harris	771	Jimmy Edwards	1581
1978	Jimmy Jones	2060	Lawrie Skolrood	661	Jimmy Edwards	840
1979	Tom Clements	2803	Leif Petterson	838	Ron Rowland	814
1980	Dave Marler	1914	Rocky DiPietro	869	Obie Graves	658
1981	Tom Clements	4536	Keith Baker	1218	Rufus Crawford	400
1982	Tom Clements	4706	Keith Baker	1282	Mark Bragagnolo	384
1983	Dieter Brock	1241	Ron Johnson	914	Johnny Shepherd	1069
1984	Dieter Brock	3966	Rocky DiPietro	1063	Kelvin Lindsey	308
1985	Ken Hobart	2522	Steve Stapler	614	Ken Hobart	928
1986	Mike Kerrigan	3193	Tony Champion	1216	Walter Bender	618
1987	Tom Porras	3293	Steve Stapler	1516	Johnnie Jones	408
1988	Mike Kerrigan	2764	Earl Winfield	1213	Martin Sartin	460
1989	Mike Kerrigan	3635	Tony Champion	1656	Derrick McAdoo	1039
1990	Mike Kerrigan	3655	Earl Winfield	1054	Derrick McAdoo	752
1991	Mike Kerrigan	2242	Earl Winfield	874	Jamie Morris	591
1992	Damon Allen	3858	Ken Evraire	1081	Damon Allen	831
1993	Don McPherson	2242	Earl Winfield	1076	Bruce Perkins	812
1994	Timm Rosenbach	2083	Earl Winfield	1150	John Hood	415
1995	Anthony Calvillo	2831	Earl Winfield	1496	Kalin Hall	581
1996	Anthony Calvillo	2571	Mac Cody	1426	Mike Saunders	352
1997	Anthony Calvillo	2177	Prince Wimbley	637	Archie Amerson	630
1998	Danny McManus	4864	Darren Flutie	1386	Ronald Williams	807
1999	Danny McManus	5318	Darren Flutie	1155	Ronald Williams	1025
2000	Danny McManus	4200	Archie Amerson	1198	Ronald Williams	1264
2001	Danny McManus	4465	Darren Flutie	1206	Ronald Williams	607
2002	Danny McManus	4531	Archie Amerson	970	Troy Davis	1143
2003	Danny McManus	2869	Archie Amerson	960	Troy Davis	1206
2004	Danny McManus	5034	Craig Yeast	1184	Troy Davis	1628
2005	Danny McManus	2544	D.J. Flick	1245	Troy Davis	792
2006	Jason Maas	3204	Terry Vaughn	695	Corey Holmes	369

COACHING HISTORY: 1950-1955 Carl Voyles 48-27-1-.638; 1956-1962 Jim Trimble 60-36-2-.622; 1963-1967 Ralph Sazio 49-20-1-.707; 1968-1970 Joe Restic 22-17-3-.560; 1971 Al Darrow 7-7-0-.500; 1972-1975 Jerry Williams 30-28-0-.517; 1975 Bob Krouse 0-1-1-.250; 1976 George Dickson 0-2-0-.000; 1976-1977 Bob Shaw 13-17-0-.433; 1978 Tom Dimitroff 1-3-1-.300; 1978-1980 John Payne 18-24-1-.430; 1981 Frank Kush 11-4-1-.719; 1982-1983 Bud Riley 12-15-1-.446; 1983-1990 Al Bruno 56-61-3-.479; 1990-1991 David Beckman 2-12-0-.143; 1991-1994 John Gregory 21-31-0-.404; 1994-1997 Don Sutherin 20-35-0-.364; 1997 Urban Bowman 1-10-0-.091; 1998-2003 Ron Lancaster 51-56-1-2-.491; 2004-2006 Greg Marshall 14-25-1-.363; 2006 Ron Lancaster 4-10-0-.286; 2007-present

HAMILTON TIGERS
(became New York Americans)

Home City: Hamilton, Ontario
Home Arena: Hamilton Arena   Capacity: 3,800
Origin of Name: Named by team executives after a senior team which won the Allan Cup in 1919.

Regular Season Record

Season	League	GP	W	L	T	GF	GA	Pts	Pct
1920-1921	NHL	24	6	18	0	92	132	12	.250
1921-1922	NHL	24	7	17	0	88	105	14	.292
1922-1923	NHL	24	6	18	0	81	110	12	.250
1923-1924	NHL	24	9	15	0	63	68	18	.375
1924-1925	NHL	30	19	10	1	90	60	39	.650
TOTAL:	5 years	126	47	78	1	414	475	95	
AVERAGE:		25	9	16	0	83	95	19	.377

Playoff Record*
*-The team's players went on strike for more money at the end of the 1924-1925 season and did not compete in the playoffs.

Regular Season Individual Leaders

Season	Goals		Points		Penalty Minutes	
1920-1921	Joe Malone	28	Joe Malone	37	Bill Couture	95
1921-1922	Joe Malone	24	Joe Malone	31	Harry Mummery	40
1922-1923	Mickey Roach	17	Mickey Roach	27	Cully Wilson	46
1923-1924	Bill Burch	16	Billy Burch	22	Ken Randall	58
1924-1925	Bill Burch	20	Red Green	34	Wilfred Green	81

COACHING HISTORY: 1920-1922 Paul Thompson 13-35-0-.271; 1922-1923 Art Ross 6-18-0-.250; 1923-1924 Percy Lesueur 3-7-0-.300; 1923-24 Ken Randall 6-8-0-.429; 1924-1925 Jim Gardner 19-10-1-.650

HAMMOND CALUMET BUCCANEERS

Home City: Hammond, Indiana
Home Court: Hammond Civic Center
Origin of Name: The team was owned by fans in Hammond, Calumet City and the surrounding area.

Regular Season Record

Season	League	GP	W	L	PPGF	PPGA	Pct	GB
1948-1949	NBL	62	21	41	61.0	64.9	.339	17

Playoff Record

Season	GP	W	L	PPGF	PPGA	Result
1948-1949	2	0	2	67.5	76.0	Lost 1st Round series to Syracuse.

Regular Season Individual Leaders

Season	Field Goals		Free Throws		Points	
1948-49	George Glamack	169	George Sobek	232	George Sobek	518

COACHING HISTORY: Bob Carpenter 11-16-.407; George Sobek 10-25-.286

HAMMOND CIESAR ALL-AMERICANS
(were Whiting Ciesar All-Americans)

Home City: Hammond, Indiana
Home Court: Hammond Civic Center
Origin of Name: The team kept the same nickname when it moved from Whiting to Hammond.

Regular Season Record

Season	League	GP	W	L	PPGF	PPGA	Pct	GB
1938-1939	NBL	28	4	24	36.0	42.1	.143	13
1939-1940	NBL	28	9	19	36.9	40.8	.321	6
1940-1941	NBL	24	6	18	38.6	44.4	.250	12
TOTAL:	3 years	80	19	61				31
AVERAGE:		27	7	20	37.2	42.4	.238	10

Regular Season Individual Leaders

Season	Field Goals		Free Throws		Points	
1938-39	Lou Boudreau	78	Joe Sotak	48	Lou Boudreau	189
1939-40	Pim Goff	68	Bobby Neu	71	Bobby Neu	159
1940-41	Dar Hutchins	70	Bobby Neu	63	Bobby Neu	195

COACHING HISTORY: 1938-1939 Whitey Wickhorst 4-24-.143; 1939-1940 Lou Boudreau 1-4-.200; 1939-1940 Eddie Ciesar 0-2-.000; 1939-1940 Leo Bereolos 8-13-.381; 1940-1941 Carl Anderson 6-18-.250

HAMMOND PROS

Home City: Hammond, Indiana
Home Stadium: Gleason Field
Origin of Name: As with all teams with the name of Pros, the name is a shortened version of professional.

Regular Season Record

Season	League	GP	W	L	T	PF	PA	Pct
1922	NFL	6	0	5	1	0	69	.000
1923	NFL	7	1	5	1	14	59	.214
1924	NFL	5	2	2	1	18	45	.500
1925	NFL	5	1	4	0	23	87	.200
1926	NFL	4	0	4	0	3	56	.000
TOTAL:	5 years	27	4	20	3	58	316	
AVERAGE:		5	1	4	0	12	63	.204

Regular Season Individual Leaders

	Passing Yards		Receiving Yards		Rushing Yards	
1922						
1923					Russ Oltz	21
1924						
1925	Jim Kendrick	12	Duncan Annan	8	Duncan Annan	18
1926	Harry Curzon	35	Dick Hudson	35	Buck Gavin	12

COACHING HISTORY: 1922 Wally Hess 0-5-1; 1923-1925 Fritz Pollard 4-10-2-.313; 1925-1926 Doc Young 0-5-0-.000

HARTFORD BICENTENNIALS
(became Connecticut Bicentennials)

Home City: Hartford, Connecticut
Home Stadium: Dillon Stadium
Origin of Name: Adopted the name because the team was formed around the time of the U.S.A.'s bicentennial.

Regular Season Record

Season	League	GP	W	L	GF	GA	BP	Pts	Pct
1975	NASL	22	6	16	27	51	25	61	.308
1976	NASL	24	12	12	37	56	35	107	.495
TOTAL:	2 years	46	18	28	64	107	60	168	
AVERAGE:		23	9	14	32	54	30	84	.406

Regular Season Individual Leaders

Season	Goals		Points		GAA (360 Min)	
1975	Emir Travljanin	5	Emir Travljanin	12	Arnold Mausser	2.24
1976	John Coyne	8	John Coyne	17	Gene DuChateau	0.92

COACHING HISTORY: 1975-1976 Manfred Schellscheidt 8-19; 1976 Bobby Thompson 10-9

HARTFORD BLUES

Home City: Hartford, Connecticut
Home Field: Hartford Baseball Grounds*
Origin of Name: The team was named after the color of their uniforms

Regular Season Record

Season	League	GP	W	L	Pct	GB	R	OR
1876	NL	68	47	21	.691	6	429	261
1877	NL	58	31	27	.534	10	341	311
TOTAL:	2 years	126	78	48		16	770	572
AVERAGE:		63	39	24	.619	8	385	286

Regular Season Individual Leaders

Season	Home Runs		RBI's		Wins	
1876	Jack Remsen	1	Tom York	39	Tommy Bond	31
	Tom York	1				
1877	Joe Start	1	Tom York	37	Terry Larkin	29
	Tom Carey	1				
	Tom York	1				
	Terry Larkin	1				

*-played all their home games in 1877 in Brooklyn, New York.

COACHING HISTORY: 1876-1877 Bob Ferguson 78-48-.619

HARTFORD BLUES

Home City: Hartford, Connecticut
Home Stadium: East Hartford Velodrome
Origin of Name:

			Regular Season Record					
Season	League	GP	W	L	T	PF	PA	Pct
1926	NFL	10	3	7	0	57	99	.300

COACHING HISTORY: Jack Keough 3-7-0-.300

HARTFORD WHALERS
(became Carolina Hurricanes)

Home City: Boston, Massachusetts (1972-1974)
    Springfield, Massachusetts (1974-1975, 1977-1979)
    Hartford, Connecticut (1974-1997)
Home Arena: Boston Garden (1972-1974)   Capacity: 14,994 [1972]
    West Springfield Big E (1974-1975)   Capacity: 5,513 [1974]
    Hartford Civic Center (1974-1978)   Capacity: 10,507 [1974]
    Springfield Civic Center (1977-1979)   Capacity: 7,725 [1977]
Home Arena: Hartford Civic Center II (1979-1997)   Capacity: 15,635 [1997]
Origin of Name: The name was chosen by team executives because of Hartford's whaling history.
Known as New England Whalers from 1972 to 1979.

			Regular Season Record						
Season	League	GP	W	L	T	GF	GA	Pts	Pct
1972-1973	WHA	78	46	30	2	318	263	94	.603
1973-1974	WHA	78	43	31	4	291	260	90	.577
1974-1975	WHA	78	43	30	5	274	279	91	.583
1975-1976	WHA	80	33	40	7	255	290	73	.456
1976-1977	WHA	81	35	40	6	275	290	76	.469
1977-1978	WHA	80	44	31	5	335	269	93	.581
1978-1979	WHA	80	37	34	9	298	287	83	.519
1979-1980	NHL	80	27	34	19	303	312	73	.456
1980-1981	NHL	80	21	41	18	222	372	60	.375
1981-1982	NHL	80	21	41	18	264	351	60	.375
1982-1983	NHL	80	19	54	7	261	403	45	.281
1983-1984	NHL	80	28	42	10	288	320	66	.413
1984-1985	NHL	80	30	41	9	268	318	69	.431
1985-1986	NHL	80	40	36	4	332	302	84	.525
1986-1987	NHL	80	43	30	7	287	270	93	.581
1987-1988	NHL	80	35	38	7	249	267	77	.481
1988-1989	NHL	80	37	38	5	299	290	79	.494
1989-1990	NHL	80	38	33	9	275	268	85	.531
1990-1991	NHL	80	31	38	11	238	276	73	.456
1991-1992	NHL	80	26	41	13	247	283	65	.406
1992-1993	NHL	84	26	52	6	284	369	58	.345

1993-1994	NHL	84	27	48	9	227	288	63	.375
1994-1995	NHL	48	19	24	5	127	141	43	.448
1995-1996	NHL	82	34	39	9	237	259	77	.470
1996-1997	NHL	82	32	39	11	226	256	75	.457
TOTAL:	25 years	1975	815	945	215	6680	7283	1845	
AVERAGE:		79	33	38	8	267	291	74	.467

Playoff Record

Season	GP	W	L	GF	GA	Result
1972-1973	15	12	3	30	48	Won WHA Championship.
1973-1974	7	3	4	23	24	Lost Quarterfinal series to Chicago.
1974-1975	6	2	4	17	28	Lost Quarterfinal series to Minnesota.
1975-1976	17	10	7	54	40	Lost Semifinal series to Houston.
1976-1977	5	1	4	14	23	Lost Quarterfinal series to Quebec.
1977-1978	14	8	6	56	47	Lost Championship series to Winnipeg.
1978-1979	10	5	5	39	42	Lost Semifinal series to Edmonton.
1979-1980	3	0	3	8	18	Lost Preliminary series to Montreal.
1985-1986	10	4	6	29	23	Lost Division Final to Montreal.
1986-1987	6	2	4	19	27	Lost Division Semifinal to Quebec.
1987-1988	6	2	4	20	23	Lost Division Semifinal to Montreal.
1988-1989	4	0	4	11	18	Lost Division Semifinal to Montreal.
1989-1990	7	3	4	21	23	Lost Division Semifinal to Boston.
1990-1991	6	2	4	17	24	Lost Division Semifinal to Boston.
1991-1992	7	3	4	18	21	Lost Division Semifinal to Montreal.
TOTAL:	123	57	66	376	429	
AVERAGE:	8	4	4	25	29	

Regular Season Individual Leaders

Season	Goals		Points		Penalty Minutes	
1972-1973	Tom Webster	53	Tom Webster	103	Brad Selwood	114
1973-1974	Tom Webster	43	John French	72	Rick Ley	148
1974-1975	Tom Webster	40	Wayne Carleton	74	Nick Fotiu	144
1975-1976	Tom Webster	33	Tom Webster	83	Gordie Roberts	102
1976-1977	George Lyle	39	Tom Webster	85	Gordie Roberts	169
1977-1978	Gordie Howe	34	Gordie Howe	96	Jack Carlson	192
1978-1979	Mark Howe	42	Mark Howe	107	Al Hangsleben	148
1979-1980	Blaine Stoughton	56	Mike Rogers	105	Nick Fotiu	107
1980-1981	Blaine Stoughton	43	Mike Rogers	105	Pat Boutette	160
1981-1982	Blaine Stoughton	52	Blaine Stoughton	91	Garry Howatt	242
1982-1983	Blaine Stoughton	45	Ron Francis	90	Greg Adams	216
1983-1984	Sylvain Turgeon	40	Mark Johnson	87	Torrie Robertson	199
1984-1985	Sylvain Turgeon	31	Ron Francis	81	Torrie Robertson	337
1985-1986	Sylvain Turgeon	45	Sylvain Turgeon	79	Torrie Robertson	358
1986-1987	Kevin Dineen	40	Ron Francis	93	Paul MacDermid	202
1987-1988	Ron Francis	25	Ron Francis	75	Torrie Robertson	293
	Kevin Dineen	25				
1988-1989	Kevin Dineen	45	Kevin Dineen	89	Ulf Samuelsson	181
1989-1990	Pat Verbeek	44	Ron Francis	101	Pat Verbeek	228
1990-1991	Pat Verbeek	43	Pat Verbeek	82	Pat Verbeek	246
1991-1992	John Cullen	26	John Cullen	77	Pat Verbeek	243
1992-1993	Geoff Sanderson	46	Geoff Sanderson	89	Nick Kypreos	325
1993-1994	Geoff Sanderson	41	Pat Verbeek	75	Marc Potvin	246
1994-1995	Geoff Sanderson	18	Andrew Cassels	37	Kelly Chase	141
1995-1996	Brendan Shanahan	44	Brendan Shanahan	78	Scott Daniels	254

Season	Goals		Points		Penalty Minutes	
1996-1997	Geoff Sanderson	36	Geoff Sanderson	67	Stu Grimson	218

COACHING HISTORY: 1972-1973 Jack Kelley 46-30-2-.603; 1973-1975 Ron Ryan 83-59-9-.579; 1974-1976 Jack Kelley 17-18-3-.487; 1975-1976 Don Blackburn 14-18-3-.443; 1975-1978 Harry Neale 84-77-12-.520; 1978-1979 Bill Dineen 37-34-9-.519; 1979-1981 Don Blackburn 42-63-35-.425; 1980-1983 Larry Pleau 31-66-21-.352; 1982-1983 Larry Kish 12-32-5-.296; 1982-1983 John Cunniff 3-9-1-.269; 1983-1988 Jack Evans 163-174-37-.485; 1987-1989 Larry Pleau 50-51-5-.495; 1989-1991 Rick Ley 69-71-20-.494; 1991-1992 Jim Roberts 26-41-13-.406; 1992-1993 Paul Holmgren 30-63-8-.337; 1993-1994 Pierre McGuire 23-37-7-.396; 1994-1996 Paul Holmgren 24-30-6-.450; 1995-1997 Paul Maurice 61-72-19-.464

HAWAIIANS, The

Home City: Honolulu, Hawaii
Home Stadium: Honolulu Stadium (1974)   Capacity: 23,000 [1974]
                Aloha Stadium (1975)
Origin of Name: The team was based in Hawaii.

Regular Season Record
Season	League	GP	W	L	T	PF	PA	Pct
1974	WFL	20	9	11	0	413	422	.450
1975	WFL	11	4	7	0	210	281	.364
TOTAL:	2 years	31	13	18	0	623	703	
AVERAGE:		16	7	9	0	312	352	.419

Playoff Record
Season	GP	W	L	PF	PA	Result
1974	2	1	1	53	36	Lost 2nd Round series to Birmingham.

Regular Season Individual Leaders
Season	Passing Yards		Receiving Yards		Rushing Yards	
1974	Norris Weese	1847	Tim Delaney	1232	Al Davis	694
1975	Sonny Kixkiller	799	Tim Delaney	594	Calvin Hill	218

COACHING HISTORY: 1974-1975 Mike Giddings 13-18-0-.419

HOUSTON AEROS

Home City: Houston, Texas
Home Arena: Sam Houston Coliseum (1972-1975)   Capacity: 9,000 [1972]
                The Summit (1975-1978)   Capacity: 15,256 [1977]
Origin of Name: The name was chosen because of Houston's association with the aerospace industry.

Regular Season Record
Season	League	GP	W	L	T	GF	GA	Pts	Pct
1972-1973	WHA	78	39	35	4	284	269	82	.526
1973-1974	WHA	78	48	25	5	318	219	101	.647
1974-1975	WHA	78	53	25	0	369	247	106	.679
1975-1976	WHA	80	53	27	0	341	263	106	.663
1976-1977	WHA	80	50	24	6	320	241	106	.663
1977-1978	WHA	80	42	34	4	296	302	88	.550
TOTAL:	6 years	474	285	170	19	1928	1541	589	
AVERAGE:		79	48	28	3	321	257	99	.621

Playoff Record

Season	GP	W	L	GF	GA	Result
1972-1973	10	4	6	26	30	Lost Semifinal series to Winnipeg.
1973-1974	14	12	2	71	35	**Won WHA Championship.**
1974-1975	13	12	1	61	26	**Won WHA Championship.**
1975-1976	17	8	9	56	63	Lost WHA Final series to Winnipeg.
1976-1977	11	6	5	43	40	Lost Semifinal series to Winnipeg.
1977-1978	6	2	4	16	29	Lost Quarterfinal series to Quebec.
TOTAL:	71	44	27	273	223	
AVERAGE:	12	7	5	46	37	

Regular Season Individual Leaders

Season	Goals		Points		Penalty Minutes	
1972-1973	Gord Labossiere	36	Gord Labossiere	96	John Schella	239
1973-1974	Frank Hughes	42	Gordie Howe	100	John Schella	170
1974-1975	Frank Hughes	48	Larry Lund	108	John Schella	176
1975-1976	Mark Howe	39	Gordie Howe	102	Glen Irwin	116
1976-1977	Rich Preston	38	Terry Ruskowski	84	Cam Connor	224
1977-1978	Morris Lukowich	40	Andre Lacroix	113	Cam Connor	217

COACHING HISTORY: 1972-1978 Bill Dineen 285-170-19-.621

HOUSTON ASTROS

Home City: Houston, Texas
Home Field: Colt Stadium (1962-1964)   Capacity: 32,601 [1962]
            The Astrodome (1965-1999)   Capacity: 54,699 [1999]
            Minute Maid Park (2000-present) **   Capacity: 40,950 [2006]
Origin of Name: The team was named Astros after the Astrodome opened in 1965. Chosen in a Name the Team Contest the name Colts was used by the franchise from 1962-1964.

Regular Season Record

Season	League	GP	W	L	Pct	GB	R	OR
1962	NL	160	64	96	.400	36.5	592	717
1963	NL	162	66	96	.407	33	464	640
1964	NL	162	66	96	.407	27	495	628
1965	NL	162	65	97	.401	32	569	711
1966	NL	162	72	90	.444	23	612	695
1967	NL	162	69	93	.426	32.5	626	742
1968	NL	162	72	90	.444	25	510	588
1969	NL	162	81	81	.500	12	676	668
1970	NL	162	79	83	.488	23	744	763
1971	NL	162	79	83	.488	11	585	567
1972	NL	153	84	69	.549	10.5	708	636
1973	NL	162	82	80	.506	17	681	672
1974	NL	162	81	81	.500	21	653	632
1975	NL	161	64	97	.398	43.5	664	711
1976	NL	162	80	82	.494	22	625	657
1977	NL	162	81	81	.500	17	680	650
1978	NL	162	74	88	.457	21	605	634
1979	NL	162	89	73	.549	1.5	583	582
1980	NL	163	93	70	.571	-	637	589

**-known as Enron Field 2000 to 2002.

1981	NL	110	61	49	.555	NA	394	331
1982	NL	162	77	85	.475	12	569	620
1983	NL	162	85	77	.525	6	643	646
1984	NL	162	80	82	.494	12	693	630
1985	NL	162	83	79	.512	12	706	691
1986	NL	162	96	66	.593	-	654	569
1987	NL	162	76	86	.469	14	648	678
1988	NL	162	82	80	.506	12.5	617	631
1989	NL	162	86	76	.531	6	647	669
1990	NL	162	75	87	.463	16	573	656
1991	NL	162	65	97	.401	29	605	717
1992	NL	162	81	81	.500	17	608	668
1993	NL	162	85	77	.525	19	716	630
1994	NL	115	66	49	.574	.5	602	503
1995	NL	144	76	68	.528	9	747	674
1996	NL	162	82	80	.506	6	753	792
1997	NL	162	84	78	.519	-	777	660
1998	NL	162	102	60	.630	-	874	620
1999	NL	162	97	65	.599	-	823	675
2000	NL	162	72	90	.444	23	938	944
2001	NL	162	93	69	.574	-	847	769
2002	NL	162	84	78	.519	13	749	695
2003	NL	162	87	75	.537	1	805	677
2004	NL	162	92	70	.568	13	803	698
2005	NL	162	89	73	.549	11	693	609
2006	NL	162	82	80	.506	1.5	735	719
TOTAL:	45 years	7162	3579	3583		642	29928	29653
AVERAGE:		159	80	80	.499	14.5	665	659

Playoff Record

Season	GP	W	L	R	OR	Result
1980	5	2	3	19	20	Lost NLCS to Philadelphia.
1981	5	2	3	6	13	Lost Division series to Los Angeles.
1986	6	2	4	17	21	Lost NLCS to New York.
1997	3	0	3	5	18	Lost Division Semifinal to Atlanta.
1998	4	1	3	8	14	Lost Division Semifinal to San Diego.
1999	4	1	3	15	18	Lost Division Semifinal to Atlanta.
2001	3	0	3	6	14	Lost Division Semifinal to Atlanta.
2004	12	7	5	67	55	Lost NLCS to St. Louis.
2005	14	7	7	61	57	Lost World Series to Chicago.
TOTAL:	56	22	34	204	230	
AVERAGE:	6	2	4	23	26	

Regular Season Individual Leaders

Season	Home Runs		RBI's		Wins	
1962	Roman Mejias	24	Roman Mejias	76	Bob Bruce	10
					Dick Farrell	10
1963	John Bateman	10	John Bateman	59	Dick Farrell	14
1964	Walt Bond	20	Walt Bond	85	Bob Bruce	15
1965	Jim Wynn	22	Jim Wynn	73	Dick Farrell	11
1966	Jim Wynn	18	Rusty Staub	81	Dave Giusti	15
1967	Jim Wynn	37	Jim Wynn	107	Mike Cuellar	16
1968	Jim Wynn	26	Rusty Staub	72	Don Wilson	13
1969	Jim Wynn	33	Denis Menke	90	Larry Dierker	20

Season	Home Runs		RBI's		Wins	
1970	Jim Wynn	27	Denis Menke	92	Larry Dierker	16
1971	Joe Morgan	13	Cesar Cedeno	81	Don Wilson	16
1972	Lee May	29	Lee May	98	Larry Dierker	15
					Don Wilson	15
1973	Lee May	28	Lee May	105	Dave Roberts	17
1974	Cesar Cedeno	26	Cesar Cedeno	102	Tom Griffin	14
1975	Cliff Johnson	20	Bob Watson	85	Larry Dierker	14
1976	Cesar Cedeno	18	Bob Watson	102	J.R. Richard	20
1977	Bob Watson	22	Bob Watson	110	J.R. Richard	18
1978	Bob Watson	14	Jose Cruz	83	J.R. Richard	18
1979	Jose Cruz	9	Jose Cruz	72	Joe Niekro	21
1980	Terry Puhl	13	Jose Cruz	91	Joe Niekro	20
1981	Jose Cruz	13	Jose Cruz	55	Nolan Ryan	11
					Don Sutton	11
1982	Phil Garner	13	Phil Garner	83	Joe Niekro	17
1983	Dickie Thon	20	Jose Cruz	92	Joe Niekro	15
1984	Jose Cruz	12	Jose Cruz	95	Joe Niekro	16
1985	Glenn Davis	20	Jose Cruz	79	Mike Scott	18
1986	Glenn Davis	31	Glenn Davis	101	Mike Scott	18
1987	Glenn Davis	27	Glenn Davis	93	Mike Scott	16
1988	Glenn Davis	30	Glenn Davis	99	Bob Knepper	14
					Mike Scott	14
1989	Glenn Davis	34	Glenn Davis	89	Mike Scott	20
1990	Franklin Stubbs	23	Franklin Stubbs	71	Danny Darwin	11
					Mark Portugal	11
1991	Jeff Bagwell	15	Jeff Bagwell	82	Pete Harnisch	12
1992	Eric Anthony	19	Jeff Bagwell	96	Doug Jones	11
1993	Craig Biggio	21	Jeff Bagwell	88	Mark Portugal	18
1994	Jeff Bagwell	39	Jeff Bagwell	116	Doug Drabek	12
1995	Craig Biggio	22	Jeff Bagwell	87	Shane Reynolds	10
					Greg Swindell	10
					Doug Drabek	10
1996	Jeff Bagwell	31	Jeff Bagwell	120	Shane Reynolds	16
1997	Jeff Bagwell	43	Jeff Bagwell	135	Darryl Kile	19
1998	Moises Alou	38	Moises Alou	124	Shane Reynolds	19
1999	Jeff Bagwell	42	Jeff Bagwell	126	Mike Hampton	22
2000	Jeff Bagwell	47	Jeff Bagwell	132	Scott Elarton	17
2001	Jeff Bagwell	39	Jeff Bagwell	130	Wade Miller	16
2002	Lance Berkman	42	Lance Berkman	128	Roy Oswalt	19
2003	Jeff Bagwell	39	Jeff Bagwell	100	Jeriome Robertson	15
2004	Lance Berkman	30	Jeff Kent	107	Roy Oswalt	20
2005	Morgan Ensberg	36	Morgan Ensberg	101	Roy Oswalt	20
2006	Lance Berkman	45	Lance Berkman	136	Roy Oswalt	15

COACHING HISTORY: 1962-1964 Harry Craft 191-280-.406; 1964-1965 Luman Harris 70-105-.400; 1966-1968 Grady Hatton 164-221-.426; 1968-1972 Harry Walker 355-353-.501; 1972 Francis Parker 1-0-1.000; 1972-1973 Leo Durocher 98-95-.508; 1974-1975 Preston Gomez 128-161-.443; 1975-1982 Bill Virdon 544-522-.510; 1982-1985 Bob Lillis 276-261-.514; 1986-1988 Hal Lanier 254-232-.523; 1989-1993 Art Howe 307-341-.474; 1994-1996 Terry Collins 224-197-.532; 1997-2001 Larry Dierker 519-426-.549; 1999 Matt Galante 13-14-.481; 2002-2004 Jimy Williams 215-197-.522; 2004-present Phil Garner

HOUSTON COMETS

Home City: Houston, Texas
Home Arena: Compaq Center   Capacity: 16,285 [2001]
                  Toyota Center   Capacity: 18,300 [2005]
Origin of Name: The name was chosen to show affiliation with the NBA's Rockets.

Regular Season Record

Season	League	GP	W	L	PPGF	PPGA	Pct	GB
1997	WNBA	28	18	10	76.0	56.0	.643	-
1998	WNBA	30	27	3	76.2	63.6	.900	-
1999	WNBA	32	26	6	74.0	64.7	.813	-
2000	WNBA	32	27	5	77.3	64.5	.844	1
2001	WNBA	32	19	13	64.1	62.3	.594	9
2002	WNBA	32	24	8	64.8	59.1	.750	1
2003	WNBA	34	20	14	66.0	63.0	.588	4
2004	WNBA	34	13	21	64.0	65.0	.382	12
2005	WNBA	34	19	15	67.9	66.6	.559	6
2006	WNBA	34	18	16	71.0	92.5	.529	7
TOTAL:	10 years	322	211	111				40
AVERAGE:		32	21	11	69.9	66.0	.655	4

Playoff Record

Season	GP	W	L	PPGF	PPGA	Result
1997	2	2	0	67.5	52.5	**Won WNBA Championship.**
1998	5	4	1	73.4	65.2	**Won WNBA Championship.**
1999	6	4	2	69.0	61.2	**Won WNBA Championship.**
2000	6	6	0	72.7	64.0	**Won WNBA Championship.**
2001	2	0	2	58.5	67.0	Lost Conference Semifinal to L.A.
2002	3	1	2	71.3	72.7	Lost Conference Semifinal to Utah.
2003	3	1	2	65.3	61.0	Lost Conf. Semifinal to Sacramento.
2005	5	2	3	68.6	68.8	Lost Conference Final to Sacramento.
2006	2	0	2	71.0	92.5	Lost Conf. Semifinal to Sacramento.
TOTAL:	34	20	14			
AVERAGE:	4	2	2	69.5	66.1	

Regular Season Individual Leaders

Season	Field Goals % (20 games min.)		Free Throws % (20 games min.)		Points per Game (20 games min.)	
1997	Cynthia Cooper	.470	Janeth Arcain	.894	Cynthia Cooper	22.2
1998	Monica Lamb	.541	Cynthia Cooper	.854	Cynthia Cooper	22.7
1999	Cynthia Cooper	.463	Cynthia Cooper	.891	Cynthia Cooper	22.1
2000	Tammy Jackson	.574	A Valdemoro	1.000	Sheryl Swoopes	20.7
2001	Tammy Jackson	.500	Janeth Arcain	.900	Tina Thompson	19.9
2002	Michelle Snow	.469	Janeth Arcain	.883	Sheryl Swoopes	18.5
	Rebecca Lobo	.469				
2003	Mfon Udoka	.500	Cynthia Cooper	.893	Tina Thompson	16.9
2004	Tiffani Johnson	.500	Sheryl Swoopes	.856	Tina Thompson	20.0
2005	Sancho Lyttle	.584	Roneeka Hodges	1.000	Sheryl Swoopes	18.6
2006	Michelle Snow	.510	Tina Thompson	.804	Sheryl Swoopes	15.5

COACHING HISTORY: 1997-present Van Chancellor

HOUSTON DYNAMO
(were San Jose Earthquakes)

Home City: Houston, Texas
Home Field: Robertson Stadium (2006-present)   Capacity: 32,000 [2006]
Origin of Name:

Season	League	GP	W	L	T	SOW	GF	GA	Pts
2006	MLS	32	11	8	13	NA	44	40	46

Playoff Record

Season	GP	W	L	T	GF	GA	Result
2006	4	2	1	1	17	4	Won MLS Cup.

Regular Season Individual Leaders

Season	Goals		Points		GAA (min. 5 games)	
2006	Brian Ching	11	Dwayne DeRosario	27	Pat Onstad	1.25
	Dwayne DeRosario	11				

COACHING HISTORY: 2006-present Dominic Kinnear

HOUSTON GAMBLERS

Home City: Houston Texas
Home Stadium: The Astrodome   Capacity: 50,496 [1984]
Origin of Name: The name was chosen by Jerry Argovitz, one of the co-owners of the team.

Regular Season Record

Season	League	GP	W	L	T	PF	PA	Pct
1984	USFL	18	13	5	0	618	400	.722
1985	USFL	18	10	8	0	544	388	.556
TOTAL:	2 years	36	23	13	0	1162	788	
AVERAGE:		18	12	6	0	581	394	.639

Playoff Record

Season	GP	W	L	PF	PA	Result
1984	1	0	1	16	17	Lost 1st Round series to Arizona.
1985	1	0	1	20	22	Lost 1st Round series to Birmingham.
TOTAL:	2	0	2	36	39	
AVERAGE:	1	0	1	18	20	

Regular Season Individual Leaders

Season	Passing Yards		Receiving Yards		Rushing Yards	
1984	Jim Kelly	5219	Richard Johnson	1455	Todd Fowler	1003
1985	Jim Kelly	4623	Richard Johnson	1384	Todd Fowler	402

COACHING HISTORY: 1984-1985 Jack Pardee 23-13-0-.639

HOUSTON HURRICANE

Home City: Houston, Texas
Home Stadium: The Astrodome   Capacity: 35,443
Origin of Name: The name was chosen in a Name the Team Contest.

Regular Season Record

Season	League	GP	W	L	GF	GA	BP	Pts	Pct
1978	NASL	30	10	20	37	61	36	96	.356
1979	NASL	30	22	8	61	46	55	187	.693
1980	NASL	32	14	18	51	52	45	129	.448
TOTAL:	3 years	92	46	46	149	159	136	412	
AVERAGE:		31	16	15	50	53	45	137	.498

Playoff Record

Season	GP	W	L	GF	GA	Result
1979	2	0	2	2	4	Lost 1st Round series to Philadelphia.
1980	3	1	2	2	3	Lost 1st Round series to Edmonton.
TOTAL:	5	1	4	4	7	
AVERAGE:	3	1	2	2	4	

Regular Season Individual Leaders

Season	Goals		Points		GAA (360 Min)	
1978	Kresten Bjerre	6	Dean Smith	19	Keith Van Eron	1.60
	Dean Smith	6				
1979	Kai Haaskivi	12	Kai Haaskivi	30	Paul Hammond	1.46
	Eduardo Marasco	12				
1980	Eduardo Marasco	13	Eduardo Marasco	33	Paul Hammond	1.57

COACHING HISTORY: 1978-1979 Timo Liekoski 32-28-.524; 1980 Eckhard Krautzun 14-18-.448

HOUSTON MAVERICKS

Home City: Houston, Texas
Home Court: Sam Houston Coliseum   Capacity: 9,300
Origin of Name: The name is synonymous with Texas. Sam Maverick was a Texan who fought for Texas independence.

Regular Season Record

Season	League	GP	W	L	PPGF	PPGA	Pct	GB
1967-1968	ABA	78	29	49	103.5	107.8	.372	19
1968-1969	ABA	78	23	55	111.3	117.0	.295	37
TOTAL:	2 years	156	52	104				56
AVERAGE:		78	26	52	107.4	112.4	.333	28

Playoff Record

Season	GP	W	L	PPGF	PPGA	Result
1967-1968	3	0	3	103.3	114.0	Lost 1st Round series to Dallas.

Regular Season Individual Leaders

Season	Field Goal % (min. 70 games)		Points		Points per Game (min. 70 games)	
1967-68	Art Becker	.468	Art Becker	1427	Art Becker	18.8
1968-69	Art Becker	.476	Stew Johnson	1421	Art Becker	13.4

COACHING HISTORY: 1967-1969 Slater Martin 32-58-.356; 1968-1969 Jim Weaver 20-46-.303

HOUSTON OILERS
(became Tennessee Oilers)

Home City: Houston, Texas
Home Stadium: Jeppesen Stadium (1960-1964)   Capacity: 23,500
          Rice University Stadium (1965-1967)   Capacity: 70,000
          The Astrodome (1968-1996))   Capacity: 59,969 [1996]
Origin of Name: The team was named by then owner Bud Adams Jr. chosen to reflect on one of
Houston's major industries.

Regular Season Record

Season	League	GP	W	L	T	PF	PA	Pct
1960	AFL	14	10	4	0	379	285	.714
1961	AFL	14	10	3	1	513	242	.750
1962	AFL	14	11	3	0	387	270	.786
1963	AFL	14	6	8	0	302	372	.429
1964	AFL	14	4	10	0	310	355	.286
1965	AFL	14	4	10	0	298	429	.286
1966	AFL	14	3	11	0	335	396	.214
1967	AFL	14	9	4	1	258	199	.679
1968	AFL	14	7	7	0	303	248	.500
1969	AFL	14	6	6	2	278	279	.500
1970	NFL	14	3	10	1	217	352	.250
1971	NFL	14	4	9	1	251	330	.321
1972	NFL	14	1	13	0	164	380	.071
1973	NFL	14	1	13	0	199	467	.071
1974	NFL	14	7	7	0	236	282	.500
1975	NFL	14	10	4	0	293	226	.714
1976	NFL	14	5	9	0	222	273	.357
1977	NFL	14	8	6	0	299	230	.571
1978	NFL	16	10	6	0	283	298	.625
1979	NFL	16	11	5	0	362	331	.688
1980	NFL	16	11	5	0	295	251	.688
1981	NFL	16	7	9	0	281	355	.438
1982	NFL	9	1	8	0	136	245	.111
1983	NFL	16	2	14	0	288	460	.125
1984	NFL	16	3	13	0	240	437	.188
1985	NFL	16	5	11	0	284	412	.313
1986	NFL	16	5	11	0	274	329	.313
1987	NFL	15	9	6	0	345	349	.600
1988	NFL	16	10	6	0	424	365	.625
1989	NFL	16	9	7	0	365	412	.563
1990	NFL	16	9	7	0	405	307	.563
1991	NFL	16	11	5	0	386	251	.688
1992	NFL	16	10	6	0	352	258	.625
1993	NFL	16	12	4	0	368	238	.750
1994	NFL	16	2	14	0	226	352	.125
1995	NFL	16	7	9	0	348	324	.438
1996	NFL	16	8	8	0	345	319	.500
TOTAL:	37 years	548	251	291	6	11251	11908	
AVERAGE:		15	7	8	0	304	322	.464

Playoff Record

Season	GP	W	L	PF	PA	Result
1960	1	1	0	24	16	**Won AFL Championship.**
1961	1	1	0	10	3	**Won AFL Championship.**
1962	1	0	1	17	20	Lost AFL Championship to Dallas.
1967	1	0	1	7	40	Lost AFL Championship to Oakland.
1969	1	0	1	7	56	Lost Divisional playoff to Oakland.
1978	3	2	1	53	74	Lost AFC Championship to Pittsburgh.
1979	3	2	1	43	48	Lost AFC Championship to Pittsburgh.
1980	1	0	1	7	27	Lost 1st Round playoff to Oakland.
1987	2	1	1	33	54	Lost Divisional playoff to Denver.
1988	2	1	1	34	40	Lost Divisional playoff to Buffalo.
1989	1	0	1	23	26	Lost Wild Card Game to Pittsburgh.
1990	1	0	1	14	41	Lost Wild Card Game to Cincinnati.
1991	2	1	1	41	36	Lost Conference Semifinal to Denver.
1992	1	0	1	38	41	Lost Wild Card Game to Buffalo.
1993	1	0	1	20	28	Lost Conference Semifinal to Kansas City.
TOTAL:	22	9	13	371	550	
AVERAGE:	2	1	1	25	37	

Regular Season Individual Leaders

Season	Passing Yards		Receiving Yards		Rushing Yards	
1960	George Blanda	2413	Bill Groman	1473	Billy Cannon	644
1961	George Blanda	3330	C. Hennigan	1746	Billy Cannon	948
1962	George Blanda	2810	C. Hennigan	867	Charley Tolar	1012
1963	George Blanda	3003	C. Hennigan	1051	Charley Tolar	659
1964	George Blanda	3287	C. Hennigan	1546	Sid Blanks	756
1965	George Blanda	2542	Charley Frazier	717	Ode Burrell	528
1966	George Blanda	1764	Charley Frazier	1129	Ode Burrell	406
1967	Pete Beathard	1114	Hoyle Granger	300	Hoyle Granger	1194
1968	Pete Beathard	1559	Alvin Reed	747	Hoyle Granger	848
1969	Pete Beathard	2455	Jerry LeVias	696	Hoyle Granger	740
1970	Charley Johnson	1652	Alvin Reed	604	Joe Dawkins	517
1971	Dan Pastorini	1702	Charlie Joiner	681	Robert Holmes	323
1972	Dan Pastorini	1711	Ken Burrough	521	Fred Willis	461
1973	Dan Pastorini	1482	Billy Parks	581	Fred Willis	579
1974	Dan Pastorini	1571	Ken Burrough	492	Willie Rodgers	413
1975	Dan Pastorini	2053	Ken Burrough	1063	Ronnie Coleman	790
1976	Dan Pastorini	1795	Ken Burrough	932	Ronnie Coleman	684
1977	Dan Pastorini	1987	Ken Burrough	816	Ronnie Coleman	660
1978	Dan Pastorini	2473	Ken Burrough	624	Earl Campbell	1450
1979	Dan Pastorini	2090	Ken Burrough	752	Earl Campbell	1697
1980	Ken Stabler	3202	Dave Casper	796	Earl Campbell	1934
1981	Ken Stabler	1988	Ken Burrough	668	Earl Campbell	1376
1982	Gifford Nielsen	1005	Dave Casper	573	Earl Campbell	538
1983	Oliver Luck	1375	Tim Smith	1176	Earl Campbell	1301
1984	Warren Moon	3338	Tim Smith	1141	Larry Moriarty	785
1985	Warren Moon	2709	Drew Hill	1169	Mike Rozier	462
1986	Warren Moon	3489	Drew Hill	1112	Mike Rozier	662
1987	Warren Moon	2806	Drew Hill	989	Mike Rozier	957
1988	Warren Moon	2327	Drew Hill	1141	Mike Rozier	1002
1989	Warren Moon	3631	Drew Hill	938	Alonzo Highsmith	531
1990	Warren Moon	4689	Haywood Jeffries	1048	Lorenzo White	702
1991	Warren Moon	4690	Haywood Jeffries	1181	Allen Pinkett	720

Season	Passing Yards		Receiving Yards		Rushing Yards	
1992	Warren Moon	2521	Curtis Duncan	954	Lorenzo White	1226
1993	Warren Moon	3485	Webster Slaughter	904	Gary Brown	1002
1994	Billy Joe Tolliver	1287	Webster Slaughter	846	Lorenzo White	757
1995	Chris Chandler	2460	Chris Sanders	823	Rodney Thomas	947
1996	Chris Chandler	2099	Chris Sanders	882	Eddie George	1368

COACHING HISTORY: 1960-1961 Lou Rymkus 11-7-1-.605; 1961 Wally Lemm 9-0-0-1.000; 1962-1963 Frank Ivy 17-11-0-.607; 1964 Sammy Baugh 4-10-0-.286; 1965 Hugh Taylor 4-10-0-.286; 1966-1970 Wally Lemm 28-38-4-.429; 1971 Ed Hughes 4-9-1-.321; 1972-1973 Bill Peterson 1-18-0-.053; 1973-1974 Sid Gillman 8-15-0-348; 1975-1980 Bum Phillips 55-35-0-.611; 1981-1983 Ed Biles 8-23-0-.258; 1983 Chuck Studley 2-8-0-.200; 1984-1985 Hugh Campbell 8-22-0-.267; 1986-1989 Jerry Glanville 33-30-0-.524; 1990-1994 Jack Pardee 43-31-0-.581; 1994-1996 Jeff Fisher 16-22-0-.421

HOUSTON ROCKETS
(were San Diego Rockets)

Home City: Houston, Texas
Home Court: Hofheinz Pavilion (1971-1975)   Capacity: 10,218
      Hofheinz Pavilion & Hemisfair Arena (1972-1973)   Capacity: 10,446
      Compaq Center (1975-2003) *   Capacity: 16,285 [2002]
      Toyota Center (2003-present)   Capacity: 18,300 [2006]
Origin of Name: The team kept the same nickname when it moved from San Diego to Houston.

Regular Season Record

Season	League	GP	W	L	PPGF	PPGA	Pct	GB
1971-1972	NBA	82	34	48	109.7	111.2	.415	35
1972-1973	NBA	82	33	49	112.8	114.5	.402	19
1973-1974	NBA	82	32	50	107.4	107.6	.390	15
1974-1975	NBA	82	41	41	103.9	102.9	.500	19
1975-1976	NBA	82	40	42	106.2	107.0	.488	9
1976-1977	NBA	82	49	33	106.4	104.8	.598	-
1977-1978	NBA	82	28	54	103.8	107.8	.341	24
1978-1979	NBA	82	47	35	113.4	112.4	.573	1
1979-1980	NBA	82	41	41	110.8	110.6	.500	9
1980-1981	NBA	82	40	42	108.3	107.9	.488	12
1981-1982	NBA	82	46	36	105.9	105.9	.561	2
1982-1983	NBA	82	14	68	99.3	110.9	.171	39
1983-1984	NBA	82	29	53	110.6	113.7	.354	16
1984-1985	NBA	82	48	34	111.2	109.5	.585	4
1985-1986	NBA	82	51	31	114.4	111.8	.622	-
1986-1987	NBA	82	42	40	106.9	105.9	.512	13
1987-1988	NBA	82	46	36	109.0	107.6	.561	8
1988-1989	NBA	82	45	37	108.5	107.5	.549	6
1989-1990	NBA	82	41	41	106.7	105.3	.500	15
1990-1991	NBA	82	52	30	106.7	103.2	.634	3
1991-1992	NBA	82	42	40	102.0	103.7	.512	13
1992-1993	NBA	82	55	27	104.0	99.8	.671	-
1993-1994	NBA	82	58	24	101.1	96.8	.707	-
1994-1995	NBA	82	47	35	103.5	101.4	.573	15
1995-1996	NBA	82	48	34	102.5	100.7	.585	11

*-known as The Summit from 1975 to 1997

1996-1997	NBA	82	57	25	100.6	96.1	.695	7
1997-1998	NBA	82	41	41	98.8	99.5	.500	21
1998-1999	NBA	50	31	19	94.2	91.9	.620	6
1999-2000	NBA	82	34	48	99.5	100.3	.415	21
2000-2001	NBA	82	45	37	97.2	94.9	.549	13
2001-2002	NBA	82	28	54	92.3	97.2	.341	30
2002-2003	NBA	82	43	39	93.8	92.3	.524	17
2003-2004	NBA	82	45	37	89.8	88.0	.549	13
2004-2005	NBA	82	51	31	95.1	91.0	.622	8
2005-2006	NBA	82	34	48	90.1	91.7	.415	29
TOTAL:	35 years	2838	1458	1380				453
AVERAGE:		81	42	39	103.7	103.4	.514	13

Playoff Record

Season	GP	W	L	PPGF	PPGA	Result
1974-1975	8	3	5	108.5	107.9	Lost Conference Semifinal to Boston.
1976-1977	12	6	6	108.9	108.8	Lost Conference Final to Philadelphia.
1978-1979	2	0	2	98.5	104.5	Lost 1st Round series to Atlanta.
1979-1980	7	2	5	102.1	109.0	Lost Conference Semifinal to Boston.
1980-1981	21	12	9	98.0	98.5	Lost Championship series to Boston.
1981-1982	3	1	2	87.0	92.0	Lost 1st Round series to Seattle.
1984-1985	5	2	3	104.0	104.2	Lost 1st Round series to Utah.
1985-1986	20	13	7	111.3	107.5	Lost Championship series to Boston.
1986-1987	10	5	5	109.7	108.1	Lost Conference Semifinal to Seattle.
1987-1988	4	1	3	104.5	107.0	Lost 1st Round series to Dallas.
1988-1989	4	1	3	106.5	106.3	Lost 1st Round series to Seattle.
1989-1990	4	1	3	97.8	105.5	Lost 1st Round series to L.A. Lakers.
1990-1991	3	0	3	93.3	99.0	Lost 1st Round series to L.A. Lakers.
1992-1993	12	6	6	97.8	96.3	Lost Conference Semifinal to Seattle.
1993-1994	23	15	8	97.1	94.0	**Won NBA Championship.**
1994-1995	22	15	7	107.0	104.2	**Won NBA Championship.**
1995-1996	8	3	5	97.8	102.6	Lost Conference Semifinal to Seattle.
1996-1997	16	9	7	101.3	94.3	Lost Conference Final to Chicago.
1997-1998	5	2	3	84.6	91.4	Lost 1st Round series to Utah.
1998-1999	4	1	3	97.0	99.3	Lost 1st Round series to Lakers.
2003-2004	5	1	4	84.6	90.0	Lost 1st Round series to Lakers.
2004-2005	7	3	4	97.6	100.3	Lost 1st Round series to Dallas.
TOTAL:	205	102	103			
AVERAGE:	9	4	5	101.7	101.2	

Regular Season Individual Leaders

Season	Field Goal % (min. 70 games)		Points		Points per Game (min. 70 games)	
1971-72	R. Tomjanovich	.495	Elvin Hayes	2063	Elvin Hayes	25.2
1972-73	Otto Moore	.487	R. Tomjanovich	1560	R. Tomjanovich	19.3
1973-74	R. Tomjanovich	.536	R. Tomjanovich	1961	R. Tomjanovich	24.5
1974-75	R. Tomjanovich	.525	R. Tomjanovich	1677	R. Tomjanovich	20.7
1975-76	R. Tomjanovich	.517	Calvin Murphy	1722	Calvin Murphy	21.0
1976-77	R. Tomjanovich	.510	R. Tomjanovich	1753	R. Tomjanovich	21.6
1977-78	Calvin Murphy	.491	Calvin Murphy	1949	Calvin Murphy	25.6
1978-79	Moses Malone	.540	Moses Malone	2031	Moses Malone	24.8
1979-80	Allen Leavell	.503	Moses Malone	2119	Moses Malone	25.8
1980-81	Moses Malone	.522	Moses Malone	2222	Moses Malone	27.8
1981-82	Moses Malone	.519	Moses Malone	2520	Moses Malone	31.1

Season	Field Goal % (min. 70 games)		Points		Points per Game (min. 70 games)	
1982-83	Elvin Hayes	.476	Allen Leavell	1167	Allen Leavell	14.8
1983-84	Ralph Sampson	.523	Ralph Sampson	1720	Ralph Sampson	21.0
1984-85	H. Olajuwon	.538	Ralph Sampson	1809	Ralph Sampson	22.1
1985-86	Rodney McCray	.537	H. Olajuwon	1597	H. Olajuwon	23.5
1986-87	Rodney McCray	.552	H. Olajuwon	1755	H. Olajuwon	23.4
1987-88	H. Olajuwon	.514	H. Olajuwon	1805	H. Olajuwon	22.8
1988-89	Otis Thorpe	.542	H. Olajuwon	2034	H. Olajuwon	24.8
1989-90	Otis Thorpe	.548	H. Olajuwon	1995	H. Olajuwon	24.3
1990-91	Otis Thorpe	.556	Otis Thorpe	1435	Kenny Smith	17.7
1991-92	Otis Thorpe	.592	H. Olajuwon	1510	H. Olajuwon	21.6
1992-93	Otis Thorpe	.558	H. Olajuwon	2140	H. Olajuwon	26.1
1993-94	Otis Thorpe	.561	H. Olajuwon	2184	H. Olajuwon	27.3
1994-95	H. Olajuwon	.517	H. Olajuwon	2005	H. Olajuwon	27.8
1995-96	Mark Bryant	.543	H. Olajuwon	1936	H. Olajuwon	26.9
1996-97	H. Olajuwon	.510	H. Olajuwon	1810	H. Olajuwon	23.2
1997-98	Kevin Willis	.510	Kevin Willis	1305	Clyde Drexler	18.4
1998-99*	H. Olajuwon	.514	H. Olajuwon	945	H. Olajuwon	18.9
1999-00	S. Anderson	.473	Steve Francis	1388	Steve Francis	18.0
2000-01	Steve Francis	.451	Steve Francis	1591	Steve Francis	19.9
2001-02	Kelvin Cato	.583	Cuttino Mobley	1606	Cuttino Mobley	21.7
2002-03	Kelvin Cato	.520	Steve Francis	1703	Steve Francis	21.0
2003-04	Yao Ming	.522	Yao Ming	1431	Yao Ming	17.5
2004-05	Yao Ming	.552	Tracy McGrady	2003	Tracy McGrady	25.7
2005-06	Juwan Howard	.459	Yao Ming	1271	Juwan Howard	11.8

COACHING HISTORY: 1971-1973 Tex Winter 51-78-.395; 1972-1976 John Egan 129-152-.459; 1976-1979 Tom Nissalke 124-122-.504; 1979-1983 Del Harris 141-187-.430; 1983-1988 Bill Fitch 216-194-.527; 1988-1992 Don Chaney 164-134-.550; 1991-203 Rudy Tomjanovich 503-397-.559; 2003-present Jeff Van Gundy

HOUSTON STARS

Home City: Houston, Texas
Home Stadium: The Astrodome   Capacity: 46,000 [1967]
Origin of Name: The team was represented by the Bangu Soccer Club of Rio de Janiero.

Season	League	GP	W	L	T	GF	GA	BP	Pts	Pct
1967	USA	12	4	4	4	19	18	NA	12	.500
1968	NASL	32	14	12	6	58	41	48	150	.521
TOTAL:	2 years	44	18	16	10	77	59	48	162	
AVERAGE:		22	9	8	5	39	30	24	81	.409

Season	Goals		Points		GAA (360 Min)	
1967	Paulo Borges	6	Paulo Borges	15	Ubirajara Motta	1.45
1968	Tibor Vigh	13	Tibor Vigh	29	Leif Nielsen	1.24

COACHING HISTORY: 1967 Matim Francisco 4-4-4; 1968 Geza Henni 14-12-6

*-minimum 40 games.

HOUSTON TEXANS
(became Shreveport Steamers)

Home City: Houston Texas
Home Stadium: The Astrodome   Capacity: 44,500 [1974]
Origin of Name: The team was based in Texas.

Regular Season Record

Season	League	GP	W	L	T	PF	PA	Pct
1974	WFL	12	3	8	1	113	269	.292

Regular Season Individual Leaders

Season	Passing Yards	Receiving Yards	Rushing Yards
1974	See Shreveport Steamers		

COACHING HISTORY: Jim Garrett 3-8-1-.292

HOUSTON TEXANS

Home City: Houston Texas
Home Stadium: Reliant Stadium (2002-present)   Capacity: 69,500 [2005]
Origin of Name:

Regular Season Record

Season	League	GP	W	L	T	PF	PA	Pct
2002	NFL	16	4	12	0	213	356	.250
2003	NFL	16	5	11	0	255	380	.313
2004	NFL	16	7	9	0	309	339	.438
2005	NFL	16	2	14	0	260	431	.125
2006	NFL	16	6	10	0	267	366	.375
TOTAL:	5 years	80	24	56	0	1304	1872	
AVERAGE:		16	5	11	0	261	374	.300

Regular Season Individual Leaders

Season	Passing Yards		Receiving Yards		Rushing Yards	
2002	David Carr	2592	Corey Bradford	697	Jonathan Wells	529
2003	David Carr	2013	Andre Johnson	976	Domanick Davis	1031
2004	David Carr	3531	Andre Johnson	1142	Domanick Davis	1188
2005	David Carr	2488	Andre Johnson	688	Domanick Davis	976
2006	David Carr	2767	Andre Johnson	1147	Ron Dayne	612

COACHING HISTORY: 2002-2005 Dom Capers 18-46-0-.281; 2006-present Gary Kubiak

INDIANA FEVER

Home City: Indianapolis, Indiana
Home Court: Conseco Fieldhouse   Capacity: 18,345 [2005]
Origin of Name: The name was developed by WNBA Creative Services along with the team.

Regular Season Record

Season	League	GP	W	L	PPGF	PPGA	Pct	GB
2000	WNBA	32	9	23	69.1	71.5	.281	11
2001	WNBA	32	10	22	67.3	70.3	.313	12
2002	WNBA	32	16	16	65.5	66.5	.500	2

2003	WNBA	34	16	18	68.7	68.3	.471	9
2004	WNBA	34	15	19	64.7	66.0	.441	3
2005	WNBA	34	21	13	63.8	62.7	.618	5
2006	WNBA	34	21	13	69.5	83.0	.618	5
TOTAL:	7 years	232	108	124				47
AVERAGE:		33	15	18	66.9	69.8	.466	7

Playoff Record

Season	GP	W	L	PPGF	PPGA	Result
2002	3	1	2	65.3	71.3	Lost Conference semifinal to N.Y.
2005	4	2	2	64.0	62.8	Lost Conference final to Connecticut.
2006	2	0	2	69.5	83.0	Lost Conference semifinal to Detroit
TOTAL:	9	3	6			
AVERAGE:	3	1	2	65.7	70.1	

Regular Season Individual Leaders

Season	Field Goal % (min. 20 games)		Free Throw % (min. 20 games)		Points per Game (min. 20 games)	
2000	Kara Walters	.561	Monica Maxwell	.862	Kara Wolters	11.9
2001	Kelly Schumacher	.495	Niele Ivey	.933	Rita Williams	11.9
2002	O. Scott-Richardson	.487	Nikki McCray	.816	T. Catchings	18.6
2003	Natalie Williams	.485	Stephanie White	.938	T. Catchings	19.7
2004	Kelly Schumacher	.469	Kelly Miller	.877	T. Catchings	16.7
2005	Jurgita Streimikyte	.461	Kelly Miller	.848	T. Catchings	14.7
2006	Tamika Whitmore	.457	T. Whitmore	.821	T. Catchings	16.3

COACHING HISTORY: 2000 Anne Donovan 9-23-.281; 2001-2003 Neil Fortner 42-56-.429; 2004-present Brian Winters

INDIANA PACERS

Home City: Indianapolis, Indiana
Home Court: State Fairgrounds (1967-1974)   Capacity: 9,147 [1974]
           Market Square Arena (1974-2000)   Capacity: 16,530 [2000]
           Conseco Fieldhouse (2000-present)   Capacity: 18,345 [2006]
Origin of Name: The name was chosen by team executives.

Regular Season Record

Season	League	GP	W	L	PPGF	PPGA	Pct	GB
1967-1968	ABA	78	38	40	109.6	109.4	.487	16
1968-1969	ABA	78	44	34	119.6	115.5	.564	-
1969-1970	ABA	84	59	25	113.2	109.8	.702	-
1970-1971	ABA	84	58	26	119.1	113.1	.690	-
1971-1972	ABA	84	47	37	112.9	110.3	.560	13
1972-1973	ABA	84	51	33	114.7	112.5	.607	4
1973-1974	ABA	84	46	38	105.8	105.0	.548	5
1974-1975	ABA	84	45	39	112.8	111.7	.536	20
1975-1976	ABA	84	39	45	112.9	112.6	.464	21
1976-1977	NBA	82	36	46	106.8	108.6	.439	14
1977-1978	NBA	82	31	51	108.6	111.1	.378	17
1978-1979	NBA	82	38	44	108.6	110.2	.463	10
1979-1980	NBA	82	37	45	111.2	111.9	.451	13
1980-1981	NBA	82	44	38	107.6	106.2	.537	16
1981-1982	NBA	82	35	47	102.2	104.0	.427	20

1982-1983	NBA	82	20	62	108.7	114.5	.244	31
1983-1984	NBA	82	26	56	104.5	109.3	.317	24
1984-1985	NBA	82	22	60	108.3	114.5	.268	37
1985-1986	NBA	82	26	56	103.9	107.2	.317	31
1986-1987	NBA	82	41	41	106.1	106.7	.500	16
1987-1988	NBA	82	38	44	104.6	105.4	.463	16
1988-1989	NBA	82	28	54	106.9	111.1	.341	35
1989-1990	NBA	82	42	40	109.3	109.1	.512	17
1990-1991	NBA	82	41	41	111.7	112.1	.500	20
1991-1992	NBA	82	40	42	112.2	110.3	.488	27
1992-1993	NBA	82	41	41	107.8	106.1	.500	16
1993-1994	NBA	82	47	35	101.0	97.5	.573	10
1994-1995	NBA	82	52	30	99.2	95.5	.634	-
1995-1996	NBA	82	52	30	99.3	96.1	.634	20
1996-1997	NBA	82	39	43	95.4	94.4	.477	30
1997-1998	NBA	82	58	24	96.0	89.9	.707	4
1998-1999	NBA	50	33	17	94.7	90.9	.660	-
1999-2000	NBA	82	56	26	101.3	96.7	.683	-
2000-2001	NBA	82	41	41	92.6	92.8	.500	11
2001-2002	NBA	82	42	40	96.8	96.5	.512	8
2002-2003	NBA	82	48	34	96.8	93.3	.585	2
2003-2004	NBA	82	61	21	91.4	85.6	.744	-
2004-2005	NBA	82	44	38	93.0	92.2	.537	10
2005-2006	NBA	82	41	41	93.9	92.0	.500	23
TOTAL:	39 years	3172	1627	1545				557
AVERAGE:		81	42	40	105.3	104.5	.513	14

Playoff Record

Season	GP	W	L	PPGF	PPGA	Result
1967-1968	3	0	3	116.3	133.3	Lost 1st Round series to Pittsburgh.
1968-1969	16	9	7	127.9	123.9	Lost Championship series to Oakland.
1969-1970	15	12	3	114.6	107.5	**Won ABA Championship.**
1970-1971	11	7	4	108.2	107.8	Lost 2nd Round series to Utah.
1971-1972	20	12	8	108.4	107.3	**Won ABA Championship.**
1972-1973	18	12	6	102.5	100.8	**Won ABA Championship.**
1973-1974	14	7	7	100.4	101.6	Lost 2nd Round series to Utah.
1974-1975	18	9	9	108.8	108.4	Won Championship series to Kentucky.
1975-1976	3	1	2	105.7	105.0	Lost 1st Round series to Kentucky.
1989-1990	3	0	3	91.7	104.0	Lost 1st Round series to Detroit.
1990-1991	5	2	3	118.4	118.8	Lost 1st Round series to Boston.
1991-1992	3	0	3	107.7	115.0	Lost 1st Round series to Boston.
1992-1993	4	1	3	102.8	102.5	Lost 1st Round series to New York.
1993-1994	16	10	6	90.3	87.4	Lost Conference Final to New York.
1994-1995	17	10	7	98.6	97.5	Lost Conference Final to Orlando.
1995-1996	5	2	3	87.0	88.0	Lost 1st Round series to Atlanta.
1997-1998	16	10	6	91.8	89.5	Lost Conference Final to Chicago.
1998-1999	13	9	4	93.6	90.0	Lost Conference Final to New York.
1999-2000	23	13	10	98.1	95.4	Lost Championship series to Lakers.
2000-2001	4	1	3	87.3	93.5	Lost 1st Round series to Philadelphia.
2001-2002	5	2	3	91.6	91.4	Lost 1st Round series to New Jersey.
2002-2003	6	2	4	91.2	96.8	Lost 1st Round series to Boston.
2003-2004	16	10	6	85.5	81.1	Lost Conference Final to Detroit.
2004-2005	13	6	7	84.0	86.9	Lost Conference Semifinal to Detroit.
2005-2006	6	2	4	89.3	93.0	Lost 1st Round series to New Jersey.

TOTAL: 273   149   124

AVERAGE: 11   6   5   100.5   99.6

Regular Season Individual Leaders

Season	Field Goal % (min. 70 games)		Points		Points per Game (min. 70 games)	
1967-68	Bob Netolicky	.504	Fred Lewis	1565	Fred Lewis	20.6
1968-69	Bob Netolicky	.509	Mel Daniels	1824	Mel Daniels	24.0
1969-70	Art Becker	.521	Roger Brown	1935	Roger Brown	23.0
1970-71	Mel Daniels	.514	Mel Daniels	1723	Mel Daniels	21.0
1971-72	Mel Daniels	.505	Mel Daniels	1513	Mel Daniels	19.2
1972-73	George McGinnis	.495	George McGinnis	2261	George McGinnis	27.6
1973-74	Darnell Hillman	.498	George McGinnis	2071	George McGinnis	25.9
1974-75	Bill Knight	.534	George McGinnis	2353	George McGinnis	29.8
1975-76	Bill Knight	.494	Bill Knight	1969	Bill Knight	28.1
1976-77	Bill Knight	.493	Bill Knight	2075	Bill Knight	26.6
1977-78	Dan Roundfield	.489	Rick Sobers	1436	Rick Sobers	18.2
1978-79	Alex English	.511	Johnny Davis	1444	Johnny Davis	18.3
1979-80	Bill Knight	.533	Mickey Johnson	1566	Mickey Johnson	19.1
1980-81	Bill Knight	.533	Bill Knight	1436	Bill Knight	17.5
1981-82	Louis Orr	.497	Johnny Davis	1396	Johnny Davis	17.0
1982-83	Bill Knight	.520	Clark Kellogg	1625	Clark Kellogg	20.1
1983-84	Jerry Sichting	.532	Clark Kellogg	1506	Clark Kellogg	19.1
1984-85	Jerry Sichting	.521	Clark Kellogg	1432	Clark Kellogg	18.6
1985-86	Wayman Tisdale	.515	Herb Williams	1549	Herb Williams	19.9
1986-87	Wayman Tisdale	.513	Chuck Person	1541	Chuck Person	18.8
1987-88	Vern Fleming	.523	Chuck Person	1341	Chuck Person	17.0
1988-89	Rik Smits	.517	Chuck Person	1728	Chuck Person	21.6
1989-90	Rik Smits	.533	Reggie Miller	2016	Reggie Miller	24.6
1990-91	Vern Fleming	.531	Reggie Miller	1855	Reggie Miller	22.6
1991-92	Detlef Schrempf	.536	Reggie Miller	1695	Reggie Miller	20.7
1992-93	Dale Davis	.568	Reggie Miller	1736	Reggie Miller	21.2
1993-94	Rik Smith	.534	Reggie Miller	1574	Reggie Miller	19.9
1994-95	Dale Davis	.563	Reggie Miller	1588	Reggie Miller	19.6
1995-96	Dale Davis	.558	Reggie Miller	1606	Reggie Miller	21.1
1996-97	Dale Davis	.538	Reggie Miller	1751	Reggie Miller	21.6
1997-98	Dale Davis	.548	Reggie Miller	1578	Reggie Miller	19.5
1998-99	Dale Davis	.533	Reggie Miller	920	Reggie Miller	18.4
1999-00	Dale Davis	.502	Reggie Miller	1470	Jalen Rose	18.2
2000-01	Jeff Foster	.469	Reggie Miller	1527	Jalen Rose	20.5
2001-02	Jermaine O'Neal	.479	Jermaine O'Neal	1371	Jermaine O'Neal	19.0
2002-03	Brad Miller	.493	Jermaine O'Neal	1600	Jermaine O'Neal	20.8
2003-04	Jeff Foster	.544	Jermaine O'Neal	1566	Jermaine O'Neal	20.1
2004-05	Fred Jones	.425	Jermaine O'Neal	1068	Jermaine O'Neal	24.3
2005-06	Danny Granger	.462	Stephen Jackson	1329	Stephen Jackson	16.4

COACHING HISTORY: 1967-1969 Larry Staverman 40-47-.460; 1968-1980 Bob Leonard 529-456-.537; 1980-1984 Jack McKinney 125-203-.381; 1984-1986 George Irvine 48-116-.293; 1986-1989 Jack Ramsay 79-92-.462; 1988-1989 Mel Daniels 0-2-.000; 1988-1989 George Irvine 6-14-.300; 1988-1991 Dick Versace 51-56-.477; 1991-1993 Bob Hill 113-108-.511; 1993-1997 Larry Brown 190-138-.579; 1997-2000 Larry Bird 147-67-.687; 2000-2003 Isiah Thomas 131-115-.533; 2003-present Rick Carlisle

INDIANAPOLIS COLTS
(were Baltimore Colts)

Home City: Indianapolis, Indiana
Home Stadium: RCA Dome *   Capacity: 56,127 [2005]
Origin of Name: The team kept the same nickname when it moved from Baltimore to
Indianapolis.

Regular Season Record

Season	League	GP	W	L	T	PF	PA	Pct
1984	NFL	16	4	12	0	239	414	.250
1985	NFL	16	5	11	0	320	386	.313
1986	NFL	16	3	13	0	229	400	.188
1987	NFL	15	9	6	0	300	238	.600
1988	NFL	16	9	7	0	354	315	.563
1989	NFL	16	8	8	0	298	301	.500
1990	NFL	16	7	9	0	281	353	.438
1991	NFL	16	1	15	0	143	381	.063
1992	NFL	16	9	7	0	216	302	.563
1993	NFL	16	4	12	0	189	378	.250
1994	NFL	16	8	8	0	307	320	.500
1995	NFL	16	9	7	0	331	316	.563
1996	NFL	16	9	7	0	317	334	.563
1997	NFL	16	3	13	0	313	401	.188
1998	NFL	16	3	13	0	310	444	.188
1999	NFL	16	13	3	0	423	333	.813
2000	NFL	16	10	6	0	429	326	.625
2001	NFL	16	6	10	0	413	486	.375
2002	NFL	16	10	6	0	349	313	.349
2003	NFL	16	12	4	0	447	336	.750
2004	NFL	16	12	4	0	522	351	.750
2005	NFL	16	14	2	0	439	247	.875
2006	NFL	16	12	4	0	427	360	.750
TOTAL:	23 years	367	180	187	0	7596	8035	
AVERAGE:		16	8	8	0	330	349	.490

Playoff Record

Season	GP	W	L	PF	PA	Result
1987	1	0	1	21	38	Lost Divisional playoff to Cleveland.
1995	3	2	1	61	47	Lost Conference Final to Pittsburgh.
1996	1	0	1	14	42	Lost Wild Card Game to Pittsburgh.
1999	1	0	1	16	19	Lost Conference Semifinal to Tennessee.
2000	1	0	1	17	23	Lost Wild Card Game to Miami.
2002	1	0	1	0	41	Lost Wild Card Game to NY Jets.
2003	3	2	1	93	65	Lost Conference Final to New England.
2004	2	1	1	52	44	Lost Conf. Semifinal to New England.
2005	1	0	1	18	21	Lost Conf. Semifinal to Pittsburgh.
2006	4	4	0	105	65	**Won super Bowl LI.**
TOTAL:	18	9	9	397	405	
AVERAGE:	2	1	1	40	41	

*-known as Hoosier Dome from 1984 to 1994.

Regular Season Individual Leaders

Season	Passing Yards		Receiving Yards		Rushing Yards	
1984	Mike Pagel	1426	Ray Butler	664	Randy McMillan	705
1985	Mike Pagel	2414	Wayne Capers	438	Randy McMillan	858
1986	Jack Trudeau	2225	Bill Brooks	1131	Randy McMillan	609
1987	Jack Trudeau	1587	Bill Brooks	722	Eric Dickerson	1288
1988	Chris Chandler	1619	Bill Brooks	867	Eric Dickerson	1659
1989	Jack Trudeau	2317	Bill Brooks	919	Eric Dickerson	1311
1990	Jeff George	2152	Jessie Hester	924	Eric Dickerson	677
1991	Jeff George	2910	Bill Brooks	888	Eric Dickerson	536
1992	Jeff George	1963	Reg Langhorne	811	Anthony Johnson	592
1993	Jeff George	2526	Reg Langhorne	1038	Roosevelt Potts	711
1994	Jim Harbaugh	1440	Sean Dawkins	742	Marshall Faulk	1282
1995	Jim Harbaugh	2575	Sean Dawkins	784	Marshall Faulk	1078
1996	Jim Harbaugh	2630	Marvin Harrison	836	Marshall Faulk	587
1997	Jim Harbaugh	2060	Marvin Harrison	866	Marshall Faulk	1054
1998	Peyton Manning	3739	Marshall Faulk	908	Marshall Faulk	1319
1999	Peyton Manning	4135	Marvin Harrison	1663	Edgerrin James	1553
2000	Peyton Manning	4413	Marvin Harrison	1413	Edgerrin James	1709
2001	Peyton Manning	4131	Marvin Harrison	1524	Dominic Rhodes	1104
2002	Peyton Manning	4200	Marvin Harrison	1722	Edgerrin James	989
2003	Peyton Manning	4267	Marvin Harrison	1272	Edgerrin James	1259
2004	Peyton Manning	4557	Reggie Wayne	1210	Edgerrin James	1548
2005	Peyton Manning	3747	Marvin Harrison	1146	Edgerrin James	1506
2006	Peyton Manning	4397	Marvin Harrison	1366	Joseph Adddai	1081

COACHING HISTORY: 1984 Frank Kush 4-11-0-.267; 1984 Hal Hunter 0-1-0-.000; 1985-1986 Rod Dowhower 5-24-0-.172: 1986-1991 Ron Meyer 36-35-0-.507; 1991 Rick Venturi 1-10-0-.090; 1992-1995 Ted Marchibroda 30-34-0-.469; 1996-1997 Lindy Infante 12-20-0-.375; 1998-2001 Jim Mora 32-32-0-.500; 2002-present Tony Dungy

INDIANAPOLIS FEDERAL HOOSIERS

Home City: Indianapolis, Indiana
Home Field: West Washington Street Park *   Capacity: 20,000 [1914]
Origin of Name: The team got its nickname because this Federal League team played in the Hoosier State.

		Regular Season Record						
Season	League	GP	W	L	Pct	GB	R	OR
1914	FL	153	88	65	.575	-	762	622

Regular Season Individual Leaders

Season	Home Runs		RBI's		Wins	
1914	Benny Kauff	8	Frank LaPorte	107	Cy Falkenberg	25

COACHING HISTORY: Bill Phillips 88-65-.575

INDIANAPOLIS HOOSIERS

Home City: Indianapolis, Indiana
Home Field: South Street Park
Origin of Name: The team played in the Hoosier State.

Regular Season Record

Season	League	GP	W	L	Pct	GB	R	OR
1878	NL	60	24	36	.400	17	293	328

Regular Season Individual Leaders

Season	Home Runs		RBI's		Wins	
1878	Russ McKelvy	2	Russ McKelvy	36	Edward Nolan	13

COACHING HISTORY: John Clapp 24-36-.400

INDIANAPOLIS HOOSIERS

Home City: Indianapolis, Indiana
Home Field: Bruce Park
Origin of Name: The team played in Indiana which is known as the Hoosier State.

Regular Season Record

Season	League	GP	W	L	Pct	GB	R	OR
1884	AA	107	29	78	.271	46	462	755

Regular Season Individual Leaders

Season	Home Runs		RBI's		Wins	
1884	John Kerins	6	Not Recorded		Larry McKeon	18

COACHING HISTORY: Jim Gifford 25-59-.298; Bill Watkins 4-19-.174

INDIANAPOLIS HOOSIERS

Home City: Indianapolis, Indiana
Home Field: Bruce Park (Sundays only in 1887)
         Tinker Park (1887-1889)**
Origin of Name: See above.

Regular Season Record

Season	League	GP	W	L	Pct	GB	R	OR
1887	NL	126	37	89	.294	43	628	965
1888	NL	135	50	85	.370	36	603	731
1889	NL	134	59	75	.440	28	819	894
TOTAL:	3 years	395	146	249		107	2050	2590
AVERAGE:		132	49	83	.370	36	683	863

Regular Season Individual Leaders

Season	Home Runs		RBI's		Wins	
1887	Jerry Denny	11	Jerry Denny	97	Henry Boyle	13
1888	Jerry Denny	12	Jerry Denny	63	Henry Boyle	15
1889	Jerry Denny	18	Jerry Denny	112	Henry Boyle	21

COACHING HISTORY: 1887 Walter Burnham 6-22-.214; 1887 Fred Thomas 11-18-.379; 1887 Horace Fogel 20-49-.290; 1888 Harry Spence 50-85-.370; 1889 Frank Bancroft 25-42-.373; 1889 Jack Glassock 34-33-.507

*-also known as Federal League Park, **-also known as 7th Street Park II

INDIANAPOLIS JETS

Home City: Indianapolis, Indiana
Home Court: Butler Field House (1948-49)
Origin of Name: The team was owned by Frank Kautsky and were known as the Indianapolis Kautskys for the first three seasons..

Regular Season Record

Season	League	GP	W	L	PPGF	PPGA	Pct	GB
1945-1946	NBL	32	10	22	46.4	49.8	.313	10
1946-1947	NBL	44	27	17	56.9	53.1	.614	1
1947-1948	NBL	59	24	35	60.2	63.2	.407	18.5
1948-1949	BAA	60	18	42	74.7	79.4	.300	27
TOTAL:	4 years	195	79	116				56.5
AVERAGE:		49	20	29	61.7	63.7	.405	14

Playoff Record

Season	GP	W	L	PPGF	PPGA	Result
1946-1947	5	2	3	63.6	68.0	Lost 1st Round to Chicago.
1947-1948	4	1	3	69.0	72.8	Lost 1st Round to Tri-Cities.
TOTAL:	9	3	6			
AVERAGE:	5	2	3	66.3	70.4	

Regular Season Individual Leaders

Season	Field Goals		Free Throws		Points	
1945-46	Jerry Steiner	106	Arnie Risen	65	Jerry Steiner	270
1946-47	Arnie Risen	204	Arnie Risen	174	Arnie Risen	582
1947-48	Leo Klier	227	George Glamack	162	Keo Klier	606
1948-49	Price Brookfield	176	Price Brookfield	442	John Mandic	151

COACHING HISTORY: 1945-1946 Nat Hickey 10-22-.313; 1946-1947 Ernie Andres 21-13-.618; 1946-1947 Bob Dietz & Herm Schaefer 6-4-.600; 1947-1948 Glenn Curtis 2-2-.500; 1947-1948 Leo Klier 1-1-.500; 1947-1949 Bruce Hale 25-45-.357; 1948-1949 Burl Friddle 14-29-.326

INDIANAPOLIS KAUTSKYS

Home City: Indianapolis, Indiana
Home Court: Butler Field House
             Cathedral High
Origin of Name: The team was named after owner Frank Kautsky.

Regular Season Record

Season	League	GP	W	L	PPGF	PPGA	Pct	GB
1937-1938	NBL	13	4	9	36.3	37.7	.308	7.5
1938-1939	NBL	26	13	13	43.3	43.6	.500	3
1939-1940	NBL	28	9	19	41.5	45.6	.321	9.5
1941-1942	NBL	23	12	11	41.5	41.2	.522	7.5
TOTAL:	4 years	90	38	52				27.5
AVERAGE:		23	10	13	41.3	42.8	.388	6.5

Playoff Record

Season	GP	W	L	PPGF	PPGA	Result
1941-1942	2	0	2	40.5	52.0	Lost 1st Round to Oshkosh.

Regular Season Individual Leaders

Season	Field Goals		Free Throws		Points	
1937-38	Bob Kessler	36	Bob Kessler	31	Bob Kessler	103
1938-39	Jewell Young	96	Jewell Young	72	Jewell Young	264
1939-40	Ernie Andres	130	Jewell Young	70	Ernie Andres	292
1941-42	Jewell Young	93	Jewell Young	77	Jewell Young	263

COACHING HISTORY: 1937-1938 Frank Kautsky 4-9-.308; 1938-1940 Bob Nipper 22-32-.407; 1941-1942-(unknown)

INDIANAPOLIS OLYMPIANS

Home City: Indianapolis, Indiana
Home Court: Butler University
Origin of Name: The team consisted of the 1948 Olympic gold medal winning team from the University of Kentucky.

Regular Season Record

Season	League	GP	W	L	PPGF	PPGA	Pct	GB
1949-1950	NBA	64	39	25	85.8	82.1	.609	-
1950-1951	NBA	68	31	37	81.7	84.1	.456	13
1951-1952	NBA	66	34	32	82.9	82.8	.515	7
1952-1953	NBA	71	28	43	74.6	77.4	.394	20.5
TOTAL:	4 years	269	132	137				40.5
AVERAGE:		67	33	34	81.3	81.6	.493	10

Playoff Record

Season	GP	W	L	PPGF	PPGA	Result
1949-1950	6	3	3	78.5	81.5	Lost Division Final to Anderson.
1950-1951	3	1	2	89.7	89.3	Lost Division Semifinal to Minneapolis.
1951-1952	2	0	2	78.5	86.0	Lost Division Semifinal to Minneapolis.
1952-1953	2	0	2	74.0	83.0	Lost Division Semifinal to Minneapolis.
TOTAL:	13	4	9			
AVERAGE:	3	1	2	80.2	85.0	

Regular Season Individual Leaders

Season	Field Goal % (min. 60 games)		Points		Points per Game (min. 60 games)	
1949-1950	Alex Groza	.478	Alex Groza	1496	Alex Groza	23.4
1950-1951	Alex Groza	.470	Alex Groza	1429	Alex Groza	21.7
1951-1952	Robert Lavoy	.397	Joe Graboski	904	Joe Graboski	13.7
1952-1953	Robert Lavoy	.402	Leo Barnhorst	967	Leo Barnhorst	13.6

COACHING HISTORY: 1949-1951 Cliff Barker 70-62-.530; 1951-1953 Herm Schaeffer 62-75-.453

INDIANAPOLIS RACERS

Home City: Indianapolis, Indiana
Home Arena: Market Square Arena   Capacity: 16,042 [1975]
Origin of Name: The name was suggested because Indianapolis is the home of the most prestigious automobile race in North America, the Indianapolis 500. The name was chosen in a Name the Team Contest in which the club received over 4,000 entries.

Regular Season Record

Season	League	GP	W	L	T	GF	GA	Pts	Pct
1974-1975	WHA	78	18	57	3	216	338	39	.250
1975-1976	WHA	80	35	39	6	245	247	76	.475
1976-1977	WHA	81	36	37	8	276	305	80	.494
1977-1978	WHA	80	24	51	5	267	353	53	.331
1978-1979	WHA	25	5	18	2	78	130	12	.240
TOTAL:	5 years	344	118	202	24	1082	1373	260	
AVERAGE:		69	24	40	5	216	275	53	.378

Playoff Record

Season	GP	W	L	GF	GA	Result
1975-1976	7	3	4	15	18	Lost Quarterfinal series to New England.
1976-1977	9	5	4	33	34	Lost Semifinal series to Quebec.
TOTAL:	16	8	8	48	52	
AVERAGE:	8	4	4	24	26	

Regular Season Individual Leaders

Season	Goals		Points		Penalty Minutes	
1974-1975	Bobby Whitlock	31	Bobby Whitlock	57	Bob Fitchner	96
1975-1976	Nick Harbaruk	23	Al Karlander	45	Kim Clackson	351
	Reg Thomas	23				
1976-1977	Blair MacDonald	34	Darryl Maggs	71	Kim Clackson	168
1977-1978	Claude St. Sauveur	36	Claude St. Sauveur	78	Kevin Devine	141
1978-1979	Don Larway	8	Don Larway	18	Glenn Irwin	124
	Gary McGregor	8				

COACHING HISTORY: 1974-1975 Gerry Moore 18-57-3-.250; 1975-1977 Jacques Demers 71-76-14-.484; 1977-1978 Ron Ingram 16-31-4-.353; 1977-1978 Bill Goldsworthy 8-20-1-.293; 1978-1979 Pat Stapleton 5-18-2-.240

JACKSONVILLE BULLS

Home City: Jacksonville, Florida
Home Stadium: Gator Bowl   Capacity: 70,000 [1984]
Origin of Name: The name was chosen in a Name the Team Contest.

Regular Season Record

Season	League	GP	W	L	T	PF	PA	Pct
1984	USFL	18	6	12	0	327	455	.333
1985	USFL	18	9	9	0	407	402	.500
TOTAL:	2 years	36	15	21	0	734	857	
AVERAGE:		18	8	10	0	367	429	.417

Regular Season Individual Leaders

Season	Passing Yards		Receiving Yards		Rushing Yards	
1984	Robbie Mahfouz	2174	Gary Clark	760	Larry Mason	495
1985	Ed Luther	2792	Alton Alexis	1118	Mike Rozier	1361

COACHING HISTORY: 1984-1985 Lindy Infante 15-21-0-.417

JACKSONVILLE EXPRESS
(were Jacksonville Sharks)

Home City: Jacksonville, Florida
Home Stadium: Gator Bowl   Capacity: 70,000 [1975]
Origin of Name: Were known as Jacksonville Sharks during the 1974 season.

Regular Season Record

Season	League	GP	W	L	T	PF	PA	Pct
1974	WFL	14	4	10	0	258	358	.286
1975	WFL	11	6	5	0	227	247	.545
TOTAL:	2 years	25	10	15	0	485	605	
AVERAGE:		13	5	8	0	243	303	.400

Regular Season Individual Leaders

Season	Passing Yards		Receiving Yards		Rushing Yards	
1974	Reggie Oliver	1415	Dennis Hughes	498	Tom Durrance	658
1975	George Mira	1675	Dennis Hughes	552	Al Haywood	687

COACHING HISTORY: 1974 Bud Asher 2-4-0-.333; 1974-1975 Charlie Tate 8-11-0-.421

JACKSONVILLE JAGUARS

Home City: Jacksonville, Florida
Home Stadium: Alltel Stadium *   Capacity: 73,000 [2005]
Origin of Name: Touchdown Jacksonville!, the ownership group responsible for securing the new franchise announced December 6, 1991 that the team would be named Jaguars.

Regular Season Record

Season	League	GP	W	L	T	PF	PA	Pct
1995	NFL	16	4	12	0	275	404	.250
1996	NFL	16	9	7	0	325	335	.563
1997	NFL	16	11	5	0	394	318	.688
1998	NFL	16	11	5	0	392	338	.688
1999	NFL	16	14	2	0	396	217	.875
2000	NFL	16	7	9	0	367	327	.438
2001	NFL	16	6	10	0	294	286	.375
2002	NFL	16	6	10	0	328	315	.375
2003	NFL	16	5	11	0	276	331	.313
2004	NFL	16	9	7	0	261	280	.563
2005	NFL	16	12	4	0	361	269	.750
2006	NFL	16	8	8	0	371	274	.500
TOTAL:	12 years	192	102	90	0	4040	3694	
AVERAGE:		16	9	7	0	337	308	.531

Playoff Record

Season	GP	W	L	PF	PA	Result
1996	3	2	1	66	74	Lost Conference Final to New England.
1997	1	0	1	17	42	Lost Wild Card Game to Denver.
1998	2	1	1	49	44	Lost Conference Semifinal to N.Y. Jets.

*-built on the site of and incorporated parts of the old Gator Bowl Stadium. Named Jacksonville Municipal Stadium from 1995 to 1996.

1999	2	1	1	76	40	Lost Conference Final to Tennessee.
2005	1	0	1	3	28	Lost 1st Round playoff to New England.
TOTAL:	9	4	5	211	228	
AVERAGE:	2	1	1	42	46	

Regular Season Individual Leaders

Season	Passing Yards		Receiving Yards		Rushing Yards	
1995	Mark Brunell	2168	Willie Jackson	589	James Stewart	525
1996	Mark Brunell	4367	Jimmy Smith	1244	James Stewart	723
1997	Mark Brunell	3281	Jimmy Smith	1324	Natrone Means	823
1998	Mark Brunell	2601	Jimmy Smith	1182	Fred Taylor	1223
1999	Mark Brunell	3060	Jimmy Smith	1636	James Stewart	931
2000	Mark Brunell	3640	Jimmy Smith	1213	Fred Taylor	1399
2001	Mark Brunell	3309	Jimmy Smith	1373	Stacey Mack	877
2002	Mark Brunell	2788	Jimmy Smith	1027	Fred Taylor	1314
2003	Byron Leftwich	2819	Jimmy Smith	805	Fred Taylor	1572
2004	Byron Leftwich	2941	Jimmy Smith	1172	Fred Taylor	1224
2005	Byron Leftwich	2123	Jimmy Smith	1023	Fred Taylor	787
2006	David Garrard	1735	Matt Jones	643	Fred Taylor	1146

COACHING HISTORY: 1995-2002 Tom Coughlin 68-60-0-.531; 2003-present Jack Del Rio

JACKSONVILLE TEAMEN
(were New England Teamen)

Home City: Jacksonville, Florida
Home Field: Gator Bowl   Capacity: 70,000 [1982]
Origin of Name: The team kept the same nickname when it moved from the New England area to Jacksonville.

Regular Season Record

Season	League	GP	W	L	GF	GA	BP	Pts	Pct
1981	NASL	32	18	14	51	46	41	141	.294
1982	NASL	32	11	21	41	71	39	105	.219
TOTAL:	2 years	64	29	35	92	117	80	246	
AVERAGE:		32	15	17	46	59	40	123	.256

Playoff Record

Season	GP	W	L	GF	GA	Result
1981	5	3	2	8	8	Lost 2nd Round series to San Diego.

Regular Season Individual Leaders

Season	Goals		Points		GAA (360 Min)	
1981	Alan Green	16	Alan Green	38	Arnold Mausser	1.21
1982	Ricardo Alonso	21	Ricardo Alonso	46		

COACHING HISTORY: 1981-1982 Noel Cantwell 29-35-.256

KANKAKEE GALLAGHER TROJANS

Home City: Kankakee, Illinois
Home Court: South Indiana Street Armory
Origin of Name: Most of the players were from the Gallagher Business School and the team adapted the name of the school as its own.

Regular Season Record

Season	League	GP	W	L	PPGF	PPGA	Pct	GB
1937-1938	NBL	14	3	11	33.3	53.3	.214	9

Regular Season Individual Leaders

Season	Field Goals		Free Throws		Points	
1937-38	Fred Grafft	33	Fred Grafft	20	Fred Grafft	86

COACHING HISTORY: Don Betourne 3-11-.214

KANSAS CITY ATHLETICS
(were Philadelphia Athletics)
(became Oakland Athletics)

Home City: Kansas City, Missouri
Home Field: Municipal Stadium   Capacity: 32,561 [1964]
Origin of Name: The team kept the same nickname when it moved from Philadelphia.

Regular Season Record

Season	League	GP	W	L	Pct	GB	R	OR
1955	AL	154	63	91	.409	33	638	911
1956	AL	154	52	102	.338	45	619	831
1957	AL	153	59	94	.386	38.5	563	710
1958	AL	154	73	81	.474	19	642	713
1959	AL	154	66	88	.429	28	681	760
1960	AL	154	58	96	.377	39	615	756
1961	AL	161	61	100	.379	47.5	683	863
1962	AL	162	72	90	.444	24	745	837
1963	AL	162	73	89	.451	31.5	615	704
1964	AL	162	57	105	.352	42	621	836
1965	AL	162	59	103	.364	43	585	755
1966	AL	160	74	86	.463	23	564	648
1967	AL	161	62	99	.385	29.5	533	660
TOTAL:	13 years	2053	829	1224		443	8104	9984
AVERAGE:		158	64	94	.404	34	623	768

Regular Season Individual Leaders

Season	Home Runs		RBI's		Wins	
1955	Gus Zernial	30	Gus Zernial	84	Art Ditmar	12
1956	Harry Simpson	21	Harry Simpson	105	Art Ditmar	12
1957	Gus Zernial	27	Gus Zernial	69	Virgil Trucks	9
					Tom Morgan	9
1958	Bob Cerv	38	Bob Cerv	104	Ned Garver	12
1959	Bob Cerv	20	Bob Cerv	87	Bud Daley	16
1960	Norm Siebern	19	Norm Siebern	69	Bud Daley	16
1961	Norm Siebern	18	Norm Siebern	98	Norm Bass	11
1962	Norm Siebern	25	Norm Siebern	117	Ed Rakow	14
1963	Norm Siebern	16	Norm Siebern	83	Dave Wickersham	12
					Orlando Pena	12
1964	Rocky Colavito	34	Rocky Colavito	102	Orlando Pena	12
1965	Ken Harrelson	23	Ken Harrelson	66	Rollie Sheldon	10
					Fred Talbot	10
1966	Roger Repoz	11	Dick Green	62	Lew Krausse	14
1967	Rick Monday	14	Rick Monday	58	James Hunter	13

COACHING HISTORY: 1955-1957 Lou Boudreau 151-260-.367; 1957-1959 Harry Craft 162-196-.453; 1960 Bob Elliot 58-96-.377; 1961 Joe Gordon 26-43-.377; 1961-1962 Hank Bauer 107-147-.421; 1963-1964 Ed Lopat 90-124-.421; 1964-1965 Mel McGaha 45-91-.331; 1965 Haywood Sullivan 54-82-.397; 1966-1967 Alvin Dark 126-155-.448: 1967 Luke Appling 10-30-.250

KANSAS CITY BLUES
(were New York Metropolitans)

Home City: Kansas City, Missouri
Home Field: Association Park I (1888)
          Exposition Park (1889)
Origin of Name: As with most teams with colors in their name the team was probably named after the color of their uniforms.

Regular Season Record

Season	League	GP	W	L	Pct	GB	R	OR
1888	AA	132	43	89	.326	47.5	579	896
1889	AA	137	55	82	.401	38	852	1031
TOTAL:	2 years	269	98	171		85.5	1431	1927
AVERAGE:		135	49	86	.364	43	716	964

Regular Season Individual Leaders

Season	Home Runs		RBI's		Wins	
1888	Jim McTamany	4	James Davis	61	Henry Porter	18
1889	James Burns	5	James Burns	97	Parke Swartzel	19
					James Conway	19

COACHING HISTORY: 1888 Dave Rowe 14-35-.286; 1888 Sam Barkley 26-43-.377; 1888-1889 Bill Watkins 58-93-.384

KANSAS CITY CHIEFS
(were Dallas Texans)

Home City: Kansas City, Missouri
Home Stadium: Municipal Stadium (1963-1971)   Capacity: 47,000 [1971]
          Arrowhead Stadium (1972-present)   Capacity: 79,451 [2005]
Origin of Name: The team was named by owner Lamar Hunt.

Regular Season Record

Season	League	GP	W	L	T	PF	PA	Pct
1963	AFL	14	5	7	2	347	263	.429
1964	AFL	14	7	7	0	366	306	.500
1965	AFL	14	7	5	2	322	285	.571
1966	AFL	14	11	2	1	448	276	.821
1967	AFL	14	9	5	0	408	254	.643
1968	AFL	14	12	2	0	371	170	.857
1969	AFL	14	11	3	0	359	177	.786
1970	NFL	14	7	5	2	272	244	.571
1971	NFL	14	10	3	1	302	208	.750
1972	NFL	14	8	6	0	287	254	.571
1973	NFL	14	7	5	2	231	192	.571
1974	NFL	14	5	9	0	233	293	.357

1975	NFL	14	5	9	0	282	341	.357
1976	NFL	14	5	9	0	290	376	.357
1977	NFL	14	2	12	0	225	349	.143
1978	NFL	16	4	12	0	243	327	.250
1979	NFL	16	7	9	0	238	262	.438
1980	NFL	16	8	8	0	319	336	.500
1981	NFL	16	9	7	0	343	290	.563
1982	NFL	9	3	6	0	176	184	.333
1983	NFL	16	6	10	0	386	367	.375
1984	NFL	16	8	8	0	314	324	.500
1985	NFL	16	6	10	0	317	360	.375
1986	NFL	16	10	6	0	358	326	.625
1987	NFL	15	4	11	0	273	388	.267
1988	NFL	16	4	11	1	254	320	.281
1989	NFL	16	8	7	1	318	286	.531
1990	NFL	16	11	5	0	369	257	.688
1991	NFL	16	10	6	0	322	252	.625
1992	NFL	16	10	6	0	348	282	.625
1993	NFL	16	11	5	0	328	291	.688
1994	NFL	16	9	7	0	319	298	.563
1995	NFL	16	13	3	0	358	241	.813
1996	NFL	16	9	7	0	297	300	.563
1997	NFL	16	13	3	0	375	232	.813
1998	NFL	16	7	9	0	327	363	.438
1999	NFL	16	9	7	0	390	322	.563
2000	NFL	16	7	9	0	355	354	.438
2001	NFL	16	6	10	0	320	344	.375
2002	NFL	16	8	8	0	467	399	.500
2003	NFL	16	13	3	0	484	332	.813
2004	NFL	16	7	9	0	483	435	.438
2005	NFL	16	10	6	0	403	325	.625
2006	NFL	16	9	7	0	331	315	.563
TOTAL:	44 years	666	350	304	12	14558	13100	
AVERAGE:		15	8	7	0	331	298	.535

Playoff Record

Season	GP	W	L	PF	PA	Result
1966	2	1	1	41	42	Lost Super Bowl to Green Bay.
1968	1	0	1	6	41	Lost Division playoff to Oakland.
1969	3	3	0	53	20	**Won Super Bowl IV.**
1971	1	0	1	24	27	Lost Division playoff to Miami.
1986	1	0	1	15	35	Lost 1st Round playoff to N.Y. Jets.
1990	1	0	1	16	17	Lost Wild Card Game to Miami.
1991	2	1	1	24	43	Lost Conference Semifinal to Buffalo.
1992	1	0	1	0	17	Lost Wild Card Game to San Diego.
1993	3	2	1	68	74	Lost Conference Final to Buffalo.
1994	1	0	1	17	27	Lost 1st Round game to Miami.
1995	1	0	1	7	10	Lost Conference Semifinal to Indianapolis.
1997	1	0	1	10	14	Lost Conference Semifinal to Denver.
2003	1	0	1	31	38	Lost Conference Semifinal to Indianapolis.
2006	1	0	1	8	23	Lost Wild Card Game to Indianapolis.
TOTAL:	20	7	13	320	428	
AVERAGE:	2	1	1	23	31	

Regular Season Individual Leaders

Season	Passing Yards		Receiving Yards		Rushing Yards	
1963	Len Dawson	2389	Chris Burford	824	Curtis McClinton	568
1964	Len Dawson	2879	Frank Jackson	943	Abner Haynes	697
1965	Len Dawson	2262	Curtis McClinton	590	Curtis McClinton	661
1966	Len Dawson	2527	Otis Taylor	1297	Mike Garrett	801
1967	Len Dawson	2651	Otis Taylor	958	Mike Garrett	1087
1968	Len Dawson	2109	Frank Pitts	655	Robert Holmes	866
1969	Len Dawson	1323	Otis Taylor	696	Mike Garrett	732
1970	Len Dawson	1876	Otis Taylor	618	Ed Podolak	749
1971	Len Dawson	2504	Otis Taylor	1110	Ed Podolak	708
1972	Len Dawson	1835	Otis Taylor	821	Ed Podolak	615
1973	Mike Livingston	916	Otis Taylor	565	Ed Podolak	721
1974	Len Dawson	1573	Barry Pearson	387	Woody Green	509
1975	Mike Livingston	1245	Barry Pearson	608	Woody Green	611
1976	Mike Livingston	2682	Walter White	808	MacArthur Lane	542
1977	Mike Livingston	1823	Walter White	674	Ed Podolak	550
1978	Mike Livingston	1573	Tony Reed	483	Tony Reed	1053
1979	Steve Fuller	1484	J.T. Smith	444	Ted McKnight	755
1980	Steve Fuller	2250	Henry Marshall	799	Ted McKnight	693
1981	Bill Kenney	1983	J.T. Smith	852	Joe Delaney	1121
1982	Bill Kenney	1192	Henry Marshall	549	Joe Delaney	380
1983	Bill Kenney	4348	Carlos Carson	1351	Billy Jackson	499
1984	Bill Kenney	2098	Carlos Carson	1078	Herman Heard	684
1985	Bill Kenney	2536	Stephone Paige	943	Herman Heard	595
1986	Bill Kenney	1922	Stephone Paige	829	Mike Pruitt	448
1987	Bill Kenney	2107	Carlos Carson	1044	Christian Okoye	660
1988	Steve DeBerg	2935	Stephone Paige	902	Christian Okoye	473
1989	Steve DeBerg	2529	Stephone Paige	759	Christian Okoye	1480
1990	Steve DeBerg	3444	Stephone Paige	1021	Barry Ward	1015
1991	Steve DeBerg	2965	Tim Barnett	564	Christian Okoye	1031
1992	Dave Krieg	3115	Willie Davis	756	Barry Ward	607
1993	Joe Montana	2144	Willie Davis	909	Marcus Allen	764
1994	Joe Montana	3283	Willie Davis	822	Marcus Allen	709
1995	Steve Bono	3121	Willie Davis	527	Marcus Allen	890
1996	Steve Bono	2572	Chris Penn	628	Marcus Allen	830
1997	Elvis Grbac	1943	Andre Rison	1092	Greg Hill	550
1998	Rich Gannon	2305	D. Alexander	992	Donnell Bennett	527
1999	Elvis Grbac	3389	Tony Gonzalez	849	Donnell Bennett	627
2000	Elvis Grbac	4169	D. Alexander	1391	Tony Richardson	697
2001	Trent Green	3783	Tony Gonzalez	917	Priest Holmes	1555
2002	Trent Green	3690	Eddie Kennison	906	Priest Holmes	1615
2003	Trent Green	4039	Tony Gonzalez	916	Priest Holmes	1420
2004	Trent Green	4591	Tony Gonzalez	1258	Priest Holmes	892
2005	Trent Green	4014	Eddie Kennison	1102	Larry Johnson	1750
2006	Damon Huard	1878	Tony Gonzalez	900	Larry Johnson	1789

COACHING HISTORY: 1963-1974 Hank Stram 99-59-10-.619; 1975-1977 Paul Wiggin 11-24-0-.314; 1977 Tom Bettio 1-6-0-.143; 1978-1982 Marv Levy 31-42-0-.425; 1983-1986 John Mackovic 30-34-0-.469; 1987-1988 Frank Gansz 8-22-1-.274; 1989-1998 Marty Schottenheimer 101-58-1-.634; 1999-2000 Gunther Cunningham 16-16-0-.500; 2001-2005 Dick Vermeil 44-36-0-.550; 2006-present Herm Edwards

KANSAS CITY COWBOYS

Home City: Kansas City, Missouri
Home Field: Association Park I
Origin of Name: The name was chosen to reflect the western heritage of the area.

		Regular Season Record						
Season	League	GP	W	L	Pct	GB	R	OR
1886	NL	121	30	91	.248	58.5	494	872

		Regular Season Individual Leaders				
Season	Home Runs		RBI's		Wins	
1886	William McQuery	4	Dave Rowe	57	Stump Weidman	12
	Al Myers	4			Jim Whitney	12

COACHING HISTORY: Dave Rowe 30-91-.248

KANSAS CITY COWBOYS

Home City: Kansas City, Missouri
Home Stadium: The team played only road games.
Origin of Name: See Above.

		Regular Season Record						
Season	League	GP	W	L	T	PF	PA	Pct
1924	NFL	9	2	7	0	46	124	.222
1925	NFL	8	2	5	1	65	97	.313
1926	NFL	11	8	3	0	76	53	.727
TOTAL:	3 years	28	12	15	1	187	274	
AVERAGE:		9	4	5	0	62	91	.446

	Regular Season Individual Leaders					
Season	Passing Yards		Receiving Yards		Rushing Yards	
1924	Roy Andrews	144	Chuck Corgan	197	Charlie Hill	121
1925	Phil White	204	Chuck Corgan	148	Charlie Hill	60
1926	Al Bloodgood	43	Glen Spears	35	Al Bloodgood	72

COACHING HISTORY: LeRoy Andrews 12-15-1-.446

KANSAS CITY KINGS
(were Kansas City-Omaha Kings)
(became Sacramento Kings)

Home City: Kansas City, Missouri
Home Court: Kemper Arena   Capacity: 16,642 [1984]
Origin of Name: The team kept the same nickname from its previous locations.

		Regular Season Record						
Season	League	GP	W	L	PPGF	PPGA	Pct	GB
1975-1976	NBA	82	31	51	103.3	106.2	.378	7
1976-1977	NBA	82	40	42	107.7	106.8	.488	10
1977-1978	NBA	82	31	51	109.5	111.4	.378	17
1978-1979	NBA	82	48	34	113.1	110.2	.585	-
1979-1980	NBA	82	47	35	108.0	104.9	.573	2
1980-1981	NBA	82	40	42	106.9	106.9	.488	12
1981-1982	NBA	82	30	52	107.1	110.2	.366	18

1982-1983	NBA	82	45	37	113.8	112.3	.549	8
1983-1984	NBA	82	38	44	110.0	111.5	.463	7
1984-1985	NBA	82	31	51	114.8	117.5	.378	21
TOTAL:	10 years	820	381	439				102
AVERAGE:		82	38	44	109.4	109.8	.465	10

Playoff Record

Season	GP	W	L	PPGF	PPGA	Result
1978-1979	5	1	4	99.2	105.8	Lost Conference Semifinal to Phoenix.
1979-1980	3	1	2	99.3	102.0	Lost 1st Round series to Phoenix.
1980-1981	15	7	8	91.7	94.9	Lost Conference Final to Houston.
1983-1984	3	0	3	103.0	111.0	Lost 1st Round series to Los Angeles.
TOTAL:	26	9	17			
AVERAGE:	6	2	4	98.3	103.4	

Regular Season Individual Leaders

Season	Field Goal % (min. 70 games)		Points		Points per Game (min. 70 games)	
1975-76	Ollie Johnson	.513	Nate Archibald	1935	Nate Archibald	24.8
1976-77	Brian Taylor	.504	Ron Boone	1818	Ron Boone	22.2
1977-78	Scott Wedman	.509	Ron Boone	1448	Scott Wedman	17.7
					Ron Boone	17.7
1978-79	Bill Robinzine	.548	Otis Birdsong	1778	Otis Birdsong	21.7
1979-80	Reggie King	.515	Otis Birdsong	1858	Otis Birdsong	22.7
1980-81	Leon Douglas	.573	Otis Birdsong	1747	Otis Birdsong	24.6
1981-82	Steve Johnson	.613	Mike Woodson	1221	Mike Woodson	16.1
1982-83	Steve Johnson	.624	Eddie Johnson	1621	Larry Drew	20.1
1983-84	Joe Meriweather	.532	Eddie Johnson	1794	Eddie Johnson	21.9
1984-85	Otis Thorpe	.600	Eddie Johnson	1876	Eddie Johnson	22.9

COACHING HISTORY: 1975-1978 Phil Johnson 84-117-.418; 1977-1978 Larry Staverman 18-27-.400; 1978-1984 Lowell "Cotton" Fitzsimmons 248-244-.504; 1984-1985 Jack McKinney 1-8-.111; 1984-1985 Phil Johnson 30-43-.411.

KANSAS CITY-OMAHA KINGS
(were Cincinnati Royals)
(became Kansas City Kings)

Home City: Kansas City, Missouri
           Omaha, Nebraska
Home Court: Municipal Auditorium (Kansas City)   Capacity: 9,929 [1975]
             Omaha Civic Auditorium (Omaha)   Capacity: 9,144 [1975]
Origin of Name: The name was chosen in a Name the Team Contest.

Regular Season Record

Season	League	GP	W	L	PPGF	PPGA	Pct	GB
1972-1973	NBA	82	36	46	107.6	110.5	.439	24
1973-1974	NBA	82	33	49	102.0	105.8	.402	26
1974-1975	NBA	82	44	38	101.4	101.6	.537	3
TOTAL:	3 years	246	113	133				53
AVERAGE:		82	38	44	103.7	106.0	.459	18

Playoff Record

Season	GP	W	L	PPGF	PPGA	Result
1974-1975	6	2	4	91.8	98.0	Lost Conference Semifinal to Chicago.

Regular Season Individual Leaders

Season	Field Goal % (min. 70 games)		Points		Points per Game (min. 70 games)	
1972-73	Matt Guokas	.570	Nate Archibald	2719	Nate Archibald	34.0
1973-74	Don Kojis	.478	Jimmy Walker	1423	Jimmy Walker	19.8
1974-75	Jimmy Walker	.475	Nate Archibald	2170	Nate Archibald	26.5

COACHING HISTORY: 1972-1974 Bob Cousy 42-60-.412; 1973-1974 Draff Young 0-4-.000; 1973-1975 Phil Johnson 71-69-.507

KANSAS CITY PACKERS

Home City: Kansas City, Missouri
Home Field: Federal League Park ** Capacity: 12,000 [1914]
Origin of Name: The name was chosen due to the fact Kansas City is the home of a major livestock show and is well known for its packing plants.

Regular Season Record

Season	League	GP	W	L	Pct	GB	R	OR
1914	FL	151	67	84	.444	20	644	683
1915	FL	153	81	72	.529	5.5	547	551
TOTAL:	2 years	304	148	156		25.5	1191	1234
AVERAGE:		152	74	78	.487	13	596	617

Regular Season Individual Leaders

Season	Home Runs		RBI's		Wins	
1914	Bill Kenworthy	15	Bill Kenworthy	91	Gene Packard	20
1915	George Perring	7	George Perring	68	Nick Cullop	22

COACHING HISTORY: 1914-1915 George Stovall 148-156-.487

KANSAS CITY ROYALS

Home City: Kansas City, Missouri
Home Field: Municipal Stadium (1969-1972) Capacity: 35,561 [1971]
Ewing Kauffman Stadium (1973-present)** Capacity: 40,793 [2006]
Origin of Name: The name was chosen in a Name the Team Contest.

Regular Season Record

Season	League	GP	W	L	Pct	GB	R	OR
1969	AL	162	69	93	.426	28	586	688
1970	AL	162	65	97	.401	33	611	705
1971	AL	161	85	76	.528	16	603	566
1972	AL	154	76	78	.494	16.5	580	545
1973	AL	162	88	74	.543	6	754	752
1974	AL	162	77	85	.475	13	667	662
1975	AL	162	91	71	.562	7	710	649

*-also known as Gordon and Koppel Field
**-known as Royals Stadium from 1973 to 1992

1976	AL	162	90	72	.556	-	713	611
1977	AL	162	102	60	.630	-	822	651
1978	AL	160	90	70	.568	-	743	634
1979	AL	162	85	77	.525	3	851	816
1980	AL	162	97	65	.599	-	809	694
1981	AL	103	50	53	.485	NA	397	405
1982	AL	162	90	72	.556	3	784	717
1983	AL	162	79	83	.488	20	696	767
1984	AL	162	84	78	.519	-	673	686
1985	AL	162	91	71	.562	-	687	639
1986	AL	162	76	86	.469	16	654	673
1987	AL	162	83	79	.512	2	715	691
1988	AL	161	84	77	.522	19.5	704	648
1989	AL	162	92	70	.568	7	690	635
1990	AL	161	75	86	.466	27.5	707	709
1991	AL	162	82	80	.506	13	727	722
1992	AL	162	72	90	.444	24	610	667
1993	AL	162	84	78	.519	10	675	694
1994	AL	115	64	51	.557	4	574	532
1995	AL	144	70	74	.486	30	629	691
1996	AL	161	75	86	.466	24	746	786
1997	AL	161	67	94	.416	19	747	820
1998	AL	161	72	89	.447	16.5	715	899
1999	AL	161	64	97	.398	32.5	856	921
2000	AL	162	77	85	.475	18	879	930
2001	AL	162	65	97	.401	26	728	859
2002	AL	162	62	100	.383	32.5	737	891
2003	AL	162	83	79	.512	7	836	867
2004	AL	162	58	104	.358	34	720	905
2005	AL	162	56	106	.346	43	701	935
2006	AL	162	62	100	.383	34	757	971
TOTAL:	38 years	6015	2932	3083		585	26793	27633
AVERAGE:		158	77	81	.487	15.5	705	727

Playoff Record

Season	GP	W	L	R	OR	Result
1976	5	2	3	24	23	Lost ALCS to New York.
1977	5	2	3	22	21	Lost ALCS to New York.
1978	4	1	3	17	19	Lost ALCS to New York.
1980	9	5	4	37	33	Lost World Series to Philadelphia.
1981	3	0	3	2	10	Lost Divisional playoff to Oakland.
1984	3	0	3	4	14	Lost ALCS to Detroit.
1985	14	8	6	54	38	**Won World Series**.
TOTAL:	43	18	25	160	158	
AVERAGE:	6	2	4	23	23	

Season	Home Runs		RBI's		Wins	
1969	Ed Kirkpatrick	14	Joe Foy	71	Wally Bunker	12
1970	Bob Oliver	27	Bob Oliver	99	Jim Rooker	10
1971	Amos Otis	15	Amos Otis	79	Dick Drago	17
1972	John Mayberry	25	John Mayberry	100	Dick Drago	12
					Paul Splittorff	12
1973	John Mayberry	26	John Mayberry	100	Paul Splittorff	20

Season	Home Runs		RBI's		Wins	
	Amos Otis	26				
1974	John Mayberry	22	Hal McRae	88	Steve Busby	22
1975	John Mayberry	34	John Mayberry	106	Steve Busby	18
1976	Amos Otis	18	John Mayberry	95	Dennis Leonard	17
1977	John Mayberry	23	Al Cowens	112	Dennis Leonard	20
	Al Cowens	23				
1978	Amos Otis	22	Amos Otis	96	Dennis Leonard	21
1979	George Brett	23	Darrell Porter	112	Paul Splittorff	15
1980	George Brett	24	George Brett	118	Dennis Leonard	20
1981	Willie Aikens	17	Amos Otis	57	Dennis Leonard	13
1982	Hal McRae	27	Hal McRae	133	Larry Gura	18
1983	George Brett	25	George Brett	93	Paul Splittorff	13
1984	Steve Balboni	28	Steve Balboni	77	Bud Black	17
1985	Steve Balboni	36	George Brett	112	Bret Saberhagen	20
1986	Steve Balboni	29	Steve Balboni	88	Charlie Leibrandt	14
1987	Danny Tartabull	34	Danny Tartabull	101	Bret Saberhagen	18
1988	Danny Tartabull	26	George Brett	103	Mark Gubicza	20
1989	Bo Jackson	32	Bo Jackson	105	Bret Saberhagen	23
1990	Bo Jackson	28	George Brett	87	Steve Farr	13
1991	Danny Tartabull	31	Danny Tartabull	100	Bret Saberhagen	13
					Kevin Appier	13
1992	Mike Macfarlane	17	Gregg Jefferies	75	Kevin Appier	15
1993	Mike Macfarlane	20	George Brett	75	Kevin Appier	18
1994	Bob Hamelin	24	Bob Hamelin	65	David Cone	16
1995	Gary Gaetti	35	Gary Gaetti	96	Kevin Appier	15
1996	Craig Paquette	22	Craig Paquette	67	Tim Belcher	15
1997	Chili Davis	30	Jeff King	112	Tim Belcher	13
1998	Dean Palmer	34	Dean Palmer	119	Tim Belcher	14
1999	Jermaine Dye	38	Jermaine Dye	119	Jeff Suppan	10
					Jose Rosado	10
2000	Jermaine Dye	33	Mike Sweeney	144	Jeff Suppan	10
2001	Mike Sweeney	29	Carlos Beltran	101	Jeff Suppan	10
2002	Carlos Beltran	29	Carlos Beltran	105	Paul Byrd	17
2003	Carlos Beltran	26	Carlos Beltran	100	Brian Anderson	14
2004	Mike Sweeney	22	Mike Sweeney	79	Jimmy Gobble	9
					Darrell May	9
2005	Mike Sweeney	21	Emil Brown	86	Runelvys Hernandez	8
2006	Mark Teahen	18	Emil Brown	81	Mark Redman	11

COACHING RECORD: 1969 Joe Gordon 69-93-.426; 1970 Charlie Metro 19-35-.352; 1970-1972 Bob Lemon 207-216-.489; 1973-1975 Jack McKeon 215-205-.512; 1975-1979 Dorrel "Whitey" Herzog 408-304-.573; 1980-1981 Jim Frey 127-105-.547; 1981-1986 Dick Howser 405-365-.526; 1986 Mike Ferraro 35-38-.479; 1987 Bill Gardner 62-64-.493; 1987-1991 John Wathan 287-270-.515; 1991 Bob Schaeffer 1-0-1.000; 1991-1994 Hal McRae 286-277-.508; 1995-1997 Bob Boone 181-206-.468; 1997-2002 Tony Muser 325-423-.434; 2002 John Mizerock 5-9-.357; 2002-2005 Tony Pena 203-296-.407; 2005-present Buddy Bell

KANSAS CITY SCOUTS
(became Colorado Rockies)

Home City: Kansas City, Missouri
Home Arena: Crosby-Kemper Arena   Capacity: 16,500 [1975]
Origin of Name: The team was named in honor of the scouts who left with the wagon trains going westward from Kansas City.

Regular Season Record

Season	League	GP	W	L	T	GF	GA	Pts	Pct
1974-1975	NHL	80	15	54	11	184	328	41	.256
1975-1976	NHL	80	12	56	12	190	351	36	.225
TOTAL:	2 years	160	27	110	23	374	679	77	
AVERAGE:		80	14	55	11	187	340	39	.241

Regular Season Individual Leaders

Season	Goals		Points		Penalty Minutes	
1974-1975	Wilf Paiement	26	Simon Nolet	58	Wilf Paiement	101
	Simon Nolet	26				
1975-1976	Guy Charron	27	Guy Charron	71	Steve Durbano	209

COACHING HISTORY: 1974-1976 Armand Guidolin 26-84-15-.268; 1975-1976 Sid Abel 0-3-0-.000; 1975-1976 Ed Bush 1-23-8-.156

KANSAS CITY SPURS
(were Chicago Spurs)

Home City: Kansas City, Missouri
Home Stadium: Municipal Stadium (1968)
                    Pembroke County Day School Stadium
Origin of Name: The team kept the same nickname after moving from Chicago.

Regular Season Record

Season	League	GP	W	L	T	GF	GA	BP	Pts	Pct
1968	NASL	32	16	11	5	61	43	47	158	.549
1969	NASL	16	10	2	4	53	28	38	110	.764
1970	NASL	24	8	10	6	42	44	34	100	.463
TOTAL:	3 years	72	34	23	15	156	115	119	368	
AVERAGE:		24	11	8	5	52	38	40	123	.568

Playoff Record

Season	GP	W	L	T	GF	GA	Result
1968	2	0	1	1	1	2	Lost Conference Final to San Diego.

Regular Season Individual Leaders

Season	Goals		Points		GAA (360 Min)	
1968	Eric Barber	16	Eric Barber	32	Bert Hoogerman	1.28
1969	Jorge Benitez	15	Jorge Benitez	35	Leonel Conde	1.75
1970	Manfred Seissler	11	Manfred Seissler	29	Leonel Conde	1.65

COACHING HISTORY: 1968-1969 Janos Bedl 26-13-9-.620; 1970 Alan Rogers 8-10-6-.463

KANSAS CITY UNIONS

Home City: Kansas City, Missouri
Home Field: Athletic Park   Capacity: 4,000
Origin of Name: Most of the teams in the league adopted the name of the league as their own.

Regular Season Record

Season	League	GP	W	L	Pct	GB	R	OR
1884	UA	79	16	63	.203	61	311	618

Regular Season Individual Leaders

Season	Home Runs	RBI's	Wins	
1884	5 tied at 1	Not Recorded	Ernie Hickman	4
			Bob Black	4

COACHING HISTORY: Ted Sullivan 16-63-.203

KANSAS CITY WIZARDS

Home City: Kansas City, Missouri
Home Field: Arrowhead Stadium (1996-present)   Capacity: 79,451 [2005]
Origin of Name: Chosen in a Name the Team Contest. Originally "Wiz" the name was expanded to Wizards before the start of the first season as an unintentional tie-in to the movie The Wizard of Oz.

Season	League	GP	W	L	T	SOW	GF	GA	Pts
1996	MLS	32	17	15	NA	5	61	63	41
1997	MLS	32	21	11	NA	7	57	51	49
1998	MLS	32	12	20	NA	2	45	50	32
1999	MLS	32	8	24	NA	2	33	53	20
2000	MLS	32	16	7	9	NA	47	29	57
2001	MLS	27	11	13	3	NA	33	53	36
2002	MLS	28	9	10	9	NA	37	45	36
2003	MLS	30	11	10	9	NA	48	44	42
2004	MLS	30	14	9	7	NA	38	30	49
2005	MLS	32	11	9	12	NA	52	44	45
2006	MLS	32	10	14	8	NA	43	45	38
TOTAL:	11 years	339	140	142	57	16	494	507	445
AVERAGE:		31	13	13	5	2	45	46	41

Playoff Record

Season	GP	W	L	T	GF	GA	Result
1996	5	2	3	0	9	10	Lost Semifinals to Los Angeles.
1997	2	0	2	0	2	6	Lost Quarterfinal to Colorado.
2000	7	4	1	2	7	4	**Won MLS Cup.**
2001	3	1	2	0	4	4	Lost Quarterfinal to Miami.
2002	3	1	2	0	8	9	Lost Quarterfinal to Los Angeles.
2003	3	1	1	1	5	4	Lost Conference Final to San Jose.
2004	4	2	2	0	7	5	Lost MLS Cup to D.C. United.
TOTAL:	27	11	13	3	42	42	
AVERAGE:	4	2	2	0	6	6	

Regular Season Individual Leaders

Season	Goals	Points		GAA (min. 5 games)	
1996	Preki	18 Preki	49	Garth Lagerwey	1.75

Season	Goals		Points		GAA (min. 5 games)	
1997	Preki	12	Preki	41	Mike Ammann	1.56
1998	Mo Johnston	11	Preki	33	Mike Ammann	1.56
1999	Preki	7	Preki	25	Tony Meola	1.18
2000	Miklos Molnar	12	Chris Henderson	27	Tony Meola	0.92
2001	Roy Lassiter	7	Roy Lassiter	15	Tony Meola	1.64
2002	Preki	7	Preki	24	Tony Meola	1.24
	Chris Klein	7				
2003	Preki	12	Preki	41	Tony Meola	1.42
2004	Josh Wolff	10	Josh Wolff	27	Bo Oshoniyi	0.89
2005	Josh Wolff	10	Josh Wolff	30	Bo Oshoniyi	1.38
2006	Scott Sealy	10	Jose Burciaga Jr.	24	Bo Oshoniyi	1.41

COACHING HISTORY: 1996-1999 Ron Newman 50-50; 1999 Ken Fogarty 0-3; 1999-2006 Bob Gansler 86-85-51; 2006-present Brian Bliss

KENOSHA MAROONS

Home City: Kenosha, Wisconsin
Home Stadium: Nash Employees' Athletic Field
Origin of Name: The team received its name from the color of their uniforms.

			Regular Season Record					
Season	League	GP	W	L	T	PF	PA	Pct
1924	NFL	6	0	5	1	18	127	.083

COACHING HISTORY: Earl Potteiger 0-5-1-.083

KENTUCKY COLONELS

Home City: Louisville, Kentucky
Home Court: Convention Center (1967-68, 1970-72)
                    Freedom Hall (1967-1973)   Capacity: 16,933 [1975]
                    University of Kentucky Memorial Coliseum (1974-1975)
Origin of Name: The name is a popular nickname in Kentucky.

			Regular Season Record					
Season	League	GP	W	L	PPGF	PPGA	Pct	GB
1967-1968	ABA	78	36	42	104.5	105.2	.462	18
1968-1969	ABA	78	42	36	111.2	111.0	.538	2
1969-1970	ABA	84	45	39	113.5	112.5	.536	14
1970-1971	ABA	84	44	40	122.3	122.1	.524	11
1971-1972	ABA	84	68	16	116.0	107.0	.810	-
1972-1973	ABA	84	56	28	111.9	105.5	.667	1
1973-1974	ABA	84	53	31	107.4	103.3	.631	2
1974-1975	ABA	84	58	26	108.9	101.7	.690	-
1975-1976	ABA	84	46	38	111.0	110.2	.548	14
TOTAL:	9 years	744	448	296				62
AVERAGE:		83	50	33	111.9	108.7	.602	7

			Playoff Record			
Season	GP	W	L	PPGF	PPGA	Result
1967-1968	5	2	3	102.2	105.2	Lost 1st Round series to Minnesota.
1968-1969	7	3	4	110.7	113.7	Lost 1st Round series to Indiana.

1969-1970	12	5	7	111.5	112.9	Lost 2nd Round series to Indiana.
1970-1971	19	11	8	120.6	121.6	Lost Championship series to Utah.
1971-1972	6	2	4	100.0	103.3	Lost 1st Round series to New York.
1972-1973	19	11	8	104.6	100.3	Lost Championship series to Indiana.
1973-1974	8	4	4	103.5	104.6	Lost 2nd Round series to New York.
1974-1975	15	12	3	106.6	99.0	**Won ABA Championship**.
1975-1976	10	5	5	113.8	113.4	Lost 2nd Round series to Denver.
TOTAL:	101	55	46			
AVERAGE:	11	6	5	108.2	108.2	

Regular Season Individual Leaders

Season	Field Goal % (min. 70 games)		Points		Points per Game (min. 70 games)	
1967-68	Goose Ligon	.454	Darrell Carrier	1765	Darrell Carrier	22.9
1968-69	Gene Moore	.453	Louie Dampier	1933	Louie Dampier	24.8
1969-70	Goose Ligon	.507	Louie Dampier	2131	Louie Dampier	26.0
1970-71	Goose Ligon	.540	Dan Issel	2480	Dan Issel	29.9
1971-72	Artis Gilmore	.598	Dan Issel	2538	Dan Issel	30.6
1972-73	Artis Gilmore	.559	Dan Issel	2292	Dan Issel	27.3
1973-74	Artis Gilmore	.493	Dan Issel	2118	Dan Issel	25.5
1974-75	Artis Gilmore	.580	Artis Gilmore	1981	Artis Gilmore	23.6
1975-76	Artis Gilmore	.552	Artis Gilmore	2067	Artis Gilmore	24.6

COACHING HISTORY: 1967-1968 John Givens 5-12-.294; 1968-1971 Gene Rhodes 128-110-.538; 1970-1971 Alex Groza 2-0-1.000; 1970-1971 Frank Ramsey 32-35-.478; 1971-1973 Joe Mullaney 124-44-.738; 1973-1974 Babe McCarthy 53-31-.631; 1974-1976 Hubie Brown 104-64-.619

LAS VEGAS POSSE

Home City: Las Vegas, Nevada
Home Stadium: Sam Boyd Stadium   Capacity: 31,000 [1994]
Origin of Name: The name was entered in a Name the Team Contest by Janet Negrete of Las Vegas because in her words when she moved to Las Vegas it was "just a cowboy town." Five other entries were received with the name Posse but Negrete was declared winner because she also chose the colors.

Regular Season Record

Season	League	GP	W	L	T	PF	PA	Pts	Pct
1994	CFL	18	5	13	0	444	622	10	.278

Regular Season Individual Leaders

Season	Passing Yards		Receiving Yards		Rushing Yards	
1994	Anthony Calvillo	2582	Curtis Mayfield	1202	Zedrick Robinson	271

COACHING HISTORY: 1994 Ron Meyer 5-13-0-.278

LAS VEGAS QUICKSILVERS
(were San Diego Jaws)
(became San Diego Sockers)

Home City: Las Vegas, Nevada
Home Field: Las Vegas Stadium   Capacity: 16,000
Origin of Name:

Regular Season Record

Season	League	GP	W	L	GF	GA	BP	Pts	Pct
1977	NASL	26	11	15	38	44	37	103	.440

Regular Season Individual Leaders

Season	Goals		Points		GAA (360 Min)	
1977	Gerry Ingram	7	Gerry Ingram	18	Alan Mayer	1.40

COACHING HISTORY: Derek Trevis 10-10; Jim Fryatt 1-5

LONDON MONARCHS

Home City: London, England
Home Stadium: Wembley Stadium   Capacity: 63,500 [1991]
Origin of Name: London is the seat of the British monarchy.

Regular Season Record

Season	League	GP	W	L	T	PF	PA	Pct
1991	WLAF	10	9	1	0	310	121	.900
1992	WFL	10	2	7	1	178	203	.250
TOTAL:	2 years	20	11	8	1	488	324	
AVERAGE:		10	6	4	0	244	162	.575

Playoff Record

Season	GP	W	L	PF	PA	Result
1991	2	2	0	63	26	**Won WLAF Championship**.

Regular Season Individual Leaders

Season	Passing Yards		Receiving Yards		Rushing Yards	
1991	Stan Gelbaugh	2655	Jon Horton	931	Jeff Alexander	391
1992			Bernard Ford	833	Jeff Alexander	501

COACHING HISTORY: 1991 Larry Kennan 9-1-0-.900; 1992 Ray Willsey 2-7-1-.250

LOS ANGELES ANGELS
(became California Angels)

Home City: Los Angeles, California
Home Field: Wrigley Field (California) (1961)   Capacity: 20,457 [1961]
           Dodger Stadium (1962-1965)   Capacity: 56,000 [1964]
Origin of Name: The team was named after the Pacific Coast League team, which was based in the "City of Angels."

Regular Season Record

Season	League	GP	W	L	Pct	GB	R	OR
1961	AL	161	70	91	.435	38.5	744	784
1962	AL	162	86	76	.531	10	718	706
1963	AL	161	70	91	.435	34	597	660

1964	AL	162	82	80	.506	17	544	551
TOTAL:	4 years	646	308	338		99.5	2603	2701
AVERAGE:		162	77	85	.477	25	651	675

Regular Season Individual Leaders

Season	Home Runs		RBI's		Wins	
1961	Leon Wagner	28	Ken Hunt	84	Ken McBride	12
1962	Leon Wagner	37	Leon Wagner	107	Dean Chance	14
1963	Leon Wagner	26	Leon Wagner	90	Ken McBride	13
					Dean Chance	13
1964	Joe Adcock	21	Jim Fregosi	72	Dean Chance	20

COACHING HISTORY: 1961-1964 Bill Rigney 308-338-.477

LOS ANGELES ANGELS OF ANAHEIM
(were Los Angeles Angels)
(were known as California Angels from 1965 to 1996)
(were Anaheim Angels from 1997 to 2004)

Home City: Anaheim, California
Home Field: Dodger Stadium (1965)   Capacity: 56,000 [1965]
            Anaheim Stadium (1966-1996)   Capacity: 64,593 [1996]
            Edison International Field (1997-present)*   Capacity: 45,113 [2006]
Origin of Name: The team kept the same name when it moved from Los Angeles to Anaheim.

Regular Season Record

Season	League	GP	W	L	Pct	GB	R	OR
1965	AL	162	75	87	.463	27	527	569
1966	AL	162	80	82	.494	18	604	643
1967	AL	161	84	77	.522	7.5	567	587
1968	AL	162	67	95	.414	36	498	615
1969	AL	162	71	91	.438	26	528	652
1970	AL	162	86	76	.531	12	631	630
1971	AL	162	76	86	.469	25.5	511	576
1972	AL	155	75	80	.484	18	454	533
1973	AL	162	79	83	.488	15	629	657
1974	AL	162	68	94	.420	22	618	657
1975	AL	161	72	89	.447	25.5	628	723
1976	AL	162	76	86	.469	14	550	631
1977	AL	162	74	88	.457	28	675	695
1978	AL	162	87	75	.537	5	691	666
1979	AL	162	88	74	.543	-	866	768
1980	AL	160	65	95	.406	31	698	797
1981	AL	110	51	59	.464	NA	476	453
1982	AL	162	93	69	.574	-	814	670
1983	AL	162	70	92	.432	29	722	779
1984	AL	162	81	81	.500	3	696	697
1985	AL	162	90	72	.556	1	732	703
1986	AL	162	92	70	.568	-	786	684
1987	AL	162	75	87	.463	10	770	803
1988	AL	162	75	87	.463	29	714	771

*-known as Anaheim Stadium in 1997

1989	AL	162	91	71	.562	8	669	578
1990	AL	162	80	82	.494	23	690	706
1991	AL	162	81	81	.500	14	653	649
1992	AL	162	72	90	.444	24	579	671
1993	AL	162	71	91	.438	23	684	770
1994	AL	115	47	68	.409	5.5	543	660
1995*	AL	144	78	66	.542	-	801	697
1996	AL	161	70	91	.435	19.5	762	943
1997	AL	162	84	78	.519	6	829	794
1998	AL	162	85	77	.525	3	787	783
1999	AL	162	70	92	.432	25	711	826
2000	AL	162	82	80	.506	9.5	864	869
2001	AL	162	75	87	.463	41	692	730
2002	AL	162	99	63	.611	4	851	644
2003	AL	162	77	85	.475	19	736	743
2004	AL	162	92	70	.568	1	836	734
2005	AL	162	95	67	.586	-	761	643
2006	AL	162	89	73	.549	4	766	732
TOTAL:	42 years	6675	3288	3387		612	28599	29131
AVERAGE:		159	78	81	.493	15	681	694

Playoff Record

Season	GP	W	L	R	OR	Result
1979	4	1	3	15	26	Lost ALCS to Baltimore.
1982	5	2	3	23	23	Lost ALCS to Milwaukee.
1986	7	3	4	30	41	Lost ALCS to Boston.
2002	16	11	5	101	81	**Won World Series.**
2004	3	0	3	12	25	Lost Divisional series to Boston.
2005	10	4	6	36	42	Lost ALCS to Chicago.
TOTAL:	45	21	24	217	238	
AVERAGE:	7	3	4	36	40	

Regular Season Individual Leaders

Season	Home Runs		RBI's		Wins	
1965	Jim Fregosi	15	Jim Fregosi	64	Dean Chance	15
1966	Joe Adcock	18	Bobby Knoop	72	Jack Sanford	13
					George Brunet	13
1967	Don Mincher	25	Don Mincher	76	Jim McGlothin	12
					Minnie Rojas	12
					Rickey Clark	12
1968	Rick Reichardt	21	Rick Reichardt	73	George Brunet	13
1969	Rick Reichardt	13	Rick Reichardt	68	Andy Messersmith	16
1970	Jim Fregosi	22	Alex Johnson	86	Clyde Wright	22
1971	Ken McMullen	21	Ken McMullen	68	Andy Messersmith	20
1972	Bob Oliver	19	Bob Oliver	70	Nolan Ryan	19
1973	Frank Robinson	30	Frank Robinson	97	Nolan Ryan	21
1974	Frank Robinson	20	Frank Robinson	63	Nolan Ryan	22
1975	Lee Stanton	14	Lee Stanton	82	Frank Tanana	16
					Ed Figueroa	16
1976	Bobby Bonds	10	Bobby Bonds	54	Frank Tanana	19
1977	Bobby Bonds	37	Bobby Bonds	115	Nolan Ryan	19
1978	Don Baylor	34	Don Baylor	99	Frank Tanana	18

*-defeated by Seattle 9 to 1 in a playoff to determine 1st place.

Season	Home Runs		RBI's		Wins	
1979	Don Baylor	36	Don Baylor	139	Dave Frost	16
					Nolan Ryan	16
1980	Jason Thompson	17	Carney Lansford	80	Mark Clear	11
					Frank Tanana	11
1981	Bobby Grich	22	Don Baylor	66	Ken Forsch	11
1982	Reggie Jackson	39	Reggie Jackson	101	Geoff Zahn	18
1983	Fred Lynn	22	Fred Lynn	74	Bruce Kison	11
					Ken Forsch	11
					Tommy John	11
1984	Reggie Jackson	25	Brian Downing	91	Mike Witt	15
1985	Reggie Jackson	27	Reggie Jackson	85	Mike Witt	15
			Brian Downing	85		
1986	Doug DeCinces	26	Wally Joyner	100	Mike Witt	18
1987	Wally Joyner	34	Wally Joyner	117	Mike Witt	16
1988	Brian Downing	25	Chili Davis	93	Mike Witt	13
1989	Chili Davis	22	Chili Davis	90	Bert Blyleven	17
1990	Lance Parrish	24	Dave Winfield	78	Chuck Finley	18
1991	Dave Winfield	28	Wally Joyner	96	Mark Langston	19
1992	Gary Gaetti	12	Junior Felix	72	Mark Langston	13
1993	Tim Salmon	31	Chili Davis	112	Chuck Finley	16
					Mark Langston	16
1994	Chili Davis	26	Chili Davis	84	Chuck Finley	10
1995	Tim Salmon	34	Jim Edmonds	107	Chuck Finley	15
					Mark Langston	15
1996	Tim Salmon	30	Tim Salmon	98	Chuck Finley	15
1997	Tim Salmon	33	Tim Salmon	129	Chuck Finley	13
					Jason Dickson	13
1998	Tim Salmon	26	Jim Edmonds	91	Chuck Finley	11
1999	Mo Vaughn	33	Mo Vaughn	108	Chuck Finley	12
2000	Troy Glaus	47	Garret Anderson	117	S. Hasegawa	10
			Bengie Molina	117		
2001	Troy Glaus	41	Garret Anderson	123	Ramon Ortiz	13
2002	Troy Glaus	30	Garret Anderson	123	Ramon Ortiz	15
2003	Garrett Anderson	29	Garrett Anderson	116	Ramon Ortiz	16
2004	Vladimir Guerrero	39	Vladimir Guerrero	126	Bartolo Colon	18
2005	Vladimir Guerrero	32	Vladimir Guerrero	108	Bartolo Colon	21
2006	Vladimir Guerrero	33	Vladimir Guerrero	116	Ervin Santana	16

COACHING HISTORY: 1965-1969 Bill Rigney 317-369-.462; 1969-1971 Harold Phillips 222-225-.497; 1972 Del Rice 75-80-.484; 1973-1974 Bobby Winkles 111-129-.463; 1974-1976 Dick Williams 147-194-.431; 1976-1977 Norm Sherry 76-71-.517; 1977-1978 Dave Garcia 60-67-.472; 1978-1981 Jim Fregosi 237-248-.489; 1981-1982 Gene Mauch 122-103-.542; 1983-1984 John McNamara 151-173-.466; 1985-1987 Gene Mauch 257-229-.529; 1988 Octavio Rojas 75-79-.487; 1988 Lawrence Stubing 0-8-.000; 1989-1991 Doug Rader 232-216-.518; 1991-1994 Buck Rodgers 140-172-.449; 1992 John Wathan 39-50-.438; 1995-1996 Marcel Lachemann 177-193-.478, 1996-John McNamara 18-32-.360; 1997-1999 Terry Collins 221-237-.483; 1999-Joe Maddon 18-10-.643, 2000-present Mike Scioscia

LOS ANGELES AZTECS

Home City: Los Angeles, California
Home Stadium: East Los Angeles College Stadium (1974)
        El Camino College Stadium (1975-76)
        Los Angeles Memorial Coliseum (1977; 1981)   Capacity: 90,000 [1977]
        Rose Bowl (1978-1980)   Capacity: 106,721 [1979]
Origin of Name: The name was chosen to attract some of the large Mexican-American population
living in Los Angeles.

Regular Season Record

Season	League	GP	W	L	T	GF	GA	BP	Pts	Pct
1974	NASL	20	11	7	2	41	36	38	110	.611
1975	NASL	22	12	10	-	42	33	35	107	.540
1976	NASL	24	12	12	-	43	44	36	108	.500
1977	NASL	26	15	11	-	65	54	57	147	.628
1978	NASL	30	9	21	-	36	69	34	88	.326
1979	NASL	30	18	12	-	62	47	54	162	.600
1980	NASL	32	20	12	-	61	52	54	174	.604
1981	NASL	32	19	13	-	53	55	48	160	.333
TOTAL:	8 years	216	116	98	2	403	390	356	1056	
AVERAGE:		27	15	12	0	50	49	45	132	.494

Playoff Record

Season	GP	W	L	GF	GA	Result
1974	2	2	0	6	3	**Won NASL Championship**.
1975	1	0	1	1	2	Lost Quarterfinal series to St. Louis.
1976	1	0	1	0	2	Lost 1st Round series to Dallas.
1977	5	3	2	11	7	Lost Conference Final to Seattle.
1979	5	3	2	10	8	Lost 2nd Round series to Vancouver.
1980	8	4	4	11	12	Lost 3rd Round series to New York.
1981	3	1	2	7	9	Lost 1st Round series to Montreal.
TOTAL:	25	13	12	46	43	
AVERAGE:	4	2	2	7	6	

Regular Season Individual Leaders

Season	Goals		Points		GAA (360 Min)	
1974	Douglas McMillan	10	Douglas McMillan	30	Blas Sanchez	1.76
1975	Uri Banhoffer	14	Uri Banhoffer	37	John Taylor	1.27
1976	George Best	15	George Best	37	Graham Horn	1.85
1977	Steve David	26	Steve David	58	Bill Mishalow	1.02
1978	Wolfgang Sunholz	5	Bob McAlinden	13	Bill Mishalow	2.14
1979	Leo Van Veen	13	Leo Van Veen	32	Bob Rigby	1.40
1980	Luis Fernando	28	Luis Fernando	60	Alfredo Anhielo	1.32
1981						

COACHING HISTORY: 1974 Alex Perolli 11-7-2-.611; 1975-1978 Terry Fisher 44-41; 1978
Tommy Smith 3-13; 1978 Peter Short 1-0; 1979-1980 Rinus Michels 38-24; 1981 Claudio
Coutinho 19-13

LOS ANGELES BUCCANEERS

Home City: Los Angeles, California
Home Stadium: The team only played road games
Origin of Name:

Regular Season Record

Season	League	GP	W	L	T	PF	PA	Pct
1926	NFL	10	6	3	1	77	57	.650

Regular Season Individual Leaders

Season	Passing Yards		Receiving Yards		Rushing Yards	
1926	Tuffy Maul	134	Tut Imlay	175	Tut Imlay	72

COACHING HISTORY: Brick Muller & Tut Imlay 6-3-1-.650

LOS ANGELES CHARGERS
(became San Diego Chargers)

Home City: Los Angeles, California
Home Stadium: Los Angeles Memorial Coliseum   Capacity: 92,604
Origin of Name: The team was originally owned by Baron Hilton the owner of the Carte Blanche credit card company.

Regular Season Record

Season	League	GP	W	L	T	PF	PA	Pct
1960	AFL	14	10	4	0	373	336	.714

Playoff Record

Season	GP	W	L	PF	PA	Result
1960	1	0	1	16	24	Lost Championship game to Houston.

Regular Season Individual Leaders

Season	Passing Yards		Receiving Yards		Rushing Yards	
1960	Jack Kemp	3018	Dave Kocourek	662	Paul Lowe	855

COACHING HISTORY: Sid Gillman 10-4-0-.714

LOS ANGELES CLIPPERS
(were San Diego Clippers)

Home City: Los Angeles, California
Home Court: Los Angeles Sports Arena (1984-1999)   Capacity: 16,021 [1998]
       Arrowhead Pond (1995-present)   Capacity: 18,211 [1998]
       Staples Center (2000-present)   Capacity: 18,694 [2006]
Origin of Name: The team kept the same nickname when it moved from San Diego.

Regular Season Record

Season	League	GP	W	L	PPGF	PPGA	Pct	GB
1984-1985	NBA	82	31	51	107.1	111.6	.378	31
1985-1986	NBA	82	32	50	108.6	115.5	.390	30
1986-1987	NBA	82	12	70	104.5	115.9	.146	53
1987-1988	NBA	82	17	65	98.8	109.1	.207	45
1988-1989	NBA	82	21	61	106.2	116.2	.256	36
1989-1990	NBA	82	30	52	103.8	107.2	.366	33
1990-1991	NBA	82	31	51	103.5	107.0	.378	32
1991-1992	NBA	82	45	37	102.9	101.9	.549	12
1992-1993	NBA	82	41	41	107.1	106.8	.500	21
1993-1994	NBA	82	27	55	103.0	108.7	.329	36
1994-1995	NBA	82	17	65	96.7	105.8	.207	42
1995-1996	NBA	82	29	53	99.4	103.0	.354	35
1996-1997	NBA	82	36	46	97.2	99.5	.439	21
1997-1998	NBA	82	17	65	95.9	103.3	.207	44

1998-1999	NBA	50	9	41	90.4	99.2	.180	26
1999-2000	NBA	82	15	67	92.0	103.5	.183	52
2000-2001	NBA	82	31	51	92.5	95.3	.378	25
2001-2002	NBA	82	39	43	95.7	96.1	.476	22
2002-2003	NBA	82	27	55	93.8	98.0	.329	32
2003-2004	NBA	82	28	54	94.8	99.4	.341	28
2004-2005	NBA	82	37	45	95.7	96.5	.451	25
2005-2006	NBA	82	47	35	97.2	95.6	.573	7
TOTAL:	22 years	1772	619	1153				688
AVERAGE:		80	28	52	104.4	104.4	.349	31

Playoff Record

Season	GP	W	L	PPGF	PPGA	Result
1991-1992	5	2	3	98.2	102.2	Lost 1st Round series to Utah.
1992-1993	5	2	3	92.2	97.0	Lost 1st Round series to Houston.
1996-1997	3	0	3	92.3	105.0	Lost 1st Round series to Utah.
2005-2006	12	7	5	105.7	101.9	Lost Conference Semifinal to Phoenix.
TOTAL:	25	11	14			
AVERAGE:	6	3	3	99.9	101.4	

Regular Season Individual Leaders

Season	Field Goal % (min. 70 games)		Points		Points per Game (min. 70 games)	
1984-85	James Donaldson	.637	Derek Smith	1767	Derek Smith	22.1
1985-86	Rory White	.519	Marques Johnson	1525	Marques Johnson	20.3
1986-87	Michael Cage	.521	Mike Woodson	1262	Mike Woodson	17.1
1987-88	Michael Cage	.470	Mike Woodson	1438	Mike Woodson	18.0
1988-89	Benoit Benjamin	.541	Ken Norman	1450	Ken Norman	18.1
1989-90	Danny Manning	.533	Charles Smith	1645	Charles Smith	21.1
1990-91	Danny Manning	.519	Charles Smith	1480	Charles Smith	20.0
1991-92	Danny Manning	.542	Danny Manning	1579	Danny Manning	19.3
1992-93	Stanley Roberts	.527	Danny Manning	1800	Danny Manning	22.8
1993-94	Loy Vaught	.537	Ron Harper	1508	Ron Harper	20.1
1994-95	Charles Outlaw	.523	Loy Vaught	1401	Loy Vaught	17.5
1995-96	Charles Outlaw	.575	Loy Vaught	1298	Loy Vaught	16.2
1996-97	Charles Outlaw	.609	Loy Vaught	1220	Loy Vaught	14.9
1997-98	Lamond Murray	.481	Rodney Rogers	1149	Lamond Murray	15.4
1998-99*	Maurice Taylor	.461	Maurice Taylor	773	Maurice Taylor	16.8
1999-00	Maurice Taylor	.464	Lamar Odom	1259	Maurice Taylor	17.1
2000-01	Darius Miles	.504	Lamar Odom	1304	Lamar Odom	17.2
2001-02	Elton Brand	.527	Elton Brand	1453	Elton Brand	18.2
2002-03	Sean Rooks	.421	Elton Brand	1146	Andre Miller	13.6
2003-04	Chris Karman	.460	Corey Maggette	1508	Corey Maggette	20.7
2004-05	Elton Brand	.503	Elton Brand	1622	Elton Brand	20.0
2005-06	Elton Brand	.527	Elton Brand	1953	Elton Brand	24.7

*-minimum 40 games.

COACHING HISTORY: 1984-1985 Jim Lynam 22-39-.361; 1984-1987 Don Chaney 53-132-.286; 1987-1989 Gene Shue 27-93-.225; 1988-1990 Don Casey 41-85-.325; 1990-1992 Mike Schuler 53-76-.411; 1991-1992 Mack Calvin 1-1-.500; 1991-1993 Larry Brown 64-53-.547; 1993-1994 Bob Weiss 27-55-.329; 1994-1998 Bill Fitch 99-229-.302; 1998-2000 Chris Ford 20-75-.211; 1999-2000 Jim Todd 4-33-.108; 2000-2003 Alvin Gentry 97-149-.394; 2003-present Mike Dunleavy

LOS ANGELES DODGERS
(were Brooklyn Dodgers)

Home City: Los Angeles, California
Home Field: Memorial Coliseum (1958-1961)   Capacity: 94,600 [1959]
             Dodger Stadium (1962-present)   Capacity: 56,000 [2006]
Origin of Name: The team kept the same nickname when it moved to Los Angeles from Brooklyn.

Regular Season Record

Season	League	GP	W	L	Pct	GB	R	OR
1958	NL	154	71	83	.461	21	668	761
1959	NL	156	88	68	.564	-	705	670
1960	NL	154	82	72	.532	13	662	593
1961	NL	154	89	65	.578	4	735	697
1962	NL	165	102	63	.618	1	842	697
1963	NL	162	99	63	.611	-	640	550
1964	NL	162	80	82	.494	13	614	572
1965	NL	162	97	65	.599	-	608	521
1966	NL	162	95	67	.586	-	606	490
1967	NL	162	73	89	.451	28.5	519	595
1968	NL	162	76	86	.469	21	470	509
1969	NL	162	85	77	.525	8	645	561
1970	NL	161	87	74	.540	14.5	749	684
1971	NL	162	89	73	.549	1	663	587
1972	NL	155	85	70	.548	10.5	584	527
1973	NL	161	95	66	.590	3.5	675	565
1974	NL	162	102	60	.630	-	798	561
1975	NL	162	88	74	.543	20	648	534
1976	NL	162	92	70	.568	10	608	543
1977	NL	162	98	64	.605	-	769	582
1978	NL	162	95	67	.586	-	727	573
1979	NL	162	79	83	.488	11.5	739	717
1980	NL	163	92	71	.564	1	663	591
1981	NL	110	63	47	.573	NA	450	356
1982	NL	162	88	74	.543	1	691	612
1983	NL	162	91	71	.562	-	654	609
1984	NL	162	79	83	.488	13	580	600
1985	NL	162	95	67	.586	-	682	579
1986	NL	162	73	89	.451	23	638	679
1987	NL	162	73	89	.451	17	635	675
1988	NL	161	94	67	.584	-	628	544
1989	NL	160	77	83	.481	14	554	536
1990	NL	161	86	75	.534	4.5	728	685
1991	NL	162	93	69	.574	1	665	565
1992	NL	162	63	99	.389	35	548	636
1993	NL	162	81	81	.500	23	675	662
1994	NL	114	58	56	.509	-	532	509
1995	NL	144	78	66	.542	-	634	609
1996	NL	162	90	72	.556	1	703	652
1997	NL	162	88	74	.543	2	742	645
1998	NL	162	83	79	.512	14.5	669	678
1999	NL	162	77	85	.475	23	793	787
2000	NL	162	86	76	.531	11	798	729
2001	NL	162	86	76	.531	6	758	744

2002	NL	162	92	70	.568	6	713	643
2003	NL	162	85	77	.525	15.5	574	556
2004	NL	162	93	69	.574	-	761	684
2005	NL	162	71	91	.438	11	685	755
2006	NL	162	88	74	.543	-	820	751
TOTAL:	49 years	7781	4170	3611		403	32647	30160
AVERAGE:		159	85	74	.536	8	666	616

Playoff Record

Season	GP	W	L	R	OR	Result
1959	6	4	2	21	23	**Won World Series.**
1963	4	4	0	12	4	**Won World Series.**
1965	7	4	3	24	20	**Won World Series.**
1966	4	0	4	2	13	Lost World Series to Baltimore.
1974	9	4	5	31	26	Lost World Series to Oakland.
1977	10	5	5	50	40	Lost World Series to New York.
1978	10	5	5	44	53	Lost World Series to New York.
1981	16	10	6	55	38	**Won World Series.**
1983	4	1	3	8	16	Lost NLCS to Philadelphia.
1985	6	2	4	23	29	Lost NLCS to St. Louis.
1988	12	8	4	52	38	**Won World Series.**
1995	3	0	3	10	22	Lost Division series to Cincinnati.
1996	3	0	3	5	10	Lost Division series to Atlanta.
2004	4	1	3	12	22	Lost Division series to St. Louis.
2006	3	0	3	11	19	Lost Division series to New York.
TOTAL:	101	48	53	360	373	
AVERAGE:	7	3	4	24	25	

Season	Home Runs		RBI's		Wins	
1958	Gil Hodges	22	Carl Furillo	83	John Podres	13
	Charlie Neal	22				
1959	Gil Hodges	25	Duke Snider	88	Don Drysdale	17
1960	Frank Howard	23	Norm Larker	78	Don Drysdale	15
1961	John Roseboro	18	Wally Moon	88	John Podres	18
					Sandy Koufax	18
1962	Frank Howard	31	Tom Davis	153	Don Drysdale	25
1963	Frank Howard	28	Tom Davis	88	Sandy Koufax	25
1964	Frank Howard	24	Tom Davis	86	Sandy Koufax	19
1965	Jim Lefebvre	12	Ron Fairly	70	Sandy Koufax	26
	Lou Johnson	12				
1966	Jim Lefebvre	24	Jim Lefebvre	74	Sandy Koufax	27
1967	Al Ferrara	16	Ron Fairly	55	Claude Osteen	17
1968	Len Gabrielson	10	Tom Haller	53	Don Drysdale	14
1969	Andy Kosco	19	Andy Kosco	74	Bill Singer	20
					Claude Osteen	20
1970	Bill Grabarkewitz	17	Wes Parker	111	Claude Osteen	16
1971	Dick Allen	23	Dick Allen	90	Al Downing	20
1972	Frank Robinson	19	Willie Davis	79	Claude Osteen	20
	Willie Davis	19				
1973	Joe Ferguson	25	Joe Ferguson	88	Don Sutton	18
1974	Jim Wynn	32	Steve Garvey	111	Andy Messersmith	20
1975	Ron Cey	25	Ron Cey	101	Andy Messersmith	19
1976	Ron Cey	23	Steve Garvey	80	Don Sutton	21
			Ron Cey	80		

Season	Home Runs		RBI's		Wins	
1977	Steve Garvey	33	Steve Garvey	115	Tommy John	20
1978	Reggie Smith	29	Steve Garvey	113	Burt Hooton	19
1979	Steve Garvey	28	Steve Garvey	110	Rick Sutcliffe	17
	Davey Lopes	28				
	Ron Cey	28				
1980	Dusty Baker	29	Steve Garvey	106	Jerry Reuss	18
1981	Ron Cey	13	Steve Garvey	64	F. Valenzuela	13
1982	Pedro Guerrero	32	Pedro Guerrero	100	F. Valenzuela	19
1983	Pedro Guerrero	32	Pedro Guerrero	103	F. Valenzuela	15
					Bob Welch	15
1984	Mike Marshall	21	Pedro Guerrero	72	Bob Welch	13
1985	Pedro Guerrero	33	Mike Marshall	95	Orel Hershiser	19
1986	Franklin Stubbs	23	Bill Madlock	60	F. Valenzuela	21
1987	Pedro Guerrero	27	Pedro Guerrero	89	Orel Hershiser	16
1988	Kirk Gibson	25	Mike Marshall	82	Orel Hershiser	23
1989	Eddie Murray	20	Eddie Murray	88	Orel Hershiser	15
					Tim Belcher	15
1990	Kal Daniels	27	Eddie Murray	95	Ramon Martinez	20
1991	Darryl Strawberry	28	Darryl Strawberry	99	Ramon Martinez	17
1992	Eric Karros	20	Eric Karros	88	Tom Candiotti	11
1993	Mike Piazza	35	Mike Piazza	112	Pedro Astacio	14
1994	Mike Piazza	24	Mike Piazza	92	Ramon Martinez	12
1995	Mike Piazza	32	Eric Karros	105	Ramon Martinez	17
	Eric Karros	32				
1996	Mike Piazza	36	Eric Karros	111	Hideo Nomo	16
1997	Mike Piazza	40	Mike Piazza	124	Chan Ho Park	14
					Hideo Nomo	14
1998	Raul Mondesi	30	Raul Mondesi	90	Chan Ho Park	15
1999	Gary Sheffield	34	Eric Karros	112	Kevin Brown	18
	Eric Karros	34				
2000	Gary Sheffield	43	Gary Sheffield	109	Chan Ho Park	18
2001	Shawn Green	49	Shawn Green	125	Chan Ho Park	15
2002	Shawn Green	42	Shawn Green	114	Hideo Nomo	16
2003	Jeromy Burnitz	31	Shawn Green	85	Hideo Nomo	16
2004	Adrian Beltre	48	Adrian Beltre	121	Kazuhisa Ishii	13
					Jose Lima	13
					Jeff Weaver	13
2005	Jeff Kent	29	Jeff Kent	105	Jeff Weaver	14
2006	Nomar Garciaparra	20	J.D. Drew	100	Derek Lowe	16
	J.D. Drew	20			Brad Penny	16

COACHING HISTORY: 1958-1976 Walter Alston 1675-1367-.551; 1977-1996 Tom Lasorda 1613-1455-.526; 1996-1998 Bill Russell 173-150-.536; 1998 Glenn Hoffman 47-40-.540; 1999-2000 Davey Johnson 163-161-.503; 2001-2005 Jim Tracy 427-383-.527; 2006-present Grady Little

LOS ANGELES DONS

Home City: Los Angeles, California
Home Stadium: Los Angeles Coliseum   Capacity: 103,000 [1946]
Origin of Name: The team's name was chosen by the owner, to reflect the Spanish heritage of the area. Perhaps not coincidentally the owner was actor Don Ameche.

Regular Season Record

Season	League	GP	W	L	T	PF	PA	Pct
1946	AAFC	14	7	5	2	305	290	.571
1947	AAFC	14	7	7	0	328	256	.500
1948	AAFC	14	7	7	0	258	305	.500
1949	AAFC	12	4	8	0	253	322	.333
TOTAL:	4 years	54	25	27	2	1144	1173	
AVERAGE:		14	6	7	1	286	293	.481

Regular Season Individual Leaders

Season	Passing Yards		Receiving Yards		Rushing Yards	
1946	Charlie O'Rourke	1250	Dale Gentry	341	John Kimbrough	473
1947	Charlie O'Rourke	1449	Dale Gentry	352	John Kimbrough	562
1948	Glenn Dobbs	2403	Joe Aguirre	599	Glenn Dobbs	539
1949	Glenn Dobbs	825	Dick Wilkins	589	Herm Wedemeyer	291

COACHING HISTORY: 1946-1947 Dud Degroot 12-10-2-.542; 1947 Mel Hein & Ted Shipkey 2-2-0-.500; 1948-1949 Jim Phelan 11-15-0-.423

LOS ANGELES EXPRESS

Home City: Los Angeles, California
Home Stadium: Los Angeles Coliseum   Capacity: 92,516 [1985]
Origin of Name: Name chosen in a Name the Team Contest.

Regular Season Record

Season	League	GP	W	L	T	PF	PA	Pct
1983	USFL	18	8	10	0	296	370	.444
1984	USFL	18	10	8	0	338	373	.556
1985	USFL	18	3	15	0	266	456	.167
TOTAL:	3 years	54	21	33	0	900	1199	
AVERAGE:		18	7	11	0	300	400	.389

Playoff Record

Season	GP	W	L	PF	PA	Result
1984	2	1	1	50	56	Lost 2nd Round game to Arizona.

Regular Season Individual Leaders

Season	Passing Yards		Receiving Yards		Rushing Yards	
1983	Tom Ramsey	1975	Ricky Ellis	716	LaRue Harrington	547
1984	Steve Young	2361	Jo Jo Townsell	889	Kevin Nelson	828
1985	Steve Young	1741	Jo Jo Townsell	777	Mel Gray 526	

COACHING HISTORY: 1983 Hugh Campbell 8-10-0-.444; 1984-1985 John Hadl 13-23-0-.361

LOS ANGELES GALAXY

Home City: Los Angeles, California
Home Field: Rose Bowl Stadium (1996-2002)   Capacity: 30,000 [2003]
             Home Depot Center (2003-present)   Capacity: 27,000 [2005]
Origin of Name: So named because Los Angeles is the home of the stars.

Season	League	GP	W	L	T	SOW	GF	GA	Pts
1996	MLS	32	19	13	NA	4	59	49	49
1997	MLS	32	16	16	NA	2	55	44	44

1998	MLS	32	24	8	NA	2	85	44	68
1999	MLS	32	20	12	NA	3	49	29	54
2000	MLS	32	14	10	8	NA	47	37	50
2001	MLS	26	14	7	5	NA	52	36	47
2002	MLS	28	16	9	3	NA	44	33	51
2003	MLS	30	9	12	9	NA	35	35	36
2004	MLS	30	11	9	10	NA	42	40	43
2005	MLS	32	13	13	6	NA	44	45	45
2006	MLS	32	11	15	6	NA	37	37	39
TOTAL:	11 years	338	167	124	47	11	549	429	526
AVERAGE:		31	15	11	4	1	50	39	48

Playoff Record

Season	GP	W	L	T	GF	GA	Result
1996	6	4	2	0	10	6	Lost MLS Cup to D.C. United.
1997	2	0	1	1	0	3	Lost Quarterfinals to Dallas.
1998	4	2	2	0	10	7	Lost Quarterfinals to Chicago.
1999	6	4	2	0	12	7	Lost MLS Cup to D.C. United.
2000	5	3	1	1	8	2	Lost Quarterfinals to Kansas City.
2001	7	3	2	2	10	10	Lost MLS Cup to San Jose.
2002	6	5	1	0	15	8	**Won MLS Cup.**
2003	2	1	1	0	2	5	Lost Conf. Semifinal to San Jose.
2004	3	1	2	0	2	3	Lost Conference Final to Kansas City.
2005	4	3	0	1	7	2	**Won MLS Cup.**
TOTAL:	45	26	14	5	76	53	
AVERAGE:	5	3	2	0	8	8	

Regular Season Individual Leaders

Season	Goals		Points		GAA (min. 5 games)	
1996	Eduardo Hurtado	21	Eduardo Hurtado	49	Jorge Campos	1.24
1997	Welton	11	Welton	26	Jorge Campos	1.31
1998	Cobi Jones	19	Cobi Jones	51	Matt Reis	1.34
1999	Cobi Jones	8	Cobi Jones	24	Kevin Hartman	0.91
	Carlos Hermosillo	8				
2000	Cobi Jones	7	Cobi Jones	20	Kevin Hartman	1.00
2001	Luis Hernandez	8	Cobi Jones	22	Kevin Hartman	1.25
2002	Carlos Ruiz	24	Carlos Ruiz	49	Joe Cannon	1.10
2003	Carlos Ruiz	15	Carlos Ruiz	35	Kevin Hartman	1.13
2004	Carlos Ruiz	11	Carlos Ruiz	24	Kevin Hartman	1.30
2005	Landon Donovan	12	Landon Donovan	34	Kevin Hartman	1.39
2006	Landon Donovan	12	Landon Donovan	31	Kevin Hartman	1.14

COACHING HISTORY: 1996-1997 Lothar Osiander 22-22; 1997-2000 Octavio Zambrano 59-30; 2000-2004 Sigi Schmid 65-43-24; 2004-2006 Steve Sampson 17-24-10; 2006-present Frank Yallop

LOS ANGELES KINGS

Home City: Inglewood, California
Home Arena: Long Beach Sports Arena (1967-1968)   Capacity: 11,168 [1968]
           Los Angeles Sports Arena (1967-1968)   Capacity: 11,325 [1968]
           The Great Western Forum (1967-1999) *   Capacity: 16,005 [1999]
           Staples Center (2000-present)   Capacity: 18,118 [2005]
Origin of Name: The name was chosen by owner Jack Kent Cooke from names submitted in a Name the Team contest.

Season	League	GP	W	L	T	OL	SL	GF	GA	Pts
1967-1968	NHL	74	31	33	10	NA	NA	200	224	72
1968-1969	NHL	76	24	42	10	NA	NA	185	260	58
1969-1970	NHL	76	14	52	10	NA	NA	168	290	38
1970-1971	NHL	78	25	40	13	NA	NA	239	303	63
1971-1972	NHL	78	20	49	9	NA	NA	206	305	49
1972-1973	NHL	78	31	36	11	NA	NA	232	245	73
1973-1974	NHL	78	33	33	12	NA	NA	233	231	78
1974-1975	NHL	80	42	17	21	NA	NA	269	185	105
1975-1976	NHL	80	38	33	9	NA	NA	263	265	85
1976-1977	NHL	80	34	31	15	NA	NA	271	241	83
1977-1978	NHL	80	31	34	15	NA	NA	243	245	77
1978-1979	NHL	80	34	34	12	NA	NA	292	286	80
1979-1980	NHL	80	30	36	14	NA	NA	290	313	74
1980-1981	NHL	80	43	24	13	NA	NA	337	290	99
1981-1982	NHL	80	24	41	15	NA	NA	314	369	63
1982-1983	NHL	80	27	41	12	NA	NA	308	365	66
1983-1984	NHL	80	23	44	13	NA	NA	309	376	59
1984-1985	NHL	80	34	32	14	NA	NA	339	326	82
1985-1986	NHL	80	23	49	8	NA	NA	284	389	54
1986-1987	NHL	80	31	41	8	NA	NA	318	341	70
1987-1988	NHL	80	30	42	8	NA	NA	318	359	70
1988-1989	NHL	80	42	31	7	NA	NA	376	335	91
1989-1990	NHL	80	34	39	7	NA	NA	338	337	75
1990-1991	NHL	80	46	24	10	NA	NA	340	254	102
1991-1992	NHL	80	35	31	14	NA	NA	287	296	84
1992-1993	NHL	84	39	35	10	NA	NA	338	340	88
1993-1994	NHL	84	27	45	12	NA	NA	294	322	66
1994-1995	NHL	48	16	23	9	NA	NA	142	174	41
1995-1996	NHL	82	24	40	18	NA	NA	256	302	66
1996-1997	NHL	82	28	43	11	NA	NA	214	268	67
1997-1998	NHL	82	38	33	11	NA	NA	227	225	87
1998-1999	NHL	82	32	45	5	NA	NA	189	222	69
1999-2000	NHL	82	39	31	12	4	NA	245	228	94
2000-2001	NHL	82	38	28	13	3	NA	252	228	92
2001-2002	NHL	82	40	27	11	4	NA	214	190	95
2002-2003	NHL	82	33	37	6	6	NA	203	221	78
2003-2004	NHL	82	28	29	16	9	NA	205	217	81
2004-2005	NHL	Season cancelled due to lockout.								
2005-2006	NHL	82	42	35	NA	4	1	249	270	89
TOTAL:	38 years	3014	1203	1360	424	30	1	9987	10637	2863
AVERAGE:		79	32	36	11	1	0	263	280	75

*-Originally known as the Forum from 1967-1988

Playoff Record

Season	GP	W	L	GF	GA	Result
1967-1968	7	3	4	21	26	Lost Quarterfinal series to Minnesota.
1968-1969	11	4	7	28	41	Lost Semifinal series to St. Louis.
1973-1974	5	1	4	7	10	Lost Quarterfinal series to Chicago.
1974-1975	3	1	2	6	7	Lost Preliminary series to Toronto.
1975-1976	9	5	4	17	27	Lost Quarterfinal series to Boston.
1976-1977	9	4	5	35	37	Lost Quarterfinal series to Boston.
1977-1978	2	0	2	3	11	Lost Preliminary series to Toronto.
1978-1979	2	0	2	2	9	Lost Preliminary series to N.Y. Rangers.
1979-1980	4	1	3	10	21	Lost Preliminary series to N.Y. Islanders.
1980-1981	4	1	3	12	23	Lost Preliminary series to N.Y. Rangers.
1981-1982	10	4	6	41	42	Lost Division Final to Vancouver.
1984-1985	3	0	3	11	7	Lost Division Semifinal to Edmonton.
1986-1987	5	1	4	20	32	Lost Division Semifinal to Edmonton.
1987-1988	5	1	4	18	30	Lost Division Semifinal to Calgary.
1988-1989	11	4	7	36	42	Lost Division Final to Calgary.
1989-1990	10	4	6	39	48	Lost Division Final to Edmonton.
1990-1991	12	6	6	46	37	Lost Division Final to Edmonton.
1991-1992	6	2	4	18	23	Lost Division Semifinal to Edmonton.
1992-1993	24	13	11	93	91	Lost Stanley Cup Final series to Montreal.
1997-1998	4	0	4	8	16	Lost Conference Quarterfinal to St. Louis.
1999-2000	4	0	4	6	15	Lost Conference Quarterfinal to Detroit.
2000-2001	13	7	6	25	34	Lost Conference Semifinal to Colorado.
2001-2002	7	3	4	13	16	Lost Conference Quarterfinal to Colorado.
TOTAL:	170	65	105	515	645	
AVERAGE:	7	3	4	22	28	

Regular Season Individual Leaders

Season	Goals		Points		Penalty Minutes	
1967-1968	Bill Flett	26	Eddie Joyal	57	Dave Amodio	101
1968-1969	Eddie Joyal	33	Eddie Joyal	52	Dale Rolfe	85
1969-1970	Eddie Shack	22	Ross Lonsberry	42	Ross Lonsberry	118
1970-1971	Mike Byers	27	Juha Widing	65	Gilles Marotte	96
1971-1972	Juha Widing	27	Juha Widing	55	Mike Corrigan	92
1972-1973	Mike Corrigan	37	Juha Widing	70	Mike Corrigan	146
1973-1974	Robert Goring	28	Robert Goring	61	Mike Corrigan	119
					Terry Harper	119
1974-1975	Bob Nevin	31	Bob Nevin	72	Dan Maloney	165
1975-1976	Marcel Dionne	40	Marcel Dionne	94	Dave Hutchison	181
1976-1977	Marcel Dionne	53	Marcel Dionne	122	Dave Schultz	232
1977-1978	Robert Goring	37	Marcel Dionne	79	Bert Wilson	127
1978-1979	Marcel Dionne	59	Marcel Dionne	130	Randy Holt	202
1979-1980	Charlie Simmer	56	Marcel Dionne	137	Jay Wells	113
1980-1981	Marcel Dionne	58	Marcel Dionne	135	Jay Wells	155
1981-1982	Marcel Dionne	50	Marcel Dionne	117	Jay Wells	145
1982-1983	Marcel Dionne	56	Marcel Dionne	107	Jay Wells	167
1983-1984	Charlie Simmer	44	Bernie Nicholls	95	Jay Wells	141
1984-1985	Marcel Dionne	46	Marcel Dionne	126	Jay Wells	185
	Bernie Nicholls	46				
1985-1986	Marcel Dionne	36	Bernie Nicholls	97	Dave Williams	320
	Bernie Nicholls	36				
1986-1987	Luc Robitaille	45	Luc Robitaille	84	Dave Williams	358
1987-1988	Jimmy Carson	55	Luc Robitaille	111	Larry Playfair	197

Season	Goals		Points		Penalty Minutes	
1988-1989	Bernie Nicholls	70	Wayne Gretzky	168	Marty McSorley	350
1989-1990	Luc Robitaille	52	Wayne Gretzky	142	Marty McSorley	322
1990-1991	Luc Robitaille	45	Wayne Gretzky	163	Jay Miller	259
	Tomas Sandstrom	45				
1991-1992	Luc Robitaille	44	Wayne Gretzky	121	Marty McSorley	268
1992-1993	Luc Robitaille	63	Luc Robitaille	125	Marty McSorley	399
1993-1994	Luc Robitaille	44	Wayne Gretzky	130	Warren Rychel	322
1994-1995	Rick Tocchet	18	Wayne Gretzky	48	Matt Johnson	102
1995-1996	Dimitri Khristich	27	Dimitri Khristich	64	Sean O'Donnell	127
1996-1997	Ray Ferraro	25	Dimitri Khristich	56	Matt Johnson	194
1997-1998	Glen Murray	29	Jozef Stumpel	79	Matt Johnson	249
1998-1999	Luc Robitaille	39	Luc Robitaille	74	Sean O'Donnell	186
1999-2000	Luc Robitaille	36	Luc Robitaille	74	Ian Laperriere	185
2000-2001	Ziggy Palffy	38	Ziggy Palffy	89	Stu Grimson	245
2001-2002	Ziggy Palffy	31	Jason Allison	73	Ian Laperriere	125
2002-2003	Ziggy Palffy	37	Ziggy Palffy	85	Ian Laperriere	122
2003-2004	Alexander Frolov	24	Luc Robitaille	51	Sean Avery	261
2004-2005	Season cancelled due to lockout.					
2005-2006	Pavol Demitra	25	L. Visnovsky	67	Sean Avery	257

COACHING HISTORY: 1967-1969 Leonard "Red" Kelly 55-75-20-.433; 1969-1970 Hal Laycoe 5-18-1-.229; 1969-1970 John Wilson 9-34-9-.260; 1970-1972 Larry Regan 27-47-14-.386; 1971-1972 Fred Glover 18-42-8-.324; 1972-1977 Bob Pulford 178-150-68-.535; 1977-1978 Ron Stewart 31-34-15-.481; 1978-1981 Bob Berry 107-94-39-.527; 1981-1982 Parker MacDonald 13-24-5-.369; 1981-1984 Don Perry 52-85-31-.402; 1983-1984 Rogatien Vachon 1-0-1-.750; 1983-1984 Roger Neilson 8-17-3-.339; 1984-1987 Pat Quinn 75-101-28-.436; 1986-1988 Mike Murphy 20-37-11-.375; 1987-1988 Rogatien Vachon 0-1-0-.000; 1987-1989 Robbie Ftorek 65-56-11-.534; 1989-1990 Cap Raeder & Rick Wilson 6-9-0-.400; 1989-1992 Tom Webster 114-92-33-.546; 1992-1995 Barry Melrose 79-101-29; 1994-1995 Rogatien Vachon 3-2-2-.571; 1995-1999 Larry Robinson 122-161-45-.441; 1999-2006 Andy Murray 215-176-58-30-1-.541; 2005-present John Torchetti

LOS ANGELES LAKERS
(were Minneapolis Lakers)

Home City: Inglewood, California
Home Arena: The Los Angeles Sports Arena (1960-1967)   Capacity: 14,781 [1966]
         The Great Western Forum (1967-1999)*   Capacity: 17,505 [1998]
         Staples Center (2000-present)   Capacity: 18,997 [2006]
Origin of Name: The team kept the same nickname when it moved to L.A. from Minneapolis.

Regular Season Record

Season	League	GP	W	L	PPGF	PPGA	Pct	GB
1960-1961	NBA	79	36	43	114.0	114.1	.456	15
1961-1962	NBA	80	54	26	118.5	120.0	.675	-
1962-1963	NBA	80	53	27	115.5	112.4	.663	-
1963-1964	NBA	80	42	38	109.7	108.7	.525	6
1964-1965	NBA	80	49	31	111.9	109.9	.613	-
1965-1966	NBA	80	45	35	119.5	116.4	.563	-
1966-1967	NBA	81	36	45	120.5	120.2	.444	8
1967-1968	NBA	82	52	30	121.2	115.6	.634	4
1968-1969	NBA	82	55	27	112.2	108.1	.671	-

*-known as the Forum from 1967-1988

1969-1970	NBA	82	46	36	113.7	111.8	.561	2
1970-1971	NBA	82	48	34	114.8	111.7	.585	-
1971-1972	NBA	82	69	13	121.0	108.7	.841	-
1972-1973	NBA	82	60	22	111.7	103.2	.732	-
1973-1974	NBA	82	47	35	109.2	108.3	.573	-
1974-1975	NBA	82	30	52	103.2	107.2	.366	18
1975-1976	NBA	82	40	42	106.9	106.8	.488	19
1976-1977	NBA	82	53	29	106.9	104.1	.646	-
1977-1978	NBA	82	45	37	110.3	107.6	.549	13
1978-1979	NBA	82	47	35	112.9	109.9	.573	5
1979-1980	NBA	82	60	22	115.1	109.2	.732	-
1980-1981	NBA	82	54	28	111.2	107.3	.659	3
1981-1982	NBA	82	57	25	114.6	109.8	.695	-
1982-1983	NBA	82	58	24	115.0	109.5	.707	-
1983-1984	NBA	82	54	28	115.6	111.8	.659	-
1984-1985	NBA	82	62	20	118.2	110.9	.756	-
1985-1986	NBA	82	62	20	117.3	109.5	.756	-
1986-1987	NBA	82	65	17	117.8	108.5	.793	-
1987-1988	NBA	82	62	20	112.8	107.0	.756	-
1988-1989	NBA	82	57	25	114.7	107.5	.695	-
1989-1990	NBA	82	63	19	110.7	103.9	.768	-
1990-1991	NBA	82	58	24	106.3	99.6	.707	5
1991-1992	NBA	82	43	39	100.4	101.5	.524	14
1992-1993	NBA	82	39	43	104.2	105.5	.476	23
1993-1994	NBA	82	33	49	100.4	104.7	.402	30
1994-1995	NBA	82	48	34	105.1	105.3	.585	11
1995-1996	NBA	82	53	29	102.9	98.5	.646	11
1996-1997	NBA	82	56	26	100.0	95.7	.683	1
1997-1998	NBA	82	61	21	105.5	97.8	.744	1
1998-1999	NBA	50	31	19	99.0	96.0	.620	4
1999-2000	NBA	82	67	15	100.8	92.3	.817	-
2000-2001	NBA	82	56	26	100.6	97.2	.683	-
2001-2002	NBA	82	58	24	101.3	94.1	.707	3
2002-2003	NBA	82	50	32	100.4	98.0	.610	9
2003-2004	NBA	82	56	26	98.2	94.3	.683	-
2004-2005	NBA	82	34	48	98.7	101.7	.415	28
2005-2006	NBA	82	45	37	99.4	96.9	.549	9
TOTAL:	46 years	3726	2349	1377				242
AVERAGE:		81	51	30	109.6	106.1	.630	5

Playoff Record

Season	GP	W	L	PPGF	PPGA	Result
1960-1961	12	6	6	117.0	115.6	Lost Division Final to St. Louis.
1961-1962	13	7	6	117.7	116.7	Lost Championship series to Boston.
1962-1963	13	6	7	113.0	110.8	Lost Championship series to Boston.
1963-1964	5	2	3	101.2	107.0	Lost Division Semifinal to St. Louis.
1964-1965	11	5	6	114.3	119.1	Lost Championship series to Boston.
1965-1966	14	7	7	116.6	116.3	Lost Championship series to Boston.
1966-1967	3	0	3	108.3	119.7	Lost Div. Semifinal to San Francisco.
1967-1968	15	10	5	113.5	108.9	Lost Championship series to Boston.
1968-1969	18	11	7	103.4	99.1	Lost Championship series to Boston.
1969-1970	18	11	7	114.0	110.1	Lost Championship series to New York.
1970-1971	12	5	7	99.7	103.8	Lost Conference Final to Milwaukee.
1971-1972	15	12	3	106.6	103.4	**Won NBA Championship.**

1972-1973	17	9	8	103.4	99.2	Lost Championship series to New York.
1973-1974	5	1	4	93.0	106.0	Lost Conference Semifinal to Milwaukee.
1976-1977	11	4	7	103.4	104.2	Lost Conference Final to Portland.
1977-1978	3	1	2	99.0	104.0	Lost 1st Round series to Seattle.
1978-1979	8	3	5	109.4	110.6	Lost Conference Semifinal to Seattle.
1979-1980	16	12	4	110.6	106.3	**Won NBA Championship.**
1980-1981	3	1	2	101.3	102.0	Lost 1st Round series to Houston.
1981-1982	14	12	2	115.4	109.4	**Won NBA Championship.**
1982-1983	15	8	7	109.7	109.1	Lost Championship series to Philadelphia.
1983-1984	22	14	8	111.8	104.8	Lost Championship series to Boston.
1984-1985	19	15	4	126.3	116.2	**Won NBA Championship.**
1985-1986	14	8	6	115.5	107.9	Lost Conference Final to Houston.
1986-1987	18	15	3	120.6	109.2	**Won NBA Championship.**
1987-1988	24	15	9	105.7	103.0	**Won NBA Championship.**
1988-1989	15	11	4	110.5	105.1	Lost Championship series to Detroit.
1989-1990	9	4	5	106.1	103.6	Lost Conference Semifinal to Phoenix.
1990-1991	16	12	4	123.2	122.1	Lost Championship series to Chicago.
1991-1992	4	1	3	94.5	109.3	Lost 1st Round series to Portland.
1992-1993	5	2	3	97.0	100.8	Lost 1st Round series to Phoenix.
1994-1995	10	5	5	92.5	96.6	Lost Conf. Semifinal to San Antonio.
1995-1996	4	1	3	94.8	96.8	Lost 1st Round series to Houston.
1996-1997	9	4	5	95.2	94.1	Lost Conference Semifinal to Utah.
1997-1998	13	7	6	100.2	99.0	Lost Conference Final to Utah.
1998-1999	8	3	5	94.0	96.9	Lost Conference Semifinal to San Antonio.
1999-2000	23	15	8	99.8	97.4	**Won NBA Championship.**
2000-2001	16	15	1	103.5	90.6	**Won NBA Championship.**
2001-2002	19	15	4	97.8	94.1	**Won NBA Championship.**
2002-2003	12	6	6	100.3	100.0	Lost Conference Semifinal to San Antonio.
2003-2004	22	13	9	88.1	86.5	Lost Championship series to Detroit.
2005-2006	7	3	4	100.6	107.3	Lost 1st Round series to Phoenix.
TOTAL:	530	317	213			
AVERAGE:	13	8	5	107.4	104.8	

Regular Season Individual Leaders

Season	Field Goal % (min. 70 games)		Points		Points per Game (min. 70 games)	
1960-61	Tom Hawkins	.431	Elgin Baylor	2538	Elgin Baylor	34.8
1961-62	Rudy LaRusso	.466	Jerry West	2310	Jerry West	30.8
1962-63	Dick Barnett	.471	Elgin Baylor	2719	Elgin Baylor	34.0
1963-64	Gene Wiley	.535	Jerry West	2064	Jerry West	28.7
1964-65	Jerry West	.497	Jerry West	2292	Jerry West	31.0
1965-66	Bob Boozer	.484	Jerry West	2476	Jerry West	31.3
1966-67	Tom Hawkins	.481	Jerry West	1892	Jerry West	28.7
1967-68	Tom Hawkins	.499	Elgin Baylor	2002	Elgin Baylor	26.0
1968-69	W. Chamberlain	.583	Elgin Baylor	1881	Elgin Baylor	24.8
1969-70	Jerry West	.497	Jerry West	2309	Jerry West	31.2
1970-71	W. Chamberlain	.545	Jerry West	1859	W. Chamberlain	20.7
1971-72	W. Chamberlain	.649	Gail Goodrich	2127	Gail Goodrich	25.9
1972-73	W. Chamberlain	.727	Gail Goodrich	1814	Gail Goodrich	23.9
1973-74	Harold Hairston	.507	Gail Goodrich	2076	Gail Goodrich	25.3
1974-75	Harold Hairston	.506	Gail Goodrich	1630	Gail Goodrich	22.6
1975-76	K. Abdul-Jabbar	.529	K. Abdul-Jabbar	2275	K. Abdul-Jabbar	27.7
1976-77	K. Abdul-Jabbar	.579	K. Abdul-Jabbar	2152	K. Abdul-Jabbar	26.2
1977-78	K. Abdul-Jabbar	.550	K. Abdul-Jabbar	1600	K. Abdul-Jabbar	25.8

Season	Field Goal % (min. 70 games)		Points		Points per Game (min. 70 games)	
1978-79	K. Abdul-Jabbar	.577	K. Abdul-Jabbar	1903	K. Abdul-Jabbar	23.8
1979-80	K. Abdul-Jabbar	.604	K. Abdul-Jabbar	2034	K. Abdul-Jabbar	24.8
1980-81	K. Abdul-Jabbar	.574	K. Abdul-Jabbar	2095	K. Abdul-Jabbar	26.2
1981-82	K. Abdul-Jabbar	.579	K. Abdul-Jabbar	1818	K. Abdul-Jabbar	23.9
1982-83	K. Abdul-Jabbar	.588	K. Abdul-Jabbar	1722	K. Abdul-Jabbar	21.8
1983-84	Mike McGee	.594	K. Abdul-Jabbar	1717	K. Abdul-Jabbar	21.5
1984-85	K. Abdul-Jabbar	.599	K. Abdul-Jabbar	1735	K. Abdul-Jabbar	22.0
1985-86	Kurt Rambis	.595	K. Abdul-Jabbar	1846	K. Abdul-Jabbar	23.4
1986-87	K. Abdul-Jabbar	.564	Earvin Johnson	1909	Earvin Johnson	23.9
1987-88	Kurt Rambis	.548	Byron Scott	1754	Byron Scott	21.7
1988-89	M. Thompson	.559	Earvin Johnson	1730	Earvin Johnson	22.5
1989-90	James Worthy	.548	Earvin Johnson	1765	Earvin Johnson	22.3
1990-91	Vlade Divac	.565	James Worthy	1670	James Worthy	21.4
1991-92	Sedale Threatt	.489	Sedale Threatt	1240	Sedale Threatt	15.1
1992-93	A.C. Green	.537	Sedale Threatt	1235	Sedale Threatt	15.1
1993-94	George Lynch	.508	Vlade Divac	1123	Vlade Divac	14.2
1994-95	Vlade Divac	.507	Nick Van Exel	1348	Nick Van Exel	16.9
1995-96	Cedric Ceballos	.530	Cedric Ceballos	1656	Cedric Ceballos	21.2
1996-97	Travis Knight	.509	Eddie Jones	1374	Eddie Jones	17.2
1997-98	Corie Blount	.572	Shaquille O'Neal	1699	Shaquille O'Neal	28.3
1998-99*	Shaquille O'Neal	.576	Shaquille O'Neal	1289	Shaquille O'Neal	26.3
1999-00	Shaquille O'Neal	.574	Shaquille O'Neal	2344	Shaquille O'Neal	29.7
2000-01	Shaquille O'Neal	.572	Shaquille O'Neal	2125	Shaquille O'Neal	28.7
2001-02	S. Medvedenko	.477	Kobe Bryant	2019	Kobe Bryant	25.2
2002-03	Kobe Bryant	.451	Kobe Bryant	2461	Kobe Bryant	30.0
2003-04	Gary Payton	.471	Kobe Bryant	1557	Gary Payton	14.6
2004-05	Chris Mihm	.507	Kobe Bryant	1819	Caron Butler	15.5
2005-06	Kwame Brown	.526	Kobe Bryant	2832	Kobe Bryant	35.4

COACHING HISTORY: 1960-1967 Fred Schaus 315-245-.563; 1967-1969 Butch van Breda Kolff 107-57-.652; 1969-1971 Joe Mullaney 94-70-.573; 1971-1976 Bill Sharman 246-164-.600; 1976-1979 Jerry West 145-101-.589; 1979-1980 Jack McKinney 10-4-.714; 1979-1982 Paul Westhead 111-50-.689; 1981-1990 Pat Riley 533-194-.733; 1990-1992 Mike Dunleavy 101-63-.616; 1992-1994 Randy Pfund 67-80-.456; 1993-1994 Earvin Johnson 5-12-.294; 1994-1999 Del Harris 224-116-.659; 1998-1999 Bill Bartka 1-0-1.000; 1998-1999 Kurt Rambis 24-13-.649; 1999-2004 Phil Jackson 287-123-.700; 2004-2005 Rudy Tomjanovich 24-19-.558; 2004-2005 Frank Hamblen 10-29-.256; 2005-present Phil Jackson

LOS ANGELES RAIDERS
(were Oakland Raiders)
(became Oakland Raiders)

Home City: Los Angeles, California
Home Stadium: Memorial Coliseum   Capacity: 67,800 [1994]
Origin of Name: The team kept the same nickname when it moved from Oakland to L.A.

			Regular Season Record					
Season	**League**	**GP**	**W**	**L**	**T**	**PF**	**PA**	**Pct**
1982	NFL	9	8	1	0	260	200	.889
1983	NFL	16	12	4	0	442	338	.750

*-minimum 40 games.

1984	NFL	16	11	5	0	371	278	.688
1985	NFL	16	12	4	0	354	308	.750
1986	NFL	16	8	8	0	323	346	.500
1987	NFL	15	5	10	0	301	289	.333
1988	NFL	16	7	9	0	325	369	.438
1989	NFL	16	8	8	0	315	297	.500
1990	NFL	16	12	4	0	337	268	.750
1991	NFL	16	9	7	0	298	297	.563
1992	NFL	16	7	9	0	249	281	.438
1993	NFL	16	10	6	0	306	326	.625
1994	NFL	16	9	7	0	303	327	.563
TOTAL:	13 years	200	118	82	0	4184	3924	
AVERAGE:		15	9	6	0	322	302	.590

Playoff Record

Season	GP	W	L	PF	PA	Result
1982	2	1	1	41	27	Lost 2nd Round playoff to N.Y. Jets.
1983	3	3	0	106	33	**Won Super Bowl XVIII.**
1984	1	0	1	7	13	Lost 1st Round playoff to Seattle.
1985	1	0	1	20	27	Lost Divisional playoff to New England.
1990	2	1	1	23	61	Lost Conference Semifinal to Cincinnati
1991	1	0	1	6	10	Lost Wild Card Game to Kansas City.
1993	2	1	1	65	53	Lost Conference Semifinal to Buffalo.
TOTAL:	12	6	6	268	224	
AVERAGE:	2	1	1	38	32	

Regular Season Individual Leaders

Season	Passing Yards		Receiving Yards		Rushing Yards	
1982	Jim Plunkett	2035	Cliff Branch	575	Marcus Allen	697
1983	Jim Plunkett	2935	Todd Christensen	1247	Marcus Allen	1014
1984	Marc Wilson	2151	Todd Christensen	1007	Marcus Allen	1168
1985	Marc Wilson	2608	Todd Christensen	987	Marcus Allen	1759
1986	Jim Plunkett	1986	Todd Christensen	1153	Marcus Allen	759
1987	Marc Wilson	2070	James Lofton	880	Marcus Allen	754
1988	Jay Schroeder	1839	M. Fernandez	805	Marcus Allen	831
1989	Steve Beuerlein	1677	M. Fernandez	1069	Bo Jackson	950
1990	Jay Schroeder	2849	Willie Gault	985	Bo Jackson	698
1991	Jay Schroeder	2562	M. Fernandez	694	Roger Craig	590
1992	Jay Schroeder	1476	Tim Brown	693	Eric Dickerson	729
1993	Jeff Hostetler	3242	Tim Brown	1180	Greg Robinson	591
1994	Jeff Hostetler	3334	Tim Brown	1309	Harvey Williams	983

COACHING HISTORY: 1982-1987 Tom Flores 56-32-0-.636; 1988-1989 Mike Shanahan 8-12-0-.400; 1989-1994 Art Shell 54-38-0-.587

LOS ANGELES RAMS
(were Cleveland Rams)
(became St. Louis Rams)

Home City: Los Angeles, California (1946-1979)
     Anaheim, California (1980-1994)
Home Stadium: Memorial Coliseum (1946-1979)   Capacity: 90,000 [1979]
     Anaheim Stadium (1980-1994)   Capacity: 69,008 [1994]
Origin of Name: The team kept the same nickname when it moved from Cleveland to California.

Regular Season Record

Season	League	GP	W	L	T	PF	PA	Pct
1946	NFL	11	6	4	1	277	257	.600
1947	NFL	12	6	6	0	259	214	.500
1948	NFL	12	6	5	1	327	269	.545
1949	NFL	12	8	2	2	360	239	.800
1950	NFL	12	9	3	0	466	309	.750
1951	NFL	12	8	4	0	392	261	.667
1952	NFL	12	9	3	0	349	234	.750
1953	NFL	12	8	3	1	366	236	.727
1954	NFL	12	6	5	1	314	285	.545
1955	NFL	12	8	3	1	260	231	.727
1956	NFL	12	4	8	0	291	307	.333
1957	NFL	12	6	6	0	307	278	.500
1958	NFL	12	8	4	0	344	278	.667
1959	NFL	12	2	10	0	242	315	.167
1960	NFL	12	4	7	1	265	297	.364
1961	NFL	14	4	10	0	263	333	.286
1962	NFL	14	1	12	1	220	334	.077
1963	NFL	14	5	9	0	210	350	.357
1964	NFL	14	5	7	2	283	339	.417
1965	NFL	14	4	10	0	269	328	.286
1966	NFL	14	8	6	0	289	212	.571
1967	NFL	14	11	1	2	398	196	.917
1968	NFL	14	10	3	1	312	200	.769
1969	NFL	14	11	3	0	320	243	.786
1970	NFL	14	9	4	1	325	202	.692
1971	NFL	14	8	5	1	313	260	.615
1972	NFL	14	6	7	1	291	286	.464
1973	NFL	14	12	2	0	388	178	.857
1974	NFL	14	10	4	0	263	181	.714
1975	NFL	14	12	2	0	312	135	.857
1976	NFL	14	10	3	1	351	190	.750
1977	NFL	14	10	4	0	302	146	.714
1978	NFL	16	12	4	0	316	245	.750
1979	NFL	16	9	7	0	323	309	.563
1980	NFL	16	11	5	0	424	289	.688
1981	NFL	16	6	10	0	303	351	.375
1982	NFL	9	2	7	0	200	250	.222
1983	NFL	16	9	7	0	361	344	.563
1984	NFL	16	10	6	0	346	316	.625
1985	NFL	16	11	5	0	340	277	.688
1986	NFL	16	10	6	0	309	267	.625
1987	NFL	15	6	9	0	317	361	.400
1988	NFL	16	10	6	0	407	293	.625
1989	NFL	16	11	5	0	426	344	.688
1990	NFL	16	5	11	0	345	412	.313
1991	NFL	16	3	13	0	234	390	.188
1992	NFL	16	6	10	0	313	383	.375
1993	NFL	16	5	11	0	221	367	.313
1994	NFL	16	4	12	0	286	385	.250
TOTAL:	49 years	681	364	299	18	15399	13706	
AVERAGE:		14	8	6	0	314	280	.548

Playoff Record

Season	GP	W	L	PF	PA	Result
1949	1	0	1	0	14	Lost Championship game to Philadelphia.
1950	2	1	1	52	44	Lost Championship game to Cleveland.
1951	1	1	0	24	17	**Won NFL Championship**.
1952	1	0	1	21	31	Lost Conference playoff to Detroit.
1955	1	0	1	14	38	Lost Championship game to Cleveland.
1967	1	0	1	7	28	Lost Conference Championship to Green Bay.
1969	1	0	1	20	23	Lost Conference Championship to Minnesota.
1973	1	0	1	16	27	Lost Divisional playoff to Dallas.
1974	2	1	1	29	24	Lost NFC Championship to Minnesota.
1975	2	1	1	42	60	Lost NFC Championship to Dallas.
1976	2	1	1	27	36	Lost NFC Championship to Minnesota.
1977	1	0	1	7	14	Lost Divisional playoff to Minnesota.
1978	2	1	1	34	38	Lost NFC Championship to Dallas.
1979	3	2	1	49	50	Lost Super Bowl game to Pittsburgh.
1980	1	0	1	13	34	Lost 1st Round playoff to Dallas.
1983	2	1	1	31	68	Lost Divisional playoff to Washington.
1984	1	0	1	13	16	Lost 1st Round playoff to N.Y. Giants.
1985	2	1	1	20	24	Lost NFC Championship to Chicago.
1986	1	0	1	7	19	Lost 1st Round playoff to Washington.
1988	1	0	1	17	28	Lost 1st Round playoff to Minnesota.
1989	3	2	1	43	50	Lost Conference Final to San Francisco.
TOTAL:	32	12	20	486	683	
AVERAGE:	2	1	1	23	33	

Regular Season Individual Leaders

Season	Passing Yards		Receiving Yards		Rushing Yards	
1946	Bob Waterfield	1747	Jim Benton	981	Fred Gehrke	371
1947	Bob Waterfield	1210	Jim Benton	511	Ken Washington	444
1948	Jim Hardy	1390	Tom Fears	698	Dick Hoermer	354
1949	Bob Waterfield	2168	Tom Fears	1013	Dick Hoermer	582
1950	N. Van Brocklin	2061	Tom Fears	1116	Glenn Davis	416
1951	N. Van Brocklin	1725	Elroy Hirsch	1495	Dan Towler	854
1952	N. Van Brocklin	1736	Tom Fears	600	Dan Towler	894
1953	N. Van Brocklin	2393	Elroy Hirsch	941	Dan Towler	879
1954	N. Van Brocklin	2637	Bob Boyd	1212	Tank Younger	610
1955	N. Van Brocklin	1890	Tom Fears	569	Ron Waller	716
1956	Billy Wade	1461	Leon Clarke	650	Ron Waller	543
1957	N. Van Brocklin	2105	Bob Boyd	534	Tom Wilson	616
1958	Billy Wade	2875	Del Shofner	1097	Jon Arnett	683
1959	Billy Wade	2001	Del Shofner	936	Ollie Matson	863
1960	Billy Wade	1294	Jim Phillips	883	Jon Arnett	436
1961	Zeke Bratkowski	1547	Jim Phillips	1092	Jon Arnett	609
1962	Zeke Bratkowski	1541	Jim Phillips	875	Dick Bass	1033
1963	Roman Gabriel	1947	Jim Phillips	793	Dick Bass	520
1964	Bill Munson	1533	Bucky Pope	786	Ben Wilson	553
1965	Bill Munson	1701	Tom McDonald	1036	Dick Bass	549
1966	Roman Gabriel	2540	Tom McDonald	714	Dick Bass	1090
1967	Roman Gabriel	2779	Bernie Casey	871	Les Josephson	800
1968	Roman Gabriel	2364	Bernie Casey	565	Willie Ellison	616
1969	Roman Gabriel	2549	Jack Snow	734	Larry Smith	599
1970	Roman Gabriel	2552	Jack Snow	859	Les Josephson	640
1971	Roman Gabriel	2238	Jack Snow	666	Willie Ellison	1000

Season	Passing Yards		Receiving Yards		Rushing Yards	
1972	Roman Gabriel	2027	Jack Snow	590	Willie Ellison	764
1973	John Hadl	2008	Harold Jackson	874	L. McCutcheon	1097
1974	James Harris	1544	Harold Jackson	514	L. McCutcheon	1109
1975	James Harris	2148	Harold Jackson	786	L. McCutcheon	911
1976	James Harris	1460	Ron Jessie	779	L. McCutcheon	1168
1977	Pat Haden	1551	Harold Jackson	666	L. McCutcheon	1238
1978	Pat Haden	2995	Willie Miller	767	Cullen Bryant	658
1979	Pat Haden	1854	Preston Dennard	766	Wendell Tyler	1109
1980	Vince Ferragamo	3199	Bill Waddy	670	Cullen Bryant	807
1981	Pat Haden	1815	Preston Dennard	821	Wendell Tyler	1074
1982	Vince Ferragamo	1609	Preston Dennard	383	Wendell Tyler	564
1983	Vince Ferragamo	3276	Mike Barber	657	Eric Dickerson	1808
1984	Jeff Kemp	2021	Henry Ellard	622	Eric Dickerson	2105
1985	Dieter Brock	2658	Henry Ellard	811	Eric Dickerson	1234
1986	Jim Everett	1018	Henry Ellard	447	Eric Dickerson	1821
1987	Jim Everett	2064	Henry Ellard	799	Charles White	1374
1988	Jim Everett	3964	Henry Ellard	1414	Greg Bell	1212
1989	Jim Everett	4310	Henry Ellard	1382	Greg Bell	1137
1990	Jim Everett	3989	Henry Ellard	1294	Cleveland Gary	808
1991	Jim Everett	3438	Henry Ellard	1052	Robert Delpino	688
1992	Jim Everett	3323	Henry Ellard	727	Cleveland Gary	1125
1993	Jim Everett	1652	Henry Ellard	945	Jerome Bettis	1429
1994	Chris Miller	2104	Willie Anderson	945	Jerome Bettis	1025

COACHING HISTORY: 1946 Adam Walsh 6-4-1-.600; 1947 Bob Snyder 6-6-0-.500; 1948-1949 Clark Shaughnessy 14-7-3-.646; 1950-1952 Joe Stydahar 17-8-0-.680; 1952-1954 Hamp Pool 23-10-2-.686; 1955-1959 Sid Gillman 28-31-1-.475; 1960-1962 Bob Waterfield 9-24-1-.279; 1962-1965 Harland Svare 14-31-3-.323; 1966-1970 George Allen 49-17-4-.729; 1971-1972 Tom Prothro 14-12-2-.536; 1973-1977 Chuck Knox 54-15-1-.779; 1978-1982 Ray Malavasi 40-33-0-.548; 1983-1991 John Robinson 88-55-.615; 1992-1994 Chuck Knox 15-33-0-.313

LOS ANGELES SHARKS
(became Michigan Stags)

Home City: Los Angeles, California
Home Arena: Los Angeles Sports Arena   Capacity: 14,700 [1972]
Origin of Name: Both the Los Angeles Aces and the San Francisco Sharks were to ice teams in the inaugural WHA season, but when the San Francisco team moved to Quebec, Los Angeles adopted the name for their own.

			Regular Season Record						
Season	League	GP	W	L	T	GF	GA	Pts	Pct
1972-1973	WHA	78	37	35	6	259	250	80	.513
1973-1974	WHA	78	25	53	0	239	339	50	.321
TOTAL:	2 years	156	62	88	6	498	589	130	
AVERAGE:		78	31	44	3	249	295	65	.417

				Playoff Record		
Season	GP	W	L	GF	GA	Result
1972-1973	6	2	4	16	23	Lost Quarterfinal series to Houston.

Regular Season Individual Leaders

Season	Goals		Points		Penalty Minutes	
1972-1973	Gary Veneruzzo	43	Gary Veneruzzo	73	Tom Gilmore	191
1973-1974	Marc Tardif	40	Marc Tardif	70	Steve Sutherland	182

COACHING HISTORY: 1972-1974 Terry Slater 42-49-6-.464; 1973-1974 Ted McCaskill 20-39-0-.339

LOS ANGELES SPARKS

Home City: Los Angeles, California
Home Arena: Great Western Forum (1997-1999)   Capacity: 17,505 [1999]
                  Staples Center (2000-present)   Capacity: 18,694 (2005)
Origin of Name:

Regular Season Record

Season	League	GP	W	L	PPGF	PPGA	Pct	GB
1997	WNBA	28	14	14	74.0	71.8	.500	2
1998	WNBA	30	12	18	70.9	72.3	.400	15
1999	WNBA	32	20	12	76.5	72.4	.625	6
2000	WNBA	32	28	4	75.5	67.7	.875	-
2001	WNBA	32	28	4	76.3	67.7	.875	-
2002	WNBA	32	25	7	76.6	69.8	.781	-
2003	WNBA	34	24	10	73.5	71.5	.706	-
2004	WNBA	34	25	9	73.4	69.4	.735	-
2005	WNBA	34	17	17	68.4	69.0	.500	8
2006	WNBA	34	25	9	67.4	70.6	.735	-
TOTAL:	10 years	322	218	104				31
AVERAGE:		32	22	10	73.2	70.2	.677	3

Playoff Record

Season	GP	W	L	PPGF	PPGA	Result
1999	4	2	2	65.8	68.3	Lost Conference final to Houston
2000	4	2	2	78.0	74.5	Lost Conference final to Houston.
2001	7	6	1	74.0	64.6	**Won WNBA Championship.**
2002	6	6	0	77.8	65.0	**Won WNBA Championship.**
2003	9	5	4	72.7	67.7	Lost final series to Detroit.
2004	3	1	2	60.3	67.3	Lost Conf. semifinal to Sacramento.
2005	2	0	2	67.5	78.0	Lost Conference semifinal to Indiana.
2006	5	3	2	67.4	70.6	Lost Conference Final to Sacramento.
TOTAL:	40	25	15			
AVERAGE:	5	3	2	71.7	68.3	

Regular Season Individual Leaders

Season	Field Goals % (20 games min.)		Free Throws % (20 games min.)		Points per Game (20 games min.)	
1997	Pamela McGee	.459	Penny Toler	.839	Lisa Leslie	15.9
1998	S. Van Embricqs	.483	Katrina Colleton	.833	Lisa Leslie	19.6
1999	DeLisha Milton	.530	Ukari Figgs	.875	Lisa Leslie	15.6
2000	C. Machanguana	.578	Allison Feaster	.833	Lisa Leslie	17.8
2001	Latasha Byears	.602	Mwadi Mabika	.861	Lisa Leslie	19.5
2002	DeLisha Milton	.487	Mwadi Mabika	.839	Lisa Leslie	16.9
2003	Rhonda Mapp	.500	Tamecka Dixon	.883	Lisa Leslie	18.4
2004	Lisa Leslie	.494	Mwadi Mabika	.824	Lisa Leslie	17.6
2005	Christi Thomas	.500	T. Whitmore	.868	C. Holdsclaw	17.0
2006	Lisa Leslie	.511	Mwadi Mabika	.889	Lisa Leslie	20.0

COACHING HISTORY: 1997 Linda Sharp 4-7-.364, 1997-1998 Julie Rousseau 22-25-.469, 1999 Orlando Woolridge 20-12-.625; 2000-2004 Michael Cooper 119-31-.793, 2004-Karleen Thompson 11-3-.786; 2005-present Joe Bryant

LOS ANGELES STARS
(were Anaheim Amigos)
(became Utah Stars)

Home City: Los Angeles, California
Home Court: Los Angeles Sports Arena Capacity: 11,325 [1968]
Origin of Name:

Regular Season Record

Season	League	GP	W	L	PPGF	PPGA	Pct	GB
1968-1969	ABA	78	33	45	114.4	117.5	.423	27
1969-1970	ABA	84	43	41	113.7	113.9	.512	8
TOTAL:	2 years	162	76	86				35
AVERAGE:		81	38	43	114.1	115.7	.469	18

Playoff Record

Season	GP	W	L	PPGF	PPGA	Result
1969-1970	17	10	7	116.5	117.7	Lost Championship series to Indiana.

Regular Season Individual Leaders

Season	Field Goal % (min. 70 games)	Points		Points per Game (min. 70 games)	
1968-69	Warren Davis	.501	Larry Miller	1328	Larry Miller	17.0
1969-70	Willie Wise	.476	Mack Calvin	1414	Mack Calvin	16.8

COACHING HISTORY: 1968-1970 Bill Sharman 76-86-.469

LOS ANGELES TOROS
(became San Diego Toros)

Home City: Los Angeles, California
Home Field: Memorial Coliseum Capacity: 103,000
Origin of Name:

Regular Season Record

Season	League	GP	W	L	T	GF	GA	Pts	Pct
1967	NPSL	32	7	15	10	42	61	114	.396

Regular Season Individual Leaders

Season	Goals	Points		GAA (360 Min)	
1967	Eli Durante	15	Eli Durante	35	Lothar Spranger	1.82

COACHING HISTORY: Max Wozniak 7-15-10-.396

LOS ANGELES WOLVES

Home City: Los Angeles, California
Home Stadium: Memorial Coliseum (1967) Capacity: 103,000
                      Rose Bowl (1968)
Origin of Name: As with most of the USA clubs the team was represented by a European professional club, Los Angeles being represented by Wolverhampton.

Regular Season Record

Season	League	GP	W	L	T	GF	GA	BP	Pts	Pct
1967	USA	12	5	2	5	21	14	-	15	.625
1968	NASL	32	11	13	8	55	52	49	139	.483
TOTAL:	2 years	44	16	15	13	76	66	49	154	
AVERAGE:		22	8	7	7	38	33	25	77	

Playoff Record

Season	GP	W	L	T	GF	GA	Result
1967	1	1	0	0	5	6	Won USA Championship.

Regular Season Individual Leaders

Season	Goals		Points		GAA (360 Min)	
1967	Ernie Hunt	4	Ernie Hunt	10	Phil Parkes	1.00
1968	Carlos Metidieri	16	Carlos Metidieri	37		

COACHING HISTORY: 1967 Ronnie Allen 5-2-5-.625; 1968 Ray Wood 11-13-8-.483

LOUISVILLE BRECKS

Home City: Louisville, Kentucky
Home Stadium: Kentucky Fairgrounds (1922)
               Parkway Field (1923)
Origin of Name: The team was originally a boys neighborhood team known as The Floyd and Brecks.

Regular Season Record

Season	League	GP	W	L	T	PF	PA	Pct
1922	NFL	4	1	3	0	13	140	.250
1923	NFL	3	0	3	0	0	83	.000
TOTAL:	2 years	7	1	6	0	13	223	
AVERAGE:		4	1	3	0	7	112	.071

Regular Season Individual Leaders

Season	Passing Yards		Receiving Yards	Rushing Yards
1922				
1923	Jim Kendrick	104		

COACHING HISTORY: 1922 Hubert Wiggs 1-3-0-.250; 1923 Jim Kendrick 0-3-0-.000

LOUISVILLE COLONELS

Home City: Louisville, Kentucky
Home Field: National League Park
Origin of Name: Colonels is a popular nickname and image in Louisville.

Regular Season Record

Season	League	GP	W	L	Pct	GB	R	OR
1876	NL	66	30	36	.455	22	280	344
1877	NL	60	35	25	.583	7	339	288
TOTAL:	2 years	126	65	61		29	619	632
AVERAGE:		63	33	30	.516	14.5	310	316

Regular Season Individual Leaders

Season	Home Runs		RBI's		Wins	
1876	Joe Gerhardt	2	Charles Fulmer	29	Jim Devlin	30
1877	George Shaffer	3	Joe Gerhardt	35	Jim Devlin	35

COACHING HISTORY: 1876 Chick Fulmer 30-36-.455; 1877 Jack Chapman 35-25-.583

LOUISVILLE COLONELS
(merged with the Pittsburgh Pirates in 1900)

Home City: Louisville, Kentucky
Home Field: Eclipse Park I (1882-1893)
           Eclipse Park II (1893-1899)
Origin of Name: Named after previous National League team. The team was first known as the Eclipse and was chosen to honor American Eclipse a famous horse retired to stud in Kentucky.

Regular Season Record

Season	League	GP	W	L	Pct	GB	R	OR
1882	AA	80	42	38	.525	13	443	352
1883	AA	97	52	45	.536	13.5	564	562
1884	AA	108	68	40	.630	7.5	573	425
1885	AA	112	53	59	.473	26	564	598
1886	AA	136	66	70	.485	25.5	833	805
1887	AA	136	76	60	.559	19.5	956	854
1888	AA	135	48	87	.356	44	689	870
1889	AA	138	27	111	.196	66.5	632	1091
1890	AA	132	88	44	.667	-	819	588
1891	AA	139	55	84	.396	40	713	890
1892	NL	152	63	89	.414	40	649	804
1893	NL	125	50	75	.400	34	759	942
1894	NL	130	36	94	.277	54	692	1001
1895	NL	131	35	96	.267	52.5	698	1090
1896	NL	131	38	93	.290	53	653	997
1897	NL	130	52	78	.400	40	669	859
1898	NL	151	70	81	.464	33	728	833
1899	NL	152	75	77	.493	28	827	775
TOTAL:	18 years	2315	994	1321		590	12461	14336
AVERAGE:		128	55	73	.429	33	692	796

Playoff Record

Season	GP	W	L	T	R	OR	Result
1890	7	3	3	1	32	42	Lost World Series to Brooklyn.

Regular Season Individual Leaders

Season	Home Runs		RBI's		Wins	
1882	Pete Browning	5	Not Recorded		Tony Mullane	30
1883	Pete Browning	4	Not Recorded		Guy Hecker	26
					Sam Weaver	26
1884	Pete Browning	4	Not Recorded		Guy Hecker	52
1885	Pete Browning	9	Not Recorded		Guy Hecker	30
1886	John Kerins	4	Not Recorded		Thomas Ramsey	38
	Guy Hecker	4				
1887	Joe Werrick	7	Not Recorded		Thomas Ramsey	37
1888	Joseph Mack	3	Pete Browning	72	Elton Chamberlain	14
	Pete Browning	3				

Season	Home Runs		RBI's		Wins	
1889	Dan Shannon	4				
	Phil Tomney	4				
	Scott Stratton	4	William Weaver	60	Philip Ehret	10
1890	William Wolf	4	Not Recorded		Scott Stratton	34
1891	Tom Cahill	3	William Wolf	82	John T. Fitzgerald	14
1892	Lew Whistler	5	Fred Pfeffer	76	Scott Stratton	21
1893	Tom Brown	5	Willard Brown	85	George Hemming	18
1894	Tom Brown	9	John Grim	70	George Hemming	13
1895	Jimmy Collins	6	Fred Clarke	82	Bert Cunningham	11
1896	Fred Clarke	9	Fred Clarke	79	Charles Fraser	12
1897	Bob Stafford	7	Perry Werden	83	Charles Fraser	15
1898	Honus Wagner	10	Honus Wagner	105	Bert Cunningham	28
1899	Honus Wagner	7	Honus Wagner	113	Charles Phillippe	21

COACHING HISTORY: 1882 John Dyler 6-7-.462; 1882-1883 Bill Reccius 36-28-.563; 1882-1883 Leech Maskrey 36-29-.554; 1883-1884 Joe Gerhardt 55-37-.598; 1884 Mike Walsh 29-22-.569; 1885-1886 Jim Hart 119-129-.480; 1887 John Kelly 76-60-.559; 1888 John Kerins 11-32-.256; 1888 Mordecai Davidson 37-55-.402; 1889 Thomas Esterbrook 2-8-.200; 1889 William Wolf 15-51-.227; 1889 Dan Shannon 9-43-.173; 1889-1892 Jack Chapman 167-172-.493; 1892 Fred Pfeffer 40-54-.426; 1893-1894 Bill Barnie 86-169-.337; 1895-1896 John McCloskey 44-130-.253; 1896 Bill McGunnigle 29-59-.330; 1897 Jim Rogers 17-26-.395; 1897-1899 Fred Clarke 180-210-.462

LOUISVILLE COLONELS

Home City: Louisville, Kentucky
Home Stadium: The team actually operated out of Chicago
Origin of Name: See Above

Regular Season Record

Season	League	GP	W	L	T	PF	PA	Pct
1926	NFL	4	0	4	0	0	108	.000

Regular Season Individual Leaders

Season	Passing Yards		Receiving Yards	Rushing Yards	
1926	Chuck Palmer	78		Lou Metzger	13

COACHING HISTORY: Len Sachs 0-4-0-.000

MEMPHIS GRIZZLIES
(were Vancouver Grizzlies)

Home City: Memphis, Tennessee
Home Court: The Pyramid (2001-2003)   Capacity: 19,342 [2003]
            FedEx Forum (2004-present)   Capacity: 18,400 [2006]
Origin of Name: The team kept the same nickname when it moved to Memphis from Vancouver.

Regular Season Record

Season	League	GP	W	L	PPGF	PPGA	Pct	GB
2001-2002	NBA	82	23	59	89.9	97.3	.280	35
2002-2003	NBA	82	28	54	97.5	100.7	.341	32
2003-2004	NBA	82	50	32	96.7	94.3	.610	8
2004-2005	NBA	82	45	37	93.4	91.1	.549	14
2005-2006	NBA	82	33	49	91.7	93.6	.402	30

AVERAGE:	5 years	410	179	231				119
TOTAL:		82	36	46	93.8	95.4	.437	24

Playoff Record

Season	GP	W	L	PPGF	PPGA	Result
2003-2004	4	0	4	83.5	97.5	Lost 1st Round series to San Antonio.
2004-2005	4	0	4	102.8	113.8	Lost 1st Round series to Phoenix.
2005-2006	4	0	4	84.3	98.3	Lost 1st Round series to Dallas.
TOTAL:	12	0	12			
AVERAGE:	4	0	4	90.2	103.2	

Regular Season Individual Leaders

Season	Field Goal % (min. 70 games)		Points		Points per Game (min. 70 games)	
2001-02	Pau Gasol	.518	Pau Gasol	1441	Pau Gasol	17.6
2002-03	Pau Gasol	.510	Pau Gasol	1555	Pau Gasol	19.0
2003-04	Bo Outlaw	.510	Pau Gasol	1381	Pau Gasol	17.7
2004-05	Mike Miller	.505	Mike Miller	1022	Mike Miller	13.4
2005-06	Pau Gasol	.503	Pau Gasol	1628	Pau Gasol	20.4

COACHING HISTORY: 2001-2003 Sidney Lowe 23-67-.256; 2002-2005 Hubie Brown 83-85-.494; 2004-2005 Lionel Hollins 0-4-.000; 2004-present Mike Fratello

MEMPHIS MAD DOGS

Home City: Memphis, Tennessee
Home Stadium: Liberty Bowl
Origin of Name:

Capacity: 63,068 [1995]

Regular Season Record

Season	League	GP	W	L	T	PF	PA	Pts	Pct
1995	CFL	18	9	9	0	346	364	18	.500

Regular Season Individual Leaders

Season	Passing Yards		Receiving Yards		Rushing Yards	
1995	Damon Allen	3211	Joseph Horn	1415	Alfred Shipman	483

COACHING HISTORY: 1995 Pepper Rodgers 9-9-0-.500

MEMPHIS ROGUES
(became Calgary Boomers)

Home City: Memphis, Tennessee
Home Field: Liberty Bowl
Origin of Name:

Capacity: 50,164 [1979]

Regular Season Record

Season	League	GP	W	L	GF	GA	BP	Pts	Pct
1978	NASL	30	10	20	43	58	41	101	.374
1979	NASL	30	6	24	38	74	37	73	.270
1980	NASL	32	14	18	49	57	42	126	.438
TOTAL:	3 years	92	30	62	130	189	120	300	
AVERAGE:		31	10	21	43	63	40	100	.362

Regular Season Individual Leaders

Season	Goals		Points		GAA (360 Min)	
1978	Jimmy Husband	9	Jimmy Husband	22	John Houska	1.83
1979	Jimmy Husband	9	Jimmy Husband	23	John Houska	2.18
1980	Paul Child	12	Paul Child	27	Bob Stetler	1.52

COACHING HISTORY: 1978-Eddie McCreadie 10-20; 1979 Eddie McCreadie and Charlie Cooke; 1980 Charlie Cooke 14-18

MEMPHIS SHOWBOATS

Home City: Memphis, Tennessee
Home Stadium: Liberty Bowl   Capacity: 50,164 [1985]
Origin of Name: The team was named after the Mississippi Riverboats which traveled through the area in the mid 1800's.

Regular Season Record

Season	League	GP	W	L	T	PF	PA	Pct
1984	USFL	18	7	11	0	320	455	.389
1985	USFL	18	11	7	0	428	337	.611
TOTAL:	2 years	36	18	18	0	748	792	
AVERAGE:		18	9	9	0	374	396	.500

Playoff Record

Season	GP	W	L	PF	PA	Result
1985	2	1	1	67	35	Lost 2nd Round series to Oakland.

Regular Season Individual Leaders

Season	Passing Yards		Receiving Yards		Rushing Yards	
1984	Walter Lewis	1862	Derrick Crawford	703	Alan Reid	723
1985	Mike Kelley	2186	Greg Moser	1145	Tim Spencer	789

COACHING HISTORY: 1984-1985 Pepper Rodgers 18-18-0-.500

MEMPHIS SOUNDS

Home City: Memphis, Tennessee
Home Court: Mid-South Coliseum   Capacity: 10,945 [1975]
Origin of Name: The name was chosen because musician Isaac Hayes was one of the owners. First known as the Memphis Pros and then the Tams. The name "Tams" was chosen in a Name the Team contest and stood for Tennessee, Arkansas and Mississippi which all surround Memphis

Regular Season Record

Season	League	GP	W	L	PPGF	PPGA	Pct	GB
1970-1971	ABA	84	41	43	109.2	109.9	.488	17
1971-1972	ABA	84	26	58	107.5	113.0	.310	34
1972-1973	ABA	84	24	60	111.5	118.1	.286	33
1973-1974	ABA	84	21	63	101.2	108.2	.250	34
1974-1975	ABA	84	27	57	103.6	108.9	.321	31
TOTAL:	5 years	420	139	281				149
AVERAGE:		84	28	56	106.6	111.6	.331	30

Playoff Record

Season	GP	W	L	PPGF	PPGA	Result
1970-1971	4	0	4	98.3	103.3	Lost 1st Round series to Indiana.

Regular Season Individual Leaders

Season	Field Goal % (min. 70 games)		Points		Points per Game (min. 70 games)	
1970-71	Jimmy Jones	.486	Steve Jones	1836	Steve Jones	22.1
1971-72	Wilbert Jones	.469	John Neumann	1409	John Neumann	18.3
1972-73	Lee Davis	.520	G. Thompson	1727	G. Thompson	21.6
1973-74	Charlie Edge	.500	G. Thompson	1498	G. Thompson	19.2
1974-75	Chuck Williams	.494	George Carter	1508	George Carter	18.4

COACHING HISTORY: 1970-1972 Babe McCarthy 67-101-.399; 1972-1973 Bob Bass 24-60-.286; 1973-1974 Butch Van Breda Kolff 21-63-.250; 1974-1975 Joe Mullaney 27-57-.321

MEMPHIS SOUTHMEN

Home City: Memphis, Tennessee
Home Stadium: Memphis Memorial Stadium   Capacity: 50,000 [1975]
Origin of Name: The team was originally to have been called the Toronto Northmen but due to opposition from the Canadian Football League, John Bassett the team's owner moved the team to Memphis and called them the Southmen.

Regular Season Record

Season	League	GP	W	L	T	PF	PA	Pct
1974	WFL	20	17	3	0	629	365	.850
1975	WFL	11	7	4	0	254	206	.636
TOTAL:	2 years	31	24	7	0	883	571	
AVERAGE:		16	12	4	0	442	286	.774

Playoff Record

Season	GP	W	L	PF	PA	Result
1974	1	0	1	15	18	Lost 2nd Round series to Florida.

Regular Season Individual Leaders

Season	Passing Yards		Receiving Yards		Rushing Yards	
1974	John Huarte	2416	Ed Marshall	1159	J.J. Jennings	1524
1975	Danny White	1445	Ed Marshall	582	Willie Spencer	581

COACHING HISTORY: 1974-1975 John McVay 24-7-0-.774

MIAMI DOLPHINS

Home City: Miami, Florida
Home Stadium: Orange Bowl (1966-1986)   Capacity: 75,206 [1986]
           Pro Player Stadium (1987-present)*   Capacity: 75,540 [2005]
Origin of Name: The team's nickname was picked in a Name the Team Contest.

Regular Season Record

Season	League	GP	W	L	T	PF	PA	Pct
1966	AFL	14	3	11	0	213	362	.214
1967	AFL	14	4	10	0	219	407	.286
1968	AFL	14	5	8	1	276	355	.385
1969	AFL	14	3	10	1	233	332	.231
1970	NFL	14	10	4	0	297	228	.714
1971	NFL	14	10	3	1	315	174	.769
1972	NFL	14	14	0	0	385	171	1.000

*-known as Joe Robbie Stadium from 1987 to 1996

1973	NFL	14	12	2	0	343	150	.857
1974	NFL	14	11	3	0	327	216	.786
1975	NFL	14	10	4	0	357	222	.714
1976	NFL	14	6	8	0	263	264	.429
1977	NFL	14	10	4	0	313	197	.714
1978	NFL	16	11	5	0	372	254	.688
1979	NFL	16	10	6	0	341	257	.625
1980	NFL	16	8	8	0	266	305	.500
1981	NFL	16	11	4	1	345	275	.719
1982	NFL	9	7	2	0	198	131	.778
1983	NFL	16	12	4	0	389	250	.750
1984	NFL	16	14	2	0	513	298	.875
1985	NFL	16	12	4	0	428	320	.750
1986	NFL	16	8	8	0	430	405	.500
1987	NFL	15	8	7	0	362	335	.533
1988	NFL	16	6	10	0	319	380	.375
1989	NFL	16	8	8	0	331	379	.500
1990	NFL	16	12	4	0	336	242	.750
1991	NFL	16	8	8	0	343	349	.500
1992	NFL	16	11	5	0	340	281	.688
1993	NFL	16	9	7	0	349	351	.563
1994	NFL	16	10	6	0	389	327	.625
1995	NFL	16	9	7	0	398	332	.563
1996	NFL	16	8	8	0	339	325	.500
1997	NFL	16	9	7	0	339	327	.563
1998	NFL	16	10	6	0	321	265	.625
1999	NFL	16	9	7	0	326	336	.563
2000	NFL	16	11	5	0	323	226	.688
2001	NFL	16	11	5	0	344	290	.688
2002	NFL	16	9	7	0	378	301	.562
2003	NFL	16	10	6	0	311	261	.625
2004	NFL	16	4	12	0	275	354	.250
2005	NFL	16	9	7	0	318	317	.562
2006	NFL	16	6	10	0	260	283	.375
TOTAL:	41 years	624	368	252	4	13524	11834	
AVERAGE:		15	9	6	0	330	289	.593

Playoff Record

Season	GP	W	L	PF	PA	Result
1970	1	0	1	14	21	Lost Divisional playoff to Oakland.
1971	3	2	1	51	48	Lost Super Bowl to Dallas.
1972	3	3	0	55	38	**Won Super Bowl VII.**
1973	3	3	0	85	33	**Won Super Bowl VIII.**
1974	1	0	1	26	28	Lost Divisional playoff to Oakland.
1978	1	0	1	9	17	Lost 1st Round playoff to Houston.
1979	1	0	1	14	34	Lost Divisional playoff to Pittsburgh.
1981	1	0	1	38	41	Lost Divisional playoff to San Diego.
1982	4	3	1	93	53	Lost Super Bowl to Washington.
1983	1	0	1	20	27	Lost Divisional playoff to Seattle.
1984	3	2	1	92	76	Lost Super Bowl to San Francisco.
1985	2	1	1	38	52	Lost AFC Championship to New England.
1990	2	1	1	51	60	Lost Conference Semifinal to Buffalo.
1992	2	1	1	41	29	Lost Conference Final to Buffalo.
1994	2	1	1	48	39	Lost Conference Semifinal to San Diego.

1995	1	0	1	22	37	Lost 1st Round playoff to Buffalo.
1997	1	0	1	3	17	Lost Wild Card Game to New England.
1998	2	1	1	27	55	Lost Conference Semifinal to Denver.
1999	2	1	1	27	79	Lost Conference Semifinal to Jacksonville.
2000	2	1	1	23	44	Lost Conference Semifinal to Oakland.
2001	1	0	1	3	20	Lost 1st Round series to Baltimore.
TOTAL:	39	20	19	780	848	
AVERAGE:	2	1	1	37	40	

Regular Season Individual Leaders

Season	Passing Yards		Receiving Yards		Rushing Yards	
1966	Dick Wood	993	Bo Roberson	519	Joe Auer	416
1967	Bob Griese	2005	Jack Clancy	868	Abner Haynes	346
1968	Bob Griese	2473	Karl Noonan	760	Jim Kiick	621
1969	Bob Griese	1695	Larry Seiple	577	Jim Kiick	575
1970	Bob Griese	2019	Paul Warfield	703	Larry Csonka	874
1971	Bob Griese	2089	Paul Warfield	996	Larry Csonka	1051
1972	Earl Morrall	1360	Paul Warfield	606	Larry Csonka	1117
1973	Bob Griese	1422	Paul Warfield	514	Larry Csonka	1003
1974	Bob Griese	1968	Nat Moore	605	Larry Csonka	749
1975	Bob Griese	1693	Nat Moore	705	Mercury Morris	875
1976	Bob Griese	2097	Nat Moore	625	Benny Malone	797
1977	Bob Griese	2252	Nat Moore	765	Benny Malone	615
1978	Bob Griese	1791	Nat Moore	645	Del Williams	1258
			Duriel Harris	645		
1979	Bob Griese	2160	Nat Moore	840	Larry Csonka	837
1980	David Woodley	1850	Tony Nathan	588	Del Williams	671
1981	David Woodley	2470	Duriel Harris	911	Tony Nathan	782
1982	David Woodley	1080	Jimmy Cefalo	357	Andra Franklin	701
1983	Dan Marino	2210	Mark Duper	1003	Andra Franklin	746
1984	Dan Marino	5084	Mark Clayton	1389	Woody Bennett	606
1985	Dan Marino	4137	Mark Clayton	996	Tony Nathan	667
1986	Dan Marino	4746	Mark Duper	1313	Lorenzo Hampton	830
1987	Dan Marino	3245	Mark Clayton	776	Troy Stradford	619
1988	Dan Marino	4434	Mark Clayton	1129	Lorenzo Hampton	414
1989	Dan Marino	3997	Mark Clayton	1011	Sammie Smith	659
1990	Dan Marino	3563	Mark Duper	810	Sammie Smith	831
1991	Dan Marino	3970	Mark Duper	1085	Mark Higgs	905
1992	Dan Marino	4116	Mark Duper	762	Mark Higgs	915
1993	Scott Mitchell	1773	Irving Fryar	1010	Mark Higgs	693
1994	Dan Marino	4453	Irving Fryar	1270	Bernie Parmalee	868
1995	Dan Marino	3668	Irving Fryar	910	Bernie Parmalee	878
1996	Dan Marino	2795	O.J. McDuffie	918	K. Abdul-Jabbar	1116
1997	Dan Marino	3780	O.J. McDuffie	943	K. Abdul-Jabbar	892
1998	Dan Marino	3497	O.J. McDuffie	1050	K. Abdul-Jabbar	960
1999	Dan Marino	2448	Tony Martin	1037	J.J. Johnson	558
2000	Jay Fiedler	2402	Oronde Gadsen	786	Lamar Smith	1139
2001	Jay Fiedler	3290	Chris Chambers	883	Lamar Smith	968
2002	Jay Fiedler	2024	Chris Chambers	734	Ricky Williams	1853
2003	Jay Fiedler	2138	Chris Chambers	963	Ricky Williams	1372
2004	A.J. Feeley	1893	Chris Chambers	898	Sammy Morris	523
2005	Gus Frerotte	2996	Chris Chambers	1118	Ronnie Brown	907
2006	Joey Harrington	2236	Marty Booker	747	Ronnie Brown	1008

COACHING HISTORY: 1966-1969 George Wilson 15-39-2-.286; 1970-1995 Don Shula 257-133-2-.658; 1996-1999 Jimmy Johnson 36-28-0-.563; 2000-2004 Dave Wannstedt 42-31-0-.575; 2004 Jim Bates 3-4-0-.429; 2005-2006 Nick Saban 15-17-0-.469; 2007-present Cam Cameron

MIAMI FUSION

Home City: Ft. Lauderdale, Florida
Home Field: Lockhart Stadium (1998-2001)   Capacity: 20,450 [2001]
Origin of Name:

Season	League	GP	W	L	T	SOW	GF	GA	Pts
1998	MLS	32	15	17	NA	5	46	68	35
1999	MLS	32	13	19	NA	5	42	59	29
2000	MLS	32	12	15	5	NA	54	52	41
2001	MLS	26	16	5	5	NA	57	36	53
TOTAL:	4 years	122	56	56	10	10	199	215	158
AVERAGE:		31	14	14	3	3	50	54	40

Playoff Record

Season	GP	W	L	T	GF	GA	Result
1998	2	0	2	0	1	3	Lost Semifinals to D.C. United.
1999	2	0	2	0	0	3	Lost Semifinals to D.C. United.
2001	6	3	3	0	5	9	Lost Quarterfinals to San Jose.
TOTAL:	10	3	7	0	6	15	
AVERAGE:	3	1	2	0	2	5	

Regular Season Individual Leaders

Season	Goals		Points		GAA (min. 5 games)	
1998	Diego Serna	11	Diego Serna	31	Jeff Cassar	1.95
1999	Diego Serna	10	Henry Gutierrez	26	Jeff Cassar	1.73
2000	Diego Serna	16	Diego Serna	42	Jeff Cassar	1.16
2001	A.P. Chacon	19	A.P. Chacon	47	Nick Rimando	1.29

COACHING HISTORY: 1998 Carlos Cordoba 8-11; 1998-2000 Ivo Wortmann 21-29-1; 2000-2001 Ray Hudson 27-16-6

MIAMI HEAT

Home City: Miami, Florida
Home Court: Miami Arena (1989-1999)   Capacity: 15,200 [1998]
            American Airlines Arena (2000-present)   Capacity: 16,500 [2006]
Origin of Name: The nickname was chosen in a Name the Team Contest.

Regular Season Record

Season	League	GP	W	L	PPGF	PPGA	Pct	GB
1988-1989	NBA	82	15	67	97.8	109.0	.183	36
1989-1990	NBA	82	18	64	100.6	110.3	.220	36
1990-1991	NBA	82	24	58	101.8	107.8	.293	32
1991-1992	NBA	82	38	44	105.0	109.2	.463	13
1992-1993	NBA	82	36	46	103.6	104.7	.439	24
1993-1994	NBA	82	42	40	103.4	100.7	.512	15
1994-1995	NBA	82	32	50	101.1	102.8	.390	25
1995-1996	NBA	82	42	40	96.5	95.0	.512	18

1996-1997	NBA	82	61	21	94.8	89.3	.744	-
1997-1998	NBA	82	55	27	95.0	90.0	.671	-
1998-1999	NBA	50	33	17	89.0	84.0	.660	-
1999-2000	NBA	82	52	30	94.4	91.3	.634	-
2000-2001	NBA	82	50	32	88.9	86.6	.610	6
2001-2002	NBA	82	36	46	87.2	88.7	.439	16
2002-2003	NBA	82	25	57	85.6	90.6	.305	24
2003-2004	NBA	82	42	40	90.3	89.7	.512	5
2004-2005	NBA	82	59	23	101.5	95.0	.720	-
2005-2006	NBA	82	52	30	99.9	96.0	.634	-
TOTAL:	18 years	1444	712	732				250
AVERAGE:		80	39	41	96.6	97.0	.493	14

Playoff Record

Season	GP	W	L	PPGF	PPGA	Result
1991-1992	3	0	3	99.3	117.3	Lost 1st Round series to Chicago.
1993-1994	5	2	3	89.8	96.6	Lost 1st Round series to Atlanta.
1995-1996	3	0	3	83.7	106.7	Lost 1st Round series to Chicago.
1996-1997	17	8	9	85.1	86.6	Lost Conference Final to Chicago.
1997-1998	5	2	3	87.4	89.6	Lost 1st Round series to New York.
1998-1999	5	2	3	79.0	83.0	Lost 1st Round series to New York.
1999-2000	10	6	4	83.2	80.7	Lost Conf. Semifinal to New York.
2000-2001	3	0	3	78.3	100.7	Lost 1st Round series to Charlotte.
2003-2004	13	6	7	84.1	84.1	Lost Conf. Semifinal to Indiana.
2004-2005	15	11	4	98.0	93.7	Lost Conference Final to Detroit.
2005-2006	23	16	7	96.3	92.5	**Won NBA Championship.**
TOTAL:	102	53	49			
AVERAGE:	9	5	4	89.4	90.4	

Regular Season Individual Leaders

Season	Field Goal % (min. 70 games)		Points		Points per Game (min. 70 games)	
1988-89	Billy Thompson	.487	Kevin Edwards	1094	Kevin Edwards	13.8
1989-90	Billy Thompson	.516	Rony Seikaly	1228	Rony Seikaly	16.6
1990-91	Sherman Douglas	.504	Sherman Douglas	1352	Sherman Douglas	18.5
1991-92	Grant Long	.494	Glen Rice	1765	Glen Rice	22.3
1992-93	Rony Seikaly	.480	Glen Rice	1554	Glen Rice	19.0
1993-94	Matt Geiger	.574	Glen Rice	1708	Glen Rice	21.1
1994-95	Matt Geiger	.536	Glen Rice	1831	Glen Rice	22.3
1995-96	A. Mourning	.523	A. Mourning	1623	A. Mourning	23.2
1996-97	Isaac Austin	.502	Tim Hardaway	1644	Tim Hardaway	20.3
1997-98	P.J. Brown	.471	Tim Hardaway	1528	Tim Hardaway	18.9
1998-99*	C. Weatherspoon	.534	A. Mourning	924	A. Mourning	20.1
1999-00	A. Mourning	.551	A. Mourning	1718	A. Mourning	21.7
2000-01	Anthony Mason	.482	Anthony Mason	1290	Anthony Mason	16.1
2001-02	A. Mourning	.516	Eddie Jones	1480	Eddie Jones	18.3
2002-03	Brian Grant	.509	Caron Butler	1201	Caron Butler	15.4
2003-04	Brian Grant	.471	Eddie Jones	1401	Eddie Jones	17.3
2004-05	Shaquille O'Neal	.601	Dwyane Wade	1854	Dwyane Wade	24.1
2005-06	Udonis Haslem	.508	Dwyane Wade	2040	Dwyane Wade	27.2

*-minimum 40 games.

COACHING HISTORY: 1988-1991 Ron Rothstein 57-189-.232; 1991-1995 Kevin Loughery 133-159-.455; 1994-1995 Alvin Gentry 15-21-.417; 1995-2003 Pat Riley 354-270-.567; 2003-2006 Stan Van Gundy 112-73-.605; 2005-present Pat Riley

MIAMI SEAHAWKS
(became Baltimore Colts)

Home City: Miami, Florida
Home Stadium: Orange Bowl Stadium
Origin of Name:

Regular Season Record

Season	League	GP	W	L	T	PF	PA	Pct
1946	AAFC	14	3	11	0	167	378	.214

Regular Season Individual Leaders

Season	Passing Yards		Receiving Yards		Rushing Yards	
1946	Marion Pugh	608	Lamar Davis	275	Jimmy Nelson	163

COACHING HISTORY: Jack Meagher 1-5-0-.167; Hamp Pool 2-6-0-.250

MIAMI SOL

Home City: Miami, Florida
Home Court: American Airlines Arena   Capacity: 19,600 [2001]
Origin of Name: The name was chosen to create an association with the Miami Heat of the NBA. Sol is Spanish for sun.

Regular Season Record

Season	League	GP	W	L	PPGF	PPGA	Pct	GB
2000	WNBA	32	13	19	57.2	62.5	.406	7
2001	WNBA	32	20	12	61.2	59.3	.625	2
2002	WNBA	32	15	17	63.9	65.3	.469	3
TOTAL:	3 years	96	48	48				12
AVERAGE:		32	16	16	60.8	62.4	.500	4

Playoff Record

Season	GP	W	L	PPGF	PPGA	Result
2001	3	1	2	53.3	61.3	Lost Conference Semifinal to New York

Regular Season Individual Leaders

Season	Field Goal %		Free Throw %		Points per Game	
	(min. 20 games)		(min 20 games)		(min. 20 games)	
2000	Sharon Manning	.478	K. Rasmussen	.844	Sheri Sam	12.8
2001	Tracy Reid	.508	Elena Baranova	.930	Sheri Sam	13.9
2002	K. Rasmussen	.552	K. Rasmussen	.848	Sheri Sam	14.5

COACHING HISTORY: 2000-2002 Ron Rothstein 48-48-.500

MIAMI TOROS
(were Washington Darts)
(became Fort Lauderdale Strikers)

Home City: Miami, Florida
Home Field: Miami Dade North Stadium (1972)
                 Orange Bowl (1973-75)   Capacity: 80,045 [1976]
                 Tamiami Stadium (1976)
Origin of Name: The team was named by owner Joe Robbie. Called Gatos during 1972 season.

Regular Season Record

Season	League	GP	W	L	T	GF	GA	BP	Pts	Pct
1972	NASL	14	3	8	3	17	32	17	44	.349
1973	NASL	19	8	5	6	26	21	22	88	.515
1974	NASL	20	9	5	6	38	24	35	107	.594
1975	NASL	22	14	8	-	47	30	39	123	.621
1976	NASL	24	6	18	-	29	58	28	63	.292
TOTAL:	5 years	99	40	44	15	157	165	141	425	
AVERAGE:		20	8	9	3	31	33	28	85	.480

Playoff Record

Season	GP	W	L	GF	GA	Result
1974	2	1	1	6	5	Lost Championship game to Los Angeles.
1975	2	1	1	2	4	Lost Semifinal series to Tampa Bay.
TOTAL:	4	2	2	8	9	
AVERAGE:	2	1	1	4	4	

Regular Season Individual Leaders

Season	Goals		Points		GAA (360 Min)	
1972	Warren Archibald	6	Warren Archibald	17	Paulo Dias	1.92
1973	Warren Archibald	12	Warren Archibald	29	Ruben Montoya	1.11
1974	Steve David	13	Steve David	26	Osvaldo Toriani	1.20
1975	Steve David	23	Steve David	52	Bill Nuttall	1.18
1976	Cliff Marshall	5	Cliff Marshall	12	Van Taylor	1.92

COACHING HISTORY: 1972 Sal DeRosa, Norm Sutherland; 1973-1974 John Young 17-10-12-.556; 1975-1976 Greg Meyers 20-26-.449

MICHIGAN PANTHERS
(merged with Oakland for the 1985 season)

Home City: Pontiac, Michigan
Home Stadium: Pontiac Silverdome Capacity: 80,638 [1984]
Origin of Name: The name was chosen to fit in with Detroit's other professional sports teams, the Lions and Tigers.

Regular Season Record

Season	League	GP	W	L	T	PF	PA	Pct
1983	USFL	18	12	6	0	451	337	.667
1984	USFL	18	10	8	0	400	382	.556
TOTAL:	2 years	36	22	14	0	851	719	
AVERAGE:		18	11	7	0	426	360	.611

Playoff Record

Season	GP	W	L	PF	PA	Result
1983	2	2	0	61	43	Won USFL Championship.
1984	1	0	1	21	27	Lost 1st Round series to Los Angeles.
TOTAL:	3	2	1	82	70	
AVERAGE:	2	1	1	41	35	

Regular Season Individual Leaders

Season	Passing Yards		Receiving Yards		Rushing Yards	
1983	Bobby Hebert	3568	Anthony Carter	1181	Ken Lacy	1180
1984	Bobby Hebert	3758	Derek Holloway	1219	John Williams	984

COACHING HISTORY: 1983-1984 Jim Stanley 22-14-0

MICHIGAN STAGS
(were Los Angeles Sharks)
(became Baltimore Blades)

Home City: Detroit, Michigan
Home Arena: Cobo Arena   Capacity: 10,500 [1975]
Origin of Name:

Regular Season Record

Season	League	GP	W	L	T	GF	GA	Pts	Pct
1974-1975	WHA	43	14	26	3	107	179	31	.360

Regular Season Individual Leaders

Season	Goals		Points		Penalty Minutes	
1974-75	Gary Veneruzzo	17	Gary Veneruzzo	29	Danny Gruen	84

COACHING HISTORY: John Wilson 14-26-3-.360

MILWAUKEE BADGERS

Home City: Milwaukee, Wisconsin
Home Stadium: Borchert Field
Origin of Name: The name was chosen because Wisconsin's nickname is the Badger State. The badger is Wisconsin's state animal.

Regular Season Record

Season	League	GP	W	L	T	PF	PA	Pct
1922	NFL	9	2	4	3	51	71	.389
1923	NFL	12	7	2	3	100	49	.708
1924	NFL	13	5	8	0	142	188	.385
1925	NFL	6	0	6	0	7	191	.000
1926	NFL	9	2	7	0	41	66	.222
TOTAL:	5 years	49	16	27	6	341	565	
AVERAGE:		10	3	6	1	68	113	.388

Regular Season Individual Leaders

Season	Passing Yards		Receiving Yards		Rushing Yards	
1922	Jim Conzelman	75	McMillin	42	Jim Conzelman	104
1923	Jim Conzelman	345	Ben Winkelman	132	Jim Conzelman	125
1924	Red Dunn	565	Evar Swanson	218	Red Dunn	36
1925	Shorty Barr	84	John Bryan	63	Hank Gillo	35
1926	John Heimsch	119	Lavie Dilweg	126	John Heimsch	112

COACHING HISTORY: 1922 Fritz Pollard 2-4-3-.389; 1923-1924 Jimmy Conzelman 12-10-5-.537; 1925-1926 John Bryan 2-13-0-.133

MILWAUKEE BRAVES
(were Boston Braves)
(became Atlanta Braves)

Home City: Milwaukee, Wisconsin
Home Field: County Stadium   Capacity: 43,911 [1953]
Origin of Name: The team kept the same nickname when it moved from Boston to Milwaukee.

Regular Season Record

Season	League	GP	W	L	Pct	GB	R	OR
1953	NL	154	92	62	.597	13	738	589

1954	NL	154	89	65	.578	8	670	556
1955	NL	154	85	69	.552	13.5	743	668
1956	NL	154	92	62	.597	1	709	569
1957	NL	154	95	59	.617	-	772	613
1958	NL	154	92	62	.597	-	675	541
1959	NL	156	86	70	.551	2	724	623
1960	NL	154	88	66	.571	7	724	658
1961	NL	154	83	71	.539	10	712	656
1962	NL	162	86	76	.531	15.5	730	665
1963	NL	162	84	78	.519	15	677	603
1964	NL	162	88	74	.543	5	803	744
1965	NL	162	86	76	.531	11	708	633
TOTAL:	13 years	2036	1146	890		101	9385	8118
AVERAGE:		157	88	68	.563	8	722	624

Playoff Record

Season	GP	W	L	R	OR	Result
1957	7	4	3	23	25	Won World Series.
1958	7	3	4	25	29	Lost World Series to New York.
TOTAL:	14	7	7	48	54	
AVERAGE:	7	4	3	24	27	

Regular Season Individual Leaders

Season	Home Runs		RBI's		Wins	
1953	Eddie Mathews	47	Eddie Mathews	135	Warren Spahn	23
1954	Eddie Mathews	40	Eddie Mathews	103	Warren Spahn	21
1955	Eddie Mathews	41	Hank Aaron	106	Warren Spahn	17
1956	Joe Adcock	38	Joe Adcock	103	Warren Spahn	20
1957	Hank Aaron	44	Hank Aaron	132	Warren Spahn	21
1958	Eddie Mathews	31	Hank Aaron	95	Warren Spahn	22
1959	Eddie Mathews	46	Hank Aaron	123	Warren Spahn	21
					Lew Burdette	21
1960	Hank Aaron	40	Hank Aaron	126	Warren Spahn	21
1961	Joe Adcock	35	Hank Aaron	120	Warren Spahn	21
1962	Hank Aaron	45	Hank Aaron	128	Warren Spahn	18
1963	Hank Aaron	44	Hank Aaron	130	Warren Spahn	23
1964	Hank Aaron	24	Joe Torre	109	Tony Cloninger	19
1965	Eddie Mathews	32	Eddie Mathews	95	Tony Cloninger	24
	Hank Aaron	32				

COACHING HISTORY: 1953-1956 Charlie Grimm 290-218-.571; 1956-1959 Fred Haney 341-231-.596; 1960-1961 Chuck Dressen 159-124-.562; 1961-1962 George Tebbetts 98-89-.524; 1963-1965 Bob Bragan 258-228-.531

MILWAUKEE BREWERS
(merged with Cincinnati in 1891)

Home City: Milwaukee, Wisconsin
Home Field: Athletic Park   Capacity: 10,000
Origin of Name: The name was chosen because Milwaukee is well known for its many breweries.

FOR RECORD SEE CINCINNATI KELLY'S KILLERS

MILWAUKEE BREWERS
(became St. Louis Browns)

Home City: Milwaukee, Wisconsin
Home Field: Milwaukee Park
Origin of Name: Named after previous baseball teams.

Regular Season Record

Season	League	GP	W	L	Pct	GB	R	OR
1901	AL	137	48	89	.350	35.5	641	828

Regular Season Individual Leaders

Season	Home Runs		RBI's		Wins	
1901	John Anderson	8	John Anderson	99	Bill Reidy	15

COACHING HISTORY: Hugh Duffy 48-89-.350

MILWAUKEE BREWERS
(were Seattle Pilots)

Home City: Milwaukee, Wisconsin
Home Field: County Stadium (1970-2000)   Capacity: 53,192 [2000]
          Miller Park (2001-present)   Capacity: 41,900 [2006]
Origin of Name: Named after previous American League team.

Regular Season Record

Season	League	GP	W	L	Pct	GB	R	OR
1970	AL	162	65	97	.401	33	613	751
1971	AL	161	69	92	.429	32	534	609
1972	AL	156	65	91	.417	21	493	595
1973	AL	162	74	88	.457	23	708	731
1974	AL	162	76	86	.469	15	647	660
1975	AL	162	68	94	.420	28	675	792
1976	AL	161	66	95	.410	32	570	655
1977	AL	162	67	95	.414	33	639	765
1978	AL	162	93	69	.574	6.5	804	650
1979	AL	161	95	66	.590	8	807	722
1980	AL	162	86	76	.531	17	811	682
1981	AL	109	62	47	.569	NA	493	459
1982	AL	162	95	67	.586	-	891	717
1983	AL	162	87	75	.537	11	764	708
1984	AL	161	67	94	.416	36.5	641	734
1985	AL	161	71	90	.441	28	690	802
1986	AL	161	77	84	.478	18	667	734
1987	AL	162	91	71	.562	7	862	817
1988	AL	162	87	75	.537	2	682	616
1989	AL	162	81	81	.500	8	707	679
1990	AL	161	73	88	.453	14.5	732	760
1991	AL	162	83	79	.512	8	799	744
1992	AL	162	92	70	.568	4	740	604
1993	AL	162	69	93	.426	26	733	792
1994	AL	115	53	62	.461	15	547	586
1995	AL	144	65	79	.451	35	740	747
1996	AL	162	80	82	.494	19.5	894	899
1997	AL	161	78	83	.484	8	681	742

1998	NL	162	74	88	.457	28	707	812
1999	NL	161	74	87	.460	22.5	815	886
2000	NL	162	73	89	.451	22	740	826
2001	NL	162	68	94	.420	25	741	807
2002	NL	162	56	106	.346	41	627	821
2003	NL	162	68	94	.420	20	714	873
2004	NL	161	67	94	.416	37.5	634	757
2005	NL	162	81	81	.500	19	726	697
2006	NL	162	75	87	.463	8.5	730	833
TOTAL:	37 years	5860	2771	3089		712.5	25998	27064
AVERAGE:		158	75	83	.473	19.5	703	731

Playoff Record

Season	GP	W	L	R	OR	Result
1981	5	2	3	13	19	Lost Divisional playoff to New York.
1982	12	6	6	56	62	Lost World Series to St. Louis.
TOTAL:	17	8	9	69	81	
AVERAGE:	9	4	5	35	41	

Regular Season Individual Leaders

Season	Home Runs		RBI's		Wins	
1970	Tom Harper	31	Tom Harper	82	Marty Pattin	14
1971	John Briggs	21	Dave May	65	Marty Pattin	14
1972	John Briggs	21	George Scott	88	Jim Lonborg	14
1973	Dave May	25	George Scott	107	Jim Colborn	20
1974	George Scott	17	George Scott	82	Jim Slaton	13
	John Briggs	17				
1975	George Scott	36	George Scott	109	Pete Broberg	14
1976	George Scott	18	George Scott	77	Bill Travers	15
1977	Don Money	25	Don Money	83	Jerry Augustine	12
1978	Larry Hisle	34	Larry Hisle	115	Mike Caldwell	22
1979	Gorman Thomas	45	Gorman Thomas	123	Mike Caldwell	16
1980	Ben Oglivie	41	Cecil Cooper	122	Bryan Haas	16
1981	Gorman Thomas	21	Ben Oglivie	72	Pete Vuckovich	14
1982	Gorman Thomas	39	Cecil Cooper	121	Pete Vuckovich	18
1983	Cecil Cooper	30	Cecil Cooper	126	Jim Slaton	14
1984	Robin Yount	16	Robin Yount	80	Don Sutton	14
1985	Cecil Cooper	16	Cecil Cooper	99	Ted Higuera	15
1986	Rob Deer	33	Rob Deer	86	Ted Higuera	20
1987	Rob Deer	28	Robin Yount	103	Ted Higuera	18
1988	Rob Deer	23	Robin Yount	91	Ted Higuera	16
1989	Rob Deer	26	Robin Yount	103	Chris Bosio	15
1990	Rob Deer	27	Dave Parker	92	Ron Robinson	12
1991	Greg Vaughn	27	Greg Vaughn	98	Bill Wegman	15
					Jaime Navarro	15
1992	Greg Vaughn	23	Paul Molitor	89	Jaime Navarro	17
1993	Greg Vaughn	30	Greg Vaughn	97	Cal Eldred	16
1994	Greg Vaughn	19	Dave Nilsson	69	Cal Eldred	11
1995	John Jaha	20	B.J. Surhoff	73	Ricky Bones	10
1996	John Jaha	34	John Jaha	118	Scott Karl	13
1997	Jeromy Burnitz	27	Jeromy Burnitz	85	Cal Eldred	13
1998	Jeromy Burnitz	38	Jeromy Burnitz	125	Steve Woodard	10
					Scott Karl	10
1999	Jeromy Burnitz	33	Jeromy Burnitz	103	Hideo Nomo	12

Season	Home Runs		RBI's		Wins	
2000	Geoff Jenkins	34	Jeromy Burnitz	98	Jeff D'Amico	12
					Jim Haynes	12
2001	Richie Sexson	45	Richie Sexson	125	Jamey Wright	11
					Ben Sheets	11
2002	Richie Sexson	29	Richie Sexson	102	Ben Sheets	11
2003	Richie Sexson	45	Richie Sexson	124	Ben Sheets	11
2004	Geoff Jenkins	27	Geoff Jenkins	93	Doug Davis	12
2005	Carlos Lee	32	Carlos Lee	114	Chris Capuano	18
2006	Bill Hall	35	Bill Hall	85	Dave Bush	12

COACHING HISTORY: 1970-1972 Dave Bristol 144-209-.408; 1972 Roy McMillan 1-1-.500; 1972-1975 Del Crandall 272-338-.446; 1976-1977 Alex Grammas 133-190-.412; 1978-1980 George Bamberger 235-180-.566; 1980-1982 Bob Rodgers 124-102-.549; 1982-1983 Harvey Kuenn 159-118-.574; 1984 Rene Lachemann 67-94-.416; 1985-1986 George Bamberger 141-171-.452; 1986-1991 Tom Trebelhorn 422-397-.515; 1992-1999 Phil Garner 585-644-.476; 2000-2002 Davey Lopes 144-195-.425; 2002 Jerry Royster 53-94-.361; 2003-present Ned Yost

MILWAUKEE BUCKS

Home City: Milwaukee, Wisconsin
Home Court: Milwaukee Arena (1968-1988)*   Capacity: 10,746 [1974]
     Bradley Center (1988-present)   Capacity: 18,717 [2006]
Origin of Name: The name was chosen in a Name the Team Contest

Regular Season Record

Season	League	GP	W	L	PPGF	PPGA	Pct	GB
1968-1969	NBA	82	27	55	110.2	115.4	.329	30
1969-1970	NBA	82	56	26	118.8	114.2	.683	4
1970-1971	NBA	82	66	16	118.4	106.2	.805	-
1971-1972	NBA	82	63	19	114.6	103.5	.768	-
1972-1973	NBA	82	60	22	107.2	99.0	.732	-
1973-1974	NBA	82	59	23	107.1	99.0	.720	-
1974-1975	NBA	82	38	44	100.7	100.5	.463	9
1975-1976	NBA	82	38	44	101.8	103.3	.463	-
1976-1977	NBA	82	30	52	108.4	111.5	.366	20
1977-1978	NBA	82	44	38	112.4	113.0	.537	4
1978-1979	NBA	82	38	44	114.1	111.8	.463	10
1979-1980	NBA	82	49	33	110.1	106.1	.598	-
1980-1981	NBA	82	60	22	113.1	105.9	.732	-
1981-1982	NBA	82	55	27	108.4	102.9	.671	-
1982-1983	NBA	82	51	31	106.6	102.2	.622	-
1983-1984	NBA	82	50	32	105.7	101.5	.610	-
1984-1985	NBA	82	59	23	110.9	104.0	.720	-
1985-1986	NBA	82	57	25	114.5	105.5	.695	-
1986-1987	NBA	82	50	32	110.4	106.5	.610	7
1987-1988	NBA	82	42	40	106.1	105.5	.512	12
1988-1989	NBA	82	49	33	108.9	105.3	.598	14
1989-1990	NBA	82	44	38	106.0	106.8	.537	15
1990-1991	NBA	82	48	34	106.4	104.0	.585	13
1991-1992	NBA	82	31	51	105.0	106.7	.378	36
1992-1993	NBA	82	28	54	102.3	106.1	.341	29

*-also known as The Mecca

1993-1994	NBA	82	20	62	96.9	103.4	.244	37
1994-1995	NBA	82	34	48	99.3	103.7	.415	17
1995-1996	NBA	82	25	57	95.6	100.9	.305	47
1996-1997	NBA	82	33	49	95.3	97.2	.402	36
1997-1998	NBA	82	36	46	94.5	96.4	.439	26
1998-1999	NBA	50	28	22	91.7	90.0	.560	5
1999-2000	NBA	82	42	40	101.2	101.0	.512	14
2000-2001	NBA	82	52	30	100.7	96.9	.634	-
2001-2002	NBA	82	41	41	97.5	97.7	.500	9
2002-2003	NBA	82	42	40	99.5	99.3	.512	8
2003-2004	NBA	82	41	41	98.0	97.0	.500	20
2004-2005	NBA	82	30	52	97.2	100.2	.366	24
2005-2006	NBA	82	40	42	97.8	98.8	.488	24
TOTAL:	38 years	3084	1656	1428				470
AVERAGE:		81	44	37	105.2	103.5	.537	12

Playoff Record

Season	GP	W	L	PPGF	PPGA	Result
1969-1970	10	5	5	113.4	113.4	Lost Division Final to New York.
1970-1971	14	12	2	109.1	94.6	**Won NBA Championship.**
1971-1972	11	6	5	108.7	102.3	Lost Conference Final to Los Angeles.
1972-1973	6	2	4	99.2	96.7	Lost Conf. Semifinal to Golden State.
1973-1974	16	11	5	101.0	95.4	Lost Championship series to Boston.
1975-1976	3	1	2	112.3	113.3	Lost 1st Round series to Detroit.
1977-1978	9	5	4	112.4	109.8	Lost Conference Semifinal to Denver.
1979-1980	7	3	4	102.3	101.4	Lost Conference Semifinal to Seattle.
1980-1981	7	3	4	107.0	104.4	Lost Conf. Semifinal to Philadelphia.
1981-1982	6	2	4	102.5	106.0	Lost Conf. Semifinal to Philadelphia.
1982-1983	9	5	4	101.6	98.8	Lost Conference Final to Philadelphia.
1983-1984	16	8	8	102.5	101.7	Lost Conference Final to Boston.
1984-1985	8	3	5	109.0	111.3	Lost Conf. Semifinal to Philadelphia.
1985-1986	14	7	7	109.8	112.2	Lost Conference Final to Boston.
1986-1987	12	6	6	118.2	117.7	Lost Conference Semifinal to Boston.
1987-1988	5	2	3	108.6	109.8	Lost 1st Round series to Atlanta.
1988-1989	9	3	6	97.2	102.1	Lost Conference Semifinal to Detroit.
1989-1990	4	1	3	101.0	110.5	Lost 1st Round series to Chicago.
1998-1999	3	0	3	95.3	105.7	Lost 1st Round series to Indiana.
1999-2000	5	2	3	96.0	94.2	Lost 1st Round series to Indiana.
2000-2001	18	9	9	95.7	94.3	Lost Conference Final to Philadelphia.
2002-2003	6	2	4	97.8	102.2	Lost 1st Round series to New Jersey.
2003-2004	5	1	4	87.6	98.2	Lost 1st Round series to Detroit.
2005-2006	5	1	4	97.6	107.2	Lost 1st Round series to Detroit.
TOTAL:	208	100	108			
AVERAGE:	9	4	5	104.3	103.5	

Regular Season Individual Leaders

Season	Field Goal % (min. 70 games)		Points		Points per Game (min. 70 games)	
1968-69	Jon McGlockin	.487	Jon McGlockin	1570	Jon McGlockin	19.6
1969-70	Jon McGlockin	.530	K. Abdul-Jabbar	2361	K. Abdul-Jabbar	28.8
1970-71	K. Abdul-Jabbar	.577	K. Abdul-Jabbar	2596	K. Abdul-Jabbar	31.7
1971-72	K. Abdul-Jabbar	.574	K. Abdul-Jabbar	2822	K. Abdul-Jabbar	34.8
1972-73	K. Abdul-Jabbar	.554	K. Abdul-Jabbar	2292	K. Abdul-Jabbar	30.2
1973-74	K. Abdul-Jabbar	.539	K. Abdul-Jabbar	2191	K. Abdul-Jabbar	27.0

Season	Field Goal % (min. 70 games)		Points		Points per Game (min. 70 games)	
1974-75	K. Abdul-Jabbar	.513	K. Abdul-Jabbar	1949	K. Abdul-Jabbar	30.0
1975-76	Elmore Smith	.518	Bob Dandridge	1571	Bob Dandridge	21.5
1976-77	Swen Nater	.528	Brian Winters	1509	Bob Dandridge	20.8
1977-78	Alex English	.542	Brian Winters	1594	Brian Winters	19.9
1978-79	Marques Johnson	.550	Marques Johnson	1972	Marques Johnson	25.6
1979-80	Marques Johnson	.544	Marques Johnson	1671	Marques Johnson	21.7
1980-81	Marques Johnson	.552	Marques Johnson	1541	Marques Johnson	20.3
1981-82	Bob Lanier	.558	Sidney Moncrief	1581	Sidney Moncrief	19.8
1982-83	Alton Lister	.529	Marques Johnson	1714	Sidney Moncrief	22.5
1983-84	Bob Lanier	.572	Sidney Moncrief	1654	Sidney Moncrief	20.9
1984-85	Alton Lister	.538	Terry Cummings	1861	Terry Cummings	23.6
1985-86	Alton Lister	.551	Terry Cummings	1627	Sidney Moncrief	20.2
1986-87	Ricky Pierce	.534	Terry Cummings	1707	Terry Cummings	20.8
1987-88	Ricky Pierce	.510	Terry Cummings	1621	Terry Cummings	21.3
1988-89	Ricky Pierce	.518	Terry Cummings	1829	Terry Cummings	22.9
1989-90	Ricky Pierce	.510	Ricky Pierce	1359	Ricky Pierce	23.0
1990-91	Fred Roberts	.533	Jay Humphries	1215	Jay Humphries	15.2
1991-92	Fred Roberts	.482	Moses Malone	1279	Dale Ellis	15.7
1992-93	Fred Roberts	.528	Blue Edwards	1382	Blue Edwards	16.9
1993-94	Vin Baker	.501	Eric Murdock	1257	Eric Murdock	15.3
1994-95	Marty Conlon	.532	Glenn Robinson	1755	Glenn Robinson	21.9
1995-96	Benoit Benjamin	.520	Vin Baker	1729	Vin Baker	21.1
1996-97	Vin Baker	.505	Glenn Robinson	1689	Glenn Robinson	21.1
1997-98	Ervin Johnson	.537	Ray Allen	1602	Ray Allen	19.5
1998-99*	Robert Traylor	.537	Glenn Robinson	865	Glenn Robinson	18.4
1999-00	Ervin Johnson	.516	Ray Allen	1809	Ray Allen	22.1
2000-01	Ervin Johnson	.545	Ray Allen	1806	Ray Allen	22.0
2001-02	Darvin Ham	.569	Ray Allen	1503	Sam Cassell	19.7
2002-03	Sam Cassell	.470	Sam Cassell	1536	Sam Cassell	19.7
2003-04	Dan Gadzuric	.524	Michael Redd	1776	Michael Redd	21.7
2004-05	Dan Gadzuric	.539	Michael Redd	1723	Michael Redd	23.0
2005-06	Dan Gadzuric	.553	Michael Redd	2028	Michael Redd	25.4

COACHING HISTORY: 1968-1977 Larry Costello 410-264-.608; 1977-1987 Don Nelson 540-344-.611; 1987-1992 Del Harris 191-154-.554; 1991-1992 Frank Hamblen 23-42-.354; 1992-1996 Mike Dunleavy 107-221-.326; 1996-1998 Chris Ford 69-95-.421; 1998-2003 George Karl 205-173-.542; 2003-2005 Terry Porter 71-93-.433; 2005-present Terry Stotts

MILWAUKEE GRAYS

Home City: Milwaukee, Wisconsin
Home Field: Milwaukee Base-Ball Grounds
Origin of Name: The team was named for the color of their uniforms.

		Regular Season Record						
Season	League	GP	W	L	Pct	GB	R	OR
1878	NL	60	15	45	.250	26	256	386

*-minimum 40 games.

Regular Season Individual Leaders

Season	Home Runs		RBI's		Wins	
1878	Jake Goodman	1	Jake Goodman	27	Sam Weaver	12
	Charlie Bennett	1				

COACHING HISTORY: Jack Chapman 15-45-.250

MILWAUKEE HAWKS
(were Tri-Cities Blackhawks)
(became St. Louis Hawks)

Home City: Milwaukee, Wisconsin
Home Court: Milwaukee Arena   Capacity: 11,000
Origin of Name: The name was a short form of Blackhawks, the team's previous nickname.

Regular Season Record

Season	League	GP	W	L	PPGF	PPGA	Pct	GB
1951-1952	NBA	66	17	49	73.2	81.2	.258	24
1952-1953	NBA	71	27	44	75.9	78.8	.380	21.5
1953-1954	NBA	72	21	51	70.0	75.3	.292	31
1954-1955	NBA	72	26	46	87.4	90.4	.361	17
TOTAL:	4 years	281	91	190				93.5
AVERAGE:		70	23	47	76.6	81.4	.324	23.5

Regular Season Individual Leaders

Season	Field Goal % (min. 50 games)		Points		Points per Game (min. 50 games)	
1951-52	Mel Hutchins	.365	Richard Mehen	703	Richard Mehen	10.8
1952-53	Mel Hutchins	.379	Leo Barnhorst	967	Leo Barnhorst	13.6
1953-54	G. Ratkovicz	.393	Don Sunderlage	760	Don Sunderlage	11.2
1954-55	Bob Pettit	.407	Bob Pettit	1466	Bob Pettit	20.4
	Charles Share	.407				

COACHING HISTORY: 1951-1952 Doxie Moore 17-49-.258; 1952-1954 Fuzzy Levane 38-79-.325; 1953-1955 Red Holzman 36-62-.367

MILWAUKEE UNIONS

Home City: Milwaukee, Wisconsin
Home Field: Wright Street Grounds
Origin of Name: Like so many teams in the Union Association this team adopted the nickname of Unions.

Regular Season Record

Season	League	GP	W	L	Pct	GB	R	OR
1884	UA	12	8	4	.667	35.5	53	34

Regular Season Individual Leaders

Season	Home Runs		RBI's	Wins	
1884		0	Not Recorded	Ed Cushman	4

COACHING HISTORY: Tom Loftus 8-4-.667

MINNEAPOLIS LAKERS
(became Los Angeles Lakers)

Home City: Minneapolis, Minnesota
Home Court: Minneapolis Auditorium (1948-1958)   Capacity: 10,000
            Minneapolis Armory (1959-1960)
Origin of Name: Named Lakers because Minnesota is well known for its 15,000 lakes.

Regular Season Record

Season	League	GP	W	L	PPGF	PPGA	Pct	GB
1947-1948	NBL	60	43	17	64.1	56.6	.717	-
1948-1949	BAA	60	44	16	84.0	76.7	.733	1
1949-1950	NBA	68	51	17	84.1	75.7	.750	-
1950-1951	NBA	68	44	24	82.8	77.4	.647	-
1951-1952	NBA	66	40	26	85.6	79.5	.606	1
1952-1953	NBA	70	48	22	85.3	79.2	.686	-
1953-1954	NBA	72	46	26	81.7	78.3	.639	-
1954-1955	NBA	72	40	32	95.6	94.5	.556	3
1955-1956	NBA	72	33	39	99.3	100.2	.458	4
1956-1957	NBA	72	34	38	102.3	103.1	.472	-
1957-1958	NBA	72	19	53	105.1	111.5	.264	22
1958-1959	NBA	72	33	39	106.0	107.3	.458	16
1959-1960	NBA	75	25	50	107.3	111.4	.333	21
TOTAL:	13 years	899	500	399				68
AVERAGE:		69	38	31	91.0	88.6	.556	5

Playoff Record

Season	GP	W	L	PPGF	PPGA	Result
1947-1948	10	8	2	75.8	67.3	**Won NBL Championship.**
1948-1949	10	8	2	80.3	73.9	**Won BAA Championship.**
1949-1950	13	11	2	84.0	75.5	**Won NBA Championship.**
1950-1951	7	3	4	79.3	82.1	Lost Division Final to Rochester.
1951-1952	13	9	4	82.3	78.9	**Won NBA Championship.**
1952-1953	12	9	3	82.9	77.7	**Won NBA Championship.**
1953-1954	13	9	4	80.3	74.1	**Won NBA Championship.**
1954-1955	7	3	4	94.9	96.0	Lost Division Final to Ft. Wayne.
1955-1956	3	1	2	121.0	102.3	Lost Division Semifinal to St. Louis.
1956-1957	5	2	3	117.8	120.4	Lost Division Final to St. Louis.
1958-1959	13	6	7	106.5	111.0	Lost Championship series to Boston.
1959-1960	9	5	4	104.1	106.0	Lost Division Final to St. Louis.
TOTAL:	115	74	41			
AVERAGE:	10	6	4	92.4	88.8	

Regular Season Individual Leaders

Season	Field Goals		Free Throws		Points	
1947-48	George Mikan	406	George Mikan	383	George Mikan	1195
1948-49	George Mikan	583	George Mikan	532	George Mikan	1698
1949-50	George Mikan	649	George Mikan	567	George Mikan	1865
1950-51	George Mikan	678	George Mikan	576	George Mikan	1932
1951-52	George Mikan	545	George Mikan	433	George Mikan	1523
1952-53	George Mikan	500	George Mikan	442	George Mikan	1442
1953-54	George Mikan	441	George Mikan	424	George Mikan	1306
1954-55	Clyde Lovellette	519	Vern Mikkelsen	447	Vern Mikkelsen	1327
1955-56	Clyde Lovellette	594	Clyde Lovellette	338	Clyde Lovellette	1526

Season	Field Goals		Free Throws		Points	
1956-57	Clyde Lovellette	574	Dick Garmaker	365	Clyde Lovellette	1434
1957-58	Vern Mikkelsen	439	Larry Foust	428	Vern Mikkelsen	1248
1958-59	Elgin Baylor	605	Elgin Baylor	532	Elgin Baylor	1742
1959-60	Elgin Baylor	755	Elgin Baylor	564	Elgin Baylor	2074

COACHING HISTORY: 1947-1959 John Kundla 466-319-.594; 1957-1958 George Mikan 9-30-.231; 1959-1960 John Castellani 11-25-.306; 1959-1960 Jim Pollard 14-25-.359

MINNEAPOLIS MARINES

Home City: Minneapolis, Minnesota
Home Stadium: Nicollet Park
Origin of Name:

			Regular Season Record					
Season	League	GP	W	L	T	PF	PA	Pct
1922	NFL	4	1	3	0	19	40	.250
1923	NFL	9	2	5	2	48	87	.333
1924	NFL	6	0	6	0	14	108	.000
TOTAL:	3 years	19	3	14	2	81	235	
AVERAGE:		6	1	4	1	27	78	.211

		Regular Season Individual Leaders				
Season	Passing Yards		Receiving Yards		Rushing Yards	
1922						
1923	Sid Kaplan	152	Paul Flynn	42	Dick Hudson	98
1924	Wilfred Houle	41	John Simon	25	Marty Norton	8

COACHING HISTORY: 1922 Russel Tollefson 1-3-0; 1923 Harry Mehre 2-5-2-.333; 1924 Joe Brandy 0-6-0-.000

MINNEAPOLIS REDJACKETS

Home City: Minneapolis, Minnesota
Home Stadium: Nicollet Park
Origin of Name:

			Regular Season Record					
Season	League	GP	W	L	T	PF	PA	Pct
1929	NFL	10	1	9	0	42	185	.100
1930	NFL	9	1	7	1	27	165	.167
TOTAL:	2 years	19	2	16	1	69	350	
AVERAGE:		10	1	8	1	35	175	.132

		Regular Season Individual Leaders				
Season	Passing Yards		Receiving Yards		Rushing Yards	
1929	Herb Joesting	135			Herb Joesting	95
1930	Kelly Rodriguez	16	Mally Nydall	16	Herb Joesting	221

COACHING HISTORY: 1929 Herb Joesting 1-9-0-.100; 1930 George Gibson 1-7-1-.167

MINNESOTA FIGHTING SAINTS

Home City: St. Paul, Minnesota
Home Arena: St. Paul Auditorium (1972-1973)   Capacity: 8,000 [1972]
       St. Paul Civic Center (1972-1976)   Capacity: 16,180 [1972]
Origin of Name:

Regular Season Record

Season	League	GP	W	L	T	GF	GA	Pts	Pct
1972-1973	WHA	78	38	37	3	250	269	79	.506
1973-1974	WHA	78	44	32	2	332	275	90	.577
1974-1975	WHA	78	42	33	3	308	279	87	.558
1975-1976	WHA	59	30	25	4	211	212	64	.542
TOTAL:	4 years	293	154	127	12	1101	1035	320	
AVERAGE:		73	38	32	3	275	259	80	.548

Playoff Record

Season	GP	W	L	GF	GA	Result
1972-1973	5	1	4	16	23	Lost Quarterfinal series to Winnipeg.
1973-1974	11	6	5	39	40	Lost Semifinal series to Houston.
1974-1975	12	6	6	44	42	Lost Quarterfinal series to Quebec.
TOTAL:	28	13	15	99	105	
AVERAGE:	9	4	5	33	35	

Regular Season Individual Leaders

Season	Goals		Points		Penalty Minutes	
1972-1973	Wayne Connelly	40	Wayne Connelly	70	Dick Paradise	189
1973-1974	Mike Walton	57	Mike Walton	117	Gord Gallant	223
1974-1975	Mike Walton	48	Mike Walton	93	Gord Gallant	203
1975-1976	Mike Walton	31	Mike Walton	71	Paul Holmgren	121

COACHING HISTORY: 1972-1973 Glen Sonmor 38-37-3-.506; 1973-1976 Harry Neale 116-90-9-.560

MINNESOTA FIGHTING SAINTS
(were Cleveland Crusaders)

Home City: St. Paul, Minnesota
Home Arena: St. Paul Civic Center   Capacity: 15,705 [1977]
Origin of Name: The team was named after the previous WHA team.

Regular Season Record

Season	League	GP	W	L	T	GF	GA	Pts	Pct
1976-1977	WHA	42	19	18	5	136	129	43	.512

Regular Season Individual Leaders

Season	Goals		Points		Penalty Minutes	
1976-77	Mike Antonovich	27	Dave Keon	51	Bill Butters	133

COACHING HISTORY: Glen Sonmor 19-18-5-.512

MINNESOTA KICKS
(were Denver Dynamos)

Home City: Minneapolis, Minnesota
Home Field: Memorial Stadium (University of Minnesota)   Capacity: 56,725 [1977]
Origin of Name: The team name was chosen in a Name the Team Contest.

Regular Season Record

Season	League	GP	W	L	GF	GA	BP	Pts	Pct
1976	NASL	24	15	9	54	33	48	138	.639
1977	NASL	26	16	10	44	36	41	136	.581
1978	NASL	30	17	13	58	43	54	156	.578
1979	NASL	30	21	9	67	48	58	184	.681

1980	NASL	32	16	16	66	56	51	147	.510
1981	NASL	32	19	13	63	57	55	163	.340
TOTAL:	6 years	174	104	70	352	273	307	924	
AVERAGE:		29	17	12	59	46	51	154	.526

Playoff Record

Season	GP	W	L	GF	GA	Result
1976	3	2	1	6	4	Lost Championship series to Toronto.
1977	2	0	2	1	3	Lost Division Final to Seattle.
1978	4	2	2	12	8	Lost Conference Semifinal to New York.
1979	2	0	2	2	4	Lost 1st Round series to Tulsa.
1980	2	0	2	0	3	Lost 1st Round series to Dallas.
1981	4	2	2	5	7	Lost 2nd Round series to Ft. Lauderdale.
TOTAL:	17	6	11	26	29	
AVERAGE:	3	1	2	4	5	

Regular Season Individual Leaders

Season	Goals		Points		GAA (360 Min)	
1976	Alan Willey	16	Alan Willey	39	Geoff Barnett	1.27
1977	Alan Willey	14	Alan Willey	29	Geoff Barnett	1.25
1978	Alan Willey	21	Alan Willey	45	Timo Lettieri	0.63
1979	Alan Willey	21	Alan Willey	49	Volkmar Gross	1.55
1980	Ace Ntsoelengoe	13	Ace Ntsoelengoe	43	Tino Lettieri	1.41
1981	Ron Futcher	14	Ron Futcher	37		

COACHING HISTORY: 1976-1978 Freddie Goodwin 48-32-.597; 1979-1980 Roy McCrohan 23-16; 1980-1981 Freddie Goodwin 33-22

MINNESOTA LYNX

Home City: Minneapolis, Minnesota
Home Arena: Target Center   Capacity: 19,006 [2005]
Origin of Name: The name was chosen to show affiliation with the NBA's Timberwolves.

Regular Season Record

Season	League	GP	W	L	PPGF	PPGA	Pct	GB
1999	WNBA	32	15	17	63.6	66.0	.469	11
2000	WNBA	32	15	17	68.5	68.3	.469	13
2001	WNBA	32	12	20	64.9	67.4	.375	16
2002	WNBA	32	10	22	62.6	65.8	.313	15
2003	WNBA	34	18	16	70.0	69.7	.529	6
2004	WNBA	34	18	16	63.7	64.4	.529	7
2005	WNBA	34	14	20	65.0	67.3	.412	11
2006	WNBA	34	10	24	74.2	80.4	.294	15
TOTAL:	8 years	264	112	152				94
AVERAGE:		33	14	19	66.6	68.7	.424	12

Playoff Record

Season	GP	W	L	PPGF	PPGA	Result
2003	3	1	2	69.0	75.3	Lost Conference semifinal to L.A.
2004	2	0	2	56.0	67.0	Lost Conference semifinal to Seattle.
TOTAL:	5	1	4			
AVERAGE:	3	1	2	63.8	72.0	

Regular Season Individual Leaders

Season	Field Goals % (20 games min.)		Free Throws % (20 games min.)		Points per Game (20 games min.)	
1999	Kristin Folkl	.479	Tonya Edwards	.806	Brandy Reed	16.1
2000	Marla Brumfield	.465	Katie Smith	.869	Katie Smith	20.2
2001	Katie Smith	.393	Katie Smith	.895	Katie Smith	23.1
2002	Tamika Williams	.561	Tamara Moore	.857	Katie Smith	16.5
2003	Tamika Williams	.668	Katie Smith	.881	Katie Smith	18.2
2004	Tamika Williams	.540	Katie Smith	.899	Nicole Ohlde	11.7
2005	Tamika Williams	.551	Nicole Ohlde	.817	Nicole Ohlde	11.2
2006	Seimone Augustus	.456	S. Augustus	.897	S. Augustus	21.9

COACHING HISTORY: 1999 to 2002 Brian Agler 52-76-.406; 2003-2005 Suzie McConnell Serio 50-52-.490; 2006-present Carolyn Jenkins

MINNESOTA MUSKIES
(became Miami Floridians)

Home City: Bloomington, Minnesota
Home Court: Metropolitan Sports Center   Capacity: 15,499
Origin of Name: The name was chosen because the Muskie (a fish) abound in the lakes of Minnesota.

Regular Season Record

Season	League	GP	W	L	PPGF	PPGA	Pct	GB
1967-1968	ABA	78	50	28	108.6	104.7	.641	4

Playoff Record

Season	GP	W	L	PPGF	PPGA	Result
1967-1968	10	4	6	109.2	109.7	Lost 2nd Round series to Pittsburgh.

Regular Season Individual Leaders

Season	Field Goal % (min. 70 games)		Points		Points per Game (min. 70 games)	
1967-68	Erv Inniger	.437	Mel Daniels	1729	Mel Daniels	22.2

COACHING HISTORY: Jim Pollard 50-28-.641

MINNESOTA NORTH STARS
(became Dallas Stars)

Home City: Bloomington, Minnesota
Home Arena: Met Center *   Capacity: 15,174 [1992]
Origin of Name: North Stars was one of the many entries submitted in a Name the Team Contest. Minnesota's official nickname is "North Star State."

Regular Season Record

Season	League	GP	W	L	T	GF	GA	Pts	Pct
1967-1968	NHL	74	27	32	15	191	226	69	.466
1968-1969	NHL	76	18	43	15	189	270	51	.336
1969-1970	NHL	76	19	35	22	224	257	60	.395
1970-1971	NHL	78	28	34	16	191	223	72	.462
1971-1972	NHL	78	37	29	12	191	191	86	.551
1972-1973	NHL	78	37	30	11	254	230	85	.549
1973-1974	NHL	78	23	38	17	235	195	63	.404

*-originally known as Metropolitan Sports Center from 1967 to 1982.

1974-1975	NHL	80	23	50	7	221	341	53	.331
1975-1976	NHL	80	20	53	7	195	303	47	.294
1976-1977	NHL	80	23	39	18	240	310	64	.400
1977-1978	NHL	80	18	53	9	218	325	45	.281
1978-1979	NHL	80	28	40	12	257	289	68	.425
1979-1980	NHL	80	36	28	16	311	253	88	.550
1980-1981	NHL	80	35	28	17	291	263	87	.544
1981-1982	NHL	80	37	23	20	346	288	94	.588
1982-1983	NHL	80	40	24	16	321	290	96	.600
1983-1984	NHL	80	39	31	10	345	344	88	.550
1984-1985	NHL	80	25	43	12	268	321	62	.388
1985-1986	NHL	80	38	33	9	327	305	85	.531
1986-1987	NHL	80	30	40	10	296	314	70	.438
1987-1988	NHL	80	19	48	13	242	349	51	.319
1988-1989	NHL	80	27	37	16	258	278	70	.438
1989-1990	NHL	80	36	40	4	284	291	76	.475
1990-1991	NHL	80	27	39	14	256	266	68	.425
1991-1992	NHL	80	32	42	6	246	278	70	.438
1992-1993	NHL	84	36	38	10	272	293	82	.488
TOTAL:	26 years	2062	758	970	334	6669	7293	1850	
AVERAGE:		79	29	37	13	257	281	71	.449

Playoff Record

Season	GP	W	L	GF	GA	Result
1967-1968	14	7	7	48	39	Lost Semifinal series to St. Louis.
1969-1970	6	2	4	16	20	Lost Quarterfinal series to St. Louis.
1970-1971	12	6	6	35	42	Lost Semifinal series o Montreal.
1971-1972	7	3	4	19	19	Lost Quarterfinal series to St. Louis.
1972-1973	6	2	4	12	14	Lost Quarterfinal series to Philadelphia.
1976-1977	2	0	2	3	11	Lost Preliminary series to Buffalo.
1979-1980	15	8	7	49	57	Lost Semifinal series to Philadelphia.
1980-1981	19	12	7	84	74	Lost Stanley Cup Final to N.Y. Islanders.
1981-1982	4	1	3	14	14	Lost Division Semifinal to Chicago.
1982-1983	9	4	5	34	40	Lost Division Final to Chicago.
1983-1984	16	7	9	47	53	Lost Conference Final to Edmonton.
1984-1985	9	5	4	38	38	Lost Division Final to Chicago.
1985-1986	5	2	3	20	18	Lost Division Semifinal to St. Louis.
1988-1989	5	1	4	15	23	Lost Division Semifinal to St. Louis.
1989-1990	7	3	4	18	21	Lost Division Semifinal to Chicago.
1990-1991	23	14	9	81	75	Lost Stanley Cup Final to Pittsburgh.
1991-1992	7	3	4	19	23	Lost Division Semifinal to Detroit.
TOTAL:	166	80	86	552	581	
AVERAGE:	10	5	5	33	34	

Regular Season Individual Leaders

Season	Goals		Points		Penalty Minutes	
1967-1968	Wayne Connelly	35	Wayne Connelly	56	Dave Balon	90
1968-1969	Danny Grant	34	Danny Grant	65	Bill Goldsworthy	151
1969-1970	Bill Goldsworthy	36	Jean-Paul Parise	72	Barry Gibbs	182
1970-1971	Bill Goldsworthy	34	Jude Drouin	68	Barry Gibbs	132
	Danny Grant	34				
1971-1972	Bill Goldsworthy	31	Bill Goldsworthy	62	Barry Gibbs	128
1972-1973	Bill Goldsworthy	32	Dennis Hextall	82	Dennis Hextall	140
1973-1974	Bill Goldsworthy	48	Dennis Hextall	82	Dennis O'Brien	166

Season	Goals		Points		Penalty Minutes	
1974-1975	Bill Goldsworthy	37	Dennis Hextall	74	Dennis Hextall	147
1975-1976	Bill Hogaboam	28	Bill Hogaboam	51	Dennis O'Brien	187
			Tim Young	51		
1976-1977	Ernie Hicke	30	Tim Young	95	Dennis O'Brien	116
1977-1978	Tim Young	23	Roland Eriksson	60	Jerry Engele	105
1978-1979	Bobby Smith	30	Bobby Smith	74	Greg Smith	147
1979-1980	Al MacAdam	42	Al MacAdam	93	Brad Maxwell	126
	Steve Payne	42				
1980-1981	Steve Payne	30	Bobby Smith	93	Greg Smith	128
1981-1982	Dino Ciccarelli	55	Bobby Smith	114	Dino Ciccarelli	138
1982-1983	Dino Ciccarelli	37	Neal Broten	77	Willi Plett	170
			Bobby Smith	77		
1983-1984	Brian Bellows	41	Neal Broten	89	Willi Plett	316
1984-1985	Steve Payne	29	Brian Bellows	62	Harold Snepsts	232
1985-1986	Dino Ciccarelli	44	Neal Broten	105	Willi Plett	231
1986-1987	Dino Ciccarelli	52	Dino Ciccarelli	103	Willi Plett	263
1987-1988	Dino Ciccarelli	41	Dino Ciccarelli	86	Basil McRae	378
1988-1989	Dave Gagner	35	Dave Gagner	78	Basil McRae	365
1989-1990	Brian Bellows	55	Brian Bellows	99	Basil McRae	351
1990-1991	Dave Gagner	40	Dave Gagner	82	Shane Churla	286
1991-1992	Ulf Dahlen	36	Mike Modano	77	Shane Churla	278
1992-1993	Russ Courtnall	36	Mike Modano	93	Shane Churla	286

COACHING HISTORY: 1967-1970 Wren Blair 48-66-33-.439; 1968-1969 John Muckler 6-22-7-.271; 1969-1970 Charlie Burns 10-22-12-.364; 1970-1975 Jack Gordon 116-124-50-.486; 1973-1974 Parker MacDonald 20-30-11-.418; 1974-1975 Charlie Burns 12-27-2-.317; 1975-1978 Ted Harris 48-104-27-.344; 1977-1978 Andre Beaulieu 6-23-3-.234; 1977-1978 Lou Nanne 7-18-4-.310; 1978-1979 Harry Howell 3-6-2-.364; 1978-1983 Glen Sonmor 155-126-72-.541; 1982-1983 Murray Oliver 18-11-7-.597; 1983-1985 Bill Mahoney 64-74-22-.469; 1985-1987 Lorne Henning 68-72-18-.487; 1986-1987 Glen Sonmor 0-1-1-.250; 1987-1988 Herb Brooks 19-48-13-.319; 1988-1990 Pierre Page 63-77-20-.456; 1990-1993 Bob Gainey 95-119-30-.451

MINNESOTA PIPERS
(were Pittsburgh Pipers)
(became Pittsburgh Pipers)

Home City: Bloomington, Minnesota
Home Court: Metropolitan Sports Center   Capacity: 15,500 [1968]
Origin of Name: The team kept the same name when it moved from Pittsburgh.

Regular Season Record

Season	League	GP	W	L	PPGF	PPGA	Pct	GB
1968-1969	ABA	78	36	42	114.3	114.2	.462	8

Playoff Record

Season	GP	W	L	PPGF	PPGA	Result
1968-1969	7	3	4	110.6	112.3	Lost 1st Round series to Miami.

Regular Season Individual Leaders

Season	Field Goal % (min. 70 games)		Points		Points per Game (min. 70 games)	
1968-69	Art Heyman	.421	Connie Hawkins	1420	Art Heyman	14.4

COACHING HISTORY: Jim Harding 20-12-.625; Vern Mikkelsen 6-7-.462; Gus Young 10-23-.303

MINNESOTA STRIKERS
(were Ft. Lauderdale Strikers)

Home City: Bloomington, Minnesota
Home Field: Hubert H. Humphrey Metrodome   Capacity: 54,711
Origin of Name: The team kept the same nickname when it moved to Bloomington from Ft. Lauderdale.

Season	League	GP	W	L	GF	GA	BP	Pts	Pct
			Regular Season Record						
1984	NASL	24	14	10	40	44	35	115	.319

Regular Season Individual Leaders

Season	Goals		Points		GAA (360 Min)	
1984	Alan Willey	15	Alan Willey	34	Tino Lettieri	1.55

COACHING HISTORY: Dave Chadwick 14-10

MINNESOTA TIMBERWOLVES

Home City: Minneapolis, Minnesota
Home Court: Hubert H. Humphrey Metrodome (1989-1990)   Capacity: 23,000 [1990]
         Target Center (1990-present)   Capacity: 19,006 [2006]
Origin of Name: The name was chosen in a Name the Team Contest.

Regular Season Record

Season	League	GP	W	L	PPGF	PPGA	Pct	GB
1989-1990	NBA	82	22	60	95.2	99.4	.268	34
1990-1991	NBA	82	29	53	99.6	103.5	.354	26
1991-1992	NBA	82	15	67	100.5	107.5	.183	40
1992-1993	NBA	82	19	63	98.1	105.9	.232	36
1993-1994	NBA	82	20	62	96.7	103.6	.244	38
1994-1995	NBA	82	21	61	94.2	103.2	.256	41
1995-1996	NBA	82	26	56	97.9	103.2	.317	33
1996-1997	NBA	82	40	42	96.1	97.6	.488	24
1997-1998	NBA	82	45	37	101.1	100.4	.549	17
1998-1999	NBA	50	25	25	92.9	92.6	.500	12
1999-2000	NBA	82	50	32	98.5	96.0	.610	5
2000-2001	NBA	82	47	35	97.3	96.0	.573	11
2001-2002	NBA	82	50	32	99.3	96.0	.610	8
2002-2003	NBA	82	51	31	98.1	96.0	.622	9
2003-2004	NBA	82	58	24	94.5	89.1	.707	-
2004-2005	NBA	82	44	38	96.8	95.3	.537	8
2005-2006	NBA	82	33	49	91.7	93.6	.402	11
TOTAL:	17 years	1362	595	767				353
AVERAGE:		80	35	45	97.1	98.9	.437	21

Playoff Record

Season	GP	W	L	PPGF	PPGA	Result
1996-1997	3	0	3	99.7	111.0	Lost 1st Round series to Houston.
1997-1998	5	2	3	90.2	96.0	Lost 1st Round series to Seattle.
1998-1999	4	1	3	80.5	86.8	Lost 1st Round series to San Antonio.
1999-2000	4	1	3	85.3	87.3	Lost 1st Round series to Portland.

2000-2001	4	1	3	82.0	88.5	Lost 1st Round series to San Antonio.
2001-2002	3	0	3	102.0	112.7	Lost 1st Round series to Dallas.
2002-2003	6	2	4	100.5	106.8	Lost 1st Round series to Lakers.
2003-2004	18	10	8	91.9	92.6	Lost Conference Final to Lakers.
TOTAL:	47	17	30		
AVERAGE:	6	2	4	91.6	95.9

Regular Season Individual Leaders

Season	Field Goal % (min. 70 games)		Points		Points per Game (min. 70 games)	
1989-90	Tyrone Corbin	.481	Tony Campbell	1903	Tony Campbell	23.2
1990-91	Felton Spencer	.512	Tony Campbell	1678	Tony Campbell	21.8
1991-92	Doug West	.518	J. Richardson	1350	Tony Campbell	16.8
1992-93	Doug West	.517	Doug West	1543	Doug West	19.3
1993-94	Thurl Bailey	.510	Isaiah Rider	1313	C. Laettner	16.8
1994-95	C. Laettner	.489	Isaiah Rider	1532	Isaiah Rider	20.4
1995-96	Kevin Garnett	.491	Isaiah Rider	1470	Isaiah Rider	19.6
1996-97	Cherokee Parks	.510	Tom Gugliotta	1672	Tom Gugliotta	20.6
1997-98	Cherokee Parks	.499	Kevin Garnett	1518	Kevin Garnett	18.5
1998-99*	Dean Garrett	.502	Kevin Garnett	977	Kevin Garnett	20.8
1999-00	Wally Szczerbiak	.511	Kevin Garnett	1857	Kevin Garnett	22.9
2000-01	Wally Szczerbiak	.510	Kevin Garnett	1784	Kevin Garnett	22.0
2001-02	Joe Smith	.511	Kevin Garnett	1714	Kevin Garnett	21.2
2002-03	Gary Trent	.535	Kevin Garnett	1883	Kevin Garnett	23.0
2003-04	Kevin Garnett	.499	Kevin Garnett	1987	Kevin Garnett	24.2
2004-05	Wally Szczerbiak	.506	Kevin Garnett	1817	Kevin Garnett	22.2
2005-06	Kevin Garnett	.526	Kevin Garnett	1656	Kevin Garnett	21.8

COACHING HISTORY: 1989-1991 Bill Musselman 51-113-.311; 1991-1993 Jimmy Rodgers 21-90-.189; 1992-1994 Sidney Lowe 33-102-.244; 1994-1996 Bill Blair 27-75-.265; 1995-2005 Flip Saunders 353-303-.538; 2004-2005 Kevin McHale 19-11-.633; 2005-present Dwane Casey

MINNESOTA TWINS
(were Washington Senators)

Home City: Bloomington, Minnesota (1960-1981)
           Minneapolis, Minnesota (1982-present)
Home Field: Metropolitan Stadium (1960-1981)   Capacity: 45,919 [1975]
           Hubert H. Humphrey Metrodome (1982-present)   Capacity: 56,144 [2006]
Origin of Name: The team was named for the twin cities of Minneapolis and St. Paul.

Regular Season Record

Season	League	GP	W	L	Pct	GB	R	OR
1961	AL	160	70	90	.438	38	707	778
1962	AL	162	91	71	.562	5	798	713
1963	AL	161	91	70	.565	13	767	602
1964	AL	162	79	83	.488	20	737	678
1965	AL	162	102	60	.630	-	774	600
1966	AL	162	89	73	.549	9	663	581
1967	AL	162	91	71	.562	1	671	590
1968	AL	162	79	83	.488	24	562	546
1969	AL	162	97	65	.599	-	790	618
1970	AL	162	98	64	.605	-	744	605

*-minimum 40 games.

1971	AL	160	74	86	.463	26.5	654	670
1972	AL	154	77	77	.500	15.5	537	535
1973	AL	162	81	81	.500	13	738	692
1974	AL	162	82	80	.506	8	673	669
1975	AL	159	76	83	.478	20.5	724	736
1976	AL	162	85	77	.525	5	743	704
1977	AL	161	84	77	.522	17.5	867	776
1978	AL	162	73	89	.451	19	666	678
1979	AL	162	82	80	.506	6	764	725
1980	AL	161	77	84	.478	19.5	670	724
1981	AL	109	41	68	.376	NA	378	486
1982	AL	162	60	102	.370	33	657	819
1983	AL	162	70	92	.432	29	709	822
1984	AL	162	81	81	.500	3	673	675
1985	AL	162	77	85	.475	14	705	782
1986	AL	162	71	91	.438	21	741	839
1987	AL	162	85	77	.525	-	786	806
1988	AL	162	91	71	.562	13	759	672
1989	AL	162	80	82	.494	19	740	738
1990	AL	162	74	88	.457	29	666	729
1991	AL	162	95	67	.586	-	776	652
1992	AL	162	90	72	.556	6	747	653
1993	AL	162	71	91	.438	23	693	830
1994	AL	113	53	60	.469	14	594	688
1995	AL	144	56	88	.389	44	703	889
1996	AL	162	78	84	.481	21.5	877	900
1997	AL	162	68	94	.420	18.5	772	861
1998	AL	162	70	92	.432	19	734	818
1999	AL	160	63	97	.394	33	686	845
2000	AL	162	69	93	.426	26	748	880
2001	AL	162	85	77	.525	6	771	766
2002	AL	161	94	67	.584	-	768	712
2003	AL	162	90	72	.556	-	801	758
2004	AL	162	92	70	.568	-	780	715
2005	AL	162	83	79	.512	16	688	662
2006	AL	162	96	66	.593	-	801	683
TOTAL:	46 years	7311	3661	3650		648.5	33002	32900
AVERAGE:		159	80	79	.501	14	717	715

Season	GP	W	L	Playoff Record R	OR	Result
1965	7	3	4	20	24	Lost World Series to Los Angeles.
1969	3	0	3	5	16	Lost ALCS to Baltimore.
1970	3	0	3	10	27	Lost ALCS to Baltimore.
1987	12	8	4	72	49	**Won World Series.**
1991	12	8	4	47	44	**Won World Series.**
2002	10	4	6	39	55	Lost ALCS to Anaheim.
2003	4	1	3	6	16	Lost Division series to Yankees.
2004	4	1	3	17	21	Lost Division series to Yankees.
2006	3	0	3	7	16	Lost Division series to Oakland.
TOTAL:	58	25	33	223	268	
AVERAGE:	7	3	4	25	30	

Regular Season Individual Leaders

Season	Home Runs		RBI's		Wins	
1961	Harmon Killebrew	46	Harmon Killebrew	122	Camilo Pascual	15
1962	Harmon Killebrew	48	Harmon Killebrew	126	Camilo Pascual	20
1963	Harmon Killebrew	45	Harmon Killebrew	96	Camilo Pascual	21
1964	Harmon Killebrew	49	Harmon Killebrew	111	Jim Kaat	17
1965	Harmon Killebrew	25	Tony Oliva	98	James Grant	21
1966	Harmon Killebrew	39	Harmon Killebrew	110	Jim Kaat	25
1967	Harmon Killebrew	44	Harmon Killebrew	113	Dean Chance	20
1968	Bob Allison	22	Tony Oliva	68	Dean Chance	16
1969	Harmon Killebrew	49	Harmon Killebrew	140	Jim Perry	20
					Dave Boswell	20
1970	Harmon Killebrew	41	Harmon Killebrew	113	Jim Perry	24
1971	Harmon Killebrew	28	Harmon Killebrew	119	Jim Perry	17
1972	Harmon Killebrew	26	Bobby Darwin	80	Bert Blyleven	17
1973	Bobby Darwin	18	Tony Oliva	92	Bert Blyleven	20
1974	Bobby Darwin	25	Bobby Darwin	94	Bert Blyleven	17
1975	Dan Ford	15	Rod Carew	80	Jim Hughes	16
1976	Dan Ford	20	Larry Hisle	96	Bill Campbell	17
1977	Larry Hisle	28	Larry Hisle	119	Dave Goltz	20
1978	Roy Smalley	19	Dan Ford	82	Dave Goltz	15
1979	Roy Smalley	24	Roy Smalley	95	Jerry Koosman	20
1980	John Castino	13	John Castino	64	Jerry Koosman	16
1981	Roy Smalley	7	Mickey Hatcher	37	Pete Redfern	9
1982	Gary Ward	28	Kent Hrbek	92	Bobby Castillo	13
1983	Tom Brunansky	28	Gary Ward	88	Ken Schrom	15
1984	Tom Brunansky	32	Kent Hrbek	107	Frank Viola	18
1985	Tom Brunansky	27	Kent Hrbek	93	Frank Viola	18
1986	Gary Gaetti	34	Gary Gaetti	108	Bert Blyleven	17
1987	Kent Hrbek	34	Gary Gaetti	109	Frank Viola	17
1988	Gary Gaetti	28	Kirby Puckett	121	Frank Viola	24
1989	Kent Hrbek	25	Kirby Puckett	85	Allan Anderson	17
1990	Kent Hrbek	22	Gary Gaetti	85	Kevin Tapani	12
1991	Chili Davis	29	Chili Davis	93	Scott Erickson	20
1992	Kirby Puckett	19	Kirby Puckett	110	John Smiley	16
					Kevin Tapani	16
1993	Kent Hrbek	25	Kirby Puckett	89	Kevin Tapani	12
1994	Kirby Puckett	20	Kirby Puckett	112	Kevin Tapani	11
1995	Marty Cordova	24	Kirby Puckett	99	Brad Radke	11
1996	Marty Cordova	16	Paul Molitor	113	Frank Rodriguez	13
1997	Marty Cordova	16	Paul Molitor	89	Brad Radke	20
1998	Matt Lawton	21	Matt Lawton	77	Brad Radke	12
1999	Ron Coomer	16	Marty Cordova	70	Brad Radke	12
2000	Jacques Jones	19	Matt Lawton	88	Eric Milton	13
2001	Torii Hunter	27	Corey Koskie	103	Joe Mays	17
2002	Torii Hunter	29	Torii Hunter	94	Rick Reed	15
2003	Torii Hunter	26	Torii Hunter	102	Brad Radke	14
					Kyle Lohse	14
2004	Corey Koskie	25	Torii Hunter	81	Johan Santana	20
2005	Jacque Jones	23	Justin Morneau	79	Johan Santana	16
2006	Justin Morneau	34	Justin Morneau	130	Johan Santana	19

COACHING HISTORY: 1961 Harry Lavagetto 29-45-.392; 1961-1967 Sam Mele 518-427-.548; 1967-1968 Cal Ermer 145-129-.529; 1969 Billy Martin 97-65-.599; 1970-1972 Bill

Rigney 208- 184-.531; 1972-1975 Frank Quilici 280-287-.494; 1976-1980 Gene Mauch 378-394-.490; 1980-1981 John Goryl 34-38-.472; 1981-1985 Bill Gardner 268-353-.432; 1985-1986 Ray Miller 109-130-.456; 1986-2001 Tom Kelly 1140-1244-.478; 2002-present Ron Gardenhire

MINNESOTA VIKINGS

Home City: Bloomington, Minnesota (1961-1981)
Minneapolis, Minnesota (1982-present)
Home Stadium: Metropolitan Stadium (1961-1981)   Capacity: 48,446 [1981]
Hubert H. Humphrey Metrodome (1982-present)   Capacity: 64,121 [2005]
Origin of Name: The team was named by the team's first G.M. Bert Rose, because of Minnesota's large Scandinavian population.

Regular Season Record

Season	League	GP	W	L	T	PF	PA	Pct
1961	NFL	14	3	11	0	285	407	.214
1962	NFL	14	2	11	1	254	410	.179
1963	NFL	14	5	8	1	309	390	.393
1964	NFL	14	8	5	1	355	296	.607
1965	NFL	14	7	7	0	383	403	.500
1966	NFL	14	4	9	1	292	304	.321
1967	NFL	14	3	8	3	233	294	.321
1968	NFL	14	8	6	0	282	242	.571
1969	NFL	14	12	2	0	379	133	.857
1970	NFL	14	12	2	0	335	143	.857
1971	NFL	14	11	3	0	245	139	.786
1972	NFL	14	7	7	0	301	252	.500
1973	NFL	14	12	2	0	296	168	.857
1974	NFL	14	10	4	0	310	195	.714
1975	NFL	14	12	2	0	377	180	.857
1976	NFL	14	11	2	1	305	176	.821
1977	NFL	14	9	5	0	231	227	.643
1978	NFL	16	8	7	1	294	306	.531
1979	NFL	16	7	9	0	259	337	.438
1980	NFL	16	9	7	0	317	308	.563
1981	NFL	16	7	9	0	325	369	.438
1982	NFL	9	5	4	0	187	198	.556
1983	NFL	16	8	8	0	316	348	.500
1984	NFL	16	3	13	0	276	484	.188
1985	NFL	16	7	9	0	346	359	.438
1986	NFL	16	9	7	0	398	273	.563
1987	NFL	15	8	7	0	336	335	.533
1988	NFL	16	11	5	0	406	233	.688
1989	NFL	16	10	6	0	351	275	.625
1990	NFL	16	6	10	0	351	326	.375
1991	NFL	16	8	8	0	301	306	.500
1992	NFL	16	11	5	0	374	249	.688
1993	NFL	16	9	7	0	277	290	.563
1994	NFL	16	10	6	0	356	314	.625
1995	NFL	16	8	8	0	412	385	.500
1996	NFL	16	9	7	0	298	315	.563
1997	NFL	16	9	7	0	354	359	.563
1998	NFL	16	15	1	0	556	296	.938

1999	NFL	16	10	6	0	399	335	.625
2000	NFL	16	11	5	0	397	371	.688
2001	NFL	16	5	11	0	290	390	.313
2002	NFL	16	6	10	0	390	442	.390
2003	NFL	16	9	7	0	416	353	.563
2004	NFL	16	8	8	0	405	395	.500
2005	NFL	16	9	7	0	306	344	.562
2006	NFL	16	6	10	0	282	327	.375
TOTAL:	46 years	694	377	308	9	15147	13981	
AVERAGE:		15	8	7	0	329	304	.550

Playoff Record

Season	GP	W	L	PF	PA	Result
1968	1	0	1	14	24	Lost Conference Championship to Baltimore.
1969	3	2	1	57	50	Lost Super Bowl to Kansas City.
1970	1	0	1	14	17	Lost Divisional playoff to San Francisco.
1971	1	0	1	12	20	Lost Divisional playoff to Dallas.
1973	3	2	1	61	54	Lost Super Bowl to Miami.
1974	3	2	1	50	40	Lost Super Bowl to Pittsburgh.
1975	1	0	1	14	17	Lost Divisional playoff to Dallas.
1976	3	2	1	73	65	Lost Super Bowl to Oakland.
1977	2	1	1	20	30	Lost NFC Championship to Dallas.
1978	1	0	1	10	34	Lost Divisional playoff to Los Angeles.
1980	1	0	1	16	31	Lost Divisional playoff to Philadelphia.
1982	2	1	1	37	45	Lost 2nd Round playoff to Washington.
1987	3	2	1	90	51	Lost NFC Championship to Washington.
1988	2	1	1	37	51	Lost Divisional playoff to San Francisco.
1989	1	0	1	13	41	Lost Conference Semifinal to San Francisco.
1992	1	0	1	7	24	Lost 1st Round game to Washington.
1993	1	0	1	10	17	Lost 1st Round game to N.Y. Giants.
1994	1	0	1	18	35	Lost 1st Round game to Chicago.
1996	1	0	1	15	40	Lost Wild Card Game to Dallas.
1997	2	1	1	45	60	Lost Conference Semifinal to San Francisco.
1998	2	1	1	68	51	Lost Conference Semifinal to Atlanta.
1999	2	1	1	64	59	Lost Conference Semifinal to St. Louis.
2000	2	1	1	34	57	Lost Conference Final to N.Y. Giants.
2004	2	1	1	45	44	Lost Conf. Semifinal to Philadelphia.
TOTAL:	42	18	24	824	957	
AVERAGE:	2	1	1	34	40	

Regular Season Individual Leaders

Season	Passing Yards		Receiving Yards		Rushing Yards	
1961	Fran Tarkenton	1997	Jerry Reichow	859	Hugh McElhenny	570
1962	Fran Tarkenton	2595	Tommy Mason	603	Tommy Mason	740
1963	Fran Tarkenton	2311	Paul Flatley	867	Tommy Mason	763
1964	Fran Tarkenton	2506	Bill Brown	703	Bill Brown	866
1965	Fran Tarkenton	2609	Paul Flatley	896	Bill Brown	699
1966	Fran Tarkenton	2561	Paul Flatley	777	Bill Brown	829
1967	Joe Kapp	1386	Gene Washington	384	Dave Osborn	972
1968	Joe Kapp	1695	Gene Washington	756	Bill Brown	805
1969	Joe Kapp	1726	Gene Washington	821	Dave Osborn	643
1970	Gary Cuozzo	1720	Gene Washington	702	Dave Osborn	681
1971	Gary Cuozzo	842	Bob Grim	691	Clint Jones	675
1972	Fran Tarkenton	2651	John Gilliam	1035	Oscar Reed	639

Season	Passing Yards		Receiving Yards		Rushing Yards	
1973	Fran Tarkenton	2113	John Gilliam	907	Chuck Foreman	801
1974	Fran Tarkenton	2598	Jim Lash	631	Chuck Foreman	777
1975	Fran Tarkenton	2994	John Gilliam	777	Chuck Foreman	1070
1976	Fran Tarkenton	2961	Sammy White	906	Chuck Foreman	1155
1977	Fran Tarkenton	1734	Sammy White	760	Chuck Foreman	1112
1978	Fran Tarkenton	3468	Ahmad Rashad	769	Chuck Foreman	749
1979	Tom Kramer	3397	Ahmad Rashad	1156	Rickey Young	708
1980	Tom Kramer	3582	Ahmad Rashad	1095	Ted Brown	912
1981	Tom Kramer	3912	Joe Senser	1004	Ted Brown	1063
1982	Tom Kramer	2037	Sammy White	503	Ted Brown	515
1983	Steve Dils	2840	Darrin Nelson	618	Darrin Nelson	642
1984	Tom Kramer	1678	Leo Lewis	830	Alfred Anderson	773
1985	Tom Kramer	3522	Anthony Carter	821	Darrin Nelson	893
1986	Tom Kramer	3000	Steve Jordan	859	Darrin Nelson	793
1987	Wade Wilson	2106	Anthony Carter	922	Darrin Nelson	642
1988	Wade Wilson	2746	Anthony Carter	1225	Darrin Nelson	380
1989	Wade Wilson	2543	Anthony Carter	1066	Herschel Walker	915
1990	Rich Gannon	2278	Anthony Carter	1008	Herschel Walker	770
1991	Rich Gannon	2166	Chris Carter	962	Herschel Walker	825
1992	Rich Gannon	1905	Chris Carter	681	Terry Allen	1201
1993	Jim McMahon	1967	Chris Carter	1071	Scott Graham	487
1994	Warren Moon	4264	Chris Carter	1256	Terry Allen	1031
1995	Warren Moon	4228	Chris Carter	1371	Robert Smith	632
1996	Brad Johnson	2258	Jake Reed	1320	Robert Smith	692
1997	Brad Johnson	3036	Jake Reed	1138	Robert Smith	1266
1998	R. Cunningham	3704	Randy Moss	1313	Robert Smith	1187
1999	Jeff George	2816	Randy Moss	1413	Robert Smith	1015
2000	Daunte Culpepper	3937	Randy Moss	1437	Robert Smith	1521
2001	Daunte Culpepper	2612	Randy Moss	1233	Michael Bennett	682
2002	Daunte Culpepper	3853	Randy Moss	1347	Michael Bennett	1296
2003	Daunte Culpepper	3479	Randy Moss	1632	Moe Williams	745
2004	Daunte Culpepper	4717	Nate Burleson	1006	Onterrio Smith	544
2005	Brad Johnson	1885	Travis Taylor	604	Mewelde Moore	662
2006	Brad Johnson	2750	Travis Taylor	651	Chester Taylor	1216

COACHING HISTORY: 1961-1966 Norm Van Brocklin 29-51-4-.369; 1967-1983 Bud Grant 151-87-5-.632; 1984 Les Steckel 3-13-0-.188; 1985 Bud Grant 7-9-0-.438; 1986-1991 Jerry Burns 52-43-0-.547; 1992-2001 Dennis Green 97-62-0-.610; 2001-2005 Mike Tice 32-33-0-.492; 2006-present Brad Childress

MINNESOTA WILD

Home City: St. Paul, Minnesota
Home Arena: Xcel Energy Center   Capacity: 18,064 [2005]
Origin of Name: The name was chosen in a Name the Team Contest in which the team received thousands of entries. As team CEO Jack Sperling said "We think it best represents what Minnesota fans hold most dear. Our rugged natural wilderness, the premier-brand hockey that's native to Minnesota and the great enthusiasm of all of our hockey fans."

Regular Season Record

Season	League	GP	W	L	T	OL	SL	GF	GA	Pts
2000-2001	NHL	82	25	39	13	5	NA	168	210	68
2001-2002	NHL	82	26	35	12	9	NA	195	238	73

2002-2003	NHL	82	42	29	10	1	NA	198	178	95
2003-2004	NHL	82	30	29	20	3	NA	188	183	83
2004-2005	NHL Season cancelled due to lockout.									
2005-2006	NHL	82	38	36	NA	5	3	231	215	84
TOTAL:	5 years	410	161	168	55	23	3	980	1024	403
AVERAGE:		82	32	34	11	5	1	196	205	81

Playoff Record

Season	GP	W	L	GF	GA	Result
2002-2003	18	8	10	43	43	Lost Conference Final to Anaheim..

Regular Season Individual Leaders

Season	Goals		Points		Penalty Minutes	
2000-2001	Marian Gaborik	18	Marian Gaborik	36	Matt Johnson	137
	D. Hendrickson	18				
	Wes Walz	18				
2001-2002	Marian Gaborik	30	Andrew Brunette	68	Matt Johnson	181
2002-2003	Marian Gaborik	30	Marian Gaborik	65	Matt Johnson	201
2003-2004	Alexander Daigle	20	Alexander Daigle	51	Matt Johnson	177
2004-2005	Season cancelled due to lockout.					
2005-2006	Marian Gaborik	38	Brian Rolston	79	Derek Boogaard	158

COACHING HISTORY: 2000-present Jacques Lemaire

MONTREAL ALOUETTES

Home City: Montreal, Quebec
Home Stadium: Molson Stadium [McGill University] (1950-1968, 1972)
         Autostade (1969-1971, 1973-1976)   Capacity: 33,212 [1974]
         Olympic Stadium (1977-1981)   Capacity: 58,500
Origin of Name: Alouette is a French word meaning lark.

Regular Season Record

Season	League	GP	W	L	T	PF	PA	Pts	Pct
1950	CRU	12	6	6	0	192	261	12	.500
1951	CRU	12	3	9	0	146	286	6	.250
1952	CRU	12	2	10	0	136	278	4	.167
1953	CRU	14	8	6	0	292	229	16	.571
1954	CRU	14	11	3	0	341	148	22	.786
1955	CRU	12	9	3	0	388	214	18	.750
1956	CFC	14	10	4	0	478	361	20	.714
1957	CFC	14	6	8	0	287	301	12	.429
1958	CFL	14	7	6	1	265	269	15	.536
1959	CFL	14	6	8	0	193	305	12	.429
1960	CFL	14	5	9	0	340	458	10	.357
1961	CFL	14	4	9	1	213	225	9	.321
1962	CFL	14	4	7	3	308	309	11	.393
1963	CFL	14	6	8	0	277	297	12	.429
1964	CFL	14	6	8	0	192	264	12	.429
1965	CFL	14	5	9	0	183	215	10	.357
1966	CFL	14	7	7	0	156	215	14	.500
1967	CFL	14	2	12	0	166	302	4	.143
1968	CFL	14	3	9	2	234	327	8	.286
1969	CFL	14	2	10	2	304	395	6	.214
1970	CFL	14	7	6	1	246	279	15	.536

1971	CFL	14	6	8	0	226	248	12	.429
1972	CFL	14	4	10	0	246	353	8	.286
1973	CFL	14	7	6	1	273	238	15	.536
1974	CFL	16	9	5	2	339	271	20	.625
1975	CFL	16	9	7	0	353	345	18	.563
1976	CFL	16	7	8	1	305	273	15	.469
1977	CFL	16	11	5	0	311	245	22	.688
1978	CFL	16	8	7	1	331	295	17	.531
1979	CFL	16	11	4	1	351	284	23	.719
1980	CFL	16	8	8	0	356	375	16	.500
1981	CFL	16	3	13	0	267	518	6	.188
TOTAL:	32 years	456	202	238	16	8695	9383	420	
AVERAGE:		14	6	8	0	272	293	13	.461

Playoff Record

Season	GP	W	L	PF	PA	Result
1953	2	0	2	23	59	Lost Division Final to Hamilton.
1954	3	2	1	63	54	Won Eastern Division Final series.
1955	2	1	1	57	70	Lost Grey Cup Final to Edmonton.
1956	3	2	1	105	112	Lost Grey Cup Final to Edmonton.
1957	3	1	2	35	71	Lost Division Final to Hamilton.
1958	1	0	1	12	26	Lost Division Semifinal to Ottawa.
1959	1	0	1	0	43	Lost Division Semifinal to Ottawa.
1960	1	0	1	14	30	Lost Division Semifinal to Ottawa.
1962	3	1	2	56	75	Lost Division Final to Hamilton.
1963	1	0	1	5	17	Lost Division Semifinal to Ottawa.
1964	1	0	1	0	27	Lost Division Semifinal to Ottawa.
1965	1	0	1	7	36	Lost Division Semifinal to Ottawa.
1966	1	0	1	14	24	Lost Division Semifinal to Hamilton.
1970	4	4	0	82	43	**Won Grey Cup**.
1972	1	0	1	11	14	Lost Division Semifinal to Ottawa.
1973	2	1	1	46	33	Lost Division Final to Ottawa.
1974	2	2	0	34	11	**Won Grey Cup**.
1975	3	2	1	63	31	Lost Grey Cup Final to Edmonton.
1976	1	0	1	0	23	Lost Division Semifinal to Hamilton.
1977	2	2	0	62	24	**Won Grey Cup**.
1978	3	2	1	69	56	Lost Grey Cup Final to Edmonton.
1979	2	1	1	26	23	Lost Grey Cup Final to Edmonton.
1980	2	1	1	38	45	Lost Division Final to Hamilton.
1981	1	0	1	16	20	Lost Division Semifinal to Ottawa.
TOTAL:	46	22	24	838	967	
AVERAGE:	2	1	1	35	40	

Regular Season Individual Leaders

Season	Passing Yards		Receiving Yards		Rushing Yards	
1950						
1951						
1952						
1953						
1954	Sam Etcheverry	3610	Red O'Quinn	1024	Alex Webster	984
1955	Sam Etcheverry	3638	Red O'Quinn	1097	Pat Abbruzzi	1248
1956	Sam Etcheverry	4723	Hal Patterson	1914	Pat Abbruzzi	1062
1957	Sam Etcheverry	3341	Red O'Quinn	1005	Pat Abbruzzi	809

Season	Passing Yards		Receiving Yards		Rushing Yards	
1958	Sam Etcheverry	3548	Red O'Quinn	962	Joey Wells	722
1959	Sam Etcheverry	3133	Red O'Quinn	692	Veryl Switzer	863
1960	Sam Etcheverry	3571	Hal Patterson	1121	George Dixon	976
1961	Gerry Thomkins	1163	Marv Luster	539	Don Clark	1143
1962	Sandy Stevens	1542	Marv Luster	725	George Dixon	1520
1963	Warren Rabb	723	Marv Luster	341	George Dixon	1270
1964	George Bork	906	Jack Gotta	262	George Dixon	594
1965	Bernie Faloney	2253	Terry Evanshen	631	J.W. Lockett	653
1966	George Bork	752	Don Davis	365	Don Lisbon	1007
1967	George Bork	936	Roger Murphy	701	Charlie Scales	370
1968	Carroll Williams	2968	Dave Lewis	794	Carroll Williams	436
1969	Sonny Wade	2719	Bill Star	686	Dennis Duncan	1037
1970	Sonny Wade	2411	Terry Evanshen	625	Dennis Duncan	823
1971	Sonny Wade	2090	Terry Evanshen	852	Bill Massey	655
1972	Sonny Wade	1637	Peter Dalla Riva	607	Ike Brown	817
1973	George Mira	1366	Johnny Rodgers	841	John Harvey	1024
1974	Jimmy Jones	2297	Johnny Rodgers	1024	Steve Ferrughelli	1134
1975	Jimmy Jones	1865	Peter Dalla Riva	733	Steve Ferrughelli	893
1976	Sonny Wade	2504	Peter Dalla Riva	763	Andy Hopkins	1075
1977	Sonny Wade	1210	Peter Dalla Riva	676	John O'Leary	859
1978	Joe Barnes	1177	Bob Gaddis	814	John O'Leary	584
1979	Joe Barnes	2456	Bob Gaddis	578	David Green	1678
1980	Gerry Dattilio	2892	Keith Baker	891	David Green	873
1981	Vince Ferragamo	2182	James Scott	1422	David Overstreet	952

COACHING HISTORY: 1950-1951 Lew Hayman 9-15-0-.375; 1952-1959 Doug "Peahead" Walker 59-48-1-.551; 1960-1962 Perry Moss 13-25-4-.357; 1963-1966 Jim Trimble 24-32-0-.429; 1967 Darrell Mudra 2-12-0-.143; 1968-1969 O. Kay Dalton 5-19-4-.250; 1970-1972 Sam Etcheverry 17-24-1-.417; 1973-1977 Marv Levy 43-31-4-.577; 1978-1981 Joe Scanella 28-28-2-.500; 1981 Jim Eddy 2-4-0-.333

MONTREAL ALOUETTES
(were Baltimore Stallions)

Home City: Montreal, Quebec
Home Stadium: Olympic Stadium (1996-1997)   Capacity: 56,245 [1997]
        Molson Stadium (1998-present)   Capacity: 20,202 [2006]
Origin of name: The name was chosen by team owner Jim Speros on February 7, 1996 and named in honor of the previous CFL team.

Regular Season Record

Season	League	GP	W	L	T	OL	PF	PA	Pts	Pct
1996	CFL	18	12	6	0	NA	534	469	24	.667
1997	CFL	18	13	5	0	NA	509	532	26	.722
1998	CFL	18	12	5	1	NA	470	435	25	.694
1999	CFL	18	12	6	0	NA	495	395	24	.667
2000	CFL	18	12	6	0	0	594	377	24	.667
2001	CFL	18	9	9	0	0	454	419	18	.500
2002	CFL	18	13	5	0	1	587	407	27	.750
2003	CFL	18	13	5	0	NA	569	414	26	.722
2004	CFL	18	14	4	0	NA	584	436	28	.778
2005	CFL	18	10	8	0	NA	592	519	20	.556
2006	CFL	18	10	8	0	NA	451	431	20	.556

TOTAL:	11 years	198	130	67	1	1	5839	4834	262	
AVERAGE:		18	12	6	0	0	531	440	24	.662

Playoff Record

Season	GP	W	L	PF	PA	Result
1996	1	0	1	7	43	Lost Division Final to Toronto.
1997	2	1	1	75	72	Lost Division Final to Toronto.
1998	2	1	1	61	50	Lost Division Final to Hamilton.
1999	1	0	1	26	27	Lost Division Final to Hamilton.
2000	2	1	1	61	52	Lost Grey Cup Final to B.C.
2001	1	0	1	12	24	Lost Division Semifinal to Hamilton.
2002	2	2	0	43	34	**Won Grey Cup.**
2003	2	1	1	52	60	Lost Grey Cup to Edmonton.
2004	1	0	1	18	26	Lost Division Semifinal to Toronto.
2005	3	2	1	98	69	Lost Grey Cup Game to Edmonton.
2006	2	1	1	47	49	Lost Grey Cup Game to B.C.
TOTAL:	19	9	10	500	506	
AVERAGE:	2	1	1	45	46	

Regular Season Individual Leaders

Season	Passing Yards		Receiving Yards		Rushing Yards	
1996	Tracy Ham	3313	Jock Climie	1209	Mike Pringle	825
1997	Tracy Ham	3687	Chris Armstrong	1411	Mike Pringle	1775
1998	Tracy Ham	2511	N. Williams	1057	Mike Pringle	2064
1999	Anthony Calvillo	2592	Ben Cahoon	846	Mike Pringle	1656
2000	Anthony Calvillo	4277	Ben Cahoon	1022	Mike Pringle	1778
2001	Anthony Calvillo	3671	Tyree Davis	874	Mike Pringle	1323
2002	Anthony Calvillo	5013	Ben Cahoon	1060	L. Phillips	1022
2003	Anthony Calvillo	5891	J. Copeland	1757	Deonce Whitaker	560
2004	Anthony Calvillo	6041	Ben Cahoon	1183	Autry Denson	772
2005	Anthony Calvillo	5556	Kerry Watkins	1364	Robert Edwards	1199
2006	Anthony Calvillo	4714	Ben Cahoon	1190	Robert Edwards	1155

COACHING HISTORY: 1996 Bob Price 12-6-0-.667; 1997-1998 Dave Ritchie 25-10-1-.708; 1999-2000 Charlie Taaffe 24-12-0-0-.667; 2001 Rod Rust 9-8-0-0-.529; 2001-Jim Popp 0-1-0-0-.000; 2002-2006 Don Matthews 58-28-0-1-.680; 2006-Jim Popp 2-2-0-.500

MONTREAL CANADIENS

Home City: Montreal, Quebec
Home Arena: Jubilee Arena   Capacity: 3,200 [1909]
Origin of Name: The team was named by club founder J. Ambrose O'Brien and was originally called "Club de Hockey Canadien".

Regular Season Record

Season	League	GP	W	L	T	GF	GA	Pts	Pct
1909-1910	NHA	12	2	10	0	59	100	4	.167

Regular Season Individual Leaders

Season	Goals		Points		GAA	
1909-1910	Art Bernier	11	Art Bernier	11	Ted Groulx	8.56
	Didier Pitre	11	Didier Pitre	11		

COACHING HISTORY:

MONTREAL CANADIENS

Home City: Montreal, Quebec
Home Arena: Jubilee Arena (1910-1913: 1918-1920)   Capacity: 3,200
          Westmount Arena (1913-1918)   Capacity: 6,000
          Mount Royal Arena (1920-1926)   Capacity: 6,750
          Montreal Forum I (1926-1968)   Capacity: 15,500
          Montreal Forum II (1968-1996)   Capacity: 17,959 [1995]
          Bell Center (1996-present)*   Capacity: 21,273 [2005]
Origin of Name: The team was named after "Club Athletique Canadien" a French Canadian sports club owned by team owner George Kennedy, and also after the previous NHA team founded and named by J. Ambrose O'Brien.

Regular Season Record

Season	League	GP	W	L	T	OL	SL	GF	GA	Pts
1910-1911	NHA	16	8	8	0	NA	NA	66	62	16
1911-1912	NHA	18	8	10	0	NA	NA	59	66	16
1912-1913	NHA	20	9	11	0	NA	NA	83	81	18
1913-1914	NHA	20	13	7	0	NA	NA	85	65	26
1914-1915	NHA	20	6	14	0	NA	NA	65	81	12
1915-1916	NHA	24	16	7	1	NA	NA	104	76	33
1916-1917	NHA	20	10	10	0	NA	NA	89	80	20
1917-1918	NHL	22	13	9	0	NA	NA	115	84	26
1918-1919	NHL	18	10	8	0	NA	NA	88	78	20
1919-1920	NHL	24	13	11	0	NA	NA	129	113	26
1920-1921	NHL	24	13	11	0	NA	NA	112	99	26
1921-1922	NHL	24	12	11	1	NA	NA	88	94	25
1922-1923	NHL	24	13	9	2	NA	NA	73	61	28
1923-1924	NHL	24	13	11	0	NA	NA	59	48	26
1924-1925	NHL	30	17	11	2	NA	NA	93	56	36
1925-1926	NHL	36	11	24	1	NA	NA	79	108	23
1926-1927	NHL	44	28	14	2	NA	NA	99	67	58
1927-1928	NHL	44	26	11	7	NA	NA	116	48	59
1928-1929	NHL	44	22	7	15	NA	NA	71	43	59
1929-1930	NHL	44	21	14	9	NA	NA	142	114	51
1930-1931	NHL	44	26	10	8	NA	NA	129	89	60
1931-1932	NHL	48	25	16	7	NA	NA	128	111	57
1932-1933	NHL	48	18	25	5	NA	NA	92	115	41
1933-1934	NHL	48	22	20	6	NA	NA	99	101	50
1934-1935	NHL	48	19	23	6	NA	NA	110	145	44
1935-1936	NHL	48	11	26	11	NA	NA	82	123	33
1936-1937	NHL	48	24	18	6	NA	NA	115	111	54
1937-1938	NHL	48	18	17	13	NA	NA	123	128	49
1938-1939	NHL	48	15	24	9	NA	NA	115	146	39
1939-1940	NHL	48	10	33	5	NA	NA	90	167	25
1940-1941	NHL	48	16	26	6	NA	NA	121	147	38
1941-1942	NHL	48	18	27	3	NA	NA	134	173	39
1942-1943	NHL	50	19	19	12	NA	NA	181	191	50
1943-1944	NHL	50	38	5	7	NA	NA	234	109	83
1944-1945	NHL	50	38	8	4	NA	NA	228	121	80
1945-1946	NHL	50	28	17	5	NA	NA	172	134	61
1946-1947	NHL	60	34	16	10	NA	NA	189	138	78

*-known as Molson Center from 1996-2002.

1947-1948	NHL	60	20	29	11	NA	NA	147	169	51
1948-1949	NHL	60	28	23	9	NA	NA	152	126	65
1949-1950	NHL	70	29	22	19	NA	NA	164	150	77
1950-1951	NHL	70	25	30	15	NA	NA	173	184	65
1951-1952	NHL	70	34	26	10	NA	NA	195	164	78
1952-1953	NHL	70	28	23	19	NA	NA	155	148	75
1953-1954	NHL	70	35	24	11	NA	NA	195	141	81
1954-1955	NHL	70	41	18	11	NA	NA	228	157	93
1955-1956	NHL	70	45	15	10	NA	NA	222	131	100
1956-1957	NHL	70	35	23	12	NA	NA	210	155	82
1957-1958	NHL	70	43	17	10	NA	NA	250	158	96
1958-1959	NHL	70	39	18	13	NA	NA	258	158	91
1959-1960	NHL	70	40	18	12	NA	NA	255	178	92
1960-1961	NHL	70	41	19	10	NA	NA	254	188	92
1961-1962	NHL	70	42	14	14	NA	NA	259	166	98
1962-1963	NHL	70	28	19	23	NA	NA	225	183	79
1963-1964	NHL	70	36	21	13	NA	NA	209	167	85
1964-1965	NHL	70	36	23	11	NA	NA	211	185	83
1965-1966	NHL	70	41	21	8	NA	NA	239	173	90
1966-1967	NHL	70	32	25	13	NA	NA	202	188	77
1967-1968	NHL	74	42	22	10	NA	NA	236	167	94
1968-1969	NHL	76	46	19	11	NA	NA	271	202	103
1969-1970	NHL	76	38	22	16	NA	NA	244	201	92
1970-1971	NHL	78	42	23	13	NA	NA	291	216	97
1971-1972	NHL	78	46	16	16	NA	NA	307	205	108
1972-1973	NHL	78	52	10	16	NA	NA	329	184	120
1973-1974	NHL	78	45	24	9	NA	NA	293	240	99
1974-1975	NHL	80	47	14	19	NA	NA	374	225	113
1975-1976	NHL	80	58	11	11	NA	NA	337	174	127
1976-1977	NHL	80	60	8	12	NA	NA	387	171	132
1977-1978	NHL	80	59	10	11	NA	NA	359	183	129
1978-1979	NHL	80	52	17	11	NA	NA	337	204	115
1979-1980	NHL	80	47	20	13	NA	NA	328	240	107
1980-1981	NHL	80	45	22	13	NA	NA	332	232	103
1981-1982	NHL	80	46	17	17	NA	NA	360	223	109
1982-1983	NHL	80	42	24	14	NA	NA	350	286	98
1983-1984	NHL	80	35	40	5	NA	NA	286	295	75
1984-1985	NHL	80	41	27	12	NA	NA	309	262	94
1985-1986	NHL	80	40	33	7	NA	NA	330	280	87
1986-1987	NHL	80	41	29	10	NA	NA	277	241	92
1987-1988	NHL	80	45	22	13	NA	NA	298	238	103
1988-1989	NHL	80	53	18	9	NA	NA	315	218	115
1989-1990	NHL	80	41	28	11	NA	NA	288	234	93
1990-1991	NHL	80	39	30	11	NA	NA	273	249	89
1991-1992	NHL	80	41	28	11	NA	NA	267	207	93
1992-1993	NHL	84	48	30	6	NA	NA	326	280	102
1993-1994	NHL	84	41	29	14	NA	NA	283	248	96
1994-1995	NHL	48	18	23	7	NA	NA	125	148	43
1995-1996	NHL	82	40	32	10	NA	NA	265	248	90
1996-1997	NHL	82	31	36	15	NA	NA	249	276	77
1997-1998	NHL	82	37	32	13	NA	NA	235	208	87
1998-1999	NHL	82	32	39	11	NA	NA	184	209	75
1999-2000	NHL	82	35	38	9	4	NA	196	194	83
2000-2001	NHL	82	28	40	8	6	NA	206	232	70

2001-2002	NHL	82	36	31	12	3	NA	207	209	87
2002-2003	NHL	82	30	35	8	9	NA	206	234	77
2003-2004	NHL	82	41	30	7	4	NA	208	192	93
2004-2005	NHL	Season cancelled due to lockout.								
2005-2006	NHL	82	42	31	NA	6	3	243	247	93
TOTAL:	95 years	5766	2961	1936	838	32	3	19071	15544	6795
AVERAGE:		61	31	20	9	0	0	201	164	72

				Playoff Record			
Season	**GP**	**W**	**L**	**T**	**GF**	**GA**	**Result**
1913-1914	2	1	1	0	2	6	Lost Championship series to Toronto.
1915-1916	5	3	2	0	15	13	**Won Stanley Cup.**
1916-1917	6	2	4	0	18	29	Lost Stanley Cup Final to Seattle.
1917-1918	2	1	1	0	7	10	Lost League playoff to Toronto.
1918-1919	10	6	3	1	36	37	Stanley Cup Final canceled.
1922-1923	2	1	1	0	2	3	Lost League playoff to Ottawa.
1923-1924	6	6	0	0	19	6	**Won Stanley Cup.**
1924-1925	6	3	3	0	13	18	Lost Stanley Cup Final to Victoria.
1926-1927	4	1	1	2	3	6	Lost Semifinal series to Ottawa.
1927-1928	2	0	1	1	2	3	Lost Semifinal series to Maroons.
1928-1929	3	0	3	0	2	5	Lost Semifinal series to Boston.
1929-1930	6	5	0	1	14	6	**Won Stanley Cup.**
1930-1931	10	6	4	0	23	21	**Won Stanley Cup.**
1931-1932	4	1	3	0	9	13	Lost Semifinal series to Rangers.
1932-1933	2	0	1	1	5	8	Lost Quarterfinal series to Rangers.
1933-1934	2	0	1	1	3	4	Lost Quarterfinal series to Chicago.
1934-1935	2	0	1	1	5	6	Lost Quarterfinal series to Rangers.
1936-1937	5	2	3	0	8	13	Lost Semifinal series to Detroit.
1937-1938	3	1	2	0	8	11	Lost Quarterfinal series to Chicago.
1938-1939	3	1	2	0	5	8	Lost Quarterfinal series to Detroit.
1940-1941	3	1	2	0	7	8	Lost Quarterfinal series to Chicago.
1941-1942	3	1	2	0	8	8	Lost Quarterfinal series to Detroit.
1942-1943	5	1	4	0	17	18	Lost Semifinal series to Boston.
1943-1944	9	8	1	0	39	14	**Won Stanley Cup.**
1944-1945	6	2	4	0	21	15	Lost Semifinal series to Toronto.
1945-1946	9	8	1	0	45	20	**Won Stanley Cup.**
1946-1947	11	6	5	0	29	23	Lost Stanley Cup Final to Toronto.
1948-1949	7	3	4	0	14	17	Lost Semifinal series to Detroit.
1949-1950	5	1	4	0	7	15	Lost Semifinal series to Rangers
1950-1951	11	5	6	0	23	25	Lost Stanley Cup Final to Toronto.
1951-1952	11	4	7	0	20	23	Lost Stanley Cup Final to Detroit.
1952-1953	12	8	4	0	34	23	**Won Stanley Cup.**
1953-1954	11	7	4	0	28	18	Lost Stanley Cup Final to Detroit.
1954-1955	12	7	5	0	36	36	Lost Stanley Cup Final to Detroit.
1955-1956	10	8	2	0	42	18	**Won Stanley Cup.**
1956-1957	10	8	2	0	37	18	**Won Stanley Cup.**
1957-1958	10	8	2	0	35	20	**Won Stanley Cup.**
1958-1959	11	8	3	0	40	25	**Won Stanley Cup.**
1959-1960	8	8	0	0	29	11	**Won Stanley Cup.**
1960-1961	6	2	4	0	15	16	Lost Semifinal series to Chicago.
1961-1962	6	2	4	0	13	19	Lost Semifinal series to Chicago.
1962-1963	5	1	4	0	6	14	Lost Semifinal series to Toronto.
1963-1964	7	3	4	0	14	17	Lost Semifinal series to Toronto.
1964-1965	13	8	5	0	35	26	**Won Stanley Cup.**

1965-1966	10	8	2	0	33	20	Won Stanley Cup.
1966-1967	10	6	4	0	30	25	Lost Stanley Cup Final to Toronto.
1967-1968	13	12	1	0	48	25	Won Stanley Cup.
1968-1969	14	12	2	0	43	26	Won Stanley Cup.
1970-1971	20	12	8	0	75	63	Won Stanley Cup.
1971-1972	6	2	4	0	14	19	Lost Quarterfinal series to Rangers.
1972-1973	17	12	5	0	73	52	Won Stanley Cup.
1973-1974	6	2	4	0	17	21	Lost Quarterfinal series to Rangers.
1974-1975	11	6	5	0	49	30	Lost Semifinal series to Buffalo.
1975-1976	13	12	1	0	44	26	Won Stanley Cup.
1976-1977	14	12	2	0	54	23	Won Stanley Cup.
1977-1978	15	12	3	0	58	29	Won Stanley Cup.
1978-1979	16	12	4	0	63	41	Won Stanley Cup.
1979-1980	10	6	4	0	39	26	Lost Quarterfinal series to Minnesota.
1980-1981	3	0	3	0	6	15	Lost Preliminary series to Edmonton.
1981-1982	5	2	3	0	16	11	Lost Division Semifinal to Quebec.
1982-1983	3	0	3	0	2	8	Lost Division Semifinal to Buffalo.
1983-1984	15	9	6	0	42	32	Lost Conference Final to Islanders
1984-1985	12	6	6	0	43	41	Lost Division Final to Quebec.
1985-1986	20	15	5	0	56	41	Won Stanley Cup.
1986-1987	17	10	7	0	67	54	Lost Conf. Final to Philadelphia.
1987-1988	11	5	6	0	33	35	Lost Division Final to Boston.
1988-1989	21	14	7	0	67	51	Lost Stanley Cup Final to Calgary.
1989-1990	11	5	6	0	31	29	Lost Division Final to Boston.
1990-1991	13	7	6	0	47	42	Lost Division Final to Boston.
1991-1992	11	4	7	0	29	32	Lost Division Final to Boston.
1992-1993	20	16	4	0	66	51	Won Stanley Cup.
1993-1994	7	3	4	0	20	22	Lost Conf. Quarterfinal to Boston.
1995-1996	6	2	4	0	17	19	Lost Conf. Quarterfinal to Rangers.
1996-1997	5	1	4	0	11	22	Lost Conf. Quarterfinal to N.J.
1997-1998	10	4	6	0	28	32	Lost Conference Semifinal to Buffalo.
2001-2002	12	6	6	0	32	39	Lost Conf. Semifinal to Carolina.
2003-2004	11	4	7	0	24	28	Lost Conf. Semifinal to Tampa Bay.
2005-2006	6	2	4	0	17	15	Lost Conf. Quarterfinal to Carolina.
TOTAL:	680	399	273	8	2087	1718	
AVERAGE:	9	5	4	0	27	22	

Season	Goals		Points		Penalty Minutes	
1910-1911	Newsy Lalonde	19	Newsy Lalonde	19	Not Recorded	
	Didier Pitre	19				
1911-1912	Didier Pitre	28	Didier Pitre	28	Not Recorded	
1912-1913	Newsy Lalonde	25	Newsy Lalonde	25	Not Recorded	
1913-1914	Newsy Lalonde	22	Newsy Lalonde	22	Not Recorded	
1914-1915	Didier Pitre	30	Didier Pitre	30	Not Recorded	
1915-1916	Newsy Lalonde	31	Newsy Lalonde	31	Not Recorded	
1916-1917	Newsy Lalonde	27	Newsy Lalonde	27	Not Recorded	
1917-1918	Joe Malone	44	Joe Malone	48	Joe Hall	100
1918-1919	Newsy Lalonde	23	Newsy Lalonde	32	Joe Hall	89
1919-1920	Newsy Lalonde	37	Newsy Lalonde	46	Billy Couture	67
1920-1921	Newsy Lalonde	33	Newsy Lalonde	43	Bert Corbeau	86
1921-1922	Odie Cleghorn	21	Sprague Cleghorn	26	Sprague Cleghorn	80
1922-1923	Billy Boucher	24	Billy Boucher	31	Billy Boucher	55
1923-1924	Billy Boucher	16	Billy Boucher	22	Billy Boucher	48
1924-1925	Howie Morenz	28	Aurel Joliat	41	Billy Boucher	92

Season	Goals		Points		Penalty Minutes	
1925-1926	Howie Morenz	23	Howie Morenz	26	Billy Boucher	112
			Aurel Joliat	26		
1926-1927	Howie Morenz	25	Howie Morenz	32	Aurel Joliat	79
1927-1928	Howie Morenz	33	Howie Morenz	51	Aurel Joliat	105
1928-1929	Howie Morenz	17	Howie Morenz	27	Albert LeDuc	79
1929-1930	Howie Morenz	40	Howie Morenz	50	Sylvio Mantha	108
1930-1931	Howie Morenz	28	Howie Morenz	51	Marty Burke	91
1931-1932	Howie Morenz	24	Howie Morenz	49	Sylvio Mantha	62
1932-1933	Aurel Joliat	18	Aurel Joliat	39	John Gagnon	64
1933-1934	Aurel Joliat	22	Aurel Joliat	37	Gerry Carson	51
1934-1935	L. Goldsworthy	20	Alfred Lepine	31	Roger Jenkins	63
1935-1936	L. Goldsworthy	15	L. Goldsworthy	26	John Gagnon	42
	Aurel Joliat	15				
1936-1937	John Gagnon	20	John Gagnon	36	John Gagnon	38
					Albert Siebert	38
1937-1938	George Mantha	23	George Mantha	42	Albert Siebert	56
1938-1939	Hector Blake	24	Hector Blake	47	Stewart Evans	58
1939-1940	Hector Blake	17	Hector Blake	36	Emile Drouin	51
1940-1941	John Quilty	18	John Quilty	34	Erwin Chamberlain	75
1941-1942	Joe Benoit	20	Hector Blake	45	Ken Reardon	93
1942-1943	Joe Benoit	30	Hector Blake	59	Leo Lamoureux	53
1943-1944	Maurice Richard	32	Elmer Lach	72	Mike McMahon	98
1944-1945	Maurice Richard	50	Elmer Lach	80	Leo Lamoureux	58
1945-1946	Hector Blake	29	Hector Blake	50	Emile Bouchard	52
1946-1947	Maurice Richard	45	Maurice Richard	71	Erwin Chamberlain	97
1947-1948	Elmer Lach	30	Elmer Lach	61	Ken Reardon	129
1948-1949	Billy Reay	22	Billy Reay	45	E. Chamberlain	111
1949-1950	Maurice Richard	43	Maurice Richard	65	Maurice Richard	114
1950-1951	Maurice Richard	42	Maurice Richard	66	Tom Johnson	128
1951-1952	Bernie Geoffrion	30	Elmer Lach	65	Doug Harvey	82
1952-1953	Maurice Richard	28	Maurice Richard	61	Maurice Richard	112
1953-1954	Maurice Richard	37	Maurice Richard	67	Maurice Richard	112
1954-1955	Maurice Richard	38	Bernie Geoffrion	75	Maurice Richard	125
	Bernie Geoffrion	38				
1955-1956	Jean Beliveau	47	Jean Beliveau	88	Jean Beliveau	143
1956-1957	Jean Beliveau	33	Jean Beliveau	84	Jean Beliveau	105
	Maurice Richard	33				
1957-1958	Dickie Moore	36	Dickie Moore	84	Doug Harvey	107
1958-1959	Jean Beliveau	45	Dickie Moore	96	Jean-Guy Talbot	77
1959-1960	Jean Beliveau	34	Jean Beliveau	74	Henri Richard	66
1960-1961	Bernie Geoffrion	50	Bernie Geoffrion	95	Jean-Guy Talbot	143
1961-1962	Claude Provost	33	Ralph Backstrom	65	Lou Fontinato	167
1962-1963	Gilles Tremblay	25	Henri Richard	73	Lou Fontinato	141
1963-1964	Jean Beliveau	28	Jean Beliveau	78	John Ferguson	125
1964-1965	Claude Provost	27	Claude Provost	64	John Ferguson	156
1965-1966	Bobby Rousseau	30	Bobby Rousseau	78	John Ferguson	153
1966-1967	Yvan Cournoyer	25	Bobby Rousseau	63	John Ferguson	177
1967-1968	Jean Beliveau	31	Jean Beliveau	68	John Ferguson	117
1968-1969	Yvan Cournoyer	43	Yvan Cournoyer	87	John Ferguson	185
1969-1970	Jacques Lemaire	32	Yvan Cournoyer	63	John Ferguson	139
1970-1971	Yvan Cournoyer	37	Jean Beliveau	76	Pete Mahovlich	181
1971-1972	Yvan Cournoyer	47	Frank Mahovlich	96	Pete Mahovlich	103
1972-1973	Jacques Lemaire	44	Jacques Lemaire	95	Guy Lapointe	117

Season	Goals		Points		Penalty Minutes	
1973-1974	Yvon Cournoyer	40	Frank Mahovlich	80	Pete Mahovlich	122
1974-1975	Guy Lafleur	53	Guy Lafleur	119	Doug Risebrough	198
1975-1976	Guy Lafleur	56	Guy Lafleur	125	Doug Risebrough	180
1976-1977	Steve Shutt	60	Guy Lafleur	136	Doug Risebrough	132
1977-1978	Guy Lafleur	60	Guy Lafleur	132	Gilles Lupien	108
1978-1979	Guy Lafleur	52	Guy Lafleur	129	Gilles Lupien	124
1979-1980	Guy Lafleur	50	Guy Lafleur	125	Gilles Lupien	117
	Pierre Larouche	50				
1980-1981	Steve Shutt	35	Steve Shutt	73	Chris Nilan	262
	Mark Napier	35				
1981-1982	Mark Napier	40	Keith Acton	88	Chris Nilan	204
1982-1983	Mark Napier	40	Guy Lafleur	76	Chris Nilan	213
1983-1984	Guy Lafleur	30	Bobby Smith	72	Chris Nilan	338
1984-1985	Mats Naslund	42	Mats Naslund	79	Chris Nilan	358
1985-1986	Mats Naslund	43	Mats Naslund	110	Chris Nilan	274
1986-1987	Bobby Smith	28	Mats Naslund	80	Chris Nilan	266
1987-1988	Stephane Richer	50	Bobby Smith	93	Chris Chelios	172
1988-1989	Mats Naslund	33	Mats Naslund	84	Shayne Corson	193
1989-1990	Stephane Richer	51	Stephane Richer	91	Todd Ewen	158
1990-1991	Stephane Richer	31	Russ Courtnall	76	Lyle Odelein	259
1991-1992	Kirk Muller	36	Kirk Muller	77	Lyle Odelein	212
1992-1993	Brian Bellows	40	V. Damphousse	97	Lyle Odelein	205
1993-1994	V. Damphousse	40	V. Damphousse	91	Lyle Odelein	276
1994-1995	Mark Recchi	14	Mark Recchi	43	Lyle Odelein	152
1995-1996	Pierre Turgeon	38	Pierre Turgeon	96	Lyle Odelein	230
	V. Damphousse	38				
1996-1997	Mark Recchi	34	V. Damphousse	81	Scott Thornton	128
1997-1998	Mark Recchi	32	Mark Recchi	74	Scott Thornton	158
1998-1999	Martin Rucinsky	17	Mark Recchi	47	Shayne Corson	147
1999-2000	Sergei Zholtok	26	Martin Rucinsky	49	Shayne Corson	115
2000-2001	Brian Savage	21	Saku Koivu	47	Sheldon Souray	92
			Oleg Petrov	47		
2001-2002	Yanic Perreault	27	Yanic Perreault	56	Gino Odjick	104
2002-2003	Richard Zednick	31	Saku Koivu	71	Richard Zednick	79
2003-2004	Richard Zednick	26	Mike Ribeiro	65	Darren Langdon	135
2004-2005	Season cancelled due to lockout.					
2005-2006	Michael Ryder	30	Alex Kovalev	65	Sheldon Souray	116
					Mike Komisarek	116

COACHING HISTORY: 1910-1917 George Kennedy 70-67-1-.511; 1917-1922 Newsy Lalonde 51-44-0-.537; 1921-1926 Leo Dandurand 64-61-6-.511; 1926-1932 Cecil Hart 148-72-48-.642; 1932-1935 Newsy Lalonde 45-53-14-.464; 1934-1935 Leo Dandurand 14-15-3-.484; 1935-1936 Sylvio Mantha 11-26-11-.344; 1936-1939 Cecil Hart 48-53-25-.480; 1938-1939 Jules Dugal 9-6-3-.583; 1939-1940 Alfred Lepine 10-33-5-.260; 1940-1955 Dick Irvin 431-313-152-.566; 1955-1968 Hector Blake 500-255-159-.634; 1968-1971 Claude Ruel 95-49-31-.631; 1970-1971 Al MacNeil 31-15-9-.645; 1971-1979 Scotty Bowman 419-110-105-.744; 1979-1980 Bernie Geoffrion 15-9-6-.600; 1979-1981 Claude Ruel 77-33-20-.669; 1981-1984 Bob Berry 116-71-36-.601; 1983-1985 Jacques Lemaire 48-37-12-.557; 1985-1988 Jean Perron 126-84-30-.588; 1988-1992 Pat Burns 174-104-42-.609; 1992-1996 Jacques Demers 107-86-27-.548; 1995-1996 Steve Shutt and Jacques Laperriere 0-1-0-.000; 1995-1997 Mario Tremblay 71-63-25-.525; 1997-2001 Alain Vigneault 109-122-35-0-.476; 2000-2003 Michel Therrien 77-76-23-14; 2002-2006 Claude Julien 72-63-10-14-1-.528; 2005-present Bob Gainey

MONTREAL CONCORDE
(became Montreal Alouettes)

Home City: Montreal, Quebec
Home Stadium: Olympic Stadium   Capacity: 58,500 [1985]
Origin of Name: The name was derived from the city of Montreal's motto, 'Concordia Salus' Latin for 'salvation from harmony'. During the 1986 season the team adopted the name of the former CFL club, the "Alouettes."

Regular Season Record

Season	League	GP	W	L	T	PF	PA	Pts	Pct
1982	CFL	16	2	14	0	267	502	4	.125
1983	CFL	16	5	10	1	367	447	11	.344
1984	CFL	16	6	9	1	386	404	13	.406
1985	CFL	16	8	8	0	284	332	16	.500
1986	CFL	18	4	14	0	320	500	8	.222
TOTAL:	5 years	82	25	55	2	1624	2185	52	
AVERAGE:		16	5	11	0	325	437	10	.317

Playoff Record

Season	GP	W	L	PF	PA	Result
1984	1	0	1	11	17	Lost Division Semifinal to Hamilton.
1985	2	1	1	56	70	Lost Division Final to Hamilton.
TOTAL:	3	1	2	67	87	
AVERAGE:	2	1	1	34	44	

Regular Season Individual Leaders

Season	Passing Yards		Receiving Yards		Rushing Yards	
1982	Johnny Evans	2242	Nick Arakgi	1062	Lester Brown	388
1983	Johnny Evans	1864	Nick Arakgi	582	Lester Brown	792
1984	Turner Gill	2673	Nick Arakgi	1078	Dwaine Wilson	1083
1985	Turner Gill	2255	Nick Arakgi	741	Dwaine Wilson	435
1986	Brian Ransom	3204	James Hood	1411	Tony Jones	366

COACHING HISTORY: 1982-1985 Joe Galat 19-41-2-.323; 1985-1986 Gary Durchik 6-14-0-.300

MONTREAL EXPOS
(became Washington Nationals)

Home City: Montreal, Quebec
Home Stadium: Jarry Park (1969-1976)   Capacity: 28,456 [1969]
               Olympic Stadium (1977-present)   Capacity: 46,500 [2004]
               Hiram Bithorn Stadium (2003-2004)   Capacity: 18,000 [2003]*
Origin of Name: The team was named after Expo '67, the World's Fair held in Montreal in 1967.

Regular Season Record

Season	League	GP	W	L	Pct	GB	R	OR
1969	NL	162	52	110	.321	48	582	791
1970	NL	162	73	89	.451	16	687	807
1971	NL	161	71	90	.441	25.5	622	729
1972	NL	156	70	86	.449	26.5	513	609
1973	NL	162	79	83	.488	3.5	668	702
1974	NL	161	79	82	.491	8.5	662	657
1975	NL	162	75	87	.463	17.5	601	690

*-the Expos played 22 games in San Juan, Puerto Rico in 2003

1976	NL	162	55	107	.340	46	531	734
1977	NL	162	75	87	.463	26	665	736
1978	NL	162	76	86	.469	14	633	611
1979	NL	160	95	65	.594	2	701	581
1980	NL	162	90	72	.556	1	694	629
1981	NL	108	60	48	.556	NA	443	394
1982	NL	162	86	76	.531	6	697	616
1983	NL	162	82	80	.506	8	677	646
1984	NL	161	78	83	.484	18	593	585
1985	NL	161	84	77	.522	16.5	633	636
1986	NL	161	78	83	.484	29.5	637	688
1987	NL	162	91	71	.562	4	741	720
1988	NL	162	81	81	.500	20	628	592
1989	NL	162	81	81	.500	12	632	630
1990	NL	162	85	77	.525	10	662	598
1991	NL	161	71	90	.441	26.5	579	655
1992	NL	162	87	75	.537	9	648	581
1993	NL	162	94	68	.580	3	732	682
1994	NL	114	74	40	.649	-	585	454
1995	NL	144	66	78	.458	24	621	638
1996	NL	162	88	74	.543	8	741	668
1997	NL	162	78	84	.481	23	691	740
1998	NL	162	65	97	.401	41	644	783
1999	NL	162	68	94	.420	35	718	853
2000	NL	162	67	95	.414	28	738	902
2001	NL	162	68	94	.420	20	669	811
2002	NL	162	83	79	.512	18	735	718
2003	NL	162	83	79	.512	18	711	716
2004	NL	162	67	95	.414	29	635	769
TOTAL:	36 years	5698	2755	2943		641	23349	24351
AVERAGE:		158	77	81	.484	18	649	676

Playoff Record

Season	GP	W	L	R	OR	Result
1981	10	5	5	26	29	Lost NLCS to Los Angeles.

Regular Season Individual Leaders

Season	Home Runs		RBI's		Wins	
1969	Rusty Staub	29	Coco Laboy	83	Bill Stoneman	11
1970	Rusty Staub	30	Rusty Staub	94	Carl Morton	18
1971	Rusty Staub	19	Rusty Staub	97	Bill Stoneman	17
1972	Ron Fairly	17	Ron Fairly	68	Mike Torrez	16
1973	Bob Bailey	26	Ken Singleton	103	Steve Renko	15
1974	Bob Bailey	20	Willie Davis	89	Mike Torrez	15
					Steve Rogers	15
1975	Mike Jorgensen	18	Gary Carter	68	Dale Murray	15
1976	Larry Parrish	11	Larry Parrish	61	Woody Fryman	13
1977	Gary Carter	31	Tony Perez	91	Steve Rogers	17
1978	Ellis Valentine	25	Tony Perez	78	Ross Grimsley	20
	Andre Dawson	25				
1979	Larry Parrish	30	Andre Dawson	92	Bill Lee	16
1980	Gary Carter	29	Gary Carter	101	Steve Rogers	16
					Scott Sanderson	16
1981	Andre Dawson	24	Gary Carter	68	Steve Rogers	12

Season	Home Runs		RBI's		Wins	
1982	Gary Carter	29	Al Oliver	109	Steve Rogers	19
1983	Andre Dawson	32	Andre Dawson	113	Steve Rogers	17
					Bill Gullickson	17
1984	Gary Carter	27	Gary Carter	106	Charlie Lea	15
1985	Andre Dawson	23	Hubie Brooks	100	Bryn Smith	18
1986	Andre Dawson	20	Andre Dawson	78	Floyd Youmans	13
1987	Tim Wallach	26	Tim Wallach	123	Neal Heaton	13
1988	Andres Galarraga	29	Andres Galarraga	92	Dennis Martinez	15
1989	Andres Galarraga	23	Andres Galarraga	85	Dennis Martinez	16
1990	Tim Wallach	21	Tim Wallach	98	Bill Sampen	12
1991	Ivan Calderon	19	Ivan Calderon	75	Dennis Martinez	14
1992	Larry Walker	23	Larry Walker	93	Dennis Martinez	16
					Ken Hill	16
1993	Larry Walker	22	Marquis Grissom	95	Dennis Martinez	15
1994	Moises Alou	22	Larry Walker	86	Ken Hill	16
1995	Sean Berry	14	David Segui	68	Pedro Martinez	14
	Moises Alou	14				
	Tony Tarasco	14				
1996	Henry Rodriguez	36	Henry Rodriguez	103	Jeff Fassero	15
1997	Rondell White	28	Henry Rodriguez	83	Pedro Martinez	17
1998	Vladimir Guerrero	38	Vladimir Guerrero	109	Dustin Hermanson	14
1999	Vladimir Guerrero	42	Vladimir Guerrero	131	Dustin Hermanson	9
					Javier Vazquez	9
2000	Vladimir Guerrero	44	Vladimir Guerrero	123	Dustin Hermanson	12
2001	Vladimir Guerrero	34	Vladimir Guerrero	108	Javier Vazquez	16
2002	Vladimir Guerrero	39	Vladimir Guerrero	111	Tomo Ohka	13
2003	Vladimir Guerrero	25	Orlando Cabrera	80	Livan Hernandez	15
2004	Tony Batista	32	Tony Batista	110	Livian Hernandez	11

COACHING HISTORY: 1969-1975 Gene Mauch 499-627-.443; 1976 Karl Kuehl 43-85-.336; 1976 Charlie Fox 12-22-.353; 1977-1981 Dick Williams 380-347-.523; 1981-1982 Jim Fanning 102-87-.540; 1983-1984 Bill Virdon 146-147-.498; 1984 Jim Fanning 14-16-.467; 1985-1991 Buck Rodgers 520-499-.510; 1991-1992 Tom Runnells 68-81-.456; 1992-2001 Felipe Alou 691-717-.491; 2001-Jeff Torborg 47-62-.431; 2002-2004 Frank Robinson 233-253-.479

MONTREAL MACHINE

Home City: Montreal, Quebec
Home Stadium: Olympic Stadium   Capacity: 61,000 [1991]
Origin of Name:

Regular Season Record

Season	League	GP	W	L	T	PF	PA	Pct
1991	WLAF	10	4	6	0	145	244	.400
1992	WFL	10	2	8	0	175	274	.200
TOTAL:	2 years	20	6	14	0	320	518	
AVERAGE:		10	3	7	0	160	259	.300

Regular Season Individual Leaders

Season	Passing Yards		Receiving Yards		Rushing Yards	
1991	Mike Proctor	1222	K.D. Dunn	321	Ricky Johnson	423
1992	Mike Proctor	1478				

COACHING HISTORY: 1991-1992 Jacques Dussault 6-14-0-.300

MONTREAL MANIC
(were Philadelphia Fury)

Home City: Montreal, Quebec
Home Field: Olympic Stadium   Capacity: 58,500
Origin of Name: The team was named for the Manicouagan River in northern Quebec.

Regular Season Record

Season	League	GP	W	L	GF	GA	BP	Pts	Pct
1981	NASL	32	15	17	63	57	55	141	.294
1982	NASL	32	19	13	60	43	49	159	.331
1983	NASL	30	12	18	58	71	52	124	.276
TOTAL:	3 years	94	46	48	181	171	156	424	
AVERAGE:		31	15	16	60	57	52	141	.301

Playoff Record

Season	GP	W	L	GF	GA	Result
1981	6	3	3	16	17	Lost 2nd Round series to Chicago.
1982	3	1	2	4	7	Lost 1st Round series to Fort Lauderdale.
1983	5	3	2	7	7	Lost 2nd Round series to Tulsa.
TOTAL:	14	7	7	27	31	
AVERAGE:	5	2	3	9	10	

Regular Season Individual Leaders

Season	Goals		Points		GAA (360 Min)	
1981	Gordon Hill	16	Gordon Hill	44	Bob Rigby	1.57
1982	Alan Willey	15	Alan Willey	37	Victor Nogueira	1.25
1983	Alan Willey	13	Alan Willey	38	Eddie Gettemeier	1.83

COACHING HISTORY: 1981-1982 Eddie Firmani 34-30; 1983 Andy Lynch 12-18

MONTREAL MAROONS

Home City: Montreal, Quebec
Home Arena: Montreal Forum   Capacity: 15,500
Origin of Name: Like many other teams, the Maroons was named after the color of their uniforms.

Regular Season Record

Season	League	GP	W	L	T	GF	GA	Pts	Pct
1924-1925	NHL	30	9	19	2	45	65	20	.333
1925-1926	NHL	36	20	11	5	91	73	45	.625
1926-1927	NHL	44	20	20	4	71	68	44	.500
1927-1928	NHL	44	24	14	6	96	77	54	.614
1928-1929	NHL	44	15	20	9	67	65	39	.443
1929-1930	NHL	44	23	16	5	141	114	51	.580
1930-1931	NHL	44	20	18	6	105	106	46	.523
1931-1932	NHL	48	19	22	7	142	139	45	.469
1932-1933	NHL	48	22	20	6	135	119	50	.521
1933-1934	NHL	48	19	18	11	117	122	49	.510
1934-1935	NHL	48	24	19	5	123	92	53	.552
1935-1936	NHL	48	22	16	10	114	106	54	.563
1936-1937	NHL	48	22	17	9	126	110	53	.552
1937-1938	NHL	48	12	30	6	101	149	30	.313
TOTAL:	14 years	622	271	260	91	1474	1405	633	
AVERAGE:		44	19	18	7	105	100	45	.509

Playoff Record

Season	GP	W	L	T	GF	GA	Result
1925-1926	8	5	1	2	18	8	**Won Stanley Cup.**
1926-1927	2	0	1	1	1	2	Lost Quarterfinal series to Canadiens.
1927-1928	9	5	3	1	12	8	Lost Stanley Cup Final to Rangers.
1929-1930	4	1	3	0	5	11	Lost Semifinal series to Boston.
1930-1931	2	0	2	0	1	8	Lost Quarterfinal series to Rangers.
1931-1932	4	1	1	2	6	5	Lost Semifinal series to Toronto.
1932-1933	2	0	2	0	2	5	Lost Quarterfinal series to Detroit.
1933-1934	4	1	2	1	4	7	Lost Semifinal series to Chicago.
1934-1935	7	5	0	2	16	8	**Won Stanley Cup.**
1935-1936	3	0	3	0	1	6	Lost Semifinal series to Detroit.
1936-1937	5	2	3	0	8	11	Lost Semifinal series to Rangers.
TOTAL:	50	20	21	9	74	79	
AVERAGE:	5	2	2	1	7	7	

Regular Season Individual Leaders

Season	Goals		Points		Penalty Minutes	
1924-1925	Harry Broadbent	14	Harry Broadbent	20	Harry Broadbent	75
1925-1926	Nels Stewart	34	Nels Stewart	42	Nels Stewart	119
1926-1927	Nels Stewart	17	Nels Stewart	21	Nels Stewart	133
1927-1928	Nels Stewart	27	Nels Stewart	34	Albert Siebert	109
1928-1929	Nels Stewart	21	Nels Stewart	29	Mervyn Dutton	139
1929-1930	Nels Stewart	39	Nels Stewart	55	Mervyn Dutton	98
1930-1931	Nels Stewart	25	Nels Stewart	39	Albert Seibert	76
1931-1932	Dave Trottier	26	Dave Trottier	44	Dave Trottier	94
			Reginald Smith	44		
1932-1933	L. Northcott	22	L. Northcott	43	Reginald Smith	66
1933-1934	L. Northcott	20	Reginald Smith	37	Reginald Smith	58
1934-1935	Herb Cain	20	Earl Robinson	35	Stewart Evans	54
1935-1936	Reginald Smith	19	Reginald Smith	38	Allan Shields	81
1936-1937	Earl Robinson	16	Bob Gracie	36	Lionel Conacher	64
1937-1938	Bob Gracie	12	Bob Gracie	31	Allan Shields	67

COACHING HISTORY: 1924-1929 Eddie Gerard 88-84-26-.510; 1929-1931 Duncan Munro 37-29-10-.553; 1930-1931 George Boucher 6-5-1-.542; 1931-1932 Sprague Cleghorn 19-22-7-.469; 1932-1934 Eddie Gerard 41-38-17-.516; 1934-1938 Tommy Gorman 74-71-29-.509; 1937-1938 "King" Clancy 6-11-1-.361

MONTREAL OLYMPIQUES

Home City: Montreal, Quebec
Home Field: The Autostade [1971,1973]   Capacity: 33,212 [1974
            Molson Stadium (McGill University) [1972]
Origin of Name: Les Olympiques de Montreal were named such because Montreal had been awarded the 1976 Olympic Games.

Regular Season Record

Season	League	GP	W	L	T	GF	GA	BP	Pts	Pct
1971	NASL	24	4	15	5	29	58	26	65	.301
1972	NASL	14	4	5	5	19	20	18	57	.452
1973	NASL	19	5	10	4	25	32	22	64	.374
TOTAL:	3 years	57	13	30	14	73	110	66	186	
AVERAGE:		19	4	10	5	24	37	22	62	.363

Regular Season Individual Leaders

Season	Goals		Points		GAA (360 Min)	
1971	Franco Gallina	10	Franco Gallina	22	Jerry Rainey	1.81
1972	Mike Dillon	8	Mike Dillon	18	Sam Nusum	1.43
1973	Tommy Ord	6	Tommy Ord	18	Sam Nusum	1.68

COACHING HISTORY: 1971 Renato Tofani 4-15-5-.301; 1972-1973 Graham Adams 9-15-9-.407

MONTREAL SHAMROCKS

Home City: Montreal, Quebec
Home Arena: Wood Avenue Arena   Capacity: 4,300
Origin of Name: The team was originally the Montreal Crystals of the Amateur Hockey Association and when the team became affiliated with the Shamrock Amateur Athletic Association they changed their name to Shamrocks.

Regular Season Record

Season	League	GP	W	L	T	GF	GA	Pts	Pct
1908-1909	ECHA	12	2	10	0	56	103	4	.167
1909-1910	NHA	12	3	8	1	52	95	7	.292
TOTAL:	2 years	24	5	18	1	108	198	11	
AVERAGE:		12	3	9	0	54	99	6	.229

Regular Season Individual Leaders

Season	Goals		Points		GAA	
1908-1909	Harry Hyland	18	Harry Hyland	18	W. Baker	8.58
1909-1910	Don Smith	15	Don Smith	15	Jack Winchester	5.20

COACHING HISTORY:

MONTREAL WANDERERS

Home City: Montreal, Quebec
Home Arena: Wood Avenue Arena   Capacity: 4,300
Origin of Name:

Regular Season Record

Season	League	GP	W	L	T	GF	GA	Pts	Pct
1908-1909	ECHA	12	9	3	0	82	61	18	.750
1909-1910	NHA	12	11	1	0	91	41	22	.917
1910-1911	NHA	16	7	9	0	73	88	14	.438
1911-1912	NHA	18	9	9	0	95	96	18	.500
1912-1913	NHA	20	10	10	0	93	90	20	.500
1913-1914	NHA	20	7	13	0	102	125	14	.350
1914-1915	NHA	20	14	6	0	127	82	28	.700
1915-1916	NHA	24	10	14	0	90	116	20	.417
1916-1917	NHA	20	5	15	0	94	137	10	.250
1917-1918	NHL	6	1	5	0	17	35	2	.167
TOTAL:	10 years	168	83	85	0	864	871	166	
AVERAGE:		17	8	9	0	86	87	16	.494

Playoff Record

Season	GP	W	L	GF	GA	Result
1908-1909	2	1	1	13	10	Won playoff series with Edmonton.

1909-1910	1	1	0	7	3	**Won Stanley Cup.**
1914-1915	2	1	1	1	4	Lost Championship series with Ottawa.
TOTAL:	5	3	2	21	17
AVERAGE:	2	1	1	7	6

Regular Season Individual Leaders

Season	Goals		Points		Penalty Minutes	
1908-1909	Frank Glass	17	Frank Glass	17	Not Recorded	
1909-1910	Ernie Russell	31	Ernie Russell	31	Not Recorded	
1910-1911	Ernie Russell	18	Ernie Russell	18	Not Recorded	
1911-1912	Ernie Russell	27	Ernie Russell	27	Not Recorded	
1912-1913	Harry Hyland	27	Harry Hyland	27	Not Recorded	
1913-1914	Harry Hyland	31	Harry Hyland	31	Not Recorded	
1914-1915	Gordon Roberts	29	Gordon Roberts	29	Not Recorded	
1915-1916	Gordon Roberts	21	Gordon Roberts	21	Not Recorded	
1916-1917	Odie Cleghorn	28	Odie Cleghorn	28	Not Recorded	
1917-1918	Harry Hyland	6	Dave Ritchie	7	Art Ross	12
			Harry Hyland	7		

COACHING HISTORY: 1910-1911 Dick Boon 7-9-0-.438; 1917-1918 Art Ross 1-5-0-.167

MOOSE JAW ORPHANS
(Saskatoon Sheiks became Moose Jaw Orphans-in mid 1921-1922 season)

Home City: Moose Jaw, Saskatchewan
Home Arena: Moose Jaw Arena   Capacity: 4,000
Origin of Name: Named Orphans because the team was homeless when they left Saskatoon.

Regular Season Record

Season	League	GP	W	L	T	GF	GA	Pts	Pct
1921-1922	WCHL	10	1	9	0	24	60	2	.100

Regular Season Individual Leaders

1921-1922   See Saskatoon Sheiks

COACHING HISTORY:

NASHVILLE PREDATORS

Home City: Nashville Tennessee
Home Arena: Gaylord Entertainment Center   Capacity: 17,113 [2005]
Origin of Name: The NHL formally accepted the name Predators, November 6, 1997. Other names considered were Fury and Tigers. The team's logo, which was chosen before the name, is a silver saber-tooth tiger head.

Regular Season Record

Season	League	GP	W	L	T	OL	SL	GF	GA	Pts
1998-1999	NHL	82	28	47	7	NA	NA	190	261	63
1999-2000	NHL	82	28	47	7	7	NA	199	240	70
2000-2001	NHL	82	34	36	9	3	NA	186	200	80
2001-2002	NHL	82	28	41	13	0	NA	196	230	69
2002-2003	NHL	82	27	35	13	7	NA	183	206	74
2003-2004	NHL	82	38	29	11	4	NA	216	217	91
2004-2005	NHL	Season cancelled due to lockout.								

*-known as Nashville Arena 1998-99

2005-2006	NHL	82	49	25	NA	5	3	259	227	106
TOTAL:	7 years	574	232	260	60	26	3	1429	1581	553
AVERAGE:		82	33	37	9	4	0	204	226	79

Playoff Record

Season	GP	W	L	GF	GA	Result
2003-2004	6	2	4	9	12	Lost Conference Quarterfinal to Detroit.
2005-2006	5	1	4	10	17	Lost Conference Quarterfinal to San Jose.
TOTAL:	11	3	8	19	29	
AVERAGE:	6	2	4	10	15	

Regular Season Individual Leaders

Season	Goals		Points		Penalty Minutes	
1998-1999	S. Krivokrasov	25	Cliff Ronning	53	Patrick Cote	242
1999-2000	Cliff Ronning	26	Cliff Ronning	62	Bob Boughner	97
2000-2001	Scott Walker	25	Cliff Ronning	62	Cale Hulse	128
2001-2002	Denis Arkhipov	20	Cliff Ronning	49	Cale Hulse	121
2002-2003	A. Johansson	20	David Legwand	48	Cale Hulse	121
2003-2004	Scott Walker	25	Scott Walker	67	Jordin Tootoo	137
2004-2005	Season cancelled due to lockout.					
2005-2006	Paul Kariya	31	Paul Kariya	85	Darcy Hordichuk	163
	Steve Sullivan	31				

COACHING HISTORY: 1998-present Barry Trotz

NEW ENGLAND PATRIOTS
(were Boston Patriots)

Home City: Foxboro, Massachusetts
Home Stadium: Foxboro Stadium (1971-2001)*   Capacity: 60,292 [2000]
                 Gillette Stadium (2002-present)   Capacity: 68,000 [2005]
Origin of Name: The team kept the same nickname after moving from Boston to Foxboro.

Regular Season Record

Season	League	GP	W	L	T	PF	PA	Pct
1971	NFL	14	6	8	0	238	325	.429
1972	NFL	14	3	11	0	192	446	.214
1973	NFL	14	5	9	0	258	300	.357
1974	NFL	14	7	7	0	348	289	.500
1975	NFL	14	3	11	0	258	358	.214
1976	NFL	14	11	3	0	376	236	.786
1977	NFL	14	9	5	0	278	217	.643
1978	NFL	16	11	5	0	358	286	.688
1979	NFL	16	9	7	0	411	326	.563
1980	NFL	16	10	6	0	441	325	.625
1981	NFL	16	2	14	0	322	370	.125
1982	NFL	9	5	4	0	143	157	.556
1983	NFL	16	8	8	0	274	289	.500
1984	NFL	16	9	7	0	362	352	.563
1985	NFL	16	11	5	0	362	290	.688
1986	NFL	16	11	5	0	412	307	.688
1987	NFL	15	8	7	0	320	293	.533
1988	NFL	16	9	7	0	250	284	.563

*-originally known as Schaefer Stadium from 1971 to 1982 and then Sullivan Stadium from 1983 to 1989.

1989	NFL	16	5	11	0	297	391	.313
1990	NFL	16	1	15	0	181	446	.063
1991	NFL	16	6	10	0	211	305	.375
1992	NFL	16	2	14	0	205	363	.125
1993	NFL	16	5	11	0	238	286	.313
1994	NFL	16	10	6	0	351	312	.625
1995	NFL	16	6	10	0	294	377	.375
1996	NFL	16	11	5	0	418	313	.687
1997	NFL	16	10	6	0	369	289	.625
1998	NFL	16	9	7	0	337	329	.563
1999	NFL	16	8	8	0	299	284	.500
2000	NFL	16	5	11	0	276	338	.312
2001	NFL	16	11	5	0	371	272	.688
2002	NFL	16	9	7	0	381	346	.381
2003	NFL	16	14	2	0	348	238	.875
2004	NFL	16	14	2	0	437	260	.875
2005	NFL	16	10	6	0	379	338	.625
2006	NFL	16	12	4	0	385	237	.750
TOTAL:	36 years	554	285	269	0	11380	11174	
AVERAGE:		15	8	7	0	316	310	.514

Playoff Record

Season	GP	W	L	PF	PA	Result
1976	1	0	1	21	24	Lost Divisional playoff to Oakland.
1978	1	0	1	14	31	Lost Divisional playoff to Houston.
1982	1	0	1	13	28	Lost 1st Round series to Miami.
1985	4	3	1	94	94	Lost Super Bowl game to Chicago.
1986	1	0	1	17	22	Lost Divisional playoff to Denver.
1994	1	0	1	13	20	Lost Wild Card Game to Cleveland.
1996	3	2	1	69	44	Lost Super Bowl to Green Bay.
1997	2	1	1	23	10	Lost Conference Semifinal to Pittsburgh.
1998	1	0	1	10	25	Lost Wild Card Game to Jacksonville.
2001	3	3	0	60	47	**Won Super Bowl XXXVI.**
2003	3	3	0	73	57	**Won Super Bowl XXXVIII.**
2004	3	3	0	85	51	**Won Super Bowl XXXIX.**
2005	2	1	1	41	30	Lost Conference Semifinal to Denver.
2006	3	2	1	95	75	Lost Conference Final to Indianapolis.
TOTAL:	29	18	11	628	558	
AVERAGE:	2	1	1	45	40	

Regular Season Individual Leaders

Season	Passing Yards		Receiving Yards		Rushing Yards	
1971	Jim Plunkett	2158	Randy Vataha	872	Carl Garrett	784
1972	Jim Plunkett	2196	Reggie Rucker	681	Josh Ashton	546
1973	Jim Plunkett	2550	Reggie Rucker	743	Sam Cunningham	516
1974	Jim Plunkett	2457	Randy Vataha	561	Mack Herron	824
1975	Steve Grogan	1976	Randy Vataha	720	Sam Cunningham	666
1976	Steve Grogan	1903	Darryl Stingley	370	Sam Cunningham	824
1977	Steve Grogan	2162	Darryl Stingley	657	Sam Cunningham	1015
1978	Steve Grogan	2824	Stanley Morgan	820	Sam Cunningham	768
1979	Steve Grogan	3286	Harold Jackson	1013	Sam Cunningham	563
1980	Steve Grogan	2475	Stanley Morgan	991	Vagas Ferguson	818
1981	Steve Grogan	1859	Stanley Morgan	1029	Tony Collins	873
1982	Steve Grogan	930	Stanley Morgan	584	Tony Collins	632

Season	Passing Yards		Receiving Yards		Rushing Yards	
1983	Steve Grogan	2411	Stanley Morgan	863	Tony Collins	1049
1984	Tony Eason	3228	Derrick Ramsey	792	Craig James	790
1985	Tony Eason	2156	Stanley Morgan	760	Craig James	1227
1986	Tony Eason	3328	Stanley Morgan	1491	Craig James	427
1987	Steve Grogan	1183	Stanley Morgan	672	Tony Collins	474
1988	Doug Flutie	1150	Stanley Morgan	502	John Stephens	1168
1989	Steve Grogan	1697	Hart Lee Dykes	795	John Stephens	833
1990	Marc Wilson	1625	Irving Fryar	856	John Stephens	808
1991	Hugh Millen	3073	Irving Fryar	1014	Leonard Russell	959
1992	Hugh Millen	1203	Irving Fryar	791	Jon Vaughn	451
1993	Drew Bledsoe	2494	Ben Coates	659	Leonard Russell	1088
1994	Drew Bledsoe	4555	Ben Coates	1174	Marion Butts	703
1995	Drew Bledsoe	3507	Vincent Brisby	974	Curtis Martin	1487
1996	Drew Bledsoe	4086	Terry Glenn	1132	Curtis Martin	1152
1997	Drew Bledsoe	3706	Shawn Jefferson	841	Curtis Martin	1160
1998	Drew Bledsoe	3633	Terry Glenn	792	Robert Edwards	1115
1999	Drew Bledsoe	3985	Terry Glenn	1147	Terry Allen	896
2000	Drew Bledsoe	3291	Terry Glenn	963	Kevin Faulk	570
2001	Tom Brady	2843	Troy Brown	1199	Antowain Smith	1157
2002	Tom Brady	3764	Troy Brown	890	Antowain Smith	982
2003	Tom Brady	3620	Deion Branch	803	Antowain Smith	642
2004	Tom Brady	3692	David Givens	874	Corey Dillon	1635
2005	Tom Brady	4110	Deion Branch	998	Corey Dillon	733
2006	Tom Brady	3529	Reche Caldwell	760	Corey Dillon	812

COACHING HISTORY: 1971-1972 John Mazur 8-15-0-.348; 1972 Phil Bengtson 1-4-0-.200; 1973-1978 Chuck Fairbanks 46-39-0-.541; 1978 Ron Erhardt & Hank Bullough 0-1-0-.000; 1979-1981 Ron Erhardt 21-27-0-.438; 1982-1984 Ron Meyer 18-15-0-.545; 1984-1989 Ray Berry 48-38-0-.558; 1990 Rod Rust 1-15-0-.063; 1991-1992 Dick MacPherson 6-18-0-.250; 1992 Dante Scarnecchia 2-6-0-.250; 1993-1996 Bill Parcells 32-32-0-.500; 1997-1999 Pete Carroll 27-21-0-.563; 2000-present Bill Belichick

NEW ENGLAND REVOLUTION

Home City: Foxboro, Massachusetts
Home Field: Foxboro Stadium (1996-2001)   Capacity: 60,292 [2002]
           Gillette Stadium (2002-present)   Capacity: 68,756 [2005]
Origin of Name:

Season	League	GP	W	L	T	SOW	GF	GA	Pts
1996	MLS	32	15	17	NA	6	43	56	33
1997	MLS	32	15	17	NA	4	40	53	37
1998	MLS	32	11	21	NA	2	53	66	29
1999	MLS	32	12	20	NA	5	38	53	26
2000	MLS	32	13	13	6	NA	47	49	45
2001	MLS	27	7	14	6	NA	35	52	27
2002	MLS	28	12	14	2	NA	49	49	38
2003	MLS	30	12	9	9	NA	55	47	45
2004	MLS	30	8	13	9	NA	42	43	33
2005	MLS	32	17	7	8	NA	55	37	59
2006	MLS	32	12	8	12	NA	39	35	48
TOTAL:	11 years	339	134	153	52	17	496	540	420
AVERAGE:		31	12	14	5	2	45	49	38

Playoff Record

Season	GP	W	L	T	GF	GA	Result
1997	2	0	1	1	2	5	Lost Quarterfinals to D.C. United.
2000	3	1	2	0	3	9	Lost Semifinals to Chicago.
2002	7	3	2	2	8	5	Lost MLS Cup to Los Angeles.
2003	3	1	1	1	3	2	Lost Conf. Final to Chicago.
2004	3	1	0	2	5	4	Lost Conf. Semifinal to D.C. United.
2005	4	2	2	0	4	3	Lost MLS Cup to Los Angeles.
2006	4	2	1	1	4	3	Lost Conf. Finals to D.C. United.
TOTAL:	26	10	9	7	29	31	
AVERAGE:	3	1	1	1	4	4	

Regular Season Individual Leaders

Season	Goals		Points		GAA (min. 5 games)	
1996	Joe Max Moore	11	Joe Max Moore	23	Aidan Heaney	1.70
1997	Alberto Naveda	7	Alberto Naveda	21	Walter Zenga	1.27
	Imad Baba	7				
1998	Raul Diaz Arce	18	Raul Diaz Arce	44	Ian Feuer	2.12
1999	Joe Max Moore	15	Joe Max Moore	38	Jeff Causey	0.95
2000	Wolde Harris	15	Wolde Harris	37	Juergen Sommer	1.38
2001	Cate	8	Cate	24	Juergen Sommer	1.68
2002	Taylor Twellman	23	Taylor Twellman	52	Adin Brown	1.23
2003	Taylor Twellman	15	Taylor Twellman	34	Adin Brown	1.42
2004	Pat Noonan	11	Pat Noonan	30	Matt Reis	1.33
2005	Taylor Twellman	17	Taylor Twellman	41	Matt Reis	1.13
2006	Taylor Twellman	11	Taylor Twellman	27	Matt Reis	1.09

COACHING HISTORY: 1996 Frank Stapleton 15-17; 1997-1998 Thomas Rongen 23-35; 1998-1999 Walter Zenga 13-23; 1999 Steve Nicol 2-0; 2000-2002 Fernando Clavijo 22-31-13; 2002-present Steve Nicol

NEW ENGLAND TEA MEN
(became Jacksonville Tea Men)

Home City: Foxboro, Massachusetts
Home Stadium: Schaefer Stadium   Capacity: 61,279 [1980]
Origin of Name: The team was owned by the Lipton Tea Company.

Regular Season Record

Season	League	GP	W	L	GF	GA	BP	Pts	Pct
1978	NASL	30	19	11	62	39	51	165	.611
1979	NASL	30	12	18	41	56	38	110	.407
1980	NASL	32	18	14	54	56	46	154	.535
TOTAL:	3 years	92	49	43	157	151	135	429	
AVERAGE:		31	16	15	52	50	45	143	.518

Playoff Record

Season	GP	W	L	GF	GA	Result
1978	1	0	1	1	3	Lost 1st Round game to Fort Lauderdale.
1980	2	0	2	0	5	Lost 1st Round game to Tampa Bay.
TOTAL:	3	0	3	1	8	
AVERAGE:	2	0	2	1	4	

Regular Season Individual Leaders

Season	Goals		Points		GAA	
					(360 Min)	
1978	Mike Flanagan	30	Mike Flanagan	68	Kevin Keelan	1.24
1979	Gerry Daly	9	Keith Weller	28	Kevin Keelan	1.61
	Keith Weller	9				
1980					Kevin Keelan	1.67

COACHING HISTORY: 1978-1980 Noel Cantwell 49-43

NEW JERSEY AMERICANS
(became New York Nets)

Home City: Teaneck, New Jersey
Home Court: Teaneck Armory   Capacity: 3,500
Origin of Name: The team adopted the league name as their own.

Regular Season Record

Season	League	GP	W	L	PPGF	PPGA	Pct	GB
1967-1968	ABA	78	36	42	110.8	112.4	.462	18

Regular Season Individual Leaders

Season	Field Goal %		Points		Points per Game	
	(min. 70 games)				(min. 70 games)	
1967-68	Dan Anderson	.494	Tony Jackson	1439	Tony Jackson	19.5

COACHING HISTORY: Max Zaslofsky 36-42-.462

NEW JERSEY DEVILS
(were Colorado Rockies)

Home City: East Rutherford, New Jersey
Home Arena: Continental Airlines Arena*   Capacity: 19,040 [2005]
Origin of Name: The team was named after the mythical Jersey Devil, a creature that first appeared in 1735. Rumors continue circulating about it to the present day.

Regular Season Record

Season	League	GP	W	L	T	OL	SL	GF	GA	Pts
1982-1983	NHL	80	17	49	14	NA	NA	230	338	48
1983-1984	NHL	80	17	56	7	NA	NA	231	350	41
1984-1985	NHL	80	22	48	10	NA	NA	264	346	54
1985-1986	NHL	80	28	49	3	NA	NA	300	374	59
1986-1987	NHL	80	29	45	6	NA	NA	293	368	64
1987-1988	NHL	80	38	36	6	NA	NA	295	296	82
1988-1989	NHL	80	27	41	12	NA	NA	281	325	66
1989-1990	NHL	80	37	34	9	NA	NA	295	288	83
1990-1991	NHL	80	32	33	15	NA	NA	272	264	79
1991-1992	NHL	80	38	31	11	NA	NA	289	259	87
1992-1993	NHL	84	40	37	7	NA	NA	308	299	87
1993-1994	NHL	84	47	25	12	NA	NA	307	220	106
1994-1995	NHL	48	22	18	8	NA	NA	136	121	52
1995-1996	NHL	82	37	33	12	NA	NA	215	202	86
1996-1997	NHL	82	45	23	14	NA	NA	231	182	104

*-known as Meadowlands Arena from 1982 to 1996.

1997-1998	NHL	82	48	23	11	NA	NA	225	166	107
1998-1999	NHL	82	47	24	11	NA	NA	248	196	105
1999-2000	NHL	82	45	29	8	5	NA	251	203	103
2000-2001	NHL	82	48	19	12	3	NA	295	195	111
2001-2002	NHL	82	41	28	9	4	NA	205	187	95
2002-2003	NHL	82	46	20	10	6	NA	216	166	108
2003-2004	NHL	82	43	25	12	2	NA	213	164	100
2004-2005	NHL	Season cancelled due to lockout.								
2005-2006	NHL	82	46	27	NA	5	4	242	229	101
TOTAL:	23 years	1836	840	753	219	25	4	5842	5738	1928
AVERAGE:		80	37	33	10	1	0	254	249	84

Playoff Record

Season	GP	W	L	GF	GA	Result
1987-1988	20	11	9	67	71	Lost Conference Final to Boston.
1989-1990	6	2	4	18	21	Lost Division Semifinal to Washington.
1990-1991	7	3	4	21	21	Lost Division Semifinal to Pittsburgh.
1991-1992	7	3	4	25	28	Lost Division Semifinal to Rangers.
1992-1993	5	1	4	13	23	Lost Division Semifinal to Pittsburgh.
1993-1994	20	11	9	52	49	Lost Conference Final to Rangers.
1994-1995	20	16	4	67	34	**Won Stanley Cup.**
1996-1997	10	5	5	27	21	Lost Conference Semifinal to Rangers.
1997-1998	6	2	4	12	13	Lost Conference Quarterfinal to Ottawa.
1998-1999	7	3	4	17	21	Lost Conference Quarterfinal to Pittsburgh.
1999-2000	23	16	7	61	36	**Won Stanley Cup.**
2000-2001	25	15	10	69	52	Lost Stanley Cup Final to Colorado.
2001-2002	6	2	4	11	9	Lost Conf. Quarterfinal to Carolina.
2002-2003	24	16	8	63	41	**Won Stanley Cup.**
2003-2004	5	1	4	9	14	Lost Conf. Quarterfinal to Philadelphia.
2005-2006	9	5	4	27	21	Lost Conference Semifinal to Carolina.
TOTAL:	200	112	88	559	475	
AVERAGE:	13	7	6	35	30	

Regular Season Individual Leaders

Season	Goals		Points		Penalty Minutes	
1982-1983	Steve Tambellini	25	Aaron Broten	55	Yvon Vautour	136
1983-1984	Mel Bridgman	23	Mel Bridgman	61	Pat Verbeek	158
1984-1985	Paul Gagne	24	Mel Bridgman	61	Pat Verbeek	162
1985-1986	Greg Adams	35	Greg Adams	77	Joe Cirella	147
1986-1987	Pat Verbeek	35	Aaron Broten	79	Ken Daneyko	183
1987-1988	Pat Verbeek	46	Kirk Muller	94	Ken Daneyko	239
1988-1989	John MacLean	42	John MacLean	87	Ken Daneyko	283
1989-1990	John MacLean	41	Kirk Muller	86	Ken Daneyko	216
1990-1991	John MacLean	45	John MacLean	78	Ken Daneyko	249
1991-1992	Claude Lemieux	41	Claude Lemieux	68	Randy McKay	246
1992-1993	Stephane Richer	38	Claude Lemieux	81	Ken Daneyko	236
1993-1994	John MacLean	37	Scott Stevens	78	Randy McKay	244
1994-1995	Stephane Richer	23	Stephane Richer	39	Mike Peluso	167
1995-1996	Steve Thomas	26	Steve Thomas	61	Mike Peluso	146
1996-1997	John MacLean	29	Bobby Holik	62	Lyle Odelein	110
	Bill Guerin	29				
1997-1998	Bobby Holik	29	Bobby Holik	65	Krzysztof Oliwa	295
1998-1999	Petr Sykora	29	Petr Sykora	72	Krzysztof Oliwa	240
1999-2000	Patrik Elias	35	Patrik Elias	72	Krzysztof Oliwa	184

Season	Goals		Points		Penalty Minutes	
2000-2001	Alex Mogilny	43	Patrik Elias	96	Colin White	155
2001-2002	Patrik Elias	29	Patrik Elias	61	Colin White	133
2002-2003	Patrik Elias	28	Patrik Elias	57	Turner Stevenson	115
2003-2004	Patrik Elias	38	Patrik Elias	81	Colin White	96
2004-2005	Season cancelled due to lockout.					
2005-2006	Brian Gionta	48	Brian Gionta	89	Colin White	91
					Cam Janssen	91

COACHING HISTORY: 1982-1984 Billy MacMillan 19-67-14-.260; 1983-1984 Tom McVie 15-38-7-.308; 1984-1988 Doug Carpenter 100-166-24-.386; 1987-1990 Jim Schoenfeld 50-59-15-.464; 1989-1991 John Cunniff 59-56-18-.511; 1991-1992 Tom McVie 42-36-15-.532; 1992-1993 Herb Brooks 40-37-7-.518; 1993-1998 Jacques Lemaire 199-122-57-.602; 1998-2000 Robbie Ftorek 88-49-19-.625; 1999-2002 Larry Robinson 73-53-19-6-.566, 2001-2002 Kevin Constantine 20-8-2-1-.694; 2002-2004 Pat Burns 89-45-22-8-.634; 2005-2006 Larry Robinson 14-13-3-2-.550; 2005-present Lou Lamoriello

NEW JERSEY GENERALS

Home City: East Rutherford, New Jersey
Home Stadium: Giants Stadium   Capacity: 76,891 [1984]
Origin of Name: The name was chosen by team executives to indicate the regional nature of the franchise.

Regular Season Record

Season	League	GP	W	L	T	PF	PA	Pct
1983	USFL	18	6	12	0	314	437	.333
1984	USFL	18	14	4	0	430	312	.778
1985	USFL	18	11	7	0	418	377	.611
TOTAL:	3 years	54	31	23	0	1162	1126	
AVERAGE:		18	10	8	0	387	375	.556

Playoff Record

Season	GP	W	L	PF	PA	Result
1984	1	0	1	17	28	Lost 1st Round game to Philadelphia.
1985	1	0	1	17	20	Lost 1st Round game to Baltimore.
TOTAL:	2	0	2	34	48	
AVERAGE:	1	0	1	17	24	

Regular Season Individual Leaders

Season	Passing Yards		Receiving Yards		Rushing Yards	
1983	Bobby Scott	2813	Sam Bowers	715	Herschel Walker	1812
1984	Brian Sipe	2540	Jeff Spek	563	M. Carthorn	1339
1985	Doug Flutie	2109	Sam Bowers	618	Herschel Walker	2411

COACHING HISTORY: 1983 Chuck Fairbanks 6-12-0-.333; 1984-1985 Walt Michaels 25-11-0-.694

NEW JERSEY KNIGHTS
(New York Golden Blades became the Knights in mid 1974 season)

Home City: Cherry Hill, New Jersey
Home Arena: Cherry Hill Arena   Capacity: 4,000
Origin of Name: The name was chosen by the league.

Regular Season Record

Season	League	GP	W	L	T	GF	GA	Pts	Pct
1973-1974	WHA	58	26	30	2	221	233	54	.466

Regular Season Individual Leaders

Season	Goals		Points		Penalty Minutes	
1973-1974	Andre Lacroix	22	Andre Lacroix	91	Kevin Morrison	100

COACHING HISTORY: Harry Howell 26-30-2-.466

NEW JERSEY NETS
(were New York Nets)

Home City: Piscataway, New Jersey (1977-1981)
          East Rutherford, New Jersey (1981-present)
Home Court: Rutgers Athletic Center (1977-1981)   Capacity: 9,050 [1980]
          Continental Airlines Arena (1981-present)*   Capacity: 20,049 [2006]
Origin of Name: The team kept the same nickname after moving from New York to New Jersey.

Regular Season Record

Season	League	GP	W	L	PPGF	PPGA	Pct	GB
1977-1978	NBA	82	24	58	106.7	112.5	.293	31
1978-1979	NBA	82	37	45	107.7	111.9	.451	17
1979-1980	NBA	82	34	48	108.3	109.5	.415	27
1980-1981	NBA	82	24	58	106.9	113.0	.293	38
1981-1982	NBA	82	44	38	106.7	106.0	.537	19
1982-1983	NBA	82	49	33	105.8	103.0	.598	16
1983-1984	NBA	82	45	37	110.0	108.9	.549	17
1984-1985	NBA	82	42	40	109.5	109.2	.512	21
1985-1986	NBA	82	39	43	109.1	111.1	.476	28
1986-1987	NBA	82	24	58	108.5	113.5	.293	35
1987-1988	NBA	82	19	63	100.4	108.5	.232	38
1988-1989	NBA	82	26	56	103.7	110.1	.317	26
1989-1990	NBA	82	17	65	100.1	108.0	.207	36
1990-1991	NBA	82	26	56	102.9	107.5	.317	30
1991-1992	NBA	82	40	42	105.4	107.1	.488	11
1992-1993	NBA	82	43	39	102.8	101.6	.524	17
1993-1994	NBA	82	45	37	103.2	101.0	.549	12
1994-1995	NBA	82	30	52	98.1	101.2	.366	27
1995-1996	NBA	82	30	52	93.7	97.9	.366	30
1996-1997	NBA	82	26	56	97.2	101.8	.317	35
1997-1998	NBA	82	43	39	99.6	98.1	.524	12
1998-1999	NBA	50	16	34	91.4	95.2	.320	17
1999-2000	NBA	82	31	51	98.0	99.0	.378	21
2000-2001	NBA	82	26	56	92.2	97.1	.317	30

*-originally the Byrne Meadowlands Arena from 1981-1996.

2001-2002	NBA	82	52	30	96.2	92.0	.634	-
2002-2003	NBA	82	49	33	95.4	90.1	.598	-
2003-2004	NBA	82	47	35	90.3	87.8	.573	-
2004-2005	NBA	82	42	40	91.4	92.9	.512	3
2005-2006	NBA	82	49	33	93.8	92.4	.598	-
TOTAL:	29 years	2346	1019	1327				594
AVERAGE:		81	35	46	101.3	103.1	.434	20

Playoff Record

Season	GP	W	L	PPGF	PPGA	Result
1978-1979	2	0	2	107.5	116.5	Lost 1st Round series to Philadelphia.
1981-1982	2	0	2	87.5	99.5	Lost 1st Round series to Washington.
1982-1983	2	0	2	103.0	111.5	Lost 1st Round series to New York.
1983-1984	11	5	6	101.2	100.7	Lost Conf. Semifinal to Milwaukee.
1984-1985	3	0	3	110.3	120.7	Lost 1st Round series to Detroit.
1985-1986	3	0	3	105.7	116.0	Lost 1st Round series to Milwaukee.
1991-1992	4	1	3	101.8	110.0	Lost 1st Round series to Cleveland.
1992-1993	5	2	3	93.6	96.8	Lost 1st Round series to Cleveland.
1993-1994	4	1	3	86.5	93.8	Lost 1st Round series to New York.
1997-1998	3	0	3	95.0	102.7	Lost 1st Round series to Chicago.
2001-2002	20	11	9	95.4	95.4	Lost NBA Final to Lakers.
2002-2003	20	14	6	93.7	90.3	Lost NBA Final to San Antonio.
2003-2004	11	7	4	88.2	85.7	Lost Conference Semifinal to Detroit.
2004-2005	4	0	4	96.8	109.5	Lost 1st Round series to Miami.
2005-2006	11	5	6	94.2	95.3	Lost Conference Semifinal to Miami.
TOTAL:	105	46	59			
AVERAGE:	7	3	4	95.6	97.4	

Regular Season Individual Leaders

Season	Field Goal % (min. 70 games)		Points		Points per Game (min. 70 games)	
1977-78	Bernard King	.479	Bernard King	1909	Bernard King	24.2
1978-79	Bernard King	.522	Bernard King	1769	John Williamson	22.2
1979-80	Cliff Robinson	.469	Mike Newlin	1634	Mike Newlin	20.9
1980-81	Bob Elliott	.511	Mike Newlin	1688	Mike Newlin	21.4
1981-82	Buck Williams	.582	Ray Williams	1674	Ray Williams	20.4
1982-83	Darryl Dawkins	.599	Buck Williams	1396	Albert King	17.0
					Buck Williams	17.0
1983-84	Darryl Dawkins	.593	Otis Birdsong	1365	Otis Birdsong	19.8
1984-85	Buck Williams	.530	M. Richardson	1649	M. Richardson	20.1
1985-86	Buck Williams	.523	Mike Gminski	1333	Mike Gminski	16.5
1986-87	Buck Williams	.557	O. Woolridge	1551	O. Woolridge	20.7
1987-88	Buck Williams	.560	Buck Williams	1279	Buck Williams	18.3
1988-89	Buck Williams	.531	Roy Hinson	1308	Roy Hinson	16.0
1989-90	C. Shackleford	.462	Dennis Hopson	1251	Dennis Hopson	15.8
1990-91	Jack Haley	.469	Reggie Theus	1510	Reggie Theus	18.6
1991-92	Drazen Petrovic	.508	Drazen Petrovic	1691	Drazen Petrovic	20.6
1992-93	Drazen Petrovic	.518	Derrick Coleman	1572	Drazen Petrovic	22.3
1993-94	Armon Gilliam	.510	Derrick Coleman	1559	Derrick Coleman	20.2
1994-95	Armon Gilliam	.503	Ken Anderson	1267	Derrick Coleman	20.5
1995-96	Armon Gilliam	.474	Armon Gilliam	1429	Armon Gilliam	18.3
1996-97	T. Massenburg	.485	Kendall Gill	1789	Kendall Gill	21.8
1997-98	Michael Cage	.512	Sam Cassell	1471	Sam Cassell	19.6

Season	Field Goal % (min. 70 games)		Points		Points per Game (min. 70 games)	
1998-99*	Keith Van Horn	.428	Stephon Marbury	1044	Keith Van Horn	21.8
	Stephon Marbury	.428				
1999-00	Johnny Newman	.446	Stephon Marbury	1640	Stephon Marbury	22.2
2000-01	Evan Eschmeyer	.460	Stephon Marbury	1598	Johnny Newman	10.9
2001-02	Aaron Williams	.526	Jason Kidd	1208	Kenyon Martin	14.9
2002-03	Richard Jefferson	.501	Jason Kidd	1495	Jason Kidd	18.7
2003-04	Aaron Williams	.503	Richard Jefferson	1515	Richard Jefferson	18.5
2004-05	Nenad Krstic	.493	Vince Carter	1886	Vince Carter	24.5
2005-06	Nenad Krstic	.507	Vince Carter	1911	Vince Carter	24.2

COACHING HISTORY: 1977-1981 Kevin Loughery 107-174-.381; 1980-1981 Bob MacKinnon 12-35-.255; 1981-1983 Larry Brown 91-67-.576; 1982-1983 Bill Blair 2-4-.333; 1983-1985 Stan Albeck 87-77-.530; 1985-1988 Dave Wohl 65-114-.363; 1987-1988 Bob MacKinnon 10-29-.256; 1987-1989 Willis Reed 33-77-.300; 1989-1992 Bill Fitch 83-163-.337; 1992-1994 Chuck Daly 88-76-.537; 1994-1996 Butch Beard 60-104-.366; 1996-1999 John Caliperi 72-112-.391; 1998-2000 Don Casey 44-68-.393; 2000-2004 Byron Scott 149-139-.517; 2003-present Lawrence Frank

NEW ORLEANS BREAKERS
(were Boston Breakers)
(became Portland Breakers)

Home City: New Orleans, Louisiana
Home Stadium: Louisiana Superdome   Capacity: 71,330 [1984]
Origin of Name: The team kept the same nickname when it moved from Boston to New Orleans.

Regular Season Record

Season	League	GP	W	L	T	PF	PA	Pct
1984	USFL	18	8	10	0	348	395	.444

Regular Season Individual Leaders

Season	Passing Yards		Receiving Yards		Rushing Yards	
1984	Johnnie Walton	3554	Frank Lockett	1199	Buford Johnson	1276

COACHING HISTORY: Dick Coury 8-10-0-.444

NEW ORLEANS BUCCANEERS
(became Memphis Pros)

Home City: New Orleans, Louisiana
Home Court: Loyola University Fieldhouse   Capacity: 6,425
            Tulane Field House (1969-70)
            Municipal Auditorium (1969-70)
Origin of Name:

Regular Season Record

Season	League	GP	W	L	PPGF	PPGA	Pct	GB
1967-1968	ABA	78	48	30	111.7	106.9	.615	-
1968-1969	ABA	78	46	32	116.1	112.7	.590	14
1969-1970	ABA	84	42	42	107.9	107.1	.500	9
TOTAL:	3 years	240	136	104				23
AVERAGE:		80	45	35	111.9	108.9	.563	8

*-minimum 40 games.

Playoff Record

Season	GP	W	L	PPGF	PPGA	Result
1967-1968	17	10	7	109.2	106.5	Lost Championship series to Pittsburgh.
1968-1969	11	4	7	115.0	119.0	Lost 2nd Round series to Oakland.
TOTAL:	28	14	14			
AVERAGE:	14	7	7	112.1	112.8	

Regular Season Individual Leaders

Season	Field Goal % (min. 70 games)		Points		Points per Game (min. 70 games)	
1967-68	"Red" Robbins	.488	Doug Moe	1884	Doug Moe	24.2
1968-69	Jimmy Jones	.535	Jimmy Jones	2050	Jimmy Jones	26.6
1969-70	Jimmy Jones	.497	Steve Jones	1805	Steve Jones	21.5

COACHING HISTORY: 1967-1970 Babe McCarthy 136-104-.563

NEW ORLEANS HORNETS
(were Charlotte Hornets)

Home City: New Orleans, Louisiana
Home Court: New Orleans Arena (2002-present)*   Capacity: 18,500 [2006]
Origin of Name: The team kept the same nickname when it moved to New Orleans from Charlotte.

Regular Season Record

Season	League	GP	W	L	PPGF	PPGA	Pct	GB
2002-2003	NBA	82	47	35	93.9	91.8	.573	3
2003-2004	NBA	82	41	41	91.8	91.9	.500	20
2004-2005	NBA	82	18	64	88.4	95.5	.220	41
2005-2006	NBA	82	38	44	92.8	95.6	.463	25
TOTAL:	4 years	328	144	184				89
AVERAGE:		82	36	46	91.7	93.7	.439	22

Playoff Record

Season	GP	W	L	PPGF	PPGA	Result
2002-2003	6	2	4	92.8	91.2	Lost 1st Round series to Philadelphia.
2003-2004	7	3	4	80.9	83.6	Lost 1st Round series to Miami.
TOTAL:	13	5	8			
AVERAGE:	7	2	4	86.4	87.1	

Regular Season Individual Leaders

Season	Field Goal % (min. 70 games)		Points		Points per Game (min. 70 games)	
2002-03	P.J. Brown	.531	Jamal Mashburn	1772	Jamal Mashburn	21.6
2003-04	Robert Traylor	.505	Baron Davis	1532	Jamaal Magloire	13.6
2004-05	P.J. Brown	.446	Lee Nailon	963	P.J. Brown	10.8
2005-06	David West	.512	David West	1262	David West	17.1

COACHING HISTORY: 2002-2003 Paul Silas 47-35-.573; 2003-2004 Tim Floyd 41-41-.500; 2004-present Byron Scott

*-due to damage to their home arena wrought by Hurricane Katrina, the Hornets played 35 games in Oklahoma City's Ford Center and 6 games in Louisiana State University's Maravich Center in Baton Rouge.

NEW ORLEANS JAZZ
(became Utah Jazz)

Home City: New Orleans, Louisiana
Home Court: Municipal Auditorium (1974-1975)   Capacity: 7,853
        Louisiana Superdome (1974-1979)   Capacity: 47,284
Origin of Name: The name was chosen in a Name the Team Contest as New Orleans is well known for its jazz music.

Regular Season Record

Season	League	GP	W	L	PPGF	PPGA	Pct	GB
1974-1975	NBA	82	23	59	101.5	109.3	.280	37
1975-1976	NBA	82	38	44	104.1	105.0	.463	11
1976-1977	NBA	82	35	47	104.6	107.4	.427	14
1977-1978	NBA	82	39	43	107.6	109.5	.476	13
1978-1979	NBA	82	26	56	108.3	114.6	.317	22
TOTAL:	5 years	410	161	249				97
AVERAGE:		82	32	50	105.2	109.2	.393	19

Regular Season Individual Leaders

Season	Field Goal % (min. 70 games)		Points		Points per Game (min. 70 games)	
1974-75	Aaron James	.477	Pete Maravich	1700	Pete Maravich	21.5
1975-76	Rich Kelley	.485	Pete Maravich	1604	Pete Maravich	25.9
1976-77	Paul Griffin	.547	Pete Maravich	2273	Pete Maravich	31.1
1977-78	Rich Kelley	.505	Truck Robinson	1862	Truck Robinson	22.7
1978-79	Rich Kelley	.506	Jim McElroy	1337	Jim McElroy	16.9

COACHING HISTORY: 1974-1975 Scotty Robertson 1-14-.067; 1974-1975 Elgin Baylor 0-1-.000; 1974-1977 Butch van Breda Kolff 74-100-.425; 1976-1979 Elgin Baylor 86-134-.391

NEW ORLEANS SAINTS

Home City: New Orleans, Louisiana
        San Antonio, Texas (2005)
Home Stadium: Tulane Stadium (1967-1974)   Capacity: 80,985 [1974]
        Louisiana Superdome (1975-present)   Capacity: 68,395 [2004]
        Alamodome (2005)*   Capacity: 91,644 [2005]
        Tiger Stadium at LSU (2005)*   Capacity: 65,000 [2005]
Origin of Name: Named Saints because the team's fight song was "When the Saints Go Marching In" and the franchise was awarded on All Saints Day in 1966.

Regular Season Record

Season	League	GP	W	L	T	PF	PA	Pct
1967	NFL	14	3	11	0	233	379	.214
1968	NFL	14	4	9	1	246	327	.321
1969	NFL	14	5	9	0	311	393	.357
1970	NFL	14	2	11	1	172	347	.179
1971	NFL	14	4	8	2	266	347	.357
1972	NFL	14	2	11	1	215	361	.179
1973	NFL	14	5	9	0	163	312	.357

*-due to Hurricane Katrina and damage to the Superdome the Saints were forced to play their home games in the Alamodome (3) and Tiger Stadium (4)

1974	NFL	14	5	9	0	166	263	.357
1975	NFL	14	2	12	0	165	360	.143
1976	NFL	14	4	10	0	253	346	.286
1977	NFL	14	3	11	0	232	336	.214
1978	NFL	16	7	9	0	281	298	.438
1979	NFL	16	8	8	0	370	360	.500
1980	NFL	16	1	15	0	291	487	.063
1981	NFL	16	4	12	0	207	378	.250
1982	NFL	9	4	5	0	129	160	.444
1983	NFL	16	8	8	0	319	337	.500
1984	NFL	16	7	9	0	298	361	.438
1985	NFL	16	5	11	0	294	401	.313
1986	NFL	16	7	9	0	288	287	.438
1987	NFL	15	12	3	0	422	283	.800
1988	NFL	16	10	6	0	312	283	.625
1989	NFL	16	9	7	0	386	301	.563
1990	NFL	16	8	8	0	274	275	.500
1991	NFL	16	11	5	0	341	211	.688
1992	NFL	16	12	4	0	330	202	.750
1993	NFL	16	8	8	0	317	343	.500
1994	NFL	16	7	9	0	348	407	.438
1995	NFL	16	7	9	0	319	348	.438
1996	NFL	16	3	13	0	229	339	.188
1997	NFL	16	6	10	0	237	327	.375
1998	NFL	16	6	10	0	305	359	.375
1999	NFL	16	3	13	0	260	434	.188
2000	NFL	16	10	6	0	354	305	.625
2001	NFL	16	7	9	0	333	409	.438
2002	NFL	16	9	7	0	432	388	.562
2003	NFL	16	8	8	0	340	326	.500
2004	NFL	16	8	8	0	348	405	.500
2005	NFL	16	3	13	0	235	398	.188
2006	NFL	16	10	6	0	413	322	.625
TOTAL:	40 years	610	247	358	5	11434	13505	
AVERAGE:		15	6	9	0	286	338	.409

Playoff Record

Season	GP	W	L	PF	PA	Result
1987	1	0	1	10	44	Lost 1st Round game to Minnesota.
1990	1	0	1	6	16	Lost Wild Card Game to Chicago.
1991	1	0	1	20	27	Lost Wild Card Game to Atlanta.
1992	1	0	1	20	36	Lost Wild Card Game to Philadelphia.
2000	2	1	1	47	62	Lost Conference Semifinal to Minnesota.
2006	2	1	1	41	45	Lost Conference Final to Chicago.
TOTAL:	8	2	5	144	230	
AVERAGE:	1	0	1	24	38	

Regular Season Individual Leaders

Season	Passing Yards		Receiving Yards		Rushing Yards	
1967	Gary Cuozzo	1562	Dan Abramowicz	721	Jim Taylor	390
1968	Billy Kilmer	2060	Dan Abramowicz	890	Don McCall	637
1969	Billy Kilmer	2532	Dan Abramowicz	1015	Andy Livingston	761
1970	Billy Kilmer	1557	Dan Abramowicz	906	Tony Baker	337
1971	Edd Hargett	1191	Dan Abramowicz	657	Jim Strong	404

Season	Passing Yards		Receiving Yards		Rushing Yards	
1972	Archie Manning	2781	Dan Abramowicz	668	Bob Gresham	381
1973	Archie Manning	1642	Bob Newland	489	Jess Phillips	663
1974	Archie Manning	1429	Bob Newland	490	Alvin Maxson	714
1975	Archie Manning	1683	Paul Seal	414	Mike Strachan	668
1976	Bobby Douglass	1288	Don Hermann	535	Chuck Muncie	659
1977	Archie Manning	1284	Henry Childs	518	Chuck Muncie	811
1978	Archie Manning	3416	Henry Childs	869	Tony Galbreath	635
1979	Archie Manning	3169	Wes Chandler	1069	Chuck Muncie	1198
1980	Archie Manning	3716	Wes Chandler	975	Jimmy Rogers	366
1981	Archie Manning	1447	Guido Merkens	458	George Rogers	1674
1982	Ken Stabler	1343	Jeff Groth	383	George Rogers	535
1983	Ken Stabler	1988	Jeff Groth	585	George Rogers	1144
1984	Richard Todd	2178	Tyrone Young	597	George Rogers	914
1985	Dave Wilson	1843	Eugene Goodlow	603	Wayne Wilson	645
1986	Dave Wilson	2353	Eric Martin	675	Rueben Mayes	1353
1987	Bobby Hebert	2119	Eric Martin	778	Rueben Mayes	917
1988	Bobby Hebert	3156	Eric Martin	1083	Dalton Hilliard	823
1989	Bobby Hebert	2686	Eric Martin	1090	Dalton Hilliard	1262
1990	Steve Walsh	2010	Eric Martin	912	Craig Heyward	599
1991	Bobby Hebert	1676	Floyd Turner	927	Fred McAfee	494
1992	Bobby Hebert	3287	Eric Martin	1041	Vaughn Dunbar	565
1993	Wade Wilson	2457	Eric Martin	950	Derek Brown	705
1994	Jim Everett	3855	Michael Haynes	985	Mario Bates	579
1995	Jim Everett	3970	Quinn Early	1087	Mario Bates	951
1996	Jim Everett	2797	Michael Haynes	786	Mario Bates	584
1997	Heath Shuler	1288	Randal Hill	761	Ray Zellars	552
1998	Danny Wuerffel	695	Sean Dawkins	823	Lamar Smith	457
1999	Billy Joe Tolliver	1916	Eddie Kennison	835	Ricky Williams	884
2000	Jeff Blake	2025	Joe Horn	1340	Ricky Williams	1000
2001	Aaron Brooks	3832	Joe Horn	1265	Ricky Williams	1245
2002	Aaron Brooks	3572	Joe Horn	1312	Deuce McAllister	1388
2003	Aaron Brooks	3546	Joe Horn	973	Deuce McAllister	1641
2004	Aaron Brooks	3810	Joe Horn	1399	Deuce McAllister	1074
2005	Aaron Brooks	2882	Donte Stallworth	945	Antowain Smith	659
2006	Drew Brees	4418	Marques Colston	1038	Deuce McAllister	1057

COACHING HISTORY: 1967-1970 Tom Fears 13-34-2-.286; 1970-1972 J.D. Roberts 7-25-3-.243; 1973-1975 John North 11-23-0-.324; 1975 Ernie Hefferle 1-7-0-.125; 1976-1977 Hank Stram 7-21-0-.250; 1978-1980 Dick Nolan 15-29-0-.341; 1980 Dick Stanfel 1-3-0-.250; 1981-1985 "Bum" Phillips 27-42-0-.391; 1985 Wade Phillips 1-3-0-.250; 1986-1996 Jim Mora 93-74-0-.557; 1996 Rick Venturi 1-7-0-.125; 1997-1999 Mike Ditka 15-33-0-.313; 2000-2005 Jim Haslett 45-51-0-.469; 2006-present Sean Payton

NEW WESTMINSTER ROYALS
(became Portland Rosebuds)

Home City: New Westminster, British Columbia
Home Arena: Vancouver Arena *   Capacity: 10,500
Origin of Name:

*-A new arena had been planned for New Westminster but it was never completed and the team played all of its home games in Vancouver.

Regular Season Record

Season	League	GP	W	L	T	GF	GA	Pts	Pct
1911-1912	PCHA	15	9	6	0	78	77	18	.600
1912-1913	PCHA	15	6	9	0	67	74	12	.400
1913-1914	PCHA	16	7	9	0	75	81	14	.438
TOTAL:	3 years	46	22	24	0	220	232	44	
AVERAGE:		15	7	8	0	73	77	14	.478

Regular Season Individual Leaders

Season	Goals		Points		GAA	
1911-1912	Harry Hyland	26	Harry Hyland	26	Hugh Lehman	5.13
1912-1913	Ran McDonald	15	Ran McDonald	15	Hugh Lehman	4.57
1913-1914	Eddie Oatman	22	Eddie Oatman	22	Hugh Lehman	5.06

COACHING HISTORY: 1911-1912 Jim Gardner 9-6-0-.600; 1912-1914 Not Available

NEW YORK AMERICANS
(were Hamilton Tigers)

Home City: New York, New York
Home Arena: Madison Square Garden III   Capacity: 15,925
Origin of Name: The team was known as the Brooklyn Americans during its final season.

Regular Season Record

Season	League	GP	W	L	T	GF	GA	Pts	Pct
1925-1926	NHL	36	12	20	4	68	89	28	.389
1926-1927	NHL	44	17	25	2	82	91	36	.409
1927-1928	NHL	44	11	27	6	63	128	28	.318
1928-1929	NHL	44	19	13	12	53	53	50	.568
1929-1930	NHL	44	14	25	5	113	161	33	.375
1930-1931	NHL	44	18	16	10	76	74	46	.523
1931-1932	NHL	48	16	24	8	95	142	40	.417
1932-1933	NHL	48	15	22	11	91	118	41	.427
1933-1934	NHL	48	15	23	10	104	132	40	.417
1934-1935	NHL	48	12	27	9	100	142	33	.344
1935-1936	NHL	48	16	25	7	109	122	39	.406
1936-1937	NHL	48	15	29	4	122	161	34	.354
1937-1938	NHL	48	19	18	11	110	111	49	.510
1938-1939	NHL	48	17	21	10	119	157	44	.458
1939-1940	NHL	48	15	29	4	196	140	34	.354
1940-1941	NHL	48	8	29	11	99	186	27	.281
1941-1942	NHL	48	16	29	3	133	175	35	.365
TOTAL:	17 years	784	255	402	127	1733	2182	637	
AVERAGE:		46	15	24	7	102	128	37	.406

Playoff Record

Season	GP	W	L	T	GF	GA	Result
1928-1929	2	0	1	1	0	1	Lost Quarterfinal series to Rangers.
1935-1936	5	2	3	0	10	11	Lost Semifinal series to Toronto.
1937-1938	6	3	3	0	13	12	Lost Semifinal series to Chicago.
1938-1939	2	0	2	0	0	6	Lost Quarterfinal series to Toronto.
1939-1940	3	1	2	0	7	9	Lost Quarterfinal series to Detroit.
TOTAL:	18	6	11	1	30	39	
AVERAGE:	3	1	2	0	6	8	

Regular Season Individual Leaders

Season	Goals		Points		Penalty Minutes	
1925-1926	Bill Burch	22	Bill Burch	25	Ken Randall	94
1926-1927	Bill Burch	19	Bill Burch	27	Lionel Conacher	81
1927-1928	Norman Himes	14	Norman Himes	19	Clarence Boucher	129
1928-1929	Bill Burch	11	Bill Burch	16	Lionel Conacher	132
1929-1930	Norman Himes	28	Norman Himes	50	Lionel Conacher	73
1930-1931	Norman Himes	15	Norman Himes	24	Mervyn Dutton	71
1931-1932	Joe Lamb	14	Norman Himes	28	George Mantha	107
					Mervyn Dutton	46
1932-1933	John Sheppard	17	Norman Himes	34	Vern Ayres	97
1933-1934	Eddie Burke	20	Eddie Burke	30	Mervyn Dutton	65
1934-1935	David Schriner	18	Art Chapman	43	Alex Smith	46
1935-1936	David Schriner	19	David Schriner	45	Mervyn Dutton	69
1936-1937	David Schriner	21	David Schriner	46	Allan Shields	79
1937-1938	David Schriner	21	David Schriner	38	Joe Jerwa	53
1938-1939	Lorne Carr	19	David Schriner	44	Joe Jerwa	52
1939-1940	M. Armstrong	16	M. Armstrong	36	Charlie Conacher	41
1940-1941	Lorne Carr	13	Lorne Carr	32	Peter Slobodzian	54
1941-1942	Norman Larson	16	Tom Anderson	41	Pat Egan	104

COACHING HISTORY: 1925-1926 Tommy Gorman 12-20-4-.389; 1926-1927 Newsy Lalonde 17-25-2-.409; 1927-1928 Wilfred Green 11-27-6-.318; 1928-1929 Tommy Gorman 19-13-12-.568; 1929-1930 Lionel Conacher 14-25-5-.375; 1930-1932 Eddie Gerard 34-40-18-.467; 1932-1935 Joe Simpson 42-72-30-.396; 1935-1942 Mervyn Dutton 106-180-50-.390

NEW YORK CELTICS
(were Brooklyn Arcadians)

Home City: New York, New York
Home Court: Madison Square Garden III   Capacity: 15,925
Origin of Name: Due to poor attendance the Brooklyn team disbanded in 1927 and its record was assumed by the powerful barnstorming New York Celtic team.

Regular Season Record

Season	League	GP	W	L	Pct
1927-1928	ABL	49	40	9	.899

Playoff Record

Season	GP	W	L	Result
1927-1928	6	5	1	Won ABL Championship

Regular Season Individual Leaders

Season	Points	
1927-28	Davey Banks	406

COACHING HISTORY: John Whitty 40-9-.899

NEW YORK COSMOS

Home City: New York, New York (1971-1976)
    East Rutherford, New Jersey (1977-1984)

Home Stadium: Yankee Stadium (1971, 1976)	Capacity: 63,800
Hofstra Stadium (1972-1973)	Capacity:
Downing Stadium (1974-1975)*	Capacity: 21,000
Giants Stadium (1977-1984)	Capacity: 76,891 [1984]

Origin of Name: The name was chosen in a Name the Team Contest. The team was known simply as the "Cosmos" from 1977 to 1984.

Regular Season Record

Season	League	GP	W	L	T	GF	GA	BP	Pts	Pct
1971	NASL	24	9	10	5	51	55	48	117	.542
1972	NASL	14	7	3	4	28	16	23	77	.611
1973	NASL	19	7	5	7	31	23	28	91	.532
1974	NASL	20	4	14	2	28	40	28	58	.322
1975	NASL	22	10	12	-	39	38	31	91	.460
1976	NASL	24	16	8	-	65	34	52	148	.685
1977	NASL	26	15	11	-	60	39	50	140	.598
1978	NASL	30	24	6	-	88	39	68	212	.785
1979	NASL	30	24	6	-	84	52	72	216	.800
1980	NASL	32	24	8	-	87	41	69	213	.740
1981	NASL	32	23	9	-	80	49	64	200	.417
1982	NASL	32	23	9	-	73	52	67	203	.423
1983	NASL	30	22	8	-	87	49	64	194	.431
1984	NASL	24	13	11	-	43	42	39	115	.319
TOTAL:	14 years	359	221	120	18	844	569	703	2075	
AVERAGE:		26	16	9	1	60	41	50	148	.527

Playoff Record

Season	GP	W	L	T	GF	GA	Result
1971	2	0	2	0	0	3	Lost Semifinal series to Atlanta.
1972	2	2	0	0	3	1	**Won NASL Championship.**
1973	1	0	1	0	0	1	Lost Semifinal game to Dallas.
1976	2	1	1	0	3	3	Lost Division Final to Tampa Bay.
1977	6	6	0	0	22	8	**Won NASL Championship.**
1978	7	6	1	0	21	12	**Won NASL Championship.**
1979	8	5	3	0	14	10	Lost 3rd Round series to Vancouver.
1980	8	7	1	0	25	9	**Won NASL Championship.**
1981	6	4	2	0	18	11	Lost Championship series to Chicago.
1982	6	5	1	0	11	3	**Won NASL Championship.**
1983	2	0	2	0	2	5	Lost 1st Round series to Montreal.
TOTAL:	50	36	14	0	119	66	
AVERAGE:	5	4	1	0	12	6	

Regular Season Individual Leaders

Season	Goals		Points		GAA (360 Min)	
1971	Randy Horton	16	Randy Horton	37	Conrad Kornek	2.15
1972	Randy Horton	9	Randy Horton	22	R. Blackmore	1.14
1973	Joe Fink	11	Randy Horton	23	Bronislaw Sularz	1.22
1974	Randy Horton	9	Randy Horton	22	Samuel Nusum	0.88

Season	Goals		Points		GAA (360 Min)	
1975	Joe Fink	6	Joe Fink	14	Samuel Nusum	1.56
	Mordechai Shpigler	6				
1976	Giorgio Chinaglia	19	Giorgio Chinaglia	49	Bob Rigby	1.14
1977	Giorgio Chinaglia	15	Giorgio Chinaglia	38	Erol Yasin	1.06
1978	Giorgio Chinaglia	34	Giorgio Chinaglia	79	Erol Yasin	1.13
1979	Giorgio Chinaglia	26	Giorgio Chinaglia	57	H. Birkenmeier	1.43
1980	Giorgio Chinaglia	32	Giorgio Chinaglia	77	H. Birkenmeier	1.14
1981	Giorgio Chinaglia	29	Giorgio Chinaglia	74	H. Birkenmeier	1.41
1982	Giorgio Chinaglia	20	Giorgio Chinaglia	55	H. Birkenmeier	1.55
1983	Roberto Cabanas	25	Roberto Cabanas	66	H. Birkenmeier	1.47
1984	Roberto Cabanas	8	Roberto Cabanas	20	H. Birkenmeier	1.50

COACHING HISTORY: 1971-1977 Gordon Bradley 57-54-18; 1976 Ken Furphy 8-6; 1977-1979 Eddie Firmani 36-11; 1979 Ray Klivecka 15-4; 1980-1981 Hennes Weisweiler 47-17; 1982-1983 Julio Mazzei 45-17; 1984 Eddie Firmani 13-11

NEW YORK GENERALS

Home City: New York, New York
Home Stadium: Yankee Stadium   Capacity: 67,000 [1967]
Origin of Name: The team was originally sponsored by RKO-GENERAL and adopted their name.

Regular Season Record

Season	League	GP	W	L	T	GF	GA	BP	Pts	Pct
1967	NPSL	32	11	13	8	60	58	NA	143	.496
1968	NASL	32	12	8	12	62	54	36	164	.569
TOTAL:	2 years	64	23	21	20	122	112	36	307	
AVERAGE:		32	12	10	10	61	56	18	154	.535

Regular Season Individual Leaders

Season	Goals		Points		GAA (360 Min)	
1967	George Kirby	14	George Kirby	30	Paul Freitag	1.65
1968	Dieter Pereau	13	Dieter Pereau	33		

COACHING HISTORY: 1967-1968 Freddie Goodwin 23-21-20-.535

NEW YORK GIANTS
(were Troy Trojans)
(became San Francisco Giants)

Home City: New York, New York
Home Field: Polo Grounds I (1883-1888)   Capacity: 21,000
            Manhattan Field (1889-1890)   Capacity:
            Polo Grounds II (1891-1957)   Capacity: 55,987
Origin of Name: The team name was coined by then manager Jim Mutrie who said his players played like "Giants" after a particularly successful road trip. Known as Gothams from 1883 to 1885.

Regular Season Record

Season	League	GP	W	L	Pct	GB	R	OR
1883	NL	96	46	50	.479	16	530	577
1884	NL	112	62	50	.554	22	693	623

1885	NL	112	85	27	.759	2	691	370
1886	NL	119	75	44	.630	12.5	692	558
1887	NL	123	68	55	.553	10.5	816	723
1888	NL	131	84	47	.641	-	659	479
1889	NL	126	83	43	.659	-	935	708
1890	NL	131	63	68	.481	24	713	698
1891	NL	132	71	61	.538	13	754	711
1892	NL	151	71	80	.470	31.5	811	826
1893	NL	132	68	64	.515	19.5	941	845
1894	NL	132	88	44	.667	3	940	789
1895	NL	131	66	65	.504	21.5	852	834
1896	NL	131	64	67	.489	27	829	821
1897	NL	131	83	48	.634	9.5	895	695
1898	NL	150	77	73	.513	25.5	837	800
1899	NL	150	60	90	.400	42	734	863
1900	NL	138	60	78	.435	23	713	823
1901	NL	137	52	85	.380	37	544	755
1902	NL	136	48	88	.353	53.5	401	589
1903	NL	139	84	55	.604	6.5	729	548
1904	NL	153	106	47	.693	-	744	476
1905	NL	153	105	48	.686	-	780	504
1906	NL	152	96	56	.632	20	625	508
1907	NL	153	82	71	.536	25.5	573	511
1908	NL	154	98	56	.636	1	652	458
1909	NL	153	92	61	.601	18.5	621	546
1910	NL	154	91	63	.591	13	715	545
1911	NL	153	99	54	.647	-	756	542
1912	NL	151	103	48	.682	-	823	571
1913	NL	152	101	51	.664	-	684	502
1914	NL	154	84	70	.545	10.5	672	576
1915	NL	152	69	83	.454	21	582	628
1916	NL	152	86	66	.566	7	597	503
1917	NL	154	98	56	.636	-	635	457
1918	NL	124	71	53	.573	10.5	480	423
1919	NL	140	87	53	.621	9	605	470
1920	NL	154	86	68	.558	7	682	543
1921	NL	153	94	59	.614	-	840	637
1922	NL	154	93	61	.604	-	852	658
1923	NL	153	95	58	.621	-	854	679
1924	NL	153	93	60	.608	-	857	641
1925	NL	152	86	66	.566	8.5	736	702
1926	NL	151	74	77	.490	13.5	663	668
1927	NL	154	92	62	.597	2	817	720
1928	NL	154	93	61	.604	2	807	653
1929	NL	151	84	67	.556	13.5	897	709
1930	NL	154	87	67	.565	5	959	814
1931	NL	152	87	65	.572	13	768	599
1932	NL	154	72	82	.468	18	755	706
1933	NL	152	91	61	.599	-	636	515
1934	NL	153	93	60	.608	2	760	583
1935	NL	153	91	62	.595	8.5	770	675
1936	NL	154	92	62	.597	-	742	621
1937	NL	152	95	57	.625	-	732	602
1938	NL	150	83	67	.553	5	705	637

1939	NL	151	77	74	.510	18.5	703	685
1940	NL	152	72	80	.474	27.5	663	659
1941	NL	153	74	79	.484	25.5	667	706
1942	NL	152	85	67	.559	20	675	600
1943	NL	153	55	98	.359	49.5	558	713
1944	NL	154	67	87	.435	38	682	773
1945	NL	152	78	74	.513	19	668	700
1946	NL	154	61	93	.396	36	612	685
1947	NL	154	81	73	.526	13	830	761
1948	NL	154	78	76	.506	13.5	780	704
1949	NL	154	73	81	.474	24	736	693
1950	NL	154	86	68	.558	5	735	643
1951	NL	157	98	59	.624	-	781	641
1952	NL	154	92	62	.597	4.5	722	639
1953	NL	154	70	84	.455	35	768	747
1954	NL	154	97	57	.630	-	732	550
1955	NL	154	80	74	.519	18.5	702	673
1956	NL	154	67	87	.435	26	540	650
1957	NL	154	69	85	.448	26	643	701
TOTAL:	75 years	10965	6067	4898		1033	54282	48140
AVERAGE:		146	81	65	.553	14	724	642

Playoff Record

Season	GP	W	L	T	R	OR	Result
1888	10	6	4	0	64	60	**Won World Series.**
1889	9	6	3	0	73	52	**Won World Series.**
1894	4	4	0	0	33	11	**Won Temple Cup.**
1905	5	4	1	0	15	3	**Won World Series.**
1911	6	2	4	0	13	27	Lost World Series to Philadelphia.
1912	8	3	4	1	31	25	Lost World Series to Boston.
1913	5	1	4	0	15	23	Lost World Series to Philadelphia.
1917	6	2	4	0	17	21	Lost World Series to Chicago.
1921	8	5	3	0	29	22	**Won World Series.**
1922	5	4	0	1	18	11	**Won World Series.**
1923	6	2	4	0	17	30	Lost World Series to Yankees.
1924	7	3	4	0	27	26	Lost World Series to Washington.
1933	5	4	1	0	16	11	**Won World Series.**
1936	6	2	4	0	23	43	Lost World Series to Yankees.
1937	5	1	4	0	12	28	Lost World Series to Yankees.
1951	6	2	4	0	18	29	Lost World Series to Yankees.
1954	4	4	0	0	21	9	**Won World Series.**
TOTAL:	105	55	48	2	442	431	
AVERAGE:	6	3	3	0	26	25	

Regular Season Individual Leaders

Season	Home Runs		RBI's		Wins	
1883	William Ewing	10	Pete Gillespie	62	Mickey Welch	25
1884	Roger Connor	4	Roger Connor	82	Mickey Welch	39
	Alex McKinnon	4				
1885	William Ewing	6	Roger Connor	65	Mickey Welch	44
1886	Roger Connor	7	Monte Ward	81	Tim Keefe	42
1887	Roger Connor	17	Roger Connor	104	Tim Keefe	35
1888	Roger Connor	14	Roger Connor	71	Tim Keefe	35
1889	Roger Connor	13	Roger Connor	130	Tim Keefe	28

Season	Home Runs		RBI's		Wins	
1890	Mike Tiernan	13	Jack Glasscock	66	Amos Rusie	29
1891	Mike Tiernan	16	Jim O'Rourke	95	Amos Rusie	33
1892	William Ewing	8	William Ewing	76	Amos Rusie	31
	Denny Lyons	8				
1893	Mike Tiernan	14	George Davis	119	Amos Rusie	33
1894	George Davis	8	G. Van Haltren	104	Amos Rusie	36
1895	G. Van Haltren	8	G. Van Haltren	103	Amos Rusie	23
1896	Mike Tiernan	7	George Davis	99	Jouett Meekin	26
1897	George Davis	10	George Davis	136	Amos Rusie	28
1898	Bill Joyce	10	Bill Joyce	91	Cy Seymour	25
1899	Tom O'Brien	6	Tom O'Brien	77	Bill Carrick	16
1900	Charles Hickman	9	Charles Hickman	91	Bill Carrick	19
1901	George Davis	7	John Ganzel	66	Christy Mathewson	20
1902	Steve Brodie	3	Bill Lauder	44	Christy Mathewson	14
1903	Sam Mertes	7	Sam Mertes	104	Joe McGinnity	31
1904	Dan McGann	6	Bill Dahlen	80	Joe McGinnity	35
1905	Bill Dahlen	7	Sam Mertes	108	Christy Mathewson	32
	Mike Donlin	7				
1906	Cy Seymour	4	Art Devlin	65	Joe McGinnity	27
	Sammy Strang	4				
1907	George Browne	5	Cy Seymour	75	Christy Mathewson	24
1908	Mike Donlin	6	Mike Donlin	106	Christy Mathewson	37
1909	John Murray	7	John Murray	91	Christy Mathewson	25
1910	Larry Doyle	8	John Murray	87	Christy Mathewson	27
1911	Larry Doyle	13	Fred Merkle	84	Christy Mathewson	26
1912	Fred Merkle	11	John Murray	92	Rube Marquard	26
1913	Larry Doyle	5	Larry Doyle	73	Christy Mathewson	25
	Tillie Shafer	5				
1914	Fred Merkle	7	Art Fletcher	79	Dick Rudolph	27
1915	Fred Merkle	4	Art Fletcher	74	Jeff Tesreau	19
	Larry Doyle	4				
1916	Dave Robertson	12	Benny Kauff	74	William Peritt	18
1917	Dave Robertson	12	H. Zimmerman	102	Ferdie Schupp	21
1918	George Burns	4	H. Zimmerman	56	James Vaughn	22
1919	Benny Kauff	10	Benny Kauff	67	Jesse Barnes	25
1920	George Kelly	11	George Kelly	94	Fred Toney	21
					Art Nehf	21
1921	George Kelly	23	George Kelly	122	Art Nehf	20
1922	George Kelly	17	Emil Meusel	132	Art Nehf	19
1923	Emil Meusel	19	Emil Meusel	125	Wilfred Ryan	16
					Jack Scott	16
1924	George Kelly	21	George Kelly	136	Jack Bentley	16
					Virgil Barnes	16
1925	Emil Meusel	21	Emil Meusel	111	Virgil Barnes	15
1926	George Kelly	13	George Kelly	80	Fred Fitzsimmons	14
1927	Rogers Hornsby	26	Rogers Hornsby	125	Burleigh Grimes	19
1928	Mel Ott	18	Fred Lindstrom	107	Larry Benton	25
1929	Mel Ott	42	Mel Ott	151	Carl Hubbell	18
1930	Mel Ott	25	Bill Terry	129	Fred Fitzsimmons	19
1931	Mel Ott	29	Mel Ott	115	Fred Fitzsimmons	18
1932	Mel Ott	38	Mel Ott	123	Carl Hubbell	18
1933	Mel Ott	23	Mel Ott	103	Carl Hubbell	23
1934	Mel Ott	35	Mel Ott	135	Hal Schumacher	23

Season	Home Runs		RBI's		Wins	
1935	Mel Ott	31	Mel Ott	114	Carl Hubbell	23
1936	Mel Ott	33	Mel Ott	135	Carl Hubbell	26
1937	Mel Ott	31	Mel Ott	95	Carl Hubbell	22
1938	Mel Ott	36	Mel Ott	116	Harry Gumbert	15
1939	Mel Ott	27	Henry Bonura	85	Harry Gumbert	18
1940	Mel Ott	19	Babe Young	101	Hal Schumacher	13
1941	Mel Ott	27	Babe Young	104	Hal Schumacher	12
1942	Mel Ott	30	Johnny Mize	110	Bill Lohrman	13
1943	Mel Ott	18	Sid Gordon	63	Ace Adams	11
1944	Mel Ott	26	Joe Medwick	85	Bill Voiselle	21
1945	Mel Ott	21	Mel Ott	79	Van Lingle Mungo	14
					Bill Voiselle	14
1946	Johnny Mize	22	Johnny Mize	70	Dave Koslo	14
1947	Johnny Mize	51	Johnny Mize	138	Larry Jansen	21
1948	Johnny Mize	40	Johnny Mize	125	Larry Jansen	18
1949	Bobby Thomson	27	Bobby Thomson	109	Sheldon Jones	15
					Larry Jansen	15
1950	Bobby Thomson	25	Hank Thompson	91	Larry Jansen	19
1951	Bobby Thomson	32	Monte Irvin	121	Sal Maglie	23
					Larry Jansen	23
1952	Bobby Thomson	24	Bobby Thomson	108	Sal Maglie	18
1953	Bobby Thomson	26	Bobby Thomson	106	Ruben Gomez	13
1954	Willie Mays	41	Willie Mays	110	John Antonelli	21
1955	Willie Mays	51	Willie Mays	127	Jim Hearn	14
					John Antonelli	14
1956	Willie Mays	36	Willie Mays	84	John Antonelli	20
1957	Willie Mays	35	Willie Mays	97	Ruben Gomez	15

COACHING HISTORY: 1883 John Clapp 46-50-.479; 1884 James Price 56-42-.571; 1884 Monte Ward 6-8-.429; 1885-1891 Jim Mutrie 529-345-.605; 1892 Pat Powers 71-80-.470; 1893-1894 Monte Ward 156-108-.591; 1895 George Davis 17-17-.500; 1895 Jack Doyle 31-31-.500; 1895 Harvey Watkins 18-17-.514; 1896 Arthur Irwin 38-53-.418; 1896-1898 Bill Joyce 177-122-.592; 1898 Cap Anson 9-13-.409; 1899 John Day 30-40-.429; 1899 Fred Hoey 30-50-.375; 1900 William Ewing 21-41-.339; 1900-1901 George Davis 91-122-.427; 1902 Horace Fogel 18-23-.439; 1902 George Smith 5-27-.156; 1902-1932 John McGraw 2658-1823-.593; 1932-1941 Bill Terry 823-661-.555; 1942-1948 Mel Ott 454-530-.461; 1948-1955 Leo Durocher 647-523-.553; 1956-1957 Bill Rigney 136-172-.442

NEW YORK GIANTS

Home City: New York, New York
Home Field: Polo Grounds IV   Capacity: 16,000 [1891]
Origin of Name: The team was named after their National League counterparts.

		Regular Season Record						
Season	League	GP	W	L	Pct	GB	R	OR
1890	PL	131	74	57	.565	8	1018	875

	Regular Season Individual Leaders					
Season	Home Runs		RBI's		Wins	
1890	Roger Connor	14	Roger Connor	103	Hank O'Day	23

COACHING HISTORY: William Ewing 74-57-.565

NEW YORK GIANTS

Home City: New York, New York (1925-1973, 1975)
　　　New Haven, Connecticut (1973-1974)
　　　East Rutherford, New Jersey (1976-
Home Stadium: Polo Grounds II (1925-1955)　　　　　　　Capacity: 55,200
　　　Yankee Stadium I (1956-1973)　　　　　　　　　　Capacity: 63,800
　　　Yale Bowl (1973-1974)　　　　　　　　　　　　　Capacity: 70,896
　　　Shea Stadium (1975)　　　　　　　　　　　　　　Capacity: 60,372
　　　Giants Stadium: (1976-present)　　　　　　　　　Capacity: 80,062 [2005]
Origin of Name: The team was named after the baseball team with which they shared the Polo Grounds.

Regular Season Record

Season	League	GP	W	L	T	PF	PA	Pct
1925	NFL	12	8	4	0	122	67	.667
1926	NFL	13	8	4	1	147	45	.654
1927	NFL	13	11	1	1	197	20	.885
1928	NFL	13	4	7	2	79	136	.385
1929	NFL	14	12	1	1	298	77	.893
1930	NFL	17	13	4	0	308	98	.765
1931	NFL	14	7	6	1	154	100	.536
1932	NFL	12	4	6	2	93	113	.417
1933	NFL	14	11	3	0	244	101	.786
1934	NFL	13	8	5	0	147	107	.615
1935	NFL	12	9	3	0	180	96	.750
1936	NFL	12	5	6	1	115	163	.458
1937	NFL	11	6	3	2	128	109	.636
1938	NFL	11	8	2	1	194	79	.773
1939	NFL	11	9	1	1	168	85	.864
1940	NFL	11	6	4	1	131	133	.591
1941	NFL	11	8	3	0	238	114	.727
1942	NFL	11	5	5	1	155	139	.500
1943	NFL	10	6	3	1	197	170	.650
1944	NFL	10	8	1	1	206	75	.850
1945	NFL	10	3	6	1	179	198	.350
1946	NFL	11	7	3	1	236	162	.682
1947	NFL	12	2	8	2	190	309	.250
1948	NFL	12	4	8	0	297	388	.333
1949	NFL	12	6	6	0	287	298	.500
1950	NFL	12	10	2	0	268	150	.833
1951	NFL	12	9	2	1	254	161	.792
1952	NFL	12	7	5	0	234	231	.583
1953	NFL	12	3	9	0	179	277	.250
1954	NFL	12	7	5	0	293	184	.583
1955	NFL	12	6	5	1	267	223	.542
1956	NFL	12	8	3	1	264	197	.708
1957	NFL	12	7	5	0	254	211	.583
1958	NFL	12	9	3	0	246	183	.750
1959	NFL	12	10	2	0	284	170	.833
1960	NFL	12	6	4	2	271	261	.600
1961	NFL	14	10	3	1	368	220	.769
1962	NFL	14	12	2	0	398	283	.857
1963	NFL	14	11	3	0	448	280	.786

1964	NFL	14	2	10	2	241	399	.167
1965	NFL	14	7	7	0	270	338	.500
1966	NFL	14	1	12	1	263	501	.077
1967	NFL	14	7	7	0	369	379	.500
1968	NFL	14	7	7	0	294	325	.500
1969	NFL	14	6	8	0	264	298	.429
1970	NFL	14	9	5	0	301	270	.643
1971	NFL	14	4	10	0	228	362	.286
1972	NFL	14	8	6	0	331	247	.571
1973	NFL	14	2	11	1	226	362	.179
1974	NFL	14	2	12	0	195	299	.143
1975	NFL	14	5	9	0	216	306	.357
1976	NFL	14	3	11	0	170	250	.214
1977	NFL	14	5	9	0	181	265	.357
1978	NFL	16	6	10	0	264	298	.375
1979	NFL	16	6	10	0	237	323	.375
1980	NFL	16	4	12	0	249	425	.250
1981	NFL	16	9	7	0	295	257	.563
1982	NFL	9	4	5	0	164	160	.444
1983	NFL	16	3	12	1	267	347	.219
1984	NFL	16	9	7	0	299	301	.563
1985	NFL	16	10	6	0	399	283	.625
1986	NFL	16	14	2	0	371	236	.875
1987	NFL	15	6	9	0	280	312	.400
1988	NFL	16	10	6	0	359	304	.625
1989	NFL	16	12	4	0	348	252	.750
1990	NFL	16	13	3	0	335	211	.813
1991	NFL	16	8	8	0	281	297	.500
1992	NFL	16	6	10	0	306	367	.375
1993	NFL	16	11	5	0	288	205	.688
1994	NFL	16	9	7	0	279	305	.563
1995	NFL	16	5	11	0	290	340	.313
1996	NFL	16	6	10	0	242	297	.375
1997	NFL	16	10	5	1	307	265	.656
1998	NFL	16	8	8	0	287	309	.500
1999	NFL	16	7	9	0	299	358	.438
2000	NFL	16	12	4	0	328	246	.750
2001	NFL	16	7	9	0	294	321	.438
2002	NFL	16	10	6	0	320	279	.625
2003	NFL	16	4	12	0	243	387	.250
2004	NFL	16	6	10	0	303	347	.375
2005	NFL	16	11	5	0	422	314	.688
2006	NFL	16	8	8	0	355	362	.500
TOTAL:	82 years	1128	595	500	33	20978	19722	
AVERAGE:		13	7	6	0	256	241	.542

Playoff Record

Season	GP	W	L	PF	PA	Result
1933	1	0	1	21	23	Lost Championship game to Bears.
1934	1	1	0	30	13	**Won NFL Championship.**
1935	1	0	1	7	26	Lost Championship game to Detroit.
1938	1	1	0	23	17	**Won NFL Championship.**
1939	1	0	1	0	27	Lost Championship game to Green Bay.
1941	1	0	1	9	37	Lost Championship game to Bears.

1943	1	0	1	0	28	Lost Divisional playoff to Washington.
1944	1	0	1	7	14	Lost Championship game to Green Bay.
1946	1	0	1	14	24	Lost Championship game to Bears.
1950	1	0	1	3	8	Lost Conference playoff to Cleveland.
1956	1	1	0	47	7	**Won NFL Championship.**
1958	2	1	1	27	23	Lost Championship game to Baltimore.
1959	1	0	1	16	35	Lost Championship game to Baltimore.
1961	1	0	1	0	37	Lost Championship game to Green Bay.
1962	1	0	1	7	16	Lost Championship game to Green Bay.
1963	1	0	1	10	14	Lost Championship game to Chicago.
1981	2	1	1	51	59	Lost Divisional playoff to San Francisco.
1984	2	1	1	26	34	Lost Divisional playoff to San Francisco.
1985	2	1	1	17	24	Lost Divisional playoff to Chicago.
1986	3	3	0	105	23	**Won Super Bowl XXI.**
1989	1	0	1	13	19	Lost Conference Semifinal to Rams.
1990	3	3	0	66	35	**Won Super Bowl XXV.**
1993	2	1	1	20	54	Lost Conference Semifinal to San Francisco.
1997	1	0	1	22	23	Lost Wild Card Game to Minnesota.
2000	3	2	1	68	47	Lost Super Bowl to Baltimore.
2002	1	0	1	38	39	Lost Wild Card Game to San Francisco.
2005	1	0	1	0	23	Lost 1st Round Playoff to Carolina.
2006	1	0	1	20	23	Lost Wild Card Game to Philadelphia.
TOTAL:	39	16	23	667	752	
AVERAGE:	2	1	1	24	27	

Regular Season Individual Leaders

Season	Passing Yards		Receiving Yards		Rushing Yards	
1925	Jack McBride	122	Lynn Bomar	102	Jack McBride	36
1926	Babe Parnell	39	Hinkey Haines	39	Hinkey Haines	75
1927	Jack McBride	357			Jack McBride	171
1928	Jack McBride	162			Mule Wilson	124
1929	Benny Friedman	985			Benny Friedman	161
1930	Benny Friedman	922			Benny Friedman	177
1931	Benny Friedman	422			Benny Friedman	188
1932	Jack McBride	463	Ray Flaherty	350	Jack McBride	302
1933	Harry Newman	973			Harry Newman	452
1934	Harry Newman	366	Red Badgro	206	Harry Newman	503
1935	Ed Danowski	795	Tod Goodwin	432	Kink Richards	449
1936	Ed Danowski	515	Dale Burnett	246	Tuffy Leemans	830
1937	Ed Danowski	814	Tuffy Leemans	157	Hank Soar	442
1938	Ed Danowski	848	Hank Soar	164	Tuffy Leemans	463
1939	Ed Danowski	437	Tuffy Leemans	185	Tuffy Leemans	429
1940	Eddie Miller	505	Jim Lee Howell	255	Tuffy Leemans	474
1941	Tuffy Leemans	475	Ward Cuff	317	Tuffy Leemans	332
1942	Tuffy Leemans	555	Ward Cuff	267	Merle Hapes	363
1943	Emery Nix	390	Will Walls	231	Bill Paschal	572
1944	Arnie Herber	651	Neal Adams	342	Bill Paschal	737
1945	Arnie Herber	641	Frank Liebel	593	Bill Paschal	247
1946	Frank Filchock	1262	Frank Liebel	360	Frank Filchock	371
1947	Paul Governali	1775	Ray Poole	395	Roberts	296
1948	Charlie Conerly	2175	Bill Swiacki	550	Roberts	491
1949	Charlie Conerly	2138	Bill Swiacki	652	Roberts	634
1950	Charlie Conerly	1000	Bob McChesney	380	Eddie Price	703
1951	Charlie Conerly	1277	Joe Scott	356	Eddie Price	971

Season	Passing Yards		Receiving Yards		Rushing Yards	
1952	Charlie Conerly	1090	Bob McChesney	430	Eddie Price	748
1953	Charlie Conerly	1711	Kyle Rote	440	Sonny Grandelius	278
1954	Charlie Conerly	1439	Kyle Rote	551	Eddie Price	555
1955	Charlie Conerly	1310	Kyle Rote	580	Alex Webster	634
1956	Charlie Conerly	1143	Frank Gifford	603	Frank Gifford	819
1957	Charlie Conerly	1712	Frank Gifford	588	Frank Gifford	528
1958	Charlie Conerly	1199	Bob Schnelker	460	Frank Gifford	468
1959	Charlie Conerly	1706	Frank Gifford	768	Frank Gifford	540
1960	George Shaw	1263	Kyle Rote	750	Mel Triplett	573
1961	Y.A. Tittle	2272	Del Shofner	1125	Alex Webster	928
1962	Y.A. Tittle	3224	Del Shofner	1133	Alex Webster	743
1963	Y.A. Tittle	3145	Del Shofner	1181	Phil King	613
1964	Y.A. Tittle	1798	Aaron Thomas	624	Ernie Wheelwright	402
1965	Earl Morrall	2446	Homer Jones	709	T. Frederickson	659
1966	Gary Wood	1142	Homer Jones	1044	Chuck Mercein	327
1967	Fran Tarkenton	3088	Homer Jones	1209	Ernie Koy	704
1968	Fran Tarkenton	2555	Homer Jones	1057	T. Frederickson	486
1969	Fran Tarkenton	2918	Homer Jones	744	Junior Coffey	511
1970	Fran Tarkenton	2777	Clifton McNeil	764	Ron Johnson	1027
1971	Fran Tarkenton	2567	Bob Tucker	791	Bobby Duhon	344
1972	Norm Snead	2307	Bob Tucker	764	Ron Johnson	1182
1973	Norm Snead	1483	Bob Tucker	681	Ron Johnson	902
1974	Craig Morton	1522	Bob Tucker	496	Joe Dawkins	561
1975	Craig Morton	2359	Walker Gillette	600	Joe Dawkins	438
1976	Craig Morton	1865	Bob Tucker	498	Doug Kotar	731
1977	Joe Pisarcik	1346	Jim Robinson	422	Bob Hammond	577
1978	Joe Pisarcik	2096	Jim Robinson	620	Doug Kotar	625
1979	Phil Simms	1743	Earnest Gray	537	Billy Taylor	700
1980	Phil Simms	2321	Earnest Gray	777	Billy Taylor	580
1981	Phil Simms	2031	Johnny Perkins	858	Rob Carpenter	822
1982	Scott Brunner	2017	Johnny Perkins	430	Butch Woolfolk	439
1983	Scott Brunner	2516	Earnest Gray	1139	Butch Woolfolk	857
1984	Phil Simms	4044	Bobby Johnson	795	Rob Carpenter	795
1985	Phil Simms	3829	Lionel Manuel	859	Joe Morris	1336
1986	Phil Simms	3487	Mark Bavaro	1001	Joe Morris	1516
1987	Phil Simms	2230	Mark Bavaro	867	Joe Morris	658
1988	Phil Simms	3359	Lionel Manuel	1029	Joe Morris	1083
1989	Phil Simms	3061	Lionel Manuel	539	Ottis Anderson	1023
1990	Phil Simms	2284	Stephen Baker	541	Ottis Anderson	784
1991	Jeff Hostetler	2032	Mark Ingram	824	R. Hampton	1059
1992	Jeff Hostetler	1225	Ed McCaffrey	610	R. Hampton	1141
1993	Phil Simms	3038	Mark Jackson	708	R. Hampton	1077
1994	Dave Brown	2536	Mike Sherrard	825	R. Hampton	1075
1995	Dave Brown	2814	Chris Calloway	796	R. Hampton	1182
1996	Dave Brown	2412	Chris Calloway	739	R. Hampton	827
1997	Danny Kanell	1740	Chris Calloway	849	Charles Way	698
1998	Danny Kanell	1603	Chris Calloway	812	Gary Brown	1063
1999	Kerry Collins	2316	Amani Toomer	1183	Joe Montgomery	348
2000	Kerry Collins	3610	Amani Toomer	1094	Tiki Barber	1006
2001	Kerry Collins	3764	Amani Toomer	1054	Tiki Barber	865
2002	Kerry Collins	4073	Amani Toomer	1343	Tiki Barber	1387
2003	Kerry Collins	3110	Amani Toomer	1057	Tiki Barber	1216
2004	Kurt Warner	2054	Amani Toomer	747	Tiki Barber	1518

Season	Passing Yards		Receiving Yards		Rushing Yards	
2005	Eli Manning	3762	Plaxico Burress	1214	Tiki Barber	1860
2006	Eli Manning	3244	Plaxico Burress	988	Tiki Barber	1662

COACHING HISTORY: 1925 Bob Folwell 8-4-0-.667; 1926 Joe Alexander 8-4-1-.654; 1927-1928 Earl Potteiger 15-8-3-.635; 1929-1930 LeRoy Andrews 24-5-1-.817; 1930 Ben Friedman 2-0-0-1.000; 1931-1953 Steve Owen 151-100-17-.595; 1954-1960 Jim Lee Howell 52-27-4-.651; 1961-1968 Allie Sherman 57-51-4-.527; 1969-1973 Alex Webster 29-40-1-.421; 1974-1976 Bill Arnsparger 7-28-0-.200; 1976-1978 John McVay 14-23-0-.378; 1979-1982 Ray Perkins 23-34-0-.404; 1983-1990 Bill Parcells 77-49-17.610; 1991-1992 Ray Handley 14-18-0-.438; 1993-1996 Dan Reeves 31-33-0-.484; 1997-2003 Jim Fassel 58-53-1-.522; 2004-present Tom Coughlin

NEW YORK GOLDEN BLADES
(became New Jersey Knights in mid 1974)

Home City: New York, New York
Home Arena: Madison Square Garden IV   Capacity: 17,500 [1973]
Origin of Name: During their initial season in the WHA the team was called the "Raiders."

Regular Season Record

Season	League	GP	W	L	T	GF	GA	Pts	Pct
1972-1973	WHA	78	33	43	2	303	334	68	.436
1973-1974	WHA	20	6	12	2	47	80	14	.350
TOTAL:	2 years	98	39	55	4	350	414	82	
AVERAGE:		49	20	27	2	175	207	41	.418

Regular Season Individual Leaders

Season	Goals		Points		Penalty Minutes	
1972-1973	Ron Ward	51	Ron Ward	118	Hal Willis	159
1973-1974	Andre Lacroix	9	Andre Lacroix	20	Ted Scharf	57

COACHING HISTORY: Camille Henry 39-55-4-.418

NEW YORK HAKOAHS

Home City: New York, New York
Home Court: St. Nicholas Arena
Origin of Name: The team played under the colors of the Hakoah Club in New York.

Regular Season Record

Season	League	GP	W	L	Pct
1928-1929	ABL	43	18	25	.419

Regular Season Individual Leaders

Season	Points	
1928-29	Davey Banks	244

COACHING HISTORY:

NEW YORK ISLANDERS

Home City: Uniondale, New York
Home Arena: Nassau Veteran's Memorial Coliseum   Capacity: 16,234 [2005]
Origin of Name: The name was chosen by owner Roy Boe.

Regular Season Record

Season	League	GP	W	L	T	OL	SL	GF	GA	Pts
1972-1973	NHL	78	12	60	6	NA	NA	170	347	30
1973-1974	NHL	78	19	41	18	NA	NA	182	247	56
1974-1975	NHL	80	33	25	22	NA	NA	264	221	88
1975-1976	NHL	80	42	21	17	NA	NA	297	190	101
1976-1977	NHL	80	47	21	12	NA	NA	288	193	106
1977-1978	NHL	80	48	17	15	NA	NA	334	210	111
1978-1979	NHL	80	51	15	14	NA	NA	358	214	116
1979-1980	NHL	80	39	28	13	NA	NA	281	247	91
1980-1981	NHL	80	48	18	14	NA	NA	355	260	110
1981-1982	NHL	80	54	16	10	NA	NA	385	250	118
1982-1983	NHL	80	42	26	12	NA	NA	302	226	96
1983-1984	NHL	80	50	26	4	NA	NA	357	269	104
1984-1985	NHL	80	40	34	6	NA	NA	345	312	86
1985-1986	NHL	80	39	29	12	NA	NA	327	284	90
1986-1987	NHL	80	35	33	12	NA	NA	279	281	82
1987-1988	NHL	80	39	31	10	NA	NA	308	267	88
1988-1989	NHL	80	28	47	5	NA	NA	265	325	61
1989-1990	NHL	80	31	38	11	NA	NA	281	288	73
1990-1991	NHL	80	25	45	10	NA	NA	223	290	60
1991-1992	NHL	80	34	35	11	NA	NA	291	299	79
1992-1993	NHL	84	40	37	7	NA	NA	335	297	87
1993-1994	NHL	84	36	36	12	NA	NA	282	264	84
1994-1995	NHL	48	15	28	5	NA	NA	126	158	35
1995-1996	NHL	82	22	50	10	NA	NA	229	315	54
1996-1997	NHL	82	29	41	12	NA	NA	240	250	70
1997-1998	NHL	82	30	41	11	NA	NA	212	225	71
1998-1999	NHL	82	24	48	10	NA	NA	194	244	58
1999-2000	NHL	82	24	49	9	1	NA	194	275	58
2000-2001	NHL	82	21	51	7	3	NA	185	268	52
2001-2002	NHL	82	42	28	8	4	NA	239	220	96
2002-2003	NHL	82	35	34	11	2	NA	224	231	83
2003-2004	NHL	82	38	29	11	4	NA	237	210	91
2004-2005	NHL	Season cancelled due to lockout.								
2005-2006	NHL	82	36	40	NA	3	3	230	278	78
TOTAL:	33 years	2632	1148	1118	347	17	3	8819	8455	2663
AVERAGE:		80	35	34	11	0	0	267	256	81

Playoff Record

Season	GP	W	L	GF	GA	Result
1974-1975	17	9	8	47	45	Lost Semifinal series to Philadelphia.
1975-1976	13	7	6	43	39	Lost Semifinal series to Montreal.
1976-1977	12	8	4	36	32	Lost Semifinal series to Montreal.
1977-1978	7	3	4	13	16	Lost Quarterfinal series to Toronto.
1978-1979	10	6	4	27	21	Lost Semifinal series to Rangers.
1979-1980	21	15	6	88	66	**Won Stanley Cup.**
1980-1981	18	15	3	97	48	**Won Stanley Cup.**
1981-1982	19	15	4	85	52	**Won Stanley Cup.**
1982-1983	20	15	5	94	53	**Won Stanley Cup.**
1983-1984	21	12	9	62	60	Lost Championship series to Edmonton.
1984-1985	10	4	6	25	28	Lost Division Final to Philadelphia.
1985-1986	3	0	3	4	11	Lost Division Semifinal to Washington.
1986-1987	14	7	7	35	42	Lost Division Final to Philadelphia.

1987-1988	6	2	4	18	23	Lost Division Semifinal to New Jersey.
1989-1990	5	1	4	13	22	Lost Division Semifinal to Rangers.
1992-1993	18	9	9	58	65	Lost Conference Final to Montreal.
1993-1994	4	0	4	3	22	Lost Conference Quarterfinal to Rangers.
2001-2002	7	3	4	21	22	Lost Conference Quarterfinal to Toronto.
2002-2003	5	1	4	7	13	Lost Conference Quarterfinal to Ottawa.
2003-2004	5	1	4	5	12	Lost Conference Quarterfinal to Tampa Bay
TOTAL:	235	133	102	781	692	
AVERAGE:	12	7	5	39	35	

Regular Season Individual Leaders

Season	Goals		Points		Penalty Minutes	
1972-1973	Billy Harris	28	Billy Harris	50	Gerry Hart	158
1973-1974	Billy Harris	23	Denis Potvin	54	Garry Howatt	204
	Ralph Stewart	23				
1974-1975	Bob Nystrom	27	Denis Potvin	76	Gerry Hart	143
1975-1976	Clark Gillies	34	Denis Potvin	98	Garry Howatt	197
1976-1977	Clark Gillies	33	Denis Potvin	80	Garry Howatt	182
1977-1978	Mike Bossy	53	Bryan Trottier	123	Garry Howatt	146
1978-1979	Mike Bossy	69	Bryan Trottier	134	Garry Howatt	205
1979-1980	Mike Bossy	51	Bryan Trottier	104	Garry Howatt	219
1980-1981	Mike Bossy	68	Mike Bossy	119	Garry Howatt	174
1981-1982	Mike Bossy	64	Mike Bossy	147	Brent Sutter	114
1982-1983	Mike Bossy	60	Mike Bossy	118	Brent Sutter	128
1983-1984	Mike Bossy	51	Mike Bossy	118	Duane Sutter	94
1984-1985	Mike Bossy	58	Mike Bossy	117	Duane Sutter	174
1985-1986	Mike Bossy	61	Mike Bossy	123	Duane Sutter	157
1986-1987	Mike Bossy	38	Bryan Trottier	87	Brian Curran	356
	Pat LaFontaine	38				
1987-1988	Pat LaFontaine	47	Pat LaFontaine	92	Alan Kerr	198
1988-1989	Pat LaFontaine	45	Pat LaFontaine	88	Richard Pilon	242
1989-1990	Pat LaFontaine	54	Pat LaFontaine	105	Mick Vukota	290
1990-1991	Pat LaFontaine	41	Pat LaFontaine	85	Ken Baumgartner	282
1991-1992	Ray Ferraro	40	Pierre Turgeon	87	Mick Vukota	293
	Derek King	40				
1992-1993	Pierre Turgeon	58	Pierre Turgeon	132	Mick Vukota	216
1993-1994	Steve Thomas	42	Pierre Turgeon	94	Mick Vukota	237
1994-1995	Ray Ferraro	22	Ray Ferraro	43	Mick Vukota	109
1995-1996	Ziggy Palffy	43	Ziggy Palffy	87	Brent Severyn	180
1996-1997	Ziggy Palffy	48	Ziggy Palffy	90	Richard Pilon	179
1997-1998	Ziggy Palffy	45	Ziggy Palffy	87	Richard Pilon	291
1998-1999	Ziggy Palffy	22	Robert Reichel	56	Gino Odjick	133
1999-2000	M. Czerkawski	35	M. Czerkawski	70	Eric Cairns	196
2000-2001	M. Czerkawski	30	M. Czerkawski	62	Zdeno Chara	155
2001-2002	Alexei Yashin	32	Alexei Yashin	75	Eric Cairns	176
2002-2003	Alexei Yashin	26	Alexei Yashin	65	Eric Cairns	124
2003-2004	M. Czerkawski	25	Oleg Kvasha	51	Eric Cairns	189
	Trent Hunter	25	Trent Hunter	51		
2004-2005	Season cancelled due to lockout.					
2005-2006	Miroslav Satan	35	Miroslav Satan	66	Eric Godard	115
			Alexei Yashin	66		

COACHING HISTORY: 1972-1973 Phil Goyette 6-40-4-.160; 1972-1973 Earl Ingarfield 6-20-2-.250; 1973-1986 Al Arbour 552-317-169-.613; 1986-1989 Terry Simpson 81-82-24-.497;

1988-1994 Al Arbour 187-220-54-.464; 1994-1995 Lorne Henning 15-28-5-.365; 1995-1997 Mike Milbury 36-73-19-.355; 1996-1998 Rick Bowness 38-50-12-.440; 1997-1999 Mike Milbury 21-38-5-.367; 1998-1999 Bill Stewart 11-19-7-.392; 1999-2001 Butch Goring 41-89-14-3-.337; 2000-2001 Lorne Henning 4-11-2-0-.294; 2001-2003 Peter Laviolette 77-62-19-6-.644; 2003-2006 Steve Stirling 56-51-11-4-2-.520; 2005-present Brad Shaw

NEW YORK JETS

Home City: New York, New York (1963-1983)
      East Rutherford, New Jersey (1984-present)
Home Stadium: Polo Grounds (1960-1963)   Capacity: 55,987
             Shea Stadium (1964-1983)   Capacity: 60,372 [1983]
             Giants Stadium (1984-present)   Capacity: 80,062 [2005]
Origin of Name: From 1960 to 1963 the team was called the "Titans." The name "Jets," adopted in 1963 was chosen by the team owners.

Regular Season Record

Season	League	GP	W	L	T	PF	PA	Pct
1960	AFL	14	7	7	0	382	399	.500
1961	AFL	14	7	7	0	301	390	.500
1962	AFL	14	5	9	0	278	423	.357
1963	AFL	14	5	8	1	249	399	.385
1964	AFL	14	5	8	1	278	315	.385
1965	AFL	14	5	8	1	285	303	.385
1966	AFL	14	6	6	2	322	312	.500
1967	AFL	14	8	5	1	371	329	.615
1968	AFL	14	11	3	0	419	280	.786
1969	AFL	14	10	4	0	353	269	.714
1970	NFL	14	4	10	0	255	286	.286
1971	NFL	14	6	8	0	212	299	.429
1972	NFL	14	7	7	0	367	324	.500
1973	NFL	14	4	10	0	240	306	.286
1974	NFL	14	7	7	0	279	300	.500
1975	NFL	14	3	11	0	258	433	.214
1976	NFL	14	3	11	0	169	383	.214
1977	NFL	14	3	11	0	191	300	.214
1978	NFL	16	8	8	0	359	364	.500
1979	NFL	16	8	8	0	337	383	.500
1980	NFL	16	4	12	0	302	395	.250
1981	NFL	16	10	5	1	355	287	.656
1982	NFL	9	6	3	0	245	166	.667
1983	NFL	16	7	9	0	313	331	.438
1984	NFL	16	7	9	0	332	364	.438
1985	NFL	16	11	5	0	393	264	.688
1986	NFL	16	10	6	0	364	386	.625
1987	NFL	15	6	9	0	334	360	.400
1988	NFL	16	8	7	1	372	354	.531
1989	NFL	16	4	12	0	253	411	.250
1990	NFL	16	6	10	0	295	345	.375
1991	NFL	16	8	8	0	314	293	.500
1992	NFL	16	4	12	0	220	315	.250
1993	NFL	16	8	8	0	270	247	.500
1994	NFL	16	6	10	0	264	320	.375
1995	NFL	16	3	13	0	233	384	.188

1996	NFL	16	1	15	0	279	454	.063
1997	NFL	16	9	7	0	348	287	.563
1998	NFL	16	12	4	0	416	266	.750
1999	NFL	16	8	8	0	308	309	.500
2000	NFL	16	9	7	0	321	321	.562
2001	NFL	16	10	6	0	308	295	.625
2002	NFL	16	9	7	0	359	336	.562
2003	NFL	16	6	10	0	283	299	.375
2004	NFL	16	10	6	0	333	261	.625
2005	NFL	16	4	12	0	240	355	.250
2006	NFL	16	10	6	0	316	295	.625
TOTAL:	47 years	708	318	382	8	14275	15497	
AVERAGE:		15	7	8	0	304	330	.455

Playoff Record

Season	GP	W	L	PF	PA	Result
1968	2	2	0	43	30	**Won Super Bowl III.**
1969	1	0	1	6	13	Lost Divisional playoff to Kansas City.
1981	1	0	1	27	31	Lost 1st Round game to Buffalo.
1982	3	2	1	61	45	Lost AFC Championship to Miami.
1985	1	0	1	14	26	Lost 1st Round game to New England.
1986	2	1	1	55	38	Lost Divisional playoff to Cleveland.
1991	1	0	1	10	17	Lost Wild Card Game to Houston.
1998	2	1	1	44	47	Lost Conference Final to Denver.
2001	1	0	1	24	38	Lost 1st Round game to Oakland.
2002	2	1	1	51	30	Lost Conference Semifinal to Oakland.
2004	2	1	1	37	37	Lost Conf. Semifinal to Pittsburgh.
2006	1	0	1	16	37	Lost Wild Card Game to New England.
TOTAL:	19	8	11	388	389	
AVERAGE:	2	1	1	32	32	

Regular Season Individual Leaders

Season	Passing Yards		Receiving Yards		Rushing Yards	
1960	Al Dorow	2748	Don Maynard	1265	Dewey Bohling	431
1961	Al Dorow	2651	Art Powell	881	Bill Mathis	846
1962	John Green	1741	Art Powell	1130	Dick Christy	535
1963	Dick Wood	2202	Bake Turner	1007	Mark Smolinski	561
1964	Dick Wood	2298	Bake Turner	974	Matt Snell	948
1965	Joe Namath	2220	Don Maynard	1218	Matt Snell	763
1966	Joe Namath	3379	George Sauer	1079	Matt Snell	644
1967	Joe Namath	4007	Don Maynard	1434	Emerson Boozer	442
1968	Joe Namath	3147	Don Maynard	1297	Matt Snell	747
1969	Joe Namath	2734	Don Maynard	938	Matt Snell	695
1970	Al Woodall	1265	Don Maynard	525	Emerson Boozer	581
1971	Bob Davis	624	Rich Caster	454	John Riggins	769
1972	Joe Namath	2816	Rich Caster	833	John Riggins	944
1973	Al Woodall	1228	Jerome Barkum	810	Emerson Boozer	831
1974	Joe Namath	2616	Rich Caster	745	John Riggins	680
1975	Joe Namath	2286	Rich Caster	820	John Riggins	1005
1976	Joe Namath	1090	David Knight	403	Clark Gaines	724
1977	Richard Todd	1863	Wesley Walker	740	Clark Gaines	595
1978	Matt Robinson	2002	Wesley Walker	1169	Kevin Long	954
1979	Richard Todd	2660	Wesley Walker	569	Clark Gaines	905
1980	Richard Todd	3329	Bruce Harper	634	Scott Dierking	567

Season	Passing Yards		Receiving Yards		Rushing Yards	
1981	Richard Todd	3231	Wesley Walker	770	Freeman McNeil	623
1982	Richard Todd	1961	Wesley Walker	620	Freeman McNeil	786
1983	Richard Todd	3478	Wesley Walker	868	Freeman McNeil	654
1984	Pat Ryan	1939	Mickey Shuler	782	Freeman McNeil	1070
1985	Ken O'Brien	3888	Mickey Shuler	879	Freeman McNeil	1331
1986	Ken O'Brien	3690	Al Toon	1176	Freeman McNeil	856
1987	Ken O'Brien	2696	Al Toon	976	Freeman McNeil	530
1988	Ken O'Brien	2567	Al Toon	1067	Freeman McNeil	944
1989	Ken O'Brien	3346	JoJo Townsell	787	John Hector	702
1990	Ken O'Brien	2855	Al Toon	757	Blair Thomas	620
1991	Ken O'Brien	3300	Rob Moore	987	Blair Thomas	728
1992	Browning Nagle	2280	Rob Moore	726	Brad Baxter	698
1993	Boomer Esiason	3421	Rob Moore	843	Johnny Johnson	821
1994	Boomer Esiason	2782	Rob Moore	1010	Johnny Johnson	931
1995	Boomer Esiason	2275	Wayne Chrebet	726	Adrian Murrell	795
1996	Frank Reich	2205	Wayne Chrebet	909	Adrian Murrell	1249
1997	Neil O'Donnell	2796	K. Johnson	963	Adrian Murrell	1086
1998	V. Testaverde	3256	K. Johnson	1131	Curtis Martin	1287
1999	Ray Lucas	1678	K. Johnson	1170	Curtis Martin	1464
2000	V. Testaverde	3732	Wayne Chrebet	937	Curtis Martin	1204
2001	V. Testaverde	2752	Laveranues Coles	868	Curtis Martin	1513
2002	Chad Pennington	3120	Laveranues Coles	1264	Curtis Martin	1094
2003	Chad Pennington	2139	Santana Moss	1105	Curtis Martin	1308
2004	Chad Pennington	2673	Santana Moss	838	Curtis Martin	1697
2005	Brooks Bollinger	1558	Laveranues Coles	845	Curtis Martin	735
2006	Chad Pennington	3352	Laveranues Coles	1098	Leon Washington	650

COACHING HISTORY: 1960-1961 Sam Baugh 14-14-0-.500; 1962 "Bulldog" Turner 5-9-0-.357; 1963-1973 Weeb Ewbank 71-77-6-.481; 1974-1975 Charley Winner 9-14-0-.391; 1975 Ken Shipp 1-4-0-.200; 1976 Lou Holtz 3-10-0-.231; 1976 Mike Holovak 0-1-0-.000; 1977-1982 Walt Michaels 39-47-1-.454; 1983-1989 Joe Walton 53-57-1-.482; 1990-1993 Bruce Coslet 26-38-0-.406; 1994 Pete Carroll 6-10-0-.375; 1995-1996 Rich Kotite 4-28-0-.125; 1997-1999 Bill Parcells 29-19-0-.604; 2000-Al Groh 9-7-0-.563; 2001-2005 Herman Edwards 39-41-0-.488; 2006-present Eric Mangini

NEW YORK KNICKERBOCKERS

Home City: New York, New York
Home Court: 69th Regiment Armory (1946-1947)   Capacity: 5,000
    Madison Square Garden III (1946-1968)   Capacity: 18,496
    Madison Square Garden IV (1968-present)   Capacity: 19,763 [2006]
Origin of Name: The name was chosen by owner Ned Irish. Knickerbockers is a name long associated with New York City.

Regular Season Record								
Season	League	GP	W	L	PPGF	PPGA	Pct	GB
1946-1947	BAA	60	33	27	64.7	64.0	.550	16
1947-1948	BAA	48	26	22	74.5	71.4	.542	1
1948-1949	BAA	60	32	28	79.2	77.7	.533	6
1949-1950	NBA	68	40	28	80.7	78.6	.588	13
1950-1951	NBA	66	36	30	85.8	85.4	.545	4
1951-1952	NBA	66	37	29	85.0	84.2	.561	3
1952-1953	NBA	70	47	23	85.5	80.3	.671	-

1953-1954	NBA	72	44	28	79.0	79.1	.611	-
1954-1955	NBA	72	38	34	92.7	92.6	.528	5
1955-1956	NBA	72	35	37	100.2	100.6	.486	10
1956-1957	NBA	72	36	36	100.8	100.9	.500	8
1957-1958	NBA	72	35	37	112.1	110.8	.486	14
1958-1959	NBA	72	40	32	110.3	110.1	.556	12
1959-1960	NBA	75	27	48	117.3	119.6	.360	32
1960-1961	NBA	79	21	58	113.7	120.1	.266	36
1961-1962	NBA	80	29	51	114.8	119.7	.363	31
1962-1963	NBA	80	21	59	110.5	117.7	.263	37
1963-1964	NBA	80	22	58	112.2	119.6	.275	37
1964-1965	NBA	80	31	49	107.4	111.1	.388	31
1965-1966	NBA	80	30	50	116.7	119.3	.375	25
1966-1967	NBA	81	36	45	116.4	119.4	.444	32
1967-1968	NBA	82	43	39	116.1	114.3	.524	19
1968-1969	NBA	82	54	28	110.8	105.2	.659	3
1969-1970	NBA	82	60	22	115.0	105.9	.732	-
1970-1971	NBA	82	52	30	110.1	105.0	.634	-
1971-1972	NBA	82	48	34	107.1	104.7	.585	8
1972-1973	NBA	82	57	25	105.0	98.2	.695	11
1973-1974	NBA	82	49	33	101.3	98.5	.598	7
1974-1975	NBA	82	40	42	100.4	101.7	.488	20
1975-1976	NBA	82	38	44	102.7	103.9	.463	16
1976-1977	NBA	82	40	42	108.6	108.6	.488	10
1977-1978	NBA	82	43	39	113.4	114.0	.524	12
1978-1979	NBA	82	31	51	107.7	111.1	.378	23
1979-1980	NBA	82	39	43	114.0	115.1	.476	22
1980-1981	NBA	82	50	32	107.9	106.3	.610	12
1981-1982	NBA	82	33	49	106.2	108.9	.402	30
1982-1983	NBA	82	44	38	100.0	97.5	.537	21
1983-1984	NBA	82	47	35	106.9	103.0	.573	15
1984-1985	NBA	82	24	58	105.2	109.8	.293	39
1985-1986	NBA	82	23	59	98.7	104.3	.280	44
1986-1987	NBA	82	24	58	103.8	110.0	.293	35
1987-1988	NBA	82	38	44	105.5	106.0	.463	19
1988-1989	NBA	82	52	30	116.7	112.9	.634	-
1989-1990	NBA	82	45	37	108.3	106.9	.549	8
1990-1991	NBA	82	39	43	103.1	103.3	.476	17
1991-1992	NBA	82	51	31	101.6	97.7	.622	-
1992-1993	NBA	82	60	22	101.6	95.4	.732	-
1993-1994	NBA	82	57	25	98.5	91.5	.695	-
1994-1995	NBA	82	55	27	98.2	95.1	.671	2
1995-1996	NBA	82	47	35	97.2	94.9	.573	13
1996-1997	NBA	82	57	25	95.4	92.2	.695	4
1997-1998	NBA	82	43	39	91.6	89.1	.524	12
1998-1999	NBA	50	27	23	86.4	85.4	.540	6
1999-2000	NBA	82	50	32	92.1	90.7	.610	2
2000-2001	NBA	82	48	34	88.7	86.1	.585	8
2001-2002	NBA	82	30	52	91.6	95.6	.366	22
2002-2003	NBA	82	37	45	95.9	97.2	.451	12
2003-2004	NBA	82	39	43	92.0	93.5	.476	8
2004-2005	NBA	82	33	49	97.3	99.7	.402	12
2005-2006	NBA	82	23	59	95.6	102.0	.280	26

TOTAL:	60 years	4671	2366	2305				871
AVERAGE:		78	40	38	101.7	101.5	.507	15

Playoff Record

Season	GP	W	L	PPGF	PPGA	Result
1946-1947	5	2	3	70.6	75.2	Lost Semifinal series to Philadelphia
1947-1948	3	1	2	79.0	79.3	Lost Quarterfinal series to Baltimore.
1948-1949	6	3	3	83.5	83.3	Lost Division Final to Washington.
1949-1950	5	3	2	87.2	85.6	Lost Division Final to Syracuse.
1950-1951	14	8	6	83.4	83.6	Lost Championship series to Rochester.
1951-1952	14	8	6	86.9	88.5	Lost Championship series to Minneapolis.
1952-1953	11	6	5	83.0	80.9	Lost Championship series to Minneapolis.
1953-1954	4	0	4	79.0	87.5	Lost playoff series to Syracuse.
1954-1955	3	1	2	104.0	111.0	Lost Division Semifinal to Boston.
1955-1956	1	0	1	77.0	82.0	Lost playoff game to Syracuse.
1958-1959	2	0	2	119.0	130.0	Lost Division Semifinal to Syracuse.
1966-1967	4	1	3	112.5	121.3	Lost Division Semifinal to Boston.
1967-1968	6	2	4	113.5	117.8	Lost Division Semifinal to Philadelphia.
1968-1969	10	6	4	106.5	103.4	Lost Division Final to Boston.
1969-1970	19	12	7	110.5	106.8	**Won NBA Championship.**
1970-1971	12	7	5	101.1	102.3	Lost Conference Final to Baltimore.
1971-1972	16	9	7	106.6	101.9	Lost Championship series to Los Angeles.
1972-1973	17	12	5	103.8	98.8	**Won NBA Championship.**
1973-1974	12	5	7	94.4	99.4	Lost Conference Final to Boston.
1974-1975	3	1	2	92.0	104.3	Lost 1st Round series to Houston.
1977-1978	6	2	4	110.7	119.8	Lost Conf. Semifinal to Philadelphia.
1980-1981	2	0	2	97.0	102.5	Lost 1st Round series to Chicago.
1982-1983	6	2	4	103.8	104.7	Lost Conf. Semifinal to Philadelphia.
1983-1984	12	6	6	106.6	111.5	Lost Conference Semifinal to Boston.
1987-1988	4	1	3	99.3	110.5	Lost 1st Round series to Boston.
1988-1989	9	5	4	106.8	108.7	Lost Conference Semifinal to Chicago.
1989-1990	10	4	6	105.0	111.0	Lost Conference Semifinal to Detroit.
1990-1991	3	0	3	86.0	106.0	Lost 1st Round series to Chicago.
1991-1992	12	6	6	90.3	89.3	Lost Conference Semifinal to Chicago.
1992-1993	15	9	6	99.0	99.5	Lost Conference Final to Chicago.
1993-1994	25	14	11	88.8	87.7	Lost Championship series to Houston.
1994-1995	11	6	5	93.3	89.4	Lost Conference Semifinal to Indiana.
1995-1996	8	4	4	88.6	88.5	Lost Conference Semifinal to Chicago.
1996-1997	10	6	4	92.7	88.0	Lost Conference Semifinal to Miami.
1997-1998	10	4	6	88.6	90.8	Lost Conference Semifinal to Indiana.
1998-1999	20	12	8	85.0	83.0	Lost NBA Finals to San Antonio.
1999-2000	16	9	7	84.4	85.5	Lost Conference Semifinal to Indiana.
2000-2001	5	2	3	89.0	92.2	Lost 1st Round series to Toronto.
2003-2004	4	0	4	84.0	96.8	Lost 1st Round series to New Jersey.
TOTAL:	355	179	176			
AVERAGE:	9	5	4	95.1	95.8	

Regular Season Individual Leaders

Season	Field Goal % (min. 70 games)		Points		Points per Game (min. 70 games)	
1946-47*	John Palmer	.307	Sidney Hertzberg	515	Sidney Hertzberg	8.7
1947-48*	Ray Kuka	.326	Carl Braun	671	Carl Braun	14.3

*-minimum 40 games

Season	Field Goal % (min. 70 games)		Points		Points per Game (min. 70 games)	
1948-49*	John Palmer	.350	Carl Braun	810	Carl Braun	14.2
1949-50*	E. Vandeweghe	.421	Carl Braun	1031	Carl Braun	15.4
1950-51#	Harry Gallatin	.416	Vincent Boryla	982	Vincent Boryla	14.9
1951-52#	Harry Gallatin	.442	Max Zaslofsky	931	Max Zaslofsky	14.1
1952-53#	Harry Gallatin	.444	Carl Braun	977	Carl Braun	14.0
1953-54#	Richard McGuire	.408	Carl Braun	1062	Carl Braun	14.8
1954-55#	Ray Felix	.438	Carl Braun	1074	Carl Braun	15.1
1955-56#	Kenny Sears	.438	Carl Braun	1112	Carl Braun	15.4
1956-57#	Kenny Sears	.418	Harry Gallatin	1079	Harry Gallatin	15.0
1957-58#	Ray Felix	.442	Kenny Sears	1342	Kenny Sears	18.6
1958-59#	Kenny Sears	.490	Kenny Sears	1488	Kenny Sears	21.0
1959-60	Jim Palmer	.429	Richie Guerin	1615	Richie Guerin	21.8
1960-61	Dick Garmaker	.440	Willie Naulls	1846	Willie Naulls	23.4
1961-62	Richie Guerin	.442	Richie Guerin	2303	Richie Guerin	29.5
1962-63	Dave Budd	.493	Richie Guerin	1701	Richie Guerin	21.5
1963-64	John Green	.470	Len Chappell	1350	Len Chappell	17.3
1964-65	John Egan	.488	Willis Reed	1560	Willis Reed	19.5
1965-66	Walt Bellamy	.512	Dick Barnett	1729	Dick Barnett	23.1
1966-67	Walt Bellamy	.521	Willis Reed	1628	Willis Reed	20.9
1967-68	Walt Bellamy	.541	Willis Reed	1685	Willis Reed	20.8
1968-69	Willis Reed	.521	Willis Reed	1733	Willis Reed	21.1
1969-70	Walt Frazier	.518	Willis Reed	1755	Willis Reed	21.7
1970-71	Walt Frazier	.494	Walt Frazier	1736	Walt Frazier	21.7
1971-72	Walt Frazier	.512	Walt Frazier	1788	Walt Frazier	23.2
	Jerry Lucas	.512				
1972-73	Dean Meminger	.515	Walt Frazier	1648	Walt Frazier	21.1
1973-74	Dean Meminger	.508	Walt Frazier	1643	Walt Frazier	20.5
1974-75	Walt Frazier	.483	Walt Frazier	1675	Walt Frazier	21.5
1975-76	Earl Monroe	.478	Earl Monroe	1574	Earl Monroe	20.7
1976-77	Earl Monroe	.517	Earl Monroe	1533	Earl Monroe	19.9
1977-78	Bob McAdoo	.520	Bob McAdoo	2097	Bob McAdoo	26.5
1978-79	Mike Glenn	.541	Ray Williams	1401	Ray Williams	17.3
1979-80	Bill Cartwright	.547	Bill Cartwright	1781	Bill Cartwright	21.7
1980-81	Mike Glenn	.558	Bill Cartwright	1646	Bill Cartwright	20.1
1981-82	Bill Cartwright	.562	M. Richardson	1469	M. Richardson	17.9
1982-83	Bill Cartwright	.566	Bernard King	1486	Bill Cartwright	15.7
1983-84	Bernard King	.572	Bernard King	2027	Bernard King	26.3
1984-85	Rory Sparrow	.492	Bernard King	1809	Darrell Walker	13.5
1985-86	Ken Bannister	.491	Gerald Wilkins	1013	Gerald Wilkins	12.5
1986-87	Gerald Wilkins	.486	Gerald Wilkins	1527	Gerald Wilkins	19.1
1987-88	Patrick Ewing	.555	Patrick Ewing	1653	Patrick Ewing	20.2
1988-89	Patrick Ewing	.567	Patrick Ewing	1815	Patrick Ewing	22.7
1989-90	Patrick Ewing	.551	Patrick Ewing	2347	Patrick Ewing	28.6
1990-91	Charles Oakley	.516	Patrick Ewing	2154	Patrick Ewing	26.6
1991-92	Patrick Ewing	.522	Patrick Ewing	1970	Patrick Ewing	24.0
	Charles Oakley	.522				
1992-93	Charles Oakley	.508	Patrick Ewing	1959	Patrick Ewing	24.2
1993-94	Anthony Bonner	.563	Patrick Ewing	1939	Patrick Ewing	24.5
1994-95	Anthony Mason	.566	Patrick Ewing	1886	Patrick Ewing	23.9
1995-96	Anthony Mason	.563	Patrick Ewing	1711	Patrick Ewing	22.5

*-minimum 40 games, #-minimum 60 games

Season	Field Goal % (min. 70 games)		Points		Points per Game (min. 70 games)	
1996-97	Buck Williams	.537	Patrick Ewing	1751	Patrick Ewing	22.4
1997-98	Larry Johnson	.485	Allan Houston	1509	Allan Houston	18.4
1998-99*	Marcus Camby	.521	Allan Houston	813	Allan Houston	16.3
1999-00	Kurt Thomas	.505	Allan Houston	1614	Allan Houston	19.7
2000-01	Kurt Thomas	.511	Allan Houston	1459	Allan Houston	18.7
2001-02	O. Harrington	.527	Latrell Sprewell	1575	Allan Houston	20.4
2002-03	O. Harrington	.508	Allan Houston	1845	Allan Houston	22.5
2003-04	Kurt Thomas	.473	Stephon Marbury	1639	Kurt Thomas	11.1
2004-05	Mike Sweetney	.531	Stephon Marbury	1781	Stephon Marbury	21.7
2005-06	Eddy Curry	.563	Jamal Crawford	1128	Jamal Crawford	14.3

COACHING HISTORY: 1946-1947 Neil Cohalan 33-27-.550; 1947-1956 Joe Lapchick 326-247-.569; 1955-1958 Vince Boryla 80-85-.485; 1958-1960 Fuzzy Levane 48-51-.485; 1959-1961 Carl Braun 40-87-.315; 1961-1965 Eddie Donovan 85-193-.306; 1964-1966 Harry Gallatin 25-38-.397; 1965-1968 Dick McGuire 75-102-.424; 1967-1977 Red Holzman 466-317-.595; 1977-1979 Willis Reed 49-47-.510; 1978-1982 Red Holzman 147-167-.468; 1982-1987 Hubert Brown 142-202-.413; 1986-1987 Bob Hill 20-46-.303; 1987-1989 Rick Pitino 90-74-.549; 1989-1991 Stu Jackson 52-45-.536; 1990-1991 John McLeod 32-35-.478; 1991-1995 Pat Riley 223-105-.680; 1995-1996 Don Nelson 34-25-.576, 1995-2002 Jeff van Gundy 251-172-.593; 2001-2004 Don Chaney 72-112-.391; 2003-2005 Lenny Wilkens 40-41-.494; 2003-2004 Don Chaney 16-24-.400; 2005-present Larry Brown

NEW YORK LIBERTY

Home City: New York, New York
Home Arena: Madison Square Garden   Capacity: 19,763 [2005]
Origin of Name: The name was probably suggested by New York's famous Statue of Liberty.

Regular Season Record

Season	League	GP	W	L	PPGF	PPGA	Pct	GB
1997	WNBA	28	17	11	68.3	65.9	.607	1
1998	WNBA	30	18	12	68.6	65.5	.600	2
1999	WNBA	32	18	14	70.0	65.3	.563	-
2000	WNBA	32	20	12	67.1	63.5	.625	-
2001	WNBA	32	21	11	67.6	65.1	.656	1
2002	WNBA	32	18	14	65.3	63.0	.563	-
2003	WNBA	34	16	18	66.0	66.4	.471	9
2004	WNBA	34	18	16	66.2	67.6	.529	-
2005	WNBA	34	18	16	68.1	67.2	.529	8
2006	WNBA	34	11	23	69.8	78.2	.324	15
TOTAL:	10 years	322	175	147				36
AVERAGE:		32	17	15	67.7	66.8	.543	4

Playoff Record

Season	GP	W	L	PPGF	PPGA	Result
1997	2	1	1	55.0	53.0	Lost WNBA Championship to Houston.
1999	6	3	3	64.2	66.8	Lost WNBA Championship to Houston.
2000	7	4	3	64.2	60.9	Lost WNBA Championship to Houston.
2001	6	3	3	57.0	54.5	Lost Conference Final to Charlotte.
2002	8	4	4	71.8	69.1	Lost WNBA Championship to L.A.

*-minimum 40 games

2004	5	2	3	63.0	64.6	Lost Conference Final to Connecticut.
2005	2	0	2	50.5	60.5	Lost Conference Semifinal to Indiana.
TOTAL:	36	17	19			
AVERAGE:	5	2	3	63.3	62.7	

Regular Season Individual Leaders

Season	Field Goals % (20 games min.)		Free Throws % (20 games min.)		Points per Game (20 games min.)	
1997	Trena Trice	.554	Vickie Johnson	.771	S. Witherspoon	14.5
1998	Rebecca Lobo	.484	Sue Wicks	.800	S. Witherspoon	13.8
1999	Crystal Robinson	.439	Becky Hammon	.882	Vickie Johnson	13.3
2000	Becky Hammon	.472	Crystal Robinson	.909	Tari Phillips	13.8
2001	Tari Phillips	.507	Crystal Robinson	.897	Tari Phillips	15.3
2002	Tari Phillips	.491	Crystal Robinson	.819	Tari Phillips	14.1
2002	Vickie Johnson	.458	Erin Thom	1.000	Vickie Johnson	13.4
2003	Elena Baranova	.463	Vickie Johnson	.886	Becky Hammon	13.5
2004	DeTrina White	.544	Crystal Robinson	.930	Becky Hammon	13.5
2005	Ann Wauters	.541	Erin Thorn	1.000	Becky Hammon	13.9
2006	C. Kraayeveld	.444	Becky Hammon	.960	S. Christon	12.4

COACHING HISTORY: 1997-1998 Nancy Darsch 35-23-.603, 1999-2004 Richie Adubato 100-78-.562, 2004-present Pat Coyle (11-7 2004)

NEW YORK METROPOLITANS
(became Kansas City Blues)

Home City: New York, New York
Home Field: Polo Grounds I (1883-1885)   Capacity: 21,000
           Metropolitan Park (1884 some games)
           St. George Ground (1886-1887)
Origin of Name: The team was owned by the Metropolitan Exhibition Company.

Regular Season Record

Season	League	GP	W	L	Pct	GB	R	OR
1883	AA	96	54	42	.563	11	498	405
1884	AA	107	75	32	.701	-	734	423
1885	AA	108	44	64	.407	33	526	688
1886	AA	135	53	82	.393	38	628	766
1887	AA	133	44	89	.331	50	754	1093
TOTAL:	5 years	579	270	309		132	3140	3375
AVERAGE:		116	54	62	.466	26.5	628	675

Playoff Record

Season	GP	W	L	R	OR	Result
1884	3	0	3	3	21	Lost World Series to Providence.

Regular Season Individual Leaders

Season	Home Runs		RBI's		Wins	
1883	John O'Rourke	2	Not Recorded		Tim Keefe	41
	Ed Kennedy	2				
1884	Dave Orr	9	Not Recorded		Tim Keefe	37
					Jack Lynch	37
1885	Dave Orr	6	Not Recorded		Jack Lynch	23
1886	Dave Orr	7	Not Recorded		Jack Lynch	20
1887	Darby O'Brien	5	Not Recorded		Al Mays	17

COACHING HISTORY: 1883-1884 Jim Mutrie 129-74-.635; 1885-1886 Jim Gifford 50-76-.397; 1886-1887 Bob Ferguson 53-94-.361; 1887 Dave Orr 28-36-.438; 1887 O.P. Caylor 10-29-.256

NEW YORK METS

Home City: New York, New York
Home Field: Polo Grounds V (1962-1963)   Capacity: 56,000 [1953]
          Shea Stadium (1964-present)   Capacity: 57,333 [2006]
Origin of Name: The name is short for Metropolitans and was named for the American Association team from the 1880's.

Regular Season Record

Season	League	GP	W	L	Pct	GB	R	OR
1962	NL	160	40	120	.250	60.5	617	948
1963	NL	162	51	111	.315	48	501	774
1964	NL	162	53	109	.327	40	569	776
1965	NL	162	50	112	.309	47	495	752
1966	NL	161	66	95	.410	28.5	587	761
1967	NL	162	61	101	.377	40.5	498	672
1968	NL	162	73	89	.451	24	473	499
1969	NL	162	100	62	.617	-	632	541
1970	NL	162	83	79	.512	6	695	630
1971	NL	162	83	79	.512	14	588	550
1972	NL	156	83	73	.532	13.5	528	578
1973	NL	161	82	79	.509	-	608	588
1974	NL	162	71	91	.438	17	572	646
1975	NL	162	82	80	.506	10.5	646	625
1976	NL	162	86	76	.531	15	615	538
1977	NL	162	64	98	.395	37	587	663
1978	NL	162	66	96	.407	24	607	690
1979	NL	162	63	99	.389	35	593	706
1980	NL	162	67	95	.414	24	611	702
1981	NL	103	41	62	.398	NA	348	432
1982	NL	162	65	97	.401	27	609	723
1983	NL	162	68	94	.420	22	575	680
1984	NL	162	90	72	.556	6.5	652	676
1985	NL	162	98	64	.605	3	695	568
1986	NL	162	108	54	.667	-	783	578
1987	NL	162	92	70	.568	3	823	698
1988	NL	160	100	60	.625	-	703	532
1989	NL	162	87	75	.537	6	683	595
1990	NL	162	91	71	.562	4	775	613
1991	NL	161	77	84	.478	20.5	640	646
1992	NL	162	72	90	.444	24	599	653
1993	NL	162	59	103	.364	38	672	744
1994	NL	113	55	58	.487	18.5	506	526
1995	NL	144	69	75	.479	21	657	618
1996	NL	162	71	91	.438	25	746	779
1997	NL	162	88	74	.543	13	709	777
1998	NL	162	88	74	.543	18	706	645
1999	NL	162	96	66	.593	7	848	711
2000	NL	162	94	68	.580	1	807	738
2001	NL	162	82	80	.506	6	643	713

2002	NL	161	75	86	.466	26.5	690	703
2003	NL	161	66	95	.410	34.5	642	754
2004	NL	162	71	91	.438	25	684	731
2005	NL	162	83	79	.512	7	722	648
2006	NL	162	97	65	.599	-	834	731
TOTAL:	45 years	7149	3407	3742		841	28773	29851
AVERAGE:		159	76	83	.477	18.5	639	663

Playoff Record

Season	GP	W	L	R	OR	Result
1969	8	7	1	42	24	**Won World Series.**
1973	12	6	6	47	29	Lost World Series to Oakland.
1986	13	8	5	53	44	**Won World Series.**
1988	7	3	4	27	31	Lost NLCS to Los Angeles.
1999	10	5	5	43	40	Lost NLCS to Atlanta.
2000	14	8	6	60	51	Lost World Series to Yankees.
2006	10	6	4	46	39	Lost NLCS to St. Louis.
TOTAL:	74	43	31	318	258	
AVERAGE:	11	6	5	45	37	

Regular Season Individual Leaders

Season	Home Runs		RBI's		Wins	
1962	Frank Thomas	34	Frank Thomas	94	Roger Craig	10
1963	Jim Hickman	17	Frank Thomas	60	Al Jackson	13
1964	Charley Smith	20	Joe Christopher	76	Al Jackson	11
1965	Ron Swoboda	19	Charley Smith	62	Al Jackson	8
					Jack Fisher	8
1966	Ed Kranepool	16	Ken Boyer	61	Dennis Ribant	11
					Bob Shaw	11
					Jack Fisher	11
1967	Tommy Davis	16	Tommy Davis	73	Tom Seaver	16
1968	Ed Charles	15	Ron Swoboda	59	Jerry Koosman	19
1969	Tommie Agee	26	Tommie Agee	76	Tom Seaver	25
1970	Tommie Agee	24	Tommie Agee	97	Tom Seaver	18
1971	Ed Kranepool	14	Cleon Jones	69	Tom Seaver	20
	Tommie Agee	14				
	Cleon Jones	14				
1972	John Milner	17	Cleon Jones	52	Tom Seaver	21
1973	John Milner	23	Rusty Staub	76	Tom Seaver	19
1974	John Milner	20	Rusty Staub	78	Jerry Koosman	15
1975	Dave Kingman	36	Rusty Staub	105	Tom Seaver	22
1976	Dave Kingman	37	Dave Kingman	86	Jerry Koosman	21
1977	John Milner	12	Steve Henderson	65	Nino Espinosa	10
	Steve Henderson	12				
	John Stearns	12				
1978	Willie Montanez	17	Willie Montanez	96	Nino Espinosa	11
1979	Joel Youngblood	16	Richie Hebner	79	Craig Swan	14
			Lee Mazzilli	79		
1980	Lee Mazzilli	16	Lee Mazzilli	76	Mark Bomback	10
1981	Dave Kingman	22	Dave Kingman	59	Neil Allen	7
					Pat Zachry	7
1982	Dave Kingman	37	Dave Kingman	99	Craig Swan	11
1983	George Foster	28	George Foster	90	Jesse Orosco	13
1984	Darryl Strawberry	26	Darryl Strawberry	97	Dwight Gooden	17

Season	Home Runs		RBI's		Wins	
1985	Gary Carter	32	Gary Carter	100	Dwight Gooden	24
1986	Darryl Strawberry	27	Gary Carter	105	Bob Ojeda	18
1987	Darryl Strawberry	39	Darryl Strawberry	104	Dwight Gooden	15
1988	Darryl Strawberry	39	Darryl Strawberry	101	David Cone	20
1989	Howard Johnson	36	Howard Johnson	101	Sid Fernandez	14
					Ron Darling	14
					David Cone	14
1990	Darryl Strawberry	37	Darryl Strawberry	108	Frank Viola	20
1991	Howard Johnson	38	Howard Johnson	117	David Cone	14
1992	Bobby Bonilla	19	Eddie Murray	93	Sid Fernandez	14
1993	Bobby Bonilla	34	Eddie Murray	100	Dwight Gooden	12
1994	Bobby Bonilla	20	Jeff Kent	68	Bret Saberhagen	14
1995	Rico Brogna	22	Rico Brogna	76	Bobby Jones	10
1996	Todd Hundley	41	Bernard Gilkey	117	Mark Clark	14
1997	Todd Hundley	30	John Olerud	102	Bobby Jones	15
1998	Mike Piazza	32	Mike Piazza	111	Al Leiter	17
1999	Mike Piazza	40	Mike Piazza	124	Orel Hershiser	13
2000	Mike Piazza	38	Mike Piazza	113	Al Leiter	16
2001	Mike Piazza	36	Mike Piazza	94	Kevin Appier	11
					Al Leiter	11
					Steve Trachsel	11
2002	Mike Piazza	33	Mike Piazza	98	Al Leiter	13
2003	Cliff Floyd	18	Ty Wigginton	71	Steve Trachsel	16
2004	Mike Cameron	30	Richard Hidalgo	82	Steve Trachsel	12
2005	Cliff Floyd	34	David Wright	102	Pedro Martinez	15
2006	Carlos Beltran	41	Carlos Beltran	116	Tom Glavine	15
			David Wright	116		

COACHING HISTORY: 1962-1965 Casey Stengel 175-404-.302; 1965-1967 Wes Westrum 142-237-.375; 1967 Francis Parker 4-7-.364; 1968-1971 Gil Hodges 339-309-.523; 1972-1975 Yogi Berra 292-296-.497; 1975 Roy McMillan 26-27-.491; 1976-1977 Joe Frazier 101-105-.490; 1977-1981 Joe Torre 286-421-.405; 1982-1983 George Bamberger 81-127-.389; 1983 Frank Howard 52-64-.448; 1984-1990 Dave Johnson 595-417-.588; 1990-1991 Bud Harrelson 145-129-.529; 1991 Mike Cubbage 3-4-.429; 1992-1993 Jeff Torborg 85-115-.425; 1993-1996 Dallas Green 229-283-.447; 1996-2002 Bobby Valentine 535-467-.534; 2003-2004 Art Howe 137-186-.424; 2005-present Willie Randolph

NEW YORK MUTUALS

Home City: New York, New York
Home Field: Capitoline Grounds
Origin of Name: The club was organized in the firehouse of the Mutual Hook and Ladder Company No. 1 in 1857.

Regular Season Record

Season	League	GP	W	L	Pct	GB	R	OR
1876	NL	56	21	35	.375	26	260	412

Regular Season Individual Leaders

Season	Home Runs		RBI's		Wins	
1876	Jimmy Hallinan	2	Jimmy Hallinan	36	Bob Mathews	21

COACHING HISTORY: Bill Cammeyer 21-35-.375

NEW YORK NETS
(were New Jersey Americans)
(became New Jersey Nets)

Home City: Commack, New York (1968-1969)
  West Hempstead, New York (1969-1971)
  Uniondale, New York (1971-1977)
Home Court: Long Island Arena (1968-1969)   Capacity: 6,500
  Island Garden (1969-1971)   Capacity: 5,200
  Nassau Veteran's Memorial Coliseum (1971-1977)   Capacity: 15,934 [1977]
Origin of Name: The name was chosen as a tie in to the other New York teams, the Jets and the Mets.

Regular Season Record

Season	League	GP	W	L	PPGF	PPGA	Pct	GB
1968-1969	ABA	78	17	61	108.5	117.2	.218	27
1969-1970	ABA	84	39	45	108.9	109.8	.464	20
1970-1971	ABA	84	40	44	111.0	111.6	.476	15
1971-1972	ABA	84	44	40	112.8	112.4	.524	24
1972-1973	ABA	84	30	54	103.6	110.1	.357	27
1973-1974	ABA	84	55	29	109.4	104.0	.655	-
1974-1975	ABA	84	58	26	111.1	103.4	.690	-
1975-1976	ABA	84	55	29	111.8	108.8	.655	5
1976-1977	NBA	82	22	60	95.9	102.7	.268	28
TOTAL:	9 years	748	360	388				146
AVERAGE:		83	40	43	108.1	108.9	.481	16

Playoff Record

Season	GP	W	L	PPGF	PPGA	Result
1969-1970	7	3	4	111.7	114.0	Lost 1st Round series to Kentucky.
1970-1971	6	2	4	119.3	121.7	Lost 1st Round series to Virginia.
1971-1972	19	10	9	107.5	109.6	Lost Championship series to Indiana.
1972-1973	5	1	4	104.4	112.8	Lost 1st Round series to Indiana.
1973-1974	14	12	2	106.9	96.1	**Won ABA Championship.**
1974-1975	5	1	4	102.4	108.2	Lost 1st Round series to St. Louis.
1975-1976	13	8	5	111.2	111.2	**Won ABA Championship.**
TOTAL:	69	37	32			
AVERAGE:	10	5	5	109.1	110.5	

Regular Season Individual Leaders

Season	Field Goal % (min. 70 games)		Points		Points per Game (min. 70 games)	
1968-69	Wilbert Frazier	.424	Walt Simon	1436	Walt Simon	21.1
1969-70	Levern Tart	.495	Levern Tart	1935	Levern Tart	24.2
1970-71	Billy Paultz	.524	Rick Barry	1734	Rick Barry	29.4
1971-72	T. Washington	.571	Rick Barry	2518	Rick Barry	31.5
1972-73	T. Washington	.539	George Carter	1578	George Carter	19.0
1973-74	Julius Erving	.512	Julius Erving	2299	Julius Erving	27.4
1974-75	Brian Taylor	.513	Julius Erving	2343	Julius Erving	27.9
1975-76	Kim Hughes	.530	Julius Erving	2462	Julius Erving	29.3
1976-77	Van Breda Kolff	.445	Robert Hawkins	1006	Al Skinner	12.6

COACHING HISTORY: 1968-1969 Max Zaslofsky 17-61-.218; 1969-1970 York Larese 39-45-.464; 1970-1973 Lou Carnesecca 114-138-.452; 1973-1977 Kevin Loughery 190-188-.503

NEW YORK-NEW JERSEY KNIGHTS

Home City: East Rutherford, New Jersey
Home Stadium: Giants Stadium   Capacity: 77,152 [1991]
Origin of Name:

Regular Season Record

Season	League	GP	W	L	T	PF	PA	Pct
1991	WLAF	10	5	5	0	257	155	.500
1992	WFL	10	6	4	0	284	188	.600
TOTAL:	2 years	20	11	9	0	541	343	
AVERAGE:		10	6	4	0	271	172	.550

Playoff Record

Season	GP	W	L	PF	PA	Result
1991	1	0	1	26	42	Lost 1st Round game to London.

Regular Season Individual Leaders

Season	Passing Yards		Receiving Yards		Rushing Yards	
1991	Jeff Graham	2407	Monty Gilbreath	643	Eric Wilkerson	717
1992	Reggie Slack	1898				

COACHING HISTORY: 1991-1992 Darrell Davis 11-9-0-.550

NEW YORK RANGERS

Home City: New York, New York
Home Arena: Madison Square Garden III (1926-1968)   Capacity: 15,925
            Madison Square Garden IV (1968-present)   Capacity: 18,200 [2005]
Origin of Name: The team was named after the Texas Rangers. The president of Madison Square Garden and one of the men responsible for bringing the Rangers to New York was Tex Rickard and the team was unofficially known as "Tex's Rangers" after Rickard's home state police.

Regular Season Record

Season	League	GP	W	L	T	OL	SL	GF	GA	Pts
1926-1927	NHL	44	25	13	6	NA	NA	95	72	56
1927-1928	NHL	44	19	16	9	NA	NA	94	79	47
1928-1929	NHL	44	21	13	10	NA	NA	72	65	52
1929-1930	NHL	44	17	17	10	NA	NA	136	143	44
1930-1931	NHL	48	23	17	8	NA	NA	134	112	54
1931-1932	NHL	48	23	17	8	NA	NA	134	112	54
1932-1933	NHL	48	23	17	8	NA	NA	135	107	54
1933-1934	NHL	48	21	19	8	NA	NA	120	113	50
1934-1935	NHL	48	22	20	6	NA	NA	137	139	50
1935-1936	NHL	48	19	17	12	NA	NA	91	96	50
1936-1937	NHL	48	19	20	9	NA	NA	117	106	47
1937-1938	NHL	48	27	15	6	NA	NA	149	96	60
1938-1939	NHL	48	26	16	6	NA	NA	149	105	58
1939-1940	NHL	48	27	11	10	NA	NA	136	77	64
1940-1941	NHL	48	21	19	8	NA	NA	143	125	50
1941-1942	NHL	48	29	17	2	NA	NA	177	143	60
1942-1943	NHL	50	11	31	8	NA	NA	161	253	30
1943-1944	NHL	50	6	39	5	NA	NA	162	310	17
1944-1945	NHL	50	11	29	10	NA	NA	154	147	32
1945-1946	NHL	50	13	28	9	NA	NA	144	191	35

1946-1947	NHL	60	22	32	6	NA	NA	167	186	50
1947-1948	NHL	60	21	26	13	NA	NA	176	201	55
1948-1949	NHL	60	18	31	11	NA	NA	133	172	47
1949-1950	NHL	70	28	31	11	NA	NA	170	189	67
1950-1951	NHL	70	20	29	21	NA	NA	169	201	61
1951-1952	NHL	70	23	34	13	NA	NA	192	219	59
1952-1953	NHL	70	17	37	16	NA	NA	152	211	50
1953-1954	NHL	70	29	31	10	NA	NA	161	182	68
1954-1955	NHL	70	17	35	18	NA	NA	150	210	52
1955-1956	NHL	70	32	28	10	NA	NA	204	203	74
1956-1957	NHL	70	26	30	14	NA	NA	184	227	66
1957-1958	NHL	70	32	25	13	NA	NA	195	188	77
1958-1959	NHL	70	26	32	12	NA	NA	201	217	64
1959-1960	NHL	70	17	38	15	NA	NA	187	247	49
1960-1961	NHL	70	22	38	10	NA	NA	204	248	54
1961-1962	NHL	70	26	32	12	NA	NA	195	207	64
1962-1963	NHL	70	22	36	12	NA	NA	211	233	56
1963-1964	NHL	70	22	38	10	NA	NA	186	242	54
1964-1965	NHL	70	20	38	12	NA	NA	179	246	52
1965-1966	NHL	70	18	41	11	NA	NA	195	261	47
1966-1967	NHL	70	30	28	12	NA	NA	188	189	72
1967-1968	NHL	74	39	23	12	NA	NA	226	183	90
1968-1969	NHL	76	41	26	9	NA	NA	231	196	91
1969-1970	NHL	76	38	22	16	NA	NA	246	189	92
1970-1971	NHL	78	49	18	11	NA	NA	259	177	109
1971-1972	NHL	78	48	17	13	NA	NA	317	192	109
1972-1973	NHL	78	47	23	8	NA	NA	298	208	102
1973-1974	NHL	78	40	24	14	NA	NA	300	251	94
1974-1975	NHL	80	37	29	14	NA	NA	319	276	88
1975-1976	NHL	80	29	42	9	NA	NA	262	333	67
1976-1977	NHL	80	29	37	14	NA	NA	272	310	72
1977-1978	NHL	80	30	37	13	NA	NA	279	280	73
1978-1979	NHL	80	40	29	11	NA	NA	316	292	91
1979-1980	NHL	80	38	32	10	NA	NA	308	284	86
1980-1981	NHL	80	30	36	14	NA	NA	312	317	74
1981-1982	NHL	80	39	27	14	NA	NA	316	306	92
1982-1983	NHL	80	35	35	10	NA	NA	306	287	80
1983-1984	NHL	80	42	29	9	NA	NA	314	304	93
1984-1985	NHL	80	26	44	10	NA	NA	295	345	62
1985-1986	NHL	80	36	38	6	NA	NA	280	276	78
1986-1987	NHL	80	34	38	8	NA	NA	307	323	76
1987-1988	NHL	80	36	34	10	NA	NA	300	283	82
1988-1989	NHL	80	37	35	8	NA	NA	310	307	82
1989-1990	NHL	80	36	31	13	NA	NA	279	267	85
1990-1991	NHL	80	36	31	13	NA	NA	297	265	85
1991-1992	NHL	80	50	25	5	NA	NA	321	246	105
1992-1993	NHL	84	34	39	11	NA	NA	304	308	79
1993-1994	NHL	84	52	24	8	NA	NA	299	231	112
1994-1995	NHL	48	22	23	3	NA	NA	139	134	47
1995-1996	NHL	82	41	27	14	NA	NA	272	237	96
1996-1997	NHL	82	38	34	10	NA	NA	258	231	86
1997-1998	NHL	82	25	39	18	NA	NA	197	231	68
1998-1999	NHL	82	33	38	11	NA	NA	217	227	77
1999-2000	NHL	82	29	41	12	3	NA	218	246	73

2000-2001	NHL	82	33	43	5	1	NA	250	290	72
2001-2002	NHL	82	36	38	4	4	NA	227	258	80
2002-2003	NHL	82	32	36	10	4	NA	210	231	78
2003-2004	NHL	82	27	40	7	8	NA	206	250	69
2004-2005	NHL	Season cancelled due to lockout.								
2005-2006	NHL	82	44	26	NA	8	4	257	215	100
TOTAL:	79 years	5406	2279	2291	807	28	4	16763	16856	5397
AVERAGE:		68	29	29	10	0	0	212	213	68

Playoff Record

Season	GP	W	L	T	GF	GA	Result
1926-1927	2	0	1	1	1	3	Lost Semifinal series to Boston.
1927-1928	9	5	3	1	16	12	**Won Stanley Cup.**
1928-1929	6	3	2	1	5	5	Lost Stanley Cup Final to Boston.
1929-1930	4	1	2	1	7	7	Lost Semifinal series to Canadiens.
1930-1931	4	2	2	0	8	4	Lost Semifinal series to Chicago.
1931-1932	7	3	4	0	23	27	Lost Stanley Cup Final to Toronto.
1932-1933	8	6	1	1	25	13	**Won Stanley Cup.**
1933-1934	2	0	1	1	1	2	Lost Quarterfinal series to Maroons.
1934-1935	4	1	1	2	10	10	Lost Semifinal series to Maroons.
1936-1937	9	6	3	0	18	10	Lost Stanley Cup Final to Detroit.
1937-1938	3	1	2	0	7	8	Lost Quarterfinal series to Americans.
1938-1939	7	3	4	0	12	14	Lost Semifinal series to Boston.
1939-1940	12	8	4	0	29	20	**Won Stanley Cup.**
1940-1941	3	1	2	0	6	6	Lost Quarterfinal series to Detroit.
1941-1942	6	2	4	0	12	13	Lost Semifinal series to Toronto.
1947-1948	6	2	4	0	12	17	Lost Semifinal series to Detroit.
1949-1950	12	7	5	0	32	29	Lost Stanley Cup Final to Detroit.
1955-1956	5	1	4	0	9	24	Lost Semifinal series to Montreal.
1956-1957	5	1	4	0	12	22	Lost Semifinal series to Montreal.
1957-1958	6	2	4	0	16	28	Lost Semifinal series to Boston.
1961-1962	6	2	4	0	15	22	Lost Semifinal series to Toronto.
1966-1967	4	0	4	0	8	14	Lost Semifinal series to Montreal.
1967-1968	6	2	4	0	12	18	Lost Quarterfinal series to Chicago.
1968-1969	4	0	4	0	7	16	Lost Quarterfinal series to Montreal.
1969-1970	6	2	4	0	16	25	Lost Quarterfinal series to Boston.
1970-1971	13	7	6	0	30	36	Lost Semifinal series to Chicago.
1971-1972	16	10	6	0	52	41	Lost Stanley Cup Final to Boston.
1972-1973	10	5	5	0	33	26	Lost Semifinal series to Chicago.
1973-1974	13	7	6	0	38	39	Lost Quarterfinal series to Philadelphia.
1974-1975	3	1	2	0	13	10	Lost Preliminary series to Islanders.
1977-1978	3	1	2	0	6	11	Lost Preliminary series to Buffalo.
1978-1979	18	11	7	0	66	42	Lost Stanley Cup Final to Montreal.
1979-1980	9	4	5	0	21	23	Lost Quarterfinal series to Philadelphia.
1980-1981	14	7	7	0	60	56	Lost Semifinal series to Islanders.
1981-1982	10	5	5	0	39	42	Lost Division Final to Islanders.
1982-1983	9	5	4	0	33	37	Lost Division Final to Islanders.
1983-1984	5	2	3	0	14	13	Lost Division Semifinal to Islanders.
1984-1985	3	0	3	0	10	14	Lost Division Semifinal to Philadelphia.
1985-1986	16	8	8	0	47	55	Lost Conference Final to Montreal.
1986-1987	6	2	4	0	13	22	Lost Division Semifinal to Philadelphia.
1988-1989	4	0	4	0	11	19	Lost Division Semifinal to Pittsburgh.
1989-1990	10	5	5	0	37	35	Lost Division Final to Washington.
1990-1991	6	2	4	0	16	16	Lost Division Semifinal to Washington.

1991-1992	13	6	7	0	47	49	Lost Division Final to Pittsburgh.
1993-1994	23	16	7	0	81	50	**Won Stanley Cup**.
1994-1995	10	4	6	0	35	37	Lost Conf. Semifinal to Philadelphia.
1995-1996	11	5	6	0	34	38	Lost Conference Semifinal to Pittsburgh.
1996-1997	15	9	6	0	36	35	Lost Conference Final to Philadelphia.
2005-2006	4	0	4	0	4	17	Lost Conf. Quarterfinal to New Jersey.
TOTAL:	390	183	199	8	1095	1132	
AVERAGE:	8	4	4	0	22	23	

Regular Season Individual Leaders

Season	Goals		Points		Penalty Minutes	
1926-1927	Bill Cook	33	Bill Cook	37	Clarence Abel	78
1927-1928	Frank Boucher	23	Frank Boucher	35	Ivan Johnson	146
1928-1929	Bill Cook	15	Frank Boucher	28	Frederick Cook	70
1929-1930	Bill Cook	29	Frank Boucher	62	Ivan Johnson	82
1930-1931	Bill Cook	30	Bill Cook	42	Ivan Johnson	77
1931-1932	Bill Cook	33	Bill Cook	47	Ivan Johnson	106
1932-1933	Bill Cook	28	Bill Cook	50	Ivan Johnson	127
1933-1934	Frederick Cook	18	Frank Boucher	44	Ivan Johnson	86
1934-1935	Cecil Dillon	25	Frank Boucher	45	Earl Seibert	86
1935-1936	Cecil Dillon	18	Cecil Dillon	32	Ivan Johnson	58
1936-1937	Butch Keeling	22	Cecil Dillon	31	Ott Heller	42
					Joe Cooper	42
1937-1938	Cecil Dillon	21	Cecil Dillon	39	Art Coulter	80
1938-1939	Alex Shibicky	24	Clint Smith	41	Murray Patrick	64
1939-1940	Bryan Hextall	24	Bryan Hextall	39	Art Coulter	68
1940-1941	Bryan Hextall	26	Bryan Hextall	44	Walter Pratt	52
			Lynn Patrick	44		
1941-1942	Lynn Patrick	32	Bryan Hextall	56	Walter Pratt	55
1942-1943	Bryan Hextall	27	Lynn Patrick	61	Vic Myles	57
1943-1944	Bryan Hextall	21	Bryan Hextall	54	Bob Dill	66
1944-1945	Ab DeMarco	24	Ab DeMarco	54	Bob Dill	59
1945-1946	Ab DeMarco	20	Ab DeMarco	47	Phil Watson	43
1946-1947	Tony Leswick	27	Tony Leswick	41	Bill Juzda	60
1947-1948	Herb O'Connor	24	Herb O'Connor	60	Tony Leswick	76
	Tony Leswick	24				
1948-1949	Edgar Laprade	18	Herb O'Connor	35	Tony Leswick	70
1949-1950	Edgar Laprade	22	Edgar Laprade	44	Gus Kyle	143
			Tony Leswick	44		
1950-1951	Nick Mickoski	20	Don Raleigh	39	Tony Leswick	112
			Reg Sinclair	39		
1951-1952	W. Hergesheimer	28	Don Raleigh	61	Hy Buller	96
1952-1953	W. Hergesheimer	30	W. Hergesheimer	59	Hy Buller	73
1953-1954	W. Hergesheimer	27	Paul Ronty	46	Ivan Irwin	109
1954-1955	Danny Lewicki	29	Danny Lewicki	53	Jack Evans	91
1955-1956	Dean Prentice	24	Andy Bathgate	66	Lou Fontinato	202
	Andy Hebenton	24				
1956-1957	Andy Bathgate	27	Andy Bathgate	77	Lou Fontinato	139
1957-1958	Camille Henry	32	Andy Bathgate	78	Lou Fontinato	152
1958-1959	Andy Bathgate	40	Andy Bathgate	88	Lou Fontinato	149
1959-1960	Dean Prentice	32	Andy Bathgate	74	Lou Fontinato	137
1960-1961	Andy Bathgate	29	Andy Bathgate	77	Lou Fontinato	100
1961-1962	Andy Bathgate	28	Andy Bathgate	84	Albert Langlois	90
1962-1963	Camille Henry	37	Andy Bathgate	81	Doug Harvey	92

Season	Goals		Points		Penalty Minutes	
1963-1964	Camille Henry	29	Phil Goyette	65	Vic Hadfield	151
1964-1965	Rod Gilbert	25	Rod Gilbert	61	Arnie Brown	145
1965-1966	Bob Nevin	29	Bob Nevin	62	Reg Fleming	124
1966-1967	Rod Gilbert	28	Phil Goyette	61	Reg Fleming	146
1967-1968	Jean Ratelle	32	Jean Ratelle	78	Reg Fleming	132
1968-1969	Jean Ratelle	32	Jean Ratelle	78	Reg Fleming	138
1969-1970	Dave Balon	33	Walt Tkaczuk	77	Dave Balon	100
1970-1971	Dave Balon	36	Walt Tkaczuk	75	Ted Irvine	137
1971-1972	Vic Hadfield	50	Jean Ratelle	109	Vic Hadfield	142
1972-1973	Jean Ratelle	41	Jean Ratelle	94	Dale Rolfe	74
1973-1974	Rod Gilbert	36	Brad Park	82	Brad Park	148
1974-1975	Steve Vickers	41	Rod Gilbert	97	Derek Sanderson	106
1975-1976	Rod Gilbert	36	Rod Gilbert	86	Carol Vadnais	104
1976-1977	Phil Esposito	34	Phil Esposito	80	Nick Fotiu	174
1977-1978	Pat Hickey	40	Phil Esposito	81	Carol Vadnais	115
1978-1979	Phil Esposito	42	Phil Esposito	78	Nick Fotiu	190
			Anders Hedberg	78		
1979-1980	Phil Esposito	34	Phil Esposito	78	Dave Maloney	186
1980-1981	Anders Hedberg	40	Anders Hedberg	70	Barry Beck	231
	Ed Johnstone	40				
1981-1982	Ron Duguay	40	Mike Rogers	103	Carol Vadnais	170
1982-1983	Mark Pavelich	37	Mike Rogers	76	Dave Maloney	132
1983-1984	Pierre Larouche	48	Mark Pavelich	82	Dave Maloney	168
1984-1985	T. Sandstrom	29	Reijo Ruotsalainen	73	George McPhee	139
1985-1986	T. Sandstrom	25	Mike Ridley	65	Bob Brooke	111
1986-1987	Walt Poddubny	40	Walt Poddubny	87	Larry Melnyk	182
	Tomas Sandstrom	40				
1987-1988	Walt Poddubny	38	Walt Poddubny	88	Michel Petit	223
1988-1989	Tony Granato	36	T. Sandstrom	88	Rudy Poeschek	199
1989-1990	John Ogrodnick	43	John Ogrodnick	74	Troy Mallette	305
1990-1991	Mike Gartner	49	Brian Leetch	88	Troy Mallette	252
1991-1992	Mike Gartner	40	Mark Messier	107	Tie Domi	246
1992-1993	Mike Gartner	45	Mark Messier	91	Jeff Beukeboom	153
1993-1994	Adam Graves	52	Sergei Zubov	89	Jeff Beukeboom	170
1994-1995	Adam Graves	17	Mark Messier	53	Nick Kypreos	93
1995-1996	Mark Messier	47	Mark Messier	99	Jeff Beukeboom	220
1996-1997	Mark Messier	36	Wayne Gretzky	97	Darren Langdon	195
1997-1998	Wayne Gretzky	23	Wayne Gretzky	90	Darren Langdon	197
	Pat LaFontaine	23				
	Alexei Kovalev	23				
	Adam Graves	23				
1998-1999	Adam Graves	38	Wayne Gretzky	62	Ulf Samuelsson	93
1999-2000	Michael York	26	Petr Nedved	68	Mathieu Schneider	78
2000-2001	Petr Nedved	32	Brian Leetch	79	Dale Purinton	180
2001-2002	Eric Lindros	37	Eric Lindros	73	Theo Fleury	216
2002-2003	Petr Nedved	27	Petr Nedved	58	Dale Purinton	161
2003-2004	Bobby Holik	25	Bobby Holik	56	Chris Simon	225
2004-2005	Season cancelled due to lockout.					
2005-2006	Jaromir Jagr	54	Jaromir Jagr	123	Darius Kasparaitis	97

COACHING HISTORY: 1926-1939 Lester Patrick 285-217-106-.556; 1939-1949 Frank Boucher 167-243-77-.422; 1948-1950 Lynn Patrick 40-51-16-.449; 1950-1952 Neil Colville 26-41-26-.419; 1951-1953 Bill Cook 34-59-24-.393; 1953-1954 Frank Boucher 12-20-6-.395;

1953-1955 Murray Patrick 34-46-22-.441; 1955-1960 Phil Watson 119-124-52-.492; 1959-1961 Alf Pike 36-67-22-.376; 1961-1962 Doug Harvey 26-32-12-.457; 1962-1963 Murray Patrick 11-19-4-.382; 1962-1966 George Sullivan 58-103-35-.385; 1965-1975 Emile Francis 347-209-98-.606; 1968-1969 Bernie Geoffrion 22-18-3-.547; 1973-1974 Larry Popein 18-14-9-.549; 1975-1976 Ron Stewart 15-20-4-.436; 1975-1977 John Ferguson 43-59-19-.434; 1977-1978 Jean-Guy Talbot 30-37-13-.456; 1978-1981 Fred Shero 82-74-25-.522; 1980-1981 Craig Patrick 26-23-10-.525; 1981-1985 Herb Brooks 131-113-41-.532; 1984-1985 Craig Patrick 11-22-2-.343; 1985-1987 Ted Sator 41-48-10-.465; 1986-1987 Tom Webster 5-7-4-.438; 1986-1987 Phil Esposito 24-21-0-.533; 1987-1989 Michel Bergeron 73-67-18-.519; 1988-1989 Phil Esposito 0-2-0-.000; 1989-1992 Roger Neilson 141-104-35-.566; 1992-1993 Ron Smith 15-22-7-.420; 1993-1994 Mike Keenan 52-24-8-.667; 1994-1998 Colin Campbell 118-108-43-.519; 1997-2000 John Muckler 70-92-24-.441; 1999-2000 John Tortorella 0-3-1-.125; 2000-2002 Ron Low 69-81-9-5-.463; 2002-2003 Bryan Trottier 21-26-6-1-.454; 2002-2004 Glen Sather 33-39-11-7-.467; 2003-2004 Tom Renney

NEW YORK RED BULLS
(Were known as New York New Jersey MetroStars from 1996-2005)

Home City: East Rutherford, New Jersey
Home Field: Giants Stadium (1996-present)   Capacity: 80,242 [2005]
Origin of Name: The team was purchased by Red Bull energy drink in 2006.

Season	League	GP	W	L	T	SOW	GF	GA	Pts
1996	MLS	32	15	17	NA	3	45	47	39
1997	MLS	32	13	19	NA	2	43	53	35
1998	MLS	32	15	17	NA	3	54	63	39
1999	MLS	32	7	25	NA	3	32	64	15
2000	MLS	32	17	12	3	NA	64	56	54
2001	MLS	26	13	10	3	NA	38	35	42
2002	MLS	28	11	15	2	NA	41	47	35
2003	MLS	30	11	10	9	NA	40	40	42
2004	MLS	30	11	12	7	NA	47	49	40
2005	MLS	32	12	9	11	NA	53	49	47
2006	MLS	32	9	11	12	NA	41	41	39
TOTAL:	11 years	338	134	157	47	11	498	544	427
AVERAGE:		31	12	14	4	1	45	50	39

Playoff Record

Season	GP	W	L	T	GF	GA	Result
1996	3	1	2	0	4	5	Lost Quarterfinals to D.C. United.
1998	2	0	2	0	4	7	Lost Semifinals to Columbus.
2000	5	3	2	0	8	8	Lost Quarterfinals to Chicago.
2001	3	1	2	0	7	5	Lost Semifinals to Los Angeles.
2003	2	0	1	1	1	3	Lost Conf. Semifinal to New England.
2004	2	0	2	0	0	4	Lost Conf. Semifinal to D.C. United.
2005	2	1	1	0	2	3	Lost Conf. Semifinal to New England.
2006	2	0	1	1	1	2	Lost Conf. Semifinal to D.C. United.
TOTAL:	21	6	13	2	27	37	
AVERAGE:	3	1	2	0	3	5	

Regular Season Individual Leaders

Season	Goals		Points		GAA (min. 5 games)	
1996	Giavanni Savarese	13	Giavanni Savarese	27	Tony Meola	1.31

Season	Goals		Points		GAA (min. 5 games)	
1997	Giavanni Savarese	14	Giavanni Savarese	32	Tony Meola	1.61
1998	Giavanni Savarese	14	Eduardo Hurtado	37	Tony Meola	2.00
1999	Eduardo Hurtado	7	Eduardo Hurtado	17	Tim Howard	1.58
2000	Adolfo Valencia	16	Adolfo Valencia	41	Tim Howard	1.59
2001	Rodrigo Faria	8	Clint Mathis	19	Tim Howard	1.33
2002	Rodrigo Faria	12	Rodrigo Faria	29	Tim Howard	1.61
	Mamadou Diallo	12	Mamadou Diallo	29		
2003	Clint Mathis	9	Clint Mathis	19	Jonny Walker	0.95
2004	Amado Guevara	10	Amado Guevara	30	Jonny Walker	1.61
	John Wolyniec	10				
2005	Amado Guevara	11	Amado Guevara	33	Zach Wells	1.24
2006	Amado Guevara	8	Amado Guevara	21	Jon Conway	1.00

COACHING HISTORY: 1996 Eddie Firmani 3-5; 1996 Carlos Queiroz 12-12; 1997 Alberto Parreira 13-19; 1998 Alfonso Mondelo 14-17; 1998-1999 Bora Mutinovic 8-25; 2000-2002 Octavio Zambrano 41-37-8; 2003-2005 Bob Bradley 32-31-26; 2005-2006 Mo Johnston 4-3-8; 2006 Richie Williams 1-3-1; 2006 Bruce Arena

NEW YORK SKYLINERS

Home City: New York, New York
Home Field: Yankee Stadium   Capacity: 67,000 [1967]
Origin of Name: May have adopted the name in tribute to the city's famous skyline. The team was represented by the Cerro club of Montevideo, Uruguay.

			Regular Season Record						
Season	League	GP	W	L	T	GF	GA	Pts	Pct
1967	USA	12	2	4	6	15	17	10	.417

		Regular Season Individual Leaders			
Season	Goals		Points		GAA (360 Min)	
1967	Bendicto Ribeiro	5	Bendicto Ribeiro	12	O. Miguelucci	1.39

COACHING HISTORY: Ondino Vierra 2-4-6-.417

NEW YORK STARS
(became Charlotte Stars)

Home City: New York, New York
Home Stadium: Downing Stadium *   Capacity: 21,000
Origin of Name: The team was named by coach Babe Parilli.

			Regular Season Record					
Season	League	GP	W	L	T	PF	PA	Pct
1974	WFL	11	3	8	0	165	278	.273

	Regular Season Individual Leaders	
Season	Passing Yards	Receiving Yards	Rushing Yards
1974	See Charlotte Stars		

COACHING HISTORY: Babe Parilli 3-8-0-.273

NEW YORK YANKEES
(were Baltimore Orioles)

Home City: New York, New York
Home Field: Hilltop Park (1903-1912)   Capacity: 15,000
      Polo Grounds V (1913-1922)   Capacity: 38,000 [1919]
      Yankee Stadium I (1923-1913)   Capacity: 67,224 [1958]
      Shea Stadium (1974-1975)   Capacity: 55,101 [1975]
      Yankee Stadium II (1976-present)   Capacity: 56,937 [2006]
Origin of Name: According to some baseball historians the team's nickname was originated by Jim Price of the *New York Press*. From 1903 to 1912 the team was known as the "Hilltops" due to the fact the team's ball park was situated on high ground.

Regular Season Record

Season	League	GP	W	L	Pct	GB	R	OR
1903	AL	134	72	62	.537	17	579	573
1904	AL	151	92	59	.609	1.5	598	526
1905	AL	149	71	78	.477	21.5	587	644
1906	AL	151	90	61	.596	3	643	544
1907	AL	148	70	78	.473	21	604	671
1908	AL	154	51	103	.331	39.5	458	700
1909	AL	151	74	77	.490	23.5	591	580
1910	AL	151	88	63	.583	14.5	629	502
1911	AL	152	76	76	.500	25.5	686	726
1912	AL	152	50	102	.329	55	632	839
1913	AL	151	57	94	.377	38	529	669
1914	AL	154	70	84	.455	30	536	550
1915	AL	152	69	83	.454	32.5	583	596
1916	AL	154	80	74	.519	11	575	561
1917	AL	153	71	82	.464	28.5	524	560
1918	AL	123	60	63	.488	13.5	491	474
1919	AL	139	80	59	.576	7.5	582	514
1920	AL	154	95	59	.617	3	839	629
1921	AL	153	98	55	.641	-	948	708
1922	AL	154	94	60	.610	-	758	618
1923	AL	152	98	54	.645	-	823	622
1924	AL	152	89	63	.586	2	798	667
1925	AL	154	69	85	.448	28.5	706	774
1926	AL	154	91	63	.591	-	847	713
1927	AL	154	110	44	.714	-	975	599
1928	AL	154	101	53	.656	-	894	685
1929	AL	154	88	66	.571	18	899	775
1930	AL	154	86	68	.558	16	1062	898
1931	AL	153	94	59	.614	13.5	1067	760
1932	AL	154	107	47	.695	-	1002	724
1933	AL	150	91	59	.607	7	927	768
1934	AL	154	94	60	.610	7	842	669
1935	AL	149	89	60	.597	3	818	632
1936	AL	153	102	51	.667	-	1065	731
1937	AL	154	102	52	.662	-	979	671

*-also known as Triborough Stadium

1938	AL	152	99	53	.651	-	966	710
1939	AL	151	106	45	.702	-	967	556
1940	AL	154	88	66	.571	2	817	671
1941	AL	154	101	53	.656	-	830	631
1942	AL	154	103	51	.669	-	801	507
1943	AL	154	98	56	.636	-	669	542
1944	AL	154	83	71	.539	6	674	617
1945	AL	152	81	71	.533	6.5	676	606
1946	AL	154	87	67	.565	17	684	547
1947	AL	154	97	57	.630	-	794	568
1948	AL	154	94	60	.610	2.5	857	633
1949	AL	154	97	57	.630	-	829	637
1950	AL	154	98	56	.636	-	914	691
1951	AL	154	98	56	.636	-	798	621
1952	AL	154	95	59	.617	-	727	557
1953	AL	151	99	52	.656	-	801	547
1954	AL	154	103	51	.669	8	805	563
1955	AL	154	96	58	.623	-	762	569
1956	AL	154	97	57	.630	-	857	631
1957	AL	154	98	56	.636	-	723	534
1958	AL	154	92	62	.597	-	759	577
1959	AL	154	79	75	.513	15	687	647
1960	AL	154	97	57	.630	-	746	627
1961	AL	162	109	53	.673	-	827	612
1962	AL	162	96	66	.593	-	817	680
1963	AL	161	104	57	.646	-	714	547
1964	AL	162	99	63	.611	-	730	577
1965	AL	162	77	85	.475	25	611	604
1966	AL	159	70	89	.440	26.5	611	612
1967	AL	162	72	90	.444	20	522	621
1968	AL	162	83	79	.512	20	536	531
1969	AL	161	80	81	.497	28.5	562	587
1970	AL	162	93	69	.574	15	680	612
1971	AL	162	82	80	.506	21	648	641
1972	AL	155	79	76	.510	6.5	557	527
1973	AL	162	80	82	.494	17	641	610
1974	AL	162	89	73	.549	2	671	623
1975	AL	160	83	77	.519	12	681	588
1976	AL	159	97	62	.610	-	730	575
1977	AL	162	100	62	.617	-	831	651
1978	AL	163	100	63	.613	-	735	582
1979	AL	160	89	71	.556	13.5	734	672
1980	AL	162	103	59	.636	-	820	662
1981	AL	107	59	48	.551	NA	421	343
1982	AL	162	79	83	.488	16	709	716
1983	AL	162	91	71	.562	7	770	703
1984	AL	162	87	75	.537	17	758	679
1985	AL	161	97	64	.602	2	839	660
1986	AL	162	90	72	.556	5.5	797	738
1987	AL	162	89	73	.549	9	788	758
1988	AL	161	85	76	.528	3.5	772	748
1989	AL	161	74	87	.460	14.5	698	792
1990	AL	162	67	95	.414	21	603	749
1991	AL	162	71	91	.438	20	674	777

1992	AL	162	76	86	.469	20	733	746
1993	AL	162	88	74	.543	7	821	761
1994	AL	113	70	43	.619	-	670	534
1995	AL	144	79	65	.549	7	745	688
1996	AL	162	92	70	.568	-	871	787
1997	AL	162	96	66	.593	2	891	688
1998	AL	162	114	48	.704	-	965	656
1999	AL	162	98	64	.605	-	900	731
2000	AL	161	87	74	.540	-	871	814
2001	AL	160	95	65	.594	-	803	712
2002	AL	161	103	58	.640	-	897	697
2003	AL	162	101	61	.623	-	877	716
2004	AL	162	101	61	.623	-	897	808
2005	AL	162	95	67	.586	-	886	789
2006	AL	162	97	65	.599	-	930	767
TOTAL:	104 years	16112	9171	6941		896.5	78463	67332
AVERAGE:		155	88	67	.569	8.5	754	647

				Playoff Record			
Season	GP	W	L	T	R	OR	Result
1921	8	3	5	0	22	29	Lost World Series to Giants.
1922	5	0	4	1	11	18	Lost World Series to Giants.
1923	6	4	2	0	30	17	**Won World Series.**
1926	7	3	4	0	21	31	Lost World Series to St. Louis.
1927	4	4	0	0	23	10	**Won World Series.**
1928	4	4	0	0	27	10	**Won World Series.**
1932	4	4	0	0	37	19	**Won World Series.**
1936	6	4	2	0	43	23	**Won World Series.**
1937	5	4	1	0	28	12	**Won World Series.**
1938	4	4	0	0	22	9	**Won World Series.**
1939	4	4	0	0	20	8	**Won World Series.**
1941	5	4	1	0	17	11	**Won World Series.**
1942	5	1	4	0	18	23	Lost World Series to St. Louis.
1943	5	4	1	0	17	9	**Won World Series.**
1947	7	4	3	0	38	29	**Won World Series.**
1949	5	4	1	0	21	14	**Won World Series.**
1950	4	4	0	0	11	5	**Won World Series.**
1951	6	4	2	0	29	18	**Won World Series.**
1952	7	4	3	0	26	20	**Won World Series.**
1953	6	4	2	0	33	27	**Won World Series.**
1955	7	3	4	0	26	31	Lost World Series to Brooklyn.
1956	7	4	3	0	33	25	**Won World Series.**
1957	7	3	4	0	25	23	Lost World Series to Milwaukee.
1958	7	4	3	0	29	25	**Won World Series.**
1960	7	3	4	0	55	27	Lost World Series to Pittsburgh.
1961	5	4	1	0	27	13	**Won World Series.**
1962	7	4	3	0	20	21	**Won World Series.**
1963	4	0	4	0	4	12	Lost World Series to Los Angeles.
1964	7	3	4	0	33	32	Lost World Series to St. Louis.
1976	9	3	6	0	31	46	Lost World Series to Cincinnati.
1977	11	7	4	0	47	50	**Won World Series.**
1978	10	7	3	0	55	40	**Won World Series.**
1980	3	0	3	0	6	14	Lost ALCS to Kansas City.
1981	14	8	6	0	61	44	Lost World Series to Los Angeles.

1995	5	2	3	0	33	35	Lost Division Series to Seattle.
1996	15	11	4	0	61	61	**Won World Series.**
1997	5	2	3	0	24	21	Lost Division playoff to Cleveland.
1998	13	11	2	0	62	34	**Won World Series.**
1999	12	11	1	0	58	31	**Won World Series.**
2000	16	11	5	0	69	57	**Won World Series.**
2001	17	10	7	0	57	71	Lost World Series to Arizona.
2002	4	1	3	0	25	31	Lost Division Series to Anaheim.
2003	17	9	8	0	67	52	Lost World Series to Florida.
2004	11	6	5	0	66	58	Lost ALCS to Boston.
2005	5	2	3	0	20	25	Lost Division Series to Los Angeles.
2006	4	1	3	0	14	22	Lost Division Series to Detroit.
TOTAL:	336	201	134	1	1502	1243	
AVERAGE:	7	4	3	0	33	27	

Regular Season Individual Leaders

Season	Home Runs		RBI's		Wins	
1903	Herm McFarland	5	Jimmy Williams	82	Jack Chesbro	21
1904	John Ganzel	6	John Anderson	82	Jack Chesbro	41
	Pat Dougherty	6				
1905	Jimmy Williams	6	Jimmy Williams	62	Jack Chesbro	20
1906	William Conroy	4	Jimmy Williams	77	Al Orth	27
1907	Danny Hoffman	5	Hal Chase	68	Al Orth	14
1908	Harry Niles	4	Charlie Hemphill	44	Jack Chesbro	14
1909	Hal Chase	4	Clyde Engle	71	Joe Lake	14
	Ray Demmitt	4				
1910	Harry Wolter	4	Hal Chase	73	Russ Ford	26
	William Cree	4	William Cree	73		
1911	Harry Wolter	4	Roy Hartzell	91	Russ Ford	22
	William Cree	4				
1912	Guy Zinn	6	Hal Chase	58	Russ Ford	13
1913	Harry Wolter	2	William Cree	63	Ray Fisher	11
	Ed Sweeney	2			Russ Ford	11
1914	Roger Peckinpaugh	3	Roger Peckinpaugh	51	Ray Caldwell	17
1915	Luke Boone	5	Wally Pipp	60	Ray Caldwell	19
	Roger Peckinpaugh	5	Roy Hartzell	60		
1916	Wally Pipp	12	Wally Pipp	93	Bob Shawkey	24
1917	Wally Pipp	9	Frank Baker	71	Bob Shawkey	13
					Ray Caldwell	13
1918	Frank Baker	6	Frank Baker	62	George Mogridge	16
1919	Frank Baker	10	George Lewis	89	Bob Shawkey	20
1920	Babe Ruth	54	Babe Ruth	137	Carl Mays	26
1921	Babe Ruth	59	Babe Ruth	171	Carl Mays	27
1922	Babe Ruth	35	Babe Ruth	99	Joe Bush	26
1923	Babe Ruth	41	Babe Ruth	131	Sam Jones	21
1924	Babe Ruth	46	Babe Ruth	121	Herb Pennock	21
1925	Bob Meusel	33	Bob Meusel	138	Herb Pennock	16
1926	Babe Ruth	47	Babe Ruth	145	Herb Pennock	23
1927	Babe Ruth	60	Lou Gehrig	175	Waite Hoyt	22
1928	Babe Ruth	54	Babe Ruth	142	George Pipgras	24
			Lou Gehrig	142		
1929	Babe Ruth	46	Babe Ruth	154	George Pipgras	18

Season	Home Runs		RBI's		Wins	
1930	Babe Ruth	49	Lou Gehrig	174	Charles Ruffing	15
					George Pipgras	15
1931	Lou Gehrig	46	Lou Gehrig	184	Lefty Gomez	21
	Babe Ruth	46				
1932	Babe Ruth	41	Lou Gehrig	151	Lefty Gomez	24
1933	Babe Ruth	34	Lou Gehrig	139	Lefty Gomez	16
1934	Lou Gehrig	49	Lou Gehrig	165	Lefty Gomez	26
1935	Lou Gehrig	30	Lou Gehrig	119	Charles Ruffing	16
1936	Lou Gehrig	49	Lou Gehrig	152	Charles Ruffing	20
1937	Joe DiMaggio	46	Joe DiMaggio	167	Lefty Gomez	21
1938	Joe DiMaggio	32	Joe DiMaggio	140	Charles Ruffing	21
1939	Joe DiMaggio	30	Joe DiMaggio	126	Charles Ruffing	21
1940	Joe DiMaggio	31	Joe DiMaggio	133	Charles Ruffing	15
1941	Charlie Keller	33	Joe DiMaggio	125	Lefty Gomez	15
					Charles Ruffing	15
1942	Charlie Keller	26	Joe DiMaggio	114	Ernie Bonham	21
1943	Charlie Keller	31	Nick Etten	107	Spud Chandler	20
1944	Nick Etten	22	John Lindell	103	Hank Borowy	17
1945	Nick Etten	18	Nick Etten	111	Bill Bevens	13
1946	Charlie Keller	30	Charlie Keller	101	Spud Chandler	20
1947	Joe DiMaggio	20	Tom Henrich	98	Allie Reynolds	19
1948	Joe DiMaggio	39	Joe DiMaggio	155	Vic Raschi	19
1949	Tom Henrich	24	Yogi Berra	91	Vic Raschi	21
1950	Joe DiMaggio	32	Yogi Berra	124	Vic Raschi	21
1951	Yogi Berra	27	Yogi Berra	88	Ed Lopat	21
					Vic Raschi	21
1952	Yogi Berra	30	Yogi Berra	98	Allie Reynolds	20
1953	Yogi Berra	27	Yogi Berra	108	Edward Ford	18
1954	Mickey Mantle	27	Yogi Berra	125	Bob Grim	20
1955	Mickey Mantle	37	Yogi Berra	108	Edward Ford	18
1956	Mickey Mantle	52	Mickey Mantle	130	Edward Ford	19
1957	Mickey Mantle	34	Mickey Mantle	94	Tom Sturdivant	16
1958	Mickey Mantle	42	Mickey Mantle	97	Bob Turley	21
1959	Mickey Mantle	31	Mickey Mantle	75	Edward Ford	16
1960	Mickey Mantle	40	Roger Maris	112	Art Ditmar	15
1961	Roger Maris	61	Roger Maris	142	Edward Ford	25
1962	Roger Maris	33	Roger Maris	100	Ralph Terry	23
1963	Elston Howard	28	Joe Pepitone	89	Edward Ford	24
1964	Mickey Mantle	35	Mickey Mantle	111	Jim Bouton	18
1965	Tom Tresh	26	Tom Tresh	74	Mel Stottlemyre	20
1966	Joe Pepitone	31	Joe Pepitone	83	Fritz Peterson	12
					Mel Stottlemyre	12
1967	Mickey Mantle	22	Joe Pepitone	64	Mel Stottlemyre	15
1968	Mickey Mantle	18	Roy White	62	Mel Stottlemyre	21
1969	Joe Pepitone	27	Bobby Murcer	82	Mel Stottlemyre	20
1970	Bobby Murcer	23	Roy White	94	Fritz Peterson	20
1971	Bobby Murcer	25	Bobby Murcer	94	Mel Stottlemyre	16
1972	Bobby Murcer	33	Bobby Murcer	96	Fritz Peterson	17
1973	Graig Nettles	22	Bobby Murcer	95	Mel Stottlemyre	16
	Bobby Murcer	22				
1974	Graig Nettles	22	Bobby Murcer	88	Pat Dobson	19
					George Medich	19
1975	Bobby Bonds	32	Thurman Munson	102	James Hunter	23

Season	Home Runs		RBI's		Wins	
1976	Graig Nettles	32	Thurman Munson	105	Ed Figueroa	19
1977	Graig Nettles	37	Reggie Jackson	110	Ron Guidry	16
					Ed Figueroa	16
1978	Graig Nettles	27	Reggie Jackson	97	Ron Guidry	25
	Reggie Jackson	27				
1979	Reggie Jackson	29	Reggie Jackson	89	Tommy John	21
1980	Reggie Jackson	41	Reggie Jackson	111	Tommy John	22
1981	Graig Nettles	15	Dave Winfield	68	Ron Guidry	11
	Reggie Jackson	15				
1982	Dave Winfield	37	Dave Winfield	106	Ron Guidry	14
1983	Dave Winfield	32	Dave Winfield	116	Ron Guidry	21
1984	Don Baylor	27	Don Mattingly	110	Phil Niekro	16
1985	Don Mattingly	35	Don Mattingly	145	Ron Guidry	22
1986	Don Mattingly	31	Don Mattingly	113	Dennis Rasmussen	18
1987	Mike Pagliarulo	32	Don Mattingly	115	Rick Rhoden	16
1988	Jack Clark	27	Dave Winfield	107	John Candelaria	13
1989	Don Mattingly	23	Don Mattingly	113	Andy Hawkins	15
	Jesse Barfield	23				
1990	Jesse Barfield	25	Jesse Barfield	78	Lee Guetterman	11
1991	Matt Nokes	24	Mel Hall	80	Scott Sanderson	16
1992	Danny Tartabull	25	Don Mattingly	86	Melido Perez	13
1993	Danny Tartabull	31	Danny Tartabull	102	Jimmy Key	18
1994	Paul O'Neill	21	Paul O'Neill	83	Jimmy Key	17
1995	Paul O'Neill	22	Paul O'Neill	26	David Cone	15
1996	Cecil Fielder	39	Cecil Fielder	117	Andy Pettitte	21
			Tino Martinez	117		
1997	Tino Martinez	44	Tino Martinez	141	Andy Pettitte	18
1998	Tino Martinez	28	Tino Martinez	123	David Cone	20
1999	Tino Martinez	28	Bernie Williams	115	Orlando Hernandez	17
2000	David Justice	41	Bernie Williams	121	Andy Pettitte	19
2001	Tino Martinez	34	Tino Martinez	113	Roger Clemens	20
2002	Jason Giambi	41	Jason Giambi	122	David Wells	19
2003	Jason Giambi	41	Jason Giambi	107	Andy Pettitte	21
2004	Alex Rodriguez	36	Gary Sheffield	121	Jon Lieber	14
	Gary Sheffield	36				
2005	Alex Rodriguez	48	Alex Rodriguez	130	Randy Johnson	17
2006	Jason Giambi	37	Alex Rodriguez	121	Chien-Ming Wang	19

COACHING HISTORY: 1903-1908 Clark Griffith 419-370-.531; 1908 Norman Elberfeld 27-71-.276; 1909-1910 George Stallings 153-138-.526; 1910-1911 Hal Chase 85-78-.521; 1912 Harry Wolverton 50-102-.329; 1913-1914 Frank Chance 118-170-.410; 1914 Roger Peckinpaugh 9-8-.529; 1915-1917 Bill Donovan 220-239-.479; 1918-1929 Miller Huggins 1067-719-.597; 1929 Art Fletcher 6-5-.545; 1930 Bob Shawkey 86-68-.558; 1931-1946 Joe McCarthy 1460-867-.627; 1946 Bill Dickey 57-48-.543; 1946 Johnny Neun 8-6-.571; 1947-1948 Stanley Harris 191-117-.620; 1949-1960 Casey Stengel 1149-696-.623; 1961-1963 Ralph Houk 309-176-.637; 1964 Yogi Berra 99-63-.611; 1965-1966 Johnny Keane 81-101-.445; 1966-1973 Ralph Houk 635-630-.502; 1974-1975 Bill Virdon 142-124-.534; 1975-1979 Billy Martin 334-232-.590; 1978 Dick Howser 0-1-.000; 1978-1979 Bob Lemon 82-51-.617; 1980 Dick Howser 103-59-.636; 1981-1982 Bob Lemon 17-22-.436; 1981-1982 Gene Michael 92-76-.548; 1982 Clyde King 29-33-.468; 1983 Billy Martin 91-71-.562; 1984-1985 Yogi Berra 93-85-.522; 1985 Billy Martin 91-54-.628; 1986-1988 Lou Pinniella 224-193-.537; 1988 Billy Martin 40-28-.588; 1989 Dallas Green 56-65-.463; 1989-1990 Bucky Dent 36-53-.404; 1990-1991 Stump Merrill 120-155-.436; 1992-1995 Buck Showalter 313-268-.539; 1996-present Joe Torre

NEW YORK YANKEES

Home City: New York, New York
Home Stadium: Yankee Stadium   Capacity: 67,224
Origin of Name: The team was called Yankees because they played in Yankee Stadium.

Regular Season Record

Season	League	GP	W	L	T	PF	PA	Pct
1927	NFL	16	7	8	1	143	174	.469
1928	NFL	13	4	8	1	103	179	.346
TOTAL:	2 years	29	11	16	2	246	353	
AVERAGE:		15	6	8	1	123	177	.414

Regular Season Individual Leaders

Season	Passing Yards		Receiving Yards	Rushing Yards	
1927	Bill Kelly	110		Larry Marks	45
1928	Bill Kelly	441		Gibby Welch	127

COACHING HISTORY: 1927 Ralph Scott 7-8-1-.469; 1928 Dick Rauch 4-8-1-.346

NEW YORK YANKEES

Home City: New York, New York
Home Stadium: Yankee Stadium I   Capacity: 63,800
Origin of Name: The team was owned by Dan Topping, the owner of the baseball Yankees, and was named after them.

Regular Season Record

Season	League	GP	W	L	T	PF	PA	Pct
1946	AAFC	14	10	3	1	270	192	.750
1947	AAFC	14	11	2	1	378	239	.821
1948	AAFC	14	6	8	0	265	301	.429
1949	AAFC	12	8	4	0	196	206	.667
TOTAL:	4 years	54	35	17	2	1109	938	
AVERAGE:		14	9	4	1	277	235	.667

Playoff Record

Season	GP	W	L	PF	PA	Result
1946	1	0	1	9	14	Lost Championship game to Cleveland.
1947	1	0	1	3	14	Lost Championship game to Cleveland.
TOTAL:	2	0	2	12	28	
AVERAGE:	1	0	1	6	14	

Regular Season Individual Leaders

Season	Passing Yards		Receiving Yards		Rushing Yards	
1946	Ace Parker	763	Spec Sanders	259	Spec Sanders	709
1947	Spec Sanders	1442	Jack Russell	368	Spec Sanders	1432
1948	Spec Sanders	918	Bruce Alford	578	Spec Sanders	759
1949	Don Panciera	801	Bruce Alford	213	Buddy Young	495

COACHING HISTORY: 1946-1948 Ray Flaherty 23-11-2-.667; 1948-1949 Red Strader 12-10-0-.545

NEW YORK YANKS
(became Dallas Texans)

Home City: New York, New York
Home Stadium: Polo Grounds (1949)   Capacity: 55,987
Home Stadium: Yankee Stadium I (1950-1951)   Capacity: 63,800
Origin of Name: Adapted from previous sports teams in the city. Were known during their first
years as the New York Bulldogs.

Regular Season Record

Season	League	GP	W	L	T	PF	PA	Pct
1949	NFL	12	1	10	1	153	368	.125
1950	NFL	12	7	5	0	366	367	.583
1951	NFL	12	1	9	2	241	382	.167
TOTAL:	3 years	36	9	24	3	760	1117	
AVERAGE:		12	3	8	1	253	372	.292

Regular Season Individual Leaders

Season	Passing Yards		Receiving Yards		Rushing Yards	
1949	Bobby Layne	1796	Bill Chipley	631	Joe Osmanski	312
1950	G. Ratterman	2251	Dan Edwards	775	Zollie Toth	636
1951	Bob Celeri	1797	Dan Edwards	509	Zollie Toth	384

COACHING HISTORY: 1949 Charley Ewart 1-10-1-.125; 1950-1951 Red Strader 8-14-2-.375

NEWARK PEPPERS

Home City: Harrison, New Jersey
Home Field: Harrison Field   Capacity: 21,000 [1915]
Origin of Name:

Regular Season Record

Season	League	GP	W	L	Pct	GB	R	OR
1915	FL	152	80	72	.526	6	585	562

Regular Season Individual Leaders

Season	Home Runs		RBI's		Wins	
1915	Jimmy Esmond	5	Jimmy Esmond	62	Ed Reulbach	21

COACHING HISTORY: Bill Phillips 26-27-.491; Bill McKechnie 54-45-.545

NEWARK TORNADOES
(were Orange Tornadoes)

Home City: Newark, New Jersey
Home Stadium: Newark Velodrome
Origin of Name: The team kept the same name when it moved from Orange to Newark.

Regular Season Record

Season	League	GP	W	L	T	PF	PA	Pct
1930	NFL	12	1	10	1	51	190	.125

Regular Season Individual Leaders

Season	Passing Yards		Receiving Yards		Rushing Yards	
1930	Frank Kirkleski	117			Frank Kirkleski	28

COACHING HISTORY: John Depler 1-10-1-.125

OAKLAND ATHLETICS
(were Kansas City Athletics)

Home City: Oakland, California
Home Field: McAfee Coliseum *   Capacity: 34,007 [2006]
Origin of Name: The team kept the same nickname when it moved from Kansas City to Oakland.

Regular Season Record

Season	League	GP	W	L	Pct	GB	R	OR
1968	AL	162	82	80	.506	21	569	544
1969	AL	162	88	74	.543	9	740	678
1970	AL	162	89	73	.549	9	678	593
1971	AL	161	101	60	.627	-	691	564
1972	AL	155	93	62	.600	-	604	457
1973	AL	162	94	68	.580	-	758	615
1974	AL	162	90	72	.556	-	689	551
1975	AL	162	98	64	.605	-	758	606
1976	AL	161	87	74	.540	2.5	686	598
1977	AL	161	63	98	.391	38.5	605	749
1978	AL	162	69	93	.426	23	532	690
1979	AL	162	54	108	.333	34	573	860
1980	AL	162	83	79	.512	14	686	642
1981	AL	109	64	45	.587	NA	458	403
1982	AL	162	68	94	.420	25	691	819
1983	AL	162	74	88	.457	25	708	782
1984	AL	162	77	85	.475	7	738	796
1985	AL	162	77	85	.475	14	757	787
1986	AL	162	76	86	.469	16	731	760
1987	AL	162	81	81	.500	4	806	789
1988	AL	162	104	58	.642	-	800	620
1989	AL	162	99	63	.611	-	712	576
1990	AL	162	103	59	.636	-	733	570
1991	AL	162	84	78	.519	11	760	776
1992	AL	162	96	66	.593	-	745	672
1993	AL	162	68	94	.420	26	715	846
1994	AL	114	51	63	.447	1	549	589
1995	AL	144	67	77	.465	11	730	761
1996	AL	162	78	84	.481	12	861	900
1997	AL	162	65	97	.401	25	763	946
1998	AL	162	74	88	.457	14	803	866
1999	AL	162	87	75	.537	8	893	846
2000	AL	161	91	70	.565	-	947	813
2001	AL	162	102	60	.630	14	884	646
2002	AL	162	103	59	.636	-	800	654
2003	AL	162	96	66	.593	-	768	643
2004	AL	162	91	71	.562	1	793	742
2005	AL	162	88	74	.543	7	772	658
2006	AL	162	93	69	.574	-	771	727
TOTAL:	39 years	6188	3248	2940		372	28257	27134
AVERAGE:		158	83	75	.525	9.5	725	696

*-known as Oakland Alameda County Coliseum 1968-1998 and Network Associates Coliseum
from 1999 to 2004.

Playoff Record

Season	GP	W	L	R	OR	Result
1971	3	0	3	7	15	Lost ALCS to Baltimore.
1972	12	7	5	29	31	**Won World Series.**
1973	12	7	5	36	39	**Won World Series.**
1974	9	7	2	27	18	**Won World Series.**
1975	3	0	3	6	18	Lost ALCS to Boston.
1981	6	3	3	14	22	Lost ALCS to New York.
1988	9	5	4	31	32	Lost World Series to Los Angeles.
1989	9	8	1	58	35	**Won World Series.**
1990	8	4	4	28	26	Lost World Series to Cincinnati.
1992	6	2	4	24	31	Lost ALCS to Toronto.
2000	5	2	3	23	19	Lost Division Semifinal to Yankees.
2001	5	2	3	12	18	Lost Division Semifinal to Yankees.
2002	5	2	3	26	27	Lost Division Semifinal to Minnesota.
2003	5	2	3	18	17	Lost Division Semifinal to Boston.
2006	7	3	4	25	29	Lost ALCS to Detroit.
TOTAL:	104	54	50	364	377	
AVERAGE:	7	4	3	24	25	

Regular Season Individual Leaders

Season	Home Runs		RBI's		Wins	
1968	Reggie Jackson	29	Reggie Jackson	74	John Odom	16
1969	Reggie Jackson	47	Reggie Jackson	118	John Odom	15
					Chuck Dobson	15
1970	Don Mincher	27	Sal Bando	75	James Hunter	18
1971	Reggie Jackson	32	Sal Bando	94	Vida Blue	24
1972	Mike Epstein	26	Sal Bando	77	James Hunter	21
1973	Reggie Jackson	32	Reggie Jackson	117	James Hunter	21
					Ken Holtzman	21
1974	Reggie Jackson	29	Sal Bando	103	James Hunter	25
1975	Reggie Jackson	36	Reggie Jackson	104	Vida Blue	22
1976	Sal Bando	27	Joe Rudi	94	Vida Blue	18
1977	Wayne Gross	22	Mitchell Page	75	Vida Blue	14
1978	Mitchell Page	17	Mitchell Page	70	John H. Johnson	11
1979	Jeff Newman	22	Dave Revering	77	Rick Langford	12
1980	Tony Armas	35	Tony Armas	109	Mike Norris	22
1981	Tony Armas	22	Tony Armas	76	Steve McCatty	14
1982	Tony Armas	28	Dwayne Murphy	94	Rick Langford	11
					Matt Keough	11
1983	Davey Lopes	17	Dwayne Murphy	75	Chris Codiroli	12
	Dwayne Murphy	17				
1984	Dave Kingman	35	Dave Kingman	118	Ray Burris	13
1985	Dave Kingman	30	Dave Kingman	91	Chris Codiroli	14
1986	Dave Kingman	35	Jose Canseco	117	Curt Young	13
1987	Mark McGwire	49	Mark McGwire	118	Dave Stewart	20
1988	Jose Canseco	42	Jose Canseco	124	Dave Stewart	21
1989	Mark McGwire	33	Dave Parker	97	Dave Stewart	21
1990	Mark McGwire	39	Mark McGwire	108	Bob Welch	27
1991	Jose Canseco	44	Jose Canseco	122	Mike Moore	17
1992	Mark McGwire	42	Mark McGwire	104	Mike Moore	17
1993	Ruben Sierra	22	Ruben Sierra	101	Bobby Witt	14
1994	Ruben Sierra	23	Ruben Sierra	92	Ron Darling	10
1995	Mark McGwire	39	Mark McGwire	90	Kevin Appier	15

Season	Home Runs		RBI's		Wins	
1996	Mark McGwire	52	Mark McGwire	113	John Wasdin	8
1997	Mark McGwire	34	Jason Giambi	81	Aaron Small	9
			Mark McGwire	81		
1998	Jason Giambi	27	Jason Giambi	110	Kenny Rogers	16
1999	Matt Stairs	38	Jason Giambi	123	Kevin Appier	16
2000	Jason Giambi	43	Jason Giambi	137	Tim Hudson	20
2001	Jason Giambi	38	Jason Giambi	120	Mark Mulder	21
2002	Eric Chavez	34	Miguel Tejada	131	Barry Zito	23
	Miguel Tejada	34				
2003	Eric Chavez	29	Miguel Tejada	106	Tim Hudson	16
2004	Eric Chavez	29	Erubiel Durazo	88	Mark Mulder	17
2005	Eric Chavez	27	Eric Chavez	101	Danny Harren	14
2006	Frank Thomas	39	Frank Thomas	114	Joe Blanton	16
					Barry Zito	16

COACHING HISTORY: 1968 Bob Kennedy 82-80-.506; 1969 Hank Bauer 80-69-.537; 1969-1970 John McNamara 97-78-.554; 1971-1973 Dick Williams 288-190-.603; 1974-1975 Alvin Dark 188-136-.580; 1976 Charles Tanner 87-74-.540; 1977-1978 Jack McKeon 71-105-.403; 1977-1978 Bobby Winkles 61-86-.415; 1979 Jim Marshall 54-108-.333; 1980-1982 Billy Martin 215-218-.497; 1983-1984 Steve Boros 94-112-.456; 1984-1986 Jackie Moore 163-190-.462; 1986 Jeff Newman 2-8-.200; 1986-1995 Tony LaRussa 798-673-.542; 1996-2002 Art Howe 600-533-.530; 2003-2005 Ken Macha

OAKLAND CLIPPERS

Home City: Oakland, California
Home Field: Oakland Coliseum   Capacity: 50,000
Origin of Name: The name was suggested by the clipper ships that made the city their home port.

Regular Season Record

Season	League	GP	W	L	T	GF	GA	BP	Pts	Pct
1967	NPSL	32	19	8	5	64	34	NA	185	.642
1968	NASL	32	18	8	6	71	38	59	185	.642
TOTAL:	2 years	64	37	16	11	135	72	59	370	
AVERAGE:		32	19	8	5	68	36	30	185	.642

Playoff Record

Season	GP	W	L	T	GF	GA	Result
1967	2	1	1	0	4	2	Won NPSL Championship.

Regular Season Individual Leaders

Season	Goals		Points		GAA (360 Min)	
1967	Ilija Mitic	13	Ilija Mitic	29	Mirko Stojanovic	1.00
1968	Ilija Mitic	18	Ilija Mitic	48	Mirko Stojanovic	1.12

COACHING HISTORY: 1967-1968 Ivan Toplak 37-16-11-.642

OAKLAND INVADERS

Home City: Oakland, California
Home Stadium: Oakland Coliseum   Capacity: 54,615 [1984]
Origin of Name: The name was adopted to rival the NFL's Raiders.

Regular Season Record

Season	League	GP	W	L	T	PF	PA	Pct
1983	USFL	18	9	9	0	319	317	.500
1984	USFL	18	7	11	0	242	348	.389
1985	USFL	18	13	4	1	473	359	.750
TOTAL:	3 years	54	29	24	1	1034	1024	
AVERAGE:		18	10	8	0	345	341	.546

Playoff Record

Season	GP	W	L	PF	PA	Result
1983	1	0	1	21	37	Lost 1st Round game to Michigan.
1985	3	2	1	100	74	Lost Championship game to Baltimore.
TOTAL:	4	2	2	121	111	
AVERAGE:	2	1	1	61	56	

Regular Season Individual Leaders

Season	Passing Yards		Receiving Yards		Rushing Yards	
1983	Fred Besana	3980	Raymond Chester	951	A. Whittington	1157
1984	Fred Besana	2792	Gordon Banks	937	Eric Jordan	744
1985	Bobby Hebert	3811	Anthony Carter	1323	Albert Bentley	1020

COACHING HISTORY: 1983-1984 John Ralston 9-12-0-.429; 1984 Chuck Hutchison 7-8-0-.467; 1985 Charlie Sumner 13-4-1-.750

OAKLAND OAKS
(became Washington Capitols)

Home City: Oakland, California
Home Court: Oakland County Coliseum   Capacity: 12,500
Origin of Name: The was name was adopted from the Pacific Coast League baseball team.

Regular Season Record

Season	League	GP	W	L	PPGF	PPGA	Pct	GB
1967-1968	ABA	78	22	56	110.8	117.4	.282	26
1968-1969	ABA	78	60	18	126.5	118.1	.769	-
TOTAL:	2 years	156	82	74				26
AVERAGE:		78	41	37	118.7	117.8	.526	13

Playoff Record

Season	GP	W	L	PPGF	PPGA	Result
1968-1969	16	12	4	124.8	117.3	Won ABA championship.

Regular Season Individual Leaders

Season	Field Goal % (min. 70 games)		Points		Points per Game (min. 70 games)	
1967-68	Jim Hadnot	.467	Jim Hadnot	1344	Jim Hadnot	17.5
1968-69	Jim Eakins	.543	W. Armstrong	1530	W. Armstrong	21.5

COACHING HISTORY: 1967-1968 Bruce Hale 22-56-.282; 1968-1969 Alex Hannum 60-18-.769

OAKLAND RAIDERS
(became Los Angeles Raiders)

Home City: San Francisco, California (1960-1961)
Oakland, California (1962-1981)
Home Stadium: Kesar Stadium (1960)   Capacity: 59,636
Candlestick Park (1961)   Capacity: 42,500
Frank Youell Field (1962-1965)   Capacity: 20,000
Oakland-Alameda County Coliseum (1966-1981)   Capacity: 54,615 [1981]
Origin of Name: The name was chosen by team executives.

Regular Season Record

Season	League	GP	W	L	T	PF	PA	Pct
1960	AFL	14	6	8	0	319	388	.429
1961	AFL	14	2	12	0	237	458	.143
1962	AFL	14	1	13	0	213	370	.071
1963	AFL	14	10	4	0	363	288	.714
1964	AFL	14	5	7	2	303	350	.417
1965	AFL	14	8	5	1	298	239	.615
1966	AFL	14	8	5	1	315	288	.615
1967	AFL	14	13	1	0	468	233	.929
1968	AFL	14	12	2	0	453	233	.857
1969	AFL	14	12	1	1	377	242	.923
1970	NFL	14	8	4	2	300	293	.667
1971	NFL	14	8	4	2	344	278	.667
1972	NFL	14	10	3	1	365	248	.750
1973	NFL	14	9	4	1	292	175	.679
1974	NFL	14	12	2	0	355	228	.857
1975	NFL	14	11	3	0	375	255	.786
1976	NFL	14	13	1	0	350	237	.929
1977	NFL	14	11	3	0	351	230	.786
1978	NFL	16	9	7	0	311	283	.563
1979	NFL	16	9	7	0	365	337	.563
1980	NFL	16	11	5	0	364	306	.688
1981	NFL	16	7	9	0	273	343	.438
TOTAL:	22 years	316	195	110	11	7391	6302	
AVERAGE:		14	9	5	0	336	286	.634

Playoff Record

Season	GP	W	L	PF	PA	Result
1967	1	1	0	40	7	Lost Super Bowl to Green Bay.
1968	2	1	1	64	33	Lost AFL Championship to N.Y. Jets.
1969	2	1	1	63	24	Lost AFL Championship to Kansas City.
1970	2	1	1	38	41	Lost AFC Championship to Baltimore.
1972	1	0	1	7	13	Lost Divisional playoff to Pittsburgh.
1973	2	1	1	43	41	Lost AFC Championship to Miami.
1974	2	1	1	41	50	Lost AFC Championship to Pittsburgh.
1975	2	1	1	41	44	Lost AFC Championship to Pittsburgh.
1976	3	3	0	80	42	**Won Super Bowl XI.**
1977	2	1	1	54	51	Lost AFC Championship to Denver.
1980	4	4	0	102	56	**Won Super Bowl XV.**
TOTAL:	23	15	8	573	402	
AVERAGE:	2	1	1	52	37	

Regular Season Individual Leaders

Season	Passing Yards		Receiving Yards		Rushing Yards	
1960	Tom Flores	1738	Billy Lott	524	Tony Teresa	608
1961	Tom Flores	2176	Doug Asad	501	Wayne Crow	490
1962	Cotton Davidson	1977	Bo Roberson	374	Clem Daniels	766
1963	Tom Flores	2101	Art Powell	1304	Clem Daniels	1099
1964	Cotton Davidson	2497	Art Powell	1361	Clem Daniels	824
1965	Tom Flores	1593	Art Powell	800	Clem Daniels	884
1966	Tom Flores	2638	Art Powell	1026	Clem Daniels	801
1967	Daryle Lamonica	3228	Fred Biletnikoff	876	Clem Daniels	575
1968	Daryle Lamonica	3245	Warren Wells	1137	Hewritt Dixon	865
1969	Daryle Lamonica	3302	Warren Wells	1260	Charlie Smith	600
1970	Daryle Lamonica	2516	Warren Wells	935	Hewritt Dixon	861
1971	Daryle Lamonica	1717	Fred Biletnikoff	929	Marv Hubbard	867
1972	Daryle Lamonica	1998	Fred Biletnikoff	802	Marv Hubbard	1100
1973	Ken Stabler	1997	Mike Siani	742	Marv Hubbard	903
1974	Ken Stabler	2469	Cliff Branch	1092	Marv Hubbard	865
1975	Ken Stabler	2296	Cliff Branch	893	Pete Banaszak	672
1976	Ken Stabler	2737	Cliff Branch	1111	Mark van Eeghen	1012
1977	Ken Stabler	2176	Dave Casper	584	Mark van Eeghen	1273
1978	Ken Stabler	2944	Dave Casper	852	Mark van Eeghen	1080
1979	Ken Stabler	3615	Cliff Branch	844	Mark van Eeghen	818
1980	Jim Plunkett	2299	Cliff Branch	858	Mark van Eeghen	838
1981	Marc Wilson	2311	Derrick Ramsey	674	Kenny King	828

COACHING HISTORY: 1960 Eddie Erdelatz 6-8-0-143; 1961-1962 Marty Feldman 2-17-0-.105; 1962 Red Conkright 1-8-0-.111; 1963-1965 Al Davis 23-16-3-.583; 1966-1968 John Rauch 33-8-1-.779; 1969-1978 John Madden 103-32-7-.750; 1979-1981 Tom Flores 27-21-0-.563

OAKLAND RAIDERS
(were Los Angeles Raiders)

Home City: Oakland, California
Home Stadium: McAfee Coliseum *   Capacity: 63,132 [2005]
Origin of Name: The team kept the same nickname when it moved from Los Angeles to Oakland.

Regular Season Record

Season	League	GP	W	L	T	PF	PA	Pct
1995	NFL	16	8	8	0	348	332	.500
1996	NFL	16	7	9	0	340	293	.438
1997	NFL	16	4	12	0	324	419	.250
1998	NFL	16	8	8	0	288	356	.500
1999	NFL	16	8	8	0	390	329	.500
2000	NFL	16	12	4	0	479	299	.750
2001	NFL	16	10	6	0	399	327	.625
2002	NFL	16	11	5	0	450	304	.688
2003	NFL	16	4	12	0	270	379	.250
2004	NFL	16	5	11	0	320	442	.313
2005	NFL	16	4	12	0	290	383	.250
2006	NFL	16	2	14	0	168	332	.125
TOTAL:	12 years	192	83	109	0	4066	4195	
AVERAGE:		16	7	9	0	339	350	.432

*-known as Oakland Alameda County Coliseum from 1995 to 1998 and Network Associates Coliseum from 1999 to 2004.

Playoff Record

Season	GP	W	L	PF	PA	Result
2000	2	1	1	30	16	Lost Conference Final to Baltimore.
2001	2	1	1	51	40	Lost Conference Final to New England.
2002	3	2	1	92	82	Lost Super Bowl to Tampa Bay.
TOTAL:	7	4	3	173	138	
AVERAGE:	2	1	1	58	46	

Regular Season Individual Leaders

Season	Passing Yards		Receiving Yards		Rushing Yards	
1995	Jeff Hostetler	1998	Tim Brown	1342	Harvey Williams	1114
1996	Jeff Hostetler	2548	Tim Brown	1104	N. Kaufman	874
1997	Jeff George	3917	Tim Brown	1408	N. Kaufman	1294
1998	Donald Hollas	1754	Tim Brown	1012	N. Kaufman	921
1999	Rich Gannon	3840	Tim Brown	1344	Tyrone Wheatley	936
2000	Rich Gannon	3430	Tim Brown	1128	Tyrone Wheatley	1046
2001	Rich Gannon	3828	Tim Brown	1165	Charlie Garner	839
2002	Rich Gannon	4689	Jerry Rice	1211	Charlie Garner	962
2003	Rich Gannon	1274	Jerry Rice	869	Tyrone Wheatley	678
2004	Kerry Collins	3495	Jerry Porter	998	Amos Zereoue	425
2005	Kerry Collins	3759	Randy Moss	1005	LaMont Jordan	1025
2006	Andrew Walter	1677	Ronald Curry	727	Justin Fargas	659

COACHING HISTORY: 1995-1996 Mike White 15-17-0-.469; 1997 Joe Bugel 4-12-0-.250; 1998-2001 Jon Gruden 38-26-0-.594; 2002-2003 Bill Callahan 15-17-0-.469; 2004-2005 Norv Turner 9-23-0-.281; 2006 Art Shell 2-14-0-.125; 2007-present

OAKLAND STOMPERS
(were Connecticut Bicentennials)
(became Edmonton Drillers)

Home City: Oakland, California
Home Field: Oakland Alameda County Coliseum   Capacity: 54,037 [1978]
Origin of Name: The name was chosen to honor California's wine making industry.

Regular Season Record

Season	League	GP	W	L	GF	GA	BP	Pts	Pct
1978	NASL	30	12	18	34	59	31	103	.381

Regular Season Individual Leaders

Season	Goals		Points		GAA (360 Min)	
1978	Charlie Mrosko	11	Charlie Mrosko	25	Gene DuChateau	1.76

COACHING HISTORY: Mirko Stojanovic 4-4; Ken Bracewell 7-13; Shep Messing & Dick Berg & Charlie Mrosko 1-1

OHIO GLORY

Home City: Columbus, Ohio
Home Stadium: Ohio Stadium (Ohio State University)   Capacity: 86,071 [1992]
Origin of Name:

Regular Season Record

Season	League	GP	W	L	T	PF	PA	Pct
1992	WFL	10	1	9	0	132	230	.100

Regular Season Individual Leaders

Season	Passing Yards	Receiving Yards		Rushing Yards	
1992		Willie Wilson	776	Amir Rasul	572

COACHING HISTORY: Larry Little 1-9-0-.100

OKLAHOMA OUTLAWS
(merged with Arizona for the 1985 season)

Home City: Tulsa, Oklahoma
Home Stadium: Skelly Stadium   Capacity: 40,235 [1984]
Origin of Name: The name was chosen by team executives.

Regular Season Record

Season	League	GP	W	L	T	PF	PA	Pct
1984	USFL	18	6	12	0	251	459	.333

Regular Season Individual Leaders

Season	Passing Yards		Receiving Yards		Rushing Yards	
1984	Doug Williams	3084	Al Williams	1087	Ernest Anderson	298

COACHING HISTORY: Woody Widenhofer 6-12-0-.333

OORANG INDIANS

Home City: Marion, Ohio
Home Stadium: Lincoln Park
Origin of Name: The team was composed entirely of native Americans.

Regular Season Record

Season	League	GP	W	L	T	PF	PA	Pct
1922	NFL	8	2	6	0	51	184	.250
1923	NFL	11	1	10	0	49	247	.045
TOTAL:	2 years	19	3	16	0	100	431	
AVERAGE:		10	2	8	0	50	216	.079

Regular Season Individual Leaders

Season	Passing Yards		Receiving Yards		Rushing Yards	
1922	Joe Guyon	101	Pete Calac	81	Joe Guyon	214
1923	Jim Thorpe	188	Joe Guyon	66	Jim Thorpe	20

COACHING HISTORY: 1922-1923 Jim Thorpe 3-16-0-.079

ORANGE TORNADOES
(became Newark Tornadoes)

Home City: Orange, New Jersey
Home Stadium: Casey Stadium
Origin of Name: The team was also known as the Orange A.C.'s.

Regular Season Record

Season	League	GP	W	L	T	PF	PA	Pct
1929	NFL	11	3	4	4	35	80	.455

Regular Season Individual Leaders

Season	Passing Yards		Receiving Yards	Rushing Yards	
1929	Frank Kirkleski	103		Carl Waite	103

COACHING HISTORY: John Depler 3-4-4-.455

ORLANDO MAGIC

Home City: Orlando, Florida
Home Court: TD Waterhouse Center **   Capacity: 17,248 [2006]
Origin of Name: The team name was chosen in a contest sponsored by the club and the *Orlando Sentinel*.

Regular Season Record

Season	League	GP	W	L	PPGF	PPGA	Pct	GB
1989-1990	NBA	82	18	64	110.9	119.8	.220	40
1990-1991	NBA	82	31	51	105.9	109.9	.378	24
1991-1992	NBA	82	21	61	101.6	108.5	.256	30
1992-1993	NBA	82	41	41	105.5	104.2	.500	19
1993-1994	NBA	82	50	32	105.7	101.8	.610	7
1994-1995	NBA	82	57	25	110.9	103.8	.695	-
1995-1996	NBA	82	60	22	104.5	99.0	.732	-
1996-1997	NBA	82	45	37	94.1	94.5	.549	16
1997-1998	NBA	82	41	41	90.1	91.2	.500	14
1998-1999	NBA	50	33	17	89.5	86.9	.660	-
1999-2000	NBA	82	41	41	100.1	99.4	.500	11
2000-2001	NBA	82	43	39	97.6	96.5	.524	13
2001-2002	NBA	82	44	38	100.5	98.9	.537	8
2002-2003	NBA	82	42	40	98.5	98.4	.512	7
2003-2004	NBA	82	21	61	94.0	101.1	.256	26
2004-2005	NBA	82	36	46	99.5	97.5	.439	23
2005-2006	NBA	82	36	46	94.9	96.0	.439	16
TOTAL:	17 years	1362	660	702				254
AVERAGE:		80	39	41	100.5	100.6	.485	15

Playoff Record

Season	GP	W	L	PPGF	PPGA	Result
1993-1994	3	0	3	91.7	97.0	Lost 1st Round series to Indiana.
1994-1995	21	11	10	102.4	101.1	Lost Championship series to Houston.
1995-1996	12	7	5	98.3	96.7	Lost Conference Final to Chicago.
1996-1997	5	2	3	84.2	92.0	Lost 1st Round series to Miami.
1998-1999	4	1	3	86.3	92.5	Lost 1st Round series to Philadelphia.
2000-2001	4	1	3	102.8	108.5	Lost 1st Round series to Milwaukee.
2001-2002	4	1	3	93.8	98.8	Lost 1st Round series to Charlotte.
2002-2003	7	3	4	87.6	94.9	Lost 1st Round series to Detroit.
TOTAL:	60	26	34			
AVERAGE:	7	3	4	96.2	98.3	

Regular Season Individual Leaders

Season	Field Goal % (min. 70 games)		Points		Points per Game (min. 70 games)	
1989-90	Michael Ansley	.497	Reggie Theus	1438	Terry Catledge	19.4
1990-91	Greg Kite	.491	Scott Skiles	1357	Scott Skiles	17.2

**-known as Orlando Arena 1989-2000.

Season	Field Goal % (min. 70 games)		Points		Points per Game (min. 70 games)	
1991-92	Terry Catledge	.496	Nick Anderson	1196	Terry Catledge	14.8
1992-93	Shaquille O'Neal	.562	Shaquille O'Neal	1893	Shaquille O'Neal	23.4
1993-94	Shaquille O'Neal	.599	Shaquille O'Neal	2377	Shaquille O'Neal	29.3
1994-95	Shaquille O'Neal	.583	Shaquille O'Neal	2315	Shaquille O'Neal	29.3
1995-96	A. Hardaway	.513	A. Hardaway	1780	A. Hardaway	21.7
1996-97	Rony Seikaly	.507	Rony Seikaly	1277	Rony Seikaly	17.3
1997-98	Bo Outlaw	.554	Horace Grant	921	Horace Grant	12.1
1998-99*	Michael Doleac	.468	A. Hardaway	791	A. Hardaway	15.8
1999-00	Bo Outlaw	.602	D. Armstrong	1330	Ron Mercer	16.9
2000-01	Bo Outlaw	.614	Tracy McGrady	2065	Tracy McGrady	26.8
2001-02	Horace Grant	.513	Tracy McGrady	1948	Tracy McGrady	25.6
2002-03	Andrew DeClercq	.534	Tracy McGrady	2407	Tracy McGrady	32.1
2003-04	Juwan Howard	.453	Tracy McGrady	1878	Juwan Howard	17.0
2004-05	Dwight Howard	.520	Steve Francis	1663	Steve Francis	21.3
2005-06	Dwight Howard	.531	Dwight Howard	1292	Dwight Howard	15.8

COACHING HISTORY: 1989-1993 Matt Guokas 111-217-.338; 1993-1997 Brian Hill 191-104-.647; 1996-1997 Richie Adubato 21-12-.636; 1997-1999 Chuck Daly 74-58-.561; 1999-2004 Doc Rivers 171-168-.504; 2003-2005 Johnny Davis 51-84-.378; 2004-2005 Chris Jent 5-13-.278; 2005-present Brian Hill

ORLANDO MIRACLE
(became Connecticut Sun)

Home City: Orlando, Florida
Home Arena: TD Waterhouse Center**   Capacity: 17,248 [2001]
Origin of Name: The name was chosen to show affiliation with the NBA's Magic.

Regular Season Record

Season	League	GP	W	L	PPGF	PPGA	Pct	GB
1999	WNBA	32	15	17	68.9	69.3	.469	3
2000	WNBA	32	16	16	69.0	69.7	.500	4
2001	WNBA	32	13	19	66.9	68.9	.406	9
2002	WNBA	32	16	16	70.4	70.5	.500	2
TOTAL:	4 years	128	60	68				18
AVERAGE:		32	15	17	68.8	69.6	.469	5

Playoff Record

Season	GP	W	L	PPGF	PPGA	Result
2000	3	1	2	53.0	63.3	Lost Conference Semifinal to Cleveland.

Regular Season Individual Leaders

Season	Field Goals % (20 games min.)		Free Throws % (20 games min.)		Points per Game (20 games min.)	
1999	A. Congreaves	.500	Carla McGhee	.833	Shannon Johnson	14.0
2000	Taj McWilliams	.524	A. Johnson	.895	Taj McWilliams	13.7
2001	Taj McWilliams	.474	Nykesha Sales	.784	Nykesha Sales	13.5
2002	C. Machanguana	.535	Katie Douglas	.866	Shannon Johnson	16.1

COACHING HISTORY: 1999-2001 Carolyn Peck 44-52-.458; 2002 Dee Brown 16-16-.500

*-minimum 40 games, **-known as Orlando Arena from 1999-2000

ORLANDO RENEGADES
(were Washington Federals)

Home City: Orlando, Florida
Home Stadium: Citrus Bowl   Capacity: 50,050 [1985]
Origin of Name: The team was named by owner Donald Dizney. In his words "Any time you comb your hair a little different you have to have a little renegade blood in you. And we hope to be a little different."

Regular Season Record

Season	League	GP	W	L	T	PF	PA	Pct
1985	USFL	18	5	13	0	308	481	.278

Regular Season Individual Leaders

Season	Passing Yards		Receiving Yards		Rushing Yards	
1985	Reggie Collier	2578	Joey Walters	784	Curtis Bledsoe	781

COACHING HISTORY: Lee Corso 5-13-0-.278

ORLANDO THUNDER

Home City: Orlando, Florida
Home Stadium: Florida Citrus Bowl   Capacity: 52,300 [1992]
Origin of Name:

Regular Season Record

Season	League	GP	W	L	T	PF	PA	Pct
1991	WLAF	10	5	5	0	242	286	.500
1992	WFL	10	8	2	0	247	127	.800
TOTAL:	2 years	20	13	7	0	489	413	
AVERAGE:		10	7	3	0	245	207	.650

Playoff Record

Season	GP	W	L	PF	PA	Result
1992	2	1	1	62	28	Lost Championship game to Sacramento.

Regular Season Individual Leaders

Season	Passing Yards		Receiving Yards		Rushing Yards	
1991	Kerwin Bell	2214	Byron Williams	811	Jones	288
1992			Darryl Clack	517	J. H. Johnson	687

COACHING HISTORY: 1991 Don Matthews 5-5-0-.500; 1992 Galen Hall 8-2-0-.800

OSHKOSH ALL-STARS

Home City: Oshkosh, Wisconsin
Home Court: South Park Junior High School Gym   Capacity: 2,200
Origin of Name:

Regular Season Record

Season	League	GP	W	L	PPGF	PPGA	Pct	GB
1937-1938	NBL	14	12	2	49.1	35.2	.857	-
1938-1939	NBL	28	17	11	41.2	36.1	.607	-
1939-1940	NBL	28	15	13	42.7	40.2	.536	-
1940-1941	NBL	24	18	6	42.2	37.1	.750	-
1941-1942	NBL	24	20	4	49.3	40.7	.833	-

1942-1943	NBL	23	11	12	44.4	44.2	.478	6
1943-1944	NBL	22	7	15	42.1	43.5	.318	11
1944-1945	NBL	30	12	18	46.9	48.2	.400	7
1945-1946	NBL	34	19	15	53.4	49.2	.559	2
1946-1947	NBL	44	28	16	58.0	55.3	.636	-
1947-1948	NBL	60	29	31	59.7	59.6	.483	14
1948-1949	NBL	64	37	27	60.9	59.0	.578	-
TOTAL:	12 years	395	225	170				40
AVERAGE:		33	19	14	49.2	45.7	.570	3

Playoff Record

Season	GP	W	L	PPGF	PPGA	Result
1937-1938	5	3	2	35.0	33.2	Lost Championship series to Akron.
1938-1939	5	2	3	36.8	40.0	Lost Championship series to Akron.
1939-1940	8	4	4	44.1	39.5	Lost Championship series to Akron.
1940-1941	5	5	0	45.6	36.2	**Won NBL Championship.**
1941-1942	5	4	1	53.4	49.6	**Won NBL Championship.**
1942-1943	2	0	2	42.5	53.0	Lost 1st Round series to Sheboygan.
1943-1944	3	1	2	30.7	34.7	Lost 1st Round series to Sheboygan.
1945-1946	5	2	3	51.6	51.6	Lost 1st Round series to Sheboygan.
1946-1947	7	3	4	50.3	50.1	Lost 2nd Round series to Chicago.
1947-1948	4	1	3	51.4	70.0	Lost 1st Round series to Minneapolis.
1948-1949	7	3	4	68.4	68.3	Lost 2nd Round series to Anderson.
TOTAL:	56	28	28			
AVERAGE:	5	3	2	46.3	47.8	

Regular Season Individual Leaders

Season	Field Goals		Free Throws		Points	
1937-38	Leroy Edwards	83	Leroy Edwards	44	Leroy Edwards	210
1938-39	Leroy Edwards	124	Leroy Edwards	86	Leroy Edwards	334
1939-40	Leroy Edwards	111	Leroy Edwards	139	Leroy Edwards	361
1940-41	Leroy Edwards	57	Leroy Edwards	76	Leroy Edwards	190
1941-42	Leroy Edwards	85	Leroy Edwards	92	Leroy Edwards	262
1942-43	Ralph Vaughn	86	Leroy Edwards	72	Ralph Vaughn	222
1943-44	Clint Wager	79	Clint Wager	72	Clint Wager	230
1944-45	Leroy Edwards	125	Leroy Edwards	157	Leroy Edwards	407
1945-46	Bob Carpenter	186	Leroy Edwards	119	Bob Carpenter	473
1946-47	Bob Carpenter	199	Leroy Edwards	144	Bob Carpenter	513
1947-48	Gene Englund	246	Gene Englund	242	Gene Englund	734
1948-49	Gene Englund	284	Gene Englund	282	Gene Englund	850

COACHING HISTORY: 1937-1949 Lon Darling 196-147-.571; 1948-1949 Gene Englund 29-23-.558

OTTAWA CIVICS
(were Denver Spurs)

Home City: Ottawa, Ontario
Home Arena: Ottawa Civic Center   Capacity: 9,355 [1976]
Origin of Name: The team was named after the arena in which they played their home games.

Regular Season Record

Season	League	GP	W	L	T	GF	GA	Pts	Pct
1975-1976	WHA	7	0	7	0	20	30	0	.000

Regular Season Individual Leaders

Season	Goals		Points		Penalty Minutes	
1975-1976	Ralph Backstrom	4	Ralph Backstrom	9	Brian Lavender	11
	Gary MacGregor	4	Gary MacGregor	9		

COACHING HISTORY: Jean-Guy Talbot 0-7-0-.000

OTTAWA NATIONALS
(became Toronto Toros)

Home City: Ottawa, Ontario
Home Arena: Ottawa Civic Center   Capacity: 9,300 [1972]
Origin of Name: The team took the name because they were in the nation's capital.

Regular Season Record

Season	League	GP	W	L	T	GF	GA	Pts	Pct
1972-1973	WHA	78	35	39	4	279	301	74	.474

Playoff Record

Season	GP	W	L	GF	GA	Result
1972-1973	5	1	4	16	24	Lost Quarterfinal series to New England.

Regular Season Individual Leaders

Season	Goals		Points		Penalty Minutes	
1972-1973	Wayne Carleton	42	Wayne Carleton	91	Rick Cunningham	121

COACHING HISTORY: Billy Harris 35-39-4-.474

OTTAWA RENEGADES

Home City: Ottawa, Ontario
Home Stadium: Frank Clair Stadium   Capacity: 27,695 [2004]
Origin of Name: The name was chosen in a Name the Team Contest and announced November 18, 2001. Renegades received 4,908 of a total of 15,931 votes. Other names considered were Beavers and Rivermen.

Regular Season Record

Season	League	GP	W	L	T	OL	PF	PA	Pts	Pct
2002	CFL	18	4	14	0	2	356	550	10	.278
2003	CFL	18	7	11	0	NA	467	581	14	.389
2004	CFL	18	5	13	0	NA	401	560	10	.278
2005	CFL	18	7	11	0	NA	458	578	14	.389
TOTAL:	4 years	72	23	49	0	2	1682	2269	48	
AVERAGE:		18	6	12	0	1	421	567	12	.333

Regular Season Individual Leaders

Season	Passing Yards		Receiving Yards		Rushing Yards	
2002	Dan Crowley	2697	Jimmy Oliver	1004	Josh Ranek	689
2003	Kerry Joseph	3694	D.J. Flick	917	Josh Ranek	1122
2004	Kerry Joseph	2762	Yo Murphy	1090	Josh Ranek	1060
2005	Kerry Joseph	4466	Jason Armstead	1307	Josh Ranek	1157

COACHING HISTORY: 2002-2005 Joe Paopao 23-49-0-.333; 2006-present

OTTAWA ROUGH RIDERS

Home City: Ottawa, Ontario
Home Stadium: Frank Clair Stadium *   Capacity: 30,927 [1996]
Origin of Name: The team adopted the name from the lumberjacks who rode the logs down the
Ottawa River.

Season	League	GP	Regular Season Record			PF	PA	Pts	Pct
			W	L	T				
1950	CRU	12	4	7	1	182	231	9	.375
1951	CRU	12	7	5	0	218	197	14	.583
1952	CRU	12	5	7	0	200	238	10	.417
1953	CRU	14	7	7	0	266	238	14	.500
1954	CRU	14	2	12	0	129	337	4	.143
1955	CRU	12	3	9	0	174	337	6	.250
1956	CFC	14	7	7	0	326	359	14	.500
1957	CFC	14	8	6	0	326	237	16	.571
1958	CFL	14	6	8	0	233	243	12	.429
1959	CFL	14	8	6	0	275	217	16	.571
1960	CFL	14	9	5	0	400	283	18	.643
1961	CFL	14	8	6	0	359	285	16	.571
1962	CFL	14	6	7	1	339	302	13	.464
1963	CFL	14	9	5	0	326	284	18	.643
1964	CFL	14	8	5	1	313	228	17	.607
1965	CFL	14	7	7	0	300	234	14	.500
1966	CFL	14	11	3	0	278	177	22	.786
1967	CFL	14	9	4	1	337	207	19	.679
1968	CFL	14	9	3	2	416	271	20	.714
1969	CFL	14	11	3	0	399	298	22	.786
1970	CFL	14	4	10	0	255	279	8	.286
1971	CFL	14	6	8	0	291	277	12	.429
1972	CFL	14	11	3	0	298	228	22	.786
1973	CFL	14	9	5	0	275	234	18	.643
1974	CFL	16	7	9	0	261	271	14	.438
1975	CFL	16	10	5	1	394	280	21	.656
1976	CFL	16	9	6	1	411	346	19	.594
1977	CFL	16	8	8	0	368	344	16	.500
1978	CFL	16	11	5	0	395	261	22	.688
1979	CFL	16	8	6	2	349	315	18	.563
1980	CFL	16	7	9	0	353	393	14	.438
1981	CFL	16	5	11	0	306	446	10	.313
1982	CFL	16	5	11	0	376	462	10	.313
1983	CFL	16	8	8	0	384	424	16	.500
1984	CFL	16	4	12	0	354	507	8	.250
1985	CFL	16	7	9	0	272	402	14	.438
1986	CFL	18	3	14	1	346	514	7	.194
1987	CFL	18	3	15	0	377	598	6	.167
1988	CFL	18	2	16	0	278	618	4	.111
1989	CFL	18	4	14	0	426	630	8	.222
1990	CFL	18	7	11	0	540	602	14	.389
1991	CFL	18	7	11	0	522	577	14	.389
1992	CFL	18	9	9	0	484	439	18	.500

*-known as Lansdowne Park from 1950 to 1992

1993	CFL	18	4	14	0	387	517	8	.222
1994	CFL	18	4	14	0	480	642	8	.222
1995	CFL	18	3	15	0	348	685	6	.167
1996	CFL	18	3	15	0	353	514	6	.167
TOTAL:	47 years	718	312	395	11	15679	17008	635	
AVERAGE:		15	7	8	0	334	362	14	.442

Playoff Record

Season	GP	W	L	T	PF	PA	Result
1951	4	4	0	0	92	47	**Won Grey Cup.**
1956	1	0	1	0	21	46	Lost Division Semifinal to Hamilton.
1957	1	0	1	0	15	24	Lost Division Semifinal to Montreal.
1958	3	1	2	0	40	66	Lost Division Final to Hamilton.
1959	3	2	1	0	67	26	Lost Division Final to Hamilton.
1960	4	4	0	0	100	61	**Won Grey Cup.**
1961	1	0	1	0	19	43	Lost Division Semifinal to Toronto.
1962	1	0	1	0	17	18	Lost Division Semifinal to Montreal.
1963	3	2	1	0	52	68	Lost Division Final to Hamilton.
1964	3	2	1	0	65	39	Lost Division Final to Hamilton.
1965	3	1	2	0	56	42	Lost Division Final to Hamilton.
1966	3	2	1	0	86	46	Lost Grey Cup Final to Saskatchewan.
1967	3	1	2	0	41	59	Lost Division Final to Hamilton.
1968	3	2	1	0	71	48	**Won Grey Cup**
1969	3	2	1	0	75	36	**Won Grey Cup.**
1971	1	0	1	0	4	23	Lost Division Semifinal to Hamilton.
1972	3	2	1	0	41	41	Lost Division Final to Hamilton.
1973	2	2	0	0	45	32	**Won Grey Cup.**
1974	2	1	1	0	25	33	Lost Division Final to Montreal.
1975	1	0	1	0	10	20	Lost Division Final to Montreal.
1976	2	2	0	0	40	35	**Won Grey Cup.**
1977	2	1	1	0	39	37	Lost Division Final to Montreal.
1978	1	0	1	0	16	21	Lost Division Final to Montreal.
1979	2	1	1	0	35	43	Lost Division Final to Montreal.
1980	1	0	1	0	21	25	Lost Division Semifinal to Montreal.
1981	3	2	1	0	60	55	Lost Grey Cup Final to Edmonton.
1982	2	1	1	0	37	64	Lost Division Final to Toronto.
1983	1	0	1	0	31	33	Lost Division Semifinal to Hamilton.
1985	1	0	1	0	20	30	Lost Division Semifinal to Montreal.
1990	1	0	1	0	25	34	Lost Division Semifinal to Toronto.
1991	1	0	1	0	8	26	Lost Division Semifinal to Winnipeg.
1992	1	0	1	0	28	29	Lost Division Semifinal to Hamilton.
1993	1	0	1	0	10	21	Lost Division Semifinal to Hamilton
1994	1	0	1	0	16	26	Lost Division Semifinal to Winnipeg.
TOTAL:	68	35	33	0	1328	1297	
AVERAGE:	2	1	1	0	39	38	

Regular Season Individual Leaders

Season	Passing Yards	Receiving Yards	Rushing Yards
1950			
1951			
1952			
1953			

Season	Passing Yards		Receiving Yards		Rushing Yards	
1954	Jim Root	851	Bob Simpson	757	Avatus Stone	410
1955						
1956			Bob Simpson	1030		
1957						
1958	Hal Ledyard	868	Bob Simpson	583	Dave Thelen	696
1959					Dave Thelen	1339
1960	Ron Lancaster	1843	Bob Simpson	607	Dave Thelen	1407
1961	Russ Jackson	1048	Bob Simpson	428	Dave Thelen	1032
1962	Russ Jackson	1427	Ernie White	758	Ernie White	804
1963	Russ Jackson	2910	Whit Tucker	967	Dave Thelen	907
1964	Russ Jackson	2156	Ted Watkins	743	Ron Stewart	867
1965	Russ Jackson	2303	Ted Watkins	724	Dave Thelen	806
1966	Russ Jackson	2400	Whit Tucker	804	Bo Scott	648
1967	Russ Jackson	3332	Whit Tucker	1171	Bo Scott	762
1968	Russ Jackson	3187	Whit Tucker	890	Bo Scott	911
1969	Russ Jackson	3641	Margene Adkins	1402	Vic Washington	717
1970	Gary Wood	2759	Hugh Oldham	1043	Gary Wood	493
1971	Rick Cassata	1100	Hugh Oldham	736	Dennis Duncan	760
1972	Rick Cassata	2548	Hugh Oldham	719	Art Cantrelle	652
1973	Rick Cassata	1255	Hugh Oldham	701	Jim Evenson	909
1974	Jerry Keeling	1841	Rhome Nixon	850	Art Green	680
1975	Tom Clements	2013	Tony Gabriel	1115	Art Green	1188
1976	Tom Clements	2856	Tony Gabriel	1320	Art Green	1257
1977	Tom Clements	2804	Tony Gabriel	1362	Richard Holmes	1016
1978	C. Holloway	1970	Tony Gabriel	1070	Richard Holmes	607
1979	C. Holloway	1965	Tony Gabriel	761	Richard Crump	581
1980	C. Holloway	1499	Tony Gabriel	850	Richard Crump	1074
1981	Jordan Case	1521	Tony Gabriel	1006	Richard Crump	440
1982	Chris Isaac	3408	Bruce Walker	608	Alvin Walker	1141
1983	J.C. Watts	3089	Alvin Walker	1431	Alvin Walker	1431
1984	J.C. Watts	3052	David Newman	896	Tim McCray	701
1985	J.C. Watts	2975	Waymon Alridge	797	J.C. Watts	710
1986	Todd Dillon	1279	Marc Lewis	1197	Lester Brown	411
1987	Todd Dillon	2901	Marc Lewis	1195	Cedric Minter	627
1988	Jeff Wickersham	1393	Gerald Alphin	1307	Orville Lee	1075
1989	Damon Allen	3093	Gerald Alphin	1471	Damon Allen	532
1990	Damon Allen	3883	Stephen Jones	1182	Reggie Barnes	1260
1991	Damon Allen	4275	Brock Smith	702	Reggie Barnes	1486
1992	Tom Burgess	4026	Stephen Jones	1400	Reggie Barnes	926
1993	Tom Burgess	5063	Jock Climie	1281	Darren Joseph	398
1994	Danny Barrett	4173	Nick Mazzoli	648	Gerry Collins	636
1995	Sammy Garza	2954	Odessa Turner	1054	Andre Ware	148
1996	David Archer	3977	Joseph Rogers	1253	Dave Dinnall	449

COACHING HISTORY: 1950 Wally Masters 4-7-1-.375; 1951-1954 Clem Crowe 21-31-0-.404; 1955 Chan Caldwell 3-9-0-.250; 1956-1969 Frank Clair 116-75-5-.605; 1970-1973 Jack Gotta 30-26-0-.536; 1974-1984 George Brancato 82-90-4-.477; 1985-1986 Joe Moss 10-23-1-.309; 1987-1988 Fred Glick 3-18-0-.167; 1988 Bob Webber 2-13-0-.111; 1989-1991 Steve Goldman 11-25-0-.306; 1991 Joe Faragalli 7-7-0-.500; 1992-1993 Ron Smeltzer 13-23-0-.361; 1994 Adam Rita 4-14-0-.222; 1995-1996 Jim Gilstrap 3-17-0; 1996 John Payne 3-13-0-.188

OTTAWA SENATORS
(became St. Louis Eagles)

Home City: Ottawa, Ontario
Home Arena: Laurier Avenue Arena (1909-1923)   Capacity: 7,500
         Ottawa Auditorium (1923-1934)   Capacity: 10,000
Origin of Name: The team was named Senators because Ottawa is the capital city of Canada.

Regular Season Record

Season	League	GP	W	L	T	GF	GA	Pts	Pct
1908-1909	ECHA	12	10	2	0	117	63	20	.833
1909-1910	NHA	12	9	3	0	89	66	18	.750
1910-1911	NHA	16	13	3	0	122	69	26	.813
1911-1912	NHA	18	9	9	0	99	93	18	.500
1912-1913	NHA	20	9	11	0	87	81	18	.450
1913-1914	NHA	20	11	9	0	65	71	22	.550
1914-1915	NHA	20	14	6	0	74	65	28	.700
1915-1916	NHA	24	13	11	0	78	72	26	.542
1916-1917	NHA	20	15	5	0	119	63	30	.750
1917-1918	NHL	22	9	13	0	102	114	18	.409
1918-1919	NHL	18	12	6	0	71	53	24	.667
1919-1920	NHL	24	19	5	0	121	64	38	.792
1920-1921	NHL	24	14	10	0	97	75	28	.583
1921-1922	NHL	24	14	8	2	106	84	30	.625
1922-1923	NHL	24	14	9	1	77	54	29	.604
1923-1924	NHL	24	16	8	0	74	54	32	.667
1924-1925	NHL	30	17	12	1	83	66	35	.583
1925-1926	NHL	36	24	8	4	77	42	52	.722
1926-1927	NHL	44	30	10	4	86	69	64	.727
1927-1928	NHL	44	20	14	10	78	57	50	.568
1928-1929	NHL	44	14	17	13	54	67	41	.466
1929-1930	NHL	44	21	15	8	138	118	50	.568
1930-1931	NHL	44	10	30	4	91	142	24	.273
1932-1933	NHL	48	11	27	10	88	131	32	.333
1933-1934	NHL	48	13	29	6	115	143	32	.333
TOTAL:	25 years	704	361	280	63	2308	1976	785	
AVERAGE:		28	14	11	3	92	79	31	.558

Playoff Record

Season	GP	W	L	T	GF	GA	Result
1909-1910	4	4	0	0	36	15	Won playoff series from Edmonton.
1910-1911	2	2	0	0	20	8	**Won Stanley Cup**.
1914-1915	5	1	4	0	12	27	Lost Stanley Cup Final to Vancouver.
1916-1917	2	1	1	0	6	7	Lost playoff series to Canadiens.
1918-1919	5	1	4	0	18	26	Lost playoff series to Canadiens.
1919-1920	5	3	2	0	15	11	**Won Stanley Cup**.
1920-1921	7	5	2	0	19	12	**Won Stanley Cup**.
1921-1922	2	0	1	1	4	5	Lost playoff series to Toronto.
1922-1923	8	6	2	0	16	10	**Won Stanley Cup**
1923-1924	2	0	2	0	2	5	Lost playoff series to Canadiens.
1925-1926	2	0	1	1	1	2	Lost playoff series to Maroons.
1926-1927	6	3	0	3	12	4	**Won Stanley Cup**.
1927-1928	2	0	2	0	1	3	Lost Quarterfinal series to Maroons.

1929-1930	2	0	1	1	3	6	Lost Quarterfinal series to Rangers.
TOTAL:	54	26	22	6	165	141
AVERAGE:	4	2	2	0	12	10

Regular Season Individual Leaders

Season	Goals		Points		Penalty Minutes	
1908-1909	Marty Walsh	38	Marty Walsh	38	Not Recorded	
1909-1910	Marty Walsh	23	Marty Walsh	23	Not Recorded	
1910-1911	Marty Walsh	37	Marty Walsh	37	Not Recorded	
1911-1912	Skene Ronan	35	Skene Ronan	35	Not Recorded	
1912-1913	Harry Broadbent	20	Harry Broadbent	20	Not Recorded	
1913-1914	Jack Darragh	23	Jack Darragh	23	Not Recorded	
1914-1915	Harry Broadbent	24	Harry Broadbent	24	Not Recorded	
1915-1916	Frank Nighbor	19	Frank Nighbor	19	Not Recorded	
1916-1917	Frank Nighbor	41	Frank Nighbor	41	Not Recorded	
1917-1918	Cy Denneny	36	Cy Denneny	46	Cy Denneny	80
1918-1919	Frank Nighbor	19	Frank Nighbor	28	Cy Denneny	58
1919-1920	Frank Nighbor	26	Frank Nighbor	41	Sprague Cleghorn	85
1920-1921	Cy Denneny	34	Cy Denneny	39	George Boucher	53
1921-1922	Harry Broadbent	32	Harry Broadbent	46	Harry Broadbent	28
1922-1923	Cy Denneny	23	Cy Denneny	34	George Boucher	58
1923-1924	Cy Denneny	22	Cy Denneny	24	Harry Broadbent	44
1924-1925	Cy Denneny	27	Cy Denneny	42	George Boucher	95
1925-1926	Cy Denneny	24	Cy Denneny	36	King Clancy	80
1926-1927	Cy Denneny	17	Cy Denneny	23	Reginald Smith	125
1927-1928	Frank Finnigan	20	Frank Finnigan	25	Alex Smith	90
1928-1929	Frank Finnigan	15	Frank Finnigan	19	Alex Smith	96
1929-1930	Hector Kilrea	36	Hector Kilrea	58	Joe Lamb	119
1930-1931	Art Gagne	19	Art Gagne	30	Joe Lamb	91
1932-1933	Ralph Weiland	16	Ralph Weiland	27	Allan Shields	119
1933-1934	Desse Roche	14	Earl Roche	29	Ralph Bowman	64

COACHING HISTORY: 1908-1909 Bruce Stuart 10-2-0-.833; 1910-1911 Pud Glass 13-3-0-.813; 1914-1915 Frank Shaughnessy 14-6-0-.700; 1915-1916 Alf Smith 13-11-0-.542; 1916-1918 Eddie Gerard 24-18-0-.571; 1918-1919 Alf Smith 12-6-0-.667; 1919-1925 Pete Green 94-52-4-.640; 1925-1926 Alex Curry 24-8-4-.722; 1926-1929 Dave Gill 64-41-27-.587; 1929-1931 Newsy Lalonde 31-45-12-.420; 1932-1933 Cy Denneny 11-27-10-.333; 1933-1934 George Boucher 13-29-6-.333

OTTAWA SENATORS

Home City: Ottawa, Ontario
Home Arena: Ottawa Civic Center (1992-1996)   Capacity: 10,575 [1995]
       Scotia Bank Place (1996-present)*   Capacity: 19,153 [2005]
Origin of Name: The team was named in honor of the previous NHL team based in Ottawa.

Regular Season Record

Season	League	GP	W	L	T	OL	SL	GF	GA	Pts
1992-1993	NHL	84	10	70	4	NA	NA	202	395	24
1993-1924	NHL	84	14	61	9	NA	NA	201	397	37
1994-1995	NHL	48	9	34	5	NA	NA	116	174	23
1995-1996	NHL	82	18	59	5	NA	NA	191	291	41
1996-1997	NHL	82	31	36	15	NA	NA	226	234	77

*-Known as Corel Center from 1996-2006

1997-1998	NHL	82	34	33	15	NA	NA	193	200	83
1998-1999	NHL	82	44	23	15	NA	NA	239	179	103
1999-2000	NHL	82	41	30	11	2	NA	244	210	95
2000-2001	NHL	82	48	21	9	4	NA	274	205	109
2001-2002	NHL	82	39	27	9	7	NA	243	208	94
2002-2003	NHL	82	52	21	8	1	NA	263	182	113
2003-2004	NHL	82	43	23	10	6	NA	262	189	102
2004-2005	NHL	Season cancelled due to lockout.								
2005-2006	NHL	82	52	21	NA	3	6	314	211	113
TOTAL:	13 years	1036	435	459	115	23	6	2968	3075	1014
AVERAGE:		80	33	35	9	2	0	228	236	78

Playoff Record

Season	GP	W	L	GF	GA	Result
1996-1997	7	3	4	13	15	Lost Conference Quarterfinal to Buffalo.
1997-1998	11	5	6	20	30	Lost Conference Semifinal to Washington.
1998-1999	4	0	4	6	12	Lost Conference Quarterfinal to Buffalo.
1999-2000	6	2	4	10	17	Lost Conference Quarterfinal to Toronto.
2000-2001	4	0	4	2	10	Lost Conference Quarterfinal to Toronto.
2001-2002	12	7	5	29	18	Lost Conference Semifinal to Toronto.
2002-2003	18	11	7	43	34	Lost Conference Final to New Jersey.
2003-2004	7	3	4	11	14	Lost Conference Quarterfinal to Toronto.
2005-2006	10	5	5	45	29	Lost Conference Semifinal to Buffalo
TOTAL:	79	36	43	179	179	
AVERAGE:	9	4	5	20	20	

Regular Season Individual Leaders

Season	Goals		Points		Penalty Minutes	
1992-1993	Sylvain Turgeon	25	Norm Maciver	63	Mike Peluso	318
1993-1924	Alexei Yashin	30	Alexei Yashin	79	Dennis Vial	214
1994-1995	Alexei Yashin	21	Alexei Yashin	44	R. Cunneyworth	68
1995-1996	Daniel Alfredsson	26	Daniel Alfredsson	61	Dennis Vial	276
1996-1997	Alexei Yashin	35	Alexei Yashin	75	Denny Lambert	217
1997-1998	Alexei Yashin	33	Alexei Yashin	72	Denny Lambert	250
1998-1999	Alexei Yashin	44	Alexei Yashin	94	Chris Murray	65
1999-2000	Shawn McEachern	29	Radek Bonk	60	Andre Roy	145
	Marian Hossa	29				
2000-2001	Alexei Yashin	40	Alexei Yashin	88	Andre Roy	169
2001-2002	Daniel Alfredsson	37	Daniel Alfredsson	71	Chris Neil	231
2002-2003	Marian Hossa	45	Marian Hossa	80	Chris Neil	147
2003-2004	Marian Hossa	36	Marian Hossa	82	Chris Neil	194
2004-2005	Season cancelled due to lockout.					
2005-2006	Dany Heatley	50	Dany Heatley	103	Chris Neil	204
			D. Alfredsson	103		

COACHING HISTORY: 1992-1996 Rick Bowness 39-178-18-.204; 1995-1996 Dave Allison 2-22-1-.100; 1995-2004 Jacques Martin; 342-238-96-20-.575; 2001-2002 Roger Neilson 1-1-0-0-.500; 2005-present Bryan Murray

PATERSON CRESCENTS

Home City: Paterson, New Jersey
Home Court: Arcola Park
Origin of Name: Were known as Paterson Whirlwinds during the first two seasons.

		Regular Season Record			
Season	League	GP	W	L	Pct
1928-1929	ABL	37	9	28	.243
1929-1930	ABL	54	18	36	.333
1930-1931	ABL	18	9	9	.500
TOTAL:	3 years	109	36	73	
AVERAGE:		36	12	24	.333

COACHING HISTORY:

PHILADELPHIA ATHLETICS

Home City: Philadelphia, Pennsylvania
Home Field: Athletics Park
Origin of Name: The team traces its roots to the mid 1800's, taking the name of a local social club.

		Regular Season Record						
Season	League	GP	W	L	Pct	GB	R	OR
1876	NL	59	14	45	.237	34.5	378	534

		Regular Season Individual Leaders			
Season	Home Runs		RBI's		Wins
1876	George Hall	5	George Hall	45	Lon Knight 10

COACHING HISTORY: Al Wright 14-45-.237

PHILADELPHIA ATHLETICS

Home City: Philadelphia, Pennsylvania
Home Field: Oakdale Park (1882)
               Athletics Park
Origin of Name: Named after previous National League team.

		Regular Season Record						
Season	League	GP	W	L	Pct	GB	R	OR
1882	AA	75	41	34	.547	11.5	406	389
1883	AA	98	66	32	.673	-	720	547
1884	AA	107	61	46	.570	14	700	546
1885	AA	112	55	57	.491	24	764	691
1886	AA	135	63	72	.467	28	772	942
1887	AA	133	64	69	.481	30	893	890
1888	AA	133	81	52	.609	10	827	594
1889	AA	133	75	58	.564	16	880	787
1890	AA	132	54	78	.409	34	702	945
1891	AA	139	73	66	.525	22	817	794
TOTAL:	10 years	1197	633	564		189.5	7481	7125
AVERAGE:		120	63	57	.529	19	748	713

		Regular Season Individual Leaders			
Season	Home Runs		RBI's		Wins
1882	Jack O'Brien	3	Not Recorded		Sam Weaver 26
1883	Harry Stovey	14	Not Recorded		Bob Mathews 30

Season	Home Runs		RBI's		Wins	
1884	Harry Stovey	10	Not Recorded		Bob Mathews	30
1885	Harry Stovey	13	Not Recorded		Bob Mathews	30
1886	Harry Stovey	7	Not Recorded		Al Atkinson	25
1887	Denny Lyons	6	Not Recorded		Gus Weyhing	26
1888	Harry Stovey	9	Henry Larkin	101	Ed Seward	35
1889	Harry Stovey	19	Harry Stovey	119	Gus Weyhing	30
1890	Denny Lyons	7	Not Recorded		John McMahon	29
1891	John Milligan	11	John Milligan	106	Gus Weyhing	31

COACHING HISTORY: 1882 Charlie Mason 21-15-.583; 1882-1883 Lew Simmons 86-51-.632; 1884-1885 Charlie Mason 45-44-.506; 1884-1891 Bill Sharsig 344-306-.529; 1885 Lon Knight 16-19-.457; 1886 Lew Simmons 41-55-.427; 1887 Frank Bancroft 22-25-.468; 1891 George Wood 54-46-.540; 1891 Bill Barnie 4-3-.571

PHILADELPHIA ATHLETICS
(became Kansas City Athletics)

Home City: Philadelphia, Pennsylvania
Home Field: Columbia Park (1901-1908)   Capacity: 9,500 [1901]
          Shibe Park (1909-1954)*   Capacity: 33,156 [1953]
Origin of Name: Named after previous National League and American Association teams.

			Regular Season Record					
Season	League	GP	W	L	Pct	GB	R	OR
1901	AL	136	74	62	.544	9	805	760
1902	AL	136	83	53	.610	-	775	636
1903	AL	135	75	60	.556	14.5	597	519
1904	AL	151	81	70	.536	12.5	557	503
1905	AL	148	92	56	.622	-	617	486
1906	AL	145	78	67	.538	12	561	536
1907	AL	145	88	57	.607	1.5	582	509
1908	AL	153	68	85	.444	22	487	554
1909	AL	153	95	58	.621	3.5	600	414
1910	AL	150	102	48	.680	-	672	439
1911	AL	151	101	50	.669	-	861	601
1912	AL	152	90	62	.592	15	780	656
1913	AL	153	96	57	.627	-	794	593
1914	AL	152	99	53	.651	-	749	520
1915	AL	152	43	109	.283	58.5	545	890
1916	AL	153	36	117	.235	54.5	447	776
1917	AL	153	55	98	.359	44.5	527	691
1918	AL	128	52	76	.406	24	412	563
1919	AL	140	36	104	.257	52	459	742
1920	AL	154	48	106	.312	50	555	831
1921	AL	153	53	100	.346	45	657	894
1922	AL	154	65	89	.422	29	705	830
1923	AL	152	69	83	.454	29	661	761
1924	AL	152	71	81	.467	20	685	778
1925	AL	152	88	64	.579	8.5	830	714
1926	AL	150	83	67	.553	6	677	570

*-known as Connie Mack Stadium from 1953 to 1954

1927	AL	154	91	63	.591	19	841	726
1928	AL	153	98	55	.641	2.5	829	615
1929	AL	150	104	46	.693	-	901	615
1930	AL	154	102	52	.662	-	951	751
1931	AL	152	107	45	.704	-	858	626
1932	AL	154	94	60	.610	13	981	752
1933	AL	151	79	72	.523	19.5	875	853
1934	AL	150	68	82	.453	31	764	838
1935	AL	149	58	91	.389	34	710	869
1936	AL	153	53	100	.346	49	714	1045
1937	AL	151	54	97	.358	46.5	699	854
1938	AL	152	53	99	.349	46	726	956
1939	AL	152	55	97	.362	51.5	711	1022
1940	AL	154	54	100	.351	36	703	932
1941	AL	154	64	90	.416	37	713	840
1942	AL	154	55	99	.357	48	549	801
1943	AL	154	49	105	.318	49	497	717
1944	AL	154	72	82	.468	17	525	594
1945	AL	150	52	98	.347	34.5	494	638
1946	AL	154	49	105	.318	55	529	680
1947	AL	154	78	76	.506	19	633	614
1948	AL	154	84	70	.545	12.5	729	735
1949	AL	154	81	73	.526	16	726	725
1950	AL	154	52	102	.338	46	670	913
1951	AL	154	70	84	.455	28	736	745
1952	AL	154	79	75	.513	16	664	723
1953	AL	154	59	95	.383	41.5	632	799
1954	AL	154	51	103	.331	60	542	875
TOTAL:	54 years	8134	3886	4248		1338.5	36499	38619
AVERAGE:		151	72	79	.478	25	676	715

				Playoff Record			
Season	**GP**	**W**	**L**	**R**	**OR**	**Result**
1905	5	1	4	3	15	Lost World Series to New York.
1910	5	4	1	35	15	**Won World Series.**
1911	6	4	2	27	13	**Won World Series.**
1913	5	4	1	23	15	**Won World Series.**
1914	4	0	4	6	16	Lost World Series to Boston.
1929	5	4	1	26	17	**Won World Series.**
1930	6	4	2	21	12	**Won World Series.**
1931	7	3	4	22	19	Lost World Series To St. Louis.
TOTAL:	43	24	19	163	122	
AVERAGE:	5	3	2	20	15	

Regular Season Individual Leaders

Season	Home Runs		RBI's		Wins	
1901	Napoleon Lajoie	14	Napoleon Lajoie	125	Charles Fraser	20
1902	Ralph Seybold	16	Lave Cross	108	Rube Waddell	24
1903	Ralph Seybold	8	Lave Cross	90	Eddie Plank	23
1904	Harry Davis	10	Daniel Murphy	77	Eddie Plank	26
					Rube Waddell	26

Season	Home Runs		RBI's		Wins	
1905	Harry Davis	8	Harry Davis	83	Rube Waddell	26
1906	Harry Davis	12	Harry Davis	96	Eddie Plank	19
1907	Harry Davis	8	Ralph Seybold	92	Eddie Plank	24
1908	Harry Davis	5	Daniel Murphy	66	Harry Vickers	18
1909	Daniel Murphy	5	Frank Baker	85	Eddie Plank	19
1910	Daniel Murphy	4	Eddie Collins	81	Jack Coombs	31
	Reuben Oldring	4				
1911	Frank Baker	11	Frank Baker	115	Jack Coombs	28
1912	Frank Baker	10	Frank Baker	130	Eddie Plank	26
1913	Frank Baker	12	Frank Baker	117	Chief Bender	21
1914	Frank Baker	9	John McInnis	95	Chief Bender	17
					Joe Bush	17
1915	Reuben Oldring	6	Napoleon Lajoie	61	Weldon Wyckoff	10
1916	Wally Schang	7	John McInnis	60	Joe Bush	15
1917	Frank Bodie	7	Frank Bodie	74	Joe Bush	11
1918	Tilly Walker	11	George Burns	70	Scott Perry	21
1919	Tilly Walker	10	Tilly Walker	64	Walt Kinney	9
					Russell Johnson	9
1920	Tilly Walker	17	Tilly Walker	82	Scott Perry	11
1921	Tilly Walker	23	Tilly Walker	101	Eddie Rommel	16
1922	Tilly Walker	37	Tilly Walker	99	Eddie Rommel	27
1923	Joe Hauser	16	Joe Hauser	94	Eddie Rommel	18
1924	Joe Hauser	27	Joe Hauser	115	Eddie Rommel	18
1925	Al Simmons	24	Al Simmons	129	Eddie Rommel	21
1926	Al Simmons	19	Al Simmons	109	Lefty Grove	13
1927	Al Simmons	15	Al Simmons	108	Lefty Grove	20
1928	Joe Hauser	16	Al Simmons	107	Lefty Grove	24
1929	Al Simmons	34	Al Simmons	157	George Earnshaw	24
1930	Jimmie Foxx	37	Al Simmons	165	Lefty Grove	28
1931	Jimmie Foxx	30	Al Simmons	128	Lefty Grove	31
1932	Jimmie Foxx	58	Jimmie Foxx	169	Lefty Grove	25
1933	Jimmie Foxx	48	Jimmie Foxx	163	Lefty Grove	24
1934	Jimmie Foxx	44	Jimmie Foxx	130	John Marcum	14
1935	Jimmie Foxx	36	Jimmie Foxx	115	John Marcum	17
1936	Bob Johnson	25	Bob Johnson	121	Harry Kelley	15
1937	Wally Moses	25	Bob Johnson	108	Harry Kelley	13
	Bob Johnson	25				
1938	Bob Johnson	30	Bob Johnson	113	George Caster	16
1939	Bob Johnson	23	Bob Johnson	114	Lynn Nelson	10
1940	Bob Johnson	31	Bob Johnson	103	John Babich	14
1941	Sam Chapman	25	Bob Johnson	107	Jack Knott	13
1942	Bob Johnson	13	Bob Johnson	80	Phil Marchildon	17
1943	Bob Estalella	11	Dick Siebert	72	Jesse Flores	12
1944	Frank Hayes	13	Frank Hayes	78	Russ Christopher	14
1945	Bob Estalella	8	George Kell	56	Russ Christopher	13
1946	Sam Chapman	20	Sam Chapman	67	Phil Marchildon	13
1947	Sam Chapman	14	Sam Chapman	83	Phil Marchildon	19
1948	Eddie Joost	16	Hank Majeski	120	Dick Fowler	15
1949	Sam Chapman	24	Sam Chapman	108	Alex Kellner	20
1950	Sam Chapman	23	Sam Chapman	95	Bob Hooper	15
1951	Gus Zernial	33	Gus Zernial	125	Bobby Shantz	18
1952	Gus Zernial	29	Gus Zernial	100	Bobby Shantz	24

Season	Home Runs		RBI's		Wins	
1953	Gus Zernial	42	Gus Zernial	108	Alex Kellner	11
					Harry Byrd	11
1954	Bill Wilson	15	Gus Zernial	62	Arnie Portocarrero	9

COACHING HISTORY: 1901-1950 Connie Mack 3627-3891-.482; 1951-1953 Jim Dykes 208-254-.450; 1954 Eddie Joost 51-103-.331

PHILADELPHIA ATOMS

Home City: Philadelphia, Pennsylvania
Home Stadium: Veterans Stadium (1973-1975)   Capacity: 55,730 [1973]
              Franklin Field (1976)   Capacity: 60,546 [1976]
Origin of Name: The name was chosen in a Name the Team Contest.

Regular Season Record

Season	League	GP	W	L	T	GF	GA	BP	Pts	Pct
1973	NASL	19	9	2	8	29	14	26	104	.608
1974	NASL	20	8	11	1	25	25	23	74	.411
1975	NASL	22	10	12	-	33	42	30	90	.455
1976	NASL	24	8	16	-	32	49	32	80	.370
TOTAL:	4 years	85	35	41	9	119	130	111	348	
AVERAGE:		21	9	10	2	30	33	28	87	.455

Playoff Record

Season	GP	W	L	T	GF	GA	Result
1973	2	2	0	0	5	0	Won NASL Championship.

Regular Season Individual Leaders

Season	Goals		Points		GAA (360 Min)	
1973	Andy Provan	11	Andy Provan	28	Bob Rigby	0.62
1974	Andy Provan	9	Andy Provan	21	Bob Rigby	1.10
1975	Chris Bahr	11	Chris Bahr	24	Bob Rigby	1.59
1976	Belisario Lopez	6	Pedro Herrara	18	Rene Vizcaino	1.78

COACHING HISTORY: 1973-1975 Al Miller 27-25-9-.488; 1976 Jesus Ponce 8-16-.370

PHILADELPHIA BELL

Home City: Philadelphia, Pennsylvania
Home Stadium: John F. Kennedy Stadium (1974)   Capacity: 90,000 [1974]
              Franklin Field (1975)
Origin of Name: The name was suggested by one of the team's investors. The name was no doubt chosen because of Philadelphia's connection to the famous Liberty Bell.

Season	League	GP	W	L	T	PF	PA	Pct
1974	WFL	19	8	11	0	491	413	.421
1975	WFL	11	4	7	0	195	237	.364
TOTAL:	2 years	30	12	18	0	686	650	
AVERAGE:		15	6	9	0	343	325	.400

Regular Season Record

Season	GP	W	L	Playoff Record PF	PA	Result
1974	1	0	1	3	18	Lost 1st Round game to Florida.

Regular Season Individual Leaders

Season	Passing Yards		Receiving Yards		Rushing Yards	
1974	King Corcoran	3632	Don Shanklin	842	John Land	1136
1975	Bob Davis	1114	Ted Kwalick	400	John Land	646

COACHING HISTORY: 1974 Ron Waller 8-11-0-.421; 1975 Willie Wood 4-7-0-.364

PHILADELPHIA BLAZERS
(became Vancouver Blazers)

Home City: Philadelphia, Pennsylvania
Home Arena: Convention Hall   Capacity: 9,000 [1972]
Origin of Name:

Regular Season Record

Season	League	GP	W	L	T	GF	GA	Pts	Pct
1972-1973	WHA	78	38	40	0	288	305	76	.487

Playoff Record

Season	GP	W	L	GF	GA	Result
1972-1973	4	0	4	6	19	Lost Quarterfinal series to Cleveland.

Regular Season Individual Leaders

Season	Goals		Points		Penalty Minutes	
1972-1973	Danny Lawson	61	Andre Lacroix	124	Jim Cardiff	185

COACHING HISTORY: John McKenzie 1-6-0-.143; Phil Watson 37-34-0-.521

PHILADELPHIA EAGLES
(Pittsburgh Steelers and Philadelphia Eagles merged for the 1943 season)

Home City: Philadelphia, Pennsylvania
Home Stadium: Baker Bowl (1933-1935)   Capacity: 18,800
                Municipal Stadium (1936-1939, 1941)   Capacity: 73,702
                Shibe Park (1940, 1942, 1944-1957)*   Capacity: 33,608
                Franklin Field (1958-1970)   Capacity: 60,546 [1970]
                Veterans Stadium (1971-2002)   Capacity: 65,352 [2002]
                Lincoln Financial Field (2003-present)   Capacity: 68,532 [2005]
Origin of Name: The team was named in honor of the eagle which was on the emblem of the
National Recovery Administration of the New Deal.

Regular Season Record

Season	League	GP	W	L	T	PF	PA	Pct
1933	NFL	9	3	5	1	77	158	.389
1934	NFL	11	4	7	0	127	85	.364
1935	NFL	11	2	9	0	60	179	.182
1936	NFL	12	1	11	0	51	206	.083

*-known as Connie Mack Stadium from 1953 to 1957

1937	NFL	11	2	8	1	86	177	.227
1938	NFL	11	5	6	0	154	164	.455
1939	NFL	11	1	9	1	105	200	.136
1940	NFL	11	1	10	0	111	211	.091
1941	NFL	11	2	8	1	119	218	.227
1942	NFL	11	2	9	0	134	239	.182
1944	NFL	10	7	1	2	267	131	.800
1945	NFL	10	7	3	0	272	133	.700
1946	NFL	11	6	5	0	231	220	.545
1947	NFL	12	8	4	0	308	242	.667
1948	NFL	12	9	2	1	376	156	.792
1949	NFL	12	11	1	0	364	134	.917
1950	NFL	12	6	6	0	254	141	.500
1951	NFL	12	4	8	0	234	264	.333
1952	NFL	12	7	5	0	252	271	.583
1953	NFL	12	7	4	1	352	215	.625
1954	NFL	12	7	4	1	284	230	.625
1955	NFL	12	4	7	1	248	231	.375
1956	NFL	12	3	8	1	143	215	.292
1957	NFL	12	4	8	0	173	230	.333
1958	NFL	12	2	9	1	235	306	.208
1959	NFL	12	7	5	0	268	278	.583
1960	NFL	12	10	2	0	321	246	.833
1961	NFL	14	10	4	0	361	297	.714
1962	NFL	14	3	10	1	282	356	.250
1963	NFL	14	2	10	2	242	381	.214
1964	NFL	14	6	8	0	312	313	.429
1965	NFL	14	5	9	0	363	359	.357
1966	NFL	14	9	5	0	326	340	.643
1967	NFL	14	6	7	1	351	409	.464
1968	NFL	14	2	12	0	202	351	.143
1969	NFL	14	4	9	1	279	377	.321
1970	NFL	14	3	10	1	241	332	.231
1971	NFL	14	6	7	1	221	302	.464
1972	NFL	14	2	11	1	145	352	.179
1973	NFL	14	5	8	1	310	393	.393
1974	NFL	14	7	7	0	242	217	.500
1975	NFL	14	4	10	0	225	302	.286
1976	NFL	14	4	10	0	165	286	.286
1977	NFL	14	5	9	0	220	207	.357
1978	NFL	16	9	7	0	270	250	.563
1979	NFL	16	11	5	0	339	282	.688
1980	NFL	16	12	4	0	384	222	.688
1981	NFL	16	10	6	0	368	221	.625
1982	NFL	9	3	6	0	191	195	.333
1983	NFL	16	5	11	0	233	322	.313
1984	NFL	16	6	9	1	278	320	.406
1985	NFL	16	7	9	0	286	310	.438
1986	NFL	16	5	10	1	256	312	.344
1987	NFL	15	7	8	0	337	380	.467
1988	NFL	16	10	6	0	379	319	.625
1989	NFL	16	11	5	0	342	274	.688
1990	NFL	16	10	6	0	396	299	.625
1991	NFL	16	10	6	0	285	244	.625

1992	NFL	16	11	5	0	354	245	.688
1993	NFL	16	8	8	0	293	315	.500
1994	NFL	16	7	9	0	308	308	.438
1995	NFL	16	10	6	0	318	338	.615
1996	NFL	16	10	6	0	363	341	.615
1997	NFL	16	6	9	1	317	372	.406
1998	NFL	16	3	13	0	161	344	.188
1999	NFL	16	5	11	0	272	357	.313
2000	NFL	16	11	5	0	351	245	.688
2001	NFL	16	11	5	0	343	208	.688
2002	NFL	16	12	4	0	415	241	.750
2003	NFL	16	12	4	0	374	287	.750
2004	NFL	16	13	3	0	386	260	.813
2005	NFL	16	6	10	0	310	388	.375
2006	NFL	16	10	6	0	398	328	.625
TOTAL:	73 years	1002	466	512	24	19400	19581	
AVERAGE:		13	6	7	0	266	268	.477

Playoff Record

Season	GP	W	L	PF	PA	Result
1947	2	1	1	42	28	Lost Championship game to Cardinals
1948	1	1	0	7	0	**Won NFL Championship.**
1949	1	1	0	14	0	**Won NFL Championship.**
1960	1	1	0	17	13	**Won NFL Championship.**
1978	1	0	1	13	14	Lost 1st Round game to Atlanta.
1979	2	1	1	44	41	Lost Divisional playoff to Tampa Bay.
1980	3	2	1	61	50	Lost Super Bowl to Oakland.
1981	1	0	1	21	27	Lost 1st Round playoff to N.Y. Giants.
1988	1	0	1	12	20	Lost Divisional playoff to Chicago.
1989	1	0	1	7	21	Lost Wild Card Game to L.A. Rams.
1990	1	0	1	6	20	Lost Wild Card Game to Washington.
1992	2	1	1	46	54	Lost Conference Semifinal to Dallas.
1995	2	1	1	69	67	Lost Conference Semifinal to Dallas.
1996	1	0	1	0	14	Lost Wild Card Game to San Francisco.
2000	2	1	1	31	23	Lost Conference Semifinal to Giants.
2001	3	2	1	88	57	Lost Conference Final to St. Louis.
2002	2	1	1	30	33	Lost Conference Final to Tampa Bay.
2003	2	1	1	23	31	Lost Conference Final to Carolina.
2004	3	2	1	75	48	Lost Super Bowl to New England.
2006	2	1	1	47	47	Lost Conf. Semifinal to New Orleans.
TOTAL:	34	17	17	653	608	
AVERAGE:	2	1	1	33	30	

Regular Season Individual Leaders

Season	Passing Yards		Receiving Yards		Rushing Yards	
1933	Reds Kirkman	354	Swede Hanson	140	Swede Hanson	494
1934	Ed Matesic	272	Joe Carter	238	Swede Hanson	805
1935	Ed Storm	372	Joe Carter	260	Swede Hanson	209
1936	Dave Smukler	345	Eggs Manske	325	Swede Hanson	359
1937	Dave Smukler	432	Joe Carter	282	Emmett Mortell	312
1938	Dave Smukler	524	Joe Carter	386	Dave Smukler	313
1939	Davey O'Brien	1324	Red Ramsey	359	Dave Smukler	218
1940	Davey O'Brien	1290	Don Looney	707	Dick Riffle	238
1941	T. Thompson	974	Dick Humbert	332	Jim Castiglia	183

Season	Passing Yards		Receiving Yards		Rushing Yards	
1942	T. Thompson	1410	Fred Meyer	304	Bob Davis	207
1944	Roy Zimmerman	785	Mel Bleeker	299	Steve Van Buren	444
1945	Roy Zimmerman	991	Jack Ferrante	474	Steve Van Buren	832
1946	T. Thompson	745	Jack Ferrante	451	Steve Van Buren	529
1947	T. Thompson	1680	Pete Pihos	382	Steve Van Buren	1008
1948	T. Thompson	1965	Pete Pihos	766	Steve Van Buren	945
1949	T. Thompson	1727	Jack Ferrante	508	Steve Van Buren	1146
1950	T. Thompson	1608	Jack Ferrante	588	Frank Ziegler	733
1951	Adrian Burke	1329	Pete Pihos	536	Frank Ziegler	418
1952	R. Thomason	1334	Bud Grant	997	John Huzvar	349
1953	R. Thomason	2462	Pete Pihos	1049	Don Johnson	439
1954	Adrian Burke	1740	Pete Pihos	872	Jim Parmer	408
1955	Adrian Burke	1359	Pete Pihos	864	Skippy Giancanelli	385
1956	R. Thomason	1119	Bobby Walston	590	Ken Keller	433
1957	R. Thomason	630	Bobby Walston	266	Billy Barnes	529
1958	N. Van Brocklin	2409	Pete Retzlaff	766	Billy Barnes	551
1959	N. Van Brocklin	2617	Tom McDonald	846	Billy Barnes	687
1960	N. Van Brocklin	2471	Pete Retzlaff	826	Clarence Peaks	465
1961	Sonny Jurgensen	3723	Tom McDonald	1144	Clarence Peaks	471
1962	Sonny Jurgensen	3261	Tom McDonald	1146	Tim Brown	545
1963	Sonny Jurgensen	1413	Pete Retzlaff	895	Tim Brown	841
1964	Norm Snead	1906	Pete Retzlaff	855	Earl Gros	748
1965	Norm Snead	2346	Pete Retzlaff	1190	Tim Brown	861
1966	Norm Snead	1275	Pete Retzlaff	653	Tim Brown	548
1967	Norm Snead	3399	Ben Hawkins	1265	Tom Woodeshick	670
1968	Norm Snead	1655	Ben Hawkins	707	Tom Woodeshick	947
1969	Norm Snead	2768	Harold Jackson	1116	Tom Woodeshick	831
1970	Norm Snead	2323	Harold Jackson	613	Cyril Pinder	657
1971	Peter Liske	1937	Harold Jackson	716	Ronnie Bull	351
1972	John Reaves	1508	Harold Jackson	1048	Po James	565
1973	Roman Gabriel	3219	H. Carmichael	1116	Tom Sullivan	968
1974	Roman Gabriel	1867	Charlie Young	696	Tom Sullivan	760
1975	Roman Gabriel	1644	Charlie Young	659	Tom Sullivan	632
1976	Mike Boryla	1247	H. Carmichael	503	Mike Hogan	561
1977	Ron Jaworski	2183	H. Carmichael	665	Mike Hogan	546
1978	Ron Jaworski	2487	H. Carmichael	1072	W. Montgomery	1220
1979	Ron Jaworski	2669	H. Carmichael	872	W. Montgomery	1512
1980	Ron Jaworski	3529	Charlie Smith	825	W. Montgomery	778
1981	Ron Jaworski	3095	H. Carmichael	1028	W. Montgomery	1402
1982	Ron Jaworski	2076	H. Carmichael	540	W. Montgomery	515
1983	Ron Jaworski	3315	Mike Quick	1409	Hubie Oliver	434
1984	Ron Jaworski	2754	Mike Quick	1052	W. Montgomery	789
1985	Ron Jaworski	3450	Mike Quick	1247	Earnest Jackson	1028
1986	Ron Jaworski	1405	Mike Quick	939	Keith Byars	577
1987	R. Cunningham	2786	Mike Quick	790	R. Cunningham	505
1988	R. Cunningham	3808	Keith Jackson	869	R. Cunningham	624
1989	R. Cunningham	3400	Keith Byars	721	R. Cunningham	621
1990	R. Cunningham	3466	Keith Byars	819	R. Cunningham	942
1991	Jim McMahon	2239	Fred Barnett	948	James Joseph	440
1992	R. Cunningham	2775	Fred Barnett	1083	Herschel Walker	1070
1993	Bubby Brister	1905	Calvin Williams	725	Herschel Walker	746
1994	R. Cunningham	3229	Fred Barnett	1127	Herschel Walker	528
1995	Rodney Peete	2326	Calvin Williams	768	Ricky Watters	1273

Season	Passing Yards		Receiving Yards		Rushing Yards	
1996	Ty Detmer	2911	Irving Fryar	1195	Ricky Watters	1411
1997	Bobby Hoying	1573	Irving Fryar	1316	Ricky Watters	1110
1998	Ty Detmer	1011	Jeff Graham	600	Duce Staley	1065
1999	Doug Pederson	1276	Torrance Small	655	Duce Staley	1273
2000	Donovan McNabb	3365	Chad Lewis	735	Donovan McNabb	629
2001	Donovan McNabb	3233	James Thrash	833	Duce Staley	604
2002	Donovan McNabb	2289	Todd Pinkston	798	Duce Staley	1029
2003	Donovan McNabb	3216	Todd Pinkston	575	Brian Westbrook	613
2004	Donovan McNabb	3875	Terrell Owens	1200	Brian Westbrook	812
2005	Donovan McNabb	2507	Terrell Owens	768	Brian Westbrook	617
2006	Donovan McNabb	2647	Reggie Brown	816	Brian Westbrook	1217

COACHING HISTORY: 1933-1935 Lud Wray 9-21-1-.306; 1936-1940 Bert Bell 10-44-2-.196; 1941-1950 Greasy Neale 58-39-4-.594; 1951 Bo McMillin 2-0-0-1.000; 1951 Wayne Millner 2-8-0-.200; 1952-1955 Jim Trimble 25-20-3-.552; 1956-1957 Hugh Devore 7-16-1-.313; 1958-1960 Buck Shaw 19-16-1-.542; 1961-1963 Nick Skorich 15-24-3-.393; 1964-1968 Joe Kuharich 28-41-1-.407; 1969-1971 Jerry Williams 7-22-2-.258; 1971-1972 Ed Khayat 8-15-2-.360; 1973-1975 Mike McCormack 16-25-1-.393; 1976-1982 Dick Vermeil 54-47-0-.535; 1983-1985 Marion Campbell 17-29-1-.372; 1985 Fred Bruney 1-0-0-1.000; 1986-1990 Buddy Ryan 43-35-1-.551; 1991-1994 Rich Kotite 36-28-0-.563; 1995-1998 Ray Rhodes 29-34-1-.461; 1999-present Andy Reid

PHILADELPHIA FLYERS

Home City: Philadelphia, Pennsylvania
Home Arena: CoreStates Spectrum* (1967-1996)   Capacity: 17,380 [1995]
              Wachovia Center** (1996-present)   Capacity: 19,523 [2005]
Origin of Name: The team was named after the Edmonton Flyers of the old Western Hockey League. Bud Poile the Flyers' first General Manager ran the Edmonton team.

Regular Season Record

Season	League	GP	W	L	T	OL	SL	GF	GA	Pts
1967-1968	NHL	74	31	32	11	NA	NA	173	179	73
1968-1969	NHL	76	20	35	21	NA	NA	174	225	61
1969 1970	NHL	76	17	35	24	NA	NA	197	225	58
1970-1971	NHL	78	28	33	17	NA	NA	207	225	73
1971-1972	NHL	78	26	38	14	NA	NA	200	236	66
1972-1973	NHL	78	37	30	11	NA	NA	296	256	85
1973-1974	NHL	78	50	16	12	NA	NA	273	164	112
1974-1975	NHL	80	51	18	11	NA	NA	293	181	113
1975-1976	NHL	80	51	13	16	NA	NA	348	209	118
1976-1977	NHL	80	48	16	16	NA	NA	323	213	112
1977-1978	NHL	80	45	20	15	NA	NA	296	200	105
1978-1979	NHL	80	40	25	15	NA	NA	281	248	95
1979-1980	NHL	80	48	12	20	NA	NA	237	254	116
1980-1981	NHL	80	41	24	15	NA	NA	313	249	97
1981-1982	NHL	80	38	31	11	NA	NA	325	313	87
1982-1983	NHL	80	49	23	8	NA	NA	326	240	106
1983-1984	NHL	80	44	26	10	NA	NA	350	290	98
1984-1985	NHL	80	53	20	7	NA	NA	348	241	113
1985-1986	NHL	80	53	23	4	NA	NA	335	241	110

*-known as The Spectrum from 1967 to 1994
**-known as CoreStates Spectrum from 1996 to 1998 and First Union Center from 1998 to 2003.

1986-1987	NHL	80	46	26	8	NA	NA	310	245	100
1987-1988	NHL	80	38	33	9	NA	NA	292	292	85
1988-1989	NHL	80	36	36	8	NA	NA	307	285	80
1989-1990	NHL	80	30	39	11	NA	NA	290	297	71
1990-1991	NHL	80	33	37	10	NA	NA	252	267	76
1991-1992	NHL	80	32	37	11	NA	NA	252	273	75
1992-1993	NHL	84	36	37	11	NA	NA	319	319	83
1993-1994	NHL	84	35	39	10	NA	NA	294	315	80
1994-1995	NHL	48	28	16	4	NA	NA	150	132	60
1995-1996	NHL	82	45	24	13	NA	NA	282	208	103
1996-1997	NHL	82	45	24	13	NA	NA	274	217	103
1997-1998	NHL	82	42	29	11	NA	NA	242	193	95
1998-1999	NHL	82	37	26	19	NA	NA	231	196	93
1999-2000	NHL	82	45	25	12	3	NA	237	179	105
2000-2001	NHL	82	43	25	11	3	NA	240	207	100
2001-2002	NHL	82	42	27	10	3	NA	234	192	97
2002-2003	NHL	82	45	20	13	4	NA	211	166	107
2003-2004	NHL	82	40	21	15	6	NA	229	186	101
2004-2005	NHL	Season cancelled due to lockout.								
2005-2006	NHL	82	45	26	NA	5	6	267	259	101
TOTAL:	38 years	3014	1513	1017	457	24	6	10208	8817	3513
AVERAGE:		79	40	27	12	1	0	269	232	92

Playoff Record

Season	GP	W	L	GF	GA	Result
1967-1968	7	3	4	17	17	Lost Quarterfinal series to St. Louis.
1968-1969	4	0	4	3	17	Lost Quarterfinal series to St. Louis.
1970-1971	4	0	4	8	20	Lost Quarterfinal series to Chicago.
1972-1973	11	5	6	27	31	Lost Semifinal series to Montreal.
1973-1974	17	12	5	54	36	**Won Stanley Cup**.
1974-1975	17	12	5	53	34	**Won Stanley Cup**.
1975-1976	16	8	8	61	49	Lost Stanley Cup Final to Montreal.
1976-1977	10	4	6	27	32	Lost Semifinal series to Boston.
1977-1978	12	7	5	37	35	Lost Semifinal series to Boston.
1978-1979	8	3	5	23	37	Lost Quarterfinal series to Rangers.
1979-1980	19	13	6	80	53	Lost Stanley Cup Final to N.Y. Islanders.
1980-1981	12	6	6	48	39	Lost Quarterfinal series to Calgary.
1981-1982	4	1	3	15	19	Lost Division Semifinal to N.Y. Rangers.
1982-1983	3	0	3	9	18	Lost Division Semifinal to N.Y. Rangers.
1983-1984	3	0	3	5	15	Lost Division Semifinal to Washington.
1984-1985	19	12	7	61	54	Lost Stanley Cup Final to Edmonton.
1985-1986	5	2	3	15	18	Lost Division Semifinal to N.Y. Rangers.
1986-1987	26	15	11	85	73	Lost Stanley Cup Final to Edmonton.
1987-1988	7	3	4	25	31	Lost Division Semifinal to Washington.
1988-1989	19	10	9	64	60	Lost Conference Final to Montreal.
1994-1995	15	10	5	50	43	Lost Conference Final to New Jersey.
1995-1996	12	6	6	37	28	Lost Conference Semifinal to Florida.
1996-1997	19	12	7	67	55	Lost Stanley Cup Final to Detroit.
1997-1998	5	1	4	9	18	Lost Conference Quarterfinal to Buffalo.
1998-1999	6	2	4	11	9	Lost Conference Quarterfinal to Toronto.
1999-2000	18	11	7	44	41	Lost Conference Final to New Jersey.
2000-2001	6	2	4	13	21	Lost Conference Quarterfinal to Buffalo.
2001-2002	5	1	4	2	11	Lost Conference Quarterfinal to Ottawa.
2002-2003	13	6	7	34	33	Lost Conference Semifinal to Ottawa.

2003-2004	18	11	7	50	43	Lost Conference Final to Tampa Bay.
2005-2006	6	2	4	14	27	Lost Conference Quarterfinal to Buffalo.
TOTAL:	346	180	166	1048	1017	
AVERAGE:	11	6	5	34	33	

Regular Season Individual Leaders

Season	Goals		Points		Penalty Minutes	
1967-1968	Leon Rochefort	21	Lou Angotti	49	Ed Van Impe	141
1968-1969	Andre Lacroix	24	Andre Lacroix	56	Forbes Kennedy	195
1969 1970	Gary Dornhoefer	26	Andre Lacroix	58	Earl Heiskala	171
1970-1971	Bobby Clarke	27	Bobby Clarke	63	Gary Dornhoefer	93
1971-1972	Bobby Clarke	35	Bobby Clarke	81	Gary Dornhoefer	183
1972-1973	Rick MacLeish	50	Bobby Clarke	104	Dave Schultz	259
1973-1974	Bobby Clarke	35	Bobby Clarke	87	Dave Schultz	348
1974-1975	Reg Leach	45	Bobby Clarke	116	Dave Schultz	472
1975-1976	Reg Leach	61	Bobby Clarke	119	Dave Schultz	307
1976-1977	Rick MacLeish	49	Rick MacLeish	97	Paul Holmgren	201
1977-1978	Bill Barber	41	Bobby Clarke	89	Andre Dupont	225
1978-1979	Bill Barber	34	Bill Barber	80	Behn Wilson	197
	Reg Leach	34				
1979-1980	Reg Leach	50	Ken Linseman	79	Paul Holmgren	267
1980-1981	Bill Barber	43	Bill Barber	85	Paul Holmgren	306
1981-1982	Bill Barber	45	Ken Linseman	92	Glen Cochrane	329
1982-1983	Darryl Sittler	43	Bobby Clarke	85	Glen Cochrane	237
1983-1984	Tim Kerr	54	Tim Kerr	93	Glen Cochrane	225
1984-1985	Tim Kerr	54	Tim Kerr	98	Rick Tocchet	181
1985-1986	Tim Kerr	58	Brian Propp	97	Rick Tocchet	284
1986-1987	Tim Kerr	58	Tim Kerr	95	Rick Tocchet	288
1987-1988	Rick Tocchet	31	Murray Craven	76	Rick Tocchet	301
			Brian Propp	76		
1988-1989	Tim Kerr	48	Tim Kerr	88	Jeff Chychrun	245
1989-1990	Rick Tocchet	37	Rick Tocchet	96	Craig Berube	291
1990-1991	Rick Tocchet	40	Rick Tocchet	71	Craig Berube	293
1991-1992	Rod Brind'Amour	33	Rod Brind'Amour	77	Terry Carkner	195
1992-1993	Mark Recchi	53	Mark Recchi	123	Ryan McGill	238
1993-1994	Eric Lindros	44	Mark Recchi	107	Dave Brown	137
1994-1995	Eric Lindros	29	Eric Lindros	70	Petr Svoboda	70
1995-1996	John LeClair	51	Eric Lindros	115	Shawn Antoski	204
1996-1997	John LeClair	50	John LeClair	97	Scott Daniels	237
1997-1998	John LeClair	51	John LeClair	87	Dan Kordic	210
1998-1999	John LeClair	43	Eric Lindros	93	Eric Lindros	120
1999-2000	John LeClair	40	Mark Recchi	91	Craig Berube	162
2000-2001	Keith Primeau	34	Mark Recchi	77	Luke Richardson	131
2001-2002	Simon Gagne	33	Jeremy Roenick	67	Todd Fedoruk	137
2002-2003	Jeremy Roenick	27	Jeremy Roenick	59	Donald Brashear	161
2003-2004	Mark Recchi	26	Mark Recchi	75	Donald Brashear	212
2004-2005	Season cancelled due to lockout.					
2005-2006	Simon Gagne	47	Simon Gagne	79	Donald Brashear	166

COACHING HISTORY: 1967-1969 Keith Allen 51-67-32-.447; 1969-1971 Vic Stasiuk 45-68-41-.425; 1971-1978 Fred Shero 308-151-95-.642; 1978-1979 Bob McCammon 22-17-11-.550; 1978-1982 Pat Quinn 141-73-48-.630; 1981-1984 Bob McCammon 97-51-20-.637; 1984-1988 Mike Keenan 190-102-28-.638; 1988-1992 Paul Holmgren 107-126-31-.464; 1991-1993 Bill Dineen 60-60-20-.500; 1993-1994 Terry Simpson

35-39-10-.476; 1994-1997 Terry Murray 118-64-30-.627; 1997-1998 Wayne Cashman 32-20-9-.598; 1997-2000 Roger Neilson 76-52-32-.575; 1999-2001 Craig Ramsay 28-20-5-0-.575; 2000-2002 Bill Barber 73-40-17-6-.621; 2002-present Ken Hitchcock

PHILADELPHIA FURY
(became Montreal Manic)

Home City: Philadelphia, Pennsylvania
Home Stadium: Veterans Stadium   Capacity: 66,052 [1980]
Origin of Name:

Regular Season Record

Season	League	GP	W	L	GF	GA	BP	Pts	Pct
1978	NASL	30	12	18	40	58	39	111	.411
1979	NASL	30	10	20	55	60	51	111	.411
1980	NASL	32	10	22	42	68	38	98	.340
TOTAL:	3 years	92	32	60	137	186	128	320	
AVERAGE:		31	11	20	46	62	43	107	.386

Playoff Record

Season	GP	W	L	GF	GA	Result
1979	4	2	2	6	6	Lost 2nd Round series to Tampa Bay.

Regular Season Individual Leaders

Season	Goals		Points		GAA (360 Min)	
1978	Pat Fidelia	8	Alan Ball	20	Jim Miller	1.72
1979	David Robb	16	David Robb	52	Keith Van Eron	1.77
1980						

COACHING HISTORY: 1978 Richard Dinnis, Alan Ball; 1978 Alan Ball 6-8; 1979 Marko Valok 10-20; 1980 Eddie Firmani 10-22

PHILADELPHIA KEYSTONES

Home City: Philadelphia, Pennsylvania
Home Field: Keystone Park
Origin of Name: The name was chosen because Pennsylvania is known as the Keystone State.

Regular Season Record

Season	League	GP	W	L	Pct	GB	R	OR
1884	UA	67	21	46	.313	50	414	545

Regular Season Individual Leaders

Season	Home Runs		RBI's	Wins	
1884	Joe Flynn	4	Not Recorded	Edward Bakely	14

COACHING HISTORY: Fergy Malone 11-30-.268; Tom Pratt 10-16-.385

PHILADELPHIA PHILLIES

Home City: Philadelphia, Pennsylvania
Home Field: Recreation Park (1883-1886)
    Philadelphia Baseball Grounds (1887-1894)
    Baker Bowl (1895-1938)   Capacity: 18,800 [1895]
    Shibe Park (1938-1970)*   Capacity: 33,608 [1961]
    Veterans Stadium (1971-2003)   Capacity: 62,418 [2003]
    Citizens Bank Park (2004-present) Capacity: 43,647 [2006]
Origin of Name: Originally called Fillies. When the team was bought in 1943 the new owners changed the name to Blue Jays but the name didn't stick and the name reverted to Phillies.

Regular Season Record

Season	League	GP	W	L	Pct	GB	R	OR
1883	NL	98	17	81	.173	46	437	887
1884	NL	112	39	73	.348	45	549	824
1885	NL	110	56	54	.509	30	513	511
1886	NL	114	71	43	.623	14	621	498
1887	NL	123	75	48	.610	3.5	901	702
1888	NL	130	69	61	.531	14.5	535	509
1889	NL	127	63	64	.496	20.5	742	748
1890	NL	132	78	54	.591	9.5	823	707
1891	NL	137	68	69	.496	18.5	756	773
1892	NL	153	87	66	.569	16.5	860	690
1893	NL	129	72	57	.558	14	1011	841
1894	NL	128	71	57	.555	18	1143	966
1895	NL	131	78	53	.595	9.5	1068	957
1896	NL	130	62	68	.477	28.5	890	891
1897	NL	132	55	77	.417	38	752	792
1898	NL	149	78	71	.523	24	823	784
1899	NL	152	94	58	.618	9	916	743
1900	NL	138	75	63	.543	8	810	792
1901	NL	140	83	57	.593	7.5	668	543
1902	NL	137	56	81	.409	46	484	649
1903	NL	135	49	86	.363	39.5	618	743
1904	NL	152	52	100	.342	53.5	571	782
1905	NL	152	83	69	.546	21.5	708	603
1906	NL	153	71	82	.464	45.5	530	568
1907	NL	147	83	64	.565	21.5	514	481
1908	NL	154	83	71	.539	16	503	446
1909	NL	153	74	79	.484	36.5	514	518
1910	NL	153	78	75	.510	25.5	674	682
1911	NL	152	79	73	.520	19.5	658	673
1912	NL	152	73	79	.480	30.5	670	689
1913	NL	151	88	63	.583	12.5	693	636
1914	NL	154	74	80	.481	20.5	651	673
1915	NL	152	90	62	.592	-	589	463
1916	NL	153	91	62	.595	2.5	581	489
1917	NL	152	87	65	.572	10	578	501
1918	NL	123	55	68	.447	26	430	507
1919	NL	137	47	90	.343	47.5	510	699
1920	NL	153	62	91	.405	30.5	565	714

*-known as Connie Mack Stadium from 1953 to 1957

1921	NL	154	51	103	.331	43.5	617	919
1922	NL	153	57	96	.373	35.5	738	920
1923	NL	154	50	104	.325	45.5	748	1008
1924	NL	151	55	96	.364	37	676	849
1925	NL	153	68	85	.444	27	812	930
1926	NL	151	58	93	.384	29.5	687	900
1927	NL	154	51	103	.331	43	678	903
1928	NL	152	43	109	.283	51	660	957
1929	NL	153	71	82	.464	27.5	897	1032
1930	NL	154	52	102	.338	40	944	1199
1931	NL	154	66	88	.429	35	684	828
1932	NL	154	78	76	.506	12	844	796
1933	NL	152	60	92	.395	31	607	760
1934	NL	149	56	93	.376	37	675	794
1935	NL	153	64	89	.418	35.5	685	871
1936	NL	154	54	100	.351	38	726	874
1937	NL	153	61	92	.399	34.5	724	869
1938	NL	150	45	105	.300	43	550	840
1939	NL	151	45	106	.298	50.5	553	856
1940	NL	153	50	103	.327	50	494	750
1941	NL	154	43	111	.279	57	501	793
1942	NL	151	42	109	.278	62.5	394	706
1943	NL	154	64	90	.416	41	571	676
1944	NL	153	61	92	.399	43.5	539	658
1945	NL	154	46	108	.299	52	548	865
1946	NL	154	69	85	.448	28	560	705
1947	NL	154	62	92	.403	32	589	687
1948	NL	154	66	88	.429	25.5	591	729
1949	NL	154	81	73	.526	16	662	668
1950	NL	154	91	63	.591	-	722	624
1951	NL	154	73	81	.474	23.5	648	644
1952	NL	154	87	67	.565	9.5	657	552
1953	NL	154	83	71	.539	22	716	666
1954	NL	154	75	79	.487	22	659	614
1955	NL	154	77	77	.500	21.5	675	666
1956	NL	154	71	83	.461	22	668	738
1957	NL	154	77	77	.500	18	623	656
1958	NL	154	69	85	.448	23	664	762
1959	NL	154	64	90	.416	23	599	725
1960	NL	154	59	95	.383	36	546	691
1961	NL	154	47	107	.305	46	584	796
1962	NL	161	81	80	.503	20	705	759
1963	NL	162	87	75	.537	12	642	578
1964	NL	162	92	70	.568	1	693	632
1965	NL	161	85	76	.528	11.5	654	667
1966	NL	162	87	75	.537	8	696	640
1967	NL	162	82	80	.506	19.5	612	581
1968	NL	162	76	86	.469	21	543	615
1969	NL	162	63	99	.389	37	645	745
1970	NL	161	73	88	.453	15.5	594	730
1971	NL	162	67	95	.414	30	558	688
1972	NL	156	59	97	.378	37.5	503	635
1973	NL	162	71	91	.438	11.5	642	717
1974	NL	162	80	82	.494	8	676	701

Year	League	G	W	L	PCT	GB	R	OR
1975	NL	162	86	76	.531	6.5	735	694
1976	NL	162	101	61	.623	-	770	557
1977	NL	162	101	61	.623	-	847	668
1978	NL	162	90	72	.556	-	708	586
1979	NL	162	84	78	.519	14	683	718
1980	NL	162	91	71	.562	-	728	639
1981	NL	107	59	48	.551	NA	491	472
1982	NL	162	89	73	.549	3	664	654
1983	NL	162	90	72	.556	-	696	635
1984	NL	162	81	81	.500	15.5	720	690
1985	NL	162	75	87	.463	26	667	673
1986	NL	162	86	76	.534	21.5	739	713
1987	NL	162	80	82	.494	15	702	749
1988	NL	161	65	96	.404	35.5	597	734
1989	NL	162	67	95	.414	26	629	735
1990	NL	162	77	85	.475	18	646	729
1991	NL	162	78	84	.481	20	629	680
1992	NL	162	70	92	.432	26	686	717
1993	NL	162	97	65	.599	-	877	740
1994	NL	115	54	61	.470	20.5	521	497
1995	NL	144	69	75	.479	21	615	658
1996	NL	162	67	95	.414	29	650	790
1997	NL	162	68	94	.420	33	668	840
1998	NL	162	75	87	.463	31	713	808
1999	NL	162	77	85	.475	26	841	846
2000	NL	162	65	97	.401	30	708	830
2001	NL	162	86	76	.531	2	746	720
2002	NL	161	80	81	.497	21.5	710	724
2003	NL	162	86	76	.531	15	791	697
2004	NL	162	86	76	.531	10	840	781
2005	NL	162	88	74	.543	2	807	726
2006	NL	162	85	77	.525	12	865	812
TOTAL:	124 years	18721	8764	9957		2962	83426	89350
AVERAGE:		151	71	80	.468	24	673	721

Playoff Record

Season	GP	W	L	R	OR	Result
1915	5	1	4	10	12	Lost World Series to Boston.
1950	4	0	4	5	11	Lost World Series to New York.
1976	3	0	3	11	19	Lost NLCS to Cincinnati.
1977	4	1	3	14	22	Lost NLCS to Los Angeles.
1978	4	1	3	17	21	Lost NLCS to Los Angeles.
1980	11	7	4	47	42	**Won World Series**.
1981	5	2	3	14	16	Lost Divisional playoff to Montreal.
1983	9	4	5	25	26	Lost World Series to Baltimore.
1993	12	6	6	59	78	Lost World Series to Toronto.
TOTAL:	57	22	35	202	247	
AVERAGE:	6	2	3	22	27	

Regular Season Individual Leaders

Season	Home Runs		RBI's		Wins	
1883	Bill McClellan	1	Jack Manning	37	John Coleman	12
	William Purcell	1				
	Emil Gross	1				

Season	Home Runs		RBI's		Wins	
1884	Jack Manning	5	Jack Manning	52	Charlie Ferguson	21
1885	Joe Mulvey	6	Joe Mulvey	64	Charlie Ferguson	26
					Ed Daily	26
1886	Sid Farrar	5	Joe Mulvey	53	Charlie Ferguson	30
1887	George Wood	14	Charlie Ferguson	85	Dan Casey	28
1888	George Wood	6	Sid Farrar	53	Charlie Buffinton	28
1889	Sam Thompson	20	Sam Thompson	111	Charlie Buffinton	28
1890	Jack Clements	7	Sam Thompson	102	William Gleason	38
1891	Sam Thompson	7	Sam Thompson	90	William Gleason	24
1892	Roger Connor	12	Sam Thompson	104	Gus Weyhing	32
1893	Ed Delahanty	19	Ed Delahanty	146	Gus Weyhing	23
1894	Sam Thompson	13	Sam Thompson	141	Jack Taylor	23
1895	Sam Thompson	18	Sam Thompson	165	Jack Taylor	26
1896	Ed Delahanty	13	Ed Delahanty	126	Jack Taylor	20
1897	Napoleon Lajoie	9	Napoleon Lajoie	127	Jack Taylor	16
1898	Elmer Flick	8	Napoleon Lajoie	127	Wiley Piatt	24
1899	Ed Delahanty	9	Ed Delahanty	137	Wiley Piatt	23
1900	Elmer Flick	11	Elmer Flick	110	Red Donahue	15
					Charles Fraser	15
					Bill Bernhard	15
1901	Elmer Flick	8	Ed Delahanty	108	Red Donahue	21
	Ed Delahanty	8				
1902	Shad Barry	3	Shad Barry	58	Guy White	16
1903	Bill Keister	3	Bill Keister	63	Bill Duggleby	13
1904	Charles Dooin	6	Sherry Magee	57	Charles Fraser	14
1905	Sherry Magee	5	Sherry Magee	98	Togie Pittinger	23
1906	Sherry Magee	6	Sherry Magee	67	Tully Sparks	19
1907	Sherry Magee	4	Sherry Magee	85	Tully Sparks	22
1908	Bill Bransfield	3	Bill Bransfield	71	George McQuillan	23
1909	John Titus	3	Sherry Magee	66	Earl Moore	18
1910	Sherry Magee	6	Sherry Magee	123	Earl Moore	22
1911	Fred Luderus	16	Fred Luderus	99	Pete Alexander	28
1912	Gavvy Cravath	11	Gavvy Cravath	70	Pete Alexander	19
1913	Gavvy Cravath	19	Gavvy Cravath	128	Tom Seaton	27
1914	Gavvy Cravath	19	Sherry Magee	103	Pete Alexander	27
1915	Gavvy Cravath	24	Gavvy Cravath	115	Pete Alexander	31
1916	Gavvy Cravath	11	Gavvy Cravath	70	Pete Alexander	33
1917	Gavvy Cravath	12	Gavvy Cravath	83	Pete Alexander	30
1918	Gavvy Cravath	8	Fred Luderus	67	Brad Hogg	13
					Mike Prendergast	13
1919	Gavvy Cravath	12	Emil Meusel	59	Lee Meadows	8
1920	Cy Williams	15	Cy Williams	72	Lee Meadows	16
1921	Cy Williams	18	Cy Williams	75	Lee Meadows	11
1922	Cy Williams	26	Cy Williams	92	Jimmy Ring	12
					Lee Meadows	12
1923	Cy Williams	41	Cy Williams	114	Jimmy Ring	18
1924	Cy Williams	24	Cy Williams	93	Bill Hubbell	10
					Jimmy Ring	10
1925	George Harper	18	George Harper	97	Jimmy Ring	14
1926	Cy Williams	18	Fred Leach	71	Hal Carlson	17
1927	Cy Williams	30	Cy Williams	98	Jack Scott	9
1928	Don Hurst	19	Art Whitney	103	Ray Benge	8
1929	Charles Klein	43	Charles Klein	145	Claude Willoughby	15

Season	Home Runs		RBI's		Wins	
1930	Charles Klein	40	Charles Klein	170	Phil Collins	16
1931	Charles Klein	31	Charles Klein	121	Jim Elliott	19
1932	Charles Klein	38	Don Hurst	143	Phil Collins	14
1933	Charles Klein	28	Charles Klein	120	Ed Holley	13
1934	Dolph Camilli	12	John Moore	93	Curt Davis	19
1935	Dolph Camilli	25	John Moore	93	Curt Davis	16
1936	Dolph Camilli	28	Dolph Camilli	102	Claude Passeau	11
					Bill Walters	11
1937	Dolph Camilli	27	Dolph Camilli	80	Wayne LaMaster	15
1938	Charles Klein	8	Morrie Arnovich	72	Claude Passeau	11
1939	Joe Marty	9	Morrie Arnovich	67	Kirby Higbe	10
	Emmett Mueller	9				
1940	Johnny Rizzo	20	Johnny Rizzo	53	Kirby Higbe	14
1941	Dan Litwhiler	18	Nick Etten	79	Tom Hughes	9
					John Podgajny	9
1942	Dan Litwhiler	9	Dan Litwhiler	56	Tom Hughes	12
1943	Ron Northey	16	Ron Northey	68	Tom Rowe	14
1944	Ron Northey	22	Ron Northey	104	Charley Schanz	13
					Ken Raffensberger	13
1945	Vince DiMaggio	19	Vince DiMaggio	84	Andy Karl	8
					Dick Barrett	8
1946	Del Ennis	17	Del Ennis	73	Tom Rowe	11
					Oscar Judd	11
1947	Andy Seminick	13	Del Ennis	81	Emil Leonard	17
1948	Del Ennis	30	Del Ennis	95	Emil Leonard	12
1949	Del Ennis	25	Del Ennis	110	Russ Meyer	17
					Ken Heintzelman	17
1950	Del Ennis	31	Del Ennis	126	Robin Roberts	20
1951	Willie Jones	22	Willie Jones	81	Robin Roberts	21
1952	Del Ennis	20	Del Ennis	107	Robin Roberts	28
1953	Del Ennis	29	Del Ennis	125	Robin Roberts	23
1954	Del Ennis	25	Del Ennis	119	Robin Roberts	23
1955	Del Ennis	29	Del Ennis	120	Robin Roberts	23
1956	Stan Lopata	32	Del Ennis	95	Robin Roberts	19
			Stan Lopata	95		
1957	Eldon Repulski	20	Ed Bouchee	76	Jack Sanford	19
1958	Harry Anderson	23	Harry Anderson	97	Robin Roberts	17
1959	Gene Freese	23	Wally Post	94	Robin Roberts	15
1960	Pancho Herrera	17	Pancho Herrera	71	Robin Roberts	12
1961	Don Demeter	20	Don Demeter	68	Art Mahaffey	11
1962	Don Demeter	29	Don Demeter	107	Art Mahaffey	19
1963	John Callison	26	Don Demeter	83	Ray Culp	14
1964	John Callison	31	John Callison	104	Jim Bunning	19
1965	John Callison	32	John Callison	101	Jim Bunning	19
1966	Dick Allen	40	Dick Allen	110	Chris Short	20
1967	Dick Allen	23	Dick Allen	77	Jim Bunning	17
1968	Dick Allen	33	Dick Allen	90	Chris Short	19
1969	Dick Allen	32	Dick Allen	89	Rick Wise	15
1970	Deron Johnson	27	Deron Johnson	93	Rick Wise	13
1971	Deron Johnson	34	Willie Montanez	99	Rick Wise	17
1972	Greg Luzinski	18	Greg Luzinski	68	Steve Carlton	27
1973	Greg Luzinski	29	Greg Luzinski	97	Wayne Twitchell	13
					Ken Brett	13

Season	Home Runs		RBI's		Wins	
					Jim Lonborg	13
					Steve Carlton	13
1974	Mike Schmidt	36	Mike Schmidt	116	Jim Lonborg	17
1975	Mike Schmidt	38	Greg Luzinski	120	Steve Carlton	15
1976	Mike Schmidt	38	Mike Schmidt	107	Steve Carlton	20
1977	Greg Luzinski	39	Greg Luzinski	130	Steve Carlton	23
1978	Greg Luzinski	35	Greg Luzinski	101	Steve Carlton	16
1979	Mike Schmidt	45	Mike Schmidt	114	Steve Carlton	18
1980	Mike Schmidt	48	Mike Schmidt	121	Steve Carlton	24
1981	Mike Schmidt	31	Mike Schmidt	91	Steve Carlton	13
1982	Mike Schmidt	35	Mike Schmidt	87	Steve Carlton	23
1983	Mike Schmidt	40	Mike Schmidt	109	John Denny	19
1984	Mike Schmidt	36	Mike Schmidt	106	Jerry Koosman	14
1985	Mike Schmidt	33	Glenn Wilson	102	Kevin Gross	15
1986	Mike Schmidt	37	Mike Schmidt	119	Kevin Gross	12
1987	Mike Schmidt	35	Mike Schmidt	113	Shane Rawley	17
1988	Chris James	19	Juan Samuel	67	Kevin Gross	12
1989	Von Hayes	26	Von Hayes	78	Jeff Parrett	12
					Ken Howell	12
1990	Dale Murphy	24	Dale Murphy	83	Pat Combs	10
1991	John Kruk	21	John Kruk	92	Terry Mulholland	16
1992	Darren Daulton	27	Darren Daulton	109	Curt Schilling	14
	Dave Hollins	27				
1993	Pete Incaviglia	24	Darren Daulton	105	Tommy Greene	16
	Darren Daulton	24			Curt Schilling	16
1994	Darren Daulton	15	Darren Daulton	56	Danny Jackson	14
1995	Gregg Jefferies	11	Charlie Hayes	85	Paul Quantril	11
	Charlie Hayes	11				
	Mark Whiten	11				
1996	Benito Santiago	30	Benito Santiago	85	Curt Schilling	9
1997	Scott Rolen	21	Scott Rolen	92	Curt Schilling	17
1998	Scott Rolen	31	Scott Rolen	110	Curt Schilling	15
1999	Mike Lieberthal	31	Rico Brogna	102	Paul Byrd	15
					Curt Schilling	15
2000	Scott Rolen	26	Scott Rolen	89	Randy Wolf	11
2001	Bobby Abreu	31	Bobby Abreu	110	Robert Person	15
2002	Pat Burrell	37	Pat Burrell	116	Vincente Padilla	14
2003	Jim Thome	47	Jim Thome	131	Randy Wolf	16
2004	Jim Thome	42	Bobby Abreu	105	Eric Milton	14
2005	Pat Burrell	32	Pat Burrell	117	Jon Lieber	17
2006	Ryan Howard	58	Ryan Howard	149	Brett Myers	12

COACHING HISTORY: 1883 Bob Ferguson 4-13-.235; 1883 Blondie Purcell 13-68-.160; 1884-1893 Harry Wright 678-589-.535; 1894-1895 Arthur Irwin 149-110-.575; 1896 Billy Nash 62-68-.477; 1897-1898 George Stallings 74-104-.416; 1898-1902 Bill Shettsline 367-303-.548; 1903 Charles Zimmer 49-86-.363; 1904-1906 Hugh Duffy 206-251-.451; 1907-1909 Bill Murray 240-214-.529; 1910-1914 Charles Dooin 392-370-.514; 1915-1918 Patrick Moran 323-257-.557; 1919 Jack Coombs 18-44-.290; 1919-1920 Gavvy Cravath 91-137-.399; 1921 Bill Donovan 31-71-.304; 1921-1922 Irvin Wilhelm 77-128-.376; 1923-1926 Art Fletcher 231-378-.379; 1927 John McInnis 51-103-.331; 1928-1933 Burt Shotton 370-549-.403; 1934-1938 Jim Wilson 280-477-.370; 1938 Hans Lobert 0-2-.000; 1939-1941 James Prothro 138-320-.301; 1942 Hans Lobert 42-109-.278; 1943 Stanley Harris 64-90-.416; 1944-1945 Fred Fitzsimmons 78-142-.355; 1945-1948 Ben Chapman 197-277-.416; 1948 Allen Cooke 6-5-.545; 1948-1952 Eddie Sawyer

296-293-.503; 1952-1954 Steve O'Neill 182-140-.565; 1954 Terry Moore 35-42-.455; 1955-1958 Mayo Smith 264-281-.484; 1958-1960 Eddie Sawyer 94-132-.416; 1960 Andy Cohen 1-0-1.000; 1960-1968 Gene Mauch 645-684-.485; 1968-1969 George Myatt 21-35-.375; 1968-1969 Bob Skinner 92-123-.428; 1970-1972 Frank Lucchesi 166-233-.416; 1972 Paul Owens 33-47-.413; 1973-1979 Danny Ozark 594-510-.538; 1979-1981 Dallas Green 169-130-.565; 1982-1983 Pat Corrales 132-115-.534; 1983-1984 Paul Owens 128-111-.536; 1985-1987 John Felske 190-195-.494; 1987-1988 Lee Elia 111-142-.439; 1988 John Vukovich 5-4-.556; 1989-1991 Nick Leyva 148-189-.439; 1991-1996 Jim Fregosi 431-463-.482; 1997-2000 Terry Francona 285-363-.440; 2001-2004 Larry Bowa 338-309-.522; 2005-present Charlie Manuel

PHILADELPHIA-PITTSBURGH
(Philadelphia Eagles and Pittsburgh Steelers merged for the 1943 season)

Home City: Philadelphia, Pennsylvania
Pittsburgh, Pennsylvania
Home Stadium: Forbes Field   Capacity: 35,000
Origin of Name: This was a merger of the Philadelphia and Pittsburgh teams.

			Regular Season Record					
Season	League	GP	W	L	T	PF	PA	Pct
1943	NFL	10	5	4	1	225	230	.550

	Regular Season Individual Leaders				
Season	Passing Yards		Receiving Yards		Rushing Yards
1943	Roy Zimmerman	846	Tony Bova	419	Jack Hinkle	571

COACHING HISTORY: Greasy Neale & Walt Kiesling 5-4-1-.550

PHILADELPHIA QUAKERS

Home City: Philadelphia, Pennsylvania
Home Field: Brotherhood Park*   Capacity: 17,200
Origin of Name: Philadelphia had been first settled primarily by Quakers.

			Regular Season Record				
Season	League	GP	W	L	Pct	GB	R	OR
1890	PL	131	68	63	.519	14	941	855

	Regular Season Individual Leaders				
Season	Home Runs		RBI's		Wins
1890	Bill Shindle	10	George Wood	102	Phil Knell	22

COACHING HISTORY: Ben Hilt 17-19-.472; Jim Fogarty 30-19-.612; Charlie Buffinton 21-25-.457

PHILADELPHIA QUAKERS
(were Pittsburgh Pirates)

Home City: Philadelphia, Pennsylvania
Home Arena: Philadelphia Arena   Capacity: 5,000
Origin of Name: The name was chosen in a bid to attract some of the large Quaker population of Pennsylvania to the games.

*-also known as Forepaugh Park

Regular Season Record

Season	League	GP	W	L	T	GF	GA	Pts	Pct
1930-1931	NHL	44	4	36	4	76	184	12	.136

Regular Season Individual Leaders

Season	Goals		Points		Penalty Minutes	
1930-1931	Hibbert Milks	17	Gerry Lowrey	27	Darcy Coulson	103

COACHING HISTORY: Cooper Smeaton 4-36-4-.136

PHILADELPHIA 76ers
(were Syracuse Nationals)

Home City: Philadelphia, Pennsylvania
Home Court: Convention Hall (1963-1967)   Capacity: 12,000
　　　　　CoreStates Spectrum (1967-1996)*   Capacity: 18,168 [1995]
　　　　　Wachovia Center (1998-present)**   Capacity: 20,444 [2006]
Origin of Name: The name was suggested because of Philadelphia's role in the founding of the United States in 1776, and submitted in a Name the Team Contest.

Regular Season Record

Season	League	GP	W	L	PPGF	PPGA	Pct	GB
1963-1964	NBA	80	34	46	112.2	116.5	.425	25
1964-1965	NBA	80	40	40	112.5	112.7	.500	22
1965-1966	NBA	80	55	25	117.3	112.7	.688	-
1966-1967	NBA	81	68	13	125.2	115.8	.840	-
1967-1968	NBA	82	62	20	122.6	114.0	.756	-
1968-1969	NBA	82	55	27	118.9	113.8	.671	2
1969-1970	NBA	82	42	40	121.9	118.5	.512	18
1970-1971	NBA	82	47	35	114.8	113.3	.573	5
1971-1972	NBA	82	30	52	112.2	115.9	.366	26
1972-1973	NBA	82	9	73	104.1	116.2	.110	59
1973-1974	NBA	82	25	57	101.2	107.5	.305	31
1974-1975	NBA	82	34	48	99.8	102.8	.415	26
1975-1976	NBA	82	46	36	106.5	106.3	.561	8
1976-1977	NBA	82	50	32	110.2	106.2	.610	-
1977-1978	NBA	82	55	27	114.7	109.6	.671	-
1978-1979	NBA	82	47	35	109.5	107.7	.573	7
1979-1980	NBA	82	59	23	109.1	104.9	.720	2
1980-1981	NBA	82	62	20	111.7	103.8	.756	-
1981-1982	NBA	82	58	24	111.2	105.5	.707	5
1982-1983	NBA	82	65	17	112.1	104.4	.793	-
1983-1984	NBA	82	52	30	107.8	105.6	.634	10
1984-1985	NBA	82	58	24	112.9	108.8	.707	5
1985-1986	NBA	82	54	28	110.4	108.0	.659	13
1986-1987	NBA	82	45	37	106.5	106.6	.549	14
1987-1988	NBA	82	36	46	105.7	107.1	.439	21
1988-1989	NBA	82	46	36	111.9	110.4	.561	6
1989-1990	NBA	82	53	29	110.2	105.2	.646	-
1990-1991	NBA	82	44	38	105.4	105.6	.537	12
1991-1992	NBA	82	35	47	101.9	103.2	.427	16
1992-1993	NBA	82	26	56	104.3	110.1	.317	34

*-known as The Spectrum from 1967 to 1994
**-known as CoreStates Center from 1996 to 1998 and First Union Center from 1998 to 2003.

1993-1994	NBA	82	25	57	98.0	105.6	.305	32
1994-1995	NBA	82	24	58	95.4	100.4	.293	33
1995-1996	NBA	82	18	64	94.5	104.5	.220	42
1996-1997	NBA	82	22	60	100.2	106.7	.268	39
1997-1998	NBA	82	31	51	93.3	95.7	.378	24
1998-1999	NBA	50	28	22	89.7	87.6	.560	5
1999-2000	NBA	82	49	33	94.8	93.4	.598	3
2000-2001	NBA	82	56	26	94.6	90.4	.683	-
2001-2002	NBA	82	43	39	91.0	89.4	.524	9
2002-2003	NBA	82	48	34	96.8	94.5	.585	1
2003-2004	NBA	82	33	49	88.0	90.5	.402	14
2004-2005	NBA	82	43	39	99.1	99.9	.524	2
2005-2006	NBA	82	38	44	99.4	101.3	.463	11
TOTAL:	43 years	3487	1850	1637				582
AVERAGE:		81	43	38	106.2	105.7	.531	14

Playoff Record

Season	GP	W	L	PPGF	PPGA	Result
1963-1964	5	2	3	113.2	118.4	Lost Division Semifinal to Cincinnati.
1964-1965	11	6	5	111.8	111.6	Lost Division Final to Boston.
1965-1966	5	1	4	104.0	113.6	Lost Division Final to Boston.
1966-1967	15	11	4	121.7	112.3	**Won NBA Championship.**
1967-1968	13	7	6	113.7	113.0	Lost Divisional Final to Boston.
1968-1969	5	1	4	106.0	116.4	Lost Division Semifinal to Boston.
1969-1970	5	1	4	113.4	123.8	Lost Division Semifinal to Milwaukee.
1970-1971	7	3	4	109.0	112.4	Lost Conference Semifinal to Baltimore.
1975-1976	3	1	2	114.3	108.3	Lost 1st Round series to Buffalo.
1976-1977	19	10	9	107.6	107.4	Lost Championship series to Portland.
1977-1978	10	6	4	114.4	108.8	Lost Conference Final to Washington.
1978-1979	9	5	4	112.7	109.2	Lost Conference Semifinal to San Antonio.
1979-1980	18	12	6	102.8	100.6	Lost Championship series to Los Angeles.
1980-1981	16	9	7	104.3	104.4	Lost Conference Final to Boston.
1981-1982	21	12	9	105.7	104.4	Lost Championship series to Los Angeles.
1982-1983	13	12	1	105.8	99.3	**Won NBA Championship.**
1983-1984	5	2	3	103.8	107.0	Lost 1st Round series to New Jersey.
1984-1985	13	8	5	107.1	104.7	Lost Conference Final to Boston
1985-1986	12	6	6	109.5	106.7	Lost Conference Semifinal to Milwaukee.
1986-1987	5	2	3	112.4	114.0	Lost 1st Round series to Milwaukee.
1988-1989	3	0	3	105.7	108.3	Lost 1st Round series to New York.
1989-1990	10	4	6	102.1	107.1	Lost Conference Semifinal to Chicago.
1990-1991	8	4	4	100.9	102.1	Lost Conference Semifinal to Chicago.
1998-1999	8	3	5	89.3	88.8	Lost Conference Semifinal to Indiana.
1999-2000	10	5	5	94.2	95.6	Lost Conference Semifinal to Indiana.
2000-2001	23	12	11	92.3	92.4	Lost Championship series to Los Angeles.
2001-2002	5	2	3	87.0	97.8	Lost 1st Round series to Boston.
2002-2003	12	6	6	90.4	91.3	Lost Conference Semifinal to Detroit.
2004-2005	5	1	4	90.8	98.8	Lost 1st Round series to Detroit.
TOTAL:	294	154	140			
AVERAGE:	10	5	5	104.8	104.6	

Regular Season Individual Leaders

Season	Field Goals (min. 70 games)		Points		Points per Game (min. 70 games)	
1963-64	Hal Greer	.444	Hal Greer	1865	Hal Greer	23.3

Season	Field Goals (min. 70 games)		Points		Points per Game (min. 70 games)	
1964-65	Hal Greer	.433	Hal Greer	1413	Hal Greer	20.2
1965-66	W. Chamberlain	.540	W. Chamberlain	2649	W. Chamberlain	33.5
1966-67	W. Chamberlain	.683	W. Chamberlain	1956	W. Chamberlain	24.1
1967-68	W. Chamberlain	.595	W. Chamberlain	1992	W. Chamberlain	24.3
1968-69	John Green	.518	Bill Cunningham	2034	Bill Cunningham	24.8
1969-70	Darrall Imhoff	.540	Bill Cunningham	2114	Bill Cunningham	26.1
1970-71	Archie Clark	.496	Bill Cunningham	1859	Bill Cunningham	23.0
1971-72	Bill Cunningham	.461	Bill Cunningham	1744	Bill Cunningham	23.3
1972-73	Dan Schlueter	.524	Fred Carter	1617	Fred Carter	20.0
1973-74	Steve Mix	.475	Fred Carter	1666	Fred Carter	21.4
1974-75	Doug Collins	.488	Fred Carter	1686	Fred Carter	21.9
1975-76	Doug Collins	.513	George McGinnis	1769	George McGinnis	23.0
1976-77	Steve Mix	.523	Julius Erving	1770	Julius Erving	21.6
1977-78	Darryl Dawkins	.575	George McGinnis	1587	Julius Erving	20.6
1978-79	Steve Mix	.538	Julius Erving	1803	Julius Erving	23.1
1979-80	Maurice Cheeks	.540	Julius Erving	2100	Julius Erving	26.9
1980-81	Darryl Dawkins	.607	Julius Erving	2014	Julius Erving	24.6
1981-82	Bobby Jones	.564	Julius Erving	1974	Julius Erving	24.4
1982-83	Bobby Jones	.543	Moses Malone	1908	Moses Malone	24.5
1983-84	Maurice Cheeks	.550	Julius Erving	1727	Moses Malone	22.7
1984-85	Maurice Cheeks	.570	Moses Malone	1941	Moses Malone	24.6
1985-86	Charles Barkley	.572	Moses Malone	1759	Moses Malone	23.8
1986-87	Charles Barkley	.594	Charles Barkley	1564	Charles Barkley	23.0
1987-88	Charles Barkley	.587	Charles Barkley	2264	Charles Barkley	28.3
1988-89	Charles Barkley	.579	Charles Barkley	2037	Charles Barkley	25.8
1989-90	Derek Smith	.508	Charles Barkley	1989	Charles Barkley	25.2
1990-91	Ron Anderson	.485	Charles Barkley	1849	Hersey Hawkins	22.1
1991-92	Charles Barkley	.552	Charles Barkley	1730	Charles Barkley	23.1
1992-93	Hersey Hawkins	.470	Hersey Hawkins	1643	Hersey Hawkins	20.3
	Jeff Hornacek	.470				
1993-94	Eric Leckner	.486	C. Weatherspoon	1506	C. Weatherspoon	18.4
1994-95	Dana Barros	.490	Dana Barros	1686	Dana Barros	20.6
1995-96	Derrick Alston	.512	Jerry Stackhouse	1384	Jerry Stackhouse	19.2
1996-97	C. Weatherspoon	.491	Allen Iverson	1787	Allen Iverson	23.5
1997-98	Allen Iverson	.461	Allen Iverson	1758	Allen Iverson	22.0
1998-99	Matt Geiger	.479	Allen Iverson	1284	Allen Iverson	26.8
1999-00	George Lynch	.461	Allen Iverson	1989	Allen Iverson	28.4
2000-01	Tyrone Hill	.474	Allen Iverson	2207	Allen Iverson	31.1
2001-02	D. Mutombo	.501	Allen Iverson	1883	Matt Harpring	11.8
2002-03	Brian Skinner	.550	Allen Iverson	2262	Allen Iverson	27.6
2003-04	Sam Dalembert	.541	Allen Iverson	1266	Kenny Thomas	13.6
2004-05	Sam Dalembert	.524	Allen Iverson	2302	Allen Iverson	30.7
2005-06	Andre Iguodala	.500	Allen Iverson	2375	Allen Iverson	33.0

COACHING HISTORY: 1963-1966 Dolph Schayes 129-111-.538; 1966-1968 Alex Hannum 130-33-.798; 1968-1972 Jack Ramsay 174-154-.530; 1972-1973 Roy Rubin 4-47-.078; 1972-1973 Kevin Loughery 5-26-.161; 1973-1978 Gene Shue 157-177-.470; 1977-1985 Bill Cunningham 454-196-.698; 1985-1988 Matt Guokas 119-88-.575; 1987-1992 Jim Lynam 194-173-.529; 1992-1993 Doug Moe 19-37-.339; 1992-1994 Fred Carter 32-76-.296; 1994-1996 John Lucas 42-122-.256; 1996-1997 Johnny Davis 22-60-.268; 1997-2003 Larry Brown 255-205-.554; 2003-2004 Randy Ayers 33-49-.402; 2004-2005 Jim O'Brien 43-39-.524; 2005-present Maurice Cheeks

PHILADELPHIA SPARTANS

Home City: Philadelphia, Pennsylvania
Home Stadium: Temple Stadium
Origin of Name:

			Regular Season Record						
Season	League	GP	W	L	T	GF	GA	Pts	Pct
1967	NPSL	32	14	9	9	53	43	157	.545

	Regular Season Individual Leaders				
Season	Goals		Points		GAA
					(360 Min)
1967	Orlando Garro	12	Orlando Garro	26	Ernesto Lopera	1.07

COACHING HISTORY: John Szep 14-9-9-.545

PHILADELPHIA STARS
(became Baltimore Stars)

Home City: Philadelphia, Pennsylvania
Home Stadium: Veterans Stadium   Capacity: 72,204 [1984]
Origin of Name: Name was chosen in a Name the Team Contest.

			Regular Season Record					
Season	League	GP	W	L	T	PF	PA	Pct
1983	USFL	18	15	3	0	379	204	.833
1984	USFL	18	16	2	0	479	225	.889
TOTAL:	2 years	36	31	5	0	858	429	
AVERAGE:		18	16	2	0	429	215	.861

			Playoff Record			
Season	GP	W	L	PF	PA	Result
1983	2	1	1	66	62	Lost Championship game to Michigan.
1984	3	3	0	71	30	**Won USFL Championship**.
TOTAL:	5	4	1	137	92	
AVERAGE:	3	2	1	69	46	

	Regular Season Individual Leaders				
Season	Passing Yards		Receiving Yards		Rushing Yards
1983	Chuck Fusina	2718	Willie Collier	771	Kelvin Bryant	1442
1984	Chuck Fusina	3837	Scott Fitzkee	895	Kelvin Bryant	1406

COACHING HISTORY: 1983-1984 Jim Mora 31-5-0-.861

PHILADELPHIA WARRIORS

Home City: Philadelphia, Pennsylvania
Home Court: Philadelphia Arena
Origin of Name:

		Regular Season Record			
Season	League	GP	W	L	Pct
1926-1927	ABL	42	24	18	.571
1927-1928	ABL	51	30	21	.588

TOTAL:	2 years	93	54	39	
AVERAGE:		47	27	20	.581

Regular Season Individual Leaders

Season	Points	
1926-27	Chick Passon	367
1927-28	Al Kellett	338

COACHING HISTORY: 1926-1927 Eddie Gottlieb 24-18-.571; 1927-1928 Not Available

PHILADELPHIA WARRIORS
(became San Francisco Warriors)

Home City: Philadelphia, Pennsylvania
Home Court: Philadelphia Arena (1946-1952)   Capacity: 7,777
        Convention Hall (1952-1962)   Capacity: 9,200
        Philadelphia Arena (1952-1962)   Capacity: 7,777
Origin of Name: The team adopted the name of previous teams which had played in Philadelphia.

Regular Season Record

Season	League	GP	W	L	PPGF	PPGA	Pct	GB
1946-1947	BAA	60	35	25	68.6	65.2	.583	14
1947-1948	BAA	48	27	21	73.4	72.1	.563	-
1948-1949	BAA	60	28	32	83.7	83.4	.467	10
1949-1950	NBA	68	26	42	73.3	76.4	.382	27
1950-1951	NBA	66	40	26	85.4	81.6	.606	-
1951-1952	NBA	66	33	33	86.5	87.8	.500	7
1952-1953	NBA	69	12	57	80.2	88.9	.174	34.5
1953-1954	NBA	72	29	43	78.2	80.4	.403	15
1954-1955	NBA	72	33	39	93.2	93.5	.458	10
1955-1956	NBA	72	45	27	103.1	98.8	.625	-
1956-1957	NBA	72	37	35	100.4	98.8	.514	7
1957-1958	NBA	72	37	35	104.3	104.4	.514	12
1958-1959	NBA	72	32	40	103.3	106.3	.444	20
1959-1960	NBA	75	49	26	118.6	116.4	.653	10
1960-1961	NBA	79	46	33	121.0	120.1	.582	11
1961-1962	NBA	80	49	31	125.4	122.7	.613	11
TOTAL:	16 years	1103	558	545				188.5
AVERAGE:		69	35	34	93.7	93.6	.506	12

Playoff Record

Season	GP	W	L	PPGF	PPGA	Result
1946-1947	10	8	2	75.3	69.4	**Won BAA Championship.**
1947-1948	13	6	7	71.7	66.0	Lost Championship series to Baltimore.
1948-1949	2	0	2	74.0	86.0	Lost Division Semifinal to Washington.
1949-1950	2	0	2	64.5	76.0	Lost Division Semifinal to Syracuse.
1950-1951	2	0	2	83.5	90.5	Lost Division Semifinal to Syracuse.
1951-1952	3	1	2	85.3	93.7	Lost Division Semifinal to Syracuse.
1955-1956	10	7	3	104.6	98.4	**Won NBA Championship.**
1956-1957	2	0	2	88.0	97.0	Lost Division Semifinal to Syracuse.
1957-1958	8	3	5	94.8	96.9	Lost Division Final to Boston.
1959-1960	9	4	5	113.9	112.0	Lost Division Final to Boston.
1960-1961	3	0	3	108.0	112.0	Lost Division Semifinal to Syracuse.
1961-1962	12	6	6	106.1	106.8	Lost Division Final to Boston.
TOTAL:	76	35	41			
AVERAGE:	6	3	3	89.1	92.1	

Regular Season Individual Leaders

Season	Field Goal % (min. 70 games)		Points		Points per Game (min. 70 games)	
1946-47*	Joe Fulks	.305	Joe Fulks	1389	Joe Fulks	23.2
1947-48*	George Senesky	.277	Joe Fulks	949	Joe Fulks	22.1
1948-49*	Ed Sadowski	.405	Joe Fulks	1560	Joe Fulks	26.0
1949-50*	Leo Mogus	.396	Joe Fulks	965	Joe Fulks	14.2
1950-51*	Paul Arizin	.407	Joe Fulks	1236	Joe Fulks	18.7
1951-52#	Neil Johnston	.472	Paul Arizin	1674	Paul Arizin	25.4
1952-53#	Neil Johnston	.452	Neil Johnston	1564	Neil Johnston	22.3
1953-54#	Neil Johnston	.449	Neil Johnston	1759	Neil Johnston	24.4
1954-55#	Neil Johnston	.440	Neil Johnston	1631	Neil Johnston	22.7
1955-56#	George Dempsey	.475	Paul Arizin	1741	Paul Arizin	24.2
1956-57#	Neil Johnston	.447	Paul Arizin	1817	Paul Arizin	25.6
1957-58#	Neil Johnston	.429	Paul Arizin	1406	Paul Arizin	20.7
1958-59#	Paul Arizin	.431	Paul Arizin	1851	Paul Arizin	26.4
1959-60	W. Chamberlain	.461	W. Chamberlain	2707	W. Chamberlain	37.6
1960-61	W. Chamberlain	.509	W. Chamberlain	3033	W. Chamberlain	38.4
1961-62	W. Chamberlain	.506	W. Chamberlain	4029	W. Chamberlain	50.4

COACHING HISTORY: 1946-1955 Eddie Gottlieb 263-318-.453; 1955-1958 George Senesky 119-97-.551; 1958-1959 Al Cervi 32-40-.444; 1959-1961 Neil Johnston 95-59-.617; 1961-1962 Frank McGuire 49-31-.613

*-40 game minimum; #-60 game minimum

PHOENIX COYOTES
(were Winnipeg Jets)

Home City: Phoenix, Arizona (1996-2003)
       Glendale, Arizona (2003-present)
Home Arena: America West Arena (1996-2002)*   Capacity: 16,210 [2004]
       Glendale Arena (2003-present)   Capacity: 17,500 [2005]
Origin of Name: The name was chosen in a Name the Team Contest in which there were over 10,000 entries.

Regular Season Record

Season	League	GP	W	L	T	OL	SL	GF	GA	Pts
1996-1997	NHL	82	38	37	7	NA	NA	240	243	83
1997-1998	NHL	82	35	35	12	NA	NA	224	227	82
1998-1999	NHL	82	39	31	12	NA	NA	205	197	90
1999-2000	NHL	82	39	35	8	4	NA	232	228	90
2000-2001	NHL	82	35	27	17	3	NA	214	212	90
2001-2002	NHL	82	40	27	9	6	NA	228	210	95
2002-2003	NHL	82	31	35	11	5	NA	204	230	78
2003-2004	NHL	82	22	36	18	6	NA	188	245	68
2004-2005	NHL	Season cancelled due to lockout.								
2005-2006	NHL	82	38	39	NA	2	3	246	271	81
TOTAL:	9 years	738	317	302	94	26	3	1981	2063	757
AVERAGE:		82	35	34	10	3	0	220	229	84

Playoff Record

Season	GP	W	L	GF	GA	Result
1996-1997	7	3	4	17	17	Lost Conference Quarterfinal to Anaheim.

*-known as Cellular One Ice Den 1998-99

1997-1998	6	2	4	20	22	Lost Conference Quarterfinal to Detroit.
1998-1999	7	3	4	19	23	Lost Conference Quarterfinal to St. Louis.
1999-2000	5	1	4	10	17	Lost Conference Quarterfinal to Colorado.
2001-2002	5	1	4	7	13	Lost Conference Quarterfinal to San Jose.
TOTAL:	30	10	20	73	92	
AVERAGE:	6	2	4	15	18	

Regular Season Individual Leaders

Season	Goals		Points		Penalty Minutes	
1996-1997	Keith Tkachuk	52	Keith Tkachuk	86	Keith Tkachuk	228
1997-1998	Keith Tkachuk	40	Keith Tkachuk	66	Rick Tocchet	157
1998-1999	Keith Tkachuk	36	Jeremy Roenick	72	Jim Cummins	190
1999-2000	Jeremy Roenick	34	Jeremy Roenick	78	Jeremy Roenick	102
2000-2001	Jeremy Roenick	30	Jeremy Roenick	76	Jeremy Roenick	114
2001-2002	Daniel Briere	32	Daymond Langkow	61	Todd Simpson	152
2002-2003	Mike Johnson	23	Mike Johnson	63	Todd Simpson	135
					Andrei Nazarov	135
2003-2004	Shane Doan	27	Shane Doan	68	Andrei Nazarov	125
2004-2005	Season cancelled due to lockout.					
2005-2006	Shane Doan	30	Shane Doan	66	Shane Doan	123
	Mike Comrie	30				

COACHING HISTORY: 1996-1997 Don Hay 38-37-7-.506; 1997-1999 Jim Schoenfeld 74-66-24-.524; 1999-2004 Bobby Francis 165-148-60-21-.522; 2003-2004 Rick Bowness 2-12-3-3-.250; 2005-present Wayne Gretzky

PHOENIX MERCURY

Home City: Phoenix, Arizona
Home Arena: America West Arena   Capacity: 19,023 [2001]
Origin of Name: The name was chosen to show affiliation with the NBA's Suns.

Regular Season Record

Season	League	GP	W	L	PPGF	PPGA	Pct	GB
1997	WNBA	28	16	12	69.2	65.2	.571	-
1998	WNBA	30	19	11	73.9	67.5	.633	8
1999	WNBA	32	15	17	68.0	68.2	.469	11
2000	WNBA	32	20	12	70.0	65.6	.625	8
2001	WNBA	32	13	19	64.5	67.8	.406	15
2002	WNBA	32	11	21	65.3	71.6	.344	14
2003	WNBA	34	8	26	61.7	66.8	.235	16
2004	WNBA	34	17	17	67.7	65.7	.500	8
2005	WNBA	34	16	18	69.4	69.2	.471	9
2006	WNBA	34	18	16	87.1	84.7	.529	7
TOTAL:	9 years	322	153	169				96
AVERAGE:		32	15	17	69.7	69.3	.475	10

Playoff Record

Season	GP	W	L	PPGF	PPGA	Result
1997	1	0	1	41.0	59.0	Lost Conference semifinal to New York.
1998	6	3	3	68.2	66.7	Lost championship series to Houston.
2000	2	0	2	73.5	93.5	Lost Conference semifinal to Los Angeles.
TOTAL:	9	3	6			
AVERAGE:	3	1	2	66.3	71.8	

Regular Season Individual Leaders

Season	Field Goals % (20 games min.)		Free Throws % (20 games min.)		Points per Game (20 games min.)	
1997	Toni Foster	.468	Bridget Pettis	.898	Jennifer Gillom	15.7
1998	Brandy Reed	.526	Bridget Pettis	.865	Jennifer Gillom	20.8
1999	Maria Stepanova	.485	Marlies Askamp	.816	Jennifer Gillom	15.2
2000	Lisa Harrison	.526	Brandy Reed	.901	Brandy Reed	19.0
2001	Maria Stepanova	.507	Lisa Harrison	.864	Jennifer Gillom	12.3
2002	Lisa Harrison	.496	Lisa Harrison	.870	Jennifer Gillom	15.3
2003	Kayte Christensen	.458	Tamicha Jackson	.810	Anna DeForge	11.9
2004	Penny Taylor	.484	Anna DeForge	.863	Diana Taurasi	17.0
2005	K. Vodichkova	.494	Belinda Snell	.889	Diana Taurasi	16.0
2006	Diana Taurasi	.452	Penny Taylor	.864	Diana Taurasi	25.3

COACHING HISTORY: 1997-2000 Cheryl Miller 70-52-.574; 2001-2002 Cynthia Cooper 24-40-.375; 2003 John Shumate 8-26-.235, 2004-2005 Carrie Graf 33-35-.485; 2006-present Paul Westhead

PHOENIX ROADRUNNERS

Home City: Phoenix, Arizona
Home Arena: Veteran's Memorial Coliseum   Capacity: 12,600 [1976]
Origin of Name: The team was named after the previous Western Hockey League team.

Regular Season Record

Season	League	GP	W	L	T	GF	GA	Pts	Pct
1974-1975	WHA	78	39	31	8	300	265	86	.551
1975-1976	WHA	80	39	35	6	302	287	84	.525
1976-1977	WHA	80	28	48	4	281	383	60	.375
TOTAL:	3 years	238	106	114	18	883	935	230	
AVERAGE:		79	35	38	6	294	312	76	.483

Playoff Record

Season	GP	W	L	GF	GA	Result
1974-1975	5	1	4	12	23	Lost Quarterfinal series to Quebec.
1975-1976	5	2	3	13	16	Lost Preliminary series to San Diego.
TOTAL:	10	3	7	25	39	
AVERAGE:	5	2	3	13	20	

Regular Season Individual Leaders

Season	Goals		Points		Penalty Minutes	
1974-1975	Michel Cormier	36	Dennis Sobchuck	77	John Hughes	201
1975-1976	Del Hall	47	Robbie Ftorek	113	Cam Connor	295
1976-1977	Robbie Ftorek	46	Robbie Ftorek	117	Jerry Rollins	186

COACHING HISTORY: 1974-1976 Sandy Hucul 78-66-14-.538; 1976-1977 Al Rollins 28-48-4-.375

PHOENIX SUNS

Home City: Phoenix, Arizona
Home Court: Arizona Veteran's Memorial Coliseum (1968-1992)   Capacity: 14,487 [1992]
                America West Arena (1992-present)   Capacity: 19,023 [2006]
Origin of Name: The name was chosen in a Name the Team Contest.

Regular Season Record

Season	League	GP	W	L	PPGF	PPGA	Pct	GB
1968-1969	NBA	82	16	66	111.7	120.5	.195	39
1969-1970	NBA	82	39	43	119.3	121.1	.476	9
1970-1971	NBA	82	48	34	113.8	111.9	.585	18
1971-1972	NBA	82	49	33	116.3	110.8	.598	14
1972-1973	NBA	82	38	44	111.6	112.9	.463	22
1973-1974	NBA	82	30	52	107.9	111.5	.366	17
1974-1975	NBA	82	32	50	101.2	103.6	.390	16
1975-1976	NBA	82	42	40	105.1	104.5	.512	17
1976-1977	NBA	82	34	48	104.9	104.2	.415	19
1977-1978	NBA	82	49	33	112.3	108.6	.598	9
1978-1979	NBA	82	50	32	115.4	111.7	.610	2
1979-1980	NBA	82	55	27	111.1	107.5	.671	5
1980-1981	NBA	82	57	25	110.0	104.5	.695	-
1981-1982	NBA	82	46	36	106.2	102.7	.561	11
1982-1983	NBA	82	53	29	107.0	102.0	.646	5
1983-1984	NBA	82	41	41	111.0	110.1	.500	13
1984-1985	NBA	82	36	46	108.0	110.1	.439	26
1985-1986	NBA	82	32	50	110.0	113.0	.390	30
1986-1987	NBA	82	36	46	111.1	113.5	.439	29
1987-1988	NBA	82	28	54	108.5	113.0	.341	34
1988-1989	NBA	82	55	27	118.6	110.9	.671	2
1989-1990	NBA	82	54	28	114.9	107.8	.659	9
1990-1991	NBA	82	55	27	114.0	107.5	.671	8
1991-1992	NBA	82	53	29	112.1	106.2	.646	4
1992-1993	NBA	82	62	20	113.4	106.7	.756	-
1993-1994	NBA	82	56	26	108.2	103.4	.683	7
1994-1995	NBA	82	59	23	110.6	106.8	.720	-
1995-1996	NBA	82	41	41	104.3	104.0	.500	23
1996-1997	NBA	82	40	42	102.8	102.2	.488	17
1997-1998	NBA	82	56	26	99.6	94.4	.683	5
1998-1999	NBA	50	27	23	95.6	93.3	.540	8
1999-2000	NBA	82	53	29	98.9	93.7	.646	14
2000-2001	NBA	82	51	31	94.0	91.8	.622	5
2001-2002	NBA	82	36	46	95.1	95.8	.439	25
2002-2003	NBA	82	44	38	95.5	94.4	.537	15
2003-2004	NBA	82	29	53	94.2	97.9	.354	27
2004-2005	NBA	82	62	20	110.4	103.3	.756	-
2005-2006	NBA	82	54	28	108.4	102.8	.659	-
TOTAL:	38 years	3084	1698	1386				504
AVERAGE:		81	45	36	107.8	105.9	.551	13

Playoff Record

Season	GP	W	L	PPGF	PPGA	Result
1969-1970	7	3	4	108.3	114.3	Lost Div. Semifinal to Los Angeles.
1975-1976	19	10	9	105.5	106.6	Lost Championship series to Boston.
1977-1978	2	0	2	96.5	102.5	Lost 1st Round series to Milwaukee.
1978-1979	15	9	6	103.1	100.3	Lost Conference Final to Seattle.
1979-1980	8	3	5	109.6	110.4	Lost Conf. Semifinal to Los Angeles.
1980-1981	7	3	4	91.7	89.0	Lost Conf. Semifinal to Kansas City.
1981-1982	7	2	5	110.0	116.6	Lost Conf. Semifinal to Los Angeles.
1982-1983	3	1	2	110.7	112.7	Lost 1st Round series to Denver.
1983-1984	17	9	8	109.0	109.2	Lost Conf. Final to Los Angeles.

1984-1985	3	0	3	115.7	136.0	Lost 1st Round series to Lakers.
1988-1989	12	7	5	118.3	111.3	Lost Conf. Final to Lakers.
1989-1990	16	9	7	108.1	105.1	Lost Conference Final to Portland.
1990-1991	4	1	3	95.8	107.3	Lost 1st Round series to Utah.
1991-1992	8	4	4	118.5	117.1	Lost Conf. Semifinal to Portland.
1992-1993	24	13	11	104.8	104.0	Lost Championship series to Chicago.
1993-1994	10	6	4	106.4	107.9	Lost Conf. Semifinal to Houston.
1994-1995	10	6	4	111.0	106.9	Lost Conf. Semifinal to Houston.
1995-1996	4	1	3	98.8	109.8	Lost 1st Round series to San Antonio.
1996-1997	5	2	3	100.2	112.8	Lost 1st Round series to Seattle.
1997-1998	4	1	3	93.0	100.5	Lost 1st Round series to San Antonio.
1998-1999	3	0	3	92.3	102.7	Lost 1st Round series to Portland.
1999-2000	9	4	5	87.3	91.0	Lost Conf. Semifinal to Lakers.
2000-2001	4	1	3	88.5	98.0	Lost 1st Round series to Sacramento.
2002-2003	6	2	4	85.2	90.5	Lost 1st Round series to San Antonio.
2003-2004	15	9	6	112.0	107.8	Lost Conf. Final to San Antonio.
2005-2006	20	10	10	107.2	106.0	Lost Conf. Final to Dallas.
TOTAL:	242	116	126			
AVERAGE:	9	4	5	105.4	106.2	

Regular Season Individual Leaders

Season	Field Goal % (min. 70 games)		Points		Points per Game (min. 70 games)	
1968-69	Neil Johnson	.481	Gail Goodrich	1931	Gail Goodrich	23.8
1969-70	Jim Fox	.524	Connie Hawkins	1995	Connie Hawkins	24.6
1970-71	Mel Counts	.457	Dick Van Arsdale	1771	Dick Van Arsdale	21.9
1971-72	Clem Haskins	.483	Dick Van Arsdale	1619	Connie Hawkins	21.0
1972-73	Connie Hawkins	.479	Charlie Scott	2048	Charlie Scott	25.3
1973-74	Dick Van Arsdale	.500	Dick Van Arsdale	1389	Dick Van Arsdale	17.8
1974-75	Curtis Perry	.477	Charlie Scott	1680	Dick Van Arsdale	16.1
1975-76	Curtis Perry	.497	Paul Westphal	1679	Paul Westphal	20.5
1976-77	Paul Westphal	.518	Paul Westphal	1726	Paul Westphal	21.3
1977-78	Walter Davis	.526	Paul Westphal	2014	Paul Westphal	25.2
1978-79	Walter Davis	.561	Paul Westphal	1941	Paul Westphal	24.0
1979-80	Walter Davis	.563	Paul Westphal	1792	Paul Westphal	21.9
1980-81	Walter Davis	.539	Truck Robinson	1543	Truck Robinson	18.8
					Dennis Johnson	18.8
1981-82	Larry Nance	.521	Dennis Johnson	1561	Dennis Johnson	19.5
1982-83	Larry Nance	.550	Walter Davis	1521	Walter Davis	19.0
1983-84	Larry Nance	.576	Walter Davis	1557	Walter Davis	20.0
1984-85	Alvan Adams	.520	Larry Nance	1211	James Edwards	14.9
	Charles Jones	.520				
1985-86	Larry Nance	.581	Walter Davis	1523	Walter Davis	21.8
1986-87	Ed Pinckney	.584	Walter Davis	1867	Walter Davis	23.6
1987-88	Jeff Hornacek	.506	Eddie Johnson	1294	Eddie Johnson	17.7
1988-89	Mark West	.653	Tom Chambers	2085	Tom Chambers	25.7
1989-90	Mark West	.625	Tom Chambers	2201	Tom Chambers	27.2
1990-91	Mark West	.647	Kevin Johnson	1710	Kevin Johnson	22.2
1991-92	Mark West	.632	Jeff Hornacek	1632	Jeff Hornacek	20.1
1992-93	Mark West	.614	Charles Barkley	1944	Charles Barkley	25.6
1993-94	Mark West	.566	Charles Barkley	1402	Charles Barkley	21.6
1994-95	Elliot Perry	.520	Charles Barkley	1561	Charles Barkley	23.0
1995-96	Charles Barkley	.500	Charles Barkley	1649	Charles Barkley	23.2
1996-97	Danny Manning	.536	Kevin Johnson	1410	Kevin Johnson	20.1

Season	Field Goal % (min. 70 games)		Points		Points per Game (min. 70 games)	
1997-98	A. McDyess	.536	A. McDyess	1225	A. McDyess	15.1
1998-99*	Danny Manning	.486	Jason Kidd	846	Tom Gugliotta	17.0
1999-00	Rodney Rogers	.486	Cliff Robinson	1478	Cliff Robinson	18.5
2000-01	Shawn Marion	.480	Shawn Marion	1369	Shawn Marion	17.3
2001-02	Bo Outlaw	.550	Stephon Marbury	1674	Stephon Marbury	20.4
2002-03	Bo Outlaw	.550	Stephon Marbury	1806	Stephon Marbury	22.3
2003-04	L. Barbarosa	.447	Shawn Marion	1498	Shawn Marion	19.0
2004-05	Steven Hunter	.614	A. Stoudemire	2080	A. Stoudemire	26.0
2005-06	Boris Diaw	.526	Shawn Marion	1769	Shawn Marion	21.8

COACHING HISTORY: 1968-1970 John Kerr 31-89-.258; 1969-1970 Jerry Colangelo 24-20-.545; 1970-1972 Lowell "Cotton" Fitzsimmons 97-67-.591; 1972-1973 Butch van Breda Kolff 3-4-.429; 1972-1973 Jerry Colangelo 35-40-.467; 1973-1987 John MacLeod 579-543-.516; 1986-1987 Dick Van Arsdale 14-12-.538; 1987-1988 John Wetzel 28-54-.341; 1988-1992 Lowell "Cotton" Fitzsimmons 217-111-.662; 1992-1996 Paul Westphal 191-88-.685; 1995-1996 Lowell "Cotton" Fitzsimmons 27-30-.474; 1996-2000 Danny Ainge 136-90-.602; 1999-2001 Scott Skiles 116-79-.595; 2001-2004 Frank Johnson 63-71-.470; 2003-present Mike D'Antoni

PITTSBURGH BURGHERS

Home City: Pittsburgh, Pennsylvania
Home Field: Exposition Park
Origin of Name:

		Regular Season Record						
Season	League	GP	W	L	Pct	GB	R	OR
1890	PL	128	60	68	.469	20.5	835	892

		Regular Season Individual Leaders			
Season	Home Runs		RBI's		Wins
1890	Jake Beckley	9	Jake Beckley	120	Harry Staley	21

COACHING HISTORY: Ned Hanlon 60-68-.469

PITTSBURGH CONDORS
(were Minnesota Pipers)
(became Minnesota Pipers)

Home City: Pittsburgh, Pennsylvania
Home Court: Civic Arena   Capacity: 12,500 [1970]
Origin of Name: The name was chosen by team General Manager Marty Blake. Were known as Pittsburgh Pipers 1968 and 1970.

		Regular Season Record						
Season	League	GP	W	L	PPGF	PPGA	Pct	GB
1967-1968	ABA	78	54	24	111.9	108.7	.692	-
1969-1970	ABA	84	29	55	112.4	117.0	.345	30
1970-1971	ABA	84	36	48	119.1	121.8	.429	19
1971-1972	ABA	84	25	59	119.2	126.4	.298	43

*-minimum 40 games.

TOTAL:	4 years	330	144	186				92
AVERAGE:		83	36	47	115.7	118.7	.436	23

Playoff Record

Season	GP	W	L	PPGF	PPGA	Result
1967-1968	15	11	4	117.4	112.4	Won ABA Championship.

Regular Season Individual Leaders

Season	Field Goal % (min. 70 games)		Points		Points per Game (min. 70 games)	
1967-68	Connie Hawkins	.519	Connie Hawkins	1875	Connie Hawkins	26.8
1969-70	Dennis Hamilton	.507	John Brisker	1617	John Brisker	21.0
1970-71	Mike Lewis	.509	John Brisker	2315	John Brisker	29.3
1971-72	Mike Lewis	.540	G. Thompson	1888	G. Thompson	27.0

COACHING HISTORY: 1967-1968 Vince Cazetta 54-24-.692; 1969-1970 John Clark 14-25-.359; 1969-1970 Buddy Jeannette 15-30-.333; 1970-1972 Jack McMahon 40-54-.426; 1971-1972 Mark Binstein 21-43-.328

PITTSBURGH IRONMEN

Home City: Pittsburgh, Pennsylvania
Home Court: Duquesne Gardens
Origin of Name: The name was suggested by Pittsburgh's large iron and steel industry.

Regular Season Record

Season	League	GP	W	L	PPGF	PPGA	Pct	GB
1946-1947	BAA	60	15	45	61.2	67.6	.250	23.5

Regular Season Individual Leaders

Season	Field Goal % (min. 40 games)		Points		Points per Game (min. 70 games)	
1946-47	Coulby Gunther	.336	Coulby Gunther	734	Coulby Gunther	14.1

COACHING HISTORY: Paul Birch 15-45-.250

PITTSBURGH MAULERS
(merged with Baltimore for the 1985 season)

Home City: Pittsburgh, Pennsylvania
Home Stadium: Three Rivers Stadium   Capacity: 50,350 [1984]
Origin of Name: The name was a tribute to the city's steelworkers.

Regular Season Record

Season	League	GP	W	L	T	PF	PA	Pct
1984	USFL	18	3	15	0	256	358	.167

Regular Season Individual Leaders

Season	Passing Yards		Receiving Yards		Rushing Yards	
1984	Glenn Carano	2368	Greg Anderson	994	Mike Rozier	792

COACHING HISTORY: Joe Pendry 3-15-0-.167

PITTSBURGH PENGUINS

Home City: Pittsburgh, Pennsylvania
Home Arena: Mellon Arena*   Capacity: 16,940 [2005]
Origin of Name: The name was picked in a Name the Team Contest.

Regular Season Record

Season	League	GP	W	L	T	OL	SL	GF	GA	Pts
1968-1969	NHL	76	20	45	11	NA	NA	189	252	51
1967-1968	NHL	74	27	34	13	NA	NA	195	216	67
1969-1970	NHL	76	26	38	12	NA	NA	182	238	64
1970-1971	NHL	78	21	37	20	NA	NA	221	240	62
1971-1972	NHL	78	26	38	14	NA	NA	220	258	66
1972-1973	NHL	78	32	37	9	NA	NA	257	265	73
1973-1974	NHL	78	28	41	9	NA	NA	242	273	65
1974-1975	NHL	80	37	28	15	NA	NA	326	289	89
1975-1976	NHL	80	35	33	12	NA	NA	339	303	82
1976-1977	NHL	80	34	33	13	NA	NA	240	252	81
1977-1978	NHL	80	25	37	18	NA	NA	254	321	68
1978-1979	NHL	80	36	31	13	NA	NA	281	279	85
1979-1980	NHL	80	30	37	13	NA	NA	251	303	73
1980-1981	NHL	80	30	37	13	NA	NA	302	345	73
1981-1982	NHL	80	31	36	13	NA	NA	310	337	75
1982-1983	NHL	80	18	53	9	NA	NA	257	394	45
1983-1984	NHL	80	16	58	6	NA	NA	254	390	38
1984-1985	NHL	80	24	51	5	NA	NA	276	385	53
1985-1986	NHL	80	34	38	8	NA	NA	313	305	76
1986-1987	NHL	80	30	38	12	NA	NA	297	290	72
1987-1988	NHL	80	36	35	9	NA	NA	319	316	81
1988-1989	NHL	80	40	33	7	NA	NA	347	349	87
1989-1990	NHL	80	32	40	8	NA	NA	318	359	72
1990-1991	NHL	80	41	33	6	NA	NA	342	305	88
1991-1992	NHL	80	39	32	9	NA	NA	343	308	87
1992-1993	NHL	84	56	21	7	NA	NA	367	268	119
1993-1994	NHL	84	44	27	13	NA	NA	299	285	101
1994-1995	NHL	48	29	16	3	NA	NA	181	158	61
1995-1996	NHL	82	49	29	4	NA	NA	362	284	102
1996-1997	NHL	82	38	36	8	NA	NA	285	280	84
1997-1998	NHL	82	40	24	18	NA	NA	228	188	98
1998-1999	NHL	82	38	30	14	NA	NA	242	225	90
1999-2000	NHL	82	37	37	8	6	NA	241	236	88
2000-2001	NHL	82	42	28	9	3	NA	281	256	96
2001-2002	NHL	82	28	41	8	5	NA	198	249	69
2002-2003	NHL	82	27	44	6	5	NA	189	255	65
2003-2004	NHL	82	23	47	8	4	NA	190	303	58
2004-2005	NHL	Season cancelled due to lockout.								
2005-2006	NHL	82	22	46	NA	8	6	244	316	58
TOTAL:	38 years	3014	1221	1379	383	31	6	10182	10875	2862
AVERAGE:		79	32	36	10	1	0	268	286	75

*-known as the Civic Arena from 1967-1999

Playoff Record

Season	GP	W	L	GF	GA	Result
1969-1970	10	6	4	22	25	Lost Semifinal series to St. Louis.
1971-1972	4	0	4	8	14	Lost Quarterfinal series to Chicago.
1974-1975	9	5	4	27	27	Lost Quarterfinal series to N.Y. Islanders.
1975-1976	3	1	2	3	8	Lost Preliminary series to Toronto.
1976-1977	3	1	2	10	13	Lost Preliminary series to Toronto.
1978-1979	7	2	5	16	25	Lost Quarterfinal series to Boston.
1979-1980	5	2	3	14	21	Lost Preliminary series to Boston.
1980-1981	5	2	3	21	20	Lost Preliminary series to St. Louis.
1981-1982	5	2	3	13	22	Lost Division Semifinal to N.Y. Islanders.
1988-1989	11	7	4	43	42	Lost Division Final to Philadelphia.
1990-1991	24	16	8	95	68	**Won Stanley Cup.**
1991-1992	21	16	5	83	63	**Won Stanley Cup.**
1992-1993	12	7	5	50	37	Lost Division Final to N.Y. Islanders.
1993-1994	6	2	4	12	20	Lost Conference Quarterfinal to Washington.
1994-1995	12	5	7	37	43	Lost Conference Semifinal to New Jersey.
1995-1996	18	11	7	57	52	Lost Conference Final to Florida.
1996-1997	5	1	4	13	20	Lost Conference Quarterfinal to Philadelphia.
1997-1998	6	2	4	15	18	Lost Conference Quarterfinal to Montreal.
1998-1999	13	6	7	35	35	Lost Conference Semifinal to Toronto.
1999-2000	11	6	5	31	23	Lost Conference Semifinal to Philadelphia.
2000-2001	18	9	9	38	44	Lost Conference Final to New Jersey.
TOTAL:	208	109	99	643	640	
AVERAGE:	10	5	5	31	30	

Regular Season Individual Leaders

Season	Goals		Points		Penalty Minutes	
1967-1968	Ab McDonald	22	Andy Bathgate	59	Leo Boivin	74
1968-1969	Keith McCreary	25	Ken Schinkel	52	Dunc McCallum	81
1969-1970	Dean Prentice	26	Dean Prentice	51	Bryan Watson	189
1970-1971	Jean Pronovost	21	Bryan Hextall	48	Bryan Hextall	133
	Dean Prentice	21				
	Keith McCreary	21				
1971-1972	Jean Pronovost	30	Syl Apps	59	Bryan Watson	212
	Greg Polis	30				
1972-1973	Al McDonough	35	Syl Apps	85	Bryan Watson	179
1973-1974	Lowell MacDonald	43	Syl Apps	85	Steve Durbano	138
1974-1975	Jean Pronovost	43	Ron Schock	86	Colin Campbell	172
1975-1976	Pierre Larouche	53	Pierre Larouche	111	Steve Durbano	161
1976-1977	Jean Pronovost	33	Jean Pronovost	64	Bob Kelly	115
1977-1978	Jean Pronovost	40	Jean Pronovost	65	Dave Schultz	378
1978-1979	Greg Malone	35	Greg Malone	65	Dave Schultz	157
1979-1980	Rick Kehoe	30	Rick Kehoe	60	Kim Clackson	166
1980-1981	Rick Kehoe	55	Rick Kehoe	88	Paul Baxter	204
1981-1982	Paul Gardner	36	Rick Kehoe	85	Paul Baxter	409
	Mike Bullard	36				
1982-1983	Rick Kehoe	29	Doug Shedden	67	Paul Baxter	238
1983-1984	Mike Bullard	51	Mike Bullard	92	Gary Rissling	297
1984-1985	Mario Lemieux	43	Mario Lemieux	100	Gary Rissling	209
1985-1986	Mario Lemieux	48	Mario Lemieux	141	Dan Frawley	174
1986-1987	Mario Lemieux	54	Mario Lemieux	107	Dan Frawley	218
1987-1988	Mario Lemieux	70	Mario Lemieux	168	Rod Buskas	206
1988-1989	Mario Lemieux	85	Mario Lemieux	199	Jay Caufield	285

Season	Goals		Points		Penalty Minutes	
1989-1990	Mario Lemieux	45	Mario Lemieux	123	Kevin Stevens	171
1990-1991	Mark Recchi	40	Mark Recchi	113	Kevin Stevens	133
	Kevin Stevens	40				
1991-1992	Kevin Stevens	54	Mario Lemieux	131	Kevin Stevens	254
1992-1993	Mario Lemieux	69	Mario Lemieux	160	Rick Tocchet	252
1993-1994	Kevin Stevens	41	Jaromir Jagr	99	Ulf Samuelsson	199
1994-1995	Jaromir Jagr	32	Jaromir Jagr	70	Francois Leroux	114
1995-1996	Mario Lemieux	69	Mario Lemieux	161	Francois Leroux	161
1996-1997	Mario Lemieux	50	Mario Lemieux	122	Dave Roche	155
1997-1998	Jaromir Jagr	35	Jaromir Jagr	102	Chris Tamer	181
1998-1999	Jaromir Jagr	44	Jaromir Jagr	127	Brad Werenka	93
1999-2000	Jaromir Jagr	42	Jaromir Jagr	96	Matthew Barnaby	197
2000-2001	Jaromir Jagr	52	Jaromir Jagr	121	Bob Boughner	145
2001-2002	Alexei Kovalev	32	Alexei Kovalev	76	Krzysztof Oliwa	150
2002-2003	Mario Lemieux	28	Mario Lemieux	91	Steve McKenna	128
2003-2004	Ryan Malone	22	Dick Tarnstrom	52	Brooks Orpik	127
2004-2005	Season cancelled due to lockout.					
2005-2006	Sidney Crosby	39	Sidney Crosby	102	Brooks Orpik	124

COACHING HISTORY: 1967-1969 George Sullivan 47-79-24-.393; 1969-1973 Leonard Kelly 90-132-52-.423; 1972-1974 Ken Schinkel 29-49-8-.384; 1973-1976 Marc Boileau 66-61-24-.517; 1975-1977 Ken Schinkel 54-43-20-.547; 1977-1980 John Wilson 91-105-44-.471; 1980-1983 Ed Johnston 79-126-35-.402; 1983-1984 Lou Angotti 16-58-6-.238; 1984-1987 Bob Berry 88-127-25-.419; 1987-1988 Pierre Creamer 36-35-9-.506; 1988-1990 Gene Ubriaco 50-47-9-.514; 1989-1990 Craig Patrick 22-26-6-.463; 1990-1991 Bob Johnson 41-33-6-.550; 1991-1993 Scotty Bowman 95-53-16-.628; 1993-1997 Ed Johnston 153-98-25-.600; 1996-1997 Craig Patrick 7-10-3-.425; 1997-2000 Kevin Constantine 86-68-35-.548; 1999-2000 Herb Brooks 29-23-5-.553; 2000-2002 Ivan Hlinka 42-32-9-3-.558, 2001-2003 Rick Kehoe 55-81-14-10-.419; 2003-2006 Ed Olczyk 31-64-8-8-2-.354; 2005-present Michel Therrien

PITTSBURGH PHANTOMS

Home City: Pittsburgh, Pennsylvania
Home Stadium: Forbes Field
Origin of Name:

		Regular Season Record							
Season	League	GP	W	L	T	GF	GA	Pts	Pct
1967	NPSL	31	10	14	7	59	74	132	.473

	Regular Season Individual Leaders				
Season	Goals		Points		GAA
					(360 Min)
1967	Manfred Rummel	14	Manfred Rummel	32	Bert Hoogerman 1.91

COACHING HISTORY: Janos Bedl, Co Prins, Pepino Gruber

PITTSBURGH PIRATES

Home City: Pittsburgh, Pennsylvania
Home Field: Recreation Park (1882-1890)   Capacity: 17,000 [1884]
Exposition Park (1891-1909)
Forbes Field (1909-1970)   Capacity: 35,000 [1960]
Three Rivers Stadium (1970-2000)   Capacity: 47,972 [2000]
PNC Park (2001-present)   Capacity: 38,496 [2006]
Origin of Name: The team was named Pirates after the team pirated two star players away from
Philadelphia of the American Association. Were also known before 1890 as the Innocents and the
Alleghenys.

Regular Season Record

Season	League	GP	W	L	Pct	GB	R	OR
1882	AA	78	39	39	.500	15	428	418
1883	AA	98	31	67	.316	35	525	728
1884	AA	108	30	78	.278	45.5	406	725
1885	AA	111	56	55	.505	22.5	547	539
1886	AA	137	80	57	.584	12	810	647
1887	NL	124	55	69	.444	24	621	750
1888	NL	134	66	68	.493	19.5	534	580
1889	NL	132	61	71	.462	25	726	801
1890	NL	136	23	113	.169	66.5	597	1235
1891	NL	135	55	80	.407	30.5	679	744
1892	NL	153	80	73	.523	23.5	802	796
1893	NL	129	81	48	.628	5	970	766
1894	NL	130	65	65	.500	25	955	972
1895	NL	132	71	61	.538	17	811	787
1896	NL	129	66	63	.512	24	787	741
1897	NL	131	60	71	.458	32.5	676	835
1898	NL	148	72	76	.486	29.5	634	694
1899	NL	149	76	73	.510	25.5	834	765
1900	NL	139	79	60	.568	4.5	733	612
1901	NL	139	90	49	.647	-	776	534
1902	NL	139	103	36	.741	-	775	440
1903	NL	140	91	49	.650	-	792	613
1904	NL	153	87	66	.569	19	675	586
1905	NL	153	96	57	.627	9	692	569
1906	NL	153	93	60	.608	23.5	622	464
1907	NL	154	91	63	.591	17	634	507
1908	NL	154	98	56	.636	1	585	474
1909	NL	152	110	42	.724	-	701	448
1910	NL	153	86	67	.562	17.5	655	576
1911	NL	154	85	69	.552	14.5	744	560
1912	NL	151	93	58	.616	10	751	565
1913	NL	149	78	71	.523	21.5	673	585
1914	NL	154	69	85	.448	25.5	503	540
1915	NL	154	73	81	.474	18	557	520
1916	NL	154	65	89	.422	29	484	586
1917	NL	154	51	103	.331	47	464	594
1918	NL	125	65	60	.520	17	466	411
1919	NL	139	71	68	.511	24.5	472	466
1920	NL	154	79	75	.513	14	530	552
1921	NL	153	90	63	.588	4	692	595

1922	NL	154	85	69	.552	8	865	736
1923	NL	154	87	67	.565	8.5	786	696
1924	NL	153	90	63	.588	3	724	588
1925	NL	153	95	58	.621	-	912	715
1926	NL	153	84	69	.549	4.5	769	689
1927	NL	154	94	60	.610	-	817	659
1928	NL	152	85	67	.559	9	837	704
1929	NL	153	88	65	.575	10.5	904	780
1930	NL	154	80	74	.519	12	891	928
1931	NL	154	75	79	.487	26	636	691
1932	NL	154	86	68	.558	4	701	711
1933	NL	154	87	67	.565	5	667	619
1934	NL	150	74	76	.493	19.5	735	713
1935	NL	153	86	67	.562	13.5	743	647
1936	NL	154	84	70	.545	8	804	718
1937	NL	154	86	68	.558	10	704	646
1938	NL	150	86	64	.573	2	707	630
1939	NL	153	68	85	.444	28.5	666	721
1940	NL	154	78	76	.506	22.5	809	783
1941	NL	154	81	73	.526	19	690	643
1942	NL	147	66	81	.449	36.5	585	631
1943	NL	154	80	74	.519	25	669	605
1944	NL	153	90	63	.588	14.5	744	662
1945	NL	154	82	72	.532	16	753	686
1946	NL	154	63	91	.409	34	552	668
1947	NL	154	62	92	.403	32	744	817
1948	NL	154	83	71	.539	8.5	706	699
1949	NL	154	71	83	.461	26	681	760
1950	NL	153	57	96	.373	33.5	681	857
1951	NL	154	64	90	.416	32.5	689	845
1952	NL	154	42	112	.273	54.5	515	793
1953	NL	154	50	104	.325	55	622	887
1954	NL	154	53	101	.344	44	557	845
1955	NL	154	60	94	.390	38.5	560	767
1956	NL	154	66	88	.429	27	588	653
1957	NL	154	62	92	.403	33	586	696
1958	NL	154	84	70	.545	8	662	607
1959	NL	154	78	76	.506	9	651	680
1960	NL	154	95	59	.617	-	734	593
1961	NL	154	75	79	.487	18	694	675
1962	NL	161	93	68	.578	8	706	626
1963	NL	162	74	88	.457	25	567	595
1964	NL	162	80	82	.494	13	663	636
1965	NL	162	90	72	.556	7	675	580
1966	NL	162	92	70	.568	3	759	641
1967	NL	162	81	81	.500	20.5	679	693
1968	NL	162	80	82	.494	17	583	532
1969	NL	162	88	74	.543	12	725	652
1970	NL	162	89	73	.549	-	729	664
1971	NL	162	97	65	.599	-	788	599
1972	NL	155	96	59	.619	-	691	512
1973	NL	162	80	82	.494	2.5	704	693
1974	NL	162	88	74	.543	-	751	657
1975	NL	161	92	69	.571	-	712	565

1976	NL	162	92	70	.568	9	708	630
1977	NL	162	96	66	.593	5	734	665
1978	NL	161	88	73	.547	1.5	684	637
1979	NL	162	98	64	.605	-	775	643
1980	NL	162	83	79	.512	8	666	646
1981	NL	102	46	56	.451	NA	407	394
1982	NL	162	84	78	.519	8	724	696
1983	NL	162	84	78	.519	6	659	648
1984	NL	162	75	87	.463	21.5	615	567
1985	NL	161	57	104	.354	43.5	568	708
1986	NL	162	64	98	.395	44	663	700
1987	NL	162	80	82	.494	15	723	744
1988	NL	160	85	75	.531	15	651	616
1989	NL	162	74	88	.457	19	637	680
1990	NL	162	95	67	.586	-	733	619
1991	NL	162	98	64	.605	-	768	632
1992	NL	162	96	66	.593	-	693	595
1993	NL	162	75	87	.463	22	707	806
1994	NL	114	53	61	.465	13	466	580
1995	NL	144	58	86	.403	27	629	736
1996	NL	162	73	89	.451	15	776	833
1997	NL	162	79	83	.488	5	724	760
1998	NL	162	69	93	.426	33	650	718
1999	NL	161	78	83	.484	18.5	775	782
2000	NL	162	69	93	.426	26	793	888
2001	NL	162	62	100	.383	31	657	857
2002	NL	161	72	89	.447	24.5	641	730
2003	NL	162	75	87	.463	13	753	801
2004	NL	161	72	89	.447	32.5	680	744
2005	NL	162	67	95	.414	33	680	769
2006	NL	162	67	95	.414	16.5	691	797
TOTAL:	125 years	18847	9556	9291		2166.5	85420	84029
AVERAGE:		151	77	74	.507	17.5	683	672

				Playoff Record		
Season	GP	W	L	R	OR	Result
1900	4	1	3	15	15	Lost NL Championship to Brooklyn.
1903	8	3	5	24	39	Lost World Series to Boston.
1909	7	4	3	34	28	**Won World Series.**
1925	7	4	3	25	26	**Won World Series.**
1927	4	0	4	10	23	Lost World Series to New York.
1960	7	4	3	27	55	**Won World Series.**
1970	3	0	3	3	9	Lost NLCS to Cincinnati.
1971	11	7	4	47	39	**Won World Series.**
1972	5	2	3	15	19	Lost NLCS to Cincinnati.
1974	4	1	3	10	20	Lost NLCS to Los Angeles.
1975	3	0	3	7	19	Lost NLCS to Cincinnati.
1979	10	7	3	47	31	**Won World Series.**
1990	6	2	4	15	20	Lost NLCS to Cincinnati.
1991	7	3	4	12	19	Lost NLCS to Atlanta.
1992	7	3	4	35	34	Lost NLCS to Atlanta.
TOTAL:	93	41	52	326	396	
AVERAGE:	6	3	3	22	26	

Regular Season Individual Leaders

Season	Home Runs		RBI's		Wins	
1882	Ed Swartwood	4	Not Recorded		Harry Salisbury	20
1883	Ed Swartwood	3	Not Recorded		Denny Driscoll	18
	Mike Mansell	3				
	Jackie Hayes	3				
1884	Charlie Eden	1	Not Recorded		Florence Sullivan	16
1885	Tom Brown	4	Not Recorded		Ed Morris	39
1886	Fred Carroll	5	Not Recorded		Ed Morris	41
1887	Fred Carroll	6	Fred Carroll	54	James Galvin	28
			Charles Smith	54		
			John Coleman	54		
1888	Charles Smith	4	Willie Kuehne	62	Ed Morris	29
1889	Jake Beckley	9	Jake Beckley	97	James Galvin	23
1890	George Miller	4	George Miller	66	Billy Gumbert	4
1891	Jake Beckley	4	Jake Beckley	73	Mark Baldwin	22
	Fred Carroll	4				
	Pete Browning	4				
	George Miller	4				
1892	Jake Beckley	10	Jake Beckley	96	Mark Baldwin	26
1893	Elmer Smith	7	Jake Beckley	106	Frank Killen	36
1894	Jake Stenzel	13	Jake Stenzel	121	Philip Ehret	19
1895	Jake Stenzel	7	Jake Beckley	110	Pink Hawley	31
1896	Elmer Smith	6	Elmer Smith	94	Frank Killen	30
1897	Elmer Smith	6	Fred Ely	74	Pink Hawley	18
1898	Jack McCarthy	4	Jack McCarthy	78	Jesse Tannehill	25
1899	Jimmy Williams	9	Jimmy Williams	116	Jesse Tannehill	24
1900	Jimmy Williams	6	Honus Wagner	100	Jesse Tannehill	20
1901	Clarence Beaumont	8	Honus Wagner	126	Charles Phillippe	22
1902	Tommy Leach	6	Honus Wagner	91	Jack Chesbro	28
1903	Tommy Leach	7	Honus Wagner	101	Sam Leever	25
	Clarence Beaumont	7				
1904	Honus Wagner	4	Honus Wagner	75	Patrick Flaherty	19
1905	Honus Wagner	6	Honus Wagner	101	Charles Phillippe	22
1906	Jim Nealon	3	Jim Nealon	83	Vic Willis	22
					Sam Leever	22
1907	Honus Wagner	6	Ed Abbaticchio	82	Vic Willis	22
			Honus Wagner	82		
1908	Honus Wagner	10	Honus Wagner	109	Nick Maddox	23
					Vic Willis	23
1909	Tommy Leach	6	Honus Wagner	100	Howie Camnitz	25
1910	Jack Flynn	6	Honus Wagner	81	Charles Adams	18
1911	Owen Wilson	12	Owen Wilson	107	Charles Adams	22
1912	Owen Wilson	11	Honus Wagner	102	Claude Hendrix	24
1913	Owen Wilson	10	John Miller	90	Charles Adams	21
1914	Ed Konetchy	4	Jim Viox	57	Wilbur Cooper	16
1915	Honus Wagner	6	Honus Wagner	78	Al Mamaux	21
1916	Max Carey	7	Bill Hinchman	76	Al Mamaux	21
1917	Bill Fischer	3	Max Carey	51	Wilbur Cooper	17
1918	George Cutshaw	5	George Cutshaw	68	Wilbur Cooper	19
1919	Casey Stengel	4	Bill Southworth	61	Wilbur Cooper	19
	Bill Southworth	4				
1920	Carson Bigbee	4	George Whitted	74	Wilbur Cooper	24
	Fred Nicholson	4				

Season	Home Runs		RBI's		Wins	
1921	Charlie Grimm	7	Charlie Grimm	71	Wilbur Cooper	22
	George Whitted	7				
	Max Carey	7				
1922	Ewell Russell	12	Carson Bigbee	99	Wilbur Cooper	23
1923	Pie Traynor	12	Pie Traynor	101	John Morrison	25
1924	Kiki Cuyler	9	Glenn Wright	111	Wilbur Cooper	20
1925	Glenn Wright	18	Glenn Wright	121	Lee Meadows	19
	Kiki Cuyler	18				
1926	George Grantham	8	Pie Traynor	92	Ray Kremer	20
	Glenn Wright	8	Kiki Kuyler	92	Lee Meadows	20
	Paul Waner	8				
	Kiki Cuyler	8				
1927	Glenn Wright	9	Paul Waner	131	Carmen Hill	22
	Paul Waner	9				
1928	George Grantham	10	Pie Traynor	124	Burleigh Grimes	25
1929	Paul Waner	15	Pie Traynor	108	Ray Kremer	18
1930	George Grantham	18	Pie Traynor	119	Ray Kremer	20
			Adam Comorosky	119		
1931	George Grantham	10	Pie Traynor	103	Henry Meine	19
1932	Paul Waner	8	Tony Piet	85	Larry French	18
	Earl Grace	8				
1933	Gus Suhr	10	Arky Vaughan	97	Larry French	18
1934	Paul Waner	14	Gus Suhr	103	Waite Hoyt	15
1935	Arky Vaughan	19	Arky Vaughan	99	Cy Blanton	18
1936	Gus Suhr	11	Gus Suhr	118	Bill Swift	16
1937	Pep Young	9	Gus Suhr	97	Cy Blanton	14
1938	Johnny Rizzo	23	Johnny Rizzo	111	Mace Brown	15
1939	Elbie Fletcher	12	Elbie Fletcher	71	Bob Klinger	14
1940	Vince DiMaggio	19	M. Van Robays	116	Truett Sewell	16
1941	Vince DiMaggio	21	Vince DiMaggio	100	Max Butcher	17
1942	Vince DiMaggio	15	Bob Elliott	89	Truett Sewell	17
1943	Vince DiMaggio	15	Bob Elliott	101	Truett Sewell	21
1944	Babe Dahlgren	12	Bob Elliott	108	Truett Sewell	21
1945	John Barrett	15	Bob Elliott	108	Nick Strincevich	16
1946	Ralph Kiner	23	Ralph Kiner	81	Fritz Ostermueller	13
1947	Ralph Kiner	51	Ralph Kiner	127	Fritz Ostermueller	12
1948	Ralph Kiner	40	Ralph Kiner	123	Bob Chesnes	14
1949	Ralph Kiner	54	Ralph Kiner	127	Cliff Chambers	13
1950	Ralph Kiner	47	Ralph Kiner	118	Cliff Chambers	12
1951	Ralph Kiner	42	Ralph Kiner	109	Murry Dickson	20
1952	Ralph Kiner	37	Ralph Kiner	87	Murry Dickson	14
1953	Frank Thomas	30	Frank Thomas	102	Murry Dickson	10
1954	Frank Thomas	23	Frank Thomas	94	Dick Littlefield	10
1955	Frank Thomas	25	Dale Long	79	Bob Friend	14
1956	Dale Long	27	Dale Long	91	Bob Friend	17
1957	Frank Thomas	23	Frank Thomas	89	Bob Friend	14
1958	Frank Thomas	35	Frank Thomas	109	Bob Friend	22
1959	Dick Stuart	27	Dick Stuart	78	Roy Face	18
					Vern Law	18
1960	Dick Stuart	23	Roberto Clemente	94	Vern Law	20
1961	Dick Stuart	35	Dick Stuart	117	Bob Friend	14
1962	Bob Skinner	20	Bill Mazeroski	81	Bob Friend	18
1963	Roberto Clemente	17	Roberto Clemente	76	Bob Friend	17

Season	Home Runs		RBI's		Wins	
1964	Willie Stargell	21	Roberto Clemente	87	Bob Veale	18
1965	Willie Stargell	27	Willie Stargell	107	Vern Law	17
					Bob Veale	17
1966	Willie Stargell	33	Roberto Clemente	119	Bob Veale	16
1967	Roberto Clemente	23	Roberto Clemente	110	Bob Veale	16
1968	Willie Stargell	24	Donn Clendendon	87	Steve Blass	18
1969	Willie Stargell	29	Willie Stargell	92	Steve Blass	16
1970	Willie Stargell	31	Willie Stargell	85	Luke Walker	15
1971	Willie Stargell	48	Willie Stargell	125	Dock Ellis	19
1972	Willie Stargell	33	Willie Stargell	112	Steve Blass	19
1973	Willie Stargell	44	Willie Stargell	119	Nelson Briles	14
1974	Willie Stargell	25	Richie Zisk	100	Jerry Reuss	16
1975	Dave Parker	25	Dave Parker	101	Jerry Reuss	18
1976	Richie Zisk	21	Dave Parker	90	John Candelaria	16
	Bill Robinson	21				
1977	Bill Robinson	26	Bill Robinson	24	John Candelaria	20
1978	Dave Parker	30	Dave Parker	117	Don Robinson	14
					Bert Blyleven	14
1979	Willie Stargell	32	Dave Parker	94	John Candelaria	14
1980	Mike Easler	21	Dave Parker	79	Jim Bibby	19
1981	Jason Thompson	15	Dave Parker	48	Rick Rhoden	9
1982	Jason Thompson	31	Jason Thompson	101	Don Robinson	15
1983	Jason Thompson	18	Jason Thompson	76	Larry McWilliams	15
					John Candelaria	15
1984	Jason Thompson	17	Tony Pena	78	Rick Rhoden	14
1985	Jason Thompson	12	Johnny Ray	70	Rick Reuschel	14
1986	Jim Morrison	23	Jim Morrison	88	Rick Rhoden	15
1987	Barry Bonds	25	Andy Van Slyke	82	Mike Dunne	13
1988	Andy Van Slyke	25	Bobby Bonilla	100	Doug Drabek	15
			Andy Van Slyke	100		
1989	Bobby Bonilla	24	Bobby Bonilla	86	Doug Drabek	14
1990	Barry Bonds	33	Bobby Bonilla	120	Doug Drabek	22
1991	Barry Bonds	25	Barry Bonds	116	John Smiley	20
1992	Barry Bonds	34	Barry Bonds	103	Doug Drabek	15
1993	Al Martin	18	Jeff King	98	Bob Walk	13
1994	Dave Clark	10	Orlando Merced	51	Zane Smith	10
1995	Jeff King	18	Jeff King	87	Denny Neagle	13
1996	Jeff King	30	Jeff King	111	Jon Lieber	9
1997	Kevin Young	18	Kevin Young	74	Esteban Loaiza	11
					Jon Lieber	11
					Francisco Cordova	11
1998	Kevin Young	27	Kevin Young	108	Francisco Cordova	13
1999	Brian Giles	39	Brian Giles	115	Todd Ritchie	15
2000	Brian Giles	35	Brian Giles	123	Jose Silva	11
2001	Brian Giles	37	Aramis Ramirez	112	Todd Ritchie	11
2002	Brian Giles	38	Brian Giles	103	Kip Wells	12
					Josh Fogg	12
2003	Reggie Sanders	31	Reggie Sanders	87	Kip Wells	10
					Josh Fogg	10
					Jeff Suppan	10
2004	Craig Wilson	29	Jayson Bay	82	Oliver Perez	12
2005	Jayson Bay	32	Jayson Bay	101	Dave Williams	10
2006	Jayson Bay	35	Jayson Bay	109	Ian Snell	14

COACHING HISTORY: 1882-1883 Al Pratt 51-59-.464; 1883 Ormond Butler 17-36-.321; 1883-1884 Joe Battin 3-14-.176; 1884 George Creamer 2-7-.222; 1884 Denny McKnight 12-17-.414; 1884 Bob Ferguson 5-21-.192; 1884-1889 Horace Phillips 295-322-.478; 1889 Fred Dunlap 7-9-.438; 1889 Ned Hanlon 26-19-.578; 1890 Guy Hecker 23-113-.169; 1891 Ned Hanlon 31-47-.397; 1891 Bill McGunnigle 24-33-.421; 1892 Tom Burns 25-30-.455; 1892-1894 Al Buckenberger 189-146-.564; 1894-1896 Connie Mack 149-134-.527; 1897 Pat Donovan 60-71-.458; 1898-1899 Bill Watkins 80-92-.465; 1899 Pat Donovan 68-57-.544; 1900-1915 Fred Clarke 1422-969-.595; 1916-1917 James Callahan 85-129-.397; 1917 Honus Wagner 1-4-.200; 1917-1919 Hugo Bezdek 166-187-.470; 1920-1922 George Gibson 201-171-.540; 1922-1926 Bill McKechnie 409-293-.583; 1927-1929 Owen Bush 246-178-.580; 1929-1931 Jewel Ens 176-167-.513; 1932-1934 George Gibson 200-159-.557; 1934-1939 Pie Traynor 457-406-.530; 1940-1946 Frank Frisch 539-528-.505; 1946 Virgil Davis 1-2-.333; 1947 Billy Herman 61-92-.399; 1947 Bill Burwell 1-0-1.000; 1948-1952 Bill Meyer 317-452-.412; 1953-1955 Fred Haney 163-299-.353; 1956-1957 Bob Bragan 102-155-.397; 1957-1964 Danny Murtaugh 605-547-.525; 1965-1967 Harry Walker 224-184-.549; 1967 Danny Murtaugh 39-39-.500; 1968-1969 Larry Shepard 164-155-.514; 1969 Alex Grammas 4-1-.800; 1970-1971 Danny Murtaugh 186-138-.574; 1972-1973 Bill Virdon 163-128-.560; 1973-1976 Danny Murtaugh 285-226-.558; 1977-1985 Charles Tanner 711-685-.509; 1986-1996 Jim Leyland 851-863-.496; 1997-present Gene Lamont 295-352-.456; 2001-2005 Lloyd McClendon 348-460-.431; 2006-present Jim Tracy

PITTSBURGH PIRATES
(became Philadelphia Quakers)

Home City: Pittsburgh, Pennsylvania
Home Arena: Duquesne Gardens
Origin of Name: The team was named after the National League baseball franchise.

Regular Season Record

Season	League	GP	W	L	T	GF	GA	Pts	Pct
1925-1926	NHL	36	19	16	1	82	70	39	.542
1926-1927	NHL	44	15	26	3	79	108	33	.375
1927-1928	NHL	44	19	17	8	67	76	46	.523
1928-1929	NHL	44	9	27	8	46	80	26	.295
1929-1930	NHL	44	5	36	3	102	185	13	.148
TOTAL:	5 years	212	67	122	23	376	519	157	
AVERAGE:		42	13	24	5	75	104	31	.370

Playoff Record

Season	GP	W	L	T	GF	GA	Result
1925-1926	2	0	1	1	4	6	Lost 1st Round series to Montreal.
1927-1928	2	1	1	0	4	6	Lost Quarterfinal series to N.Y. Rangers.
TOTAL:	4	1	2	1	8	12	
AVERAGE:	2	1	1	0	2	6	

Regular Season Individual Leaders

Season	Goals		Points		Penalty Minutes	
1925-1926	Hibbert Milks	14	Hibbert Milks	19	Lionel Conacher	64
1926-1927	Hibbert Milks	16	Hibbert Milks	22	Herb Drury	48
1927-1928	Hibbert Milks	18	Hibbert Milks	21	Duke McCurry	60
1928-1929	Hibbert Milks	9	Hibbert Milks	12	Herb Drury	49
	Harold Darragh	9	Harold Darragh	12	Roger Smith	49
1929-1930	Gerry Lowrey	16	Harold Darragh	32	Roger Smith	65

COACHING HISTORY: 1925-1929 Odie Cleghorn 62-86-20-.429; 1929-1930 Frank Fredrickson 5-36-3-.148

PITTSBURGH PIRATES

Home City: Pittsburgh, Pennsylvania
Home Court: Duquesne University Gymnasium
Origin of Name: The owners showed great originality by naming their team Pirates. It was named after the National League baseball team.

			Regular Season Record					
Season	**League**	**GP**	**W**	**L**	**PPGF**	**PPGA**	**Pct**	**GB**
1937-1938	NBL	13	8	5	37.3	33.4	.615	3.5
1938-1939	NBL	27	13	14	36.9	39.3	.481	11
TOTAL:	2 years	40	21	19				14.5
AVERAGE:		20	11	9	37.1	36.4	.525	7

	Regular Season Individual Leaders						
Season	**Field Goals**		**Free Throws**		**Points**	
1937-38	Hymie Ginsburg	36	Eddie Wisbar	22	Hymie Ginsburg	92
1938-39	Paul Birch	85	Paul Birch	51	Paul Birch	221

COACHING HISTORY: 1937-1939 Dudey Moore 21-19-.525

PITTSBURGH RAIDERS

Home City: Pittsburgh, Pennsylvania
Home Court: Duquesne University Gymnasium
Origin of Name:

			Regular Season Record					
Season	**League**	**GP**	**W**	**L**	**PPGF**	**PPGA**	**Pct**	**GB**
1944-1945	NBL	30	7	23	48.7	55.5	.233	18

	Regular Season Individual Leaders						
Season	**Field Goals**		**Free Throws**		**Points**	
1944-45	Huck Hartman	127	Huck Hartman	73	Huck Hartman	327

COACHING HISTORY: Joe Urso 7-23-.233

PITTSBURGH REBELS

Home City: Pittsburgh, Pennsylvania
Home Stadium: Exposition Park
Origin of Name: The team changed its name when it changed managers from Harry Gessler to Ennis "Rebel" Oakes.

			Regular Season Record					
Season	**League**	**GP**	**W**	**L**	**Pct**	**GB**	**R**	**OR**
1914	FL	150	64	86	.427	22.5	605	698
1915	FL	153	86	67	.562	.5	592	524
TOTAL:	2 years	303	150	153		23	1197	1222
AVERAGE:		152	75	77	.493	11.5	599	611

Regular Season Individual Leaders

Season	Home Runs		RBI's		Wins	
1914	Ed Lennox	11	Ed Lennox	84	Elmer Knetzer	20
1915	Ed Konetchy	10	Ed Konetchy	93	Frank Allen	23

COACHING HISTORY: 1914 Harry Gessler 6-12-.333; 1914-1915 Ennis Oakes 144-141-.505

PITTSBURGH STEELERS
(Pittsburgh merged with Philadelphia in 1943 and Chicago in 1944)

Home City: Pittsburgh, Pennsylvania

Home Stadium:		
Forbes Field * (1933-1963)	Capacity: 35,000
Pitt Stadium * (1958-1969)	Capacity: 54,500
Three Rivers Stadium (1970-2000)	Capacity: 59,600 [2000]
Heinz Field (2002-present)	Capacity: 64,450 [2005]

Origin of Name: The team name was chosen in a contest sponsored by the owners. For their first six years the team was called Pirates.

Regular Season Record

Season	League	GP	W	L	T	PF	PA	Pct
1933	NFL	11	3	6	2	67	208	.364
1934	NFL	12	2	10	0	51	206	.167
1935	NFL	12	4	8	0	100	209	.333
1936	NFL	12	6	6	0	98	187	.500
1937	NFL	11	4	7	0	122	145	.364
1938	NFL	11	2	9	0	79	169	.182
1939	NFL	11	1	9	1	114	216	.136
1940	NFL	11	2	7	2	60	178	.273
1941	NFL	11	1	9	1	103	276	.136
1942	NFL	11	7	4	0	167	119	.636
1945	NFL	10	2	8	0	79	220	.200
1946	NFL	11	5	5	1	136	117	.500
1947	NFL	12	8	4	0	240	259	.667
1948	NFL	12	4	8	0	200	243	.333
1949	NFL	12	6	5	1	224	214	.542
1950	NFL	12	6	6	0	180	195	.500
1951	NFL	12	4	7	1	183	235	.375
1952	NFL	12	5	7	0	300	273	.417
1953	NFL	12	6	6	0	211	263	.500
1954	NFL	12	5	7	0	219	263	.417
1955	NFL	12	4	8	0	195	285	.333
1956	NFL	12	5	7	0	217	250	.417
1957	NFL	12	6	6	0	161	178	.500
1958	NFL	12	7	4	1	261	230	.625
1959	NFL	12	6	5	1	257	216	.542
1960	NFL	12	5	6	1	240	275	.458
1961	NFL	14	6	8	0	295	287	.429
1962	NFL	14	9	5	0	312	363	.643
1963	NFL	14	7	4	3	321	295	.607
1964	NFL	14	5	9	0	253	315	.357
1965	NFL	14	2	12	0	202	397	.143
1966	NFL	14	5	8	1	316	347	.393
1967	NFL	14	4	9	1	281	320	.321

*-The Steelers played games in both Forbes Field and Pitt Stadium from 1958 to 1963

1968	NFL	14	2	11	1	244	397	.179
1969	NFL	14	1	13	0	218	404	.071
1970	NFL	14	5	9	0	210	272	.357
1971	NFL	14	6	8	0	246	292	.429
1972	NFL	14	11	3	0	343	175	.786
1973	NFL	14	10	4	0	347	210	.714
1974	NFL	14	10	3	1	305	189	.750
1975	NFL	14	12	2	0	373	162	.857
1976	NFL	14	10	4	0	342	138	.714
1977	NFL	14	9	5	0	283	243	.643
1978	NFL	16	14	2	0	356	195	.875
1979	NFL	16	12	4	0	416	262	.750
1980	NFL	16	9	7	0	352	313	.563
1981	NFL	16	8	8	0	356	297	.500
1982	NFL	9	6	3	0	204	146	.667
1983	NFL	16	10	6	0	355	303	.625
1984	NFL	16	9	7	0	387	310	.563
1985	NFL	16	7	9	0	379	355	.438
1986	NFL	16	6	10	0	307	336	.375
1987	NFL	15	8	7	0	285	299	.533
1988	NFL	16	5	11	0	336	421	.313
1989	NFL	16	9	7	0	265	326	.563
1990	NFL	16	9	7	0	292	240	.563
1991	NFL	16	7	9	0	292	344	.438
1992	NFL	16	11	5	0	299	225	.688
1993	NFL	16	9	7	0	308	281	.563
1994	NFL	16	12	4	0	316	234	.750
1995	NFL	16	11	5	0	407	327	.689
1996	NFL	16	10	6	0	344	257	.625
1997	NFL	16	11	5	0	372	307	.688
1998	NFL	16	7	9	0	263	303	.438
1999	NFL	16	6	10	0	317	320	.375
2000	NFL	16	9	7	0	321	255	.562
2001	NFL	16	13	3	0	352	212	.813
2002	NFL	16	10	5	1	390	345	.656
2003	NFL	16	6	10	0	300	327	.375
2004	NFL	16	15	1	0	372	251	.938
2005	NFL	16	11	5	0	389	258	.688
2006	NFL	16	8	8	0	353	315	.500
TOTAL:	72 years	996	498	478	20	18840	18799	
AVERAGE:		14	7	7	0	262	261	.510

Playoff Record

Season	GP	W	L	PF	PA	Result
1947	1	0	1	0	21	Lost Division playoff to Philadelphia.
1972	2	1	1	30	28	Lost AFC Championship to Miami.
1973	1	0	1	14	33	Lost Division playoff to Oakland.
1974	3	3	0	72	33	**Won Super Bowl IX.**
1975	3	3	0	65	37	**Won Super Bowl X.**
1976	2	1	1	47	38	Lost AFC Championship to Oakland.
1977	1	0	1	21	34	Lost Division playoff to Denver.
1978	3	3	0	102	46	**Won Super Bowl XIII.**
1979	3	3	0	92	46	**Won Super Bowl XIV.**
1982	1	0	1	28	31	Lost 1st Round playoff to San Diego.

1983	1	0	1	10	38	Lost Division playoff to L.A. Raiders.
1984	2	1	1	52	62	Lost AFC Championship to Miami.
1989	2	1	1	49	47	Lost Conference Semifinal to Denver.
1992	1	0	1	3	24	Lost Conference Semifinal to Buffalo.
1993	1	0	1	24	27	Lost Wild Card Game to Kansas City.
1994	2	1	1	42	26	Lost Conference Final to San Diego.
1995	3	2	1	77	64	Lost Super Bowl to Dallas.
1996	2	1	1	45	42	Lost Division Semifinal to New England.
1997	2	1	1	28	30	Lost Conference Final to Denver.
2001	2	1	1	44	34	Lost Conference Final to New England.
2002	2	1	1	67	67	Lost Conference Semifinal to Tennessee.
2004	2	1	1	47	58	Lost Conference Final to New England.
2005	4	4	0	107	55	**Won Super Bowl XL.**
TOTAL:	46	28	18	1066	921	
AVERAGE:	2	1	1	46	40	

Regular Season Individual Leaders

Season	Passing Yards		Receiving Yards		Rushing Yards	
1933	Tony Holm	406	Paul Moss	383		
1934	Warren Heller	511			Warren Heller	528
1935	John Gildea	529	Ben Smith	166	Art Strutt	323
1936	Ed Matesic	850	Bill Sortet	197	Warren Heller	332
1937	Max Fiske	318	Bill Davidson	169	Bull Karcis	511
1938	Frank Filchock	469	Eggs Manske	310	Whizzer White	567
1939	Hugh McCullough	443	Sam Boyd	423	Boyd Brumbaugh	343
1940	Billy Patterson	529	George Platukas	290	Lou Tomasetti	246
1941	Boyd Brumbaugh	260	Don Looney	186	Dick Riffle	388
1942	Bill Dudley	438	Walt Kichefski	189	Bill Dudley	696
1945	Busit Warren	368	Tony Bova	220	Busit Warren	285
1946	Bill Dudley	452	Tony Bova	171	Bill Dudley	604
1947	Johnny Clement	1004	Val Jansante	599	Johnny Clement	670
1948	Ray Evans	924	Val Jansante	623	Bob Cifers	361
1949	Joe Geri	554	Elbie Nickel	633	Jerry Nuzum	611
1950	Joe Geri	866	Elbie Nickel	527	Joe Geri	705
1951	Chuck Ortmann	671	Lynn Chandnois	490	Fran Rogel	385
1952	Jim Finks	2307	Elbie Nickel	884	Ray Mathews	315
1953	Jim Finks	1484	Elbie Nickel	743	Fran Rogel	527
1954	Jim Finks	2003	Ray Mathews	652	Fran Rogel	415
1955	Jim Finks	2270	Ray Mathews	762	Fran Rogel	588
1956	Ted Marchibroda	1585	Ray Mathews	540	Fran Rogel	476
1957	Earl Morrall	1900	Jack McClairen	630	Billy Wells	532
1958	Bobby Layne	2510	Jim Orr	910	Tom Tracy	714
1959	Bobby Layne	1986	Jim Orr	604	Tom Tracy	794
1960	Bobby Layne	1814	Buddy Dial	972	Tom Tracy	680
1961	Rudy Bukich	1253	Buddy Dial	1047	John H. Johnson	787
1962	Bobby Layne	1686	Buddy Dial	981	John H. Johnson	1141
1963	Ed Brown	2982	Buddy Dial	1295	John H. Johnson	773
1964	Ed Brown	1990	Gary Ballman	935	John H. Johnson	1048
1965	Bill Nelsen	1917	Gary Ballman	859	Dick Hoak	426
1966	Ron Smith	1249	Roy Jefferson	772	Willie Asbury	544
1967	Kent Nix	1587	J.R. Wilburn	767	Don Shy	341
1968	Dick Shiner	1856	Roy Jefferson	1074	Dick Hoak	858
1969	Dick Shiner	1422	Roy Jefferson	1079	Dick Hoak	531
1970	Terry Bradshaw	1410	Ron Shanklin	691	John Fugua	691

Season	Passing Yards		Receiving Yards		Rushing Yards	
1971	Terry Bradshaw	2259	Dave Smith	663	John Fugua	625
1972	Terry Bradshaw	1887	Ron Shanklin	669	Franco Harris	1055
1973	Terry Bradshaw	1183	Ron Shanklin	711	Franco Harris	698
1974	Joe Gilliam	1274	Frank Lewis	365	Franco Harris	1006
1975	Terry Bradshaw	2055	Lynn Swann	781	Franco Harris	1246
1976	Terry Bradshaw	1177	Lynn Swann	516	Franco Harris	1128
1977	Terry Bradshaw	2523	Lynn Swann	789	Franco Harris	1162
1978	Terry Bradshaw	2915	Lynn Swann	880	Franco Harris	1082
1979	Terry Bradshaw	3724	John Stallworth	1183	Franco Harris	1186
1980	Terry Bradshaw	3339	Theo Bell	748	Franco Harris	789
1981	Terry Bradshaw	2887	John Stallworth	1098	Franco Harris	987
1982	Terry Bradshaw	1768	John Stallworth	441	Franco Harris	604
1983	Cliff Stoudt	2553	Calvin Sweeney	577	Franco Harris	1007
1984	Mark Malone	2137	John Stallworth	1395	Frank Pollard	851
1985	Mark Malone	1428	Louis Lipps	1134	Frank Pollard	991
1986	Mark Malone	2444	Louis Lipps	590	Earnest Jackson	910
1987	Mark Malone	1896	John Stallworth	521	Earnest Jackson	696
1988	Bubby Brister	2634	Louis Lipps	973	Merril Hoge	705
1989	Bubby Brister	2365	Louis Lipps	944	Tim Worley	770
1990	Bubby Brister	2725	Louis Lipps	682	Merril Hoge	772
1991	Neil O'Donnell	1963	Louis Lipps	671	Merril Hoge	610
1992	Neil O'Donnell	2283	Jeff Graham	711	Barry Foster	1690
1993	Neil O'Donnell	3208	Eric Green	942	Leroy Thompson	763
1994	Neil O'Donnell	2443	Eric Green	618	Barry Foster	851
1995	Neil O'Donnell	2970	Yancey Thigpen	1307	Erric Pegram	813
1996	Mike Tomczak	2767	Charles Johnson	1008	Jerome Bettis	1431
1997	Kordell Stewart	3020	Yancey Thigpen	1398	Jerome Bettis	1665
1998	Kordell Stewart	2560	Charles Johnson	815	Jerome Bettis	1185
1999	Mike Tomczak	1625	Troy Edwards	714	Jerome Bettis	1091
2000	Kordell Stewart	1860	Bobby Shaw	672	Jerome Bettis	1341
			Hines Ward	672		
2001	Kordell Stewart	3109	Plaxico Burress	1008	Jerome Bettis	1072
2002	Tommy Maddox	2836	Hines Ward	1329	Amos Zereoue	762
2003	Tommy Maddox	3414	Hines Ward	1163	Jerome Bettis	811
2004	B. Roethlisberger	2621	Hines Ward	1004	Jerome Bettis	941
2005	B. Roethlisberger	2385	Hines Ward	975	Willie Parker	1202
2006	B. Roethlisberger	3513	Hines Ward	975	Willie Parker	1494

COACHING HISTORY: 1933 Tap Dauds 3-6-2-.364; 1934 Luby DiMelio 2-10-0-.167; 1935-1936 Joe Bach 10-14-0-.417; 1937-1939 Johnny Blood 6-19-0-.240; 1939-1940 Walt Kiesling 3-13-3-.237; 1941 Bert Bell 0-2-0-.000; 1941 Buff Donelli 0-5-0-.000; 1941-1942 Walt Kiesling 1-2-1-.375; 1945 Jim Leonard 2-8-0-.200; 1946-1947 Jock Sutherland 13-10-1-.563; 1948-1951 John Michelosen 20-26-2-.438; 1952-1953 Joe Bach 11-13-0-.458; 1954-1956 Walt Kiesling 14-22-0-.389; 1957-1964 Buddy Parker 51-47-6-.519; 1965 Mike Nixon 2-12-0-.143; 1966-1968 Bill Austin 11-28-3-.298; 1969-1991 Chuck Noll 193-148-1-.566; 1992-2006 Bill Cowher 149-90-1-.623; 2007-present Mike Tomlin

PORTLAND BREAKERS
(were New Orleans Breakers)

Home City: Portland, Oregon
Home Stadium: Civic Stadium   Capacity: 32,500 [1985]
Origin of Name: The team kept the same nickname when it moved from New Orleans to Portland.

Regular Season Record

Season	League	GP	W	L	T	PF	PA	Pct
1985	USFL	18	6	12	0	275	422	.333

Regular Season Individual Leaders

Season	Passing Yards		Receiving Yards		Rushing Yards	
1985	Matt Robinson	2182	Frank Lockett	794	Buford Jordan	817

COACHING HISTORY: Dick Coury 6-12-0-.333

PORTLAND FIRE

Home City: Portland, Oregon
Home Court: The Rose Garden   Capacity: 19,980 [2001]
Origin of Name: The name was created by NBA Creative Services along with the team.

Regular Season Record

Season	League	GP	W	L	PPGF	PPGA	Pct	GB
2000	WNBA	32	10	22	67.3	71.9	.313	18
2001	WNBA	32	11	21	65.3	68.8	.344	17
2002	WNBA	32	16	16	68.6	69.6	.500	9
TOTAL:	3 years	96	37	59				44
AVERAGE:		32	12	20	67.1	70.1	.385	15

Regular Season Individual Leaders

Season	Field Goal % (min. 20 games)		Free Throw % (min. 20 games)		Points per Game (min. 20 games)	
2000	Alisa Burras	.587	S. Witherspoon	.871	S. Witherspoon	16.8
2001	Alisa Burras	.530	S. Witherspoon	.849	Jackie Stiles	14.9
2002	Alisa Burras	.629	Ukari Figgs	.908	Demya Walker	10.9

COACHING HISTORY: 2000-2002 Linda Hargrove 37-59-.385

PORTLAND ROSEBUDS
(were New Westminster Royals)
(became Victoria Aristocrats)

Home City: Portland, Oregon
Home Arena: Marshall Street Arena
Origin of Name: Portland has long been known as "The Rose City".

Regular Season Record

Season	League	GP	W	L	T	GF	GA	Pts	Pct
1914-1915	PCHA	18	9	9	0	91	83	18	.500
1915-1916	PCHA	18	13	5	0	71	50	26	.722
1916-1917	PCHA	24	9	15	0	114	112	18	.375
1917-1918	PCHA	18	7	11	0	63	75	14	.389
TOTAL:	4 years	78	38	40	0	339	320	76	
AVERAGE:		20	10	10	0	85	80	19	.487

Playoff Record

Season	GP	W	L	T	GF	GA	Result
1915-1916	5	2	3	0	13	15	Lost Stanley Cup Final to Canadiens.

Regular Season Individual Leaders

Season	Goals		Points		GAA	
1914-1915	Eddie Oatman	22	Eddie Oatman	22	Mike Mitchell	4.61
	Ran McDonald	22	Ran McDonald	22		
1915-1916	Charles Tobin	21	Charles Tobin	21	Tom Murray	2.78
1916-1917	Dick Irvin	35	Dick Irvin	35	Tom Murray	4.67
1917-1918	Tom Dunderdale	14	Tom Dunderdale	14	Tom Murray	4.17

COACHING HISTORY: 1914-1917 Pete Muldoon; 1916-1917 Tom Scott; 1917-1918 Not Available

PORTLAND ROSEBUDS
(were Regina Capitals)

Home City: Portland, Oregon
Home Arena: Portland Arena
Origin of Name: Named after previous PCHA team.

Regular Season Record

Season	League	GP	W	L	T	GF	GA	Pts	Pct
1925-1926	WHL	30	12	16	2	84	110	26	.433

Regular Season Individual Leaders

Season	Goals		Points		GAA	
1925-1926	Dick Irvin	31	Dick Irvin	31	Red McCusker	3.67

COACHING HISTORY: Pete Muldoon 12-16-2-.433

PORTLAND THUNDER

Home City: Portland, Oregon
Home Stadium: Portland Civic Stadium   Capacity: 33,000 [1975]
Origin of Name: Team executives announced May 14, 1975 that the name of the team would be changed to Thunder from Storm, the name the team had been known as the previous year.

Regular Season Record

Season	League	GP	W	L	T	PF	PA	Pct
1974	WFL	20	7	12	1	264	426	.375
1975	WFL	11	4	7	0	213	239	.364
TOTAL:	2 years	31	11	19	1	477	665	
AVERAGE:		16	6	9	1	239	333	.371

Regular Season Individual Leaders

Season	Passing Yards		Receiving Yards		Rushing Yards	
1974	Pete Beathard	1247	Jeff Baker	444	Rufus Ferguson	1086
1975	Don Horn	1742	Bob Christiansen	456	Rufus Ferguson	768

COACHING HISTORY: 1974 Dick Coury 7-12-1-.375; 1975 Greg Barton 1-5-0-.167; 1975 Bob Brodhead 1-1-0-.500; 1975 Joe Gardi 2-1-0-.667

PORTLAND TIMBERS

Home City: Portland, Oregon
Home Field: Portland Civic Stadium   Capacity: 33,000 [1978]
Origin of Name: Named by team officials because of the Portland area's large forest industry.

Regular Season Record

Season	League	GP	W	L	GF	GA	BP	Pts	Pct
1975	NASL	22	16	6	43	27	42	138	.697
1976	NASL	24	8	16	23	40	23	71	.329
1977	NASL	26	10	16	39	42	38	98	.419
1978	NASL	30	20	10	50	36	47	167	.619
1979	NASL	30	11	19	50	75	46	112	.415
1980	NASL	32	15	17	50	53	43	133	.462
1981	NASL	32	17	15	52	49	45	141	.294
1982	NASL	32	14	18	49	44	42	122	.254
TOTAL:	8 years	228	111	117	356	366	326	982	
AVERAGE:		29	14	15	45	46	41	123	.403

Playoff Record

Season	GP	W	L	T	GF	GA	Result
1975	3	2	1	0	3	3	Lost Championship series to Tampa Bay.
1978	5	3	2	0	5	8	Lost Conference Final to New York.
1981	3	1	2	0	3	8	Lost 1st Round series to San Diego.
TOTAL:	11	6	5	0	11	19	
AVERAGE:	4	2	2	0	4	6	

Regular Season Individual Leaders

Season	Goals		Points		GAA	
1975	Peter Withe	16	Peter Withe	38	Graham Brown	1.20
1976	Tony Betts	5	Tony Betts	10	Jim Cumbes	1.51
1977	Stewart Scullion	11	Stewart Scullion	25	Mick Poole	1.40
1978	Clyde Best	12	Clyde Best	33	Mick Poole	1.16
1979	Clyde Best	8	John Bain	27	Mick Poole	2.30
	John Bain	8				
1980	Clyde Best	11	Clyde Best	28	Mick Poole	1.67
1981	John Bain	11	John Bain	34	Keith MacRae	1.52
1982	Ron Futcher	13	John Bain	35	Bill Irwin	1.32

COACHING HISTORY: 1975-1976 Vic Crowe 24-22-.505; 1977 Brian Tiler 10-16-.419; 1978-1980 Don Megson 35-35; 1980 Pete Warner 11-11; 1981-1982 Vic Crowe 31-33

PORTLAND TRAIL BLAZERS

Home City: Portland, Oregon
Home Court: Memorial Coliseum (1970-1995)   Capacity: 12,888 [1994]
        Rose Garden (1995-present)   Capacity: 19,980 [2006]
Origin of Name: The name was chosen in a Name the Team Contest.

Regular Season Record

Season	League	GP	W	L	PPGF	PPGA	Pct	GB
1970-1971	NBA	82	29	53	115.5	120.0	.354	19
1971-1972	NBA	82	18	64	106.8	116.5	.220	51
1972-1973	NBA	82	21	61	106.2	112.4	.256	39
1973-1974	NBA	82	27	55	106.8	111.6	.329	20
1974-1975	NBA	82	38	44	103.8	103.3	.463	10
1975-1976	NBA	82	37	45	104.1	105.3	.451	22
1976-1977	NBA	82	49	33	111.7	106.2	.598	4
1977-1978	NBA	82	58	24	107.7	101.5	.707	-
1978-1979	NBA	82	45	37	108.4	107.1	.549	7
1979-1980	NBA	82	38	44	102.5	103.3	.463	22

1980-1981	NBA	82	45	37	110.7	109.8	.549	12
1981-1982	NBA	82	42	40	109.8	109.2	.512	15
1982-1983	NBA	82	46	36	107.4	105.3	.561	12
1983-1984	NBA	82	48	34	113.1	109.6	.585	6
1984-1985	NBA	82	42	40	115.5	112.1	.512	20
1985-1986	NBA	82	40	42	115.1	114.0	.488	22
1986-1987	NBA	82	49	33	117.9	114.8	.598	16
1987-1988	NBA	82	53	29	116.1	111.5	.646	9
1988-1989	NBA	82	39	43	114.6	113.1	.476	18
1989-1990	NBA	82	59	23	114.2	107.9	.720	42
1990-1991	NBA	82	63	19	114.7	106.0	.768	-
1991-1992	NBA	82	57	25	111.4	104.1	.695	-
1992-1993	NBA	82	51	31	108.5	105.4	.622	11
1993-1994	NBA	82	47	35	107.3	104.6	.573	16
1994-1995	NBA	82	44	38	103.1	99.2	.537	15
1995-1996	NBA	82	44	38	99.3	97.0	.537	20
1996-1997	NBA	82	49	33	99.0	94.8	.598	8
1997-1998	NBA	82	46	36	94.3	92.9	.561	15
1998-1999	NBA	50	35	15	94.8	88.5	.700	-
1999-2000	NBA	82	59	23	97.5	91.0	.720	8
2000-2001	NBA	82	50	32	95.4	91.2	.610	6
2001-2002	NBA	82	49	33	96.6	93.7	.598	12
2002-2003	NBA	82	50	32	95.2	92.5	.610	9
2003-2004	NBA	82	41	41	90.7	92.0	.500	15
2004-2005	NBA	82	27	55	92.9	96.9	.329	25
2005-2006	NBA	82	21	61	88.8	98.3	.256	23
TOTAL:	36 years	2920	1556	1364				549
AVERAGE:		81	43	38	105.6	104.1	.533	15

Playoff Record

Season	GP	W	L	PPGF	PPGA	Result
1976-1977	19	14	5	107.4	102.7	**Won NBA Championship.**
1977-1978	6	2	4	96.7	98.3	Lost Conference Semifinal to Seattle.
1978-1979	3	1	2	96.7	100.0	Lost 1st Round series to Phoenix.
1979-1980	3	1	2	100.3	106.0	Lost 1st Round series to Seattle.
1980-1981	3	1	2	105.3	107.0	Lost 1st Round series to Kansas City.
1982-1983	7	3	4	105.9	107.0	Lost Conf. Semifinal to Los Angeles.
1983-1984	5	2	3	109.8	112.4	Lost 1st Round series to Phoenix.
1984-1985	9	4	5	119.1	124.1	Lost Conf. Semifinal to Los Angeles.
1985-1986	4	1	3	112.5	117.5	Lost 1st Round series to Denver.
1986-1987	4	1	3	108.8	113.3	Lost 1st Round series to Houston.
1987-1988	4	1	3	104.3	108.5	Lost 1st Round series to Utah.
1988-1989	3	0	3	107.0	119.0	Lost 1st Round series to Lakers.
1989-1990	11	2	9	107.1	109.4	Lost NBA Final to Detroit.
1990-1991	16	9	7	103.9	102.6	Lost Conference Final to Lakers.
1991-1992	21	13	8	110.0	106.6	Lost NBA Final to Chicago.
1992-1993	4	1	3	97.3	97.5	Lost 1st Round series to San Antonio.
1993-1994	4	1	3	103.8	109.0	Lost 1st Round series to Houston.
1994-1995	3	0	3	101.7	116.3	Lost 1st Round series to Phoenix
1995-1996	5	2	3	89.6	99.6	Lost 1st Round series to Utah.
1996-1997	4	1	3	89.8	96.8	Lost 1st Round series to Lakers.
1997-1998	4	1	3	99.8	104.0	Lost 1st Round series to Lakers.
1998-1999	13	7	6	86.2	86.6	Lost Conference Final to San Antonio.
1999-2000	16	10	6	92.5	88.4	Lost Conference Final to Lakers.

2000-2001	3	0	3	89.0	104.3	Lost 1st Round series to Lakers.
2001-2002	3	0	3	91.3	96.7	Lost 1st Round series to Lakers.
2002-2003	7	3	4	101.3	100.3	Lost 1st Round series to Dallas.
TOTAL:	184	81	103			
AVERAGE:	7	3	4	102.3	103.4	

Regular Season Individual Leaders

Season	Field Goal % (min. 70 games)		Points		Points per Game (min. 70 games)	
1970-71	Dale Schlueter	.488	Geoff Petrie	2031	Geoff Petrie	24.8
1971-72	Dale Schlueter	.525	Sidney Wicks	2009	Sidney Wicks	24.5
1972-73	Ollie Johnson	.497	Geoff Petrie	1970	Geoff Petrie	24.9
1973-74	Lloyd Neal	.490	Geoff Petrie	1771	Geoff Petrie	24.3
1974-75	Larry Steele	.548	Sidney Wicks	1778	Sidney Wicks	21.7
1975-76	Bob Gross	.523	Sidney Wicks	1505	Sidney Wicks	19.1
1976-77	Dave Twardzik	.612	Maurice Lucas	1599	Maurice Lucas	20.2
1977-78	Dave Twardzik	.592	Lionel Hollins	1285	Lionel Hollins	15.9
1978-79	Tom Owens	.548	Tom Owens	1520	Tom Owens	18.5
1979-80	K. Washington	.553	Ron Brewer	1286	Tom Owens	16.4
1980-81	K. Washington	.569	Jim Paxson	1354	Jim Paxson	17.1
1981-82	Calvin Natt	.576	M. Thompson	1642	M. Thompson	20.8
1982-83	Calvin Natt	.543	Jim Paxson	1756	Jim Paxson	21.7
1983-84	Calvin Natt	.583	Jim Paxson	1722	Jim Paxson	21.3
1984-85	Audie Norris	.543	Kiki Vandeweghe	1616	Kiki Vandeweghe	22.4
1985-86	Jerome Kersey	.549	Kiki Vandeweghe	1962	Kiki Vandeweghe	24.8
1986-87	Steve Johnson	.556	Kiki Vandeweghe	2122	Kiki Vandeweghe	26.9
1987-88	Terry Porter	.519	Clyde Drexler	2185	Clyde Drexler	27.0
1988-89	Steve Johnson	.524	Clyde Drexler	2123	Clyde Drexler	27.2
1989-90	Buck Williams	.548	Clyde Drexler	1703	Clyde Drexler	23.3
1990-91	Buck Williams	.602	Clyde Drexler	1767	Clyde Drexler	21.5
1991-92	Buck Williams	.604	Clyde Drexler	1903	Clyde Drexler	25.0
1992-93	Buck Williams	.511	Cliff Robinson	1570	Cliff Robinson	19.1
1993-94	Buck Williams	.555	Cliff Robinson	1647	Cliff Robinson	20.1
1994-95	Buck Williams	.512	Cliff Robinson	1601	Cliff Robinson	21.3
1995-96	Aryvdas Sabonis	.545	Cliff Robinson	1644	Cliff Robinson	21.1
1996-97	Gary Trent	.536	Ken Anderson	1436	Ken Anderson	17.5
1997-98	Rasheed Wallace	.533	Isaiah Rider	1458	Isaiah Rider	19.7
1998-99*	Rasheed Wallace	.508	Isaiah Rider	651	Isaiah Rider	13.9
1999-00	Rasheed Wallace	.519	Rasheed Wallace	1325	Rasheed Wallace	16.4
2000-01	Bonzi Wells	.533	Rasheed Wallace	1477	Rasheed Wallace	19.2
2001-02	Ruben Patterson	.515	Rasheed Wallace	1521	Rasheed Wallace	19.3
2002-03	Dale Davis	.541	Rasheed Wallace	1340	Rasheed Wallace	18.1
2003-04	Ruben Patterson	.506	Zach Randolph	1626	Zach Randolph	20.1
2004-05	Joel Przybilla	.598	D. Stoudemire	1277	D. Stoudemire	15.8
2005-06	Jarrett Jack	.442	Zach Randolph	1333	Zach Randolph	18.0

COACHING HISTORY: 1970-1972 Rolland Todd 41-97-.297; 1971-1972 Stu Inman 6-20-.231; 1972-1974 Jack McCloskey 48-116-.293; 1974-1976 Lenny Wilkens 75-89-.457; 1976-1986 Jack Ramsay 453-367-.552; 1986-1989 Mike Schuler 127-84-.602; 1988-1994 Rick Adelman 291-154-.654; 1994-1997 P.J. Carlesimo 137-109-.557; 1997-2001 Mike Dunleavy 190-106-.642; 2001-2005 Maurice Cheeks 162-139-.538; 2004-2005 Kevin Prtchard 5-22-.185; Nate McMillan 2005-present

*-minimum 40 games

PORTSMOUTH SPARTANS
(became Detroit Lions)

Home City: Portsmouth, Ohio
Home Stadium: Spartan Stadium   Capacity: 8,200
Origin of Name: The team may have been named after the stadium in which they played their home games.

Regular Season Record

Season	League	GP	W	L	T	PF	PA	Pct
1930	NFL	14	5	6	3	176	161	.464
1931	NFL	14	11	3	0	175	77	.786
1932	NFL	12	6	2	4	116	71	.667
1933	NFL	11	6	5	0	128	87	.545
TOTAL:	4 years	51	28	16	7	595	396	
AVERAGE:		13	7	4	2	149	99	.618

Regular Season Individual Leaders

Season	Passing Yards		Receiving Yards		Rushing Yards	
1930	Will Glasgow	192			Chuck Bennett	144
1931	Glenn Presnell	651			Glenn Presnell	518
1932	Glenn Presnell	290			Dutch Clark	546
1933	Glenn Presnell	774			Glenn Presnell	522

COACHING HISTORY: 1930 Hal Griffen 5-6-3-.464; 1931-1933 Potsy Clark 23-10-4-.676

POTTSVILLE MAROONS
(became Boston Bulldogs)

Home City: Pottsville, Pennsylvania
Home Stadium: Minersville Park
Origin of Name: The name was chosen because of the color of the players' uniforms.

Regular Season Record

Season	League	GP	W	L	T	PF	PA	Pct
1925	NFL	12	10	2	0	270	45	.833
1926	NFL	13	10	2	1	155	29	.808
1927	NFL	13	5	8	0	80	163	.385
1928	NFL	10	2	8	0	74	134	.200
TOTAL:	4 years	48	27	20	1	579	371	
AVERAGE:		12	7	5	0	145	93	.573

Regular Season Individual Leaders

Season	Passing Yards		Receiving Yards		Rushing Yards	
1925	Jack Ernst	693	Charlie Berry	349	Barney Wentz	628
1926	Jack Ernst	729	Charlie Berry	330	Barney Wentz	727
1927	Frank Kirkleski	730			Tony Latone	407
1928	Jack Ernst	457			Tony Latone	482

COACHING HISTORY: 1925-1927 Dick Rauch 25-12-1-.671; 1928 Pete Henry 2-8-0-.200

PROVIDENCE GRAYS

Home City: Providence, Rhode Island
Home Field: Messer Park
Origin of Name: The players wore gray uniforms.

Regular Season Record

Season	League	GP	W	L	Pct	GB	R	OR
1878	NL	60	33	27	.550	8	353	337
1879	NL	84	59	25	.702	-	612	355
1880	NL	84	52	32	.619	15	419	299
1881	NL	84	47	37	.560	9	447	426
1882	NL	84	52	32	.619	3	463	356
1883	NL	98	58	40	.592	5	636	436
1884	NL	112	84	28	.750	-	665	388
1885	NL	110	53	57	.482	33	442	531
TOTAL:	8 years	716	438	278		73	4037	3128
AVERAGE:		90	55	35	.612	9	505	391

Playoff Record

Season	GP	W	L	R	OR	Result
1884	3	3	0	21	3	Won World Series.

Regular Season Individual Leaders

Season	Home Runs		RBI's		Wins	
1878	Paul Hines	4	Paul Hines	50	Monte Ward	22
1879	Joe Start	2	Paul Hines	52	Monte Ward	47
	Paul Hines	2				
	Lew Brown	2				
	Monte Ward	2				
1880	Jack Farrell	3	Jack Farrell	36	Monte Ward	39
	Paul Hines	3				
1881	Jack Farrell	5	Monte Ward	53	Charles Radbourn	25
1882	Paul Hines	4	Joe Start	48	Charles Radbourn	33
1883	Jerry Denny	8	Jack Farrell	61	Charles Radbourn	48
1884	Jerry Denny	6	Jerry Denny	59	Charles Radbourn	59
1885	Jerry Denny	3	Joe Start	41	Charles Radbourn	28

COACHING HISTORY: 1878 George Ware 33-27-.550; 1879 George Wright 59-25-.702; 1880-1881 Jim Bullock 69-49-.585; 1881 Bob Morrow 30-20-.600; 1882-1883 Harry Wright 110-72-.604; 1884-1885 Frank Bancroft 137-85-.617

PROVIDENCE STEAM ROLLERS

Home City: Providence, Rhode Island
Home Stadium: Providence Cycledrome   Capacity: 14,000
Origin of Name: The name was chosen by co-founder Charles Coppen when he overheard a fan say Providence steamrolled its foes.

Regular Season Record

Season	League	GP	W	L	T	PF	PA	Pct
1925	NFL	12	6	5	1	111	101	.542
1926	NFL	13	5	7	1	83	103	.423
1927	NFL	14	8	5	1	105	88	.607
1928	NFL	11	8	1	2	128	42	.818

1929	NFL	12	4	6	2	107	117	.417
1930	NFL	11	6	4	1	90	125	.591
1931	NFL	11	4	4	3	78	127	.500
TOTAL:	7 years	84	41	32	11	702	703	
AVERAGE:		12	6	5	1	100	100	.542

Regular Season Individual Leaders

Season	Passing Yards		Receiving Yards		Rushing Yards	
1925	Cy Wentworth	50	Frank Garvey	43	Jim Laird	124
1926					Jack Keefer	88
1927	Wildcat Wilson	544			Curly Oden	199
1928	Wildcat Wilson	837			Wildcat Wilson	372
1929	Wildcat Wilson	279			Wildcat Wilson	99
1930					Tony Latone	223
1931	Deck Shelley	555			Deck Shelley	117

COACHING HISTORY: 1925 Archie Golembeski 6-5-1-.542; 1926 Jim Laird 5-7-1-.423; 1927-1930 Jimmy Conzelman 26-16-6-.604; 1931 Ed Robinson 4-4-3-.500

PROVIDENCE STEAMROLLERS

Home City: Providence, Rhode Island
Home Court: Providence Auditorium
Origin of Name: Named after previous NFL team.

Regular Season Record

Season	League	GP	W	L	PPGF	PPGA	Pct	GB
1946-1947	BAA	60	28	32	72.5	74.2	.467	21
1947-1948	BAA	48	6	42	69.1	80.7	.125	21
1948-1949	BAA	60	12	48	78.5	87.6	.200	26
TOTAL:	3 years	168	46	122				68
AVERAGE:		56	15	41	73.4	80.8	.274	23

Regular Season Individual Leaders

Season	Field Goal % (min. 40 games)		Points		Points per Game (min. 40 games)	
1946-47	Earl Shannon	.339	Ernie Calverly	845	Ernie Calverly	14.3
1947-48	George Nostrand	.299	Ernie Calverly	559	Ernie Calverly	11.9
1948-49	Howie Shannon	.364	Kenny Sailors	899	Kenny Sailors	15.8

COACHING HISTORY: 1946-1947 Bob Morris 28-32-.467; 1947-1948 Hank Soar 2-17-.105; 1947-1948 Nat Hickey 4-25-.138; 1948-1949 Ken Loeffler 12-48-.200

QUEBEC BULLDOGS

Home City: Quebec City, Quebec
Home Arena: Quebec Coliseum
Origin of Name.

Regular Season Record

Season	League	GP	W	L	T	GF	GA	Pts	Pct
1908-1909	ECHA	12	3	9	0	78	106	6	.250

Regular Season Individual Leaders

Season	Goals		Points		GAA	
1908-1909	Herb Jordan	29	Herb Jordan	29	Paddy Moran	8.83

COACHING HISTORY:

QUEBEC BULLDOGS

Home City: Quebec City, Quebec
Home Arena: Quebec Coliseum
Origin of Name: Named after previous ECHA team.

Regular Season Record

Season	League	GP	W	L	T	GF	GA	Pts	Pct
1910-1911	NHA	16	4	12	0	65	97	8	.250
1911-1912	NHA	18	10	8	0	81	79	20	.556
1912-1913	NHA	20	16	4	0	112	75	32	.800
1913-1914	NHA	20	12	8	0	111	73	24	.600
1914-1915	NHA	20	11	9	0	85	85	22	.550
1915-1916	NHA	24	10	12	2	91	98	22	.458
1916-1917	NHA	20	10	10	0	97	126	20	.500
TOTAL:	7 years	138	73	63	2	642	633	148	
AVERAGE:		20	10	9	1	92	90	21	.536

Playoff Record

Season	GP	W	L	T	GF	GA	Result
1911-1912	2	2	0	0	17	3	Won Stanley Cup.
1912-1913	2	2	0	0	20	5	Won Stanley Cup.
TOTAL:	4	4	0	0	37	8	
AVERAGE:	2	2	0	0	19	4	

Regular Season Individual Leaders

Season	Goals		Points		GAA	
1910-1911	Jack McDonald	14	Jack McDonald	14	Paddy Moran	6.06
	Ken Mallen	14	Ken Mallen	14		
1911-1912	Joe Malone	21	Joe Malone	21	Paddy Moran	4.39
1912-1913	Joe Malone	43	Joe Malone	43	Paddy Moran	3.75
1913-1914	Tommy Smith	39	Tommy Smith	39	Paddy Moran	3.65
1914-1915	Tommy Smith		Tommy Smith		Paddy Moran	4.25
1915-1916	Joe Malone	26	Joe Malone	26	Paddy Moran	3.73
1916-1917	Joe Malone	41	Joe Malone	41	Sam Hebert	5.43

COACHING HISTORY: 1910-1911 Not Available; 1911-1912 C. Nolan 10-8-0-.556; 1912-1913 Joe Malone 16-4-0-.800; 1913-1917 Not Available

QUEBEC BULLDOGS
(became Hamilton Tigers)

Home City: Quebec City, Quebec
Home Arena: Quebec Coliseum
Origin of Name: According to *NHL 75th Anniversary Commemorative Book* the team was formally called the Athletics but was more often referred to as the Bulldogs by the press and fans.

Regular Season Record

Season	League	GP	W	L	T	GF	GA	Pts	Pct
1919-1920	NHL	24	4	20	0	91	177	8	.167

Regular Season Individual Leaders

Season	Goals		Points		Penalty Minutes	
1919-1920	Joe Malone	39	Joe Malone	49	Harry Mummery	42

COACHING HISTORY: Mike Quinn 4-20-0-.167

QUEBEC NORDIQUES
(became Colorado Avalanche)

Home City: Quebec City, Quebec
Home Arena: Le Colisee de Quebec   Capacity: 15,399 [1995]
Origin of Name: The name was chosen in a contest sponsored by a local sportsmen's club.

Regular Season Record

Season	League	GP	W	L	T	GF	GA	Pts	Pct
1972-1973	WHA	78	33	40	5	276	313	71	.455
1973-1974	WHA	78	38	36	4	306	280	80	.513
1974-1975	WHA	78	46	32	0	331	299	92	.590
1975-1976	WHA	81	50	27	4	371	316	104	.642
1976-1977	WHA	81	47	31	3	353	295	97	.599
1977-1978	WHA	80	40	37	3	349	347	83	.519
1978-1979	WHA	80	41	34	5	288	271	87	.544
1979-1980	NHL	80	25	44	11	248	313	61	.381
1980-1981	NHL	80	30	32	18	314	318	78	.488
1981-1982	NHL	80	33	31	16	356	345	82	.513
1982-1983	NHL	80	34	34	12	343	336	80	.500
1983-1984	NHL	80	42	28	10	360	278	94	.588
1984-1985	NHL	80	41	30	9	323	275	91	.569
1985-1986	NHL	80	43	31	6	330	289	92	.575
1986-1987	NHL	80	31	39	10	267	276	72	.450
1987-1988	NHL	80	32	43	5	271	306	69	.431
1988-1989	NHL	80	27	46	7	269	342	61	.381
1989-1990	NHL	80	12	61	7	240	407	31	.194
1990-1991	NHL	80	16	50	14	236	354	46	.288
1991-1992	NHL	80	20	48	12	255	318	52	.325
1992-1993	NHL	84	47	27	10	351	300	104	.619
1993-1994	NHL	84	34	42	8	277	292	76	.452
1994-1995	NHL	48	30	13	5	185	134	65	.677
TOTAL:	23 years	1812	792	836	184	6899	7004	1768	
AVERAGE:		78	34	36	8	300	305	77	.488

Playoff Record

Season	GP	W	L	GF	GA	Result
1974-1975	15	8	7	55	48	Lost WHA Final to Houston.
1975-1976	5	1	4	15	23	Lost Quarterfinal series to Calgary.
1976-1977	17	12	5	79	56	**Won WHA Championship.**
1977-1978	11	5	6	43	41	Lost Semifinal series to New England.
1978-1979	4	0	4	30	12	Lost Semifinal series to Winnipeg.
1980-1981	5	2	3	17	22	Lost Preliminary series to Philadelphia.
1981-1982	16	7	9	48	60	Lost Conference Final to N.Y. Islanders.
1982-1983	4	1	3	8	11	Lost Division Semifinal to Boston.
1983-1984	9	5	4	26	25	Lost Division Final to Montreal.
1984-1985	18	9	9	58	63	Lost Conference Final to Philadelphia.
1985-1986	3	0	3	7	16	Lost Division Semifinal to Hartford.
1986-1987	13	7	6	48	45	Lost Division Final to Montreal.
1992-1993	6	2	4	16	19	Lost Division Semifinal to Montreal.
1994-1995	6	2	4	19	25	Lost Conference Quarterfinal to Rangers.
TOTAL:	132	61	71	469	466	
AVERAGE:	9	4	5	34	34	

Regular Season Individual Leaders

Season	Goals		Points		Penalty Minutes	
1972-1973	Alain Caron	36	J.C. Tremblay	89	Pierre Roy	167
1973-1974	Serge Bernier	37	Serge Bernier	86	Pierre Roy	137
1974-1975	Serge Bernier	54	Serge Bernier	122	Pierre Roy	118
1975-1976	Marc Tardif	71	Marc Tardif	148	Gord Gallant	297
1976-1977	Real Cloutier	66	Real Cloutier	141	Paul Baxter	244
1977-1978	Marc Tardif	65	Marc Tardif	154	Paul Baxter	240
1978-1979	Real Cloutier	75	Real Cloutier	129	Paul Baxter	240
1979-1980	Real Cloutier	42	Real Cloutier	88	Paul Baxter	145
1980-1981	Jacques Richard	52	Peter Stastny	109	Dale Hunter	226
1981-1982	Peter Stastny	46	Peter Stastny	139	Dale Hunter	272
1982-1983	Michel Goulet	57	Peter Stastny	124	Dale Hunter	206
1983-1984	Michel Goulet	56	Michel Goulet	121	Dale Hunter	232
1984-1985	Michel Goulet	55	Peter Stastny	100	Dale Hunter	209
1985-1986	Michel Goulet	53	Peter Stastny	122	Dale Hunter	265
1986-1987	Michel Goulet	49	Michel Goulet	96	Basil McRae	342
1987-1988	Michel Goulet	48	Peter Stastny	111	Gord Donnelly	301
1988-1989	Walt Poddubny	38	Peter Stastny	85	Steve Finn	235
1989-1990	Joe Sakic	39	Joe Sakic	102	Paul Gillis	234
1990-1991	Joe Sakic	48	Joe Sakic	109	Steve Finn	238
1991-1992	Owen Nolan	42	Joe Sakic	94	Steve Finn	194
1992-1993	Joe Sakic	48	Mats Sundin	114	Owen Nolan	185
1993-1994	Mats Sundin	32	Joe Sakic	92	Steve Finn	159
1994-1995	Owen Nolan	30	Joe Sakic	62	Chris Simon	106

COACHING HISTORY: 1972-1973 Maurice Richard 1-1-0-.500; 1972-1973 Maurice Filion 32-39-5-.454; 1973-1974 Jacques Plante 38-36-4-.513; 1974-1976 Jean-Guy Gendron 96-59-4-.616; 1976-1978 Marc Boileau 74-61-5-.546; 1977-1978 Maurice Filion 13-7-1-.643; 1978-1980 Jacques Demers 66-78-16-.463; 1980-1981 Maurice Filion 1-3-2-.333; 1980-1987 Michel Bergeron 253-222-79-.528; 1987-1988 Andre Savard 10-13-1-.438; 1987-1989 Ron LaPointe 33-50-6-.404; 1988-1989 Jean Perron 16-26-5-.394; 1989-1990 Michel Bergeron 12-61-7-.194; 1990-1992 Dave Chambers 19-64-15-.270; 1991-1994 Pierre Page 98-103-29-.489; 1994-1995 Marc Crawford 30-13-5-.677.

RACINE LEGIONS

Home City: Racine, Wisconsin
Home Stadium: Racine Baseball Association Field
Origin of Name: The team was sponsored by the local American Legion.

Regular Season Record

Season	League	GP	W	L	T	PF	PA	Pct
1922	NFL	11	6	4	1	122	56	.591
1923	NFL	10	4	4	2	86	86	.500
1924	NFL	10	4	4	3	69	47	.500
TOTAL:	3 years	31	14	12	6	277	189	
AVERAGE:		11	5	4	2	92	63	.548

Regular Season Individual Leaders

Season	Passing Yards		Receiving Yards		Rushing Yards	
1922	Al Elliott	57	Irv Langhoff	70	Al Elliott 175	
1923	Shorty Barr	412	Al Elliott	168	Hank Gillo	287
1924	Shorty Barr	199	John Mohardt	88	Hank Gillo	128

COACHING HISTORY: Babe Ruetz 14-12-6-.548

RACINE TORNADOES

Home City: Racine, Wisconsin
Home Stadium: Racine Baseball Association Field
Origin of Name:

			Regular Season Record					
Season	League	GP	W	L	T	PF	PA	Pct
1926	NFL	5	1	4	0	8	92	.200

Regular Season Individual Leaders

Season	Passing Yards		Receiving Yards	Rushing Yards	
1926	Shorty Barr		84	Charlie Reichow	105

COACHING HISTORY: Hank Gillo & Wallace Barr 1-4-0-.200

RALEIGH-DURHAM SKYHAWKS

Home City: Raleigh, North Carolina
Home Stadium: Carter-Finley Stadium   Capacity: 53,500 [1991]
Origin of Name:

			Regular Season Record					
Season	League	GP	W	L	T	PF	PA	Pct
1991	WLAF	10	0	10	0	123	300	.000

COACHING HISTORY: Roman Gabriel 0-10-0-.000

REAL SALT LAKE

Home City: Salt Lake City, Utah
Home Field: Rice Eccles Stadium (2005-present)   Capacity: 45,634 [2005]
Origin of Name:

Season	League	GP	W	L	T	SOW	GF	GA	Pts
2005	MLS	32	5	22	5	NA	30	65	20
2006	MLS	32	10	13	9	NA	45	49	39
TOTAL:	2 years	64	15	35	14	0	75	114	59
AVERAGE:		32	8	17	7	0	38	57	30

Regular Season Individual Leaders

Season	Goals		Points		GAA	
2005	Jason Kreis	9	Jason Kreis	22	D.J. Countess	2.01
2006	Jeff Cunningham	16	Jeff Cunningham	43	Scott Garlick	1.41

COACHING HISTORY: 2005-present John Ellinger

REGINA CAPITALS
(became Portland Rosebuds)

Home City: Regina, Saskatchewan
Home Arena: Regina Stadium
Origin of Name: The team may have been named Capitals because Regina is the capital city of Saskatchewan.

Regular Season Record

Season	League	GP	W	L	T	GF	GA	Pts	Pct
1921-1922	WCHL	24	14	10	0	94	78	28	.583
1922-1923	WCHL	30	16	14	0	93	97	32	.533
1923-1924	WCHL	30	17	11	2	83	67	36	.600
1924-1925	WCHL	28	8	20	0	82	123	16	.286
TOTAL:	4 years	112	55	55	2	352	365	112	
AVERAGE:		28	14	14	0	88	91	28	.500

Playoff Record

Season	GP	W	L	T	GF	GA	Result
1921-1922	6	3	2	1	7	8	Lost playoff series to Vancouver.
1922-1923	2	0	1	1	3	4	Lost WCHL playoff to Edmonton.
1923-1924	2	0	1	1	2	4	Lost WCHL playoff to Calgary.
TOTAL:	10	3	4	3	12	16	
AVERAGE:	3	1	1	1	4	5	

Regular Season Individual Leaders

Season	Goals		Points		GAA	
1921-1922	George Hay	23	George Hay	23	Bill Laird	3.12
1922-1923	George Hay	28	George Hay	28	Bill Laird	3.04
1923-1924	George Hay	20	George Hay	20	Red McCusker	2.23
1924-1925	George Hay	16	George Hay	16	Red McCusker	4.39

COACHING HISTORY: 1921-1922 Wes Champ 14-10-0-.583; 1922-1925 Barney Stanley 41-45-2-.466

RENFREW CREAMERY KINGS

Home City: Renfrew, Ontario
Home Arena: Renfrew Arena   Capacity: 2,500
Origin of Name: The team acquired its name because Renfrew was a well known dairy town.

Regular Season Record

Season	League	GP	W	L	T	GF	GA	Pts	Pct
1909-1910	NHA	12	8	3	1	96	54	17	.708
1910-1911	NHA	16	8	8	0	91	101	16	.500
TOTAL:	2 years	28	16	11	1	187	155	33	
AVERAGE:		14	8	6	0	94	78	16	.589

Regular Season Individual Leaders

Season	Goals		Points		GAA	
1909-1910	Newsy Lalonde	36	Newsy Lalonde	36	Bert Lindsay	4.50
1910-1911	Don Smith	28	Don Smith	28	Bert Lindsay	6.31

COACHING HISTORY: 1909-1910 Lester Patrick 8-3-1-.708

RICHMOND KING CLOTHIERS
(merged with Cincinnati Comellos in 1938)

Home City: Richmond, Indiana
Home Court: Richmond Coliseum
Origin of Name: The team was sponsored by King Clothiers.

Regular Season Record

Season	League	GP	W	L	PPGF	PPGA	Pct	GB
1937-1938	NBL	3	1	2	29.1	37.6	.333	5.5

COACHING HISTORY: Bob McConachie 1-2-.333

RICHMOND VIRGINIAS

Home City: Richmond, Virginia
Home Field: Virginia Park
Origin of Name: The team adopted the state's name as its own.

Regular Season Record

Season	League	GP	W	L	Pct	GB	R	OR
1884	AA	42	12	30	.286	30.5	194	294

Regular Season Individual Leaders

Season	Home Runs		RBI's		Wins	
1884	Bill Schenck	3	Not Recorded		Pete Meegan	7

COACHING HISTORY: Felix Moses 12-30-.286

ROCHESTER BEAU BRUMMELS

Home City: Rochester, New York
Home Field: Culver Field   Capacity: 4,200
Origin of Name: The team acquired its name because of the attractiveness of its uniforms.

Regular Season Record

Season	League	GP	W	L	Pct	GB	R	OR
1890	AA	126	63	63	.500	22	709	711

Regular Season Individual Leaders

Season	Home Runs		RBI's		Wins	
1890	Jim Knowles	5	Not Recorded		Bob Barr	28
	Sandy Griffin	5				

COACHING HISTORY: Pat Powers 63-63-.500

ROCHESTER CENTRALS

Home City: Rochester, New York
Home Court: New York State Armory
Origin of Name: The team was originally formed by a group of boys who attended school in the Central Avenue area of Rochester.

Regular Season Record

Season	League	GP	W	L	Pct
1925-1926	ABL	30	18	12	.600
1926-1927	ABL	42	14	28	.333
1927-1928	ABL	52	24	28	.462
1928-1929	ABL	40	18	22	.450
1929-1930	ABL	54	33	21	.611
1930-1931	ABL	34	15	19	.441
TOTAL:	6 years	252	122	130	
AVERAGE:		42	20	22	.484

Playoff Record

Season	GP	W	L	PF	PA	Result
1929-1930	5	1	4	81	96	Lost Championship series to Cleveland.

Regular Season Individual Leaders

Season	Points	
1925-26	Marty Barry	179
1926-27	Harry Topel	253
1927-28	Harry Topel	402
1928-29	Lou Rabin	274
1929-30	G. Chizmadia	343
1930-31	Manny Hirsch	211

COACHING HISTORY: 1925-1929 Not Available; 1929-1930 Frank Morgenweck 33-21; 1930-1931 Not Available

ROCHESTER JEFFERSONS

Home City: Rochester, New York
Home Stadium: Edgarton Park
Origin of Name:

Regular Season Record

Season	League	GP	W	L	T	PF	PA	Pct
1922	NFL	5	0	4	1	13	76	.100
1923	NFL	2	0	2	0	0	116	.000
1924	NFL	7	0	7	0	7	156	.000
1925	NFL	7	0	6	1	26	111	.071
TOTAL:	4 years	21	0	19	2	46	459	
AVERAGE:		5	0	5	0	11	115	.048

Regular Season Individual Leaders

Season	Passing Yards		Receiving Yards		Rushing Yards	
1922	Chet Wynne	78	Eddie Anderson	57	Chet Wynne	78
1923	Al Sheard	46	Elmer Roy	25	Leo Peyton	27
1924	Ben Boynton	65	Gerry Noonan	55	Al Sheard	6
1925	Lou Smythe	314	Al Sheard	118	Tex Grigg	65

COACHING HISTORY: 1922-1923 Leo Lyons 0-6-1-.071; 1924-1925 Jerry Noonan 0-13-1-.036

ROCHESTER LANCERS

Home City: Rochester, New York
Home Stadium: Aquinas Stadium (1970-73)
              Holleder Stadium (1974-1980)   Capacity: 20,000
Origin of Name: The team kept the same name when it moved from the American Soccer League
to the North American Soccer League.

Regular Season Record

Season	League	GP	W	L	T	GF	GA	BP	Pts	Pct
1970	NASL	24	9	9	6	41	45	39	111	.514
1971	NASL	24	13	5	6	48	31	45	141	.653
1972	NASL	14	6	5	3	20	22	19	64	.508
1973	NASL	19	4	9	6	17	27	17	59	.345
1974	NASL	20	8	10	2	23	30	23	77	.428
1975	NASL	22	6	16	-	29	49	28	64	.323
1976	NASL	24	13	11	-	36	32	36	114	.528
1977	NASL	26	11	15	-	34	41	33	99	.423
1978	NASL	30	14	16	-	47	52	47	131	.485
1979	NASL	30	15	15	-	43	57	42	132	.489
1980	NASL	32	12	20	-	42	67	37	109	.378
TOTAL:	11 years	265	111	131	23	380	453	366	1101	
AVERAGE:		24	10	12	2	35	41	33	100	.462

Playoff Record

Season	GP	W	L	T	GF	GA	Result
1970	2	1	1	0	4	3	Lost Championship series to Washington.
1971	3	1	2	0	4	6	Lost Semifinal series to Dallas.
1972	1	0	1	0	0	2	Lost Semifinal series to St. Louis.
1976	1	0	1	0	1	2	Lost 1st Round series to Toronto.
1977	5	3	2	0	5	6	Lost Conference Final to New York.
TOTAL:	12	5	7	0	14	19	
AVERAGE:	2	1	1	0	3	4	

Regular Season Individual Leaders

Season	Goals		Points		GAA	
1970	Carlos Metidieri	14	Carlos Metidieri	35	Dick Howard	1.80
1971	Carlos Metidieri	19	Carlos Metidieri	46	Claude Campos	1.11
1972	Carlos Metidieri	5	Carlos Metidieri	11	Claude Campos	1.43
1973	Tony Esposito	3	Tony Esposito	8	Danville Clarke	1.09
	Floriano Galassin	3	Carlos Metidieri	8		
	Antun Runac	3				
1974	Tommy Ord	7	Tommy Ord	16	Claude Campos	1.14
1975						
1976	Mike Stojanovic	17	Mike Stojanovic	41	B. Tamindzic	1.28
1977	Mike Stojanovic	14	Mike Stojanovic	33	Jack Brand	1.48
1978	Francisco Bolota	12	Francisco Bolota	27	Ratko Svilar	1.67
1979	Branko Segota	14	Branko Segota	32	Shep Messing	1.90
1980	Branko Segota	11	Branko Segota	28		

COACHING HISTORY: 1970 Alex Perolli; 1970 Charles Schiano; 1970-1971 Sal DeRosa; 1972 Adolfo Gori 6-5-3-.508; 1973 Sal DeRosa 4-9-6-.345; 1974 Billy Hughes; 1974 John Petrossi; 1974-1975 Ted Dumitru; 1976-1979 Don Popovic 53-57; 1980 Ray Klivecka 3-4; 1980 Alex Perolli 9-16

ROCHESTER ROYALS
(became Cincinnati Royals)

Home City: Rochester, New York
Home Court: Edgarton Park Arena (1946-1955)   Capacity: 5,000
Rochester War Memorial (1955-1957)   Capacity: 10,000
Origin of Name: The name was chosen in a Name the Team Contest.

Regular Season Record

Season	League	GP	W	L	PPGF	PPGA	Pct	GB
1945-1946	NBL	34	24	10	56.8	50.8	.706	2
1946-1947	NBL	44	31	13	62.9	56.5	.705	-
1947-1948	NBL	60	44	16	64.6	58.2	.733	-
1948-1949	BAA	60	45	15	84.0	77.4	.750	-
1949-1950	NBA	68	51	17	82.4	74.6	.750	-
1950-1951	NBA	68	41	27	84.6	81.7	.603	3
1951-1952	NBA	66	41	25	86.2	82.9	.621	-
1952-1953	NBA	70	44	26	86.3	83.5	.629	4
1953-1954	NBA	72	44	28	79.8	77.3	.611	2
1954-1955	NBA	72	29	43	90.8	92.4	.403	14
1955-1956	NBA	72	31	41	95.8	98.7	.431	6
1956-1957	NBA	72	31	41	93.4	95.6	.431	3
TOTAL:	12 years	758	456	302				34
AVERAGE:		63	38	25	80.6	77.5	.602	3

Playoff Record

Season	GP	W	L	PPGF	PPGA	Result
1945-1946	7	6	1	59.6	52.0	**Won NBL Championship**
1946-1947	11	6	5	63.5	61.3	Lost Championship series to Chicago.
1947-1948	11	6	5	68.7	65.5	Lost Championship series to Minneapolis.
1948-1949	4	2	2	73.3	68.8	Lost Division Final to Minneapolis.
1949-1950	3	0	3	79.3	82.3	Lost Division Semifinal to Ft. Wayne.
1950-1951	14	9	5	83.9	77.2	**Won NBA Championship.**
1951-1952	6	3	3	83.3	80.7	Lost Division Final to Minneapolis.
1952-1953	3	1	2	75.0	74.0	Lost Division Semifinal to Ft. Wayne.
1953-1954	6	3	3	80.2	83.2	Lost Division Final to Minneapolis.
1954-1955	3	1	2	94.0	97.7	Lost Division Semifinal to Minneapolis.
TOTAL:	68	37	31			
AVERAGE:	7	4	3	76.1	74.5	

Regular Season Individual Leaders

Season	Field Goals		Free Throws		Points	
1945-46	George Glamack	151	George Glamack	115	George Glamack	417
1946-47	Al Cervi	228	Al Cervi	176	Al Cervi	632
1947-48	Red Holzman	246	Al Cervi	187	Al Cervi	655
1948-49	Arnie Risen	345	Arnie Risen	305	Arnie Risen	995
1949-50	Bob Davies	317	Bobby Wanzer	283	Bob Davies	895
1950-51	Arnie Risen	377	Arnie Risen	323	Arnie Risen	1077
1951-52	Bob Davies	379	Bobby Wanzer	377	Bob Davies	1052
1952-53	Bob Davies	339	Bobby Wanzer	384	Bob Davies	1029
1953-54	Bobby Wanzer	322	Bobby Wanzer	314	Bobby Wanzer	958
1954-55	Jack Coleman	400	Bobby Wanzer	294	Bobby Wanzer	942
1955-56	Jack Twyman	417	Maurice Stokes	319	Maurice Stokes	1125
1956-57	Jack Twyman	449	Jack Twyman	276	Jack Twyman	1174

COACHING HISTORY: 1945-1946 Les Harrison 24-10-.765; 1946-1947 Ed Malanowicz & Les Harrison 31-13-.705; 1947-1948 Ed Malanowicz 44-16-.733; 1948-1955 Les Harrison 295-181-.620; 1955-1957 Bobby Wanzer 62-82-.431

ROCK ISLAND INDEPENDENTS

Home City: Rock Island, Illinois
Home Stadium: Douglas Park
Origin of Name:

Season	League	GP	Regular Season Record W	L	T	PF	PA	Pct
1922	NFL	7	4	2	1	154	27	.643
1923	NFL	8	2	3	3	84	62	.438
1924	NFL	10	6	2	2	98	44	.700
1925	NFL	11	5	3	3	99	58	.591
TOTAL:	4 years	36	17	10	9	435	191	
AVERAGE:		9	4	3	2	109	48	.597

Season	Regular Season Individual Leaders Passing Yards		Receiving Yards		Rushing Yards	
1922	Jim Conzelman	399	Tillie Voss	204	Jim Conzelman	290
1923	John Armstrong	778	Waddy Kuehl	257	Bob Phelan	190
1924	John Armstrong	20	Jim Thorpe	18	Buck Gavin	55
1925	John Armstrong	347	Joe Little Twig	140	Roddy Lamb	378

COACHING HISTORY: 1922 Jimmy Conzelman 4-2-1-.643; 1923 Dale Sies 2-3-3-.438; 1924 John Armstrong 6-2-2-.700; 1925 Rube Ursella 5-3-3-.591

SACRAMENTO GOLD MINERS
(became San Antonio Texans)

Home City: Sacramento, California
Home Stadium: Hornet Field   Capacity: 24,000 [1994]
Origin of Name: The name was chosen by the team owners.

Season	League	GP	Regular Season Record W	L	T	PF	PA	Pts	Pct
1993	CFL	18	6	12	0	498	509	12	.333
1994	CFL	18	9	8	1	436	436	19	.528
TOTAL:	2 years	36	15	20	1	934	945	31	
AVERAGE:		18	8	10	0	467	473	16	.431

Season	Regular Season Individual Leaders Passing Yards		Receiving Yards		Rushing Yards	
1993	David Archer	6023	Rod Harris	1379	Mike Oliphant	760
1994	David Archer	3340	Rod Harris	1280	Troy Mills	1230

COACHING HISTORY: 1993-1994 Kay Stephenson 15-20-1-.431

SACRAMENTO KINGS
(were Kansas City Kings)

Home City: Sacramento, California
Home Court: ARCO Arena I (1985-1988)   Capacity: 10,333 [1987]
     ARCO Arena II (1988-present)   Capacity: 17,317 [2006]
Origin of Name: The team kept the same nickname when it moved from Kansas City to
Sacramento.

Regular Season Record

Season	League	GP	W	L	PPGF	PPGA	Pct	GB
1985-1986	NBA	82	37	45	108.8	111.9	.451	14
1986-1987	NBA	82	29	53	110.9	114.1	.354	26
1987-1988	NBA	82	24	58	108.0	113.7	.293	30
1988-1989	NBA	82	27	55	105.5	111.0	.329	30
1989-1990	NBA	82	23	59	101.7	106.8	.280	40
1990-1991	NBA	82	25	57	96.7	103.5	.305	38
1991-1992	NBA	82	29	53	104.3	110.3	.347	28
1992-1993	NBA	82	25	57	107.9	111.1	.305	37
1993-1994	NBA	82	28	54	101.1	106.9	.341	35
1994-1995	NBA	82	39	43	98.2	99.2	.476	20
1995-1996	NBA	82	39	43	99.5	102.3	.476	25
1996-1997	NBA	82	34	48	96.4	99.8	.415	23
1997-1998	NBA	82	27	55	93.1	98.7	.329	34
1998-1999	NBA	50	27	23	100.2	100.6	.540	8
1999-2000	NBA	82	44	38	105.0	102.0	.537	23
2000-2001	NBA	82	55	27	101.7	95.9	.671	1
2001-2002	NBA	82	61	21	104.6	97.0	.744	-
2002-2003	NBA	82	59	23	101.7	95.2	.720	-
2003-2004	NBA	82	55	27	102.8	97.8	.671	1
2004-2005	NBA	82	50	32	103.7	101.6	.610	12
2005-2006	NBA	82	44	38	98.9	97.3	.537	10
TOTAL:	21 years	1690	781	909				435
AVERAGE:		80	37	43	102.5	103.7	.462	21

Playoff Record

Season	GP	W	L	PPGF	PPGA	Result
1985-1986	3	0	3	96.0	110.3	Lost 1st Round series to Houston.
1995-1996	4	1	3	87.8	93.8	Lost 1st Round series to Seattle.
1998-1999	5	2	3	90.6	95.4	Lost 1st Round series to Utah.
1999-2000	5	2	3	96.4	104.4	Lost 1st Round series to Lakers.
2000-2001	8	3	5	97.6	97.5	Lost Conference Semifinal to Lakers.
2001-2002	16	10	6	101.1	98.8	Lost Conference Final to Lakers.
2002-2003	12	7	5	107.9	105.6	Lost Conference Semifinal to Dallas.
2003-2004	12	7	5	93.0	91.9	Lost Conference Semifinal to Minnesota.
2004-2005	5	1	4	102.2	106.6	Lost 1st Round series to Seattle.
2005-2006	6	2	4	97.3	106.8	Lost 1st Round series to San Antonio.
TOTAL	76	35	41			
AVERAGE	8	4	4	98.4	100.1	

Regular Season Individual Leaders

Season	Field Goal % (min. 70 games)		Points		Points per Game (min. 70 games)	
1985-86	Otis Thorpe	.587	Eddie Johnson	1530	Eddie Johnson	18.7
1986-87	Otis Thorpe	.540	Reggie Theus	1600	Reggie Theus	20.3

Season	Field Goal % (min. 70 games)		Points		Points per Game (min. 70 games)	
1987-88	Ed Pinckney	.522	Otis Thorpe	1704	Reggie Theus	21.6
1988-89	Vinny Del Negro	.475	Kenny Smith	1403	Kenny Smith	17.3
1989-90	Wayman Tisdale	.525	Wayman Tisdale	1758	Wayman Tisdale	22.3
1990-91	Antoine Carr	.511	Antoine Carr	1551	Antoine Carr	20.1
1991-92	Duane Causwell	.549	Mitch Richmond	1803	Mitch Richmond	22.5
1992-93	Wayman Tisdale	.509	Wayman Tisdale	1263	Wayman Tisdale	16.6
1993-94	Wayman Tisdale	.501	Mitch Richmond	1823	Mitch Richmond	23.4
1994-95	Olden Polynice	.544	Mitch Richmond	1867	Mitch Richmond	22.8
1995-96	Olden Polynice	.527	Mitch Richmond	1872	Mitch Richmond	23.1
1996-97	Michael Smith	.539	Mitch Richmond	2095	Mitch Richmond	25.9
1997-98	C. Williamson	.495	Mitch Richmond	1623	Mitch Richmond	23.2
1998-99*	L. Funderburke	.559	Chris Webber	839	Chris Webber	20.0
1999-00	Scott Pollard	.527	Chris Webber	1834	Chris Webber	24.5
2000-01	Vlade Divac	.482	Chris Webber	1898	Chris Webber	27.1
2001-02	Scott Pollard	.550	P. Stojakovic	1506	Chris Webber	24.5
2002-03	Keon Clark	.501	Chris Webber	1542	P. Stojakovic	19.2
2003-04	Brad Miller	.510	P. Stojakovic	1964	P. Stojakovic	24.2
2004-05	Darius Songaila	.527	Mike Bibby	1571	Mike Bibby	19.6
2005-06	S. Abdur-Rahim	.525	Mike Bibby	1728	Mike Bibby	21.1

COACHING HISTORY: 1985-1987 Phil Johnson 51-77-.398; 1986-1990 Jerry Reynolds 56-113-.331; 1987-1988 Bill Russell 17-41-.293; 1989-1992 Dick Motta 48-114-.296; 1991-1992 Rex Hughes 22-35-.386; 1992-1997 Garry St. Jean 159-236-.403; 1996-1998 Eddie Jordan 33-64-.340; 1998-present Rick Adelman

SACRAMENTO MONARCHS

Home City: Sacramento, California
Home Arena: ARCO Arena   Capacity: 17,317 [2005]
Origin of Name: The team was named to show affiliation with the NBA's Kings.

Regular Season Record

Season	League	GP	W	L	PPGF	PPGA	Pct	GB
1997	WNBA	28	10	18	67.9	75.4	.357	6
1998	WNBA	30	8	22	63.9	69.4	.267	19
1999	WNBA	32	19	13	74.8	70.6	.594	7
2000	WNBA	32	10	22	67.3	71.9	.313	18
2001	WNBA	32	20	12	71.7	66.8	.625	8
2002	WNBA	32	14	18	67.7	71.7	.438	11
2003	WNBA	34	19	15	67.6	65.2	.559	5
2004	WNBA	34	18	16	68.0	65.9	.529	7
2005	WNBA	34	25	9	68.5	61.6	.735	-
2006	WNBA	34	21	13	77.2	69.6	.618	4
TOTAL:	10 years	322	164	158				85
AVERAGE:		32	16	16	69.5	68.6	.509	9

Playoff Record

Season	GP	W	L	PPGF	PPGA	Result
1999	1	0	1	58.0	71.0	Lost Conference semifinal to L.A.
2000	2	0	2	67.0	73.5	Lost Conference semifinal Houston.
2001	5	3	2	75.0	71.6	Lost Conference final to Los Angeles.

*-minimum 40 games.

2003	6	3	3	62.8	68.3	Lost Conference final to Los Angeles.
2004	6	3	3	65.3	66.8	Lost Conference final to Seattle.
2005	8	5	3	71.3	65.6	**Won WNBA Championship.**
2006	9	6	3	77.2	69.6	Lost Final Series to Detroit.
TOTAL:	37	20	17			
AVERAGE:	5	3	2	70.3	68.6	

Regular Season Individual Leaders

Season	Field Goals % (20 games min.)		Free Throws % (20 games min.)		Points per Game (20 games min.)	
1997	Linda Burgess	.541	Bridgette Gordon	.785	R. Bolton-Holifield	15.7
1998	Lady Hardmon	.487	Linda Burgess	.763	Latasha Byears	14.2
1999	Y. Griffith	.541	Kate Starbird	.815	Y. Griffith	18.8
2000	Y. Griffith	.535	Stacy Clinesmith	.824	Y. Griffith	16.3
2001	Y. Griffith	.522	La'Keshia Frett	.857	Y. Griffith	16.2
2002	La'Keshia Frett	.449	Lady Grooms	.855	Tangela Smith	14.7
2003	Y. Griffith	.485	Lady Grooms	.808	Y. Griffith	13.8
2004	Y. Griffith	.519	Lady Grooms	.917	Y. Griffith	14.5
2005	Erin Buescher	.700	Kara Lawson	.839	DeMya Walker	14.1
2006	Erin Buescher	.537	Ticha Penicheiro	.792	Y. Griffith	12.0

COACHING HISTORY: 1997 Mary Murphy 5-10-.333, 1997-98 Heidi Van Derveer 13-30-.302; 1999-2001 Sonny Allen 35-41-.461; 2001-2002 Maura McHugh 28-24-.538; 2003-present John Whisenant

SACRAMENTO SURGE

Home City: Sacramento, California
Home Stadium: Charles Hughes Stadium (1991)   Capacity: 23,000 [1991]
        Hornet Stadium (1992)   Capacity: 29,500 [1992]
Origin of Name:

Regular Season Record

Season	League	GP	W	L	T	PF	PA	Pct
1991	WLAF	10	3	7	0	179	226	.300
1992	WFL	10	8	2	0	250	152	.800
TOTAL:	2 years	20	11	9	0	429	378	
AVERAGE:		10	6	4	0	215	189	.550

Playoff Record

Season	GP	W	L	PF	PA	Result
1992	2	2	0	38	32	Won WLAF Championship.

Regular Season Individual Leaders

Season	Passing Yards		Receiving Yards		Rushing Yards	
1991	Mike Elkins	2068	Carl Parker	801	Victor Floyd	406
1992	David Archer	2964	Eddie Brown	1011	Mike Pringle	507

COACHING HISTORY: 1991-1992 Kay Stephenson 11-9-0-.550

ST. LOUIS BLUES

Home City: St. Louis, Missouri
Home Arena: St. Louis Arena (1967-1994)*   Capacity: 17,188 [1994]
          Savvis Center (1994-present)**   Capacity: 19,022 [2005]
Origin of Name: The team name was suggested by the W.C. Handy ballad "The St. Louis Blues"
and chosen by team owner Sid Solomon Jr.

Regular Season Record

Season	League	GP	W	L	T	OL	SL	GF	GA	Pts
1967-1968	NHL	74	27	31	16	NA	NA	177	191	70
1968-1969	NHL	76	37	25	14	NA	NA	204	157	88
1969-1970	NHL	76	37	27	12	NA	NA	224	179	86
1970-1971	NHL	78	34	25	19	NA	NA	223	208	87
1971-1972	NHL	78	28	39	11	NA	NA	247	247	67
1972-1973	NHL	78	32	34	12	NA	NA	233	251	76
1973-1974	NHL	78	26	40	12	NA	NA	206	248	64
1974-1975	NHL	80	35	31	14	NA	NA	269	267	84
1975-1976	NHL	80	29	37	14	NA	NA	249	290	72
1976-1977	NHL	80	32	39	9	NA	NA	239	276	73
1977-1978	NHL	80	20	47	13	NA	NA	195	304	53
1978-1979	NHL	80	18	50	12	NA	NA	249	348	48
1979-1980	NHL	80	34	34	12	NA	NA	266	278	80
1980-1981	NHL	80	45	18	17	NA	NA	352	281	107
1981-1982	NHL	80	32	40	8	NA	NA	315	349	72
1982-1983	NHL	80	25	40	15	NA	NA	285	316	65
1983-1984	NHL	80	32	41	7	NA	NA	293	316	71
1984-1985	NHL	80	37	31	12	NA	NA	299	288	86
1985-1986	NHL	80	37	34	9	NA	NA	302	291	83
1986-1987	NHL	80	32	33	15	NA	NA	281	293	79
1987-1988	NHL	80	34	38	8	NA	NA	278	294	76
1988-1989	NHL	80	33	35	12	NA	NA	275	285	78
1989-1990	NHL	80	37	34	9	NA	NA	295	279	83
1990-1991	NHL	80	47	22	11	NA	NA	310	250	105
1991-1992	NHL	80	36	33	11	NA	NA	279	266	83
1992-1993	NHL	84	37	36	11	NA	NA	282	278	85
1993-1994	NHL	84	40	33	11	NA	NA	270	283	91
1994-1995	NHL	48	28	15	5	NA	NA	178	135	61
1995-1996	NHL	82	32	34	16	NA	NA	219	248	80
1996-1997	NHL	82	36	35	11	NA	NA	236	239	83
1997-1998	NHL	82	45	29	8	NA	NA	256	204	98
1998-1999	NHL	82	37	32	13	NA	NA	237	209	87
1999-2000	NHL	82	51	20	11	1	NA	248	165	114
2000-2001	NHL	82	43	22	12	5	NA	249	195	103
2001-2002	NHL	82	43	27	8	4	NA	227	188	98
2002-2003	NHL	82	41	24	11	6	NA	253	222	99
2003-2004	NHL	82	39	30	11	2	NA	191	198	91
2004-2005	NHL			Season cancelled due to lockout.						
2005-2006	NHL	82	21	46	NA	6	9	197	292	57
TOTAL:	38 years	3014	1309	1241	432	24	9	9588	9608	3083
AVERAGE:		79	34	33	11	1	0	252	253	81

*-St. Louis Arena was known as the Checkerdome from 1977-1982 while the team was owned by
the Ralston-Purina Company. **-known as Kiel Center 1994-2000

Playoff Record

Season	GP	W	L	GF	GA	Result
1967-1968	18	8	10	42	50	Lost Stanley Cup Final to Montreal.
1968-1969	12	8	4	36	20	Lost Stanley Cup Final to Montreal.
1969-1970	16	8	8	46	46	Lost Stanley Cup Final to Boston.
1970-1971	6	2	4	15	16	Lost Quarterfinal series to Minnesota.
1971-1972	11	4	7	27	47	Lost Semifinal series to Boston.
1972-1973	5	1	4	9	22	Lost Quarterfinal series to Chicago.
1974-1975	2	0	2	6	9	Lost Preliminary series to Pittsburgh.
1975-1976	3	1	2	8	7	Lost Preliminary series to Buffalo.
1976-1977	4	0	4	4	19	Lost Quarterfinal series to Montreal.
1979-1980	3	0	3	4	12	Lost Preliminary series to Chicago.
1980-1981	11	5	6	42	50	Lost Quarterfinal series to N.Y. Rangers.
1981-1982	10	5	5	39	36	Lost Division Final to Chicago.
1982-1983	4	1	3	10	16	Lost Division Semifinal to Chicago.
1983-1984	11	6	5	30	31	Lost Division Final to Minnesota.
1984-1985	3	0	3	5	9	Lost Division Semifinal to Minnesota.
1985-1986	19	10	9	64	70	Lost Conference Final to Calgary.
1986-1987	6	2	4	12	15	Lost Division Semifinal to Toronto.
1987-1988	10	5	5	36	38	Lost Division Final to Detroit.
1988-1989	10	5	5	35	34	Lost Division Final to Chicago.
1989-1990	12	7	5	42	44	Lost Division Final to Chicago.
1990-1991	13	6	7	41	42	Lost Division Final to Minnesota.
1991-1992	6	2	4	19	23	Lost Division Semifinal to Chicago.
1992-1993	11	7	4	24	28	Lost Division Final to Toronto.
1993-1994	4	0	4	10	16	Lost Conference Quarterfinal to Dallas.
1994-1995	7	3	4	27	27	Lost Conference Quarterfinal to Vancouver.
1995-1996	13	7	6	37	37	Lost Conference Semifinal to Detroit.
1996-1997	6	2	4	12	13	Lost Conference Quarterfinal to Detroit.
1997-1998	10	6	4	29	31	Lost Conference Semifinal to Detroit.
1998-1999	13	6	7	35	36	Lost Conference Semifinal to Dallas.
1999-2000	7	3	4	22	20	Lost Conference Quarterfinal to San Jose.
2000-2001	15	9	6	40	34	Lost Conference Final to Colorado.
2001-2002	10	5	5	24	19	Lost Conference Semifinal to Detroit.
2002-2003	7	3	4	21	17	Lost Conference Quarterfinal to Vancouver.
2003-2004	5	1	4	9	12	Lost Conference Quarterfinal to San Jose.
TOTAL:	303	138	165	862	946	
AVERAGE:	9	4	5	25	28	

Regular Season Individual Leaders

Season	Goals		Points		Penalty Minutes	
1967-1968	Red Berenson	22	Red Berenson	51	Barclay Plager	153
1968-1969	Red Berenson	35	Red Berenson	82	Noel Picard	131
1969-1970	Red Berenson	33	Phil Goyette	78	Barclay Plager	128
1970-1971	Chris Bordeleau	21	Chris Bordeleau	53	Barclay Plager	172
1971-1972	Garry Unger	36	Garry Unger	70	Barclay Plager	176
1972-1973	Garry Unger	41	Garry Unger	80	Steve Durbano	231
1973-1974	Garry Unger	33	Garry Unger	68	Steve Durbano	144
1974-1975	Garry Unger	36	Garry Unger	80	Bob Gassoff	222
1975-1976	Chuck Lefley	43	Chuck Lefley	85	Bob Gassoff	306
1976-1977	Garry Unger	30	Bob MacMillan	58	Bob Gassoff	254
1977-1978	Garry Unger	32	Garry Unger	52	Brian Sutter	123
1978-1979	Brian Sutter	41	Bernie Federko	95	Brian Sutter	165
1979-1980	Bernie Federko	38	Bernie Federko	94	Brian Sutter	156

Season	Goals		Points		Penalty Minutes	
1980-1981	Wayne Babych	54	Bernie Federko	104	Brian Sutter	232
1981-1982	Brian Sutter	39	Bernie Federko	92	Brian Sutter	239
1982-1983	Brian Sutter	46	Bernie Federko	84	Brian Sutter	254
1983-1984	Bernie Federko	41	Bernie Federko	107	Dwight Schofield	219
	Joe Mullen	41				
1984-1985	Joe Mullen	40	Bernie Federko	103	Dwight Schofield	184
1985-1986	Mark Hunter	44	Bernie Federko	102	Mark Hunter	171
					Rob Ramage	171
1986-1987	Doug Gilmour	42	Doug Gilmour	105	Mark Hunter	167
1987-1988	Tony McKegny	40	Bernie Federko	89	Todd Ewen	227
1988-1989	Brett Hull	41	Brett Hull	84	Todd Ewen	171
1989-1990	Brett Hull	72	Brett Hull	113	Kelly Chase	244
1990-1991	Brett Hull	86	Brett Hull	131	Glen Featherstone	204
1991-1992	Brett Hull	70	Brett Hull	109	Kelly Chase	264
1992-1993	Brett Hull	54	Craig Janney	106	Garth Butcher	211
1993-1994	Brett Hull	57	B. Shanahan	102	Kelly Chase	278
1994-1995	Brett Hull	29	Brett Hull	50	Brendan Shanahan	136
1995-1996	Brett Hull	43	Brett Hull	83	Shayne Corson	192
1996-1997	Brett Hull	42	Brett Hull	82	Mike Peluso	158
1997-1998	Geoff Courtnall	31	Brett Hull	72	Kelly Chase	231
1998-1999	Pavol Demitra	37	Pavol Demitra	89	Tony Twist	149
1999-2000	Pavol Demitra	28	Pavol Demitra	75	Tyson Nash	150
2000-2001	Scott Young	40	Pierre Turgeon	82	Reed Low	159
2001-2002	Keith Tkachuk	38	Pavol Demitra	77	Reed Low	158
2002-2003	Pavol Demitra	36	Pavol Demitra	93	Reed Low	234
2003-2004	Keith Tkachuk	33	Keith Tkachuk	71	Mike Danton	141
					Reed Low	141
2004-2005	Season cancelled due to lockout.					
2005-2006	Mike Sillinger	22	Scott Young	49	Barret Jackman	156

COACHING HISTORY: 1967-1968 Lynn Patrick 4-10-2-.313; 1967-1971 Scotty Bowman 110-83-45-.557; 1970-1973 Al Arbour 42-40-25-.509; 1971-1972 Sid Abel 3-6-1-.350; 1971-1972 Bill McCreary 6-14-4-.333; 1972-1974 Jean-Guy Talbot 52-53-15-.496; 1973-1975 Lou Angotti 6-20-6-.281; 1974-1976 Lynn Patrick 4-5-1-.450; 1974-1976 Garry Young 41-41-16-.500; 1975-1976 Leo Boivin 17-17-9-.500; 1976-1977 Emile Francis 32-39-9-.456; 1977-1978 Leo Boivin 11-36-7-.269; 1977-1980 Barclay Plager 35-77-22-.343; 1979-1982 Gordon Berenson 99-71-31-.570; 1981-1983 Emile Francis 14-24-5-.384; 1982-1983 Barclay Plager 15-21-12-.438; 1983-1986 Jacques Demers 106-106-28-.500; 1986-1988 Jacques Martin 66-71-23-.484; 1988-1992 Brian Sutter 153-124-43-.545; 1992-1993 Bob Plager 4-6-1-.409; 1992-1994 Bob Berry 73-63-21-.532; 1994-1996 Mike Keenan 75-66-22-.528; 1996-1997 Jim Roberts 3-3-3-.500; 1996-2004 Joel Quenneville 307-192-77-17-.598; 2003-present Mike Kitchen

ST. LOUIS BOMBERS

Home City: St. Louis, Missouri
Home Court: St. Louis Arena
Origin of Name:

			Regular Season Record					
Season	League	GP	W	L	PPGF	PPGA	Pct	GB
1946-1947	BAA	61	38	23	66.6	64.1	.623	1
1947-1948	BAA	48	29	19	71.5	69.5	.604	-
1948-1949	BAA	60	29	31	75.8	79.4	.483	16

1949-1950	NBA	68	26	42	73.7	76.5	.382	25
TOTAL:	4 years	237	122	115				42
AVERAGE:		59	30	29	71.9	72.4	.515	11

Playoff Record

Season	GP	W	L	PPGF	PPGA	Result
1946-1947	3	1	2	66.7	66.3	Lost Quarterfinal series to Philadelphia.
1947-1948	7	3	4	58.9	69.9	Lost Semifinal series to Philadelphia.
1948-1949	2	0	2	64.0	79.5	Lost Division Semifinal to Rochester.
TOTAL:	12	4	8			
AVERAGE:	4	1	3	63.2	71.9	

Regular Season Individual Leaders

Season	Field Goal % (min. 40 games)		Points		Points per Game (min. 40 games)	
1946-47	Cecil Hankins	.299	John Logan	770	John Logan	12.6
1947-48	Red Rocha	.314	John Logan	644	John Logan	13.4
1948-49	Red Rocha	.389	Belus Smawley	914	Belus Smawley	15.5
1949-50	Red Rocha	.405	Ed Macauley	1081	Ed Macauley	16.1

COACHING HISTORY: 1946-1948 Ken Loeffler 67-42-.615; 1948-1950 Grady Lewis 55-73-.430

ST. LOUIS BROWNS
(were Milwaukee Brewers)
(became Baltimore Orioles)

Home City: St. Louis, Missouri
Home Field: Sportsman's Park II (1902-1908)   Capacity: 18,000 [1907]
            Sportsman's Park III (1909-1953)   Capacity: 34,450 [1953]
Origin of Name: The team was so named because of the brown trim on their uniforms.

Regular Season Record

Season	League	GP	W	L	Pct	GB	R	OR
1902	AL	136	78	58	.574	5	619	607
1903	AL	139	65	74	.468	26.5	500	525
1904	AL	152	65	87	.428	29	481	604
1905	AL	153	54	99	.353	40.5	509	606
1906	AL	149	76	73	.510	16	565	501
1907	AL	152	69	83	.454	24	538	560
1908	AL	152	83	69	.546	6.5	543	478
1909	AL	150	61	89	.407	36	443	574
1910	AL	154	47	107	.305	57	454	778
1911	AL	152	45	107	.296	56.5	567	810
1912	AL	154	53	101	.344	53	556	790
1913	AL	153	57	96	.373	39	528	642
1914	AL	153	71	82	.464	28.5	523	614
1915	AL	154	63	91	.409	39.5	521	693
1916	AL	154	79	75	.513	12	591	545
1917	AL	154	57	97	.370	43	511	687
1918	AL	124	60	64	.484	14	426	448
1919	AL	139	67	72	.482	20.5	535	567
1920	AL	153	76	77	.497	21.5	797	766
1921	AL	154	81	73	.526	17.5	835	845

1922	AL	154	93	61	.604	1	867	643
1923	AL	152	74	78	.487	24	688	720
1924	AL	152	74	78	.487	17	764	797
1925	AL	153	82	71	.536	15	897	909
1926	AL	154	62	92	.403	29	682	845
1927	AL	153	59	94	.386	50.5	724	904
1928	AL	154	82	72	.532	19	772	742
1929	AL	152	79	73	.520	26	733	713
1930	AL	154	64	90	.416	38	751	886
1931	AL	154	63	91	.409	45	722	870
1932	AL	154	63	91	.409	44	736	898
1933	AL	151	55	96	.364	43.5	669	820
1934	AL	152	67	85	.441	33	674	800
1935	AL	152	65	87	.428	28.5	718	930
1936	AL	152	57	95	.375	44.5	804	1064
1937	AL	154	46	108	.299	56	715	1023
1938	AL	152	55	97	.362	44	755	962
1939	AL	154	43	111	.279	64.5	733	1035
1940	AL	154	67	87	.435	23	757	882
1941	AL	154	70	84	.455	31	765	823
1942	AL	151	82	69	.543	19.5	730	637
1943	AL	152	72	80	.474	25	596	604
1944	AL	154	89	65	.578	-	684	587
1945	AL	151	81	70	.536	6	597	548
1946	AL	154	66	88	.429	38	621	711
1947	AL	154	59	95	.383	38	564	744
1948	AL	153	59	94	.386	37	671	849
1949	AL	154	53	101	.344	44	667	913
1950	AL	154	58	96	.377	40	684	916
1951	AL	154	52	102	.338	46	611	882
1952	AL	154	64	90	.416	31	604	733
1953	AL	154	54	100	.351	46.5	555	778
TOTAL:	52 years	7881	3416	4465		1633	33552	38808
AVERAGE:		152	66	86	.433	31.5	645	746

				Playoff Record		
Season	**GP**	**W**	**L**	**R**	**OR**	**Result**
1944	6	2	4	12	16	Lost World Series to Cardinals.

Regular Season Individual Leaders

Season	Home Runs		RBI's		Wins	
1902	Charles Hemphill	6	John Anderson	85	Red Donahue	22
					Jack Powell	22
1903	Charles Hemphill	3	John Anderson	78	Willie Sudhoff	21
	Jesse Burkett	3				
1904	Tom Jones	2	Bobby Wallace	69	Fred Glade	18
	Bobby Wallace	2				
	Charles Hemphill	2				
	Jesse Burkett	2				
1905	George Stone	7	Bobby Wallace	59	Harry Howell	14
1906	George Stone	6	George Stone	71	Barney Pelty	17
1907	George Stone	4	Bobby Wallace	70	Harry Howell	16
1908	George Stone	5	Albert Ferris	74	Rube Waddell	19

Season	Home Runs		RBI's		Wins	
1909	Albert Ferris	3	Albert Ferris	58	Jack Powell	12
	Jim Stephens	3				
1910	Pat Newnam	2	George Stone	40	Joe Lake	11
	Roy Hartzell	2				
	Al Schweitzer	2				
	Art Griggs	2				
1911	Paul Meloan	3	Frank LaPorte	82	Joe Lake	10
	Jim Murray	3				
	Joe Kutina	3				
1912	Del Pratt	5	Del Pratt	69	G. Baumgardner	11
					Earl Hamilton	11
1913	Gus Williams	5	Del Pratt	87	Earl Hamilton	13
					Roy Mitchell	13
1914	Tilly Walker	6	Tilly Walker	78	Carl Weilman	18
1915	Tilly Walker	5	Del Pratt	78	Carl Weilman	18
1916	Del Pratt	5	Del Pratt	103	Carl Weilman	17
1917	William Jacobson	4	Hank Severeid	57	Dave Davenport	17
1918	George Sisler	2	Ray Demmitt	61	Allan Sothoron	13
1919	George Sisler	10	George Sisler	83	Allan Sothoron	20
1920	George Sisler	19	George Sisler	122	Urban Shocker	20
			William Jacobson	122		
1921	Ken Williams	24	Ken Williams	117	Urban Shocker	27
1922	Ken Williams	39	Ken Williams	155	Urban Shocker	24
1923	Ken Williams	29	Marty McManus	94	Urban Shocker	20
1924	William Jacobson	19	William Jacobson	97	Urban Shocker	16
1925	Ken Williams	25	Ken Williams	105	Milt Gaston	15
			George Sisler	105		
1926	Ken Williams	17	Ken Williams	74	Tom Zachary	14
1927	Ken Williams	17	George Sisler	97	Milt Gaston	13
1928	Lu Blue	14	Henry Manush	108	Alvin Crowder	21
1929	Ralph Kress	9	Ralph Kress	107	Sam Gray	18
1930	Leon Goslin	30	Ralph Kress	112	Walter Stewart	20
1931	Leon Goslin	24	Ralph Kress	114	Walter Stewart	14
1932	Leon Goslin	17	Leon Goslin	104	George Blaeholder	14
					Walter Stewart	14
1933	Bruce Campbell	16	Bruce Campbell	106	George Blaeholder	15
					Irving Hadley	15
1934	Harlond Clift	14	Ray Pepper	101	Bobo Newsom	16
1935	Julius Solters	18	Julius Solters	104	Ivy Andrews	13
1936	Harlond Clift	20	Julius Solters	134	Chester Hogsett	13
1937	Harlond Clift	29	Harlond Clift	118	Jim Walkup	9
1938	Harlond Clift	34	Harlond Clift	118	Bobo Newsom	20
1939	George McQuinn	20	George McQuinn	94	Vern Kennedy	9
					Jack Kramer	9
1940	Walt Judnich	24	Walt Judnich	89	Eldon Auker	16
1941	George McQuinn	18	Roy Cullenbine	98	Eldon Auker	14
1942	Chet Laabs	27	Chet Laabs	99	John Niggeling	15
1943	Vern Stephens	22	Vern Stephens	91	Steve Sundra	15
1944	Vern Stephens	20	Vern Stephens	109	Nelson Potter	19
1945	Vern Stephens	24	Vern Stephens	89	Nelson Potter	15
1946	Chet Laabs	16	Walt Judnich	72	Jack Kramer	13
1947	Jeff Heath	27	Jeff Heath	85	Jack Kramer	11
1948	Les Moss	14	Whitey Platt	82	Fred Sanford	12

Season	Home Runs		RBI's		Wins	
1949	Jack Graham	24	Roy Sievers	91	Ned Garver	12
1950	Don Lenhardt	22	Don Lenhardt	81	Ned Garver	13
1951	Ken Wood	15	Ray Coleman	55	Ned Garver	20
1952	Bob Nieman	18	Bob Nieman	74	Satchel Paige	12
					Bob Cain	12
1953	Vic Wertz	19	Vic Wertz	70	Marlin Stuart	8

COACHING HISTORY: 1902-1909 Jim McAleer 551-632-.466; 1910 Jack O'Connor 47-107-.305; 1911-1912 Bobby Wallace 57-134-.298; 1912-1913 George Stovall 91-158-.365; 1913 Jimmy Austin 2-6-.250; 1913-1915 Branch Rickey 139-179-.437; 1916-1918 Fielder Jones 159-196-.448; 1918 Jimmy Austin 6-8-.429; 1918-1920 Jimmy Burke 172-181-.487; 1921-1923 Lee Fohl 225-183-.551; 1923 Jimmy Austin 23-29-.442; 1924-1926 George Sisler 218-241-.475; 1927-1929 Dan Howley 220-239-.479; 1930-1933 Bill Killefer 224-331-.404; 1933 Allen Sothoron 1-3-.250; 1933-1937 Rogers Hornsby 234-351-.400; 1937 Jim Bottomley 21-58-.266; 1938 Charles Street 55-97-.362; 1939-1941 Fred Haney 125-227-.355; 1941-1946 Luke Sewell 432-410-.513; 1947 Herold Ruel 59-95-.383; 1948-1951 Zack Taylor 222-393-.361; 1952 Rogers Hornsby 22-28-.440; 1952-1953 Marty Marion 96-162-.372

ST. LOUIS BROWNS

Home City: St. Louis, Missouri
Home Stadium: Sportsman's Park
Origin of Name: Named after the American League baseball team.

Regular Season Record

Season	League	GP	W	L	T	PF	PA	Pct
1923	NFL	7	1	4	2	14	39	.286

Regular Season Individual Leaders

Season	Passing Yards		Receiving Yards		Rushing Yards	
1923	Eber Simpson	156	Bub Weller	50	Dick King	96

COACHING HISTORY: Ollie Kraehe 1-4-2-.286

ST. LOUIS CARDINALS

Home City: St. Louis, Missouri
Home Field: Sportsman's Park (1882-1891) — Capacity: 12,000 [1886]
Robison Field (1892-1920) — Capacity: 15,200 [1899]
Sportsman's Park II (1920-1966) * — Capacity: 30,500 [1954]
Busch Stadium (1966-present) ** — Capacity: 46,700 [2006]
Origin of Name: Named by St. Louis sports writer Willie McHale because the team wore uniforms with red trim on them. Known as the Browns from 1882 to 1897.

Regular Season Record

Season	League	GP	W	L	Pct	GB	R	OR
1882	AA	80	37	43	.463	18	399	496
1883	AA	98	65	33	.663	1	549	409
1884	AA	107	67	40	.626	8	658	539
1885	AA	112	79	33	.705	-	677	461

*-Sportsman's Park II named Busch Stadium from 1953-1966
**-Busch Stadium was known as Busch Memorial Stadium from 1966 to 1982

1886	AA	139	93	46	.669	-	944	592
1887	AA	135	95	40	.704	-	1131	761
1888	AA	135	92	43	.681	-	789	501
1889	AA	135	90	45	.667	2	957	680
1890	AA	136	78	58	.574	12	870	736
1891	AA	138	86	52	.623	8.5	976	753
1892	NL	150	56	94	.373	46	703	922
1893	NL	132	57	75	.432	30.5	745	829
1894	NL	132	56	76	.424	35	771	954
1895	NL	131	39	92	.298	48.5	747	1032
1896	NL	130	40	90	.308	50.5	593	929
1897	NL	131	29	102	.221	63.5	588	1083
1898	NL	150	39	111	.260	63.5	571	929
1899	NL	151	84	67	.556	18.5	819	739
1900	NL	140	65	75	.464	19	744	748
1901	NL	140	76	64	.543	14.5	792	689
1902	NL	134	56	78	.418	44.5	517	695
1903	NL	137	43	94	.314	46.5	505	762
1904	NL	154	75	79	.487	31.5	602	595
1905	NL	154	58	96	.377	47.5	534	741
1906	NL	150	52	98	.347	63	475	620
1907	NL	153	52	101	.340	55.5	419	607
1908	NL	154	49	105	.318	50	372	624
1909	NL	152	54	98	.355	56	583	728
1910	NL	153	63	90	.412	40.5	637	717
1911	NL	149	75	74	.503	22	671	745
1912	NL	153	63	90	.412	41	659	825
1913	NL	150	51	99	.340	49	523	756
1914	NL	153	81	72	.529	13	558	540
1915	NL	153	72	81	.471	18.5	590	601
1916	NL	153	60	93	.392	33.5	476	629
1917	NL	152	82	70	.539	15	531	568
1918	NL	129	51	78	.395	33	454	534
1919	NL	137	54	83	.394	40.5	463	552
1920	NL	154	75	79	.487	18	675	682
1921	NL	153	87	66	.569	7	809	681
1922	NL	154	85	69	.552	8	863	819
1923	NL	153	79	74	.516	16	746	732
1924	NL	154	65	89	.422	28.5	740	750
1925	NL	153	77	76	.503	18	828	764
1926	NL	154	89	65	.578	-	817	678
1927	NL	153	92	61	.601	1.5	754	665
1928	NL	154	95	59	.617	-	807	636
1929	NL	152	78	74	.513	20	831	806
1930	NL	154	92	62	.597	-	1004	784
1931	NL	154	101	53	.656	-	815	614
1932	NL	154	72	82	.468	18	684	717
1933	NL	153	82	71	.536	9.5	687	609
1934	NL	153	95	58	.621	-	799	656
1935	NL	154	96	58	.623	4	829	625
1936	NL	154	87	67	.565	5	795	794
1937	NL	154	81	73	.526	15	789	733
1938	NL	151	71	80	.470	17.5	725	721
1939	NL	153	92	61	.601	4.5	779	633

1940	NL	153	84	69	.549	16	747	699
1941	NL	153	97	56	.634	2.5	734	589
1942	NL	154	106	48	.688	-	755	482
1943	NL	154	105	49	.682	-	679	475
1944	NL	154	105	49	.682	-	772	490
1945	NL	154	95	59	.617	3	756	583
1946	NL	156	98	58	.628	-	712	545
1947	NL	154	89	65	.578	5	780	634
1948	NL	154	85	69	.552	6.5	742	646
1949	NL	154	96	58	.623	1	766	616
1950	NL	153	78	75	.510	12.5	693	670
1951	NL	154	81	73	.526	15.5	683	671
1952	NL	154	88	66	.571	8.5	677	630
1953	NL	154	83	71	.539	22	768	713
1954	NL	154	72	82	.468	25	799	790
1955	NL	154	68	86	.442	30.5	654	757
1956	NL	154	76	78	.494	17	678	698
1957	NL	154	87	67	.565	8	737	666
1958	NL	154	72	82	.468	20	619	704
1959	NL	154	71	83	.461	16	641	725
1960	NL	154	86	68	.558	9	639	616
1961	NL	154	80	74	.519	13	703	668
1962	NL	162	84	78	.519	17.5	774	664
1963	NL	162	93	69	.574	6	747	628
1964	NL	162	93	69	.574	-	715	652
1965	NL	161	80	81	.497	16.5	707	674
1966	NL	162	83	79	.512	12	571	577
1967	NL	161	101	60	.627	-	695	557
1968	NL	162	97	65	.599	-	583	472
1969	NL	162	87	75	.537	13	595	540
1970	NL	162	76	86	.469	13	744	747
1971	NL	162	90	72	.556	7	739	699
1972	NL	156	75	81	.481	21.5	568	600
1973	NL	162	81	81	.500	1.5	643	603
1974	NL	161	86	75	.534	1.5	677	643
1975	NL	162	82	80	.506	10.5	662	689
1976	NL	162	72	90	.444	29	629	671
1977	NL	162	83	79	.512	18	737	688
1978	NL	162	69	93	.426	21	600	657
1979	NL	162	86	76	.531	12	731	693
1980	NL	162	74	88	.457	17	738	710
1981	NL	102	59	43	.578	NA	464	417
1982	NL	162	92	70	.568	-	685	609
1983	NL	162	79	83	.488	11	679	710
1984	NL	162	84	78	.519	12.5	652	645
1985	NL	162	101	61	.623	-	747	572
1986	NL	161	79	82	.491	28.5	601	611
1987	NL	162	95	67	.586	-	798	693
1988	NL	162	76	86	.469	25	578	633
1989	NL	162	86	76	.531	7	632	608
1990	NL	162	70	92	.432	25	599	698
1991	NL	162	84	78	.519	14	651	648
1992	NL	162	83	79	.512	13	631	604
1993	NL	162	87	75	.537	10	758	744

1994	NL	114	53	61	.465	13	535	621
1995	NL	143	62	81	.434	22.5	563	658
1996	NL	162	88	74	.543	-	759	706
1997	NL	162	73	89	.451	11	689	711
1998	NL	162	83	79	.512	19	810	782
1999	NL	161	75	86	.466	21.5	809	838
2000	NL	162	95	67	.586	-	887	771
2001	NL	162	93	69	.574	-	814	684
2002	NL	162	97	65	.599	-	787	648
2003	NL	162	85	77	.525	3	876	796
2004	NL	162	105	57	.648	-	855	659
2005	NL	162	100	62	.617	-	805	634
2006	NL	161	83	78	.516	-	781	762
TOTAL:	125 years	18878	9766	9112		2014	87402	84413
AVERAGE:		151	78	73	.517	16	699	675

Playoff Record

Season	GP	W	L	T	R	OR	Result
1885	7	3	3	1	36	38	**Co-Winner of World Series.**
1886	6	4	2	0	38	28	**Won World Series.**
1887	15	5	10	0	54	73	Lost World Series to Detroit.
1888	10	4	6	0	60	64	Lost World series to N.Y. Giants
1926	7	4	3	0	31	21	**Won World Series.**
1928	4	0	4	0	10	27	Lost World Series to New York.
1930	6	2	4	0	12	21	Lost World Series to Philadelphia.
1931	7	4	3	0	19	22	**Won World Series.**
1934	7	4	3	0	34	23	**Won World Series.**
1942	5	4	1	0	23	18	**Won World Series.**
1943	5	1	4	0	9	17	Lost World Series to New York.
1944	6	4	2	0	16	12	**Won World Series.**
1946	7	4	3	0	28	20	**Won World Series.**
1964	7	4	3	0	32	33	**Won World Series.**
1967	7	4	3	0	25	21	**Won World Series.**
1968	7	3	4	0	27	34	Lost World Series to Detroit.
1982	10	7	3	0	56	38	**Won World Series.**
1985	13	7	6	0	42	51	Lost World Series to Kansas City.
1987	14	7	7	0	49	61	Lost World Series to Minnesota.
1996	10	6	4	0	33	54	Lost NLCS to Atlanta.
2000	8	4	4	0	45	41	Lost NLCS to New York Mets.
2001	5	2	3	0	12	10	Lost Division Semifinal to Arizona.
2002	8	4	4	0	36	29	Lost NLCS to San Francisco.
2004	15	7	8	0	68	67	Lost World Series to Boston.
2005	9	5	4	0	37	33	Lost NLCS to Houston.
2006	16	11	5	0	64	44	**Won World Series.**
TOTAL:	221	114	106	1	896	900	
AVERAGE:	8	4	4	0	34	35	

Regular Season Individual Leaders

Season	Home Runs		RBI's		Wins	
1882	Oscar Walker	7	Not Recorded		George McGinnis	25
1883	Charlie Comiskey	2	Not Recorded		Tony Mullane	35
	Bill Gleason	2				
1884	James O'Neill	3	Not Recorded		George McGinnis	24
1885	James O'Neill	3	Not Recorded		Bob Caruthers	40

Season	Home Runs		RBI's		Wins	
1886	Bob Caruthers	4	Not Recorded		Dave Foutz	41
1887	James O'Neill	14	Not Recorded		Charles King	32
1888	Charlie Comiskey	6	James O'Neill	98	Charles King	45
1889	Charles Duffee	15	James O'Neill	110	Charles King	35
1890	Charles Campau	9	Not Recorded		Jack Stivetts	27
1891	Denny Lyons	11	Tom McCarthy	95	Jack Stivetts	33
1892	Perry Werden	8	Perry Werden	84	William Gleason	20
1893	Steve Brodie	2	Perry Werden	94	William Gleason	21
1894	Frederick Ely	12	Frederick Ely	89	Ted Breitenstein	27
1895	Roger Connor	8	Roger Connor	77	Ted Breitenstein	19
1896	Roger Connor	11	Roger Connor	72	Ted Breitenstein	18
1897	Mike Grady	7	Fred Hartman	67	Red Donahue	10
1898	Lave Cross	3	Lave Cross	79	Jack Taylor	15
	Jack Clements	3				
1899	Bobby Wallace	12	Bobby Wallace	108	Cy Young	26
1900	Mike Donlin	10	Bill Keister	72	Cy Young	19
1901	Jesse Burkett	10	Bobby Wallace	91	Jack Harper	23
1902	Homer Smoot	3	George Barclay	53	Mike O'Neill	16
	George Barclay	3				
1903	Homer Smoot	4	Dave Brain	60	Mordecai Brown	9
					Charles McFarland	9
1904	Dave Brain	7	Dave Brain	72	Jack Taylor	21
					Kid Nichols	21
1905	Homer Smoot	4	Homer Smoot	58	Jake Thielman	15
	Mike Grady	4			Jack Taylor	15
1906	Mike Grady	3	Jake Beckley	44	Fred Beebe	9
1907	John Murray	7	John Murray	46	Ed Karger	15
1908	John Murray	7	John Murray	62	Arthur Raymond	15
1909	Ed Konetchy	4	Ed Konetchy	80	Fred Beebe	15
1910	George Ellis	4	Ed Konetchy	78	John Lush	14
1911	Ed Konetchy	6	Ed Konetchy	88	Bob Harmon	23
1912	Ed Konetchy	8	Ed Konetchy	82	Bob Harmon	18
1913	Ed Konetchy	7	Ed Konetchy	68	Harry Sallee	18
1914	Owen Wilson	9	John Miller	88	Bill Doak	19
1915	Bob Bescher	4	John Miller	72	Bill Doak	16
1916	Rogers Hornsby	6	Rogers Hornsby	65	Bill Doak	12
	Jack Smith	6			Lee Meadows	12
	Bob Bescher	6				
1917	Rogers Hornsby	8	Rogers Hornsby	66	Bill Doak	16
1918	Walton Cruise	6	Rogers Hornsby	60	Gene Packard	12
1919	Rogers Hornsby	8	Rogers Hornsby	71	Bill Doak	13
1920	Austin McHenry	10	Rogers Hornsby	94	Bill Doak	20
1921	Rogers Hornsby	21	Rogers Hornsby	126	Jesse Haines	18
1922	Rogers Hornsby	42	Rogers Hornsby	152	Jeff Pfeffer	19
1923	Rogers Hornsby	17	Milt Stock	96	Jesse Haines	20
1924	Rogers Hornsby	25	Jim Bottomley	111	Allan Sothoron	10
1925	Rogers Hornsby	39	Rogers Hornsby	143	Bill Sherdel	15
1926	Jim Bottomley	19	Jim Bottomley	120	Flint Rhem	20
1927	Jim Bottomley	19	Jim Bottomley	124	Jesse Haines	24
1928	Jim Bottomley	31	Jim Bottomley	136	Bill Sherdel	21
1929	Jim Bottomley	29	Jim Bottomley	137	Syl Johnson	13
	Charles Hafey	29			Jesse Haines	13
1930	Charles Hafey	26	Frank Frisch	114	Bill Hallahan	15

Season	Home Runs		RBI's		Wins	
1931	Charles Hafey	16	Charles Hafey	95	Bill Hallahan	19
1932	James Collins	21	James Collins	91	Jay Dean	18
1933	Joe Medwick	18	Joe Medwick	98	Jay Dean	20
1934	James Collins	35	James Collins	128	Jay Dean	30
1935	James Collins	23	Joe Medwick	126	Jay Dean	28
	Joe Medwick	23				
1936	Johnny Mize	19	Joe Medwick	138	Jay Dean	24
1937	Joe Medwick	31	Joe Medwick	154	Lon Warneke	18
1938	Johnny Mize	27	Joe Medwick	122	Bob Weiland	16
1939	Johnny Mize	28	Joe Medwick	117	Curt Davis	22
1940	Johnny Mize	43	Johnny Mize	137	Bill McGee	16
					Lon Warneke	16
1941	Johnny Mize	16	Johnny Mize	100	Ernie White	17
					Lon Warneke	17
1942	Enos Slaughter	13	Enos Slaughter	98	Mort Cooper	22
1943	George Kurowski	13	Stan Musial	81	Mort Cooper	21
	Stan Musial	13	Walker Cooper	81		
1944	George Kurowski	20	Ray Snaders	102	Mort Cooper	22
1945	George Kurowski	21	George Kurowski	102	Charles Barrett	21
1946	Enos Slaughter	18	Enos Slaughter	130	Howie Pollet	21
1947	George Kurowski	27	George Kurowski	104	George Munger	16
					Harry Brecheen	16
1948	Stan Musial	39	Stan Musial	131	Harry Brecheen	20
1949	Stan Musial	36	Stan Musial	123	Howie Pollet	20
1950	Stan Musial	28	Stan Musial	109	Howie Pollet	14
1951	Stan Musial	32	Stan Musial	108	Gerry Staley	19
1952	Stan Musial	21	Enos Slaughter	101	Gerry Staley	17
1953	Stan Musial	30	Stan Musial	113	Harvey Haddix	20
1954	Stan Musial	35	Stan Musial	126	Harvey Haddix	18
1955	Stan Musial	33	Stan Musial	108	Harvey Haddix	12
1956	Stan Musial	27	Stan Musial	109	Wilmer Mizell	14
1957	Stan Musial	29	Del Ennis	105	Larry Jackson	15
					Lindy McDaniel	15
1958	Ken Boyer	23	Ken Boyer	90	Sam Jones	14
1959	Ken Boyer	28	Ken Boyer	94	Lindy McDaniel	14
					Larry Jackson	14
1960	Ken Boyer	32	Ken Boyer	97	Ernie Broglio	21
1961	Ken Boyer	24	Ken Boyer	95	Ray Sadecki	14
					Larry Jackson	14
1962	Ken Boyer	24	Bill White	102	Larry Jackson	16
1963	Bill White	27	Ken Boyer	111	Ernie Broglio	18
					Bob Gibson	18
1964	Ken Boyer	24	Ken Boyer	119	Ray Sadecki	20
1965	Bill White	24	Curt Flood	83	Bob Gibson	20
1966	Orlando Cepeda	17	Curt Flood	78	Bob Gibson	21
1967	Orlando Cepeda	25	Orlando Cepeda	111	Dick Hughes	16
1968	Orlando Cepeda	16	Mike Shannon	79	Bob Gibson	22
1969	Joe Torre	18	Joe Torre	101	Bob Gibson	20
1970	Dick Allen	34	Dick Allen	101	Bob Gibson	23
1971	Joe Torre	24	Joe Torre	137	Steve Carlton	20
1972	Ted Simmons	16	Ted Simmons	96	Bob Gibson	19
1973	Joe Torre	13	Ted Simmons	91	Rick Wise	16
	Ted Simmons	13				

Season	Home Runs		RBI's		Wins	
1974	Reggie Smith	23	Ted Simmons	103	Lynn McGlothen	16
1975	Reggie Smith	19	Ted Simmons	100	Bob Forsch	15
					Lynn McGlothen	15
1976	Hector Cruz	13	Ted Simmons	75	Lynn McGlothen	13
1977	Ted Simmons	21	Ted Simmons	95	Bob Forsch	20
1978	Ted Simmons	22	Ted Simmons	80	John Denny	14
1979	Ted Simmons	26	Keith Hernandez	105	Silvio Martinez	15
					Pete Vuckovich	15
1980	George Hendrick	25	George Hendrick	109	Pete Vuckovich	12
1981	George Hendrick	18	George Hendrick	61	Bob Forsch	10
1982	George Hendrick	19	George Hendrick	104	Bob Forsch	15
					Joaquin Andujar	15
1983	George Hendrick	18	George Hendrick	97	Dave LaPoint	12
					John Stuper	12
1984	David Green	15	George Hendrick	69	Joaquin Andujar	20
1985	Jack Clark	22	Tommy Herr	110	Joaquin Andujar	21
					John Tudor	21
1986	Andy Van Slyke	13	Tommy Herr	61	Bob Forsch	14
			Andy Van Slyke	61		
1987	Jack Clark	35	Jack Clark	106	Bob Forsch	11
					Danny Cox	11
					Greg Mathews	11
1988	Tom Brunansky	22	Tom Brunansky	79	Jose DeLeon	13
1989	Tom Brunansky	20	Pedro Guerrero	117	Joe Magrane	18
1990	Todd Zeile	15	Pedro Guerrero	80	John Tudor	12
1991	Todd Zeile	11	Todd Zeile	81	Bryn Smith	12
1992	Ray Lankford	20	Ray Lankford	86	Bob Tewksbury	16
1993	Mark Whiten	25	Todd Zeile	103	Bob Tewksbury	17
1994	Todd Zeile	19	Todd Zeile	75	Bob Tewksbury	12
	Ray Lankford	19				
1995	Ray Lankford	25	Ray Lankford	82	Rich DeLucia	8
1996	Ron Gant	30	Brian Jordan	104	Andy Benes	18
1997	Ray Lankford	31	Ray Lankford	98	Matt Morris	12
					Todd Stottlemyre	12
1998	Mark McGwire	70	Mark McGwire	147	Kent Mercker	11
1999	Mark McGwire	65	Mark McGwire	147	Kent Bottenfield	18
2000	Jim Edmonds	42	Jim Edmonds	108	Darryl Kile	20
2001	Albert Pujols	37	Albert Pujols	130	Matt Morris	22
2002	Albert Pujols	34	Albert Pujols	127	Matt Morris	17
2003	Albert Pujols	43	Albert Pujols	124	Woody Williams	18
2004	Albert Pujols	46	Scott Rolen	124	Jeff Suppan	16
2005	Albert Pujols	41	Albert Pujols	117	Chris Carpenter	21
2006	Albert Pujols	49	Albert Pujols	137	Chris Carpenter	15

COACHING HISTORY: 1882 Ned Cuthbert 37-43-.463; 1882 Ed Brown 10-11-.476; 1883 Ted Sullivan 53-27-.663; 1883 Charlie Comiskey 12-6-.667; 1884 Jimmy Williams 67-40-.626; 1885-1889 Charlie Comiskey 449-207-.684; 1890 Tom McCarthy 13-13-.500; 1890 James Roseman 32-19-.627; 1890 Charles Campau 33-26-.559; 1891 Charlie Comiskey 86-52-.623; 1892 Chris Von Der Ahe 56-94-.373; 1893 Bill Watkins 57-75-.432; 1894 George Miller 56-76-.424; 1895 Al Buckenberger 16-23-.410; 1895 Joe Quinn 13-27-.325; 1895 Lew Phelan 8-21-.276; 1895-1897 Chris Von Der Ahe 3-16-.158; 1896 Harry Diddlebock 7-11-.389; 1896 Arlie Latham 0-2-.000; 1896 Roger Connor 9-37-.196; 1896-1897 Tommy Dowd 30-63-.323; 1897 Hugh Nicol 9-29-.237; 1897 Bill Hallman 13-46-.220; 1898 Tim Hurst 39-111-.260;

1899-1900 Patsy Tebeau 132-122-.520; 1900 Louie Heilbroner 17-20-.459; 1901-1903 Patrick Donovan 175-236-.426; 1904-1905 Kid Nichols 94-108-.465; 1905 Jimmy Burke 17-32-.347; 1905 Stanley Robison 22-35-.386; 1906-1908 John McCloskey 153-304-.335; 1909-1912 Roger Bresnahan 255-352-.420; 1913-1917 Miller Huggins 346-415-.455; 1918 Jack Hendricks 51-78-.395; 1919-1925 Branch Rickey 458-485-.486; 1925-1926 Rogers Hornsby 153-116-.569; 1927 Bob O'Farrell 92-61-.601; 1928-1929 Bill McKechnie 128-88-.593; 1929 Bill Southworth 43-45-.489; 1929-1933 Charles Street 313-242-.564; 1933-1938 Frank Frisch 457-354-.564; 1938 Mike Gonzalez 9-8-.529; 1939-1940 Ray Blades 107-85-.557; 1940 Mike Gonzalez 0-5-.000; 1940-1945 Bill Southworth 577-301-.657; 1946-1950 Eddie Dyer 446-325-.578; 1951 Marty Marion 81-73-.526; 1952-1955 Eddie Stanky 260-238-.522; 1955 Harry Walker 51-67-.432; 1956-1958 Fred Hutchinson 232-220-.513; 1958 Stank Hack 3-7-.300; 1959-1961 Solomon Hemus 190-192-.497; 1961-1964 Johnny Keane 317-249-.560; 1965-1976 Albert Schoendienst 1010-925-.522; 1977-1978 Vern Rapp 89-89-.500; 1978 Jack Krol 1-1-.500; 1978-1980 Ken Boyer 166-191-.465; 1980 Jack Krol 0-1-.000; 1980 Albert Schoendienst 18-19-.486; 1980-1990 Dorrel "Whitey" Herzog 822-728-.530; 1990 Albert Schoendienst 13-11-.542; 1990-1995 Joe Torre 393-408-.491; 1996-present Tony LaRussa

ST. LOUIS CARDINALS
(were Chicago Cardinals)
(became Phoenix Cardinals)

Home City: St. Louis, Missouri
Home Stadium: Busch Stadium (1960-1965)   Capacity: 34,000
          Busch Memorial Stadium (1966-1987)   Capacity: 51,392 [1986]
Origin of Name: The team kept the same name when it moved from Chicago to St. Louis.

Regular Season Record

Season	League	GP	W	L	T	PF	PA	Pct
1960	NFL	12	6	5	1	288	230	.542
1961	NFL	14	7	7	0	279	267	.500
1962	NFL	14	4	9	1	287	361	.321
1963	NFL	14	9	5	0	341	283	.643
1964	NFL	14	9	3	2	357	331	.714
1965	NFL	14	5	9	0	296	309	.357
1966	NFL	14	8	5	1	264	265	.607
1967	NFL	14	6	7	1	333	356	.464
1968	NFL	14	9	4	1	325	289	.679
1969	NFL	14	4	9	1	314	389	.321
1970	NFL	14	8	5	1	325	228	.607
1971	NFL	14	4	9	1	231	279	.321
1972	NFL	14	4	9	1	193	303	.321
1973	NFL	14	4	9	1	286	365	.321
1974	NFL	14	10	4	0	285	218	.714
1975	NFL	14	11	3	0	356	276	.786
1976	NFL	14	10	4	0	309	267	.714
1977	NFL	14	7	7	0	272	287	.500
1978	NFL	16	6	10	0	248	296	.375
1979	NFL	16	5	11	0	307	358	.313
1980	NFL	16	5	11	0	299	350	.313
1981	NFL	16	7	9	0	315	408	.438
1982	NFL	9	5	4	0	135	170	.556
1983	NFL	16	8	7	1	374	428	.531
1984	NFL	16	9	7	0	423	345	.563
1985	NFL	16	5	11	0	278	414	.313

1986	NFL	16	4	11	1	218	351	.281
1987	NFL	15	7	8	0	362	368	.467
TOTAL:	28 years	402	186	202	14	8300	8791	
AVERAGE:		14	7	7	0	296	314	.480

Playoff Record

Season	GP	W	L	PF	PA	Result
1974	1	0	1	14	30	Lost Divisional playoff to Minnesota.
1975	1	0	1	23	35	Lost Divisional playoff to Los Angeles.
1982	1	0	1	16	41	Lost 1st Round playoff to Green Bay.
TOTAL:	3	0	3	53	106	
AVERAGE:	1	0	1	18	35	

Regular Season Individual Leaders

Season	Passing Yards		Receiving Yards		Rushing Yards	
1960	John Roach	1423	Sonny Randle	893	John Crow	1071
1961	Sam Etcheverry	1275	Sonny Randle	591	Prentice Gautt	523
1962	Charley Johnson	2440	Sonny Randle	1158	John Crow	751
1963	Charley Johnson	3280	Sonny Randle	1014	Joe Childress	701
1964	Charley Johnson	3045	Bobby Joe Conrad	780	John Crow	554
1965	Charley Johnson	2439	Bobby Joe Conrad	909	Bill Triplett	617
1966	Charley Johnson	1334	Jackie Smith	810	John Roland	695
1967	Jim Hart	3008	Jackie Smith	1205	John Roland	876
1968	Jim Hart	2059	Jackie Smith	789	Willie Crenshaw	813
1969	Charley Johnson	1847	John Gilliam	997	Cid Edwards	504
1970	Jim Hart	2575	John Gilliam	952	MacArthur Lane	977
1971	Jim Hart	1626	John Gilliam	837	MacArthur Lane	592
1972	Gary Cuozzo	897	Walker Gillette	550	Don Anderson	536
1973	Jim Hart	2223	Jackie Smith	600	Don Anderson	679
1974	Jim Hart	2411	Mel Gray	770	Terry Metcalf	718
1975	Jim Hart	2507	Mel Gray	926	Jim Otis	1076
1976	Jim Hart	2946	Ike Harris	782	Jim Otis	891
1977	Jim Hart	2542	Mel Gray	782	Terry Metcalf	739
1978	Jim Hart	3121	Pat Tilley	900	Jim Otis	664
1979	Jim Hart	2218	Pat Tilley	938	Ottis Anderson	1605
1980	Jim Hart	2946	Pat Tilley	966	Ottis Anderson	1352
1981	Jim Hart	1694	Pat Tilley	1040	Ottis Anderson	1376
1982	Neil Lomax	1367	Pat Tilley	465	Ottis Anderson	587
1983	Neil Lomax	2636	Roy Green	1227	Ottis Anderson	1270
1984	Neil Lomax	4614	Roy Green	1555	Ottis Anderson	1174
1985	Neil Lomax	3214	Pat Tilley	726	Stump Mitchell	1006
1986	Neil Lomax	2583	J.T. Smith	1014	Stump Mitchell	800
1987	Neil Lomax	3387	J.T. Smith	1117	Stump Mitchell	781

COACHING HISTORY: 1960-1961 Frank Ivy 11-12-1-.479; 1961 Chuck Drulis & Ray Prochaska & Ray Willsey 2-0-0-1.000; 1962-1965 Wally Lemm 27-26-3-.509; 1966-1970 Charley Winner 35-30-5-.536; 1971-1972 Bob Hollway 8-18-2-.321; 1973-1977 Don Coryell 42-27-1-.607; 1978-1979 Bud Wilkinson 9-20-0-.310; 1979 Larry Wilson 2-1-0-.667; 1980-1985 Jim Hanifan 39-49-1-.444; 1986-1987 Gene Stallings 11-19-1-.371

ST. LOUIS EAGLES
(were Ottawa Senators)

Home City: St. Louis, Missouri
Home Arena: St. Louis Arena   Capacity: 12,600
Origin of Name:

Regular Season Record

Season	League	GP	W	L	T	GF	GA	Pts	Pct
1934-1935	NHL	48	11	31	6	86	144	28	.292

Regular Season Individual Leaders

Season	Goals		Points		Penalty Minutes	
1934-1935	Syd Howe	27	Carl Voss	31	Irvine Frew	89

COACHING HISTORY: Eddie Gerard 2-11-0-.154; George Boucher 9-20-6-.343

ST. LOUIS GUNNERS
(Cincinnati Reds folded with 3 games remaining in 1934 season and the Gunners were formed)

Home City: St. Louis, Missouri
Home Stadium: Sportsman's Park
Origin of Name: The team was purchased from its Cincinnati owners by the St. Louis Gunners, an independent team operating in the area.

Regular Season Record

Season	League	GP	W	L	T	PF	PA	Pct
1934	NFL	3	1	2	0	27	61	.333

COACHING HISTORY: Mike Palm 1-2-0-.333

ST. LOUIS HAWKS
(were Milwaukee Hawks)
(became Atlanta Hawks)

Home City: St. Louis, Missouri
Home Court: Kiel Auditorium   Capacity: 10,000
Origin of Name: The team kept the same name when it moved from Milwaukee to St. Louis.

Regular Season Record

Season	League	GP	W	L	PPGF	PPGA	Pct	GB
1955-1956	NBA	72	33	39	96.6	98.0	.458	4
1956-1957	NBA	72	34	38	98.5	98.6	.472	-
1957-1958	NBA	72	41	31	107.5	106.2	.569	-
1958-1959	NBA	72	49	23	108.8	105.1	.681	-
1959-1960	NBA	75	46	29	113.4	110.7	.613	-
1960-1961	NBA	79	51	28	118.8	114.1	.646	-
1961-1962	NBA	80	29	51	118.9	122.1	.363	25
1962-1963	NBA	80	48	32	109.6	107.8	.600	5
1963-1964	NBA	80	46	34	110.0	108.4	.575	2
1964-1965	NBA	80	45	35	108.8	105.8	.563	4
1965-1966	NBA	80	36	44	111.4	112.0	.450	9
1966-1967	NBA	81	39	42	113.6	115.2	.481	5
1967-1968	NBA	82	56	26	113.0	110.3	.683	-

TOTAL:	13 years	1005	553	452				54
AVERAGE:		77	42	35	109.9	108.8	.550	4

Playoff Record

Season	GP	W	L	PPGF	PPGA	Result
1955-1956	9	4	5	93.2	103.0	Lost Division Final to Ft. Wayne.
1956-1957	10	6	4	113.8	115.4	Lost Championship series to Boston.
1957-1958	11	8	3	109.5	107.0	**Won NBA Championship.**
1958-1959	6	2	4	108.0	100.8	Lost Divisional Final to Minneapolis.
1959-1960	14	7	7	105.7	107.3	Lost Championship series to Boston.
1960-1961	12	5	7	111.9	117.1	Lost Championship series to Boston.
1962-1963	11	6	5	110.9	109.5	Lost Division Final to Los Angeles.
1963-1964	12	6	6	106.1	106.5	Lost Division Final to San Francisco.
1964-1965	4	1	3	109.0	113.3	Lost Division Semifinal to Baltimore.
1965-1966	10	6	4	114.0	115.4	Lost Division Final to Los Angeles.
1966-1967	9	5	4	114.4	113.4	Lost Division Final to San Francisco.
1967-1968	6	2	4	111.3	110.0	Lost Division Semifinal to San Francisco.
TOTAL:	114	58	56			
AVERAGE:	10	5	5	109.0	109.8	

Regular Season Individual Leaders

Season	Field Goal % (min. 70 games)		Points		Points per Game (min. 70 games)	
1955-56*	Charles Share	.430	Bob Pettit	1849	Bob Pettit	25.7
1956-57*	Charles Share	.439	Bob Pettit	1755	Bob Pettit	24.7
1957-58*	Cliff Hagan	.443	Bob Pettit	1719	Bob Pettit	24.6
1958-59*	Cliff Hagan	.456	Bob Pettit	2105	Bob Pettit	29.2
1959-60	Cliff Hagan	.464	Bob Pettit	1882	Bob Pettit	26.1
1960-61	Bob Pettit	.447	Bob Pettit	2120	Bob Pettit	27.9
1961-62	Cliff Hagan	.470	Bob Pettit	2429	Bob Pettit	31.1
1962-63	Cliff Hagan	.465	Bob Pettit	2241	Bob Pettit	28.4
1963-64	Bob Pettit	.463	Bob Pettit	2190	Bob Pettit	27.4
1964-65	Zelmo Beaty	.482	Zelmo Beaty	1351	Zelmo Beaty	16.9
1965-66	Zelmo Beaty	.473	Zelmo Beaty	1656	Zelmo Beaty	20.7
1966-67	Lou Hudson	.467	Lou Hudson	1471	Lou Hudson	18.4
1967-68	Zelmo Beaty	.488	Zelmo Beaty	1733	Zelmo Beaty	21.1

COACHING HISTORY: 1955-1957 Red Holzman 47-58-.448; 1956-1957 Slater Martin 5-3-.625; 1956-1958 Alex Hannum 56-47-.544; 1958-1959 Andy Phillip 6-4-.600; 1958-1960 Ed MacAuley 89-48-.650; 1960-1962 Paul Seymour 56-37-.602; 1961-1962 Fuzzy Levane 20-40-.333; 1961-1962 Bob Pettit 4-2-.667; 1962-1965 Harry Gallatin 111-82-.575; 1964-1968 Richie Guerin 159-131-.548

ST. LOUIS MAROONS

Home City: St. Louis, Missouri
Home Field: Lucas Park (1884)   Capacity: 10,000 [1884]
          Robison Field (1885-1886)   Capacity: 18,000
Origin of Name: The team was named for the color of their uniforms.

*-minimum 60 games

Regular Season Record

Season	League	GP	W	L	Pct	GB	R	OR
1884	UA	113	94	19	.832	-	887	429
1885	NL	108	36	72	.333	49	390	593
1886	NL	122	43	79	.352	46	547	712
TOTAL:	3 years	343	173	170		95	1824	1734
AVERAGE:		114	58	56	.504	32	608	578

Regular Season Individual Leaders

Season	Home Runs		RBI's		Wins	
1884	Fred Dunlap	13	Not Recorded		Billy Taylor	25
1885	Fred Dunlap	2	Alex McKinnon	44	Henry Boyle	16
1886	Jerry Denny	9	Alex McKinnon	72	John Healy	17

COACHING HISTORY: 1884-1885 Henry Lucas 130-91-.588; 1886 Gus Schmelz 43-79-.352

ST. LOUIS RAMS
(were Los Angeles Rams)

Home City: St. Louis, Missouri
Home Stadium: Busch Stadium (1995)   Capacity: 59,022 [1995]
Edward Jones Dome (1995-present)   Capacity: 66,000 [2005]
Origin of Name: The team kept the same nickname when it moved from Los Angeles to St. Louis.

Regular Season Record

Season	League	GP	W	L	T	PF	PA	Pct
1995	NFL	16	7	9	0	309	418	.438
1996	NFL	16	6	10	0	303	409	.375
1997	NFL	16	5	11	0	299	359	.313
1998	NFL	16	4	12	0	285	378	.250
1999	NFL	16	13	3	0	526	242	.813
2000	NFL	16	10	6	0	540	471	.625
2001	NFL	16	14	2	0	503	273	.875
2002	NFL	16	7	9	0	316	369	.438
2003	NFL	16	12	4	0	447	328	.750
2004	NFL	16	8	8	0	319	392	.500
2005	NFL	16	6	10	0	363	429	.375
2006	NFL	16	8	8	0	367	381	.500
TOTAL:	12 years	192	100	92	0	4577	4449	
AVERAGE:		16	8	8	0	381	371	.521

Playoff Record

Season	GP	W	L	PF	PA	Result
1999	3	3	0	83	59	**Won Super Bowl XXXIV.**
2000	1	0	1	28	31	Lost Wild Card Game to New Orleans.
2001	3	2	1	91	61	Lost Super Bowl to New England.
2003	1	0	1	23	29	Lost Conference Semifinal to Carolina.
2004	2	1	1	44	67	Lost Conference Semifinal to Atlanta.
TOTAL:	10	6	4	269	247	
AVERAGE:	2	1	1	54	49	

*-known as Trans World Dome from 1995-99, then The Dome at America's Center 2000-01

Regular Season Individual Leaders

Season	Passing Yards		Receiving Yards		Rushing Yards	
1995	Chris Miller	2623	Isaac Bruce	1781	Jerome Bettis	637
1996	Tony Banks	2544	Isaac Bruce	1338	Lawrence Phillips	632
1997	Tony Banks	3254	Amp Lee	825	Jerald Moore	380
1998	Tony Banks	2535	Ricky Proehl	771	June Henley	538
1999	Kurt Warner	4353	Marshall Faulk	1048	Marshall Faulk	1381
2000	Kurt Warner	3429	Torry Holt	1635	Marshall Faulk	1359
2001	Kurt Warner	4830	Torry Holt	1363	Marshall Faulk	1382
2002	Marc Bulger	1826	Torry Holt	1302	Marshall Faulk	953
2003	Marc Bulger	3845	Torry Holt	1696	Marshall Faulk	818
2004	Marc Bulger	3964	Torry Holt	1372	Marshall Faulk	774
2005	Marc Bulger	2297	Torry Holt	1331	Steven Jackson	1046
2006	Marc Bulger	4301	Torry Holt	1188	Steven Jackson	1528

COACHING HISTORY: 1995-1996 Rich Brooks 13-19-0-.406; 1997-1999 Dick Vermeil 22-26-0-.458; 2000-2005 Mike Martz 57-39-0-.594; 2006-present Scott Linehan

ST. LOUIS REDS

Home City: St. Louis, Missouri
Home Field: Sportsman's Park   Capacity 18,000
       Athletic Park   Capacity: 9,000
Origin of Name: The team may have been named for the color of their uniforms.

Regular Season Record

Season	League	GP	W	L	Pct	GB	R	OR
1876	NL	64	45	19	.703	6	386	229
1877	NL	60	28	32	.467	14	284	318
TOTAL:	2 years	124	73	51		20	670	547
AVERAGE:		62	37	25	.589	10	335	274

Regular Season Individual Leaders

Season	Home Runs		RBI's		Wins	
1876	Dennis Mack	1	Lip Pike	50	George Bradley	45
	Lip Pike	1				
1877	Joe Battin	1	John Clapp	34	Fred Nichols	18

COACHING HISTORY: 1876 Harmon Dehlman 45-19-.703; 1877 John Lucas 14-12-.538; 1877 George McManus 14-20-.412

ST. LOUIS SPIRITS
(also known as Spirits of St. Louis)

Home City: St. Louis, Missouri
Home Court: St. Louis Arena   Capacity: 18,006
Origin of Name: The team was named by club executives.

Regular Season Record

Season	League	GP	W	L	PPGF	PPGA	Pct	GB
1974-1975	ABA	84	32	52	109.0	113.4	.381	26
1975-1976	ABA	84	35	49	108.9	112.1	.417	25
TOTAL:	2 years	168	67	101				51
AVERAGE:		84	34	50	109.0	112.8	.399	26

Playoff Record

Season	GP	W	L	PPGF	PPGA	Result
1974-1975	10	5	5	116.0	117.7	Lost 2nd Round series to Kentucky.

Regular Season Individual Leaders

Season	Field Goal % (min. 70 games)		Points		Points per Game (min. 70 games)	
1974-75	Goo Kennedy	.524	Marvin Barnes	1849	Marvin Barnes	24.0
1975-1976	Ron Boone	.486	Ron Boone	1719	Marvin Barnes	24.1

COACHING HISTORY: 1974-1975 Bob MacKinnon 32-52-.381; 1975-1976 Rod Thorn 20-27-.426; 1975-1976 Joe Mullaney 15-22-.405

ST. LOUIS STARS
(became California Surf)

Home City: St. Louis, Missouri
Home Field: Francis Field (1969-70, 1975-77)   Capacity: 10,000 [1967]
                  Busch Stadium (1967-68, 1971-74)   Capacity: 49,450 [1968]
Origin of Name: The team name was chosen in a Name the Team Contest.

Regular Season Record

Season	League	GP	W	L	T	GF	GA	BP	Pts	Pct
1967	NPSL	32	14	11	7	54	57	NA	156	.542
1968	NASL	32	14	12	6	58	41	48	150	.521
1969	NASL	16	3	11	2	24	47	23	47	.326
1970	NASL	24	5	17	2	26	71	24	60	.278
1971	NASL	24	6	13	5	37	47	35	86	.398
1972	NASL	14	7	4	3	20	14	18	69	.548
1973	NASL	19	7	7	5	27	27	25	82	.480
1974	NASL	20	4	15	1	27	42	27	54	.300
1975	NASL	22	13	9	-	38	34	37	115	.581
1976	NASL	24	5	19	-	28	57	28	58	.269
1977	NASL	26	12	14	-	33	35	32	104	.444
TOTAL:	11 years	253	90	132	31	372	472	297	981	
AVERAGE:		23	8	12	3	34	43	27	89	.431

Playoff Record

Season	GP	W	L	GF	GA	Result
1972	2	1	1	3	2	Lost Championship series to New York.
1975	2	1	1	2	2	Lost Semifinal game to Portland.
1977	1	0	1	0	1	Lost 1st Round game to Rochester.
TOTAL:	5	2	3	5	5	
AVERAGE:	2	1	1	2	2	

Regular Season Individual Leaders

Season	Goals		Points		GAA	
1967	Rudolf Kobl	13	Rudolf Kobl	34	Miguel DeLima	1.74
	Bora Kostic	13				
1968	Casey Frankiewicz	14	Casey Frankiewicz	37		
1969	Tom Ferguson	7	Tom Ferguson	15	Dave Jokerst	2.78
1970	Pat McBride	9	Pat McBride	19	Miguel DeLima	2.41
1971	Casey Frankiewicz	14	Casey Frankiewicz	33	Orest Banach	1.31
1972	Willy Roy	7	Willy Roy	16	Mike Winter	1.00
1973	Gene Geimer	10	Gene Geimer	25	Mike Winter	1.41

Season	Goals		Points		GAA	
1974	Al Trost	6	Dennis Vaninger	18	Mike Winter	1.89
	Dennis Vaninger	6				
1975	John Hawley	11	John Hawley	24	Peter Bonetti	1.38
1976	Al Trost	12	Al Trost	27	Dave Jokerst	1.79
1977	Fred Binney	9	Fred Binney	20	John Jackson	1.18

COACHING HISTORY: 1967-1968 Rudi Gutendorf 28-23-13; 1969-1970 Robert Kehoe; 1970 Don Range; 1971 George Meyer 1971-1973 Casey Frankiewicz; 1974-1977 John Sewell 34-57-1

ST. LOUIS TERRIERS

Home City: St. Louis, Missouri
Home Field: Handlan's Park   Capacity: 15,000 [1915]
Origin of Name:

Regular Season Record

Season	League	GP	W	L	Pct	GB	R	OR
1914	FL	151	62	89	.411	25	565	697
1915	FL	154	87	67	.565	-	634	528
TOTAL:	2 years	305	149	156		25	1199	1225
AVERAGE:		153	75	78	.489	12.5	600	613

Regular Season Individual Leaders

Season	Home Runs		RBI's		Wins	
1914	Jack Tobin	7	Ward Miller	50	James Crandall	13
					Bob Groom	13
1915	Ernie Johnson	7	William Borton	83	Dave Davenport	22

COACHING HISTORY: 1914 Mordecai "Three Finger" Brown 50-63-.442; 1914-1915 Fielder Jones 99-93-.516

ST. PAUL SAINTS

Home City: St. Paul, Minnesota
Home Field: The team played only road games
Origin of Name:

Regular Season Record

Season	League	GP	W	L	Pct	GB	R	OR
1884	UA	8	2	6	.250	39.5	24	57

Regular Season Individual Leaders

Season	Home Runs		RBI's		Wins	
1884		0	Not Recorded		James Brown	1
					Billy O'Brien	1

COACHING HISTORY: A.M. Thompson 2-6-.250

SAN ANTONIO GUNSLINGERS

Home City: San Antonio, Texas
Home Stadium: Alamo Stadium   Capacity: 32,000 [1984]
Origin of Name: The name was picked in a Name the Team Contest

Regular Season Record

Season	League	GP	W	L	T	PF	PA	Pct
1984	USFL	18	7	11	0	309	325	.389
1985	USFL	18	5	13	0	296	436	.278
TOTAL:	2 years	36	12	24	0	605	761	
AVERAGE:		18	6	12	0	303	381	.333

Regular Season Individual Leaders

Season	Passing Yards		Receiving Yards		Rushing Yards	
1984	Rick Neuheisel	2542	Jerry Gordon	648	Scott Stamper	500
1985	Rick Neuheisel	3068	Frank Lockett	794	George Works	542

COACHING HISTORY: 1984-1985 Gil Steinke 9-15-0-.375; 1985 Jim Bates 3-9-0-.250

SAN ANTONIO RIDERS

Home City: San Antonio, Texas
Home Stadium: Alamo Stadium (1991) (San Marcos)   Capacity: 25,000 [1991]
                       Bobcat Field (1992)   Capacity: 23,000 [1992]
Origin of Name:

Regular Season Record

Season	League	GP	W	L	T	PF	PA	Pct
1991	WLAF	10	4	6	0	176	196	.400
1992	WFL	10	7	3	0	195	150	.700
TOTAL:	2 years	20	11	9	0	371	346	
AVERAGE:		10	6	4	0	186	173	.550

Regular Season Individual Leaders

Season	Passing Yards		Receiving Yards		Rushing Yards	
1991	Mike Johnson	1137	Lee Morris	409	Rickey Blake	554
1992	Mike Johnson	1760			Brown	767

COACHING HISTORY: 1991-1992 Mike Riley 11-9-0-.550

SAN ANTONIO SILVER STARS
(were Utah Starzz)

Home City: San Antonio, Texas
Home Arena: SBC Center   Capacity: 18,500 [2005]
Origin of Name: The team was named for the "Lone Star State" of Texas and for the silver color of their uniforms.

Regular Season Record

Season	League	GP	W	L	PPGF	PPGA	Pct	GB
2003	WNBA	34	12	22	65.1	71.4	.353	12
2004	WNBA	34	9	25	64.4	69.5	.265	16
2005	WNBA	34	7	27	63.0	70.6	.206	18
2006	WNBA	34	13	21	74.2	76.6	.382	12
TOTAL:	4 years	136	41	95				58
AVERAGE:		34	10	24	66.8	72.0	.301	15

Regular Season Individual Leaders

Season	Field Goals % (20 games min.)		Free Throws % (20 games min.)		Points per Game (20 games min.)	
2003	Margo Dydek	.451	LaQuanda Quick	1.000	Marie Ferdinand	13.8

Season	Field Goals % (20 games min.)		Free Throws % (20 games min.)		Points per Game (20 games min.)	
2004	L. Thomas	.489	LaToya Thomas	.841	LaToya Thomas	14.2
2005	B. Ngoyisa	.568	Edna Campbell	1.000	Marie Ferdinand	12.5
2006	Katie Feenstra	.467	Vicki Johnson	.844	Sophia Young	12.0

COACHING HISTORY: 2003-Candi Harvey 6-16-.273; 2003 Shell Dailey 6-6-.500, 2004 Dee Browne 6-18-.250, 2004 Shell Dailey & Vonn Read 3-7-.300; 2005-present Dan Hughes

SAN ANTONIO SPURS
(were Dallas Chaparrals)

Home City: San Antonio, Texas
Home Court: HemisFair Arena (1973-1993)   Capacity: 15,908 [1992]
         Alamodome (1993-2002)   Capacity: 20,557 [2002]
         SBC Center (2002-present)   Capacity: 18,500 [2006]
Origin of Name: The name was chosen in a Name the Team Contest.

			Regular Season Record					
Season	League	GP	W	L	PPGF	PPGA	Pct	GB
1973-1974	ABA	84	45	39	97.6	96.7	.536	6
1974-1975	ABA	84	51	33	113.4	109.2	.607	14
1975-1976	ABA	84	50	34	115.6	111.6	.595	10
1976-1977	NBA	82	44	38	115.0	114.4	.537	5
1977-1978	NBA	82	52	30	114.5	111.1	.634	-
1978-1979	NBA	82	48	34	119.3	114.1	.585	-
1979-1980	NBA	82	41	41	119.4	119.7	.500	9
1980-1981	NBA	82	52	30	112.3	109.4	.634	-
1981-1982	NBA	82	48	34	113.1	110.8	.585	-
1982-1983	NBA	82	53	29	114.3	110.7	.646	-
1983-1984	NBA	82	37	45	120.3	120.5	.451	8
1984-1985	NBA	82	41	41	114.8	113.9	.500	11
1985-1986	NBA	82	35	47	111.2	113.1	.427	16
1986-1987	NBA	82	28	54	108.3	113.4	.341	27
1987-1988	NBA	82	31	51	113.6	118.5	.378	23
1988-1989	NBA	82	21	61	105.5	112.3	.256	30
1989-1990	NBA	82	56	26	106.3	102.8	.683	-
1990-1991	NBA	82	55	27	107.1	102.6	.671	-
1991-1992	NBA	82	47	35	104.0	100.6	.573	8
1992-1993	NBA	82	49	33	105.5	102.8	.598	6
1993-1994	NBA	82	55	27	100.0	94.8	.671	3
1994-1995	NBA	82	62	20	106.6	100.6	.756	-
1995-1996	NBA	82	59	23	103.4	97.1	.720	-
1996-1997	NBA	82	20	62	90.5	98.3	.244	44
1997-1998	NBA	82	56	26	92.5	88.5	.683	6
1998-1999	NBA	50	37	13	92.8	84.7	.740	-
1999-2000	NBA	82	53	29	96.2	90.2	.646	2
2000-2001	NBA	82	58	24	96.2	88.4	.707	-
2001-2002	NBA	82	58	24	96.7	90.5	.707	-
2002-2003	NBA	82	60	22	95.8	90.4	.732	-
2003-2004	NBA	82	57	25	91.5	84.3	.695	1
2004-2005	NBA	82	59	23	96.2	88.4	.720	-
2005-2006	NBA	82	63	19	95.6	88.8	.768	-
TOTAL:	33 years	2680	1581	1099				229
AVERAGE:		81	48	33	105.8	103.0	.590	7

Playoff Record

Season	GP	W	L	PPGF	PPGA	Result
1973-1974	7	3	4	100.9	101.7	Lost 1st Round series to Indiana.
1974-1975	6	2	4	108.0	112.3	Lost 1st Round series to Indiana.
1975-1976	7	3	4	107.6	106.3	Lost 1st Round series to New York.
1976-1977	2	0	2	101.5	108.5	Lost 1st Round series to Boston.
1977-1978	6	2	4	107.8	108.0	Lost Conference Semifinal to Washington.
1978-1979	14	7	7	108.8	109.4	Lost Conference Final to Washington.
1979-1980	3	1	2	103.7	112.3	Lost 1st Round series to Houston.
1980-1981	7	3	4	107.7	109.7	Lost Conference Semifinal to Houston.
1981-1982	9	4	5	107.3	111.6	Lost Conference Final to Los Angeles.
1982-1983	11	6	5	121.0	116.7	Lost Conference Final to Los Angeles.
1984-1985	5	2	3	110.2	120.8	Lost 1st Round series to Denver.
1985-1986	3	0	3	92.0	123.7	Lost 1st Round series to Lakers.
1987-1988	3	0	3	109.7	120.3	Lost 1st Round series to Lakers.
1989-1990	10	6	4	117.0	111.8	Lost Conference Semifinal to Portland.
1990-1991	4	1	3	107.8	112.8	Lost 1st Round series to Golden State.
1991-1992	3	0	3	103.3	112.3	Lost 1st Round series to Phoenix.
1992-1993	10	5	5	100.7	100.6	Lost Conference Semifinal to Phoenix.
1993-1994	4	1	3	88.0	96.3	Lost 1st Round series to Utah.
1994-1995	15	9	6	99.1	94.9	Lost Conference Final to Houston.
1995-1996	10	5	5	94.2	96.8	Lost Conference Semifinal to Utah.
1997-1998	9	4	5	91.8	88.6	Lost Conference Semifinal to Utah.
1998-1999	17	15	2	88.4	81.2	**Won NBA Championship.**
1999-2000	4	1	3	81.8	83.0	Lost 1st round series to Phoenix.
2000-2001	13	7	6	91.6	91.9	Lost Conference Final to Lakers.
2001-2002	10	4	6	91.1	88.1	Lost Conference Semifinal to Lakers.
2002-2003	24	16	8	89.3	94.8	**Won NBA Championship.**
2003-2004	10	6	4	89.3	86.2	Lost Conference Semifinal to Lakers.
2004-2005	23	16	7	96.9	92.6	**Won NBA Championship.**
2005-2006	13	7	6	103.1	100.8	Lost Conference Semifinal to Dallas.
TOTAL:	262	136	126			
AVERAGE:	9	5	4	99.5	99.6	

Regular Season Individual Leaders

Season	Field Goal % (min. 70 games)		Points		Points per Game (min. 70 games)	
1973-74	Goo Kennedy	.551	James Silas	1321	James Silas	15.7
1974-75	Swen Nater	.542	George Gervin	1965	George Gervin	23.4
1975-76	James Silas	.519	James Silas	2000	James Silas	23.8
1976-77	George Gervin	.544	George Gervin	1895	George Gervin	23.1
1977-78	George Gervin	.536	George Gervin	2232	George Gervin	27.2
1978-79	George Gervin	.541	George Gervin	2365	George Gervin	29.6
1979-80	Paul Griffin	.553	George Gervin	2585	George Gervin	33.1
1980-81	Paul Griffin	.511	George Gervin	2221	George Gervin	27.1
1981-82	Dave Corzine	.519	George Gervin	2551	George Gervin	32.3
1982-83	Artis Gilmore	.626	George Gervin	2043	George Gervin	26.2
1983-84	Mark McNamara	.621	George Gervin	1967	George Gervin	25.9
1984-85	Artis Gilmore	.623	Mike Mitchell	1824	Mike Mitchell	22.2
1985-86	Steve Johnson	.632	Mike Mitchell	1921	Mike Mitchell	23.4
1986-87	Artis Gilmore	.597	Alvin Robertson	1435	Alvin Robertson	17.7
1987-88	Walter Berry	.563	Alvin Robertson	1610	Alvin Robertson	19.6
1988-89	Greg Anderson	.503	Willie Anderson	1508	Willie Anderson	18.6
1989-90	Frank Brickowski	.545	David Robinson	1993	David Robinson	24.3

Season	Field Goal % (min. 70 games)		Points		Points per Game (min. 70 games)	
1990-91	David Robinson	.552	David Robinson	2101	David Robinson	25.6
1991-92	Sean Elliott	.494	David Robinson	1578	Terry Cummings	17.3
1992-93	Antoine Carr	.538	David Robinson	1916	David Robinson	23.4
1993-94	Dennis Rodman	.534	David Robinson	2383	David Robinson	29.8
1994-95	David Robinson	.530	David Robinson	2238	David Robinson	27.6
1995-96	Will Perdue	.523	David Robinson	2051	David Robinson	25.0
1996-97	Greg Anderson	.496	D. Wilkins	1145	Vernon Maxwell	12.9
1997-98	Tim Duncan	.549	Tim Duncan	1731	David Robinson	21.6
	Will Purdue	.549				
1998-99*	David Robinson	.509	Tim Duncan	1084	Tim Duncan	21.7
1999-00	David Robinson	.512	Tim Duncan	1716	Tim Duncan	23.2
2000-01	Tim Duncan	.499	Tim Duncan	1820	Tim Duncan	22.2
2001-02	Tim Duncan	.508	Tim Duncan	2089	Tim Duncan	25.5
2002-03	Tim Duncan	.513	Tim Duncan	1884	Tim Duncan	23.3
2003-04	R. Nesterovic	.469	Tim Duncan	1538	Tony Parker	14.7
2004-05	Tony Parker	.482	Tim Duncan	1342	Tony Parker	16.6
2005-06	Tony Parker	.548	Tony Parker	1510	Tony Parker	18.9

COACHING HISTORY: 1973-1975 Tom Nissalke 62-49-.559; 1974-1976 Bob Bass 84-57-.596; 1976-1980 Doug Moe 177-135-.567; 1979-1980 Bob Bass 8-8-.500; 1980-1983 Stan Albeck 153-93-.622; 1983-1984 Morris McHone 11-20-.355; 1983-1984 Bob Bass 26-25-.510; 1984-1986 Lowell "Cotton" Fitzsimmons 76-88-.463; 1986-1988 Bob Weiss 59-105-.360; 1988-1992 Larry Brown 153-131-.539; 1991-1992 Bob Bass 26-18-.591; 1992-1993 Jerry Tarkanian 9-11-.450; 1992-1993 Rex Hughes 1-0-1.000; 1992-1994 John Lucas 94-49-.657; 1994-1996 Bob Hill 124-58-.681; 1996-present Gregg Popovich

SAN ANTONIO TEXANS
(were Sacramento Gold Miners)

Home City: San Antonio, Texas
Home Stadium: The Alamodome   Capacity: 59,000 [1995]
Origin of Name: The team adopted the state's name as its own.

Regular Season Record

Season	League	GP	W	L	T	PF	PA	Pts	Pct
1995	CFL	18	12	6	0	630	457	24	.667

Playoff Record

Season	GP	W	L	PF	PA	Result
1995	2	1	1	63	30	Lost Division Final to Baltimore.

Regular Season Individual Leaders

Season	Passing Yards		Receiving Yards		Rushing Yards	
1995	David Archer	4471	Mark Stock	949	Mike Saunders	1030

COACHING HISTORY: 1995 Kay Stephenson 12-6-0-.667

*-minimum 40 games.

SAN ANTONIO THUNDER
(became Team Hawaii)

Home City: San Antonio, Texas
Home Stadium: North East Stadium (1975)
           Alamo Stadium (1976)   Capacity: 22,500 [1975]
Origin of Name: The name was chosen in a Name the Team Contest.

Regular Season Record

Season	League	GP	W	L	GF	GA	BP	Pts	Pct
1975	NASL	22	6	16	24	46	23	59	.298
1976	NASL	24	12	12	38	32	35	107	.495
TOTAL:	2 years	46	18	28	62	78	58	166	
AVERAGE:		23	9	14	31	39	29	83	.401

Regular Season Individual Leaders

Season	Goals		Points		GAA (360 Min)	
1975	Jose Berico	5	Jose Marcio	13	Roberto Blanco	1.79
	Jose Marcio	5				
1976	Harry Hood	9	Harry Hood	25	Peter Mannos	1.18

COACHING HISTORY: 1975 Alex Perolli 1-8; 1975-1976 Don Batie 17-20

SAN ANTONIO WINGS

Home City: San Antonio, Texas
Home Stadium: Alamo Stadium   Capacity: 22,500 [1975]
Origin of Name:

Regular Season Record

Season	League	GP	W	L	T	PF	PA	Pct
1975	WFL	13	7	6	0	364	268	.538

Regular Season Individual Leaders

Season	Passing Yards		Receiving Yards		Rushing Yards	
1975	John Walton	2405	Eddie Richardson	682	Jim Strong	576

COACHING HISTORY: Perry Moss 7-6-0-.538

SAN DIEGO CHARGERS
(were Los Angeles Chargers)

Home City: San Diego, California
Home Stadium: Balboa Stadium (1961-1966)   Capacity: 34,000
           Qualcomm Stadium (1967-2003)*   Capacity: 71,000 [2005]
           PETCO Park (2004-present)   Capacity: 46,000 [2004]
Origin of Name: The team kept the same nickname when it moved from Los Angeles to San Diego.

Regular Season Record

Season	League	GP	W	L	T	PF	PA	Pct
1961	AFL	14	12	2	0	396	219	.857
1962	AFL	14	4	10	0	314	392	.286
1963	AFL	14	11	3	0	399	256	.785
1964	AFL	14	8	5	1	341	300	.607
1965	AFL	14	9	2	3	340	227	.750

*-San Diego/Jack Murphy Stadium from 1967 to 1996.

1966	AFL	14	7	6	1	335	284	.536
1967	AFL	14	8	5	1	360	352	.607
1968	AFL	14	9	5	0	382	310	.643
1969	AFL	14	8	6	0	288	276	.571
1970	NFL	14	5	6	3	282	278	.464
1971	NFL	14	6	8	0	311	341	.429
1972	NFL	14	4	9	1	264	344	.321
1973	NFL	14	2	11	1	188	386	.179
1974	NFL	14	5	9	0	212	285	.357
1975	NFL	14	2	12	0	189	345	.143
1976	NFL	14	6	8	0	248	285	.429
1977	NFL	14	7	7	0	222	205	.500
1978	NFL	16	9	7	0	355	309	.563
1979	NFL	16	12	4	0	411	246	.750
1980	NFL	16	11	5	0	418	327	.688
1981	NFL	16	10	6	0	478	390	.625
1982	NFL	9	6	3	0	288	221	.667
1983	NFL	16	6	10	0	358	462	.375
1984	NFL	16	7	9	0	394	413	.438
1985	NFL	16	8	8	0	467	435	.500
1986	NFL	16	4	12	0	335	396	.250
1987	NFL	15	8	7	0	253	317	.533
1988	NFL	16	6	10	0	231	332	.375
1989	NFL	16	6	10	0	266	290	.375
1990	NFL	16	6	10	0	315	281	.375
1991	NFL	16	4	12	0	274	342	.250
1992	NFL	16	11	5	0	335	241	.688
1993	NFL	16	8	8	0	322	290	.500
1994	NFL	16	11	5	0	381	306	.688
1995	NFL	16	9	7	0	321	323	.563
1996	NFL	16	8	8	0	310	376	.500
1997	NFL	16	4	12	0	266	425	.250
1998	NFL	16	5	11	0	241	342	.313
1999	NFL	16	8	8	0	269	316	.500
2000	NFL	16	1	15	0	269	440	.062
2001	NFL	16	5	11	0	332	321	.313
2002	NFL	16	8	8	0	333	367	.500
2003	NFL	16	4	12	0	313	441	.250
2004	NFL	16	12	4	0	446	313	.750
2005	NFL	16	9	7	0	418	312	.562
2006	NFL	16	14	2	0	492	303	.875
TOTAL:	46 years	694	333	350	11	14962	14962	
AVERAGE:		15	7	8	0	325	325	.488

Playoff Record

Season	GP	W	L	PF	PA	Result
1961	1	0	1	3	10	Lost Championship game to Houston.
1963	1	1	0	51	10	**Won AFL Championship**.
1964	1	0	1	7	20	Lost Championship game to Buffalo.
1965	1	0	1	0	23	Lost Championship game to Buffalo.
1979	1	0	1	14	17	Lost Divisional playoff to Houston.
1980	2	1	1	47	48	Lost AFC Championship to Oakland.
1981	2	1	1	48	65	Lost AFC Championship to Cincinnati.
1982	2	1	1	44	62	Lost 2nd Round series to Miami.

1992	2	1	1	17	31	Lost Conference Semifinal to Miami.
1994	3	2	1	65	83	Lost Super Bowl game to San Francisco.
1995	1	0	1	20	35	Lost Wild Card Game to Indianapolis.
2004	1	0	1	17	20	Lost Wild Card Game to Jets.
2006	1	0	1	21	24	Lost Conf. Semifinal to New England.
TOTAL:	19	7	12	354	448	
AVERAGE:	2	1	1	27	34	

Regular Season Individual Leaders

Season	Passing Yards		Receiving Yards		Rushing Yards	
1961	Jack Kemp	2686	Dave Kocourek	1055	Paul Lowe	767
1962	John Hadl	1632	Don Norton	771	Keith Lincoln	574
1963	Tobin Rote	2510	Lance Alworth	1205	Paul Lowe	1010
1964	John Hadl	2157	Lance Alworth	1235	Keith Lincoln	632
1965	John Hadl	2798	Lance Alworth	1602	Paul Lowe	1121
1966	John Hadl	2846	Lance Alworth	1383	Paul Lowe	643
1967	John Hadl	3365	Lance Alworth	1010	Dick Post	663
1968	John Hadl	3473	Lance Alworth	1312	Dick Post	758
1969	John Hadl	2253	Lance Alworth	1003	Dick Post	873
1970	John Hadl	2388	Gary Garrison	1006	Jeff Queen	261
1971	John Hadl	3075	Gary Garrison	889	Mike Garrett	591
1972	John Hadl	2449	Gary Garrsion	744	Mike Garrett	1031
1973	Dan Fouts	1126	Jerry LeVias	536	Cid Edwards	609
1974	Dan Fouts	1732	Gary Garrison	785	Don Woods	1162
1975	Dan Fouts	1396	Pat Curran	619	Rickey Young	577
1976	Dan Fouts	2535	Charlie Joiner	1056	Rickey Young	802
1977	James Harris	1240	Charlie Joiner	542	Rickey Young	543
1978	Dan Fouts	2999	John Jefferson	1001	Lydell Mitchell	820
1979	Dan Fouts	4082	John Jefferson	1090	Clarence Williams	752
1980	Dan Fouts	4715	John Jefferson	1340	Chuck Muncie	827
1981	Dan Fouts	4802	Charlie Joiner	1188	Chuck Muncie	1144
1982	Dan Fouts	2883	Wes Chandler	1032	Chuck Muncie	569
1983	Dan Fouts	2975	Kellen Winslow	1172	Chuck Muncie	886
1984	Dan Fouts	3740	Charlie Joiner	793	Earnest Jackson	1179
1985	Dan Fouts	3638	Wes Chandler	1199	Lionel James	516
1986	Dan Fouts	3031	Wes Chandler	874	Gary Anderson	442
1987	Dan Fouts	2517	Wes Chandler	617	Curtis Adams	343
1988	Mark Malone	1580	Jamie Holland	536	Gary Anderson	1119
1989	Jim McMahon	2132	Anthony Miller	1252	Marion Butts	683
1990	Billy Joe Tolliver	2574	Anthony Miller	933	Marion Butts	1225
1991	John Friesz	2896	Anthony Miller	649	Marion Butts	834
1992	Stan Humphries	3356	Anthony Miller	1060	Marion Butts	809
1993	Stan Humphries	1981	Anthony Miller	1162	Marion Butts	746
1994	Stan Humphries	3209	Tony Martin	885	Natrone Means	1350
1995	Stan Humphries	3381	Tony Martin	1224	Natrone Means	730
1996	Stan Humphries	2670	Tony Martin	1171	Leonard Russell	713
1997	Stan Humphries	1488	Tony Martin	904	Gary Brown	945
1998	Craig Whelihan	1803	Charlie Jones	699	Natrone Means	883
1999	Jim Harbaugh	2761	Jeff Graham	968	Jermaine Fazande	365
2000	Ryan Leaf	1883	Jeff Graham	907	Terrell Fletcher	384
2001	Doug Flutie	3464	Curtis Conway	1125	L Tomlinson	1236
2002	Drew Brees	3284	Curtis Conway	852	L. Tomlinson	1683
2003	Drew Brees	2108	David Boston	880	L. Tomlinson	1645
2004	Drew Brees	3159	Antonio Gates	964	L. Tomlinson	1335

Season	Passing Yards		Receiving Yards		Rushing Yards	
2005	Drew Brees	3576	Antonio Gates	1101	L. Tomlinson	1462
2006	Philip Rivers	3388	Antonio Gates	924	L. Tomlinson	1815

COACHING HISTORY: 1961-1969 Sid Gillman 82-48-6-.625; 1969-1970 Charlie Waller 9-7-3-.553; 1971 Sid Gillman 4-6-0-.400; 1971-1973 Harland Svare 7-17-2-.308; 1973 Ron Waller 1-5-0-.167; 1974-1978 Tom Prothro 21-39-0-.350; 1978-1986 Don Coryell 69-56-0-.552; 1986-1988 Al Saunders 17-22-0-.436; 1989-1991 Dan Henning 16-32-0-.333; 1992-1996 Bobby Ross 47-33-0-.588; 1997-1998 Kevin Gilbride 6-16-0-.273; 1998 June Jones 3-7-0-.300; 1999-2001 Mike Riley 14-34-0-.292; 2002-present Marty Schottenheimer

SAN DIEGO CLIPPERS
(were Buffalo Braves)
(became Los Angeles Clippers)

Home City: San Diego, California
Home Court: San Diego Sports Arena   Capacity: 13,841 [1984]
Origin of Name: The name was chosen in a Name the Team Contest

Regular Season Record

Season	League	GP	W	L	PPGF	PPGA	Pct	GB
1978-1979	NBA	82	43	39	113.1	114.9	.524	9
1979-1980	NBA	82	35	47	107.6	111.7	.427	25
1980-1981	NBA	82	36	46	106.5	108.1	.439	21
1981-1982	NBA	82	17	65	108.5	115.9	.207	40
1982-1983	NBA	82	25	57	108.6	113.4	.305	33
1983-1984	NBA	82	30	52	110.7	114.0	.366	24
TOTAL:	6 years	492	186	306				152
AVERAGE:		82	31	51	109.2	113.0	.378	25

Regular Season Individual Leaders

Season	Field Goal % (min. 70 games)		Points		Points per Game (min. 70 games)	
1978-79	Swen Nater	.569	World B. Free	2244	World B. Free	28.8
1979-80	Swen Nater	.554	World B. Free	2055	World B. Free	30.2
1980-81	Swen Nater	.553	F. Williams	1585	F. Williams	19.3
1981-82	J. Whitehead	.559	Tom Chambers	1392	Tom Chambers	17.2
1982-83	Terry Cummings	.523	Terry Cummings	1660	Terry Cummings	23.7
1983-84	James Donaldson	.596	Terry Cummings	1854	Terry Cummings	22.9

COACHING HISTORY: 1978-1980 Gene Shue 78-86-.476; 1980-1983 Paul Silas 78-168-.317; 1983-1984 Jim Lynam 30-52-.366

SAN DIEGO JAWS
(were Baltimore Comets)
(became Las Vegas Quicksilvers)

Home City: San Diego, California
Home Stadium: Aztec Bowl
Origin of Name: The name was no doubt suggested by Steven Spielberg's hit movie *Jaws* which had been released the previous year.

Regular Season Record

Season	League	GP	W	L	GF	GA	BP	Pts	Pct
1976	NASL	24	9	15	29	47	28	82	.380

Regular Season Individual Leaders

Season	Goals		Points		GAA (360 Min)	
1976	Hilary Carlyle	5	Hilary Carlyle	12	Alan Mayer	1.77

COACHING HISTORY: Derek Trevis 9-15-.380

SAN DIEGO MARINERS
(were New Jersey Knights)

Home City: San Diego, California
Home Arena: San Diego Sports Arena   Capacity: 13,039
Origin of Name: The name was chosen to reflect the city's maritime heritage.

Regular Season Record

Season	League	GP	W	L	T	GF	GA	Pts	Pct
1974-1975	WHA	78	43	31	4	326	268	90	.577
1975-1976	WHA	80	36	38	6	303	290	78	.488
1976-1977	WHA	81	40	37	4	284	283	84	.519
TOTAL:	3 years	239	119	106	14	913	841	252	
AVERAGE:		80	40	35	5	304	280	84	.527

Playoff Record

Season	GP	W	L	GF	GA	Result
1974-1975	10	4	6	34	44	Lost Semifinal series to Houston.
1975-1976	11	5	6	33	39	Lost Quarterfinal series to Houston.
1976-1977	7	3	4	19	28	Lost Quarterfinal series to Winnipeg.
TOTAL:	28	12	16	86	111	
AVERAGE:	9	4	5	29	37	

Regular Season Individual Leaders

Season	Goals		Points		Penalty Minutes	
1974-1975	Wayne Rivers	54	Andre Lacroix	147	Kevin Morrison	143
1975-1976	Norm Ferguson	37	Andre Lacroix	101	Kevin Devine	102
	Gene Peacosh	37				
1976-1977	Norm Ferguson	39	Andre Lacroix	114	Kevin Devine	114

COACHING HISTORY: 1974-1975 Harry Howell 43-31-4-.577; 1975-1977 Ron Ingram 76-75-10-.503

SAN DIEGO PADRES

Home City: San Diego, California
Home Field: Qualcomm Stadium* (1969-2003)   Capacity: 66,083 [2003]
            PETCO Park (2004-present)   Capacity: 42,500 [2006]
Origin of Name: The team was named after the previous Pacific Coast League team.

Regular Season Record

Season	League	GP	W	L	Pct	GB	R	OR
1969	NL	162	52	110	.321	41	468	746
1970	NL	162	63	99	.389	39	681	788
1971	NL	161	61	100	.379	28.5	486	610
1972	NL	153	58	95	.379	36.5	488	665

*-known as San Diego Stadium from 1969 to 1981 and San Diego/Jack Murphy Stadium from 1981 to 1996.

1973	NL	162	60	102	.370	39	548	770
1974	NL	162	60	102	.370	42	541	830
1975	NL	162	71	91	.438	37	552	683
1976	NL	162	73	89	.451	29	570	662
1977	NL	162	69	93	.426	29	692	834
1978	NL	162	84	78	.519	11	591	598
1979	NL	161	68	93	.422	22	603	681
1980	NL	162	73	89	.451	19.5	591	654
1981	NL	110	41	69	.373	NA	382	455
1982	NL	162	81	81	.500	8	675	658
1983	NL	162	81	81	.500	10	653	653
1984	NL	162	92	70	.568	-	686	634
1985	NL	162	83	79	.512	12	650	622
1986	NL	162	74	88	.457	22	656	723
1987	NL	162	65	97	.401	25	668	763
1988	NL	161	83	78	.516	11	594	583
1989	NL	162	89	73	.549	3	642	626
1990	NL	161	74	87	.460	16.5	673	673
1991	NL	162	84	78	.519	10	636	646
1992	NL	162	82	80	.506	16	617	636
1993	NL	162	61	101	.377	43	679	772
1994	NL	117	47	70	.402	12.5	479	531
1995	NL	144	70	74	.486	8	668	672
1996	NL	162	91	71	.562	-	771	682
1997	NL	162	76	86	.469	14	891	795
1998	NL	162	98	64	.605	-	749	635
1999	NL	162	74	88	.457	26	710	781
2000	NL	162	76	86	.469	21	752	815
2001	NL	162	79	83	.488	13	789	812
2002	NL	162	66	96	.407	32	662	815
2003	NL	162	64	98	.395	36.5	678	831
2004	NL	162	87	75	.537	6	768	705
2005	NL	162	82	80	.506	-	684	726
2006	NL	162	88	74	.543	-	731	679
TOTAL:	38 years	6028	2780	3248		719	24354	26444
AVERAGE:		159	73	86	.461	19	641	696

Playoff Record

Season	GP	W	L	R	OR	Result
1984	10	4	6	37	49	Lost World Series to Detroit.
1996	3	0	3	10	15	Lost Division Semifinal to St. Louis.
1998	14	7	7	51	52	Lost World Series to Yankees.
2005	3	0	3	11	21	Lost Division Semifinal to St. Louis.
2006	4	1	3	6	14	Lost Division Semifinal to St. Louis.
TOTAL:	34	12	22	115	151	
AVERAGE:	7	3	4	23	30	

Regular Season Individual Leaders

Season	Home Runs		RBI's		Wins	
1969	Nate Colbert	24	Nate Colbert	66	Al Santorini	8
					Joe Niekro	8
1970	Nate Colbert	38	Cito Gaston	93	Pat Dobson	14
1971	Nate Colbert	27	Nate Colbert	84	Clay Kirby	15
1972	Nate Colbert	38	Nate Colbert	111	Clay Kirby	12

Season	Home Runs		RBI's		Wins	
1973	Nate Colbert	22	Nate Colbert	80	Steve Arlin	11
1974	Willie McCovey	22	Dave Winfield	75	Larry Hardy	9
					Dan Spillner	9
					Dave Freisleben	9
					Bill Greif	9
1975	Willie McCovey	23	Dave Winfield	76	Randy Jones	20
1976	Dave Winfield	13	Mike Ivie	70	Randy Jones	22
1977	Dave Winfield	25	Dave Winfield	92	Bob Shirley	12
1978	Dave Winfield	24	Dave Winfield	97	Gaylord Perry	21
1979	Dave Winfield	34	Dave Winfield	118	Gaylord Perry	12
1980	Dave Winfield	20	Dave Winfield	87	Rollie Fingers	11
					Bob Shirley	11
1981	Joe Lefebvre	8	Gene Richards	42	Juan Eichelberger	8
1982	Terry Kennedy	21	Terry Kennedy	21	Tim Lollar	16
1983	Terry Kennedy	17	Terry Kennedy	98	Eric Show	15
1984	Graig Nettles	20	Steve Garvey	86	Eric Show	15
	Kevin McReynolds	20				
1985	Carmelo Martinez	21	Steve Garvey	81	Andy Hawkins	18
1986	Kevin McReynolds	26	Kevin McReynolds	96	Andy Hawkins	10
					Lance McCullers	10
1987	John Kruk	20	John Kruk	91	Ed Whitson	10
1988	Carmelo Martinez	18	Tony Gwynn	70	Eric Show	16
1989	Jack Clark	26	Jack Clark	94	Ed Whitson	16
1990	Jack Clark	25	Joe Carter	115	Ed Whitson	14
1991	Fred McGriff	31	Fred McGriff	106	Andy Benes	15
					Bruce Hurst	15
1992	Fred McGriff	35	Fred McGriff	104	Bruce Hurst	14
1993	Phil Plantier	34	Phil Plantier	100	Andy Benes	15
1994	Phil Plantier	18	Tony Gwynn	64	Joey Hamilton	9
1995	Ken Caminiti	26	Ken Caminiti	94	Andy Ashby	12
1996	Ken Caminiti	40	Ken Caminiti	130	Joey Hamilton	15
1997	Steve Finley	28	Tony Gwynn	119	Joey Hamilton	12
1998	Greg Vaughn	50	Greg Vaughn	119	Kevin Brown	18
1999	Reggie Sanders	26	Phil Nevin	85	Andy Ashby	14
2000	Phil Nevin	31	Phil Nevin	107	Matt Clement	13
2001	Phil Nevin	41	Phil Nevin	126	Kevin Jarvis	12
2002	Ryan Klesko	29	Ryan Klesko	95	Brian Lawrence	12
2003	Ryan Klesko	21	Brian Giles	88	Jake Peavy	12
2004	Phil Nevin	26	Phil Nevin	105	Brian Lawrence	15
2005	Ryann Klesko	18	Brian Giles	83	Jake Peavy	13
2006	Adrian Gonzalez	24	Mike Cameron	83	Woody Williams	12
			Brian Giles	83		

COACHING HISTORY: 1969-1972 Preston Gomez 180-316-.363; 1972-1973 Don Zimmer 114-190-.375; 1974-1977 John McNamara 224-310-.419; 1977 Alvin Dark 49-55-.471; 1978-1979 Roger Craig 152-171-.471; 1980 Jerry Coleman 73-89-.451; 1981 Frank Howard 41-69-.373; 1982-1985 Dick Williams 337-311-.520; 1986 Steve Boros 74-88-.457; 1987-1988 Larry Bowa 81-127-.389; 1988-1990 Jack McKeon 193-164-.541; 1990-1992 Greg Riddoch 200-194-.508; 1992-1994 Jim Riggleman 112-179-.385; 1995-present Bruce Bochy

SAN DIEGO ROCKETS
(became Houston Rockets)

Home City: San Diego, California
Home Court: San Diego Sports Arena   Capacity: 14,000
Origin of Name: The name was chosen in a Name the Team Contest.

Regular Season Record

Season	League	GP	W	L	PPGF	PPGA	Pct	GB
1967-1968	NBA	82	15	67	112.4	121.0	.183	41
1968-1969	NBA	82	37	45	115.3	115.5	.451	18
1969-1970	NBA	82	27	55	118.7	121.8	.329	21
1970-1971	NBA	82	40	42	113.2	113.4	.488	8
TOTAL:	4 years	328	119	209				88
AVERAGE:		82	30	52	114.9	117.9	.363	22

Playoff Record

Season	GP	W	L	PPGF	PPGA	Result
1968-1969	6	2	4	106.2	108.7	Lost Division Semifinal to Atlanta.

Regular Season Individual Leaders

Season	Field Goal % (min. 70 games)		Points		Points per Game (min. 70 games)	
1967-68	Don Kojis	.446	Don Kojis	1360	Don Kojis	19.7
1968-69	Stu Lantz	.456	Elvin Hayes	2327	Elvin Hayes	28.4
1969-70	Elvin Hayes	.452	Elvin Hayes	2256	Elvin Hayes	27.5
1970-71	Calvin Murphy	.458	Elvin Hayes	2350	Elvin Hayes	28.7

COACHING HISTORY: 1967-1970 Jack McMahon 61-129-.321; 1970-1971 Alex Hannum 58-80-.420

SAN DIEGO SAILS

Home City: San Diego, California
Home Court: Peterson Gym at San Diego State (1972-73)   Capacity: 4,200 [1972]
　　　　　Golden Hall (1973-74)
　　　　　San Diego Sports Arena (1974-1976)   Capacity: 14,000 [1976]
Origin of Name: The name was chosen because of the area's maritime history. For the first three seasons the team was known as the Conquistadors, a name which was submitted in a Name the Team Contest.

Regular Season Record

Season	League	GP	W	L	PPGF	PPGA	Pct	GB
1972-1973	ABA	84	30	54	109.0	113.3	.357	25
1973-1974	ABA	84	37	47	107.0	107.5	.440	14
1974-1975	ABA	84	31	53	109.0	115.5	.369	34
1975-1976	ABA	11	3	8	98.8	103.5	.273	36.5
TOTAL:	4 years	263	101	162				109.5
AVERAGE:		66	25	41	107.9	111.7	.384	27

Playoff Record

Season	GP	W	L	PPGF	PPGA	Result
1972-1973	4	0	4	94.8	106.8	Lost 1st Round series to Utah.

Regular Season Individual Leaders

Season	Field Goal % (min. 70 games)		Points		Points per Game (min. 70 games)	
1972-73	Gene Moore	.498	Stew Johnson	1770	Stew Johnson	22.1
1973-74	George Adams	.500	Bo Lamar	1713	Bo Lamar	20.4
1974-75	Lee Davis	.528	Bo Lamar	1606	Bo Lamar	20.9
1975-76	Pat McFarland	.458	Pat McFarland	132	Pat McFarland	12.0

COACHING HISTORY: 1972-1973 K.C. Jones 30-54-.357; 1973-1974 Wilt Chamberlain 37-47-.440; 1974-1975 Alex Groza 15-23-.395; 1974-1975 Beryl Shipley 16-30-.348; 1975-1976 Bill Musselman 3-8-.273

SAN DIEGO SOCKERS
(were Las Vegas Quicksilvers)

Home City: San Diego, California
Home Stadium: San Diego/Jack Murphy Stadium   Capacity: 52,675 [1984]
Origin of Name: The word socker is a variation of the word soccer and was probably chosen for that reason.

Regular Season Record

Season	League	GP	W	L	GF	GA	BP	Pts	Pct
1978	NASL	30	18	12	63	56	56	164	.607
1979	NASL	30	15	15	59	55	50	140	.519
1980	NASL	32	16	16	53	51	44	140	.486
1981	NASL	32	21	11	68	49	55	173	.360
1982	NASL	32	19	13	71	54	54	162	.338
1983	NASL	30	11	19	53	65	42	106	.236
1984	NASL	24	14	10	51	42	40	118	.328
TOTAL:	7 years	210	114	96	418	372	341	1003	
AVERAGE:		30	16	14	60	53	49	143	.386

Playoff Record

Season	GP	W	L	GF	GA	Result
1978	4	2	2	4	4	Lost Conference Semifinal to Tampa Bay.
1979	7	5	2	18	9	Lost 3rd Round series to Tampa Bay.
1980	9	5	4	19	21	Lost 3rd Round series to Ft. Lauderdale.
1981	9	5	4	17	13	Lost 3rd Round series to Chicago.
1982	5	2	3	9	7	Lost 2nd Round series to New York.
1984	2	0	2	1	3	Lost 1st Round series to Toronto.
TOTAL:	36	19	17	68	57	
AVERAGE:	6	3	3	11	9	

Regular Season Individual Leaders

Season	Goals		Points		GAA (360 Min)	
1978	Walker McCall	11	Jean Willrich	31	Alan Mayer	1.77
1979	Julie Veee	10	Julie Veee	28	Alan Mayer	1.77
1980	Hugo Sanchez	7	Leo Cuellar	27	Volkmar Gross	1.38
1981	Mike Stojanovic	23	Mike Stojanovic	52	Volkmar Gross	1.36
1982	Ade Coker	13	Ade Coker	35	Volkmar Gross	1.40
			Lorenz Hilkes	35		
1983	Kaz Deyna	15	Kaz Deyna	46		
1984	Ade Coker	16	Ade Coker	39		

COACHING HISTORY: 1978-1980 Hubert Vogelsinger 33-31; 1980 Hank Liotart 3-1; 1980-1984 Ron Newman 78-64

SAN DIEGO TOROS
(were Los Angeles Toros)

Home City: San Diego, California
Home Stadium: Balboa Stadium
Origin of Name: The team kept the same nickname after moving to San Diego from Los Angeles.

Regular Season Record

Season	League	GP	W	L	T	GF	GA	BP	Pts	Pct
1968	NASL	32	18	8	6	65	38	60	186	.646

Playoff Record

Season	GP	W	L	T	GF	GA	Result
1968	4	1	1	2	2	4	Lost Championship series to Atlanta.

Regular Season Individual Leaders

Season	Goals		Points		GAA (360 Min)	
1968	Cirilo Fernandez	30	Cirilo Fernandez	67	Ataulfo Sanchez	0.93

COACHING HISTORY: George Curtis, Angel Papadopolus

SAN FRANCISCO 49ers

Home City: San Francisco, California
Home Stadium: Kezar Stadium (1946-1970)   Capacity: 59,636
           Monster Park* (2005-present)   Capacity: 69,400 [2005]
Origin of Name: The team was named by the team owners and was suggested by the California Gold Rush of 1849.

Regular Season Record

Season	League	GP	W	L	T	PF	PA	Pct
1946	AAFC	14	9	5	0	307	189	.643
1947	AAFC	14	8	4	2	327	264	.643
1948	AAFC	14	12	2	0	495	248	.857
1949	AAFC	12	9	3	0	416	227	.750
1950	NFL	12	3	9	0	213	300	.250
1951	NFL	12	7	4	1	255	205	.625
1952	NFL	12	7	5	0	285	221	.583
1953	NFL	12	9	3	0	372	237	.750
1954	NFL	12	7	4	1	313	251	.625
1955	NFL	12	4	8	0	216	298	.333
1956	NFL	12	5	6	1	233	284	.458
1957	NFL	12	8	4	0	260	264	.667
1958	NFL	12	6	6	0	257	324	.500
1959	NFL	12	7	5	0	255	237	.583
1960	NFL	12	7	5	0	208	205	.583
1961	NFL	14	7	6	1	346	272	.538
1962	NFL	14	6	8	0	282	331	.429
1963	NFL	14	2	12	0	198	391	.143

*-known as Candlestick Park from 1971 to 1994, and 2002 to 2004, and 3Com Park from 1995 to 2001

1964	NFL	14	4	10	0	236	330	.286
1965	NFL	14	7	6	1	421	402	.536
1966	NFL	14	6	6	2	320	325	.500
1967	NFL	14	7	7	0	273	337	.500
1968	NFL	14	7	6	1	303	310	.536
1969	NFL	14	4	8	2	277	319	.357
1970	NFL	14	10	3	1	352	267	.750
1971	NFL	14	9	5	0	300	216	.643
1972	NFL	14	8	5	1	353	249	.607
1973	NFL	14	5	9	0	262	319	.357
1974	NFL	14	6	8	0	226	236	.429
1975	NFL	14	5	9	0	255	286	.357
1976	NFL	14	8	6	0	270	190	.571
1977	NFL	14	5	9	0	220	260	.357
1978	NFL	16	2	14	0	219	350	.125
1979	NFL	16	2	14	0	308	416	.125
1980	NFL	16	6	10	0	320	415	.375
1981	NFL	16	13	3	0	357	250	.813
1982	NFL	9	3	6	0	209	206	.333
1983	NFL	16	10	6	0	432	293	.625
1984	NFL	16	15	1	0	475	227	.938
1985	NFL	16	10	6	0	411	263	.625
1986	NFL	16	10	5	1	374	247	.656
1987	NFL	15	13	2	0	459	253	.867
1988	NFL	16	10	6	0	369	294	.625
1989	NFL	16	14	2	0	442	253	.875
1990	NFL	16	14	2	0	353	239	.875
1991	NFL	16	10	6	0	393	239	.625
1992	NFL	16	14	2	0	431	236	.875
1993	NFL	16	10	6	0	473	295	.625
1994	NFL	16	13	3	0	505	296	.813
1995	NFL	16	11	5	0	457	258	.688
1996	NFL	16	12	4	0	398	257	.750
1997	NFL	16	13	3	0	375	265	.813
1998	NFL	16	12	4	0	479	328	.750
1999	NFL	16	4	12	0	295	453	.250
2000	NFL	16	6	10	0	388	422	.375
2001	NFL	16	12	4	0	409	282	.750
2002	NFL	16	10	6	0	367	351	.625
2003	NFL	16	7	9	0	384	337	.438
2004	NFL	16	2	14	0	259	452	.125
2005	NFL	16	4	12	0	239	428	.250
2006	NFL	16	7	9	0	298	412	.438
TOTAL:	61 years	880	483	382	15	20184	17811	
AVERAGE:		14	8	6	0	331	292	.557

Playoff Record

Season	GP	W	L	PF	PA	Result
1949	1	0	1	7	21	Lost Championship game to Cleveland.
1957	1	0	1	27	31	Lost Conference playoff to Detroit.
1970	2	1	1	27	31	Lost NFC Championship to Dallas.
1971	2	1	1	27	34	Lost NFC Championship to Dallas.
1972	1	0	1	28	30	Lost Divisional playoff to Dallas.
1981	3	3	0	92	72	**Won Super Bowl XVI.**

1983	2	1	1	45	47	Lost NFC Championship to Washington.
1984	3	3	0	82	26	**Won Super Bowl XIX.**
1985	1	0	1	3	17	Lost 1st Round playoff to Giants.
1986	1	0	1	3	49	Lost Divisional playoff to Giants.
1987	1	0	1	24	36	Lost Divisional playoff to Minnesota.
1988	3	3	0	82	28	**Won Super Bowl XXIII.**
1989	3	3	0	126	26	**Won Super Bowl XXIV.**
1990	2	1	1	41	25	Lost Conference Final to Giants.
1992	2	1	1	40	43	Lost Conference Final to Dallas.
1993	2	1	1	65	41	Lost Conference Final to Dallas.
1994	3	3	0	131	69	**Won Super Bowl XXIX.**
1995	1	0	1	17	27	Lost Conference Semifinal to Green Bay.
1996	2	1	1	28	35	Lost Divisional Semifinal to Green Bay.
1997	2	1	1	48	45	Lost Conference Final to Green Bay.
1998	2	1	1	48	47	Lost Conference Semifinal to Atlanta.
2001	1	0	1	15	25	Lost 1st Round game to Green Bay.
2002	2	1	1	45	69	Lost Conference Semifinal to Tampa Bay.
TOTAL:	43	25	18	1051	874	
AVERAGE:	2	1	1	46	38	

Regular Season Individual Leaders

Season	Passing Yards		Receiving Yards		Rushing Yards	
1946	Frankie Albert	1404	Alyn Beals	586	Norm Standlee	651
1947	Frankie Albert	1692	Alyn Beals	655	John Strzykalski	906
1948	Frankie Albert	1990	Alyn Beals	591	John Strzykalski	915
1949	Frankie Albert	1862	Alyn Beals	678	Joe Perry	783
1950	Frankie Albert	1767	Alex Loyd	402	Joe Perry	647
1951	Frankie Albert	1116	Gordon Soltau	826	Joe Perry	677
1952	Y.A. Tittle	1407	Gordon Soltau	774	Joe Perry	725
1953	Y.A. Tittle	2121	Billy Wilson	840	Joe Perry	1018
1954	Y.A. Tittle	2205	Billy Wilson	830	Joe Perry	1049
1955	Y.A. Tittle	2185	Billy Wilson	831	Joe Perry	701
1956	Y.A. Tittle	1641	Billy Wilson	889	Hugh McElhenny	916
1957	Y.A. Tittle	2157	Billy Wilson	757	Hugh McElhenny	478
1958	Y.A. Tittle	1467	R.C. Owens	620	Joe Perry	758
1959	Y.A. Tittle	1331	Billy Wilson	540	J.D. Smith	1036
1960	John Brodie	1111	R.C. Owens	532	J.D. Smith	780
1961	John Brodie	2588	R.C. Owens	1032	J.D. Smith	823
1962	John Brodie	2272	Bernie Casey	819	J.D. Smith	907
1963	Lemar McHan	1243	Bernie Casey	762	J.D. Smith	560
1964	John Brodie	2498	Bernie Casey	808	Dave Kopay	271
1965	John Brodie	3112	Dave Parks	1344	Ken Willard	778
1966	John Brodie	2810	Dave Parks	974	Ken Willard	763
1967	John Brodie	2013	Dick Witcher	705	Ken Willard	510
1968	John Brodie	3020	Clifton McNeil	994	Ken Willard	967
1969	John Brodie	2405	G. Washington	711	Ken Willard	557
1970	John Brodie	2941	G. Washington	1100	Ken Willard	789
1971	John Brodie	2642	G. Washington	884	Ken Willard	855
1972	Steve Spurrier	1983	G. Washington	918	Vic Washington	468
1973	John Brodie	1126	Ted Kwalick	729	Vic Washington	543
1974	Tom Owen	1327	G. Washington	615	Wilbur Jackson	705
1975	Norm Snead	1337	G. Washington	735	Del Williams	631
1976	Jim Plunkett	1592	G. Washington	457	Del Williams	1203
1977	Jim Plunkett	1693	G. Washington	638	Del Williams	931

Season	Passing Yards		Receiving Yards		Rushing Yards	
1978	Steve DeBerg	1570	Fred Solomon	458	O.J. Simpson	593
1979	Steve DeBerg	3652	Fred Solomon	807	Paul Hofer	615
1980	Steve DeBerg	1998	Dwight Clark	991	Earl Cooper	720
1981	Joe Montana	3565	Dwight Clark	1105	Ricky Patton	543
1982	Joe Montana	2613	Dwight Clark	913	Jeff Moore	281
1983	Joe Montana	3910	Dwight Clark	840	Wendell Tyler	856
1984	Joe Montana	3630	Dwight Clark	880	Wendell Tyler	1262
1985	Joe Montana	3653	Roger Craig	1016	Roger Craig	1050
1986	Joe Montana	2236	Jerry Rice	1570	Roger Craig	830
1987	Joe Montana	3054	Jerry Rice	1078	Roger Craig	815
1988	Joe Montana	2981	Jerry Rice	1306	Roger Craig	1502
1989	Joe Montana	3521	Jerry Rice	1483	Roger Craig	1054
1990	Joe Montana	3944	Jerry Rice	1502	Dexter Carter	460
1991	Steve Young	2517	Jerry Rice	1206	Keith Henderson	561
1992	Steve Young	3465	Jerry Rice	1201	Ricky Watters	1013
1993	Steve Young	4023	Jerry Rice	1503	Ricky Watters	950
1994	Steve Young	3969	Jerry Rice	1499	Ricky Watters	877
1995	Steve Young	3200	Jerry Rice	1848	Derek Loville	723
1996	Steve Young	2410	Jerry Rice	1254	Terry Kirby	559
1997	Steve Young	3029	Terrell Owens	936	Garrison Hearst	1019
1998	Steve Young	4170	Jerry Rice	1157	Garrison Hearst	1570
1999	Jeff Garcia	2171	Terrell Owens	723	Charlie Garner	1200
2000	Jeff Garcia	4278	Terrell Owens	1451	Charlie Garner	1142
2001	Jeff Garcia	3538	Terrell Owens	1412	Garrison Hearst	1206
2002	Jeff Garcia	3344	Terrell Owens	1300	Garrison Hearst	972
2003	Jeff Garcia	2704	Terrell Owens	1102	Kevan Barlow	1024
2004	Tim Rattay	2169	Eric Johnson	825	Kevan Barlow	822
2005	Alex Smith	875	Brandon Lloyd	733	Frank Gore	608
2006	Alex Smith	2890	Antonio Bryant	733	Frank Gore	1695

COACHING HISTORY: 1946-1954 Buck Shaw 71-39-4-.640; 1955 Red Strader 4-8-0-.333; 1956-1958 Frank Albert 19-16-1-.542; 1959-1963 Red Hickey 27-27-1-.500; 1963-1967 Jack Christainsen 26-38-3-.410; 1968-1975 Dick Nolan 54-53-5-.504; 1976 Monte Clark 8-6-0-.571; 1977 Ken Meyer 5-9-0-.357; 1978 Pete McCulley 1-8-0-.111; 1978 Fred O'Connor 1-6-0-.143; 1979-1988 Bill Walsh 92-59-1-.609; 1989-1996 George Seifert 98-30-0-.766; 1997-2002 Steve Mariucci 57-39-0-.594; 2003-2004 Dennis Erickson 9-23-0-.281; 2005-present Mike Nolan

SAN FRANCISCO GIANTS
(were New York Giants)

Home City: San Francisco, California
Home Field: Seals Stadium (1958-1959)   Capacity: 22,900 [1958]
     3Com Park (1960-1999)*   Capacity: 63,000 [1999]
     SBC Park (2000-present) **   Capacity: 41,600 [2006]
Origin of Name: The team kept the same nickname when it moved from New York to San Francisco.

Regular Season Record

Season	League	GP	W	L	Pct	GB	R	OR
1958	NL	154	80	74	.519	12	727	698

*-known as Candlestick Park from 1960 to 1995
**-known as Pacific Bell Park from 2000-2003

1959	NL	154	83	71	.539	4	705	613
1960	NL	154	79	75	.513	16	671	631
1961	NL	154	85	69	.552	8	773	655
1962	NL	165	103	62	.624	-	878	690
1963	NL	162	88	74	.543	11	725	641
1964	NL	162	90	72	.556	3	656	587
1965	NL	162	95	67	.586	2	682	593
1966	NL	161	93	68	.578	1.5	675	626
1967	NL	162	91	71	.562	10.5	652	551
1968	NL	162	88	74	.543	9	599	529
1969	NL	162	90	72	.556	3	713	636
1970	NL	162	86	76	.531	16	831	826
1971	NL	162	90	72	.556	-	706	644
1972	NL	155	69	86	.445	26.5	662	649
1973	NL	162	88	74	.543	11	739	702
1974	NL	162	72	90	.444	30	634	723
1975	NL	161	80	81	.497	27.5	659	671
1976	NL	162	74	88	.457	28	595	686
1977	NL	162	75	87	.463	23	673	711
1978	NL	162	89	73	.549	6	613	594
1979	NL	162	71	91	.438	19.5	672	751
1980	NL	161	75	86	.466	17	573	634
1981	NL	111	56	55	.505	NA	427	414
1982	NL	162	87	75	.537	2	673	687
1983	NL	162	79	83	.488	12	687	697
1984	NL	162	66	96	.407	26	682	807
1985	NL	162	62	100	.383	33	556	674
1986	NL	162	83	79	.512	13	698	618
1987	NL	162	90	72	.556	-	783	669
1988	NL	162	83	79	.512	11.5	670	626
1989	NL	162	92	70	.568	-	699	600
1990	NL	162	85	77	.525	6	719	710
1991	NL	162	75	87	.463	19	649	697
1992	NL	162	72	90	.444	26	574	647
1993	NL	162	103	59	.636	1	808	636
1994	NL	115	55	60	.478	3.5	504	500
1995	NL	144	67	77	.465	11	652	776
1996	NL	162	68	94	.420	23	752	862
1997	NL	162	90	72	.556	-	784	790
1998	NL	163	89	74	.546	9.5	845	739
1999	NL	162	86	76	.531	14	872	838
2000	NL	162	97	65	.599	-	925	747
2001	NL	162	90	72	.556	2	799	748
2002	NL	161	95	66	.590	2.5	783	616
2003	NL	161	100	61	.621	-	755	638
2004	NL	162	91	71	.562	2	850	770
2005	NL	162	75	87	.463	7	649	745
2006	NL	161	76	85	.472	11.5	746	790
TOTAL:	49 years	7781	4046	3735		520	34354	33082
AVERAGE:		159	83	76	.520	10.5	701	675

Playoff Record

Season	GP	W	L	R	OR	Result
1962	7	3	4	21	20	Lost World Series to New York.

1971	4	1	3	15	24	Lost NLCS to Pittsburgh.
1987	7	3	4	23	23	Lost NLCS to St. Louis.
1989	9	4	5	44	54	Lost World Series to Oakland.
1997	3	0	3	9	15	Lost Division Semifinal to Florida.
2000	4	1	3	11	13	Lost Division Series to Mets.
2002	17	10	7	91	83	Lost World Series to Anaheim.
2003	4	1	3	16	20	Lost Division Series to Florida.
TOTAL:	55	23	32	230	252	
AVERAGE:	7	3	4	29	32	

Regular Season Individual Leaders

Season	Home Runs		RBI's		Wins	
1958	Willie Mays	29	Willie Mays	96	John Antonelli	16
			Orlando Cepeda	96		
1959	Willie Mays	34	Orlando Cepeda	105	Sam Jones	21
1960	Willie Mays	29	Willie Mays	103	Sam Jones	18
1961	Orlando Cepeda	46	Orlando Cepeda	142	Stu Miller	14
1962	Willie Mays	49	Willie Mays	141	Jack Sanford	24
1963	Willie McCovey	44	Willie Mays	103	Juan Marichal	25
1964	Willie Mays	47	Willie Mays	111	Juan Marichal	21
1965	Willie Mays	52	Willie Mays	112	Juan Marichal	22
1966	Willie Mays	37	Willie Mays	103	Juan Marichal	25
1967	Willie McCovey	31	Jim Ray Hart	99	Mike McCormick	22
1968	Willie McCovey	38	Willie McCovey	105	Juan Marichal	26
1969	Willie McCovey	45	Willie McCovey	126	Juan Marichal	21
1970	Willie McCovey	39	Willie McCovey	126	Gaylord Perry	23
1971	Bobby Bonds	33	Bobby Bonds	102	Juan Marichal	18
1972	Dave Kingman	29	Dave Kingman	83	Ron Bryant	14
1973	Bobby Bonds	39	Bobby Bonds	96	Ron Bryant	24
1974	Bobby Bonds	21	Gary Matthews	82	Mike Caldwell	14
1975	Gary Matthews	12	Bobby Murcer	91	John Montefusco	15
1976	Bobby Murcer	23	Bobby Murcer	90	John Montefusco	16
1977	Willie McCovey	28	Willie McCovey	86	Ed Halicki	16
1978	Jack Clark	25	Jack Clark	98	Vida Blue	18
1979	Mike Ivie	27	Mike Ivie	89	Vida Blue	14
1980	Jack Clark	22	Jack Clark	82	Vida Blue	14
1981	Jack Clark	17	Jack Clark	53	Doyle Alexander	11
1982	Jack Clark	27	Jack Clark	103	Bill Laskey	13
1983	Darrell Evans	30	Jeff Leonard	87	Bill Laskey	13
1984	Chili Davis	21	Jeff Leonard	86	Mike Krukow	11
	Jeff Leonard	21				
1985	Bob Brenley	19	Jeff Leonard	62	Scott Garretts	9
1986	Candy Maldonado	18	Candy Maldonado	85	Mike Krukow	20
1987	Will Clark	35	Will Clark	91	Mike LaCoss	13
1988	Will Clark	29	Will Clark	109	Rick Reuschel	19
1989	Kevin Mitchell	47	Kevin Mitchell	125	Rick Reuschel	17
1990	Kevin Mitchell	35	Matt Williams	122	John Burkett	14
1991	Matt Williams	34	Will Clark	116	Trevor Wilson	13
1992	Matt Williams	20	Will Clark	73	John Burkett	13
1993	Barry Bonds	46	Barry Bonds	123	John Burkett	22
1994	Matt Williams	43	Matt Williams	96	Mark Portugal	10
1995	Barry Bonds	33	Barry Bonds	104	Mark Leiter	10
1996	Barry Bonds	42	Barry Bonds	129	Mark Gardner	12

Regular Season Individual Leaders

Season	Home Runs		RBI's		Wins	
1997	Barry Bonds	40	Jeff Kent	121	Shawn Estes	19
1998	Barry Bonds	37	Jeff Kent	128	Kirk Rueter	16
1999	Barry Bonds	34	Jeff Kent	101	Russ Ortiz	18
2000	Barry Bonds	49	Jeff Kent	125	Livan Hernandez	17
2001	Barry Bonds	73	Barry Bonds	137	Russ Ortiz	17
2002	Barry Bonds	46	Barry Bonds	110	Russ Ortiz	14
					Kirk Rueter	14
2003	Barry Bonds	45	Barry Bonds	90	Jason Schmidt	17
2004	Barry Bonds	45	Barry Bonds	101	Jason Schmidt	18
2005	Pedro Feliz	20	Pedro Feliz	81	Noah Lowry	13
2006	Barry Bonds	26	Pedro Feliz	98	Matt Cain	13

COACHING HISTORY: 1958-1960 Bill Rigney 196-170-.536; 1960 Tom Sheehan 46-50-.479; 1961-1964 Alvin Dark 366-277-.569; 1965-1968 Herman Franks 367-280-.567; 1969-1970 Clyde King 109-97-.529; 1970-1974 Charlie Fox 348-325-.517; 1974-1975 Wes Westrum 118-129-.478; 1976 Bill Rigney 74-88-.457; 1977-1979 Joe Altobelli 245-239-.506; 1979-1980 Dave Bristol 85-98-.464; 1981-1984 Frank Robinson 264-277-.488; 1984 Danny Ozark 24-32-.429; 1985 Jim Davenport 56-88-.389; 1985-1992 Roger Craig 586-566-.509; 1993-2002 Dusty Baker 840-715-.540; 2003-present Felipe Alou

SAN FRANCISCO GOLDEN GATE GALES

Home City: San Francisco, California
Home Stadium: Kezar Stadium
Origin of Name: The name was suggested by the city's famous Golden Gate Bridge. The club was represented by the ADO Club from the Netherlands.

Regular Season Record

Season	League	GP	W	L	T	GF	GA	Pts	Pct
1967	USA	12	5	4	3	25	19	13	.542

Season	Goals		Points		GAA (360 Min)	
1967	Henk Houwaart	9	Henk Houwaart	20	Ton Thie	1.57

COACHING HISTORY: Ernst Happel 5-4-3-.542

SAN FRANCISCO WARRIORS
(were Philadelphia Warriors)
(became Golden State Warriors)

Home City: San Francisco, California

Home Court: Cow Palace (1962-1964)	Capacity: 13,862
Civic Auditorium (1964-1966)	Capacity: 7,500
USF Memorial Gym (1964-1966)	Capacity: 6,000
Cow Palace (1966-1967)	Capacity: 13,862
Civic Auditorium (1966-1967)	Capacity: 7,500
Oakland Coliseum Arena (1966-1967)	Capacity: 15,000
Cow Palace (1967-1971)	Capacity: 14,500

Origin of Name: The team kept the same nickname when they moved to San Francisco from Philadelphia.

Regular Season Record

Season	League	GP	W	L	PPGF	PPGA	Pct	GB
1962-1963	NBA	80	31	49	118.5	120.6	.388	22
1963-1964	NBA	80	48	32	107.7	102.6	.600	-
1964-1965	NBA	80	17	63	105.8	112.0	.213	32
1965-1966	NBA	80	35	45	115.5	118.2	.438	10
1966-1967	NBA	81	44	37	122.4	119.5	.543	-
1967-1968	NBA	82	43	39	117.0	117.6	.524	13
1968-1969	NBA	82	41	41	109.1	110.7	.500	14
1969-1970	NBA	82	30	52	111.1	115.6	.366	18
1970-1971	NBA	82	41	41	107.1	108.5	.500	7
TOTAL:	9 years	729	330	399				116
AVERAGE:		81	37	44	112.7	113.9	.453	13

Playoff Record

Season	GP	W	L	PPGF	PPGA	Result
1963-1964	12	5	7	106.5	105.3	Lost Championship series to Boston.
1966-1967	15	9	6	118.3	117.1	Lost Championship series to Philadelphia.
1967-1968	10	4	6	110.1	115.0	Lost Division Final to Los Angeles.
1968-1969	6	2	4	94.7	105.7	Lost Division Semifinal to Los Angeles.
1970-1971	5	1	4	96.0	113.0	Lost Conference Semifinal to Milwaukee.
TOTAL:	48	21	27			
AVERAGE:	10	4	6	105.1	111.2	

Regular Season Individual Leaders

Season	Field Goal % (min. 70 games)		Points		Points per Game (min. 70 games)	
1962-63	Kenny Sears	.530	W. Chamberlain	3586	W. Chamberlain	44.8
1963-64	W. Chamberlain	.524	W. Chamberlain	2948	W. Chamberlain	36.9
1964-65	Nate Thurmond	.419	W. Chamberlain	1480	Nate Thurmond	16.5
1965-66	Al Attles	.503	Rick Barry	2059	Rick Barry	25.7
1966-67	Jeff Mullins	.458	Rick Barry	2775	Rick Barry	35.6
1967-68	Jeff Mullins	.439	Rudy LaRusso	1726	Rudy LaRusso	21.8
1968-69	Jeff Mullins	.459	Jeff Mullins	1775	Jeff Mullins	22.8
1969-70	Jeff Mullins	.460	Jeff Mullins	1632	Jeff Mullins	22.1
1970-71	Jerry Lucas	.498	Nate Thurmond	1641	Jeff Mullins	20.8

COACHING HISTORY: 1962-1963 Bob Feerick 31-49-.388; 1963-1966 Alex Hannum 100-140-.417; 1966-1968 Bill Sharman 87-76-.534; 1968-1970 George Lee 63-71-.470; 1969-1971 Al Attles 49-63-.438

SAN JOSE EARTHQUAKES
(were known as San Jose Clash from 1996-1999)
(became Houston Dynamo)

Home City: San Jose, California
Home Field: Spartan Stadium (2000-present)   Capacity: 30,578 [2005]
Origin of Name:

Season	League	GP	W	L	T	SOW	GF	GA	Pts
1996	MLS	32	15	17	NA	3	50	50	39
1997	MLS	32	12	20	NA	3	55	59	30
1998	MLS	32	13	19	NA	3	48	60	33
1999	MLS	32	19	13	NA	10	48	49	37

2000	MLS	32	7	17	8	NA	35	50	29
2001	MLS	26	13	7	6	NA	47	29	45
2002	MLS	28	14	11	3	NA	45	35	45
2003	MLS	30	14	7	9	NA	45	35	51
2004	MLS	30	9	10	11	NA	41	35	38
2005	MLS	32	18	4	10	NA	53	31	64
TOTAL:	6 years	178	75	56	47	0	266	215	272
AVERAGE:		30	13	9	8	0	44	36	45

Playoff Record

Season	GP	W	L	T	GF	GA	Result
1996	3	1	2	0	1	4	Lost Quarterfinals to Los Angeles.
2001	6	5	1	0	13	3	**Won MLS Cup.**
2002	2	0	2	0	2	4	Lost Quarterfinals to Columbus.
2003	4	3	1	0	12	8	**Won MLS Cup.**
2004	2	1	1	0	2	3	Lost Conf. Semifinal to Kansas City.
2005	2	0	1	1	2	4	Lost Conf. Semifinal to Los Angeles.
TOTAL:	16	9	6	1	31	22	
AVERAGE:	3	2	1	0	6	4	

Regular Season Individual Leaders

Season	Goals		Points		GAA (min. 5 games)	
1996	Paul Bravo	13	Eric Wynalda	33	Dave Salzwedel	1.31
1997	Ronald Cerritos	12	Ronald Cerritos	34	David Kramer	1.62
1998	Ronald Cerritos	13	Ronald Cerritos	38	David Kramer	1.65
1999	Ronald Cerritos	15	Ronald Cerritos	39	Joe Cannon	1.33
2000	A.T. Conteh	8	A.T. Conteh	19	Joe Cannon	1.49
2001	Ronald Cerritos	11	Ronald Cerritos	28	Joe Cannon	1.09
2002	Ariel Graziani	14	Ariel Graziani	33	Joe Cannon	1.10
2003	Landon Donovan	12	Landon Donovan	30	Pat Onstad	1.04
2004	Brian Ching	12	Brian Ching	28	Jon Conway	0.60
2005	Dwayne De Rosario	9	Dwayne De Rosario	31	Pat Onstad	0.97

COACHING HISTORY: 1996-1997 Laurie Calloway 20-27-.426; 1997-1999 Brian Quinn 35-41-.461; 1999 Jorge Espinoza 4-1-.800

SAN JOSE SHARKS

Home City: Daly City, California (1991-1993)
    San Jose, California (1993-present)
Home Arena: Cow Palace (1991-1993)   Capacity: 10,800 [1992]
    HP Pavilion (1993-present) *   Capacity: 17,496 [2005]
Origin of Name: The name was chosen in a Name the Team Contest.

Regular Season Record

Season	League	GP	W	L	T	OL	SL	GF	GA	Pts
1991-1992	NHL	80	17	58	5	NA	NA	219	359	39
1992-1993	NHL	84	11	71	2	NA	NA	218	414	24
1993-1994	NHL	84	33	35	16	NA	NA	252	265	82
1994-1995	NHL	48	19	25	4	NA	NA	129	161	42
1995-1996	NHL	82	20	55	7	NA	NA	252	357	47

*-known as San Jose Arena from 1993-2001 and Compaq Center from 2001-2003.

1996-1997	NHL	82	27	47	8	NA	NA	211	278	62
1997-1998	NHL	82	34	38	10	NA	NA	210	216	78
1998-1999	NHL	82	31	33	18	NA	NA	196	191	80
1999-2000	NHL	82	35	37	10	7	NA	225	214	87
2000-2001	NHL	82	40	27	12	3	NA	217	192	95
2001-2002	NHL	82	44	27	8	3	NA	248	199	99
2002-2003	NHL	82	28	37	9	8	NA	214	239	73
2003-2004	NHL	82	43	21	12	6	NA	219	183	104
2004-2005	NHL	Season cancelled due to lockout.								
2005-2006	NHL	82	44	27	NA	4	7	266	242	99
TOTAL:	14 years	1116	426	538	121	31	7	3076	3510	1011
AVERAGE:		80	30	38	9	2	0	220	251	72

Playoff Record

Season	GP	W	L	GF	GA	Result
1993-1994	14	7	7	42	53	Lost Conference Semifinal to Toronto.
1994-1995	11	4	7	32	59	Lost Conference Semifinal to Detroit.
1997-1998	6	2	4	12	16	Lost Conference Quarterfinal to Dallas.
1998-1999	7	3	4	17	19	Lost Conference Quarterfinal to Colorado.
1999-2000	12	5	7	27	37	Lost Conference Semifinal to Dallas.
2000-2001	6	2	4	11	16	Lost Conference Quarterfinal to St. Louis.
2001-2002	12	7	5	34	32	Lost Conference Semifinal to Colorado.
2003-2004	17	10	7	38	32	Lost Conference Final to Calgary.
2005-2006	11	6	5	29	29	Lost Conference Semifinal to Edmonton.
TOTAL:	96	46	50	242	293	
AVERAGE:	11	5	6	27	33	

Regular Season Individual Leaders

Season	Goals		Points		Penalty Minutes	
1991-1992	Pat Falloon	25	Pat Falloon	59	Link Gaetz	326
1992-1993	Kelly Kisio	26	Kelly Kisio	78	Jeff Odgers	253
1993-1994	Sergei Makarov	30	Sergei Makarov	68	Jeff Odgers	222
1994-1995	Jeff Friesen	15	Ulf Dahlen	34	Jeff Odgers	117
1995-1996	Owen Nolan	29	Owen Nolan	61	Jeff Odgers	192
1996-1997	Owen Nolan	31	Owen Nolan	63	Andrei Nazarov	222
1997-1998	Jeff Friesen	31	Jeff Friesen	63	Owen Nolan	144
1998-1999	Joe Murphy	25	Jeff Friesen	57	Ronnie Stern	158
1999-2000	Owen Nolan	44	Owen Nolan	84	Ronnie Stern	151
2000-2001	Patrick Marleau	25	Patrick Marleau	52	Bryan Marchment	204
2001-2002	Teemu Selanne	29	Owen Nolan	66	Bryan Marchment	178
2002-2003	Teemu Selanne	28	Teemu Selanne	64	Bryan Marchment	108
	Patrick Marleau	28				
	Marco Sturm	28				
2003-2004	Patrick Marleau	28	Patrick Marleau	57	Scott Parker	101
	J. Cheechoo	28				
2004-2005	Season cancelled due to lockout.					
2005-2006	J. Cheechoo	56	J. Cheechoo	93	Mark Smith	97

COACHING HISTORY: 1991-1993 George Kingston 28-129-7-.192; 1993-1996 Kevin Constantine 55-78-24-.427; 1995-1996 Jim Wiley 17-37-3-.325; 1996-1997 Al Sims 27-47-8-.378; 1997-2003 Darryl Sutter 192-180-60-23-.513; 2002-2003 Cap Raeder 1-0-0-0-1.000; 2002-present Ron Wilson

SASKATCHEWAN ROUGHRIDERS

Home City: Regina, Saskatchewan
Home Stadium: Mosaic Stadium*   Capacity: 27,732 [2006]
Origin of Name: The name was adopted because a contingent of North West Mounted Police officers who played two rugby matches in Winnipeg in 1890 were referred to as "Roughriders" due to their occupation of breaking horses used by the force. The name survived the various primitive early teams and leagues.

Regular Season Record

Season	League	GP	W	L	T	OT	PF	PA	Pts	Pct
1950	CRU	14	7	7	0	NA	207	177	14	.500
1951	CRU	14	8	6	0	NA	277	219	16	.571
1952	CRU	16	3	13	0	NA	216	363	6	.188
1953	CRU	16	8	7	1	NA	243	239	17	.531
1954	CRU	16	10	4	2	NA	239	204	22	.688
1955	CRU	16	10	6	0	NA	270	245	20	.625
1956	CFC	16	10	6	0	NA	353	272	20	.625
1957	CFC	16	3	12	1	NA	276	438	7	.219
1958	CFL	16	7	7	2	NA	320	324	16	.500
1959	CFL	16	1	15	0	NA	212	567	2	.063
1960	CFL	16	2	12	2	NA	205	422	6	.188
1961	CFL	16	5	10	1	NA	211	314	11	.344
1962	CFL	16	8	7	1	NA	268	336	17	.531
1963	CFL	16	7	7	2	NA	223	266	16	.500
1964	CFL	16	9	7	0	NA	330	282	18	.563
1965	CFL	16	8	7	1	NA	276	277	17	.531
1966	CFL	16	9	6	1	NA	351	318	19	.594
1967	CFL	16	12	4	0	NA	346	282	24	.750
1968	CFL	16	12	3	1	NA	345	223	25	.781
1969	CFL	16	13	3	0	NA	392	261	26	.813
1970	CFL	16	14	2	0	NA	369	206	28	.875
1971	CFL	16	9	6	1	NA	347	316	19	.594
1972	CFL	16	8	8	0	NA	330	283	16	.500
1973	CFL	16	10	6	0	NA	360	287	20	.625
1974	CFL	16	9	7	0	NA	305	289	18	.563
1975	CFL	16	10	5	1	NA	373	390	21	.656
1976	CFL	16	11	5	0	NA	427	238	22	.688
1977	CFL	16	8	8	0	NA	330	389	16	.500
1978	CFL	16	4	11	1	NA	330	459	9	.281
1979	CFL	16	2	14	0	NA	194	437	4	.125
1980	CFL	16	2	14	0	NA	284	469	4	.125
1981	CFL	16	9	7	0	NA	431	371	18	.563
1982	CFL	16	6	9	1	NA	427	436	13	.406
1983	CFL	16	5	11	0	NA	360	536	10	.313
1984	CFL	16	6	9	1	NA	348	479	13	.406
1985	CFL	16	5	11	0	NA	320	462	10	.313
1986	CFL	18	6	11	1	NA	382	517	13	.361
1987	CFL	18	5	12	1	NA	364	529	11	.306
1988	CFL	18	11	7	0	NA	525	452	22	.611
1989	CFL	18	9	9	0	NA	547	567	18	.500
1990	CFL	18	9	9	0	NA	557	592	18	.500

*-known as Taylor Field from 1950 to 2005

1991	CFL	18	6	12	0	NA	606	710	12	.333
1992	CFL	18	9	9	0	NA	505	545	18	.500
1993	CFL	18	11	7	0	NA	511	495	22	.611
1994	CFL	18	12	6	0	NA	508	453	24	.667
1995	CFL	18	6	12	0	NA	422	451	12	.333
1996	CFL	18	5	13	0	NA	363	498	10	.278
1997	CFL	18	8	10	0	NA	413	479	16	.444
1998	CFL	18	5	13	0	NA	411	525	10	.278
1999	CFL	18	3	15	0	NA	370	592	6	.167
2000	CFL	18	5	12	1	0	516	626	11	.306
2001	CFL	18	6	12	0	0	308	416	12	.333
2002	CFL	18	8	10	0	2	435	393	18	500
2003	CFL	18	11	7	0	NA	535	430	22	.611
2004	CFL	18	9	9	0	NA	476	444	18	.500
2005	CFL	18	9	9	0	NA	441	433	18	.500
2006	CFL	18	9	9	0	NA	465	434	18	.500
TOTAL:	57 years	950	432	495	23	2	20755	22657	889	
AVERAGE:		17	8	9	0	0	364	397	16	.468

Playoff Record

Season	GP	W	L	T	PF	PA	Result
1950	1	0	1	0	1	24	Lost Division Final to Edmonton.
1951	4	2	2	0	56	59	Lost Grey Cup Final to Ottawa.
1953	2	1	1	0	23	60	Lost Division Final to Winnipeg.
1954	2	0	1	1	25	27	Lost Division Semifinal to Winnipeg.
1955	2	1	1	0	16	24	Lost Division Semifinal to Winnipeg.
1956	5	2	3	0	92	119	Lost Division Final to Edmonton.
1958	2	0	2	0	12	58	Lost Division Semifinal to Edmonton.
1962	2	0	2	0	7	43	Lost Division Semifinal to Calgary.
1963	5	2	3	0	69	110	Lost Division Final to B.C.
1964	2	1	1	0	40	76	Lost Division Semifinal to Calgary.
1965	1	0	1	0	9	15	Lost Division Semifinal to Winnipeg.
1966	3	3	0	0	64	40	**Won Grey Cup.**
1967	5	3	2	0	61	66	Lost Grey Cup Final to Hamilton.
1968	2	0	2	0	12	57	Lost Division Final to Calgary.
1969	3	2	1	0	64	53	Lost Grey Cup Final to Ottawa.
1970	3	1	2	0	36	46	Lost Division Final to Calgary.
1971	3	1	2	0	76	76	Lost Division Final to Calgary.
1972	3	2	1	0	45	43	Lost Grey Cup Final to Hamilton.
1973	2	1	1	0	56	38	Lost Division Final to Edmonton.
1974	2	1	1	0	51	45	Lost Division Final to Edmonton.
1975	2	1	1	0	60	54	Lost Division Final to Edmonton.
1976	2	1	1	0	43	36	Lost Grey Cup Final to Ottawa.
1988	1	0	1	0	18	42	Lost Division Semifinal to B.C.
1989	3	3	0	0	108	87	**Won Grey Cup.**
1990	1	0	1	0	27	43	Lost Division Semifinal to Edmonton.
1992	1	0	1	0	20	22	Lost Division Semifinal to Edmonton.
1993	1	0	1	0	13	51	Lost Division Semifinal to Edmonton.
1994	1	0	1	0	3	36	Lost Division Semifinal to Calgary.
1997	3	2	1	0	87	107	Lost Grey Cup Final to Toronto.
2002	1	0	1	0	14	24	Lost Cross-Over Game to Toronto.
2003	2	1	1	0	60	51	Lost Division Final to Edmonton.
2004	2	1	1	0	39	33	Lost Division Final to B.C.
2005	1	0	1	0	14	30	Lost Cross-Over Game to Montreal.

2006	2	1	1	0	48	66	Lost Division Final to B.C.
TOTAL:	77	33	43	1	1369	1761	
AVERAGE:	2	1	1	0	40	52	

Regular Season Individual Leaders

Season	Passing Yards		Receiving Yards		Rushing Yards	
1950	Jack Hartman	1217	Matt Anthony	390	Sammy Pierce	502
1951	Glenn Dobbs	2313	Jack Russell	818	Ken Charlton	356
1952	Glenn Dobbs	1977	Holland Aplin	810	Sully Glasser	267
1953	Frank Filchock	925	Mac Speedie	817	Bobby Marlow	563
1954	Frank Tripucka	2003	Ken Carpenter	523	Bobby Marlow	882
1955	Frank Tripucka	2306	Ken Carpenter	678	Bobby Marlow	690
1956	Frank Tripucka	3274	Ken Carpenter	784	Ken Carpenter	727
1957	Frank Tripucka	2589	Ron Dundas	625	Bobby Marlow	749
1958	Frank Tripucka	2766	Jack Hill	1065	Cookie Gilchrist	1254
1959	Don Allard	1170	Vernon Vaughn	511	Ferd Burket	423
1960	Bob Ptacek	1469	Bob Renn	695	Ferd Burket	544
1961	Dave Grosz	1341	Jack Gotta	618	Ferd Burket	583
1962	Bob Ptacek	2317	Jack Gotta	779	Ray Purdin	809
1963	Ron Lancaster	1727	Jack Gotta	478	George Reed	751
1964	Ron Lancaster	2257	Hugh Campbell	1000	Ed Buchanan	1390
1965	Ron Lancaster	2586	Hugh Campbell	1329	George Reed	1768
1966	Ron Lancaster	2976	Hugh Campbell	1109	George Reed	1409
1967	Ron Lancaster	2809	Hugh Campbell	710	George Reed	1471
1968	Ron Lancaster	2969	Gord Barwell	783	George Reed	1222
1969	Ron Lancaster	3104	Bobby Thompson	891	George Reed	1353
1970	Ron Lancaster	2779	Silas McKinnie	682	George Reed	821
1971	Ron Lancaster	2759	Bobby Thompson	774	George Reed	1146
1972	Ron Lancaster	2942	Bobby Thompson	821	George Reed	1069
1973	Ron Lancaster	3767	Tom Campana	910	George Reed	1193
1974	Ron Lancaster	2873	Bobby Thompson	711	George Reed	1447
1975	Ron Lancaster	3545	Rhett Dawson	1191	George Reed	1454
1976	Ron Lancaster	3869	Rhett Dawson	996	Steve Molnar	822
1977	Ron Lancaster	3072	Molly McGee	548	Molly McGee	600
1978	Ron Lancaster	2677	Mike Strickland	243	Mike Strickland	1306
1979	Danny Sanders	1024	Mike Strickland	406	Mike Strickland	770
1980	John Hufnagel	1576	Steve Mazurak	537	Lester Brown	590
1981	John Hufnagel	2743	Joey Walters	1715	Lester Brown	804
1982	Joe Adams	3312	Joey Walters	1692	Mike Washington	614
1983	John Hufnagel	1649	Chris DeFrance	1165	Mike Washington	639
1984	Joe Paopao	3270	Craig Ellis	871	Craig Ellis	690
1985	Joe Paopao	3420	Craig Ellis	977	Craig Ellis	569
1986	Joe Paopao	2647	Ray Elgaard	1003	Bobby Johnson	869
1987	Tom Burgess	1691	Ray Elgaard	865	Walter Bender	525
1988	Tom Burgess	2575	Ray Elgaard	1290	Tim McCray	751
1989	Kent Austin	2650	Don Narcisse	1419	Tim McCray	1285
1990	Kent Austin	4604	Ray Elgaard	1494	Milson Jones	765
1991	Kent Austin	4137	Jeff Fairholm	1239	Lucius Floyd	677
1992	Kent Austin	6225	Ray Elgaard	1444	Lucius Floyd	373
1993	Kent Austin	5754	Ray Elgaard	1393	Mike Saunders	683
1994	Tom Burgess	3442	Ray Elgaard	1100	Mike Saunders	1205
1995	Warren Jones	2958	Don Narcisse	1288	Darren Joseph	590
1996	Warren Jones	1372	Curtis Mayfield	963	Robert Mimbs	1403
1997	Reggie Slack	2423	Dan Farthing	959	Mike Saunders	586

Season	Passing Yards		Receiving Yards		Rushing Yards	
1998	Reggie Slack	3721	Don Narcisse	1215	Mike Saunders	897
1999	Steve Sarkisian	2290	Curtis Mayfield	863	Mike Saunders	971
2000	Henry Burris	4647	Curtis Marsh	1560	Darren Davis	1024
2001	Marvin Graves	1534	D. Bendross	674	Darren Davis	1243
2002	Nealon Greene	2621	D. Armstrong	1104	Sedrick Shaw	950
2003	Nealon Greene	3398	Matt Dominguez	1071	Nealon Greene	723
2004	Henry Burris	4267	Travis Moore	1025	Kenton Keith	1154
2005	Marcus Crandell	2295	Elijah Thurmon	1048	Kenton Keith	911
2006	Kerry Joseph	3489	Matt Dominguez	1169	Kenton Keith	1037

COACHING HISTORY: 1950 Fred Grant 7-7-0-.500; 1951 Harry Smith 8-6-0-.571; 1952 Glenn Dobbs 3-13-0-.188; 1953-1957 Frankie Filchock 41-35-4-.538; 1958-1959 George Terlep 7-16-2-.320; 1959 Frank Tripucka 1-6-0-.143; 1960 Ken Carpenter 2-12-2-.188; 1961-1962 Steve Owen 13-17-2-.438; 1963-1964 Bob Shaw 16-14-2-.531; 1965-1970 Eagle Keys 68-25-3-.724; 1971-1972 Dave Skrien 17-14-1-.547; 1973-1976 John Payne 40-23-1-.633; 1977-1978 Jim Eddy 8-14-0-.364; 1978 Walt Posadowski 4-5-1-.450; 1979-1980 Ron Lancaster 4-28-0-.125; 1981-1983 Joe Faragalli 16-21-1-.434; 1983-1984 Rueben Berry 10-15-1-.404; 1985-1986 Jack Gotta 11-22-1-.338; 1987-1991 John Gregory 35-43-1-.449; 1991-1993 Don Matthews 25-22-0-.532; 1994-1995 Ray Jauch 18-18-0-.500; 1996-1998 Jim Daley 18-36-0-.333; 1999 Cal Murphy 3-15-0-.167; 2000-present Danny Barrett

SASKATOON CRESCENTS
(became Moose Jaw Orphans mid way through the 1921-1922 season)

Home City: Saskatoon, Saskatchewan
Home Arena: Saskatoon Arena
Origin of Name: Were known as Saskatoon Sheiks the first two seasons.

Regular Season Record

Season	League	GP	W	L	T	GF	GA	Pts	Pct
1921-1922	WCHL	14	4	10	0	43	77	8	.286
1922-1923	WCHL	30	8	20	2	91	125	18	.300
1923-1924	WCHL	30	15	12	3	91	73	33	.550
1924-1925	WCHL	28	16	11	1	102	75	33	.589
1925-1926	WHL	30	18	11	1	93	64	37	.617
TOTAL:	5 years	132	61	64	7	420	414	129	
AVERAGE:		26	12	13	1	84	83	26	.489

Playoff Record

Season	GP	W	L	T	GF	GA	Result
1924-1925	2	0	1	1	4	6	Lost WCHL playoff to Victoria.
1925-1926	2	0	1	1	3	4	Lost WHL playoff to Victoria.
TOTAL:	4	0	2	2	7	10	
AVERAGE:	2	0	1	1	4	5	

Regular Season Individual Leaders

Season	Goals		Points		GAA	
1921-1922	Duke Dutkowski	12	Duke Dutkowski	12	Sam Hebert	5.70
1922-1923	Newsy Lalonde	29	Newsy Lalonde	29	Sam Hebert	4.17
					Tom Murray	4.17
1923-1924	Bill Cook	26	Bill Cook	26	G. Hainsworth	2.43
1924-1925	Bill Cook	21	Bill Cook	21	G. Hainsworth	2.68
1925-1926	Bill Cook	31	Bill Cook	31	G. Hainsworth	2.13

COACHING HISTORY: 1921-1922 Bob Pinder 4-10-0-.286; 1922-1926 Newsy Lalonde 57-54-7-.513

SEATTLE MARINERS

Home City: Seattle, Washington
Home Field: The Kingdome (1977-1999)   Capacity: 59,084 [1998]
          SAFECO Field (1999-present)   Capacity: 47,447 [2006]
Origin of Name: The name was chosen in a Name the Team Contest and was adopted to honor the nautical tradition of the area.

Regular Season Record

Season	League	GP	W	L	Pct	GB	R	OR
1977	AL	162	64	98	.395	38	624	855
1978	AL	160	56	104	.350	35	614	834
1979	AL	162	67	95	.414	21	711	820
1980	AL	162	59	103	.364	38	610	793
1981	AL	109	44	65	.404	NA	426	521
1982	AL	162	76	86	.469	17	651	712
1983	AL	162	60	102	.370	39	558	740
1984	AL	162	74	88	.457	10	682	774
1985	AL	162	74	88	.457	17	719	818
1986	AL	162	67	95	.414	25	718	835
1987	AL	162	78	84	.481	7	760	801
1988	AL	161	68	93	.422	35.5	664	744
1989	AL	162	73	89	.451	26	694	728
1990	AL	162	77	85	.475	26	640	680
1991	AL	162	83	79	.512	12	702	674
1992	AL	162	64	98	.395	32	679	799
1993	AL	162	82	80	.506	12	734	731
1994	AL	112	49	63	.438	2	569	616
1995	AL	144	78	66	.542	-	796	708
1996	AL	161	85	76	.528	4.5	993	895
1997	AL	162	90	72	.556	-	925	833
1998	AL	161	76	85	.472	11.5	859	855
1999	AL	162	79	83	.488	16	859	905
2000	AL	162	91	71	.562	.5	907	780
2001	AL	162	116	46	.716	-	928	627
2002	AL	162	93	69	.574	10	814	699
2003	AL	162	93	69	.574	3	795	637
2004	AL	162	63	99	.389	29	698	823
2005	AL	162	69	93	.426	26	699	751
2006	AL	162	78	84	.481	15	756	792
TOTAL:	30 years	4734	2226	2508		508	21784	22780
AVERAGE:		158	74	84	.470	17	726	759

Playoff Record

Season	GP	W	L	R	OR	Result
1995	11	5	6	47	56	Lost ALCS to Cleveland.
1997	4	1	3	11	23	Lost Division Semifinal to Baltimore.
2000	9	5	4	32	38	Lost ALCS to New York Yankees.
2001	10	4	6	38	51	Lost ALCS to New York Yankees.
TOTAL:	34	15	19	128	168	
AVERAGE:	9	4	5	32	42	

Regular Season Individual Leaders

Season	Home Runs		RBI's		Wins	
1977	Lee Stanton	27	Dan Meyer	90	Glenn Abbott	12
			Lee Stanton	90		
1978	Leon Roberts	22	Leon Roberts	92	Enrique Romo	11
1979	Willie Horton	29	Willie Horton	106	Mike Parrott	14
1980	Tom Paciorek	15	Bruce Bochte	78	Glenn Abbott	12
1981	Richie Zisk	16	Tom Paciorek	66	Floyd Bannister	9
1982	Richie Zisk	21	Al Cowens	78	Bill Caudill	12
					Floyd Bannister	12
1983	Pat Putnam	19	Pat Putnam	67	Matt Young	11
1984	Alvin Davis	27	Alvin Davis	116	Mark Langston	17
1985	Gorman Thomas	32	Phil Bradley	88	Mike Moore	17
1986	Jim Presley	27	Jim Presley	107	Mark Langston	12
1987	Alvin Davis	29	Alvin Davis	100	Mark Langston	19
1988	Steve Balboni	21	Alvin Davis	69	Mark Langston	15
1989	Jeffrey Leonard	24	Alvin Davis	95	Scott Bankhead	14
1990	Ken Griffey Jr.	22	Ken Griffey Jr.	80	Erik Hanson	18
1991	Jay Buhner	27	Ken Griffey Jr.	100	Brian Holman	13
					Randy Johnson	13
1992	Ken Griffey Jr.	27	Ken Griffey Jr.	103	Dave Fleming	17
1993	Ken Griffey Jr.	45	Ken Griffey Jr.	109	Randy Johnson	19
1994	Ken Griffey Jr.	40	Ken Griffey Jr.	90	Randy Johnson	13
1995	Jay Buhner	40	Jay Buhner	121	Randy Johnson	18
1996	Ken Griffey Jr.	49	Ken Griffey Jr.	140	Jamie Moyer	13
					Sterling Hitchcock	13
1997	Ken Griffey Jr.	56	Ken Griffey Jr.	147	Randy Johnson	20
1998	Ken Griffey Jr.	56	Ken Griffey Jr.	146	Jamie Moyer	15
1999	Ken Griffey Jr.	48	Ken Griffey Jr.	134	F. Garcia	17
2000	Alex Rodriguez	41	Edgar Martinez	145	Aaron Sele	17
2001	Bret Boone	37	Bret Boone	141	Jamie Moyer	20
2002	Mike Cameron	25	Bret Boone	107	Freddy Garcia	16
2003	Bret Boone	35	Bret Boone	117	Jamie Moyer	21
2004	Bret Boone	24	Bret Boone	83	Ron Villone	8
2005	Richie Sexson	39	Richie Sexson	121	Jamie Moyer	13
2006	Richie Sexson	34	Raul Ibanez	123	Felix Hernandez	12

COACHING HISTORY: 1977-1980 Darrell Johnson 226-362-.384; 1980-1981 Maury Wills 26-56-.317; 1981-1983 Rene Lachemann 140-180-.438; 1983-1984 Del Crandall 93-131-.415; 1984-1986 Chuck Cottier 98-119-.452; 1986 Marty Martinez 0-1-.000; 1986-1988 Dick Williams 159-192-.453; 1988 Jimmy Snyder 45-60-.429; 1989-1991 Jim Lefebvre 233-253-.479; 1992 Bill Plummer 64-98-.395; 1993-2002 Lou Piniella 839-711-.541; 2003-2004 Bob Melvin 156-168-.481; 2005-present Mike Hargrove

SEATTLE METROPOLITANS

Home City: Seattle, Washington
Home Arena: Seattle Arena
Origin of Name:

Regular Season Record

Season	League	GP	W	L	T	GF	GA	Pts	Pct
1915-1916	PCHA	18	9	9	0	68	67	18	.500
1916-1917	PCHA	24	16	8	0	125	80	32	.667

Season	League	GP	W	L	T	GF	GA		Pct
1917-1918	PCHA	18	11	7	0	67	65	22	.611
1918-1919	PCHA	20	11	9	0	66	46	22	.550
1919-1920	PCHA	22	12	10	0	59	55	24	.545
1920-1921	PCHA	24	12	11	1	77	68	25	.521
1921-1922	PCHA	24	12	11	1	65	64	25	.521
1922-1923	PCHA	30	15	15	0	100	106	30	.500
1923-1924	PCHA	30	14	16	0	84	99	28	.467
TOTAL:	9 years	210	112	96	2	711	650	226	
AVERAGE:		23	12	11	0	79	72	24	.538

Playoff Record

Season	GP	W	L	T	GF	GA	Result
1916-1917	4	3	1	0	23	11	**Won Stanley Cup.**
1917-1918	2	0	1	1	2	3	Lost PCHA playoff to Vancouver.
1918-1919	7	3	3	1	26	15	Stanley Cup Final canceled.
1919-1920	7	3	4	0	18	18	Lost Stanley Cup Final to Ottawa.
1920-1921	2	0	2	0	2	13	Lost PCHA playoff to Vancouver.
1921-1922	2	0	2	0	0	2	Lost PCHA playoff to Vancouver.
1923-1924	2	0	1	1	3	4	Lost PCHA playoff to Vancouver.
TOTAL:	26	9	14	3	74	66	
AVERAGE:	4	1	2	1	11	9	

Regular Season Individual Leaders

Season	Goals		Points		GAA	
1915-1916	Bernie Morris	23	Bernie Morris	23	Harry Holmes	3.72
1916-1917	Bernie Morris	37	Bernie Morris	37	Harry Holmes	3.33
1917-1918	Gordon Roberts	20	Gordon Roberts	20	Norm Fowler	3.61
	Bernie Morris	20	Bernie Morris	20		
1918-1919	Bernie Morris	22	Bernie Morris	22	Harry Holmes	2.30
1919-1920	Frank Foyston	26	Frank Foyston	26	Harry Holmes	2.50
1920-1921	Frank Foyston	24	Frank Foyston	24	Harry Holmes	2.83
1921-1922	Frank Foyston	16	Frank Foyston	16	Harry Holmes	2.67
	Jim Riley	16	Jim Riley	16		
1922-1923	Jim Riley	22	Jim Riley	22	Harry Holmes	3.53
1923-1924	Frank Foyston	19	Frank Foyston	19	Harry Holmes	3.30

COACHING HISTORY: 1915-1916 Not Available; 1916-1924 Pete Muldoon 103-87-2-.542

SEATTLE PILOTS
(became Milwaukee Brewers)

Home City: Seattle, Washington
Home Field: Sick's Stadium   Capacity: 25,420 [1969]
Origin of Name: The name was chosen in a Name the Team Contest.

Regular Season Record

Season	League	GP	W	L	Pct	GB	R	OR
1969	AL	162	64	98	.395	33	639	799

Regular Season Individual Leaders

Season	Home Runs		RBI's		Wins	
1969	Don Mincher	25	Tommy Davis	80	Gene Brabender	13

COACHING HISTORY: Joseph Schultz 64-98-.395

SEATTLE SEAHAWKS

Home City: Seattle, Washington
Home Stadium: The Kingdome (1976-1999)   Capacity: 66,400 [1999]
    Husky Stadium (1994, 2000-2001)   Capacity: 72,500 [2000]
    Qwest Field (2002-present)*   Capacity: 67,000 [2005]
Origin of Name: The name was chosen in a Name the Team Contest.

Regular Season Record

Season	League	GP	W	L	T	PF	PA	Pct
1976	NFL	14	2	12	0	229	429	.143
1977	NFL	14	5	9	0	282	373	.357
1978	NFL	16	9	7	0	345	358	.563
1979	NFL	16	9	7	0	378	372	.563
1980	NFL	16	4	12	0	291	408	.250
1981	NFL	16	6	10	0	322	388	.375
1982	NFL	9	4	5	0	127	147	.444
1983	NFL	16	9	7	0	403	397	.562
1984	NFL	16	12	4	0	418	282	.750
1985	NFL	16	8	8	0	349	303	.500
1986	NFL	16	10	6	0	366	293	.625
1987	NFL	15	9	6	0	371	314	.600
1988	NFL	16	9	7	0	339	329	.563
1989	NFL	16	7	9	0	241	327	.438
1990	NFL	16	9	7	0	306	286	.563
1991	NFL	16	7	9	0	276	261	.438
1992	NFL	16	2	14	0	140	312	.125
1993	NFL	16	6	10	0	280	314	.375
1994	NFL	16	6	10	0	287	323	.375
1995	NFL	16	8	8	0	363	366	.500
1996	NFL	16	7	9	0	317	376	.438
1997	NFL	16	8	8	0	365	362	.500
1998	NFL	16	8	8	0	372	310	.500
1999	NFL	16	9	7	0	338	298	.563
2000	NFL	16	6	10	0	320	405	.375
2001	NFL	16	9	7	0	301	324	.563
2002	NFL	16	7	9	0	355	369	.438
2003	NFL	16	10	6	0	404	327	.625
2004	NFL	16	9	7	0	371	373	.563
2005	NFL	16	13	3	0	452	271	.812
2006	NFL	16	9	7	0	335	341	.563
TOTAL:	31 years	484	236	248	0	10043	10338	
AVERAGE:		16	8	8	0	324	333	.488

Playoff Record

Season	GP	W	L	PF	PA	Result
1983	3	2	1	72	57	Lost AFC Championship to Raiders.
1984	2	1	1	23	38	Lost Divisional playoff to Miami.
1987	1	0	1	20	23	Lost 1st Round playoff to Houston.
1988	1	0	1	13	23	Lost Divisional playoff to Cincinnati.
1999	1	0	1	17	20	Lost Wild Card Game to Miami.
2003	1	0	1	27	33	Lost Wild Card Game to Green Bay.

*-known as Seahawks Stadium 2002-2003.

2004	1	0	1	20	27	Lost Wild Card Game to St. Louis.
2005	3	2	1	64	45	Lost Super Bowl to Pittsburgh.
2006	2	1	1	45	47	Lost Divisional playoff to Chicago.
TOTAL:	15	6	9	301	313	
AVERAGE:	2	1	1	33	35	

Regular Season Individual Leaders

Season	Passing Yards		Receiving Yards		Rushing Yards	
1976	Jim Zorn	2571	Steve Largent	705	Sherman Smith	537
1977	Jim Zorn	1687	Steve Largent	643	Sherman Smith	763
1978	Jim Zorn	3283	Steve Largent	1168	Sherman Smith	805
1979	Jim Zorn	3661	Steve Largent	1237	Sherman Smith	775
1980	Jim Zorn	3346	Steve Largent	1064	Jim Jodat	632
1981	Jim Zorn	2788	Steve Largent	1224	Theotis Brown	583
1982	Jim Zorn	1540	Steve Largent	493	Sherman Smith	202
1983	Dave Krieg	2139	Steve Largent	1074	Curt Warner	1449
1984	Dave Krieg	3671	Steve Largent	1164	David Hughes	327
1985	Dave Krieg	3602	Steve Largent	1287	Curt Warner	1094
1986	Dave Krieg	2921	Steve Largent	1070	Curt Warner	1481
1987	Dave Krieg	2131	Steve Largent	912	Curt Warner	985
1988	Dave Krieg	1741	Brian Blades	682	Curt Warner	1025
1989	Dave Krieg	3309	Brian Blades	1063	Curt Warner	631
1990	Dave Krieg	3194	Tommy Kane	776	Derrick Fenner	859
1991	Dave Krieg	2080	Brian Blades	1003	John Williams	741
1992	Stan Gelbaugh	1307	John Williams	556	Chris Warren	1017
1993	Rick Mirer	2833	Brian Blades	945	Chris Warren	1072
1994	Rick Mirer	2151	Brian Blades	1086	Chris Warren	1545
1995	Rick Mirer	2564	Joey Galloway	1039	Chris Warren	1346
1996	John Friesz	1629	Joey Galloway	987	Chris Warren	855
1997	Warren Moon	3678	Joey Galloway	1049	Chris Warren	847
1998	Warren Moon	1632	Joey Galloway	1047	Ricky Watters	1239
1999	Jon Kitna	3346	Sean Dawkins	992	Ricky Watters	1210
2000	Jon Kitna	2658	Sean Dawkins	731	Ricky Watters	1242
2001	Matt Hasselbeck	2023	Darrell Jackson	1081	Shaun Alexander	1318
2002	Matt Hasselbeck	3075	Koren Robinson	1240	Shaun Alexander	1175
2003	Matt Hasselbeck	3841	Darrell Jackson	1137	Shaun Alexander	1435
2004	Matt Hasselbeck	3382	Darrell Jackson	1199	Shaun Alexander	1696
2005	Matt Hasselbeck	3459	Bobby Engram	778	Shaun Alexander	1880
2006	Matt Hasselbeck	2442	Darrell Jackson	956	Shaun Alexander	896

COACHING HISTORY: 1976-1982 Jack Patera 35-59-0-.372; 1982 Mike McCormack 4-3-0-.571; 1983-1991 Chuck Knox 35-108-0-.245; 1992-1994 Tom Flores 14-34-0-.292; 1995-1998 Dennis Erickson 31-33-0-.484; 1999-present Mike Holmgren

SEATTLE SOUNDERS

Home City: Seattle, Washington
Home Stadium: Memorial Stadium (1974-1975)   Capacity: 18,000 [1975]
             Seattle Kingdome (1976-1983)   Capacity: 64,752 [1983]
Origin of Name: The name was chosen in a Name the Team Contest and suggested by the fact Seattle is on Puget Sound.

Regular Season Record

Season	League	GP	W	L	T	GF	GA	BP	Pts	Pct
1974	NASL	20	10	7	3	37	17	32	101	.561

1975	NASL	22	15	7	-	42	28	39	129	.652
1976	NASL	24	14	10	-	40	31	39	123	.569
1977	NASL	26	14	12	-	43	34	39	123	.526
1978	NASL	30	15	15	-	50	45	48	138	.511
1979	NASL	30	13	17	-	58	52	47	125	.463
1980	NASL	32	25	7	-	74	31	57	207	.719
1981	NASL	32	15	17	-	60	62	51	137	.285
1982	NASL	32	18	14	-	64	74	57	163	.340
1983	NASL	30	12	18	-	62	61	51	119	.264
TOTAL:	10 years	278	151	124	3	530	435	460	1365	
AVERAGE:		28	15	13	0	53	44	46	137	.445

Playoff Record

Season	GP	W	L	GF	GA	Result
1975	1	0	1	1	2	Lost Quarterfinal game to Portland.
1976	2	1	1	1	3	Lost Division Final to Minnesota.
1977	6	5	1	10	4	Lost Championship series to New York.
1978	1	0	1	2	5	Lost 1st Round series to New York.
1980	5	3	2	10	7	Lost 2nd Round series to Los Angeles.
1981	3	1	2	6	6	Lost 1st Round series to Chicago.
1982	7	4	3	14	12	Lost Preliminary series to New York.
TOTAL:	25	14	11	44	39	
AVERAGE:	4	2	2	6	6	

Regular Season Individual Leaders

Season	Goals		Points		GAA (360 Min)	
1974	Dave Butler	10	John Rowlands	28	Barry Watling	0.80
	John Rowlands	10				
1975	John Rowlands	10	John Rowlands	25	Barry Watling	1.15
1976	Gordon Wallace	12	Gordon Wallace	28	Tony Chursky	0.91
1977	Micky Cave	12	Micky Cave	30	Tony Chursky	1.27
1978	Micky Cave	13	Micky Cave	32	Tony Chursky	1.41
1979	Derek Smethurst	13	Derek Smethurst	28	Mike Ivanow	1.39
1980	Roger Davies	25	Roger Davies	61	Jack Brand	0.91
1981	Kevin Bond	16	Kevin Bond	36	Jack Brand	1.60
1982	Peter Ward	18	Peter Ward	49	Paul Hammond	1.29
1983	Peter Ward	13	Peter Ward	34		

COACHING HISTORY: 1974-1976 John Best 39-24-3-.594; 1977-1979 Jim Gabriel 42-44-.499; 1980-1982 Alan Hinton 58-38; 1983 Laurie Calloway 12-18

SEATTLE STORM

Home City: Seattle, Washington
Home Court: Key Arena at Seattle Center   Capacity: 17,072 [2005]
Origin of Name: The name was created by NBA Creative Services in co-operation with the team.

Regular Season Record

Season	League	GP	W	L	PPGF	PPGA	Pct	GB
2000	WNBA	32	6	26	56.9	67.8	.188	22
2001	WNBA	32	10	22	60.0	64.0	.313	18
2002	WNBA	32	17	15	68.4	65.7	.531	8
2003	WNBA	34	18	16	70.2	66.9	.529	6
2004	WNBA	34	20	14	71.7	66.6	.588	5

2005	WNBA	34	20	14	73.5	70.8	.588	5
2006	WNBA	34	18	16	72.3	72.7	.529	7
TOTAL:	7 years	232	109	123				71
AVERAGE:		33	16	17	67.7	67.8	.470	10

Playoff Record

Season	GP	W	L	PPGF	PPGA	Result
2002	2	0	2	60.0	73.5	Lost Conference semifinal to L.A.
2004	8	6	2	69.9	61.9	**Won WNBA championship.**
2005	3	1	2	65.7	69.7	Lost Conference semifinal to Houston.
2006	3	1	2	72.3	72.7	Lost Conference semifinal to L.A.
TOTAL:	16	8	8			
AVERAGE:	4	2	2	68.3	66.8	

Regular Season Individual Leaders

Season	Field Goal % (min. 20 games)		Free Throw %		Points per Game (min. 20 games)	
2000	C. Sampson	.468	C. Sampson	.893	Edna Campbell	13.9
2001	Simone Edwards	.479	K. Vodichkova	.864	Lauren Jackson	15.2
2002	K. Vodichkova	.465	Sue Bird	.911	Lauren Jackson	17.2
2003	Lauren Jackson	.483	Sue Bird	.884	Lauren Jackson	21.2
2004	Lauren Jackson	.478	Sue Bird	.859	Lauren Jackson	20.5
2005	Simone Edwards	.585	Betty Lennox	.874	Lauren Jackson	17.6
2006	Lauren Jackson	.535	Lauren Jackson	.899	Lauren Jackson	19.5

COACHING HISTORY: 2000-2002 Lin Dunn 33-63-.344; 2003-present Anne Donovan

SEATTLE SUPERSONICS

Home City: Seattle, Washington

Home Court: Seattle Center Coliseum (1967-1978)	Capacity: 14,098 [1978]
Kingdome (1978-1985)	Capacity: 40,192 [1985]
The Coliseum (1985-1995)	Capacity: 14,250 [1993]
Tacoma Dome (1994-1995)	Capacity: 19,000 [1994]
Key Arena at Seattle Center (1995-present)	Capacity: 17,072 [2006]

Origin of Name: The name was chosen in a Name the Team Contest.

Regular Season Record

Season	League	GP	W	L	PPGF	PPGA	Pct	GB
1967-1968	NBA	82	23	59	118.7	125.1	.280	33
1968-1969	NBA	82	30	52	112.1	116.6	.366	25
1969-1970	NBA	82	36	46	116.9	119.5	.439	12
1970-1971	NBA	82	38	44	115.0	117.0	.463	10
1971-1972	NBA	82	47	35	109.2	108.8	.573	22
1972-1973	NBA	82	26	56	103.7	109.6	.317	34
1973-1974	NBA	82	36	46	107.0	109.5	.439	11
1974-1975	NBA	82	43	39	103.1	103.1	.524	5
1975-1976	NBA	82	43	39	106.4	106.7	.524	16
1976-1977	NBA	82	40	42	104.0	105.5	.488	13
1977-1978	NBA	82	47	35	104.5	102.9	.573	11
1978-1979	NBA	82	52	30	106.6	103.9	.634	-
1979-1980	NBA	82	56	26	108.5	103.8	.683	4
1980-1981	NBA	82	34	48	104.0	105.7	.415	23
1981-1982	NBA	82	52	30	107.3	103.1	.634	5
1982-1983	NBA	82	48	34	110.0	106.8	.585	10

1983-1984	NBA	82	42	40	108.1	108.3	.512	12
1984-1985	NBA	82	31	51	102.1	107.6	.378	31
1985-1986	NBA	82	31	51	104.4	104.5	.378	31
1986-1987	NBA	82	39	43	113.7	113.3	.476	26
1987-1988	NBA	82	44	38	111.4	109.3	.537	18
1988-1989	NBA	82	47	35	112.1	109.2	.573	10
1989-1990	NBA	82	41	41	106.9	105.9	.500	22
1990-1991	NBA	82	41	41	106.6	105.4	.500	22
1991-1992	NBA	82	47	35	106.5	104.7	.573	10
1992-1993	NBA	82	55	27	108.3	101.3	.671	7
1993-1994	NBA	82	63	19	105.9	96.9	.768	-
1994-1995	NBA	82	57	25	110.4	102.2	.695	2
1995-1996	NBA	82	64	18	104.5	96.7	.780	-
1996-1997	NBA	82	57	25	100.9	93.2	.695	-
1997-1998	NBA	82	61	21	100.6	93.4	.744	-
1998-1999	NBA	50	25	25	94.9	95.9	.500	10
1999-2000	NBA	82	45	37	99.1	98.1	.549	22
2000-2001	NBA	82	44	38	97.3	97.3	.537	12
2001-2002	NBA	82	45	37	97.7	94.7	.549	16
2002-2003	NBA	82	40	42	92.1	92.3	.488	19
2003-2004	NBA	82	37	45	97.1	97.8	.451	19
2004-2005	NBA	82	52	30	98.9	96.6	.634	-
2005-2006	NBA	82	35	47	102.6	105.6	.427	9
TOTAL:	39 years	3166	1694	1472				532
AVERAGE:		81	43	38	105.7	104.6	.535	14

Playoff Record

Season	GP	W	L	PPGF	PPGA	Result
1974-1975	9	4	5	99.4	104.7	Lost Conference Semifinal to Golden Bay.
1975-1976	6	2	4	107.3	113.2	Lost Conference Semifinal to Phoenix.
1977-1978	22	13	9	102.9	102.5	Lost Championship series to Washington.
1978-1979	17	12	5	104.6	102.1	**Won NBA Championship.**
1979-1980	15	7	8	102.2	103.0	Lost Conference Final to Los Angeles.
1981-1982	8	3	5	99.5	97.3	Lost Conference Semifinal to San Antonio.
1982-1983	2	0	2	96.5	106.5	Lost 1st Round series to Portland.
1983-1984	5	2	3	97.0	97.2	Lost 1st Round series to Dallas.
1986-1987	14	7	7	110.1	112.1	Lost Conference Final to Lakers.
1987-1988	5	2	3	114.2	114.8	Lost 1st Round series to Denver.
1988-1989	8	3	5	102.0	107.1	Lost Conference Semifinal to Lakers.
1990-1991	5	2	3	103.6	106.4	Lost 1st Round series to Portland.
1991-1992	9	4	5	105.6	108.6	Lost Conference Semifinal to Utah.
1992-1993	18	10	8	105.8	104.3	Lost Conference Final to Phoenix.
1993-1994	5	2	3	95.0	94.2	Lost 1st Round series to Denver.
1994-1995	4	1	3	97.3	93.5	Lost 1st Round series to Lakers.
1995-1996	21	13	8	94.0	92.7	Lost Championship series to Chicago.
1996-1997	12	6	6	105.1	100.6	Lost Conference Semifinal to Houston.
1997-1998	10	4	6	95.2	97.6	Lost Conference Semifinal to Lakers.
1999-2000	5	2	3	95.2	97.6	Lost 1st Round Series to Utah.
2001-2002	5	2	3	86.2	96.4	Lost 1st Round series to San Antonio.
2004-2005	11	6	5	98.5	100.3	Lost Conference Semifinal to San Antonio.
TOTAL:	216	107	109			
AVERAGE:	10	5	5	101.5	102.2	

Season	Field Goal % (min. 70 games)		Points		Points per Game (min. 70 games)	
1967-68	Bob Rule	.489	Walt Hazzard	1894	Walt Hazzard	23.9
1968-69	Bob Rule	.469	Bob Rule	1965	Bob Rule	24.0
1969-70	Dick Snyder	.531	Bob Rule	1965	Bob Rule	24.6
1970-71	Dick Snyder	.531	Dick Snyder	1592	Lenny Wilkens	19.8
1971-72	Dick Snyder	.529	S. Haywood	1914	S. Haywood	26.2
1972-73	Jim Fox	.515	S. Haywood	2251	S. Haywood	29.2
1973-74	Dick Snyder	.481	S. Haywood	1761	S. Haywood	23.5
1974-75	Archie Clark	.495	Fred Brown	1700	Fred Brown	21.0
1975-76	Fred Brown	.488	Fred Brown	1757	Fred Brown	23.1
1976-77	Dennis Johnson	.504	Fred Brown	1236	Fred Brown	17.2
1977-78	Marvin Webster	.502	Gus Williams	1431	Gus Williams	18.1
1978-79	Lonnie Shelton	.519	Gus Williams	1457	Gus Williams	19.2
1979-80	Lonnie Shelton	.530	Gus Williams	1816	Gus Williams	22.1
1980-81	Vinnie Johnson	.534	Jack Sikma	1530	Jack Sikma	18.7
1981-82	James Donaldson	.609	Gus Williams	1875	Gus Williams	23.4
1982-83	James Donaldson	.583	Gus Williams	1600	Gus Williams	20.0
1983-84	Danny Vranes	.521	Jack Sikma	1563	Jack Sikma	19.1
1984-85	Tim McCormick	.557	Tom Chambers	1739	Tom Chambers	21.5
1985-86	Tim McCormick	.570	Xavier McDaniel	1404	Jack Sikma	17.1
					Xavier McDaniel	17.1
1986-87	Dale Ellis	.516	Dale Ellis	2041	Dale Ellis	24.9
1987-88	Alton Lister	.504	Dale Ellis	1938	Dale Ellis	25.8
1988-89	Olden Polynice	.506	Dale Ellis	2253	Dale Ellis	27.5
1989-90	Olden Polynice	.540	Xavier McDaniel	1471	Derrick McKey	15.7
1990-91	Sedale Threatt	.519	Shawn Kemp	1214	Derrick McKey	15.3
1991-92	Michael Cage	.566	Ricky Pierce	1690	Ricky Pierce	21.7
1992-93	Michael Cage	.526	Ricky Pierce	1403	Ricky Pierce	18.2
1993-94	Michael Cage	.545	Shawn Kemp	1431	Shawn Kemp	18.1
1994-95	Shawn Kemp	.547	Gary Payton	1689	Gary Payton	20.6
1995-96	Shawn Kemp	.561	Gary Payton	1563	Shawn Kemp	19.6
1996-97	Shawn Kemp	.510	Gary Payton	1785	Gary Payton	21.8
1997-98	Vin Baker	.542	Vin Baker	1574	Vin Baker	19.2
					Gary Payton	19.2
1998-99*	Detlef Schrempf	.472	Gary Payton	1084	Gary Payton	21.7
	Olden Polynice	.472				
1999-00	Ruben Patterson	.536	Gary Payton	1982	Gary Payton	24.2
2000-01	Jelani McCoy	.523	Gary Payton	1823	Gary Payton	23.1
2001-02	Brent Barry	.508	Gary Payton	1815	Gary Payton	22.1
2002-03	Brent Barry	.458	Rashard Lewis	1396	Rashard Lewis	18.1
2003-04	Antonio Daniels	.470	Rashard Lewis	1421	Rashard Lewis	17.8
2004-05	Nick Collison	.537	Ray Allen	1867	Ray Allen	23.9
2005-06	Rashard Lewis	.467	Ray Allen	1955	Ray Allen	25.1

*-minimum 40 games.

COACHING HISTORY: 1967-1969 Al Bianchi 53-111-.323; 1969-1972 Lenny Wilkens 121-125-.492; 1972-1973 Tom Nissalke 13-32-.289; 1972-1973 Bucky Buckwalter 13-24-.351; 1973-1977 Bill Russell 162-166-.494; 1977-1978 Bob Hopkins 5-17-.227; 1977-1985 Lenny Wilkens 357-277-.563; 1985-1990 Bernie Bickerstaff 202-208-.493; 1990-1992 K.C. Jones 59-59-.500; 1991-1992 Bob Kloppenburg 2-2-.500; 1991-1998 George Karl 384-150-.719; 1998-2001 Paul Westphal 76-71-.517, 2000-2005 Nate McMillan 212-183-.537; 2005-present Bob Weiss

SHEBOYGAN REDSKINS

Home City: Sheboygan, Wisconsin
Home Court: Eagle Auditorium
　　　　　Municipal Auditorium
Origin of Name:

Regular Season Record

Season	League	GP	W	L	PPGF	PPGA	Pct	GB
1938-1939	NBL	28	11	17	35.6	37.5	.393	6
1939-1940	NBL	28	15	13	36.7	38.3	.536	-
1940-1941	NBL	24	13	11	36.1	34.7	.542	5
1941-1942	NBL	24	10	14	39.3	42.4	.417	10
1942-1943	NBL	23	12	11	43.2	43.7	.522	5
1943-1944	NBL	22	14	8	41.5	40.9	.636	4
1944-1945	NBL	30	19	11	49.8	46.0	.633	-
1945-1946	NBL	34	21	13	51.0	48.2	.618	-
1946-1947	NBL	44	26	18	54.5	53.0	.591	2
1947-1948	NBL	60	23	37	56.8	60.9	.383	20
1948-1949	NBL	64	35	29	62.0	61.7	.547	2
1949-1950	NBA	62	22	40	82.4	87.8	.355	16
TOTAL:	12 years	443	221	222				70
AVERAGE:		37	18	19	49.5	49.6	.499	6

Playoff Record

Season	GP	W	L	PPGF	PPGA	Result
1939-1940	3	1	2	32.0	38.0	Lost 1st Round series to Oshkosh.
1940-1941	6	2	4	36.7	42.2	Lost Championship series to Oshkosh.
1942-1943	5	4	1	47.2	42.8	**Won NBL Championship.**
1943-1944	6	2	4	36.8	38.5	Lost Championship series to Ft. Wayne.
1944-1945	8	4	4	50.9	48.5	Lost Championship series to Ft. Wayne.
1945-1946	8	3	5	50.5	56.4	Lost Championship series to Rochester.
1946-1947	5	2	3	46.0	47.6	Lost 1st Round series to Oshkosh.
1948-1949	2	0	2	55.5	67.0	Lost 1st Round series to Tri-Cities.
1949-1950	3	1	2	88.0	87.3	Lost 1st Round series to Indianapolis.
TOTAL:	46	19	27			
AVERAGE:	5	2	3	49.3	52.0	

Regular Season Individual Leaders

Season	Field Goals		Free Throws		Points	
1938-39	Paul Sokody	88	Paul Sokody	47	Paul Sokody	223
1939-40	R. Lautenschlager	76	George Hesik	49	R. Lautenschlager	184
1940-41	Dave Quabius	56	Kenny Seusens	41	Dave Quabius	152
1941-42	Ed Dancker	98	Ed Dancker	47	Ed Dancker	243
1942-43	Ed Dancker	96	Ed Dancker	48	Ed Dancker	240
1943-44	Ed Dancker	70	Ed Dancker	52	Ed Dancker	192
1944-45	Ed Dancker	111	Dick Schulz	71	Ed Dancker	283
1945-46	Ed Dancker	162	Mike Novak	88	Ed Dancker	393
1946-47	Fred Lewis	230	Ed Dancker	131	Fred Lewis	585
1947-48	M. Todorovich	277	Mike Todorovich	223	Mike Todorovich	777
1948-49	M. Todorovich	239	Noble Jorgensen	194	Mike Todorovich	648
1949-50	Max Morris	252	Max Morris	277	Max Morris	781

COACHING HISTORY: 1938-1939 Doc Schutte 11-17-.393; 1939-1942 Frank Zummach 38-38-.500; 1942-1944 Carl Roth 26-19-.578; 1944-1946 Dutch Dehnert 40-24-.625; 1946-1948 Doxie Moore 49-55-.471; 1948-1950 Ken Suesens 57-69-.452

SHREVEPORT PIRATES

Home City: Shreveport, Louisiana
Home Stadium: Independence Stadium   Capacity: 40,000 [1995]
Origin of Name: In the words of team president, Lonie Glieberman, the name was chosen because he considered them to be a "pirate team in a pirate league." (This even though the CFL can trace its roots much further back than can the NFL.)

Regular Season Record

Season	League	GP	W	L	T	PF	PA	Pts	Pct
1994	CFL	18	3	15	0	330	662	6	.167
1995	CFL	18	5	13	0	465	514	10	.278
TOTAL:	2 Years	36	8	28	0	795	1176	16	
AVERAGE:		18	4	14	0	398	588	8	.222

Regular Season Individual Leaders

Season	Passing Yards		Receiving Yards		Rushing Yards	
1994	Mike Johnson	1259	C. Thompson	641	Martin Patton	659
1995	Billy Joe Tolliver	3767	Curtis Mayfield	846	Martin Patton	1040

COACHING HISTORY: 1994-1995 Forrest Gregg 8-28-0-.222

SHREVEPORT STEAMERS
(were Houston Texans)

Home City: Shreveport, Louisiana
Home Stadium: State Fair Stadium   Capacity: 48,000
Origin of Name: Name chosen in a Name the Team Contest in which the club reportedly received over 40,000 entries.

Regular Season Record

Season	League	GP	W	L	T	PF	PA	Pct
1974	WFL	8	4	4	0	127	146	.500
1975	WFL	12	5	7	0	276	313	.417
TOTAL:	2 years	20	9	11	0	403	459	
AVERAGE:		10	5	5	0	202	230	.450

Regular Season Individual Leaders

Season	Passing Yards		Receiving Yards		Rushing Yards	
1974	David Mays	997	Rick Eber	771	Jim Nance	1240
1975	Edd Hargett	2100	Ricky Scales	505	Jim Nance	767

COACHING HISTORY: 1974 Jim Garret 4-4-0-.500; 1975 Marshall Taylor 5-7-0-.417

SOUTHERN CALIFORNIA SUN

Home City: Anaheim, California
Home Stadium: Anaheim Stadium   Capacity: 69,008
Origin of Name: The name was chosen in a Name the Team Contest.

Regular Season Record

Season	League	GP	W	L	T	PF	PA	Pct
1974	WFL	20	13	7	0	486	341	.650

1975	WFL	12	7	5	0	354	341	.583
TOTAL:	2 years	32	20	12	0	840	682	
AVERAGE:		16	10	6	0	420	341	.625

Playoff Record

Season	GP	W	L	PF	PA	Result
1974	1	0	1	14	34	Lost 1st Round series to Hawaiians.

Regular Season Individual Leaders

Season	Passing Yards		Receiving Yards		Rushing Yards	
1974	Tony Adams	3905	Dave Williams	979	Kermit Johnson	1008
1975	Pat Haden	1404	Terry Lindsay	669	Anthony Davis	1200

COACHING HISTORY: 1974-1975 Tom Fears 20-12-0-.625

SOVIET "B" TEAM

Home City: Moscow, USSR
Home Arena: The team only played road games.
Origin of Name:

Regular Season Record

Season	League	GP	W	L	T	GF	GA	Pts	Pct
1977-1978	WHA	8	3	4	1	27	36	7	.438

COACHING HISTORY: Vladimir Yurzinov 3-4-1-.438

SOVIET NATIONAL TEAM

Home City: Moscow, USSR
Home Arena: The team only played road games.
Origin of Name: This was the Soviet National team which would compete in the Olympics in 1980.

Regular Season Record

Season	League	GP	W	L	T	GF	GA	Pts	Pct
1978-1979	WHA	6	4	1	1	26	20	9	.750

COACHING HISTORY: Boris Mayorov 4-1-1-.750

SPOKANE CANARIES
(were Victoria Aristocrats)

Home City: Spokane, Washington
Home Arena: Spokane Arena
Origin of Name:

Regular Season Record

Season	League	GP	W	L	T	GF	GA	Pts	Pct
1916-1917	PCHA	23	8	15	0	89	143	16	.348

Regular Season Individual Leaders

Season	Goals		Points		GAA	
1916-1917	Albert Kerr	20	Albert Kerr	20	Norm Fowler	6.22

COACHING HISTORY: Lester Patrick 8-15-0-.348

STATEN ISLAND STAPLETONS

Home City: New York, New York
Home Field: Thompson Athletic Stadium   Capacity: 12,000
Origin of Name: Stapleton is one of the communities making up the New York City borough of
Staten Island.

			Regular Season Record					
Season	League	GP	W	L	T	PF	PA	Pct
1929	NFL	10	3	4	3	89	65	.450
1930	NFL	12	5	5	2	95	112	.500
1931	NFL	11	4	6	1	79	118	.409
1932	NFL	12	2	7	3	77	173	.292
TOTAL:	4 years	45	14	22	9	340	468	
AVERAGE:		11	4	5	2	85	117	.411

	Regular Season Individual Leaders			
Season	Passing Yards		Receiving Yards	Rushing Yards
1929	Ken Strong	291		Ken Strong	527
1930	Doug Wycoff	625		Doug Wycoff	383
1931	Ken Strong	118		Ken Strong	348
1932	Grassy Hinton	119		Bob Campiglio	366

COACHING HISTORY: 1929-1930 Doug Wycoff 8-9-5-.477; 1931 Hinky Haines 4-6-1-.409;
1932 Hal Hanson 2-7-3-.292

SYRACUSE ALL-AMERICANS

Home City: Syracuse, New York
Home Court: New York State Armory
Origin of Name:

		Regular Season Record			
Season	League	GP	W	L	Pct
1929-1930	ABL	24	4	20	.167

COACHING HISTORY:

SYRACUSE NATIONALS
(became Philadelphia 76ers)

Home City: Syracuse, New York
Home Court: State Fair Coliseum (1949-1951)   Capacity: 7,500
             Onodaga County War Memorial (1951-1963)   Capacity: 8,000
Origin of Name: The club used the league's nickname as it's own.

			Regular Season Record					
Season	League	GP	W	L	PPGF	PPGA	Pct	GB
1946-1947	NBL	44	21	23	55.8	55.5	.477	10

1947-1948	NBL	60	24	36	59.3	62.5	.400	20
1948-1949	NBL	63	40	23	66.5	63.8	.635	8.5
1949-1950	NBA	64	51	13	84.8	76.7	.797	-
1950-1951	NBA	66	32	34	86.1	85.5	.485	8
1951-1952	NBA	66	40	26	86.7	82.2	.606	-
1952-1953	NBA	71	47	24	85.6	81.3	.662	12
1953-1954	NBA	72	42	30	83.5	78.6	.583	2
1954-1955	NBA	72	43	29	91.1	89.7	.597	-
1955-1956	NBA	72	35	37	96.9	96.9	.486	10
1956-1957	NBA	72	38	34	99.7	101.1	.528	6
1957-1958	NBA	72	41	31	107.2	105.1	.569	8
1958-1959	NBA	72	35	37	113.1	109.1	.486	17
1959-1960	NBA	75	45	30	118.9	116.4	.600	14
1960-1961	NBA	79	38	41	121.3	119.2	.481	19
1961-1962	NBA	80	41	39	120.7	118.4	.513	19
1962-1963	NBA	80	48	32	121.6	117.8	.600	10
TOTAL:	17 years	1180	661	519				163.5
AVERAGE:		69	39	30	94.0	91.8	.560	10

Playoff Record

Season	GP	W	L	PPGF	PPGA	Result
1946-1947	4	1	3	58.3	60.8	Lost 1st Round series to Rochester.
1947-1948	3	0	3	59.3	74.7	Lost 1st Round series to Anderson.
1948-1949	6	3	3	74.8	75.3	Lost Championship series to Anderson.
1949-1950	11	6	5	81.0	79.9	Lost Championship series to Minneapolis.
1950-1951	7	4	3	88.7	87.6	Lost Division Final to New York.
1951-1952	7	3	4	93.3	90.6	Lost Division Final to New York.
1952-1953	2	0	2	93.0	99.0	Lost Division Semifinal to Boston.
1953-1954	13	9	4	81.5	80.0	Lost Championship series to Minneapolis.
1954-1955	11	7	4	97.2	94.0	**Won NBA Championship.**
1955-1956	8	4	4	101.6	108.0	Lost Division Final to Philadelphia.
1956-1957	5	2	3	93.8	97.4	Lost Division Final to Boston.
1957-1958	3	1	2	89.0	92.7	Lost Division Semifinal to Philadelphia.
1958-1959	9	5	4	120.6	123.0	Lost Division Final to Boston.
1959-1960	3	1	2	109.7	122.0	Lost Division Semifinal to Philadelphia.
1960-1961	8	4	4	108.4	117.9	Lost Division Final to Boston.
1961-1962	5	2	3	99.2	105.4	Lost Division Semifinal to Philadelphia.
1962-1963	5	2	3	120.8	125.2	Lost Division Semifinal to Cincinnati.
TOTAL:	110	54	56			
AVERAGE:	6	3	3	92.4	96.1	

Regular Season Individual Leaders

Season	Field Goals		Free Throws		Points	
1946-47	Jerry Rizzo	155	Jerry Rizzo	169	Jerry Rizzo	479
1947-48	Jim Homer	250	Jerry Rizzo	217	Jim Homer	698
1948-49	Dolph Schayes	271	Al Cervi	287	Dolph Schayes	809
1949-50	Dolph Schayes	348	Dolph Schayes	376	Dolph Schayes	1072
1950-51	Dolph Schayes	332	Dolph Schayes	457	Dolph Schayes	1121
1951-52	Red Rocha	300	Dolph Schayes	342	Dolph Schayes	868
1952-53	Dolph Schayes	375	Dolph Schayes	512	Dolph Schayes	1262
1953-54	Dolph Schayes	370	Dolph Schayes	488	Dolph Schayes	1228
1954-55	Dolph Schayes	422	Dolph Schayes	489	Dolph Schayes	1333

Season	Field Goals		Free Throws		Points	
1955-56	Dolph Schayes	465	Dolph Schayes	542	Dolph Schayes	1472
1956-57	Dolph Schayes	496	Dolph Schayes	625	Dolph Schayes	1617
1957-58	Dolph Schayes	581	Dolph Schayes	629	Dolph Schayes	1791
1958-59	Dolph Schayes	504	Dolph Schayes	526	Dolph Schayes	1534
1959-60	Dolph Schayes	578	Dolph Schayes	533	Dolph Schayes	1689
1960-61	Hal Greer	623	Dolph Schayes	680	Dolph Schayes	1868
1961-62	Hal Greer	644	Dave Gambee	384	Hal Greer	1619
1962-63	Hal Greer	600	Hal Greer	362	Hal Greer	1562

COACHING HISTORY: 1946-1948 Benny Borgmann 45-59-.433; 1948-1957 Al Cervi 334-224-.599; 1956-1960 Paul Seymour 155-124-.556; 1960-1963 Alex Hannum 127-112-.531

SYRACUSE STARS

Home City: Syracuse, New York
Home Field: Newell Park
      Lakeside Park (Sundays only)
Origin of Name:

Regular Season Record

Season	League	GP	W	L	Pct	GB	R	OR
1879	NL	70	22	48	.314	30	276	462

Regular Season Individual Leaders

Season	Home Runs		RBI's		Wins	
1879	5 tied at 1		Blondie Purcell	25	Harry McCormick	18

COACHING HISTORY: Mike Dorgan 22-48-.314

SYRACUSE STARS

Home City: Syracuse, New York
Home Field: Star Park
Origin of Name:

Regular Season Record

Season	League	GP	W	L	Pct	GB	R	OR
1890	AA	127	55	72	.433	30.5	698	831

Regular Season Individual Leaders

Season	Home Runs		RBI's		Wins	
1890	Pat Friel	3	Not Recorded		Dan Casey	19

COACHING HISTORY: George Frazer 55-72-.433

TAMPA BAY BANDITS

Home City: Tampa, Florida
Home Stadium: Tampa Stadium   Capacity: 72,126 [1984]
Origin of Name: Named by team owner John Bassett.

Regular Season Record

Season	League	GP	W	L	T	PF	PA	Pct
1983	USFL	18	11	7	0	363	378	.611

1984	USFL	18	14	4	0	498	347	.778
1985	USFL	18	10	8	0	405	422	.556
TOTAL:	3 years	54	35	19	0	1266	1147	
AVERAGE:		18	12	6	0	422	382	.648

Playoff Record

Season	GP	W	L	PF	PA	Result
1984	1	0	1	17	36	Lost 1st Round series to Birmingham.
1985	1	0	1	27	48	Lost 1st Round series to Oakland.
TOTAL:	2	0	2	44	84	
AVERAGE:	1	0	1	22	42	

Regular Season Individual Leaders

Season	Passing Yards		Receiving Yards		Rushing Yards	
1983	Jimmy Jordan	1831	Danny Buggs	1146	Greg Boone	694
1984	John Reaves	4092	Eric Truvillion	1044	Greg Boone	1009
1985	John Reaves	4193	Larry Brodsky	1071	Gary Anderson	1207

COACHING HISTORY: 1983-1985 Steve Spurrier 35-19-0-.648

TAMPA BAY BUCCANEERS

Home City: Tampa, Florida
Home Stadium: Houlihan's Stadium (1976-1997)*   Capacity: 74,300 [1997]
          Raymond James Stadium (1998-present)   Capacity: 65,657 [2005]
Origin of Name: The name was picked in a Name the Team Contest.

Regular Season Record

Season	League	GP	W	L	T	PF	PA	Pct
1976	NFL	14	0	14	0	125	412	.000
1977	NFL	14	2	12	0	103	223	.143
1978	NFL	16	5	11	0	241	259	.313
1979	NFL	16	10	6	0	273	237	.625
1980	NFL	16	5	10	1	271	341	.344
1981	NFL	16	9	7	0	315	268	.563
1982	NFL	9	5	4	0	158	178	.556
1983	NFL	16	2	14	0	241	380	.125
1984	NFL	16	6	10	0	335	380	.375
1985	NFL	16	2	14	0	294	448	.125
1986	NFL	16	2	14	0	239	473	.125
1987	NFL	15	4	11	0	286	360	.267
1988	NFL	16	5	11	0	261	350	.313
1989	NFL	16	5	11	0	320	393	.313
1990	NFL	16	6	10	0	264	367	.375
1991	NFL	16	3	13	0	199	365	.188
1992	NFL	16	5	11	0	267	365	.313
1993	NFL	16	5	11	0	237	376	.313
1994	NFL	16	6	10	0	251	351	.375
1995	NFL	16	7	9	0	238	335	.438
1996	NFL	16	6	10	0	221	293	.375
1997	NFL	16	10	6	0	299	263	.625

*-known as Tampa Stadium from 1976 to 1996

1998	NFL	16	8	8	0	314	295	.500
1999	NFL	16	11	5	0	270	235	.688
2000	NFL	16	10	6	0	388	269	.625
2001	NFL	16	9	7	0	324	280	.563
2002	NFL	16	12	4	0	346	196	.750
2003	NFL	16	7	9	0	301	264	.438
2004	NFL	16	5	11	0	301	304	.313
2005	NFL	16	11	5	0	300	274	.688
2006	NFL	16	4	12	0	211	353	.250
TOTAL:	31 years	484	187	296	1	8193	9887	
AVERAGE:		16	6	10	0	264	319	.387

Playoff Record

Season	GP	W	L	PF	PA	Result
1979	2	1	1	24	26	Lost NFC Championship to Los Angeles.
1981	1	0	1	0	38	Lost Divisional playoff to Dallas.
1982	1	0	1	17	30	Lost 1st Round playoff to Dallas.
1997	2	1	1	27	31	Lost Conference Semifinal to Green Bay.
1999	2	1	1	20	24	Lost Conference Final to St. Louis.
2000	1	0	1	3	21	Lost Wild Card Game to Philadelphia.
2001	1	0	1	9	31	Lost 1st Round playoff to Philadelphia.
2002	3	3	0	106	37	**Won Super Bowl XXXVII.**
2005	1	0	1	10	17	Lost 1st Round playoff to Washington.
TOTAL:	14	6	8	216	255	
AVERAGE:	2	1	1	24	28	

Regular Season Individual Leaders

Season	Passing Yards		Receiving Yards		Rushing Yards	
1976	Steve Spurrier	1628	Morris Owens	390	Louis Carter	321
1977	Gary Huff	889	Morris Owens	655	Ricky Bell	436
1978	Doug Williams	1170	Morris Owens	640	Ricky Bell	679
1979	Doug Williams	2448	Isaac Hagins	692	Ricky Bell	1263
1980	Doug Williams	3396	Gordon Jones	669	Ricky Bell	599
1981	Doug Williams	3563	Kevin House	1176	Jerry Eckwood	651
1982	Doug Williams	2071	Jimmie Giles	499	James Wilder	324
1983	Jack Thompson	2906	Kevin House	769	James Wilder	640
1984	Steve DeBerg	3554	Kevin House	1005	James Wilder	1544
1985	Steve DeBerg	2488	Kevin House	803	James Wilder	1300
1986	Steve Young	2382	Gerald Carter	640	James Wilder	704
1987	Steve DeBerg	1891	Gerald Carter	586	James Wilder	488
1988	V. Testaverde	3240	Bruce Hill	1040	Lars Tate	467
1989	V. Testaverde	3133	Mark Carrier	1422	Lars Tate	589
1990	V. Testaverde	2818	Mark Carrier	813	Gary Anderson	646
1991	V. Testaverde	1994	Lawrence Dawsey	818	Reggie Cobb	752
1992	V. Testaverde	2554	Lawrence Dawsey	776	Reggie Cobb	1171
1993	Craig Erickson	3054	Courtney Hawkins	933	Reggie Cobb	658
1994	Craig Erickson	2919	Lawrence Dawsey	673	Errict Rhett	1011
1995	Trent Dilfer	2774	Jackie Harris	751	Errict Rhett	1207
1996	Trent Dilfer	2859	Mike Alstott	557	Errict Rhett	539
1997	Trent Dilfer	2555	Karl Williams	486	Warrick Dunn	978
1998	Trent Dilfer	2729	Reidel Anthony	708	Warrick Dunn	1026
1999	Trent Dilfer	1619	Jacquez Green	791	Mike Alstott	949
2000	Shaun King	2769	Keyshawn Johnson	874	Warrick Dunn	1133

Season	Passing Yards		Receiving Yards		Rushing Yards	
2001	Brad Johnson	3406	Keyshawn Johnson	1266	Mike Alstott	680
2002	Brad Johnson	3049	Keyshawn Johnson	1088	Michael Pittman	718
2003	Brad Johnson	3811	Keenan McCardell	1174	Michael Pittman	751
2004	Brian Griese	2632	Michael Clayton	1193	Michael Pittman	926
2005	Chris Simms	2035	Joey Galloway	1287	Carnell Williams	1178
2006	B. Gradkowski	1661	Joey Galloway	1057	Carnell Williams	798

COACHING HISTORY: 1976-1984 John McKay 44-88-1-.335; 1985-1986 Leeman Bennett 4-28-0-.125; 1987-1990 Ray Perkins 19-41-0-.317; 1990-1991 Richard Williamson 4-15-0-.211; 1992-1995 Sam Wyche 23-41-0-.359; 1996-2001 Tony Dungy 54-42-0-.563; 2002-present Jon Gruden

TAMPA BAY DEVIL RAYS

Home City: Tampa Bay, Florida
Home Stadium: Tropicana Field (St. Petersburg, Florida)   Capacity: 43,772 [2006]
Origin of Name: The name was chosen in a Name the Team Contest because the owners wanted a name which would reflect the geographical area.

Regular Season Record

Season	League	GP	W	L	Pct	GB	R	OR
1998	AL	162	63	99	.389	51	620	751
1999	AL	162	69	93	.426	29	772	913
2000	AL	161	69	92	.429	18	733	842
2001	AL	162	62	100	.383	34	673	887
2002	AL	161	55	106	.342	48	673	918
2003	AL	162	63	99	.389	38	715	852
2004	AL	161	70	91	.435	33.5	714	842
2005	AL	162	67	95	.414	28	750	936
2006	AL	162	61	101	.377	36	689	856
TOTAL:	9 years	1455	579	876		315.5	6339	7797
AVERAGE:		162	65	97	.398	35	704	866

Regular Season Individual Leaders

Season	Home Runs		RBI's		Wins	
1998	Fred McGriff	19	Fred McGriff	81	Rolando Arrojo	14
1999	Jose Canseco	34	Fred McGriff	104	Wilson Alvarez	9
2000	Greg Vaughn	28	Fred McGriff	103	Albie Lopez	11
2001	Greg Vaughn	24	Greg Vaughn	82	Tanyon Sturtze	11
2002	Aubrey Huff	23	Randy Winn	75	Joe Kennedy	8
					Victor Zambrano	8
2003	Aubrey Huff	34	Aubrey Huff	107	Victor Zambrano	12
2004	Aubrey Huff	29	Aubrey Huff	104	Mark Hendrickson	10
2005	Jorge Cantu	28	Jorge Cantu	117	Mark Hendrickson	11
2006	Ty Wigginton	24	Ty Wigginton	79	Scott Kazmir	10

COACHING HISTORY: 1998-2001 Larry Rothschild 205-295-.410; 2001-2002 Hal McRae 113-195-.367; 2003-2005 Lou Piniella 200-285-.412; 2006-present Joe Maddon

TAMPA BAY LIGHTNING

Home City: Tampa, Florida (1992-1993)
   St. Petersburg, Florida (1993-present)
Home Arena: Expo Hall (1992-1993)   Capacity: 10,400 [1993]
          ThunderDome (1993-1996)   Capacity: 26,000 [1995]
          St. Pete Times Forum (1996-present)* Capacity: 19,758 [2005]
Origin of Name: The name was chosen by G. M. Phil Esposito after witnessing an electrical storm.

Regular Season Record

Season	League	GP	W	L	T	OL	SL	GF	GA	Pts
1992-1993	NHL	84	23	54	7	NA	NA	245	332	53
1993-1994	NHL	84	30	43	11	NA	NA	224	251	71
1994-1995	NHL	48	17	28	3	NA	NA	120	144	37
1995-1996	NHL	82	38	32	12	NA	NA	238	248	88
1996-1997	NHL	82	32	40	10	NA	NA	217	247	74
1997-1998	NHL	82	17	55	10	NA	NA	151	269	44
1998-1999	NHL	82	19	54	9	NA	NA	179	292	47
1999-2000	NHL	82	19	54	9	7	NA	204	310	54
2000-2001	NHL	82	24	47	6	5	NA	201	280	59
2001-2002	NHL	82	27	40	11	4	NA	178	219	69
2002-2003	NHL	82	36	25	16	5	NA	219	210	93
2003-2004	NHL	82	46	22	8	6	NA	245	192	106
2004-2005	NHL	Season cancelled due to lockout.								
2005-2006	NHL	82	43	33	NA	2	4	252	260	92
TOTAL:	13 years	1036	371	527	112	29	4	2673	3254	887
AVERAGE:		80	29	41	9	2	0	206	250	68

Playoff Record

Season	GP	W	L	GF	GA	Result
1995-1996	6	2	4	13	26	Lost Conference Quarterfinal to Philadelphia
2002-2003	11	5	6	22	29	Lost Conference Semifinal to New Jersey.
2003-2004	23	16	7	60	43	**Won Stanley Cup.**
2005-2006	5	1	4	13	23	Lost Conference Quarterfinal to Ottawa.
TOTAL:	45	24	21	108	121	
AVERAGE:	11	6	5	27	40	

Regular Season Individual Leaders

Season	Goals		Points		Penalty Minutes	
1992-1993	Brian Bradley	42	Brian Bradley	86	Mike Hartman	154
1993-1994	Petr Klima	28	Brian Bradley	64	Roman Hamrlik	135
1994-1995	Brian Bradley	13	Brian Bradley	40	Enrico Ciccone	225
	Petr Klima	13				
1995-1996	Alex Selivanov	31	Brian Bradley	79	Enrico Ciccone	258
1996-1997	Dino Ciccarelli	35	Chris Gratton	62	Chris Gratton	201
1997-1998	Mikael Renberg	16	Paul Ysebaert	40	Louie Debrusk	166
	Alex Selivanov	16				
1998-1999	Wendel Clark	28	Darcy Tucker	43	Darcy Tucker	176
1999-2000	Vincent Lecavalier	25	Vincent Lecavalier	67	Petr Svoboda	170
2000-2001	Fredrik Modin	32	Brad Richards	71	Cory Sarich	106
2001-2002	Brad Richards	20	Brad Richards	62	Dave Andreychuk	109
	Dave Andreychuk	20				
2002-2003	Vincent Lecavalier	34	Vaclav Prospal	79	Andre Roy	119

*-known as The Ice Palace from 1996-2003

Season	Goals		Points		Penalty Minutes	
2003-2004	Martin St. Louis	38	Martin St. Louis	94	Chris Dingman	140
2004-2005	Season cancelled due to lockout.					
2005-2006	Vincent Lecavalier	35	Brad Richards	91	Pavel Kubina	96

COACHING HISTORY: 1992-1998 Terry Crisp 142-204-45-.421; 1997-1998 Rick Paterson 0-6-0-.000; 1997-1999 Jacques Demers 34-96-11-.280; 1999-2001 Steve Ludzik 41-74-14-2-.374; 2000-present John Tortorella

TAMPA BAY MUTINY

Home City: Tampa Bay, Florida
Home Field: Houlihan's Stadium (1996-1998)   Capacity: 74,301 [1998]
           Raymond James Stadium (1998-2001)   Capacity: 66,321 [2001]
Origin of Name:

Regular Season Record

Season	League	GP	W	L	T	SOW	GF	GA	Pts
1996	MLS	32	20	12	NA	1	66	51	68
1997	MLS	32	17	15	NA	3	55	60	45
1998	MLS	32	12	20	NA	1	46	57	34
1999	MLS	32	14	18	NA	5	51	50	32
2000	MLS	32	16	12	4	NA	62	50	52
2001	MLS	27	4	21	2	NA	32	68	14
TOTAL:	6 years	187	83	98	6	10	312	336	245
AVERAGE:		31	14	16	1	2	52	56	41

Playoff Record

Season	GP	W	L	T	GF	GA	Result
1996	5	2	3	0	10	9	Lost Quarterfinals to D.C. United.
1997	2	0	2	0	1	4	Lost Semifinals to Columbus.
1999	2	0	2	0	0	4	Lost Semifinals to Columbus.
2000	2	0	2	0	0	6	Lost Semifinals to Los Angeles.
TOTAL:	11	2	9	0	11	23	
AVERAGE:	3	1	2	0	3	6	

Regular Season Individual Leaders

Season	Goals		Points		GAA (min. 5 games)	
1996	Roy Lassiter	27	Roy Lassiter	58	Mark Dougherty	1.71
1997	Roy Lassiter	10	Carlos Valderrama	25	Scott Budnick	1.83
1998	Mauricio Ramos	9	Mauricio Ramos	27	Thomas Ravelli	1.67
1999	Musa Shannon	12	Musa Shannon	29	Scott Garlick	1.31
2000	Mamadou Diallo	26	Mamadou Diallo	56	Scott Garlick	1.53
2001	Mamadou Diallo	9	Mamadou Diallo	23	Adin Brown	2.27

COACHING HISTORY: 1996 Thomas Rongen 20-12-.625; 1997-1999 John Kowalski 32-47-.405; 1999 Tim Hankinson

TAMPA BAY ROWDIES

Home City: Tampa, Florida
Home Stadium: Tampa Stadium   Capacity: 72,126 [1984]
Origin of Name: The name was chosen in a Name the Team Contest.

Regular Season Record

Season	League	GP	W	L	GF	GA	BP	Pts	Pct
1975	NASL	22	16	6	46	27	39	135	.682
1976	NASL	24	18	6	58	30	46	154	.713
1977	NASL	26	14	12	55	45	47	131	.560
1978	NASL	30	18	12	63	48	57	165	.611
1979	NASL	30	19	11	67	46	55	169	.626
1980	NASL	32	19	13	61	50	54	168	.583
1981	NASL	32	15	17	63	64	53	139	.290
1982	NASL	32	12	20	47	77	42	112	.233
1983	NASL	30	7	23	48	87	41	83	.184
1984	NASL	24	9	15	43	61	35	87	.242
TOTAL:	10 years	282	147	135	551	535	469	1343	
AVERAGE:		28	15	13	55	54	47	134	.414

Playoff Record

Season	GP	W	L	GF	GA	Result
1975	3	3	0	6	0	**Won NASL Championship.**
1976	2	1	1	3	3	Lost Conference Final to Toronto.
1977	1	0	1	0	3	Lost 1st Round series to New York.
1978	8	5	3	13	10	Lost Championship series to New York.
1979	8	6	2	14	9	Lost Championship series to New York.
1980	5	3	2	15	8	Lost 2nd Round series to San Diego.
1981	5	3	2	11	11	Lost 2nd Round series to New York.
TOTAL:	32	21	11	62	44	
AVERAGE:	5	3	2	9	6	

Regular Season Individual Leaders

Season	Goals		Points		GAA (360 Min)	
1975	Derek Smethurst	18	Derek Smethurst	39	Paul Hammond	1.15
1976	Derek Smethurst	20	Derek Smethurst	45	Arnold Mausser	1.17
1977	Derek Smethurst	19	Derek Smethurst	42	Paul Hammond	1.69
1978	Rodney Marsh	18	Rodney Marsh	52	Winston DuBose	1.26
1979	Oscar Fabbiani	25	Oscar Fabbiani	58	Zeljko Bilecki	1.28
1980	Oscar Fabbiani	13	Steve Wegerle	33	Winston DuBose	1.49
1981	Frank Worthington	11	Frank Worthington	38		
1982	Luis Fernando	16	Luis Fernando	35		
1983	Manny Rojas	8	Manny Rojas	32		
1984	Roy Wegerle	9	Roy Wegerle	25		

COACHING HISTORY: 1975-1977 Eddie Firmani 41-15; 1977 John Boyle 7-9; 1978-1982 Gordon Jago 83-73; 1983 Al Miller 7-23; 1984 Rodney Marsh 9-15

TEAM AMERICA

Home City: Washington, D.C.
Home Stadium: Robert F. Kennedy Memorial Stadium   Capacity: 55,031 [1983]
Origin of Name: The team was to have been the nucleus of the next American national team.

Regular Season Record

Season	League	GP	W	L	GF	GA	BP	Pts	Pct
1983	NASL	30	10	20	33	54	25	79	.176

COACHING HISTORY: Alkis Panagoulas 10-20

TEAM HAWAII
(were San Antonio Thunder)
(became Tulsa Roughnecks)

Home City: Honolulu, Hawaii
Home Stadium: Aloha Stadium (University of Hawaii)   Capacity: 50,000 [1977]
Origin of Name: The team was based in Hawaii

Regular Season Record

Season	League	GP	W	L	GF	GA	BP	Pts	Pct
1977	NASL	26	11	15	45	59	41	106	.453

COACHING HISTORY: Hubert Vogelsinger 8-9; Charlie Mitchell 3-6

TENNESSEE TITANS
(were Houston Oilers)

Home City: Memphis, Tennessee (1997)
        Nashville, Tennessee (1998-present)
Home Stadium: Liberty Bowl Stadium (1997)   Capacity: 62,380 [1997]
        Vanderbilt Stadium (1998)   Capacity: 41,600 [1998]
        The Coliseum (1999-present)*   Capacity: 68,798 [2005]
Origin of Name: The team was named by owner "Bud" Adams. The name was chosen to reflect strength, leadership and other heroic qualities. Titans comes from Greek mythology and Nashville is known as the "Athens of the South". Were known as the Tennessee Oilers from 1997-1998.

Regular Season Record

Season	League	GP	W	L	T	PF	PA	Pct.
1997	NFL	16	8	8	0	333	310	.500
1998	NFL	16	8	8	0	330	320	.500
1999	NFL	16	13	3	0	392	324	.813
2000	NFL	16	13	3	0	346	191	.813
2001	NFL	16	7	9	0	336	388	.438
2002	NFL	16	11	5	0	367	324	.688
2003	NFL	16	12	4	0	435	324	.750
2004	NFL	16	5	11	0	344	439	.313
2005	NFL	16	4	12	0	299	421	.250
2006	NFL	16	8	8	0	324	400	.500
TOTAL:	10 years	160	89	71	0	3506	3441	
AVERAGE:		16	9	7	0	351	344	.556

Playoff Record

Season	GP	W	L	PF	PA	Result
1999	4	3	1	90	69	Lost Super Bowl to St. Louis.
2000	1	0	1	10	24	Lost Conference Semifinal to Baltimore
2002	2	1	1	58	72	Lost Conference Final to Oakland.
2003	2	1	1	34	34	Lost Conference Semifinal to New England.
TOTAL:	9	5	4	192	199	
AVERAGE:	2	1	1	48	50	

*-known as Adelphia Coliseum from 1999-2001

Regular Season Individual Leaders

Season	Passing Yards		Receiving Yards		Rushing Yards	
1997	Steve McNair	2665	Frank Wycheck	748	Eddie George	1399
1998	Steve McNair	3228	Frank Wycheck	768	Eddie George	1294
1999	Steve McNair	2179	Kevin Dyson	658	Eddie George	1304
2000	Steve McNair	2847	Derrick Mason	895	Eddie George	1509
2001	Steve McNair	3350	Derrick Mason	1128	Eddie George	939
2002	Steve McNair	3387	Derrick Mason	1012	Eddie George	1165
2003	Steve McNair	3215	Derrick Mason	1303	Eddie George	1031
2004	Billy Volek	2486	Drew Bennett	1247	Chris Brown	1067
2005	Steve McNair	3161	Drew Bennett	738	Chris Brown	851
2006	Vince Young	2199	Drew Bennett	737	Travis Henry	1211

COACHING HISTORY: 1997-present Jeff Fisher

TEXAS RANGERS
(were Washington Senators)

Home City: Arlington, Texas
Home Field: Arlington Stadium (1972-1993)   Capacity: 43,521 [1993]
    Ameriquest Field in Arlington (1994-present) *   Capacity: 48,911 [2006]
Origin of Name: The name was chosen in honor of the famous law enforcement agency.

Regular Season Record

Season	League	GP	W	L	Pct	GB	R	OR
1972	AL	154	54	100	.351	38.5	461	628
1973	AL	162	57	105	.352	37	619	844
1974	AL	160	84	76	.525	5	690	698
1975	AL	162	79	83	.488	19	714	733
1976	AL	162	76	86	.469	14	616	652
1977	AL	162	94	68	.580	8	767	657
1978	AL	162	87	75	.537	5	692	632
1979	AL	162	83	79	.512	5	750	698
1980	AL	161	76	85	.472	20.5	756	752
1981	AL	105	57	48	.543	NA	452	389
1982	AL	162	64	98	.395	29	590	749
1983	AL	162	77	85	.475	22	639	609
1984	AL	161	69	92	.429	14.5	656	714
1985	AL	161	62	99	.385	28.5	617	785
1986	AL	162	87	75	.537	5	771	743
1987	AL	162	75	87	.463	10	823	849
1988	AL	161	70	91	.435	33.5	637	735
1989	AL	162	83	79	.512	16	695	714
1990	AL	161	83	78	.516	19.5	676	696
1991	AL	162	85	77	.525	10	829	814
1992	AL	162	77	85	.475	19	682	753
1993	AL	162	86	76	.531	8	835	751
1994	AL	114	52	62	.456	-	613	697
1995	AL	144	74	70	.514	4	691	720
1996	AL	162	90	72	.556	-	928	799
1997	AL	162	77	85	.475	13	807	821
1998	AL	162	88	74	.543	-	940	871

*-known as The Ballpark in Arlington from 1994-2004

1999	AL	162	95	67	.586	-	945	859
2000	AL	162	71	91	.438	20.5	848	974
2001	AL	162	73	89	.451	43	890	969
2002	AL	162	72	90	.444	31	843	882
2003	AL	162	71	91	.438	25	826	969
2004	AL	162	89	73	.549	3	860	794
2005	AL	162	79	83	.488	16	865	858
2006	AL	162	80	82	.494	13	835	784
TOTAL:	35 years	5532	2676	2856		535.5	25858	26592
AVERAGE:		158	76	82	.484	15.5	739	760

Playoff Record

Season	GP	W	L	R	OR	Result
1996	4	1	3	16	16	Lost Division Semifinal to Yankees.
1998	3	0	3	1	9	Lost Division Semifinal to Yankees.
1999	3	0	3	1	14	Lost Division Semifinal to Yankees.
TOTAL:	10	1	9	18	39	
AVERAGE:	3	0	3	6	13	

Regular Season Individual Leaders

Season	Home Runs		RBI's		Wins	
1972	Ted Ford	14	Dick Billings	58	Rich Hand	10
1973	Jeff Burroughs	30	Jeff Burroughs	85	Jim Bibby	9
1974	Jeff Burroughs	25	Jeff Burroughs	118	Ferguson Jenkins	25
1975	Jeff Burroughs	29	Jeff Burroughs	94	Ferguson Jenkins	17
1976	Tommy Grieve	20	Jeff Burroughs	86	Gaylord Perry	15
1977	Toby Harrah	27	Toby Harrah	87	Doyle Alexander	17
1978	Bobby Bonds	29	Al Oliver	89	Ferguson Jenkins	18
1979	Pat Putnam	18	Buddy Bell	101	Steve Comer	17
	Buddy Bell	18				
	Richie Zisk	18				
1980	Al Oliver	19	Al Oliver	117	George Medich	14
	Richie Zisk	19				
1981	Buddy Bell	10	Buddy Bell	64	Rick Honeycutt	11
1982	Dave Hostetler	22	Dave Hostetler	67	Charlie Hough	16
			Buddy Bell	67		
1983	Larry Parrish	26	Larry Parrish	88	Charlie Hough	15
1984	Larry Parrish	22	Larry Parrish	101	Charlie Hough	16
1985	Pete O'Brien	22	Pete O'Brien	92	Charlie Hough	14
1986	Pete Incaviglia	30	Larry Parrish	94	Charlie Hough	17
1987	Larry Parrish	32	Ruben Sierra	109	Charlie Hough	18
1988	Ruben Sierra	23	Ruben Sierra	91	Charlie Hough	15
1989	Ruben Sierra	29	Ruben Sierra	119	Nolan Ryan	16
1990	Pete Incaviglia	24	Ruben Sierra	96	Bobby Witt	17
1991	Juan Gonzalez	27	Ruben Sierra	116	Jose Guzman	13
1992	Juan Gonzalez	43	Juan Gonzalez	109	Kevin Brown	21
1993	Juan Gonzalez	46	Juan Gonzalez	118	Kenny Rogers	16
1994	Jose Canseco	31	Jose Canseco	90	Kenny Rogers	11
1995	Mickey Tettleton	32	Will Clark	92	Kenny Rogers	17
1996	Juan Gonzalez	47	Juan Gonzalez	144	Ken Hill	16
					Bobby Witt	16
1997	Juan Gonzalez	42	Juan Gonzalez	131	Darren Oliver	13
1998	Juan Gonzalez	45	Juan Gonzalez	157	Rick Helling	20
1999	Rafael Palmiero	47	Rafael Palmiero	148	Aaron Sele	18

Season	Home Runs		RBI's		Wins	
2000	Rafael Palmiero	39	Rafael Palmiero	120	Rick Helling	16
2001	Alex Rodriguez	52	Alex Rodriguez	135	Rick Helling	12
2002	Alex Rodriguez	57	Alex Rodriguez	142	Kenny Rogers	13
2003	Alex Rodriguez	47	Alex Rodriguez	118	John Thomson	13
2004	Mark Teixera	38	Mark Teixera	112	Kenny Rogers	18
2005	Mark Texeira	43	Mark Texeira	144	Kenny Rogers	14
2006	Mark Texeira	33	Mark Texeira	110	Kevin Millwood	16

COACHING HISTORY: 1972 Ted Williams 54-100-.351; 1973 Dorrel "Whitey" Herzog 47-91-.341; 1973 Del Wilber 1-0-1.000; 1973-1975 Billy Martin 137-141-.493; 1975-1977 Frank Lucchesi 142-149-.488; 1977 Eddie Stanky 1-0-1.000; 1977 Connie Ryan 2-4-.333; 1977-1978 Bill Hunter 146-108-.575; 1978-1980 Pat Corrales 160-164-.494; 1981-1982 Don Zimmer 95-106-.473; 1982 Darrell Johnson 26-40-.394; 1983-1985 Doug Rader 155-200-.437; 1985-1992 Bobby Valentine 581-604-.490; 1992 Toby Harrah 32-44-.421; 1993-1994 Kevin Kennedy 138-138-.500; 1995-2001 John Oates 506-476-.515; 2001-2002 Jerry Narron 134-162-.453; 2003-present Buck Showalter

TOLEDO BLUE STOCKINGS

Home City: Toledo, Ohio
Home Field: League Park   Capacity: 4,000
                Tri-State Fairgrounds
Origin of Name: The team wore blue stockings.

Regular Season Record

Season	League	GP	W	L	Pct	GB	R	OR
1884	AA	104	46	58	.442	27.5	463	571

Regular Season Individual Leaders

Season	Home Runs		RBI's	Wins	
1884	Tony Mullane	3	Not Recorded	Tony Mullane	36

COACHING HISTORY: Charlie Morton 46-58-.442

TOLEDO JEEPS

Home City: Toledo, Ohio
Home Court: Toledo Sports Arena
Origin of Name: The team was sponsored by the workers' recreation program of Willys Jeep factory in Toledo.

Regular Season Record

Season	League	GP	W	L	PPGF	PPGA	Pct	GB
1946-1947	NBL	44	21	23	57.3	56.0	.477	10
1947-1948	NBL	59	22	37	55.8	57.1	.373	21.5
TOTAL:	2 years	103	43	60				31.5
AVERAGE:		52	22	30	56.6	56.6	.417	16

Playoff Record

Season	GP	W	L	PPGF	PPGA	Result
1946-1947	5	2	3	45.8	56.4	Lost 1st Round series to Ft. Wayne.

Regular Season Individual Leaders

Season	Field Goals		Free Throws		Points	
1946-47	Hal Tidrick	232	George Sobek	179	Hal Tidrick	579
1947-48	Hal Tidrick	267	Hal Tidrick	189	Hal Tidrick	723

COACHING HISTORY: 1946-1948 Julie Rivlin 43-60-.417

TOLEDO JIM WHITE CHEVROLETS

Home City: Toledo, Ohio
Home Court: Toledo Civic Auditorium
Origin of Name: The team was sponsored by a local Chevrolet dealership.

Regular Season Record

Season	League	GP	W	L	PPGF	PPGA	Pct	GB
1941-1942	NBL	24	3	21	39.7	51.2	.125	17
1942-1943	NBL	4	0	4	38.8	48.0	.000	7.5
TOTAL:	2 years	28	3	25				24.5
AVERAGE:		14	2	12	39.3	49.6	.107	12

Regular Season Individual Leaders

Season	Field Goals		Free Throws		Points	
1941-42	C. Chuckovitz	143	Chuck Chuckovitz	120	Chuck Chuckovitz	293
1942-43	Pat Hintz	18	5 tied with 4		Pat Hintz	40

COACHING HISTORY: 1941-1942 Tommy Edwards 3-21-.125; 1942-1943 Sid Goldberg 0-4-.000

TOLEDO MAROONS

Home City: Toledo, Ohio
Home Stadium: Swayne Field [1922]
　　　　　　　　Armory Park [1923]
Origin of Name: The team received its name from the color of their jerseys.

Regular Season Record

Season	League	GP	W	L	T	PF	PA	Pct
1922	NFL	9	5	2	2	94	59	.667
1923	NFL	7	2	3	2	23	60	.429
TOTAL:	2 years	16	7	5	4	117	119	
AVERAGE:		8	4	2	2	59	60	.563

Regular Season Individual Leaders

Season	Passing Yards		Receiving Yards		Rushing Yards	
1922	Rat Watson	58	Truck Myers	47	Gil Falcon	23
1923	Cowboy Hill	33	Tillie Voss	23	Cowboy Hill	48

COACHING HISTORY: 1922 Gil Falcon 5-2-2-.667; 1923 Clarence Horning 2-3-2-.429

TOLEDO MAUMEES

Home City: Toledo, Ohio
Home Field: Speranza Park　　　　　　　　　　　　　Capacity: 5,500
Origin of Name: Speranza Park was located near the mouth of the Maumee River.

Regular Season Record

Season	League	GP	W	L	Pct	GB	R	OR
1890	AA	132	68	64	.515	20	739	689

Regular Season Individual Leaders

Season	Home Runs	RBI's		Wins	
1890	Perry Werden	6	Not Recorded	John Healy	22

COACHING HISTORY: Charlie Morton 68-64-.515

TOLEDO REDMAN TOBACCOS

Home City: Toledo, Ohio
Home Court: Toledo Convention Hall
Origin of Name: The team was sponsored by the Pinkerton Tobacco Co. one of their brands being Red Man Tobacco.

Regular Season Record

Season	League	GP	W	L	Pct
1930-1931	ABL	36	12	24	.333

Regular Season Individual Leaders

Season	Points	
1930-31	Davey Banks	254

COACHING HISTORY:

TORONTO ARGONAUTS

Home City: Toronto, Ontario
Home Stadium: Varsity Stadium (1950-1958)   Capacity: 27,000
          Exhibition Stadium* (1959-1988)   Capacity: 54,530 [1987]
          Rogers Center** (1989-present)   Capacity: 44,921 [2006]
Origin of Name: The team was formed in 1873 by the Toronto Argonaut Rowing Club

Regular Season Record

Season	League	GP	W	L	T	OT	PF	PA	Pts	Pct
1950	CRU	12	6	5	1	NA	291	187	13	.542
1951	CRU	12	7	5	0	NA	226	205	14	.583
1952	CRU	12	7	4	1	NA	265	191	15	.625
1953	CRU	14	5	9	0	NA	172	249	10	.357
1954	CRU	14	6	8	0	NA	212	265	12	.429
1955	CRU	12	4	8	0	NA	239	328	8	.333
1956	CFC	14	4	10	0	NA	331	413	8	.286
1957	CFC	14	4	10	0	NA	274	410	8	.286
1958	CFL	14	4	10	0	NA	266	308	8	.286
1959	CFL	14	4	10	0	NA	192	274	8	.286
1960	CFL	14	10	4	0	NA	370	265	20	.714
1961	CFL	14	7	6	1	NA	255	258	15	.536
1962	CFL	14	4	10	0	NA	259	378	8	.286
1963	CFL	14	3	11	0	NA	202	310	6	.214
1964	CFL	14	4	10	0	NA	243	332	8	.286
1965	CFL	14	3	11	0	NA	193	360	6	.214
1966	CFL	14	5	9	0	NA	182	271	10	.357
1967	CFL	14	5	8	1	NA	252	266	11	.393
1968	CFL	14	9	5	0	NA	284	266	18	.643

*-known as C.N.E. Stadium until 1973
**-known as SkyDome from 1999 to 2004

1969	CFL	14	10	4	0	NA	406	280	20	.714
1970	CFL	14	8	6	0	NA	329	290	16	.571
1971	CFL	14	10	4	0	NA	289	248	20	.714
1972	CFL	14	3	11	0	NA	254	298	6	.214
1973	CFL	14	7	5	2	NA	265	231	16	.571
1974	CFL	16	6	9	1	NA	281	314	13	.406
1975	CFL	16	5	10	1	NA	261	324	11	.343
1976	CFL	16	7	8	1	NA	289	354	15	.469
1977	CFL	16	6	10	0	NA	251	266	12	.375
1978	CFL	16	4	12	0	NA	234	389	8	.250
1979	CFL	16	5	11	0	NA	234	352	10	.313
1980	CFL	16	6	10	0	NA	334	358	12	.375
1981	CFL	16	2	14	0	NA	241	506	4	.125
1982	CFL	16	6	9	1	NA	426	426	13	.594
1983	CFL	16	12	4	0	NA	452	328	24	.750
1984	CFL	16	9	6	1	NA	461	361	19	.594
1985	CFL	16	6	10	0	NA	344	397	12	.375
1986	CFL	18	10	8	0	NA	417	441	20	.556
1987	CFL	18	11	6	1	NA	484	427	23	.639
1988	CFL	18	14	4	0	NA	571	326	28	.778
1989	CFL	18	7	11	0	NA	369	428	14	.389
1990	CFL	18	10	8	0	NA	689	538	20	.556
1991	CFL	18	13	5	0	NA	647	526	26	.722
1992	CFL	18	6	12	0	NA	469	523	12	.333
1993	CFL	18	3	15	0	NA	390	593	6	.167
1994	CFL	18	7	11	0	NA	504	578	14	.389
1995	CFL	18	4	14	0	NA	376	519	8	.222
1996	CFL	18	15	3	0	NA	556	359	30	.833
1997	CFL	18	15	3	0	NA	660	327	30	.833
1998	CFL	18	9	9	0	NA	452	408	18	.500
1999	CFL	18	9	9	0	NA	386	373	18	.500
2000	CFL	18	7	10	1	0	390	562	15	.417
2001	CFL	18	7	11	0	1	432	455	15	.417
2002	CFL	18	8	10	0	0	344	482	16	.444
2003	CFL	18	9	9	0	NA	473	433	18	.528
2004	CFL	18	10	7	1	NA	422	414	21	.583
2005	CFL	18	11	7	0	NA	486	387	22	.611
2006	CFL	18	10	8	0	NA	359	343	20	.556
TOTAL:	57 years	898	408	476	14	1	19935	20700	831	
AVERAGE:		15	7	8	0	0	350	363	15	.463

				Playoff Record			
Season	GP	W	L	T	PF	PA	Result
1950	4	3	1	0	91	32	**Won Grey Cup.**
1951	2	1	1	0	28	31	Lost Division Semifinal to Hamilton.
1952	5	4	1	0	100	66	**Won Grey Cup.**
1955	2	1	1	0	68	66	Lost Division Final to Montreal.
1960	2	0	2	0	41	54	Lost Division Final to Ottawa.
1961	3	2	1	0	70	74	Lost Division Semifinal to Ottawa.
1967	1	0	1	0	22	38	Lost Division Semifinal to Ottawa.
1968	3	2	1	0	60	68	Lost Division Final to Ottawa.
1969	3	2	1	0	40	55	Lost Division Final to Ottawa.
1970	1	0	1	0	7	16	Lost Division Semifinal to Montreal.
1971	3	1	1	1	51	39	Lost Grey Cup Final to Calgary.

Year							Result
1973	1	0	1	0	10	32	Lost Division Semifinal to Montreal.
1977	1	0	1	0	16	21	Lost Division Semifinal to Ottawa.
1982	2	1	1	0	60	39	Lost Grey Cup Final to Edmonton.
1983	2	2	0	0	59	53	**Won Grey Cup.**
1984	1	0	1	0	13	14	Lost Division Final to Hamilton.
1986	2	1	1	0	56	59	Lost Division Final to Hamilton.
1987	3	2	1	0	84	54	Lost Grey Cup Final to Edmonton.
1988	1	0	1	0	11	27	Lost Division Final to Winnipeg.
1989	1	0	1	0	7	30	Lost Division Semifinal to Winnipeg.
1990	2	1	1	0	51	45	Lost Division Final to Winnipeg.
1991	2	2	0	0	78	24	**Won Grey Cup.**
1994	1	0	1	0	15	34	Lost Division Semifinal to Baltimore.
1996	2	2	0	0	86	44	**Won Grey Cup.**
1997	2	2	0	0	84	53	**Won Grey Cup.**
1998	1	0	1	0	28	41	Lost Division Semifinal to Montreal.
1999	1	0	1	0	6	27	Lost Division Semifinal to Hamilton.
2002	2	1	1	0	42	32	Lost Division Final to Montreal.
2003	2	1	1	0	54	37	Lost Division Final to Montreal.
2004	3	3	0	0	77	43	**Won Grey Cup.**
2005	1	0	1	0	17	33	Lost Division Final to Montreal.
2006	2	1	1	0	55	60	Lost Division Final to Montreal.
TOTAL:	64	35	28	1	1487	1341	
AVERAGE:	2	1	1	0	46	42	

Regular Season Individual Leaders

Season	Passing Yards		Receiving Yards		Rushing Yards	
1950						
1951						
1952					Ulysses Curtis	994
1953						
1954	N. Wirkowski	3000	Al Pfeifer	1142	Gene Wilson	984
1955	Tom Dublinski	3547	Al Pfeifer	1342		
1956						
1957			Tex Schriewer	691		
1958	Ron Knox	1658	Dick Shatto	536	Dick Shatto	969
1959						
1960	Tobin Rote	4247	Dave Mann	1382	Dick Shatto	708
1961	Tobin Rote	3093	Dave Mann	659	Cookie Gilchrist	708
1962	Tobin Rote	2532	Dick Shatto	808	Gerry McDougall	811
1963	Jackie Parker	1603	Dick Shatto	945	Dick Shatto	570
1964	Jackie Parker	1841	Dick Shatto	859	Jim Vollenweider	464
1965	Peter Liske	1847	Pat Brosnan	452	Dave Thelen	801
1966	Wally Gabler	1659	Bobby Taylor	827	Dave Thelen	745
1967	Wally Gabler	2057	Bobby Taylor	965	Jim Dillard	670
1968	Wally Gabler	3242	Bobby Taylor	985	Bill Symons	1107
1969	Tom Wilkinson	2331	Bobby Taylor	1183	Bill Symons	905
1970	Don Jonas	2041	Jim Thorpe	671	Bill Symons	908
1971	Joe Theismann	2440	Mel Profit	725	Leon McQuay	977
1972	Wally Gabler	1689	Eric Allen	1067	Leon McQuay	745
1973	Joe Theismann	2496	Eric Allen	797	Bill Symons	358
1974	Mike Rae	2501	Peter Muller	615	Doyle Orange	870
1975	Bill Bynum	923	Mike Eben	729	Doyle Orange	1055
1976	Chuck Ealey	1846	Mike Eben	681	Chuck Ealey	613
1977	Chuck Ealey	1653	Peter Muller	475	Neil Lumsden	680

Season	Passing Yards		Receiving Yards		Rushing Yards	
1978	Chuck Ealey	1420	Peter Muller	585	Terry Metcalf	669
1979	Tony Adams	2692	Terry Metcalf	568	Terry Metcalf	691
1980	Mark Jackson	3041	Bob Gaddis	1112	Terry Metcalf	554
1981	C. Holloway	2578	Paul Pearson	796	Cedric Minter	815
1982	C. Holloway	4661	Terry Greer	1466	Cedric Minter	563
1983	C. Holloway	3184	Terry Greer	2003	Cedric Minter	599
1984	Joe Barnes	3128	Terry Greer	1189	Lester Brown	594
1985	C. Holloway	1735	Terry Greer	1323	Ricky Turner	284
1986	C. Holloway	2230	Chris Woods	1163	Craig Ellis	381
1987	Gilbert Renfroe	1686	Darrell K. Smith	1392	Gill Fenerty	879
1988	Gilbert Renfroe	4113	Darrell K. Smith	1306	Gill Fenerty	968
1989	John Congemi	1472	Darrell K. Smith	959	Gill Fenerty	1247
1990	Matt Dunigan	2028	Darrell K. Smith	1826	Rickey Foggie	674
1991	Rickey Foggie	3108	Darrell K. Smith	1399	Rickey Foggie	644
1992	Rickey Foggie	3507	Paul Masotti	801	Mike Clemons	572
1993	Tracy Ham	2147	Manny Hazard	1033	Tracy Ham	605
1994	Mike Kerrigan	2224	Paul Masotti	1280	Mike Clemons	787
1995	Kent Austin	3076	Paul Masotti	1336	Mike Clemons	836
1996	Doug Flutie	5720	Mike Clemons	1268	R. Drummond	935
1997	Doug Flutie	5505	Derrell Mitchell	1457	R. Drummond	1134
1998	Kerwin Bell	4983	Derrell Mitchell	2004	Mike Clemons	610
1999	Jay Barker	2023	Tyrone Brown	911	Ryan Terry	762
2000	Kerwin Bell	2180	Derrell Mitchell	1399	Michael Jenkins	1050
2001	Jimmy Kemp	2838	Derrell Mitchell	1376	Michael Jenkins	1484
2002	Jim Ballard	1083	Derrell Mitchell	1027	R. Drummond	778
2003	Damon Allen	3395	Tony Miles	1005	Michael Jenkins	814
2004	Damon Allen	2438	Robert Baker	1086	John Avery	974
2005	Damon Allen	5082	Tony Miles	1275	John Avery	526
2006	Damon Allen	2567	Arland Bruce	1370	Ricky Williams	526

COACHING HISTORY: 1950-1954 Frank Clair 31-31-2-.500; 1955-1956 Bill Swiacki 8-18-0-.308; 1957-1959 Hamp Pool 9-23-0-.281; 1959 Steve Owen 3-7-0-.300; 1960-1962 Lou Agase 17-13-1-.565; 1962-1964 Nobby Wirkowski 11-28-0-.282; 1965-1966 Bob Shaw 8-20-0-.286; 1967-1972 Leo Cahill 45-38-1-.542; 1973-1974 John Rauch 10-9-2-.524; 1974 Joe Moss 3-5-1-.389; 1975-1976 Russ Jackson 12-18-2-.406; 1977-1978 Leo Cahill 9-16-0-.360; 1978 Bud Riley 1-6-0-.143; 1979 Forrest Gregg 5-11-0-.313; 1980-1981 Willie Wood 6-20-0-.231; 1981 Tom Hudspeth 2-4-0-.333; 1982-1989 Bob O'Billovich 75-58-3-.563; 1990 Don Matthews 10-8-0-.556; 1991-1992 Adam Rita 16-13-0-.552; 1992-1993 Dennis Meyer 4-13-0-.235; 1993-1994 Bob O'Billovich 9-17-0-.346; 1995 Mike Faragalli 2-7-0-.222; 1995 Bob O'Billovich 2-7-0-.222; 1996-1998 Don Matthews 39-15-0-.722; 1999 Jim Barker 9-9-0-.500; 2000-John Huard 1-6-1-.188; 2002-Gary Etcheverry 4-8-0-0-.333; 2000-present Michael Clemons

TORONTO BLIZZARD

Home City: Toronto, Ontario
Home Stadium: Varsity Stadium [1971-1978, 1984]   Capacity: 27,000
          Lamport Stadium [1976]   Capacity: 9,000
          Exhibition Stadium (1979-1983)   Capacity: 54,472 [1980]
The name was to the games. Previously known as the Metros and Metro Croatias (an attempt by the team management to draw upon the large ethnic population of Toronto). The name "Blizzards" was chosen by team officials.

Regular Season Record

Season	League	GP	W	L	T	GF	GA	BP	Pts	Pct
1971	NASL	24	5	10	9	32	47	32	89	.412
1972	NASL	14	4	6	4	18	22	17	53	.421
1973	NASL	19	6	4	9	32	18	26	89	.520
1974	NASL	20	9	10	1	30	31	30	87	.483
1975	NASL	22	13	9	0	39	28	36	114	.576
1976	NASL	24	15	9	0	38	30	33	123	.569
1977	NASL	26	13	13	0	42	38	37	115	.491
1978	NASL	30	16	14	0	58	47	48	144	.533
1979	NASL	30	14	16	0	52	65	49	133	.493
1980	NASL	32	14	18	0	49	65	44	128	.444
1981	NASL	32	7	25	0	39	82	37	77	.160
1982	NASL	32	17	15	0	64	47	49	151	.315
1983	NASL	30	16	14	0	51	48	45	135	.300
1984	NASL	24	14	10	0	46	33	35	117	.325
TOTAL:	14 years	359	163	173	23	590	601	518	1555	
AVERAGE:		26	12	12	2	42	43	37	.111	.486

Playoff Record

Season	GP	W	L	GF	GA	Result
1973	1	0	1	0	3	Lost Semifinal series to Philadelphia
1975	1	0	1	0	1	Lost Quarterfinal to Tampa Bay.
1976	4	4	0	10	3	**Won NASL Championship.**
1977	2	0	2	2	0	Lost Division Final to Rochester.
1978	1	0	1	0	4	Lost 1st Round series to Vancouver.
1979	2	0	2	1	5	Lost 1st Round series to New York.
1982	3	1	2	6	9	Lost 1st Round series to Seattle.
1983	6	4	2	8	6	Lost Championship series to Tulsa.
1984	4	2	2	6	6	Lost Championship series to Chicago.
TOTAL:	24	11	13	33	37	
AVERAGE:	3	1	2	4	4	

Regular Season Individual Leaders

Season	Goals		Points		GAA (360 Min)	
1971	Ian MacHattie	8	Ian MacHattie	21	Jose Rodrigues	1.88
1972	Paolo Barison	3	Jose Moraes	8	Dick Howard	1.31
	John Fahy	3				
	Jose Moraes	3				
1973	Miguel Perrichon	9	Miguel Perrichon	22	Dick Howard	1.00
1974	Bruno Pilas	5	Bruno Pilas	11	Jack Brand	1.43
1975	Ivan Lukacevic	8	John Coyne	25	Zeljko Bilecki	1.25
1976	Eusebio Ferreira	16	Eusebio Ferreira	36	Paolo Cimpiel	0.96
1977	Drago Vabec	11	Drago Vabec	26	Zeljko Bilecki	1.21
1978	Ivan Lukacevic	16	Ivan Lukacevic	37	Zeljko Bilecki	1.34
1979	Ivan Lukacevic	12	Ivan Lukacevic	31	Zeljko Bilecki	1.28
			Peter Lorimer	31		
1980	Jomo Sono	14	Jomo Sono	35	Tony Chursky	1.72
1981	Jomo Sono	8	Jomo Sono	20	Tony Chursky	2.45
1982	Neill Roberts	17	Neill Roberts	42	Jan Moller	1.37
1983	David Byrne	13	David Byrne	44	Jan Moller	1.57
1984	David Byrne	12	David Byrne	37	Paul Hammond	1.16

COACHING HISTORY: 1971-1972 Graham Leggat 9-16-13-.415; 1973-1974 Arthur Rodrigues 15-14-10-.501; 1975-1976 Ivan Markovic 23-15; 1976 Domagoj Kapetanovic 5-3; 1977 Ivan Sangullian 13-13-.491; 1978 Domagoj Kapetanovic 16-14-.533; 1979-1981 Keith Eddy 35-59; 1981 Dave Turnet 3-10; 1982-1984 Bobby Houghton 47-39

TORONTO BLUE JAYS

Home City: Toronto, Ontario
Home Field: Exhibition Stadium (1977-1989)   Capacity: 43,737 [1978]
           Rogers Center (1989-present) *   Capacity: 50,516 [2006]
Origin of Name: The club's name was picked in a Name the Team Contest.

Regular Season Record

Season	League	GP	W	L	Pct	GB	R	OR
1977	AL	161	54	107	.335	45.5	605	822
1978	AL	161	59	102	.366	40	590	775
1979	AL	162	53	109	.327	50.5	613	862
1980	AL	162	67	95	.414	36	624	762
1981	AL	106	37	69	.349	NA	329	466
1982	AL	162	78	84	.481	17	651	701
1983	AL	162	89	73	.549	9	795	726
1984	AL	162	89	73	.549	15	750	696
1985	AL	161	99	62	.615	-	759	588
1986	AL	162	86	76	.531	9.5	889	733
1987	AL	162	96	66	.593	2	845	655
1988	AL	162	87	75	.537	2	763	680
1989	AL	162	89	73	.549	-	731	651
1990	AL	162	86	76	.531	2	767	661
1991	AL	162	91	71	.562	-	684	622
1992	AL	162	96	66	.593	-	780	682
1993	AL	162	95	67	.586	-	847	742
1994	AL	115	55	60	.478	16	566	579
1995	AL	144	56	88	.389	30	642	777
1996	AL	162	74	88	.457	18	766	809
1997	AL	162	76	86	.469	22	655	694
1998	AL	162	88	74	.543	26	816	768
1999	AL	162	84	78	.518	14	883	862
2000	AL	162	83	79	.512	4.5	851	908
2001	AL	162	80	82	.494	16	767	753
2002	AL	162	78	84	.481	25.5	813	828
2003	AL	162	86	76	.531	15	894	826
2004	AL	161	67	94	.416	30.5	719	823
2005	AL	162	80	82	.494	15	775	705
2006	AL	162	87	75	.537	10	809	754
TOTAL:	30 years	4735	2345	2390		471	21978	21910
AVERAGE:		158	78	80	.495	16	733	730

Season	GP	W	L	R	OR	Result
1985	7	3	4	25	26	Lost ALCS to Kansas City.
1989	5	1	4	21	26	Lost ALCS to Oakland.
1991	5	1	4	19	27	Lost ALCS to Minnesota.
1992	12	8	4	48	44	**Won World Series.**

*-known as The Skydome from 1989 to 2004

Playoff Record

1993	12	8	4	71	59	Won World Series.
TOTAL:	41	21	20	184	182	
AVERAGE:	8	4	4	37	36	

Regular Season Individual Leaders

Season	Home Runs		RBI's		Wins	
1977	Ron Fairly	19	Ron Fairly	64	Dave Lemanczyk	13
			Doug Ault	64		
1978	John Mayberry	22	John Mayberry	70	Jim Clancy	10
1979	John Mayberry	21	John Mayberry	74	Tom Underwood	9
1980	John Mayberry	30	John Mayberry	82	Jim Clancy	13
1981	John Mayberry	17	Jon Mayberry	43	Dave Stieb	11
			Lloyd Moseby	43		
1982	Willie Upshaw	21	Willie Upshaw	75	Dave Stieb	17
1983	Willie Upshaw	27	Willie Upshaw	104	Dave Stieb	17
	Jesse Barfield	27				
1984	George Bell	26	Lloyd Moseby	92	Doyle Alexander	17
1985	George Bell	28	George Bell	95	Doyle Alexander	17
1986	Jesse Barfield	40	Jesse Barfield	108	Mark Eichhorn	14
			George Bell	108	Jimmy Key	14
					Jim Clancy	14
1987	George Bell	47	George Bell	134	Jimmy Key	17
1988	Fred McGriff	34	George Bell	97	Dave Stieb	16
1989	Fred McGriff	36	George Bell	104	Dave Stieb	17
1990	Fred McGriff	35	Kelly Gruber	118	Dave Stieb	18
1991	Joe Carter	33	Joe Carter	108	Jimmy Key	16
1992	Joe Carter	34	Joe Carter	119	Jack Morris	21
1993	Joe Carter	33	Joe Carter	121	Pat Hentgen	19
1994	Joe Carter	27	Joe Carter	103	Pat Hentgen	13
1995	Joe Carter	25	Joe Carter	76	Al Leiter	11
1996	Ed Sprague	30	Joe Carter	107	Pat Hentgen	20
1997	Carlos Delgado	30	Joe Carter	102	Roger Clemens	21
1998	Jose Canseco	46	Carlos Delgado	115	Roger Clemens	20
1999	Carlos Delgado	44	Carlos Delgado	134	David Wells	17
2000	Carlos Delgado	41	Carlos Delgado	137	David Wells	20
	Tony Batista	41				
2001	Carlos Delgado	39	Carlos Delgado	102	Chris Carpenter	11
					Esteban Loaiza	11
					Paul Quantrill	11
2002	Carlos Delgado	33	Carlos Delgado	108	Roy Halladay	19
2003	Carlos Delgado	42	Carlos Delgado	145	Roy Halladay	22
2004	Carlos Delgado	32	Carlos Delgado	99	Ted Lilly	12
2005	Vernon Wells	28	Vernon Wells	97	Gustavo Chachin	13
2006	Troy Glaus	38	Vernon Wells	106	Roy Halladay	16

COACHING HISTORY: 1977-1979 Roy Hartsfield 166-318-.343; 1980-1981 Bob Mattick 104-164-.388; 1982-1985 Bobby Cox 355-292-.549; 1986-1989 Jimy Williams 281-241-.538; 1991 Gene Tenace 19-14-.576; 1989-1997 Cito Gaston 687-637-.519; 1998 Tim Johnson 88-74-.543; 1999-2000 Jim Fregosi 167-157-.515; 2001-2002 Buck Martinez 100-115-.465; 2002-2004 Carlos Tosca 191-191-.500; 2004-present John Gibbons

TORONTO CITY

Home City: Toronto, Ontario
Home Stadium: Varsity Stadium
Origin of Name: The team played its home games in Toronto and was represented by the Hibernian team of Edinburgh, Scotland.

Regular Season Record

Season	League	GP	W	L	T	GF	GA	Pts	Pct
1967	USA	12	4	3	5	23	17	13	.542

Regular Season Individual Leaders

Season	Goals		Points		GAA (360 Min)	
1967	Peter Cormack	6	Peter Cormack	13	Allan Thomson	1.43

COACHING HISTORY: Bob Shankly 4-3-5-.542

TORONTO FALCONS

Home City: Toronto, Ontario
Home Stadium: Varsity Stadium
Origin of Name: The team was named after the Toronto Italia-Falcons of the Eastern Canada Professional Soccer League.

Regular Season Record

Season	League	GP	W	L	T	GF	GA	BP	Pts	Pct
1967	NPSL	32	10	17	5	59	70	NA	127	.441
1968	NASL	32	13	13	6	55	69	48	144	.500
TOTAL:	2 years	64	23	30	11	114	139	48	271	
AVERAGE:		32	12	15	5	57	70	24	136	.470

Regular Season Individual Leaders

Season	Goals		Points		GAA (360 Min)	
1967	Yanko Daucik	20	Yanko Daucik	48	Bill Brown	2.12
1968	Iris DeBrito	20	Iris DeBrito	42	Raul Magana	1.78

COACHING HISTORY: 1967 Hector Mariano 10-17-5-.441; 1968 Laddie Kubala 13-13-6-.500

TORONTO HUSKIES

Home City: Toronto, Ontario
Home Court: Maple Leaf Gardens   Capacity: 14,640 [1947]
Origin of Name:

Regular Season Record

Season	League	GP	W	L	PPGF	PPGA	Pct	GB
1946-1947	BAA	60	22	38	66.6	71.0	.367	27

Regular Season Individual Leaders

Season	Field Goal % (min. 40 games)	Points		Points per Game (min. 40 games)
1946-47		Mike McCarron	649	

COACHING HISTORY: Ed Sadowski 3-9-.250; Lew Hayman 0-1-.000; Dick Fitzgerald 2-1-.667; Red Rolfe 17-27-.386

TORONTO MAPLE LEAFS

Home City: Toronto, Ontario
Home Arena: Mutual Street Arena (1912-1931)   Capacity: 8,000
            Maple Leaf Gardens (1931-1999)   Capacity: 15,846 [1998]
            Air Canada Center (1999-present)   Capacity: 18,819 [2005]
Origin of Name: First known as the Blueshirts and then the Toronto Arenas when the team was purchased by the directors of the Mutual Street Arena. The team then changed its name to St. Patricks in an attempt to attract Toronto's large Irish population to the games. In 1926 team owner Conn Smythe changed the name to "Maple Leafs" as it was emblematic of Canada and previous Canadian Olympic hockey teams had worn it on their uniforms.

Regular Season Record

Season	League	GP	W	L	T	OL	SL	GF	GA	Pts
1912-1913	NHA	20	9	11	0	NA	NA	86	95	18
1913-1914	NHA	20	13	7	0	NA	NA	93	65	26
1914-1915	NHA	20	8	12	0	NA	NA	66	84	16
1915-1916	NHA	24	9	14	1	NA	NA	97	98	19
1916-1917	NHA	14	7	7	0	NA	NA	64	61	14
1917-1918	NHL	22	13	9	0	NA	NA	108	109	26
1918-1919	NHL	18	5	13	0	NA	NA	64	92	10
1919-1920	NHL	24	12	12	0	NA	NA	119	106	24
1920-1921	NHL	24	15	9	0	NA	NA	105	100	30
1921-1922	NHL	24	13	10	1	NA	NA	98	97	27
1922-1923	NHL	24	13	10	1	NA	NA	82	88	27
1923-1924	NHL	24	10	14	0	NA	NA	59	85	20
1924-1925	NHL	30	19	11	0	NA	NA	90	84	38
1925-1926	NHL	36	12	21	3	NA	NA	92	114	27
1926-1927	NHL	44	15	24	5	NA	NA	79	94	35
1927-1928	NHL	44	18	18	8	NA	NA	89	88	44
1928-1929	NHL	44	21	18	5	NA	NA	85	69	47
1929-1930	NHL	44	17	21	6	NA	NA	116	124	40
1930-1931	NHL	44	22	13	9	NA	NA	118	99	53
1931-1932	NHL	48	23	18	7	NA	NA	133	127	53
1932-1933	NHL	48	24	18	6	NA	NA	119	111	54
1933-1934	NHL	48	26	13	9	NA	NA	174	119	61
1934-1935	NHL	48	30	14	4	NA	NA	157	111	64
1935-1936	NHL	48	23	19	6	NA	NA	126	106	52
1936-1937	NHL	48	22	21	5	NA	NA	119	115	49
1937-1938	NHL	48	24	15	9	NA	NA	151	127	57
1938-1939	NHL	48	19	20	9	NA	NA	114	107	47
1939-1940	NHL	48	25	17	6	NA	NA	134	110	56
1940-1941	NHL	48	28	14	6	NA	NA	145	99	62
1941-1942	NHL	48	27	18	3	NA	NA	158	136	57
1942-1943	NHL	50	22	19	9	NA	NA	198	159	53
1943-1944	NHL	50	23	23	4	NA	NA	214	174	50
1944-1945	NHL	50	24	22	4	NA	NA	183	161	52
1945-1946	NHL	50	19	24	7	NA	NA	174	185	45
1946-1947	NHL	60	31	19	10	NA	NA	209	172	72
1947-1948	NHL	60	32	15	13	NA	NA	182	143	77
1948-1949	NHL	60	22	25	13	NA	NA	147	161	57

1949-1950	NHL	70	31	27	12	NA	NA	176	173	74
1950-1951	NHL	70	41	16	13	NA	NA	212	138	95
1951-1952	NHL	70	29	25	16	NA	NA	168	157	74
1952-1953	NHL	70	27	30	13	NA	NA	156	167	67
1953-1954	NHL	70	32	24	14	NA	NA	152	131	78
1954-1955	NHL	70	24	24	22	NA	NA	147	135	70
1955-1956	NHL	70	24	33	13	NA	NA	153	181	61
1956-1957	NHL	70	21	34	15	NA	NA	174	192	57
1957-1958	NHL	70	21	38	11	NA	NA	192	226	53
1958-1959	NHL	70	27	32	11	NA	NA	189	201	65
1959-1960	NHL	70	35	26	9	NA	NA	199	195	79
1960-1961	NHL	70	39	19	12	NA	NA	234	176	90
1961-1962	NHL	70	37	22	11	NA	NA	232	180	85
1962-1963	NHL	70	35	23	12	NA	NA	221	180	82
1963-1964	NHL	70	33	25	12	NA	NA	192	172	78
1964-1965	NHL	70	30	26	14	NA	NA	204	173	74
1965-1966	NHL	70	34	25	11	NA	NA	208	187	79
1966-1967	NHL	70	32	27	11	NA	NA	204	211	75
1967-1968	NHL	74	33	31	10	NA	NA	209	176	76
1968-1969	NHL	76	35	26	15	NA	NA	234	217	85
1969-1970	NHL	76	29	34	13	NA	NA	222	242	71
1970-1971	NHL	78	37	33	8	NA	NA	248	211	82
1971-1972	NHL	78	33	31	14	NA	NA	209	208	80
1972-1973	NHL	78	27	41	10	NA	NA	247	279	64
1973-1974	NHL	78	35	27	16	NA	NA	274	230	86
1974-1975	NHL	80	31	33	16	NA	NA	280	309	78
1975-1976	NHL	80	34	31	15	NA	NA	294	276	83
1976-1977	NHL	80	33	32	15	NA	NA	301	285	81
1977-1978	NHL	80	41	29	10	NA	NA	271	237	92
1978-1979	NHL	80	34	33	13	NA	NA	267	252	81
1979-1980	NHL	80	35	40	5	NA	NA	304	327	75
1980-1981	NHL	80	28	37	15	NA	NA	322	367	71
1981-1982	NHL	80	20	44	16	NA	NA	298	380	56
1982-1983	NHL	80	28	40	12	NA	NA	293	330	68
1983-1984	NHL	80	26	45	9	NA	NA	303	387	61
1984-1985	NHL	80	20	52	8	NA	NA	253	358	48
1985-1986	NHL	80	25	48	7	NA	NA	311	386	57
1986-1987	NHL	80	32	42	6	NA	NA	286	319	70
1987-1988	NHL	80	21	49	10	NA	NA	273	345	52
1988-1989	NHL	80	28	46	6	NA	NA	259	342	62
1989-1990	NHL	80	38	38	4	NA	NA	337	358	80
1990-1991	NHL	80	23	46	11	NA	NA	241	318	57
1991-1992	NHL	80	30	43	7	NA	NA	234	294	67
1992-1993	NHL	84	44	29	11	NA	NA	288	241	99
1993-1994	NHL	84	43	29	12	NA	NA	280	243	98
1994-1995	NHL	48	21	19	8	NA	NA	135	146	50
1995-1996	NHL	82	34	36	12	NA	NA	247	252	80
1996-1997	NHL	82	30	44	8	NA	NA	230	273	68
1997-1998	NHL	82	30	43	9	NA	NA	194	237	69
1998-1999	NHL	82	45	30	7	NA	NA	268	231	97
1999-2000	NHL	82	45	30	7	3	NA	246	222	100
2000-2001	NHL	82	37	29	11	5	NA	232	207	90
2001-2002	NHL	82	43	25	10	4	NA	249	207	100
2002-2003	NHL	82	44	28	7	3	NA	236	208	98

2003-2004	NHL	82	45	24	10	3	NA	242	204	103
2004-2005	NHL	Season cancelled due to lockout.								
2005-2006	NHL	82	41	33	NA	1	7	257	270	90
TOTAL:	93 years	5726	2505	2414	784	19	7	17834	17724	5820
AVERAGE:		62	27	26	8	0	0	192	191	63

Playoff Record

Season	GP	W	L	T	GF	GA	Result
1913-1914	5	4	1	0	19	10	**Won Stanley Cup.**
1917-1918	7	4	3	0	28	28	**Won Stanley Cup.**
1920-1921	2	0	2	0	0	7	Lost NHL playoff series to Ottawa.
1921-1922	7	4	2	1	21	13	**Won Stanley Cup.**
1924-1925	2	0	2	0	2	5	Lost NHL playoff series to Canadiens.
1928-1929	4	2	2	0	8	5	Lost Semifinal series to Rangers.
1930-1931	2	0	1	1	3	4	Lost Quarterfinal series to Chicago.
1931-1932	7	5	1	1	28	15	**Won Stanley Cup.**
1932-1933	9	4	5	0	14	18	Lost Stanley Cup to Rangers.
1933-1934	5	2	3	0	12	11	Lost Semifinal series to Detroit.
1934-1935	7	3	4	0	11	12	Lost Stanley Cup to Maroons.
1935-1936	9	4	5	0	25	27	Lost Stanley Cup to Detroit.
1936-1937	2	0	2	0	1	5	Lost Quarterfinal series to Rangers.
1937-1938	7	4	3	0	14	13	Lost Stanley Cup to Chicago.
1938-1939	10	5	5	0	22	20	Lost Stanley Cup to Boston.
1939-1940	10	6	4	0	21	19	Lost Stanley Cup to Rangers.
1940-1941	7	3	4	0	17	15	Lost Semifinal series to Boston.
1941-1942	13	8	5	0	25	31	**Won Stanley Cup.**
1942-1943	6	2	4	0	17	20	Lost Semifinal series to Detroit.
1943-1944	5	1	4	0	6	23	Lost Semifinal series to Montreal.
1944-1945	13	8	5	0	24	30	**Won Stanley Cup.**
1946-1947	11	8	3	0	31	27	**Won Stanley Cup.**
1947-1948	9	8	1	0	38	20	**Won Stanley Cup.**
1948-1949	9	8	1	0	28	15	**Won Stanley Cup.**
1949-1950	7	3	4	0	11	10	Lost Semifinal series to Detroit.
1950-1951	11	8	2	1	30	15	**Won Stanley Cup.**
1951-1952	4	0	4	0	3	13	Lost Semifinal series to Detroit.
1953-1954	5	1	4	0	8	15	Lost Semifinal series to Detroit.
1954-1955	4	0	4	0	6	14	Lost Semifinal series to Detroit.
1955-1956	5	1	4	0	10	14	Lost Semifinal series to Detroit.
1958-1959	12	5	7	0	32	39	Lost Stanley Cup to Montreal.
1959-1960	10	4	6	0	25	31	Lost Stanley Cup to Montreal.
1960-1961	5	1	4	0	8	15	Lost Semifinal series to Detroit.
1961-1962	12	8	4	0	40	30	**Won Stanley Cup.**
1962-1963	10	8	2	0	31	16	**Won Stanley Cup.**
1963-1964	14	8	6	0	39	31	**Won Stanley Cup.**
1964-1965	6	2	4	0	14	17	Lost Semifinal series to Montreal.
1965-1966	4	0	4	0	6	15	Lost Semifinal series to Montreal.
1966-1967	12	8	4	0	35	30	**Won Stanley Cup.**
1968-1969	4	0	4	0	5	24	Lost Quarterfinal series to Boston.
1970-1971	6	2	4	0	15	16	Lost Quarterfinal series to Rangers.
1971-1972	5	1	4	0	10	18	Lost Quarterfinal series to Boston.
1973-1974	4	0	4	0	9	17	Lost Quarterfinal series to Boston.
1974-1975	7	2	5	0	13	21	Lost Quarterfinal series to Philadelphia.
1975-1976	10	5	5	0	31	36	Lost Quarterfinal series to Philadelphia.
1976-1977	9	4	5	0	31	29	Lost Quarterfinal series to Philadelphia

1977-1978	13	6	7	0	33	32	Lost Semifinal series to Montreal.
1978-1979	6	2	4	0	19	24	Lost Quarterfinal series to Montreal.
1979-1980	3	0	3	0	8	17	Lost Preliminary series to Minnesota.
1980-1981	3	0	3	0	4	20	Lost Preliminary series to Islanders.
1982-1983	4	1	3	0	18	18	Lost Division Semifinal to Minnesota.
1985-1986	10	6	4	0	40	33	Lost Division Final to St. Louis.
1986-1987	13	7	6	0	33	32	Lost Division Final to Detroit.
1987-1988	6	2	4	0	20	32	Lost Division Semifinal to Detroit.
1989-1990	5	1	4	0	16	20	Lost Division Semifinal to St. Louis.
1992-1993	21	11	10	0	69	63	Lost Conf. Final to Los Angeles.
1993-1994	18	9	9	0	50	47	Lost Conf. Final to Vancouver.
1994-1995	7	3	4	0	20	22	Lost Conf. Quarterfinal to Chicago.
1995-1996	6	2	4	0	15	21	Lost Conf. Quarterfinal to St. Louis.
1998-1999	17	9	8	0	43	46	Lost Conf. Final to Buffalo.
1999-2000	12	6	6	0	26	26	Lost Conf. Semifinal to New Jersey.
2000-2001	11	7	4	0	28	23	Lost Conf. Semifinal to New Jersey.
2001-2002	20	10	10	0	44	49	Lost Conf. Final to Carolina.
2002-2003	7	3	4	0	16	24	Lost Conf. Quarterfinal to Philadelphia.
2003-2004	13	6	7	0	27	28	Lost Conf. Semifinal to Philadelphia.
TOTAL:	529	255	270	4	1356	1436	
AVERAGE:	8	4	4	0	21	22	

Regular Season Individual Leaders

Season	Goals		Points		Penalty Minutes	
1912-1913	Frank Nighbor	25	Frank Nighbor	25	Not Recorded	
1913-1914	Allan Davidson	23	Allan Davidson	23	Not Recorded	
1914-1915	Cully Wilson	21	Cully Wilson	21	Not Recorded	
1915-1916	Cy Denneny	26	Cy Denneny	26	Not Recorded	
1916-1917					Not Recorded	
1917-1918	Reg Noble	30	Reg Noble	40	Ken Randall	96
1918-1919	Alf Skinner	12	Alf Skinner	16	Russell Crawford	51
1919-1920	Reg Noble	24	Corb Denneny	36	Cully Wilson	86
	Corb Denneny	24				
1920-1921	Cecil Dye	33	Cecil Dye	38	Ken Randall	74
1921-1922	Cecil Dye	31	Cecil Dye	38	Cecil Dye	39
1922-1923	Cecil Dye	26	Cecil Dye	37	Jack Adams	64
1923-1924	Cecil Dye	16	Cecil Dye	19	Reg Noble	79
1924-1925	Cecil Dye	38	Cecil Dye	46	Bert Corbeau	74
1925-1926	Jack Adams	21	Jack Adams	26	Bert Corbeau	121
1926-1927	Bill Carson	16	Irvine Bailey	28	Bert Corbeau	88
1927-1928	Bill Carson	20	Bill Carson	26	Clarence Day	82
1928-1929	Irvine Bailey	22	Irvine Bailey	32	Art Smith	91
1929-1930	Irvine Bailey	22	Irvine Bailey	43	Red Horner	96
1930-1931	Charlie Conacher	31	Charlie Conacher	43	Harvey Jackson	81
1931-1932	Charlie Conacher	34	Harvey Jackson	53	Red Horner	97
1932-1933	Harvey Jackson	27	Harvey Jackson	44	Red Horner	144
1933-1934	Charlie Conacher	32	Charlie Conacher	52	Red Horner	146
1934-1935	Charlie Conacher	36	Charlie Conacher	57	Red Horner	125
1935-1936	Charlie Conacher	23	Charlie Conacher	38	Red Horner	167
	Bill Thoms	23	Bill Thoms	38		
1936-1937	Harvey Jackson	21	Syl Apps	45	Red Horner	124
1937-1938	Gord Drillon	26	Gord Drillon	52	Red Horner	92
1938-1939	Gord Drillon	18	Syl Apps	40	Red Horner	85
1939-1940	Gord Drillon	21	Gord Drillon	40	Red Horner	87

Season	Goals		Points		Penalty Minutes	
1940-1941	David Schriner	24	Gord Drillon	44	Reg Hamilton	59
1941-1942	Gord Drillon	23	Gord Drillon	41	Bingo Kampman	67
1942-1943	Lorne Carr	27	Lorne Carr	60	Reg Hamilton	68
			Billy Taylor	60		
1943-1944	Lorne Carr	36	Lorne Carr	74	Reg Hamilton	32
1944-1945	Ted Kennedy	29	Ted Kennedy	54	Bob Davidson	49
1945-1946	Gaye Stewart	37	Gaye Stewart	52	Bob Goldham	44
1946-1947	Ted Kennedy	28	Ted Kennedy	60	Gus Mortson	133
1947-1948	Syl Apps	26	Syl Apps	53	Bill Barilko	147
1948-1949	Harry Watson	26	Harry Watson	45	Bill Ezinicki	145
1949-1950	Max Bentley	23	Sid Smith	45	Bill Ezinicki	144
1950-1951	Sid Smith	30	Max Bentley	62	Gus Mortson	142
1951-1952	Sid Smith	27	Sid Smith	57	Fern Flaman	110
1952-1953	Sid Smith	20	Sid Smith	39	Fern Flaman	110
1953-1954	Sid Smith	22	Tod Sloan	43	Tod Sloan	100
1954-1955	Sid Smith	33	Sid Smith	54	Jim Thomson	87
1955-1956	Tod Sloan	37	Tod Sloan	66	Tod Sloan	100
1956-1957	Dick Duff	26	George Armstrong	44	Gerry James	90
1957-1958	Dick Duff	26	Dick Duff	49	George Armstrong	93
1958-1959	Dick Duff	29	Dick Duff	53	Carl Brewer	125
1959-1960	Bob Pulford	24	Bob Pulford	52	Carl Brewer	153
1960-1961	Frank Mahovlich	48	Frank Mahovlich	84	Carl Brewer	92
1961-1962	Frank Mahovlich	33	Frank Mahovlich	71	Bob Pulford	98
1962-1963	Frank Mahovlich	36	Frank Mahovlich	73	Carl Brewer	168
1963-1964	Frank Mahovlich	26	Dave Keon	60	Eddie Shack	128
1964-1965	Frank Mahovlich	23	Frank Mahovlich	51	Carl Brewer	177
1965-1966	Frank Mahovlich	32	Frank Mahovlich	56	Kent Douglas	97
			Bob Pulford	56		
1966-1967	Ron Ellis	22	Dave Keon	52	Jim Pappin	89
1967-1968	Mike Walton	30	Mike Walton	59	Tim Horton	82
1968-1969	Norm Ullman	35	Norm Ullman	77	Jim Dorey	200
1969-1970	Ron Ellis	35	Dave Keon	62	Rick Ley	102
1970-1971	Dave Keon	38	Norm Ullman	85	Jim Dorey	198
1971-1972	Paul Henderson	38	Norm Ullman	73	Rick Ley	124
1972-1973	Dave Keon	37	Darryl Sittler	77	Mike Pelyk	118
1973-1974	Darryl Sittler	38	Darryl Sittler	84	Brian Glennie	100
1974-1975	Darryl Sittler	36	Darryl Sittler	80	Dave Williams	187
1975-1976	Errol Thompson	43	Darryl Sittler	100	Dave Williams	299
1976-1977	Lanny McDonald	48	Darryl Sittler	90	Dave Williams	338
			Lanny McDonald	90		
1977-1978	Lanny McDonald	47	Darryl Sittler	117	Dave Williams	351
1978-1979	Lanny McDonald	43	Darryl Sittler	87	Dave Williams	298
1979-1980	Darryl Sittler	40	Darryl Sittler	97	Rick Vaive	265
1980-1981	Darryl Sittler	43	Wilf Paiement	97	Rick Vaive	229
1981-1982	Rick Vaive	54	Rick Vaive	89	Bob McGill	263
1982-1983	Rick Vaive	51	John Anderson	80	Jim Korn	238
1983-1984	Rick Vaive	52	Rick Vaive	93	Jim Korn	257
1984-1985	Rick Vaive	35	Rick Vaive	68	Bob McGill	250
1985-1986	Wendel Clark	34	Miroslav Frycer	75	Wendel Clark	227
1986-1987	Wendel Clark	37	Russ Courtnall	73	Wendel Clark	271
1987-1988	Ed Olczyk	42	Ed Olczyk	75	Al Secord	221
1988-1989	Ed Olczyk	38	Ed Olczyk	90	Brian Curran	185
					John Kordic	185

Season	Goals		Points		Penalty Minutes	
1989-1990	Gary Leeman	51	Gary Leeman	95	Brian Curran	301
1990-1991	V. Damphousse	26	Vince Damphousse	73	Luke Richardson	238
1991-1992	Glenn Anderson	24	Glenn Anderson	57	Bob Halkidis	145
1992-1993	N. Borschevsky	34	Doug Gilmour	127	Rob Pearson	211
1993-1994	D. Andreychuk	53	Doug Gilmour	111	Rob Pearson	189
1994-1995	Mats Sundin	23	Mats Sundin	47	Warren Rychel	101
1995-1996	Mike Gartner	35	Mats Sundin	83	Tie Domi	297
1996-1997	Mats Sundin	41	Mats Sundin	94	Tie Domi	275
1997-1998	Mats Sundin	33	Mats Sundin	74	Tie Domi	365
1998-1999	Sergei Berezin	37	Mats Sundin	83	Tie Domi	198
1999-2000	Mats Sundin	32	Mats Sundin	73	Tie Domi	198
2000-2001	Gary Roberts	29	Mats Sundin	74	Tie Domi	214
2001-2002	Mats Sundin	41	Mats Sundin	80	Tie Domi	157
2002-2003	Mats Sundin	37	Alex Mogilny	79	Wade Belak	196
2003-2004	Mats Sundin	31	Mats Sundin	75	Tie Domi	208
2004-2005	Season cancelled due to lockout.					
2005-2006	Mats Sundin	31	Mats Sundin	78	Bryan McCabe	116

COACHING HISTORY: 1912-1913 Bruce Ridpath 0-3-0-.000; 1912-1915 Jack Marshall 30-27-0-.526; 1915-1917 Not Available; 1917-1919 Dick Carroll 18-22-0-.450; 1919-1920 Frank Heffernan 5-7-0-.417; 1919-1920 Harry Sproule 7-5-0-.583; 1920-1921 Frank Carroll 15-9-0.625; 1921-1923 George O'Donoghue 15-13-1-.534; 1922-1924 Charlie Querrie 21-21-1-.500; 1924-1926 Eddie Powers 31-32-3-.492; 1926-1927 Charlie Querrie 8-17-4-.345; 1926-1927 Mike Rodden 0-2-0-.000; 1926-1927 Alex Romeril 7-5-1-.577; 1927-1931 Conn Smythe 57-57-20-.500; 1930-1932 Art Duncan 21-16-10-.553; 1931-1940 Dick Irvin 216-152-59-.575; 1940-1950 Clarence Day 259-206-81-.549; 1950-1953 Joe Primeau 97-71-42-.562; 1953-1956 Francis "King" Clancy 80-90-40-.476; 1956-1957 Howie Meeker 21-34-15-.407; 1957-1959 Billy Reay 26-50-14-.367; 1958-1969 George Imlach 358-269-123-.559; 1966-1967 Francis "King" Clancy 7-1-2-.800; 1969-1973 John McLellan 117-136-42-.468; 1971-1972 Francis "King" Clancy 9-3-3-.700; 1973-1977 Leonard Kelly 129-129-62-.500; 1977-1979 Roger Neilson 75-62-23-.541; 1979-1980 Floyd Smith 30-33-5-.478; 1979-1980 Dick Duff 0-2-0-.000; 1979-1980 George Imlach 5-5-0-.500; 1980-1981 Joe Crozier 13-22-5-.388; 1980-1984 Mike Nykoluk 89-144-47-.402; 1984-1986 Dan Maloney 45-100-15-.328; 1986-1989 John Brophy 64-111-18-.378; 1988-1989 George Armstrong 17-26-4-.404; 1989-1991 Doug Carpenter 39-47-5-.456; 1990-1992 Tom Watt 52-80-17-.406; 1992-1996 Pat Burns 133-107-41-.546; 1995-1996 Nick Beverley 9-6-2-.588; 1996-1998 Mike Murphy 60-87-17-.418; 1998-2006 Pat Quinn 300-196-52-19-7-.591; 2006-present

TORONTO ONTARIOS
(changed name to Shamrocks in mid 1914-1915)

Home City: Toronto, Ontario
Home Arena: Arena Gardens   Capacity: 8,000
Origin of Name: In their first season the team was named the "Tecumsehs" after an American Indian leader who fought on the British side during the War of 1812.

		Regular Season Record							
Season	League	GP	W	L	T	GF	GA	Pts	Pct
1912-1913	NHA	20	7	13	0	59	98	14	.350
1913-1914	NHA	20	4	16	0	61	118	8	.200
1914-1915	NHA	20	7	13	0	76	96	14	.350
TOTAL:	2 years	60	18	42	0	196	312	36	
AVERAGE:		20	6	14	0	65	104	12	.300

Regular Season Individual Leaders

Season	Goals		Points		GAA	
1912-1913	Harry Smith	14	Harry Smith	14	Bill Nicholson	4.90
1913-1914	Jack McDonald	26	Jack McDonald	26	Sam Hebert	5.68
1914-1915	Tommy Smith		Tommy Smith		Percy Lesueur	5.05

COACHING HISTORY: 1912-1913 Unknown; 1913-1915 Jim Murphy 11-29-0-.275

TORONTO RAPTORS

Home City: Toronto, Ontario
Home Court: The Skydome [1995-1999]   Capacity: 20,125 [1998]
      Air Canada Center [1999-present]   Capacity: 19,800 [2006]
Origin of Name: The name was officially chosen in a Name the Team Contest, but it was reported the name was registered the same day that the contest was announced. The name was an attempt to cash in on the dinosaur craze of the 1990's brought on by director Steven Spielberg's mega movie hit *Jurassic Park*.

Regular Season Record

Season	League	GP	W	L	PPGF	PPGA	Pct	GB
1995-1996	NBA	82	21	61	97.5	105.0	.256	51
1996-1997	NBA	82	30	52	95.5	98.6	.366	39
1997-1998	NBA	82	16	66	94.9	104.2	.195	46
1998-1999	NBA	50	23	27	91.1	92.8	.460	10
1999-2000	NBA	82	45	37	97.2	97.3	.549	11
2000-2001	NBA	82	47	35	97.6	95.4	.573	5
2001-2002	NBA	82	42	40	91.4	91.8	.512	8
2002-2003	NBA	82	24	58	90.9	96.7	.293	26
2003-2004	NBA	82	33	49	85.4	88.5	.402	28
2004-2005	NBA	82	33	49	99.7	101.4	.402	12
2005-2006	NBA	82	27	55	101.1	104.0	.329	22
TOTAL:	11 years	870	341	529				258
AVERAGE:		79	31	48	94.9	98.0	.392	23

Playoff Record

Season	GP	W	L	PPGF	PPGA	Result
1999-2000	3	0	3	83.7	87.7	Lost 1st Round series to New York.
2000-2001	12	6	6	92.2	91.3	Lost Conference Semifinal to Philadelphia.
2001-2002	5	2	3	83.8	86.6	Lost 1st Round series to Detroit.
TOTAL:	20	8	12			
AVERAGE:	7	3	4	88.8	89.6	

Regular Season Individual Leaders

Season	Field Goal % (min. 70 games)		Points		Points per Game (min. 70 games)	
1995-96	Oliver Miller	.526	D. Stoudamire	1331	D. Stoudamire	19.0
1996-97	Popeye Jones	.580	D. Stoudamire	1634	D. Stoudamire	20.2
1997-98	John Wallace	.478	Doug Christie	1287	Doug Christie	16.5
1998-99*	Vince Carter	.450	Vince Carter	913	Vince Carter	18.3
1999-00	Vince Carter	.465	Vince Carter	2107	Vince Carter	25.7
2000-01	Keon Clark	.480	Vince Carter	2070	Vince Carter	27.6
2001-02	Keon Clark	.490	Vince Carter	1484	Antonio Davis	14.5
2002-03	Jerome Williams	.499	Morris Peterson	1153	Morris Peterson	14.1

*-minimum 40 games.

Season	Field Goal % (min. 70 games)		Points		Points per Game (min. 70 games)	
2003-04	Chris Bosh	.459	Vince Carter	1645	Vince Carter	22.5
2004-05	Matt Bonner	.533	Jalen Rose	1495	Jalen Rose	18.5
2005-06	Chris Bosh	.505	Mike James	1604	Chris Bosh	22.4

COACHING HISTORY: 1995-1996 Brendan Malone 21-61-.256; 1996-1998 Darrell Walker 41-90-313; 1997-2000 Butch Carter 73-92-.442; 2000-2003 Lenny Wilkens 113-133-.459; 2003-2004 Kevin O'Neill 33-49-.402; 2004-present Sam Mitchell

TORONTO SHAMROCKS
(see Toronto Ontarios)

TORONTO TOROS
(were Ottawa Nationals)
(became Birmingham Bulls)

Home City: Toronto, Ontario
Home Arena: Maple Leaf Gardens   Capacity: 16,316 [1975]
Origin of Name: The name was chosen because Toros is a shortened form of the name Toronto.

Regular Season Record

Season	League	GP	W	L	T	GF	GA	Pts	Pct
1973-1974	WHA	78	41	33	4	304	272	86	.551
1974-1975	WHA	78	43	33	2	349	304	88	.564
1975-1976	WHA	81	24	52	5	335	398	53	.327
TOTAL:	3 years	237	108	118	11	988	974	227	
AVERAGE:		79	36	39	4	329	325	76	.479

Playoff Record

Season	GP	W	L	GF	GA	Result
1973-1974	12	7	5	45	43	Lost Semifinal series to Chicago.
1974-1975	6	2	4	27	29	Lost Quarterfinal series to San Diego.
TOTAL:	18	9	9	72	72	
AVERAGE:	9	5	4	36	36	

Regular Season Individual Leaders

Season	Goals		Points		Penalty Minutes	
1973-1974	Wayne Dillon	39	Wayne Carleton	92	Rick Cunningham	88
1974-1975	Tom Simpson	52	Wayne Dillon	95	Rick Cunningham	117
1975-1976	V. Nedomansky	56	V. Nedomansky	98	Jerry Rollins	185

COACHING HISTORY: 1973-1975 Billy Harris 63-50-5-.555; 1974-1975 Bob LeDuc 21-16-1-.566; 1975-1976 Bob Baun 15-35-5-.318; 1975-1976 Gilles Leger 9-17-0-.346

TRENTON BENGALS

Home City: Trenton, New Jersey
Home Court: Trenton Arena
Origin of Name: The team was originally the Passaic Bengal Tigers, a local basketball team which had played in the area in the preceding year.

Regular Season Record

Season	League	GP	W	L	Pct
1928-1929	ABL	40	16	24	.400

Regular Season Individual Leaders

Season	Points		
1928-29	Tom Barlow	274

COACHING HISTORY:

TRI-CITIES BLACKHAWKS
(merged with Buffalo in mid 1946-1947)
(became Milwaukee Hawks)

Home City: Moline, Illinois
         Rock Island, Illinois
         Davenport, Iowa
Home Court: Wharton Field House (Moline)   Capacity: 6,000
Origin of Name:

Regular Season Record

Season	League	GP	W	L	PPGF	PPGA	Pct	GB
1946-1947	NBL	32	15	17	49.1	51.8	.469	10
1947-1948	NBL	60	30	30	60.9	61.1	.500	13
1948-1949	NBL	64	36	28	65.1	62.4	.563	1
1949-1950	NBA	64	29	35	83.0	83.6	.453	10
1950-1951	NBA	68	25	43	84.3	88.1	.368	19
TOTAL:	5 years	288	135	153				53
AVERAGE:		58	27	31	68.5	69.4	.469	11

Playoff Record

Season	GP	W	L	PPGF	PPGA	Result
1947-1948	6	3	3	71.5	76.2	Lost 2nd Round series to Minneapolis.
1948-1949	6	3	3	66.3	64.3	Lost 2nd Round series to Oshkosh.
1949-1950	3	1	2	74.7	86.0	Lost Division Semifinal to Anderson.
TOTAL:	15	7	8			
AVERAGE:	5	2	3	70.8	75.5	

Regular Season Individual Leaders

Season	Field Goals		Free Throws		Points	
1946-47	Don Otten	200	Don Otten	169	Don Otten	569
1947-48	Don Otten	282	Don Otten	260	Don Otten	824
1948-49	Don Otten	301	Don Otten	297	Don Otten	899
1949-50	Dwight Eddleman	332	Mike Todorovich	266	Dwight Eddleman	826
1950-51	Dwight Eddleman	398	Frank Brian	418	Frank Brian	1144

COACHING HISTORY: **1946**-1948 Nat Hickey 23-29-.442; 1947-1949 Bobby McDermott 47-38-.553; 1948-1950 Roger Potter 12-14-.462; 1949-1950 Red Auerbach 28-29-.491; 1950-1951 Dave McMillan 9-14-.391; 1950-1951 John Logan 2-1-.667; 1950-1951 Mike Todorovich 14-28-.333

TROY TROJANS
(became New York Gothams)

Home City: Troy, New York
Home Field: Putnam Grounds (1879)
    Center Island Grounds (1880-1881)
    Troy Ball Club Grounds (1882)   Capacity: 3,000
Origin of Name: The residents of Troy are called Trojans.

Regular Season Record

Season	League	GP	W	L	Pct	GB	R	OR
1879	NL	75	19	56	.253	35.5	321	543
1880	NL	83	41	42	.494	25.5	392	438
1881	NL	84	39	45	.464	17	399	429
1882	NL	83	35	48	.422	19.5	430	522
TOTAL:	4 years	325	134	191		97.5	1542	1932
AVERAGE:		81	33	48	.412	24.5	386	483

Regular Season Individual Leaders

Season	Home Runs		RBI's		Wins	
1879	Dan Brouthers	4	George Bradley	23	George Bradley	13
1880	Roger Connor	3	Roger Connor	47	Mickey Welch	34
1881	Roger Connor	2	Pete Gillespie	41	Mickey Welch	21
1882	Roger Connor	4	Roger Connor	42	Tim Keefe	17

COACHING HISTORY: 1879 Horace Phillips 12-46-.207; 1879-1882 Bob Ferguson 122-145-.457

TULSA ROUGHNECKS
(were Team Hawaii)

Home City: Tulsa, Oklahoma
Home Stadium: Skelly Stadium   Capacity: 40,235 [1984]
Origin of Name: The name was chosen to honor Oklahoma's oil industry.

Regular Season Record

Season	League	GP	W	L	GF	GA	BP	Pts	Pct
1978	NASL	30	15	15	49	46	42	132	.489
1979	NASL	30	14	16	61	56	55	139	.515
1980	NASL	32	15	17	56	62	49	139	.483
1981	NASL	32	17	15	60	49	54	154	.321
1982	NASL	32	16	16	69	57	59	151	.315
1983	NASL	30	17	13	56	49	47	145	.322
1984	NASL	24	10	14	42	46	38	98	.272
TOTAL:	7 years	210	104	106	393	365	344	958	
AVERAGE:		30	15	15	56	52	49	137	.369

Playoff Record

Season	GP	W	L	GF	GA	Result
1978	1	0	1	1	3	Lost 1st Round series to Minnesota.
1979	5	3	2	8	8	Lost 2nd Round series to New York.
1980	2	0	2	2	11	Lost 1st Round series to New York.
1981	2	0	2	1	4	Lost 1st Round series to Minnesota.
1982	3	1	2	1	6	Lost 1st Round series to New York.
1983	6	5	1	14	6	**Won NASL Championship.**

TOTAL:	19	9	10	27	38
AVERAGE:	3	1	2	4	6

Regular Season Individual Leaders

Season	Goals		Points		GAA (360 Min)	
1978	Billy Caskey	11	Billy Caskey	30	Colin Boulton	1.39
1979					Colin Boulton	1.61
1980					Gene DuChateau	1.55
1981	Duncan McKenzie	14	Duncan McKenzie	44	Zeljko Bilecki	1.33
1982	Laurie Abrahams	17	Laurie Abrahams	44	Winston DuBose	1.67
1983	Ron Futcher	15	Ron Futcher	40		
1984	Ron Futcher	18	Ron Futcher	44		

COACHING HISTORY: 1978 Bill Foulkes 8-9; 1978 Alex Skotarek 7-6; 1979 Alan Hinton 14-16; 1980-1981 Charlie Mitchell 32-32; 1982-1983 Terry Hennessey 33-29; 1984 Wim Suurbier 10-14

228th BATTALION

Home City: Toronto, Ontario
Home Arena: Mutual Street Arena
Origin of Name: The Northern Fusiliers (228th Battalion) recruited several hockey stars from Ontario and formed a team which competed in the National Hockey Association in the 1916-1917 season. The regiment was called overseas during the season and didn't complete the schedule.

Regular Season Record

Season	League	GP	W	L	T	GF	GA	Pts	Pct
1916-1917	NHA	14	6	8	0	73	69	12	.429

Regular Season Individual Leaders

Season	Goals		Points		GAA	
1916-1917	Eddie Oatman	17	Eddie Oatman	17	Howard Lockhart	5.75

COACHING HISTORY: L.W. Reade 6-8-0-.429

UTAH JAZZ
(were New Orleans Jazz)

Home City: Salt Lake City, Utah
     Las Vegas, Nevada (1983-1984)
Home Court: Salt Palace (1979-1983)   Capacity: 12,201 [1980]
             Salt Palace (1983-1984)   Capacity: 12,201 [1980]
             Thomas-Mack Center (1983-1984)   Capacity: 18,500 [1984]
             Salt Palace (1985-1991)   Capacity: 12,616 [1991]
             Delta Center (1991-present)   Capacity: 19,911 [2006]
Origin of Name: The team kept the same nickname when it moved to Salt Lake City from New Orleans.

Regular Season Record

Season	League	GP	W	L	PPGF	PPGA	Pct	GB
1979-1980	NBA	82	24	58	102.4	108.4	.293	25
1980-1981	NBA	82	28	54	101.2	107.1	.341	24
1981-1982	NBA	82	25	57	110.9	116.6	.305	23
1982-1983	NBA	82	30	52	109.0	113.2	.366	23
1983-1984	NBA	82	45	37	115.0	113.8	.549	-

1984-1985	NBA	82	41	41	109.0	109.1	.500	11
1985-1986	NBA	82	42	40	108.2	108.5	.512	9
1986-1987	NBA	82	44	38	107.9	107.5	.537	11
1987-1988	NBA	82	47	35	108.5	104.8	.573	7
1988-1989	NBA	82	51	31	104.7	99.7	.622	-
1989-1990	NBA	82	55	27	106.8	102.0	.671	1
1990-1991	NBA	82	54	28	104.0	100.7	.659	1
1991-1992	NBA	82	55	27	108.3	101.9	.671	-
1992-1993	NBA	82	47	35	106.2	104.0	.573	8
1993-1994	NBA	82	53	29	101.9	97.7	.646	5
1994-1995	NBA	82	60	22	106.4	98.4	.732	2
1995-1996	NBA	82	55	27	102.5	95.9	.671	4
1996-1997	NBA	82	64	18	103.1	94.3	.780	-
1997-1998	NBA	82	62	20	101.0	94.4	.756	-
1998-1999	NBA	50	37	13	93.3	86.8	.740	-
1999-2000	NBA	82	55	27	96.5	92.0	.671	-
2000-2001	NBA	82	53	29	97.1	92.4	.646	5
2001-2002	NBA	82	44	38	96.0	95.1	.537	14
2002-2003	NBA	82	47	35	94.7	92.3	.573	13
2003-2004	NBA	82	42	40	88.7	89.9	.512	16
2004-2005	NBA	82	26	56	93.0	97.3	.317	26
2005-2006	NBA	82	41	41	92.4	95.0	.500	3
TOTAL:	27 years	2182	1227	955				231
AVERAGE:		81	45	36	102.7	100.9	.562	9

Playoff Record

Season	GP	W	L	PPGF	PPGA	Result
1983-1984	11	5	6	110.7	111.9	Lost Conference Semifinal to Phoenix.
1984-1985	10	4	6	111.0	114.5	Lost Conference Semifinal to Denver.
1985-1986	4	1	3	103.0	107.3	Lost 1st Round series to Dallas.
1986-1987	5	2	3	100.8	102.2	Lost 1st Round series to Golden State.
1987-1988	11	6	5	103.4	102.4	Lost Conference Semifinal to Los Angeles.
1988-1989	3	0	3	105.3	114.0	Lost 1st Round series to Golden State.
1989-1990	5	2	3	102.4	103.8	Lost 1st Round series to Phoenix.
1990-1991	9	4	5	105.1	102.9	Lost Conference Semifinal to Portland.
1991-1992	16	9	7	102.9	102.5	Lost Conference Final to Portland.
1992-1993	5	2	3	87.2	91.4	Lost 1st Round series to Seattle.
1993-1994	16	8	8	94.3	92.3	Lost Conference Final to Houston.
1994-1995	5	2	3	104.0	108.0	Lost 1st Round series to Houston.
1995-1996	18	10	8	95.2	87.6	Lost Conference Final to Seattle.
1996-1997	20	13	7	96.1	92.8	Lost Championship series to Chicago.
1997-1998	20	13	7	89.0	86.9	Lost Championship series to Chicago.
1998-1999	10	4	6	98.1	96.1	Lost Conference Semifinal to Portland.
1999-2000	10	4	6	87.7	93.8	Lost Conference Semifinal to Portland.
2000-2001	5	2	3	89.6	93.8	Lost 1st Round series to Dallas.
2001-2002	4	1	3	88.0	89.0	Lost 1st Round series to Sacramento.
2002-2003	5	1	4	93.0	103.6	Lost 1st Round series to Sacramento.
TOTAL:	192	93	99			
AVERAGE:	10	5	5	97.9	97.7	

Regular Season Individual Leaders

Season	Field Goal % (min. 70 games)		Points		Points per Game (min. 70 games)	
1979-80	Ben Poquette	.523	Adrian Dantley	1903	Adrian Dantley	28.0

Regular Season Individual Leaders

Season	Field Goal % (min. 70 games)		Points		Points per Game (min. 70 games)	
1980-81	Adrian Dantley	.559	Adrian Dantley	2452	Adrian Dantley	30.7
1981-82	Adrian Dantley	.570	Adrian Dantley	2457	Adrian Dantley	30.3
1982-83	Rickey Green	.493	Darrell Griffith	1709	Darrell Griffith	22.2
1983-84	Adrian Dantley	.558	Adrian Dantley	2418	Adrian Dantley	30.6
1984-85	Jeff Wilkins	.490	Darrell Griffith	1764	Darrell Griffith	22.6
	Thurl Bailey	.490				
1985-86	Adrian Dantley	.563	Adrian Dantley	2267	Adrian Dantley	29.8
1986-87	Karl Malone	.512	Karl Malone	1779	Karl Malone	21.7
1987-88	John Stockton	.574	Karl Malone	2268	Karl Malone	27.7
1988-89	Eric Leckner	.545	Karl Malone	2326	Karl Malone	29.1
1989-90	Eric Leckner	.563	Karl Malone	2540	Karl Malone	31.0
1990-91	Mark Eaton	.579	Karl Malone	2382	Karl Malone	29.0
1991-92	Karl Malone	.526	Karl Malone	2272	Karl Malone	28.0
1992-93	Karl Malone	.552	Karl Malone	2217	Karl Malone	27.0
1993-94	John Stockton	.528	Karl Malone	2063	Karl Malone	25.2
1994-95	Adam Keefe	.577	Karl Malone	2187	Karl Malone	26.7
1995-96	John Stockton	.538	Karl Malone	2106	Karl Malone	25.7
1996-97	Karl Malone	.550	Karl Malone	2249	Karl Malone	27.4
1997-98	Adam Keefe	.540	Karl Malone	2190	Karl Malone	27.0
1998-99*	Karl Malone	.493	Karl Malone	1164	Karl Malone	23.8
1999-00	Olden Polynice	.510	Karl Malone	2095	Karl Malone	25.5
2000-01	John Stockton	.504	Karl Malone	1878	Karl Malone	23.2
2001-02	Donyell Marshall	.519	Karl Malone	1788	Karl Malone	22.4
2002-03	Greg Ostertag	.518	Karl Malone	1667	Karl Malone	20.6
2003-04	Jarron Collins	.498	Andrei Kirilenko	1284	Andrei Kirilenko	16.5
2004-05	Matt Harpring	.489	Matt Harpring	1090	Matt Harpring	14.0
2005-06	Matt Harpring	.475	Mehmet Okur	1472	Mehmet Okur	18.0

COACHING HISTORY: 1979-1982 Tom Nissalke 60-124-.326; 1981-1989 Frank Layden 277-294-.485; 1988-present Jerry Sloan

UTAH STARS
(were Los Angeles Stars)

Home City: Salt Lake City, Utah
Home Court: Salt Palace   Capacity: 12,201 [1975]
Origin of Name: The team kept the same nickname when it moved to Salt Lake City from Los Angeles.

Regular Season Record

Season	League	GP	W	L	PPGF	PPGA	Pct	GB
1970-1971	ABA	84	57	27	119.0	111.9	.679	1
1971-1972	ABA	84	60	24	117.8	112.1	.714	-
1972-1973	ABA	84	55	29	115.6	110.0	.655	-
1973-1974	ABA	84	51	33	105.1	104.7	.607	-
1974-1975	ABA	84	38	46	101.3	102.9	.452	27
1975-1976	ABA	16	4	12	114.9	116.6	.125	34
TOTAL:	6 years	436	265	171				62
AVERAGE:		73	44	29	112.3	109.7	.608	10

*-minimum 40 games.

Playoff Record

Season	GP	W	L	PPGF	PPGA	Result
1970-1971	18	12	6	120.8	113.7	Won ABA Championship.
1971-1972	11	7	4	110.3	107.8	Lost 2nd Round series to Indiana.
1972-1973	10	6	4	107.3	103.4	Lost 2nd Round series to Indiana.
1973-1974	18	9	9	102.3	99.8	Lost Championship series to New York.
1974-1975	6	2	4	118.8	118.5	Lost 1st Round series to Denver.
TOTAL:	63	36	27			
AVERAGE:	12	7	5	111.9	108.6	

Regular Season Individual Leaders

Season	Field Goal % (min. 70 games)		Points		Points per Game (min. 70 games)	
1970-71	Zelmo Beaty	.555	Zelmo Beaty	1744	Zelmo Beaty	22.9
1971-72	Zelmo Beaty	.539	Zelmo Beaty	1980	Zelmo Beaty	23.6
1972-73	Jimmy Jones	.523	Ron Boone	1557	Willie Wise	22.0
1973-74	Jimmy Jones	.550	Willie Wise	1826	Willie Wise	22.3
1974-75	Moses Malone	.571	Ron Boone	2117	Ron Boone	25.2
1975-76	Don Washington	.667	John Roche	264	John Roche	16.5

COACHING HISTORY: 1970-1971 Bill Sharman 57-27-.679; 1971-1973 LaDell Andersen 115-53-.685; 1973-1974 Joe Mullaney 51-33-.607; 1974-1975 Bucky Buckwalter 24-32-.429; 1974-1976 Tom Nissalke 18-26-.409

UTAH STARZZ
(became San Antonio Silver Stars)

Home City: Salt Lake City, Utah
Home Arena: Delta Center   Capacity: 19,911 [2001]
Origin of Name: The Starzz (with two z's) was named to show affiliation with the NBA's Jazz (with two z's).

Regular Season Record

Season	League	GP	W	L	PPGF	PPGA	Pct	GB
1997	WNBA	28	7	21	64.6	75.1	.250	9
1998	WNBA	30	8	22	69.8	76.5	.267	19
1999	WNBA	32	15	17	74.0	77.1	.469	11
2000	WNBA	32	18	14	75.4	75.2	.563	10
2001	WNBA	32	19	13	69.0	68.5	.594	9
2002	WNBA	32	20	12	75.6	73.3	.625	5
TOTAL:	6 years	186	87	99				63
AVERAGE:		31	15	16	71.6	74.2	.468	10

Playoff Record

Season	GP	W	L	PPGF	PPGA	Result
2001	2	0	2	65.5	80.0	Lost Conference semifinal to Sacramento
2002	5	2	3	72.2	78.4	Lost Conference final to L.A.
TOTAL:	7	2	5			
AVERAGE:	3	1	2	70.4	78.9	

Regular Season Individual Leaders

Season	Field Goals % (20 games min.)		Free Throws % (20 games min.)		Points per Game (20 games min.)	
1997	Jessie Hicks	.463	Dena Head	.844	Wendy Palmer	15.8
1998	Malgorzata Dydek	.482	Elena Baranova	.831	Wendy Palmer	13.5

Season	Field Goals % (20 games min.)		Free Throws % (20 games min.)		Points per Game (20 games min.)	
1999	Natalie Williams	.519	Krystyna Lara	1.000	Natalie Williams	18.0
			C. Tremitiere	1.000		
2000	N. Mulitauaopele	.594	Jennifer Azzi	.930	Natalie Williams	18.7
2001	Marie Ferdinand	.493	Jennifer Azzi	.917	Natalie Williams	14.2
2002	Marie Ferdinand	.474	Margo Dydek	.844	A. Goodson	15.7

COACHING HISTORY: 1997-98 Denise Taylor 13-34-.277, 1998 Frank Layden 2-9-.182, 1999-2001 Fred Williams 38-39-.494; 2001-2002 Candi Harvey 34-17-.667

VANCOUVER BLAZERS
(were Philadelphia Blazers)
(became Calgary Cowboys)

Home City: Vancouver, British Columbia
Home Arena: Pacific Coliseum   Capacity: 15,569 [1975]
Origin of Name: The team kept the same nickname when it moved to Vancouver from Philadelphia.

Regular Season Record

Season	League	GP	W	L	T	GF	GA	Pts	Pct
1973-1974	WHA	78	27	50	1	278	345	55	.353
1974-1975	WHA	78	37	39	2	256	270	76	.487
TOTAL:	2 years	156	64	89	3	534	615	131	
AVERAGE:		78	32	45	1	267	308	65	.420

Regular Season Individual Leaders

Season	Goals		Points		Penalty Minutes	
1973-1974	Danny Lawson	50	Danny Lawson	88	Colin Campbell	193
			Bryan Campbell	88		
1974-1975	Danny Lawson	33	Danny Lawson	76	Rick Jodzio	159

COACHING HISTORY: 1973-1974 John McKenzie 3-4-0-.429; 1973-1974 Phil Watson 3-9-0-.250; 1973-1974 Andy Bathgate 21-37-1-.364; 1974-1975 Joe Crozier 37-39-2-.487

VANCOUVER CANUCKS

Home City: Vancouver, British Columbia
Home Arena: Pacific Coliseum (1970-1995)   Capacity: 16,150 [1994]
               General Motors Place (1995-present)   Capacity: 18,630 [2005]
Origin of Name: The team was named after the minor pro Western Hockey League team of the 1960's.

Regular Season Record

Season	League	GP	W	L	T	OL	SL	GF	GA	Pts
1970-1971	NHL	78	24	46	8	NA	NA	229	296	56
1971-1972	NHL	78	20	50	8	NA	NA	203	297	48
1972-1973	NHL	78	22	47	9	NA	NA	233	339	53
1973-1974	NHL	78	24	43	11	NA	NA	224	296	59
1974-1975	NHL	80	38	32	10	NA	NA	271	254	86
1975-1976	NHL	80	33	32	15	NA	NA	271	272	81
1976-1977	NHL	80	25	42	13	NA	NA	235	294	63
1977-1978	NHL	80	20	43	17	NA	NA	239	320	57
1978-1979	NHL	80	25	42	13	NA	NA	217	291	63

1979-1980	NHL	80	27	37	16	NA	NA	256	281	70
1980-1981	NHL	80	28	32	20	NA	NA	289	301	76
1981-1982	NHL	80	30	33	17	NA	NA	290	286	77
1982-1983	NHL	80	30	35	15	NA	NA	303	309	75
1983-1984	NHL	80	32	39	9	NA	NA	306	328	73
1984-1985	NHL	80	25	46	9	NA	NA	284	401	59
1985-1986	NHL	80	23	44	13	NA	NA	282	333	59
1986-1987	NHL	80	29	43	8	NA	NA	282	314	66
1987-1988	NHL	80	25	46	9	NA	NA	272	320	59
1988-1989	NHL	80	33	39	8	NA	NA	251	253	74
1989-1990	NHL	80	25	41	14	NA	NA	245	306	64
1990-1991	NHL	80	28	43	9	NA	NA	243	315	65
1991-1992	NHL	80	42	26	12	NA	NA	285	250	96
1992-1993	NHL	84	46	29	9	NA	NA	346	278	101
1993-1994	NHL	84	41	40	3	NA	NA	279	276	85
1994-1995	NHL	48	18	18	12	NA	NA	153	148	48
1995-1996	NHL	82	32	35	15	NA	NA	278	278	79
1996-1997	NHL	82	35	40	7	NA	NA	257	273	77
1997-1998	NHL	82	25	43	14	NA	NA	224	273	64
1998-1999	NHL	82	23	47	12	NA	NA	192	258	58
1999-2000	NHL	82	30	37	15	8	NA	227	237	83
2000-2001	NHL	82	36	28	11	7	NA	239	238	90
2001-2002	NHL	82	42	30	7	3	NA	254	211	94
2002-2003	NHL	82	45	23	13	1	NA	264	208	104
2003-2004	NHL	82	43	24	10	5	NA	235	194	101
2004-2005	NHL	Season cancelled due to lockout.								
2005-2006	NHL	82	42	32	NA	4	4	256	255	92
TOTAL:	35 years	2788	1066	1307	391	28	4	8914	9783	2555
AVERAGE:		80	31	37	11	1	0	255	280	73

Playoff Record

Season	GP	W	L	GF	GA	Result
1974-1975	5	1	4	9	20	Lost Quarterfinal series to Montreal.
1975-1976	2	0	2	4	8	Lost Preliminary series to Islanders.
1978-1979	3	1	2	9	15	Lost Preliminary series to Philadelphia.
1979-1980	4	1	3	7	15	Lost Preliminary series to Buffalo.
1980-1981	3	0	3	7	13	Lost Preliminary series to Buffalo.
1981-1982	17	11	6	57	50	Lost Stanley Cup Final to Islanders.
1982-1983	4	1	3	14	17	Lost Division Semifinal to Calgary.
1983-1984	4	1	3	13	14	Lost Division Semifinal to Calgary.
1985-1986	3	0	3	5	17	Lost Division Semifinal to Edmonton.
1988-1989	7	3	4	20	26	Lost Division Semifinal to Calgary.
1990-1991	6	2	4	16	26	Lost Division Semifinal to Los Angeles.
1991-1992	13	6	7	44	35	Lost Division Final to Edmonton.
1992-1993	12	6	6	46	43	Lost Division Final to Los Angeles.
1993-1994	24	15	9	78	61	Lost Stanley Cup Final to Rangers.
1994-1995	11	4	7	33	38	Lost Conference Semifinal to Chicago.
1995-1996	6	2	4	17	24	Lost Conference Quarterfinal to Colorado.
2000-2001	4	0	4	9	16	Lost Conference Quarterfinal to Colorado.
2001-2002	6	2	4	19	20	Lost Conference Quarterfinal to Detroit.
2002-2003	14	7	7	34	47	Lost Conference Seminal to Minnesota.
2003-2004	7	3	4	16	19	Lost Conference Quarterfinal to Calgary.
TOTAL:	155	66	89	457	524	
AVERAGE:	7	3	4	23	26	

Regular Season Individual Leaders

Season	Goals		Points		Penalty Minutes	
1970-1971	Rosaire Paiement	34	Andre Boudrias	66	Rosaire Paiement	152
1971-1972	Andre Boudrias	27	Andre Boudrias	61	John Schella	166
			Orland Kurtenbach	61		
1972-1973	Bobby Schmautz	38	Bobby Schmautz	38	Bobby Schmautz	137
1973-1974	D. Ververgaert	26	Andre Boudrias	75	Bob Dailey	143
1974-1975	Don Lever	38	Andre Boudrias	78	Tracy Pratt	145
1975-1976	D. Ververgaert	37	D. Ververgaert	71	Harold Snepsts	125
1976-1977	Rick Blight	28	Rick Blight	68	Harold Snepsts	149
1977-1978	Mike Walton	29	Mike Walton	66	Jack McIlhargey	172
1978-1979	Ron Sedlbauer	40	Ron Sedlbauer	56	Harold Snepsts	130
1979-1980	Stan Smyl	30	Stan Smyl	78	Stan Smyl	204
1980-1981	Dave Williams	35	Thomas Gradin	69	Dave Williams	343
1981-1982	Thomas Gradin	37	Thomas Gradin	86	Dave Williams	341
1982-1983	Darcy Rota	42	Stan Smyl	88	Dave Williams	265
1983-1984	Tony Tanti	45	Patrik Sundstrom	91	Dave Williams	294
1984-1985	Tony Tanti	39	Patrik Sundstrom	68	Garth Butcher	152
1985-1986	Tony Tanti	39	Petri Skriko	78	Garth Butcher	188
1986-1987	Tony Tanti	41	Tony Tanti	79	Garth Butcher	207
1987-1988	Tony Tanti	40	Tony Tanti	77	Garth Butcher	285
1988-1989	Petri Skriko	30	Petri Skriko	66	Garth Butcher	227
	Trevor Linden	30				
1989-1990	Greg Adams	30	Paul Reinhart	57	Ronnie Stern	208
1990-1991	Trevor Linden	33	Trevor Linden	70	Gino Odjick	296
1991-1992	Pavel Bure	34	Trevor Linden	75	Gino Odjick	348
1992-1993	Pavel Bure	60	Pavel Bure	110	Gino Odjick	370
1993-1994	Pavel Bure	60	Pavel Bure	107	Gino Odjick	271
1994-1995	Pavel Bure	20	Pavel Bure	43	Dana Murzyn	129
1995-1996	A. Mogilny	55	A. Mogilny	107	Gino Odjick	181
1996-1997	Martin Gelinas	35	A. Mogilny	73	Gino Odjick	371
1997-1998	Pavel Bure	51	Pavel Bure	90	Donald Brashear	372
1998-1999	Markus Naslund	36	Markus Naslund	66	Donald Brashear	209
1999-2000	Markus Naslund	27	Markus Naslund	65	Donald Brashear	136
2000-2001	Markus Naslund	41	Markus Naslund	75	Donald Brashear	145
2001-2002	Markus Naslund	40	Markus Naslund	90	Matt Cooke	111
2002-2003	Markus Naslund	48	Markus Naslund	104	Todd Bertuzzi	144
2003-2004	Markus Naslund	35	Markus Naslund	84	Brad May	137
2004-2005	Season cancelled due to lockout.					
2005-2006	Anson Carter	33	Markus Naslund	79	Jarkko Ruutu	142

COACHING HISTORY: 1970-1972 Hal Laycoe 44-96-16-.333; 1972-1973 Vic Stasiuk 22-47-9-.340; 1973-1974 Bill McCreary 9-25-7-.305; 1973-1977 Phil Maloney 95-105-32-.478; 1976-1978 Orland Kurtenbach 36-62-27-.396; 1978-1982 Harry Neale 106-144-65-.440; 1981-1984 Roger Neilson 51-61-21-.462; 1983-1985 Harry Neale 36-45-11-.451; 1984-1985 Bill LaForge 4-14-2-.250; 1985-1987 Tom Watt 52-87-21-.391; 1987-1991 Bob McCammon 102-156-36-.408; 1990-1994 Pat Quinn 138-108-28-.555; 1994-1996 Rick Ley 47-50-27-.488, 1995-1996 Pat Quinn 3-3-0-.500; 1996-1998 Tom Renney 39-53-9-.431; 1997-1998 Mike Keenan 36-54-18-.417; 1998-2006 Marc Crawford 246-189-62-28-4-.554; 2006-present

VANCOUVER GRIZZLIES
(became Memphis Grizzlies)

Home City: Vancouver, British Columbia
Home Court: General Motors Place (1995-present)   Capacity: 19,193 [2001]
Origin of Name: According to team general manager Stu Jackson, the name was chosen to reflect "the powerful nature of the team, the culture, geography and heritage of Western Canada and an indigenous species."

Regular Season Record

Season	League	GP	W	L	PPGF	PPGA	Pct	GB
1995-1996	NBA	82	15	67	89.8	99.8	.183	44
1996-1997	NBA	82	14	68	89.2	99.4	.171	50
1997-1998	NBA	82	19	63	96.6	103.9	.232	43
1998-1999	NBA	50	8	42	88.9	97.5	.160	29
1999-2000	NBA	82	22	60	93.9	99.5	.268	33
2000-2001	NBA	82	23	59	91.7	97.5	.280	35
TOTAL:	6 years	460	101	359				234
AVERAGE:		77	17	60	91.9	99.7	.220	39

Regular Season Individual Leaders

Season	Field Goal % (min. 70 games)		Points		Points per Game (min. 70 games)	
1995-96	Bryant Reeves	.457	Blue Edwards	1043	Bryant Reeves	13.3
1996-97	Roy Rogers	.505	S. Abdur-Rahim	1494	S. Abdur-Rahim	18.7
1997-98	Bryant Reeves	.523	S. Abdur-Rahim	1829	S. Abdur-Rahim	22.3
1998-99*	Michael Smith	.535	S. Abdur-Rahim	1152	S. Abdur-Rahim	23.0
1999-00	O. Harrington	.506	S. Abdur-Rahim	1663	S. Abdur-Rahim	20.3
2000-01	S. Abdur-Rahim	.472	S. Abdur-Rahim	1663	S. Abdur-Rahim	20.5

COACHING HISTORY: 1995-1997 Brian Winters 23-102-.184; 1996-1997 Stu Jackson 6-33-.154; 1997-2000 Brian Hill 31-123-.201; 1999-2000 Lionel Hollins 18-42-.300; 2000-present Sidney Lowe

VANCOUVER MAROONS
(were Vancouver Millionaires)

Home City: Vancouver, British Columbia
Home Arena: Denman Street Arena   Capacity: 10,500
Origin of Name: As with most clubs with "colorful" names the team was named after their uniform color. Known as Millionaires from 1911 to 1922, a name they adopted from the Renfrew team of the NHA who were sometimes known as the Millionaires because of their high payroll.

Regular Season Record

Season	League	GP	W	L	T	GF	GA	Pts	Pct
1911-1912	PCHA	15	7	8	0	102	94	14	.467
1912-1913	PCHA	16	7	9	0	84	89	14	.438
1913-1914	PCHA	15	6	9	0	76	83	12	.400
1914-1915	PCHA	17	13	4	0	115	71	26	.765
1915-1916	PCHA	18	9	9	0	75	69	18	.500
1916-1917	PCHA	23	14	9	0	131	124	28	.607
1917-1918	PCHA	18	9	9	0	70	60	18	.500

*-minimum 40 games.

1918-1919	PCHA	20	12	8	0	72	55	24	.600
1919-1920	PCHA	22	11	11	0	75	65	22	.500
1920-1921	PCHA	24	13	11	0	86	78	26	.542
1921-1922	PCHA	24	12	12	0	77	68	24	.500
1922-1923	PCHA	30	17	12	1	116	88	35	.583
1923-1924	PCHA	30	13	16	1	87	80	27	.450
1924-1925	WCHL	28	12	16	0	91	102	24	.429
1925-1926	WHL	30	10	18	2	64	90	22	.367
TOTAL:	15 years	330	165	161	4	1321	1216	334	
AVERAGE:		22	11	11	0	88	81	22	.506

Playoff Record

Season	GP	W	L	T	GF	GA	Result
1914-1915	3	3	0	0	26	8	Won Stanley Cup.
1917-1918	7	3	3	1	24	20	Lost Stanley Cup Final to Toronto.
1918-1919	2	1	1	0	5	7	Lost PCHA Championship to Seattle.
1919-1920	2	1	1	0	3	7	Lost PCHA Championship to Seattle.
1920-1921	7	4	3	0	25	14	Lost Stanley Cup Final to Ottawa.
1921-1922	9	5	4	0	16	18	Lost Stanley Cup Final to Toronto.
1922-1923	6	2	4	0	12	13	Lost playoff series to Ottawa.
1923-1924	7	2	4	1	14	18	Lost playoff series to Canadiens.
TOTAL:	43	21	20	2	125	105	
AVERAGE:	5	2	3	0	16	13	

Regular Season Individual Leaders

Season	Goals		Points		GAA	
1911-1912	Newsy Lalonde	27	Newsy Lalonde	27	Allan Parr	6.27
1912-1913	Carl Kendall	16	Carl Kendall	16	Allan Parr	5.56
1913-1914	Fred Taylor	18	Fred Taylor	18	Allan Parr	5.53
1914-1915	Mickey Mackay	34	Mickey Mackay	34	Hugh Lehman	4.18
1915-1916	Fred Taylor	22	Fred Taylor	22	Hugh Lehman	3.83
1916-1917	Gordon Roberts	43	Gordon Roberts	43	Hugh Lehman	5.39
1917-1918	Fred Taylor	32	Fred Taylor	32	Hugh Lehman	3.33
1918-1919	Fred Taylor	23	Fred Taylor	23	Hugh Lehman	2.75
1919-1920	Alf Skinner	16	Alf Skinner	16	Hugh Lehman	2.95
1920-1921	Alf Skinner	20	Alf Skinner	20	Hugh Lehman	3.25
1921-1922	Jack Adams	25	Jack Adams	25	Hugh Lehman	2.82
1922-1923	Mickey Mackay	27	Mickey Mackay	27	Hugh Lehman	2.44
1923-1924	Mickey Mackay	23	Mickey Mackay	23	Hugh Lehman	2.67
1924-1925	Mickey Mackay	27	Mickey Mackay	27	Hugh Lehman	2.73
1925-1926	Frank Boucher	16	Frank Boucher	16	Hugh Lehman	3.00

COACHING HISTORY: 1911-1926 Frank Patrick 165-161-4-.506

VANCOUVER ROYALS

Home City: Vancouver, British Columbia
Home Stadium: Empire Stadium
Origin of Name: The team was represented by the Sunderland Club of the English League.

Regular Season Record

Season	League	GP	W	L	T	GF	GA	BP	Pts	Pct
1967	USA	12	3	4	5	20	28	-	11	.458
1968	NASL	32	12	15	5	51	60	49	136	.472

TOTAL:	2 years	44	15	19	10	71	88	49	147	
AVERAGE:		22	8	9	5	36	44	25	74	.471

Regular Season Individual Leaders

Season	Goals		Points		GAA (360 Min)	
1967	George Herd	3	George Herd	8	Derek Forster	2.31
	George Mulhall	3				
	Colin Suggett	3				
1968	Henry Klein	20	Henry Klein	44		

COACHING HISTORY: 1967 Ian McCall 3-4-5-.458; 1968 Ferenc Puskas 12-15-5-.472

VANCOUVER WHITECAPS

Home City: Vancouver, British Columbia
Home Stadium: Empire Stadium (1974-1982)   Capacity: 32,759 [1975]
       B.C. Place Stadium (1983-1984)   Capacity: 59,421 [1984]
Origin of Name: The name was chosen due to the fact Vancouver is surrounded by white capped mountains and white capped ocean waves.

Regular Season Record

Season	League	GP	W	L	T	GF	GA	BP	Pts	Pct
1974	NASL	20	5	11	4	29	30	28	70	.389
1975	NASL	22	11	11	-	38	28	33	99	.500
1976	NASL	24	14	10	-	38	30	36	120	.556
1977	NASL	26	14	12	-	43	46	40	124	.530
1978	NASL	30	24	6	-	68	29	55	199	.737
1979	NASL	30	20	10	-	54	34	52	172	.637
1980	NASL	32	16	16	-	52	47	43	139	.483
1981	NASL	32	21	11	-	74	43	62	186	.388
1982	NASL	32	20	12	-	58	48	46	160	.333
1983	NASL	30	24	6	-	63	34	51	187	.416
1984	NASL	24	13	11	-	51	48	43	117	.325
TOTAL:	11 years	302	182	116	4	568	417	489	1573	
AVERAGE:		28	17	11	-	52	38	44	143	.459

Playoff Record

Season	GP	W	L	GF	GA	Result
1976	1	0	1	0	1	Lost 1st Round series to Seattle.
1977	1	0	1	0	2	Lost 1st Round series to Seattle.
1978	3	1	2	5	3	Lost Conference Semifinal to Portland.
1979	9	7	2	16	10	**Won NASL Championship.**
1980	2	0	2	2	5	Lost 1st Round series to Seattle.
1981	2	0	2	1	5	Lost 1st Round series to Tampa Bay.
1982	3	1	2	3	7	Lost 1st Round series to San Diego.
1983	3	1	2	4	5	Lost 1st Round series to Toronto.
1984	3	1	2	5	7	Lost 1st Round series to Chicago.
TOTAL:	27	11	16	36	45	
AVERAGE:	3	1	2	4	5	

Regular Season Individual Leaders

Season	Goals		Points		GAA (360 Min)	
1974	Brian Gant	6	George McLean	15		

Season	Goals		Points		GAA (360 Min)	
1975	Glen Johnson	8	Glen Johnson	23	Peter Greco	1.13
1976	Tony McAndrew	6	Billy Woof	14	Greg Weber	1.17
1977	Derek Possee	11	Derek Possee	27	Arnold Mausser	1.66
1978	Kevin Hector	21	Kevin Hector	52	Phil Parkes	0.95
1979	Kevin Hector	15	Kevin Hector	36	Phil Parkes	0.96
1980	Trevor Whymark	15	Trevor Whymark	33	Bruce Grobbelaar	1.19
1981	Carl Valentine	10	Carl Valentine	34	Barry Siddall 1.30	
1982	Ray Hankin	11	Ray Hankin	30	Tino Lettieri	1.23
			Peter Lorimer	30		
1983	David Cross	19	David Cross	42		
1984	Peter Ward	16	Peter Ward	42		

COACHING HISTORY: 1974-1975 Jim Easton 16-22-4-.447; 1976-1977 Eckhard Krautzun 17-13; 1977 Holger Osieck 0-3; 1978-1980 Tony Waiters 60-32; 1981-1983 John Giles 65-29; 1984 Alan Hinton 13-11

VICTORIA ARISTOCRATS
(became Spokane Canaries)

Home City: Victoria, British Columbia
Home Arena: Victoria Arena   Capacity: 4,000
Origin of Name: Known during the 1911-12 season as the Senators.

Regular Season Record

Season	League	GP	W	L	T	GF	GA	Pts	Pct
1911-1912	PCHA	16	7	9	0	81	90	14	.438
1912-1913	PCHA	15	10	5	0	68	56	20	.667
1913-1914	PCHA	15	10	5	0	80	67	20	.667
1914-1915	PCHA	17	4	13	0	64	116	8	.235
1915-1916	PCHA	18	5	13	0	74	102	10	.278
TOTAL:	5 years	81	36	45	0	367	431	72	
AVERAGE:		16	7	9	0	73	86	14	.444

Playoff Record

Season	GP	W	L	T	GF	GA	Result
1913-1914	3	0	3	0	8	13	Lost Stanley Cup Final to Toronto.

Regular Season Individual Leaders

Season	Goals		Points		GAA	
1911-1912	Tom Dunderdale	24	Tom Dunderdale	24	Bert Lindsay	5.13
1912-1913	Tom Dunderdale	24	Tom Dunderdale	24	Bert Lindsay	3.73
1913-1914	Tom Dunderdale	23	Tom Dunderdale	23	Bert Lindsay	4.47
1914-1915	Tom Dunderdale	17	Tom Dunderdale	17	Bert Lindsay	6.82
1915-1916	Albert Kerr	16	Albert Kerr	16	Fred McCulloch	5.67

COACHING HISTORY: 1911-1916 Lester Patrick 36-45-0-.444

VICTORIA COUGARS
(were Portland Rosebuds)

Home City: Victoria, British Columbia
Home Arena: Victoria Arena   Capacity: 4,000
Origin of Name: Known from 1918 to 1920 as the "Aristocrats."

Regular Season Record

Season	League	GP	W	L	T	GF	GA	Pts	Pct
1918-1919	PCHA	20	7	13	0	44	81	14	.350
1919-1920	PCHA	22	10	12	0	57	71	20	.455
1920-1921	PCHA	24	10	13	1	71	88	21	.438
1921-1922	PCHA	24	11	12	1	61	71	23	.479
1922-1923	PCHA	30	16	14	0	94	85	32	.533
1923-1924	PCHA	30	11	18	1	78	103	23	.383
1924-1925	WCHL	28	16	12	0	84	63	32	.571
1925-1926	WHL	30	15	11	4	68	53	34	.567
TOTAL:	8 years	208	96	105	7	557	615	199	
AVERAGE:		26	12	13	1	70	77	25	.478

Playoff Record

Season	GP	W	L	T	GF	GA	Result
1922-1923	2	1	1	0	3	5	Lost PCHA playoff to Vancouver.
1924-1925	8	5	1	2	25	13	**Won Stanley Cup.**
1925-1926	8	3	3	2	12	16	Lost Stanley Cup Final to Maroons.
TOTAL:	18	9	5	4	40	34	
AVERAGE:	6	3	2	1	13	11	

Regular Season Individual Leaders

Season	Goals		Points		GAA	
1918-1919	Eddie Oatman	11	Eddie Oatman	11	Tom Murray	4.05
1919-1920	Tom Dunderdale	25	Tom Dunderdale	25	Norm Fowler	3.23
1920-1921	Frank Fredrickson	19	Frank Fredrickson	19	Norm Fowler	3.67
1921-1922	Frank Fredrickson	15	Frank Fredrickson	15	Norm Fowler	2.82
1922-1923	Frank Fredrickson	41	Frank Fredrickson	41	Norm Fowler	2.83
1923-1924	Frank Fredrickson	19	Frank Fredrickson	19	Norm Fowler	3.43
1924-1925	Frank Fredrickson	21	Frank Fredrickson	21	Harry Holmes	2.25
1925-1926	Frank Fredrickson	16	Frank Fredrickson	16	Harry Holmes	1.77

COACHING HISTORY: 1918-1926 Lester Patrick 96-105-7-.478

VIRGINIA SQUIRES
(were Washington Capitols)

Home City: Norfolk, Virginia and Richmond, Virginia
Home Court: Old Dominion University Gym (1970-71)
   Hampton Roads Coliseum (1970-76)
   Richmond Arena (1970-71)
   Roanoke Civic Center (1970-72)
   Richmond Coliseum (1971-1974, 1975-76)
   Norfolk Scope (1971-1976)   Capacity: 10,600 [1975]
Origin of Name:

Regular Season Record

Season	League	GP	W	L	PPGF	PPGA	Pct	GB
1970-1971	ABA	84	55	29	123.3	119.7	.655	-
1971-1972	ABA	84	45	39	118.9	118.0	.536	23
1972-1973	ABA	84	42	42	115.4	115.8	.500	15
1973-1974	ABA	84	28	56	106.4	111.3	.333	27
1974-1975	ABA	84	15	69	99.0	109.5	.179	43
1975-1976	ABA	83	15	68	106.9	116.6	.181	44.5

TOTAL:	6 years	503	200	303				152.5
AVERAGE:		84	33	51	111.7	115.2	.398	25

Playoff Record

Season	GP	W	L	PPGF	PPGA	Result
1970-1971	12	6	6	124.0	123.6	Lost 2nd Round series to Kentucky.
1971-1972	11	7	4	117.2	109.7	Lost 2nd Round series to New York.
1972-1973	5	1	4	103.2	112.0	Lost 1st Round series to Kentucky.
TOTAL:	28	14	14			
AVERAGE:	9	5	4	114.8	115.1	

Regular Season Individual Leaders

Season	Field Goal % (min. 70 games)		Points		Points per Game (min. 70 games)	
1970-71	Neil Johnson	.525	Charlie Scott	2276	Charlie Scott	27.1
1971-72	George Irvine	.504	Charlie Scott	2524	Charlie Scott	34.6
1972-73	George Irvine	.527	Julius Erving	2268	Julius Erving	31.9
1973-74	Jim Eakins	.520	George Carter	1546	George Carter	19.3
1974-75	Dave Twardzik	.546	Dave Twardzik	1036	Dave Twardzik	13.6
1975-76			Luther Burden	1413	Luther Burden	19.9

COACHING HISTORY: 1970-1976 Al Bianchi 186-241-.436; 1975-1976 Mack Calvin 0-6-.000; 1975-1976 Bill Musselman 4-22-.154; 1975-1976 Jack Ankerson 1-1-.500; 1975-1976 Zelmo Beaty 9-33-.214

WARREN PENN OILERS
(became Cleveland White Horses)

Home City: Warren, Pennsylvania
Home Court: Beaty Junior High School Gym   Capacity: 900
Origin of Name: The team received its name because it was sponsored by the Hyvis Oil Company.

Regular Season Record

Season	League	GP	W	L	PPGF	PPGA	Pct	GB
1937-1938	NBL	12	3	9	26.5	38.6	.250	8
1938-1939	NBL	19	9	10	38.1	39.6	.474	11
TOTAL:	2 years	31	12	19				19
AVERAGE:		16	6	10	32.3	39.1	.387	9.5

Regular Season Individual Leaders

Season	Field Goals		Free Throws		Points	
1937-38	Frank Maury	31	Walt Stankey	17	Frank Maury	75

COACHING HISTORY: 1937-1939 Gerry Archibald 12-19-.387

WASHINGTON CAPITALS

Home City: Landover, Maryland
Home Arena: U.S. Air Arena * (1974-1997)   Capacity: 18,130 [1997]
           MCI Center (1997-present)   Capacity: 18,277 [2005]
Origin of Name: The name was chosen in a Name the Team Contest.

*-known as Capital Center from 1974 to 1993

Regular Season Record

Season	League	GP	W	L	T	OL	SL	GF	GA	Pts
1974-1975	NHL	80	8	67	5	NA	NA	181	446	21
1975-1976	NHL	80	11	59	10	NA	NA	224	394	32
1976-1977	NHL	80	24	42	14	NA	NA	221	307	62
1977-1978	NHL	80	17	49	14	NA	NA	195	321	48
1978-1979	NHL	80	24	41	15	NA	NA	273	338	63
1979-1980	NHL	80	27	40	13	NA	NA	261	293	67
1980-1981	NHL	80	26	36	18	NA	NA	286	317	70
1981-1982	NHL	80	26	41	13	NA	NA	319	338	65
1982-1983	NHL	80	39	25	16	NA	NA	306	283	94
1983-1984	NHL	80	48	27	5	NA	NA	308	226	101
1984-1985	NHL	80	46	25	9	NA	NA	322	240	101
1985-1986	NHL	80	50	23	7	NA	NA	315	272	107
1986-1987	NHL	80	38	32	10	NA	NA	285	278	86
1987-1988	NHL	80	38	33	9	NA	NA	281	249	85
1988-1989	NHL	80	41	29	10	NA	NA	305	259	92
1989-1990	NHL	80	36	38	6	NA	NA	284	275	78
1990-1991	NHL	80	37	36	7	NA	NA	258	258	81
1991-1992	NHL	80	45	27	8	NA	NA	330	275	98
1992-1993	NHL	84	43	34	7	NA	NA	325	286	93
1993-1994	NHL	84	39	35	10	NA	NA	277	263	88
1994-1995	NHL	48	22	18	8	NA	NA	136	120	52
1995-1996	NHL	82	39	32	11	NA	NA	234	204	89
1996-1997	NHL	82	33	40	9	NA	NA	214	231	75
1997-1998	NHL	82	40	30	12	NA	NA	219	202	92
1998-1999	NHL	82	31	45	6	NA	NA	200	218	68
1999-2000	NHL	82	44	26	12	2	NA	227	194	102
2000-2001	NHL	82	41	27	10	4	NA	233	211	96
2001-2002	NHL	82	36	33	11	2	NA	228	240	85
2002-2003	NHL	82	39	29	8	6	NA	224	220	92
2003-2004	NHL	82	23	45	10	4	NA	186	253	60
2004-2005	NHL	Season cancelled due to lockout.								
2005-2006	NHL	82	29	41	NA	6	6	237	306	70
TOTAL:	31 years	2476	1040	1105	303	24	6	7894	8317	2413
AVERAGE:		80	34	36	10	1	0	255	268	78

Playoff Record

Season	GP	W	L	GF	GA	Result
1982-1983	4	1	3	11	19	Lost Division Semifinal to Islanders.
1983-1984	8	4	4	28	25	Lost Division Final to Islanders.
1984-1985	5	2	3	12	14	Lost Division Semifinal to Islanders.
1985-1986	9	5	4	36	24	Lost Division Final to Rangers.
1986-1987	7	3	4	19	19	Lost Division Semifinal to Islanders.
1987-1988	14	7	7	54	50	Lost Division Final to New Jersey.
1988-1989	6	2	4	19	25	Lost Division Semifinal to Philadelphia.
1989-1990	15	8	7	49	48	Lost Conference Final to Boston.
1990-1991	11	5	6	29	35	Lost Division Final to Pittsburgh.
1991-1992	7	3	4	27	25	Lost Division Semifinal to Pittsburgh.
1992-1993	6	2	4	22	23	Lost Division Semifinal to Islanders.
1993-1994	11	5	6	32	32	Lost Conference Semifinal to Rangers.
1994-1995	7	3	4	26	29	Lost Conference Quarterfinal to Pittsburgh.
1995-1996	6	2	4	17	21	Lost Conference Quarterfinal to Pittsburgh.
1997-1998	21	12	9	53	44	Lost Stanley Cup Final to Detroit.

1999-2000	5	1	4	8	17	Lost Conference Quarterfinal to Pittsburgh.
2000-2001	6	2	4	10	14	Lost Conference Quarterfinal to Pittsburgh.
2002-2003	6	2	4	15	14	Lost Conference Quarterfinal to Tampa
TOTAL:	154	69	85	467	478	
AVERAGE:	9	4	5	26	27	

Regular Season Individual Leaders

Season	Goals		Points		Penalty Minutes	
1974-1975	Nelson Pyatt	26	Nelson Pyatt	49	Yvon Labre	146
1975-1976	Gerry Meehan	28	Gerry Meehan	64	Gordie Lane	207
1976-1977	Guy Charron	36	Guy Charron	82	Gordie Lane	207
1977-1978	Guy Charron	38	Guy Charron	73	Gordie Lane	195
1978-1979	Dennis Maruk	31	Dennis Maruk	90	Gordie Lane	147
	Tom Rowe	31				
1979-1980	Mike Gartner	36	Mike Gartner	68	Paul Mulvey	240
1980-1981	Dennis Maruk	50	Dennis Maruk	97	Al Hangsleben	198
1981-1982	Dennis Maruk	60	Dennis Maruk	136	Randy Holt	250
1982-1983	Mike Gartner	38	Dennis Maruk	81	Randy Holt	275
1983-1984	Mike Gartner	40	Mike Gartner	85	Scott Stevens	201
1984-1985	Bob Carpenter	53	Mike Gartner	102	Scott Stevens	221
1985-1986	Dave Christian	41	Dave Christian	83	Scott Stevens	165
1986-1987	Mike Gartner	41	Larry Murphy	81	Scott Stevens	283
1987-1988	Mike Gartner	48	Mike Gartner	81	Dale Hunter	238
1988-1989	Geoff Courtnall	42	Mike Ridley	89	Scott Stevens	225
1989-1990	Dino Ciccarelli	41	Dino Ciccarelli	79	Alan May	339
1990-1991	Kevin Hatcher	24	Kevin Hatcher	74	Alan May	264
1991-1992	Dino Ciccarelli	38	Michal Pivonka	80	Alan May	221
1992-1993	Peter Bondra	37	Peter Bondra	85	Alan May	268
1993-1994	Dimitri Kristich	29	Mike Ridley	70	Craig Berube	305
1994-1995	Peter Bondra	34	Peter Bondra	43	Craig Berube	173
			Joe Juneau	43		
1995-1996	Peter Bondra	52	Michal Pivonka	81	Kevin Kaminski	164
1996-1997	Peter Bondra	46	Peter Bondra	77	Craig Berube	218
1997-1998	Peter Bondra	52	Peter Bondra	78	Craig Berube	189
1998-1999	Peter Bondra	31	Peter Bondra	55	Craig Berube	166
1999-2000	Chris Simon	29	Adam Oates	71	Chris Simon	146
2000-2001	Peter Bondra	45	Adam Oates	82	Chris Simon	117
2001-2002	Peter Bondra	39	Jaromir Jagr	79	Chris Simon	137
2002-2003	Jaromir Jagr	36	Jaromir Jagr	77	Jason Doig	108
2003-2004	Robert Lang	29	Robert Lang	74	Darcy Verot	135
2004-2005	Season cancelled due to lockout.					
2005-2005	A. Ovechkin	52	A. Ovechkin	106	Brendan Witt	141

COACHING HISTORY: 1974-1975 Jim Anderson 4-45-5-.120; 1974-1975 George Sullivan 2-17-0-.105; 1974-1976 Milt Schmidt 5-33-5-.174; 1975-1978 Tom McVie 49-122-33-.321; 1978-1980 Danny Belisle 28-51-17-.380; 1979-1982 Gary Green 50-78-29-.411; 1981-1982 Roger Crozier 0-1-0-.000; 1981-1990 Bryan Murray 343-246-83-.572; 1989-1994 Terry Murray 163-134-28-.545; 1994-1997 Jim Schoenfeld 113-102-34-.522; 1997-2002 Ron Wilson 192-161-51-8-.538; 2002-2004 Bruce Cassidy 47-47-9-7-.500; 2003-present Glen Hanlon

WASHINGTON CAPITOLS

Home City: Washington, D.C.
Home Court: Uline Arena
Origin of Name: As with other teams based in Washington and Ottawa the team seems to have been named because of the fact the cities were the seats of national government.

Regular Season Record

Season	League	GP	W	L	PPGF	PPGA	Pct	GB
1946-1947	BAA	60	49	11	73.8	63.9	.817	-
1947-1948	BAA	48	28	20	73.7	71.1	.583	1
1948-1949	BAA	60	38	22	81.8	79.4	.633	-
1949-1950	NBA	68	32	36	76.5	77.4	.471	21
1950-1951	NBA	35	10	25	81.3	86.0	.286	14.5
TOTAL:	5 years	271	157	114				36.5
AVERAGE:		54	31	23	77.4	75.6	.579	7

Playoff Record

Season	GP	W	L	PPGF	PPGA	Result
1946-1947	6	2	4	62.8	67.8	Lost Semifinal series to Chicago.
1947-1948	1	1	0	72.0	75.0	Lost Division tiebreaker to Chicago.
1948-1949	11	6	5	77.3	77.5	Lost Championship series to Minneapolis.
1949-1950	2	0	2	85.0	96.5	Lost Division Semifinal to New York.
TOTAL:	20	9	11			
AVERAGE:	5	2	3	74.3	79.2	

Regular Season Individual Leaders

Season	Field Goal % (min. 40 games)		Points		Points per Game (min. 40 games)	
1946-47	Bob Feerick	.401	Bob Feerick	926	Bob Feerick	16.8
1947-48	Bob Feerick	.340	Bob Feerick	775	Bob Feerick	16.1
1948-49	John Norlander	.361	Bob Feerick	752	Bob Feerick	13.0
1949-50	Chick Halbert	.380	Fred Scolari	860	Fred Scolari	13.0
1950-51*	Alan Sawyer	.405	Bill Sharman	378	Bill Sharman	12.2

*-minimum 30 games

COACHING HISTORY: 1946-1949 Red Auerbach 115-53-.685; 1949-1950 Bob Feerick 32-36-.471; 1950-1951 Bones McKinney 10-25-.286

WASHINGTON CAPITOLS
(were Oakland Oaks)
(became Virginia Squires)

Home City: Washington, D.C.
Home Court: Washington Arena
Origin of Name: Named by team owner Earl Foreman.

Regular Season Record

Season	League	GP	W	L	PPGF	PPGA	Pct	GB
1969-1970	ABA	84	44	40	118.2	118.8	.524	7

Playoff Record

Season	GP	W	L	PPGF	PPGA	Result
1969-1970	7	3	4	120.7	127.6	Lost 1st Round series to Denver.

Regular Season Individual Leaders

Season	Field Goal % (min. 70 games)		Points		Points per Game (min. 70 games)	
1969-70	Frank Card	.527	Rick Barry	1442	Mike Barrett	14.9

COACHING HISTORY: Al Bianchi 44-40-.524

WASHINGTON DARTS
(became Miami Gatos)

Home City: Washington, D.C.
Home Field: Catholic University Stadium (some games)
Origin of Name: The team kept the same nickname when it transferred from the semi-professional American Soccer League to the NASL.

Regular Season Record

Season	League	GP	W	L	T	GF	GA	BP	Pts	Pct
1970	NASL	24	14	6	4	52	29	41	137	.634
1971	NASL	24	8	6	10	36	34	33	111	.514
TOTAL:	2 years	48	22	12	14	88	63	74	248	
AVERAGE:		24	11	6	7	44	32	37	124	.574

Playoff Record

Season	GP	W	L	GF	GA	Result
1970	2	1	1	3	4	Lost Championship series to Rochester.

Regular Season Individual Leaders

Season	Goals		Points		GAA (360 Min)	
1970	Leroy Deleon	16	Leroy Deleon	33	Lincoln Phillips	0.95
1971	Leroy Deleon	8	Leroy Deleon	23	Leonel Conde	1.38

COACHING HISTORY: 1970 Lincoln Phillips 14-6-4-.634; 1971 Alan Rogers 8-6-10-.514

WASHINGTON DIPLOMATS

Home City: Washington, D.C.
Home Stadium: RFK Memorial Stadium (1974-75, 1977-81)   Capacity: 55,031 [1975]
          Woodson Stadium (1976)
Origin of Name: The name was chosen by the wife of the team president.

Regular Season Record

Season	League	GP	W	L	T	GF	GA	BP	Pts	Pct
1974	NASL	20	7	12	1	29	36	25	70	.389
1975	NASL	22	12	10	-	42	47	40	112	.566
1976	NASL	24	14	10	-	46	38	42	126	.583
1977	NASL	26	10	16	-	32	49	32	92	.393
1978	NASL	30	16	14	-	55	47	49	145	.537
1979	NASL	30	19	11	-	68	50	59	172	.637
1980	NASL	32	17	15	-	72	61	57	159	.552
1981	NASL	32	15	17	-	59	58	51	135	.281
TOTAL:	8 years	216	110	105	1	403	386	355	1011	
AVERAGE:		27	14	13	0	50	48	44	126	.473

Playoff Record

Season	GP	W	L	T	GF	GA	Result
1976	1	0	1	0	0	2	Lost 1st Round series to New York.
1978	1	0	1	0	0	1	Lost 1st Round series to Portland.
1979	2	0	2	0	4	7	Lost 1st Round series to Los Angeles.
1980	3	1	2	0	2	4	Lost 1st Round series to Los Angeles.
TOTAL:	7	1	6	0	6	14	
AVERAGE:	2	0	2	0	2	3	

Regular Season Individual Leaders

Season	Goals		Points		GAA (360 Min)	
1974	Gary Darrell	9	Gary Darrell	20	Kurt Kuykendall	1.78
1975			Mike Barry	21	Peter Thomas	1.05
1976	Paul Cannell	13	Paul Cannell	28	Eric Martin	1.51
1977	Alan Green	9	Alan Green	23	Eric Martin	1.68
1978	Paul Cannell	14	Paul Cannell	35	Bob Stetler	1.34
1979	Alan Green	16	Alan Green	41	Bill Irwin	1.45
1980	Alan Green	25	Alan Green	59	Bill Irwin	1.85
1981					Jim Brown	1.54

COACHING HISTORY: 1974-1977 Dennis Viollet 39-41-1; 1977 Alan Spavin 4-7; 1978-1980 Gordon Bradley 52-40; 1981 Ken Furphy 15-17

WASHINGTON FEDERALS

Home City: Washington, D.C.
Home Stadium: RFK Memorial Stadium   Capacity: 55,031 [1984]
Origin of Name: The name was chosen because Washington is sometimes called the Federal City.

Regular Season Record

Season	League	GP	W	L	T	PF	PA	Pct
1983	USFL	18	4	14	0	297	442	.222
1984	USFL	18	3	15	0	270	482	.167
TOTAL:	2 years	36	7	29	0	567	924	
AVERAGE:		18	4	14	0	284	462	.194

Regular Season Individual Leaders

Season	Passing Yards		Receiving Yards		Rushing Yards	
1983	Kim McQuilken	1912	Joey Walters	959	Craig James	823
1984	Mike Hohensee	2766	Joey Walters	1410	Curtis Bledsoe	1080

COACHING HISTORY: 1983-1984 Ray Jauch 4-15-0-.211; 1984 Dick Bielske 3-14-0-.176

WASHINGTON MYSTICS

Home City: Washington, D.C.
Home Arena: MCI Center   Capacity: 20,674 [2005]
Origin of Name: The name was chosen to show affiliation with the NBA's Wizards.

Regular Season Record

Season	League	GP	W	L	PPGF	PPGA	Pct	GB
1998	WNBA	30	3	27	65.1	80.5	.100	17
1999	WNBA	32	12	20	65.6	70.2	.375	6
2000	WNBA	32	14	18	68.0	69.4	.438	6

2001	WNBA	32	10	22	60.3	64.8	.313	12
2002	WNBA	32	17	15	66.7	66.1	.531	1
2003	WNBA	34	9	25	68.5	73.5	.265	16
2004	WNBA	34	17	17	68.4	70.1	.500	1
2005	WNBA	34	16	18	66.6	67.8	.471	10
2006	WNBA	34	18	16	63.0	72.0	.529	8
TOTAL:	9 year	294	116	178				77
AVERAGE:		33	13	20	65.8	70.4	.395	9

Playoff Record

Season	GP	W	L	PPGF	PPGA	Result
2000	2	0	2	60.0	75.0	Lost Conference Semifinal to New York.
2002	5	3	2	70.2	71.0	Lost Conference final to New York.
2004	3	1	2	64.3	71.7	Lost Conf. Semifinal to Connecticut.
2006	2	0	2	63.0	72.0	Lost Conf. Semifinal to Connecticut.
TOTAL:	12	4	8			
AVERAGE:	3	1	2	65.8	72.0	

Regular Season Individual Leaders

Season	Field Goals % (20 games min.)		Free Throws % (20 games min.)		Points per Game (20 games min.)	
1998	Heidi Burge	.509	Adrienne Shuler	.824	Nikki McCray	17.7
1999	Murriel Page	.574	Nikki McCray	.806	Nikki McCray	17.5
2000	Murriel Page	.590	B. Cunningham	.842	C. Holdsclaw	17.5
2001	Murriel Page	.433	Helen Luz	.880	C. Holdsclaw	16.8
2002	Vicky Bullett	.462	C. Holdsclaw	.830	C. Holdsclaw	19.9
2003	Coco Miller	.450	C. Holdsclaw	.903	C. Holdsclaw	20.5
2004	Nakia Sanford	.500	Kiesha Brown	.875	C. Holdsclaw	19.0
2005	Chasity Melvin	.492	Murriel Page	1.000	Alana Beard	14.1
2006	Chasity Melvin	.520	Nikki Teasley	.826	Alana Beard	19.2

COACHING HISTORY: 1998 Jim Lewis 2-16-.111, 1998 Cathy Parson 1-11-.083, 1999-2000 Nancy Darsch 21-31-.404, 2000-Darrell Walker 14-18-.438; 2001 Tom Maher 10-22-.313; 2002-2003 Marianne Stanley 26-40-.394, 2004-Michael Adams 17-17-.500; 2005-present Richie Adubato

WASHINGTON NATIONALS

Home City: Washington, D.C.
Home Field: Union Association Park*   Capacity: 6,000
Origin of Name: Most teams in the city adopted names which reflected its role in the National government.

Regular Season Record

Season	League	GP	W	L	Pct	GB	R	OR
1884	UA	112	47	65	.420	46.5	572	679

Regular Season Individual Leaders

Season	Home Runs		RBI's	Wins	
1884	Bill Wise	2	Not Recorded	Bill Wise	23

COACHING HISTORY: Mike Scanlon 47-65-.420

WASHINGTON NATIONALS

Home City: Washington, D.C.
Home Field: Athletic Park
Origin of Name: See above

Regular Season Record

Season	League	GP	W	L	Pct	GB	R	OR
1884	AA	63	12	51	.190	41	248	481

Regular Season Individual Leaders

Season	Home Runs		RBI's		Wins	
1884	Frank Fennelly	2	Not Recorded		Bob Barr	9
	Bob Barr	2				

COACHING HISTORY: Holly Hollingshead 12-51-.190

WASHINGTON NATIONALS
(were Montreal Expos)

Home City: Washington, D.C.
Home Field: RFK Stadium   Capacity: 46,382 [2006]
Origin of Name:

Regular Season Record

Season	League	GP	W	L	Pct	GB	R	OR
2005	NL	162	81	81	.500	9	639	673
2006	NL	162	71	91	.438	26	746	872
TOTAL:	2 years	324	152	172		35	1385	1545
AVERAGE:		162	76	86	.469	17.5	693	773

Regular Season Individual Leaders

Season	Home Runs		RBI's		Wins	
2005	Jose Guillen	24	Jose Guillen	76	Livan Hernandez	15
2006	Alfonso Soriano	46	Ryan Zimmerman	110	Ramon Ortiz	11

COACHING HISTORY: 2005-present Frank Robinson

WASHINGTON PALACE FIVE
(merged with Brooklyn in mid 1927-1928)

Home City: Washington, D.C.
Home Court: Arcadia Hall
Origin of Name: The name was chosen because the team was owned by George Marshall, owner
of the Palace Laundry.

Regular Season Record

Season	League	GP	W	L	Pct
1925-1926	ABL	30	22	8	.733
1926-1927	ABL	42	30	12	.714
1927-1928	ABL	20	6	14	.300
TOTAL:	3 years	92	58	34	
AVERAGE:		31	19	12	.630

*-also known as Capitol Grounds

Regular Season Individual Leaders

Season	Points		
1925-26	Ray Kennedy	220	
1926-27	Rusty Saunders	399	
1927-28			

COACHING HISTORY: 1925-1926 Ray Kennedy 22-8-.733; 1926-1928 Not Available

WASHINGTON REDSKINS
(were Boston Redskins)

Home City: Washington, D.C.
Home Stadium: Griffith Stadium (1937-1960)   Capacity: 35,000
RFK Stadium (1960-1997)   Capacity: 56,454 [1996]
FedEx Field (1997-present)*   Capacity: 86,484 [2005]
Origin of Name: The team kept the same nickname when it moved from Boston to Washington.

Regular Season Record

Season	League	GP	W	L	T	PF	PA	Pct
1937	NFL	11	8	3	0	195	120	.727
1938	NFL	11	6	3	2	148	154	.636
1939	NFL	11	8	2	1	242	94	.773
1940	NFL	11	9	2	0	245	142	.818
1941	NFL	11	6	5	0	176	174	.545
1942	NFL	11	10	1	0	227	102	.909
1943	NFL	10	6	3	1	229	137	.650
1944	NFL	10	6	3	1	169	180	.650
1945	NFL	10	8	2	0	209	121	.800
1946	NFL	11	5	5	1	171	191	.500
1947	NFL	12	4	8	0	295	367	.333
1948	NFL	12	7	5	0	291	287	.583
1949	NFL	12	4	7	1	268	339	.375
1950	NFL	12	3	9	0	232	326	.250
1951	NFL	12	5	7	0	183	296	.833
1952	NFL	12	4	8	0	240	287	.333
1953	NFL	12	6	5	1	208	215	.542
1954	NFL	12	3	9	0	207	432	.250
1955	NFL	12	8	4	0	246	222	.667
1956	NFL	12	6	6	0	183	225	.500
1957	NFL	12	5	6	1	251	230	.458
1958	NFL	12	4	7	1	214	268	.375
1959	NFL	12	3	9	0	185	350	.250
1960	NFL	12	1	9	2	178	309	.167
1961	NFL	14	1	12	1	174	392	.107
1962	NFL	14	5	7	2	305	376	.429
1963	NFL	14	3	11	0	279	398	.214
1964	NFL	14	6	8	0	307	305	.429
1965	NFL	14	6	8	0	257	301	.429
1966	NFL	14	7	7	0	351	355	.500
1967	NFL	14	5	6	3	347	353	.464
1968	NFL	14	5	9	0	249	358	.357
1969	NFL	14	7	5	2	307	319	.571
1970	NFL	14	6	8	0	297	314	.429

*-known as Jack Kent Cooke Stadium 1997 to 1999.

1971	NFL	14	9	4	1	276	190	.679
1972	NFL	14	11	3	0	336	218	.786
1973	NFL	14	10	4	0	325	198	.714
1974	NFL	14	10	4	0	320	196	.714
1975	NFL	14	8	6	0	325	276	.571
1976	NFL	14	10	4	0	291	217	.714
1977	NFL	14	9	5	0	196	189	.643
1978	NFL	16	8	8	0	273	283	.500
1979	NFL	16	10	6	0	348	295	.625
1980	NFL	16	6	10	0	261	293	.375
1981	NFL	16	8	8	0	347	349	.500
1982	NFL	9	8	1	0	190	128	.889
1983	NFL	16	14	2	0	541	332	.875
1984	NFL	16	11	5	0	426	310	.688
1985	NFL	16	10	6	0	297	312	.625
1986	NFL	16	12	4	0	368	296	.750
1987	NFL	15	11	4	0	379	285	.733
1988	NFL	16	7	9	0	345	387	.438
1989	NFL	16	10	6	0	386	308	.625
1990	NFL	16	10	6	0	381	301	.625
1991	NFL	16	14	2	0	485	224	.875
1992	NFL	16	9	7	0	300	255	.563
1993	NFL	16	4	12	0	230	345	.250
1994	NFL	16	3	13	0	320	412	.188
1995	NFL	16	6	10	0	326	359	.375
1996	NFL	16	9	7	0	364	312	.563
1997	NFL	16	8	7	1	327	289	.532
1998	NFL	16	6	10	0	319	421	.375
1999	NFL	16	10	6	0	443	377	.625
2000	NFL	16	8	8	0	281	269	.500
2001	NFL	16	8	8	0	256	303	.500
2002	NFL	16	7	9	0	307	365	.438
2003	NFL	16	5	11	0	287	372	.313
2004	NFL	16	6	10	0	240	265	.375
2005	NFL	16	10	6	0	359	293	.625
2006	NFL	16	5	11	0	307	376	.313
TOTAL:	70 years	969	496	451	22	19827	19639	
AVERAGE:		14	7	7	0	283	281	.523

Playoff Record

Season	GP	W	L	PF	PA	Result
1937	1	1	0	28	21	**Won NFL Championship.**
1940	1	0	1	0	73	Lost Championship game to Bears.
1942	1	1	0	14	6	**Won NFL Championship.**
1943	2	1	1	49	41	Lost Championship game to Bears.
1945	1	0	1	14	15	Lost Championship game to Cleveland.
1971	1	0	1	20	24	Lost Divisional playoff to San Francisco.
1972	3	2	1	49	20	Lost Super Bowl to Miami.
1973	1	0	1	20	27	Lost Divisional playoff to Minnesota.
1974	1	0	1	10	19	Lost Divisional playoff to Los Angeles.
1976	1	0	1	20	35	Lost Divisional playoff to Minnesota.
1982	4	4	0	110	48	**Won Super Bowl XVII.**
1983	3	2	1	84	66	Lost Super Bowl to Raiders.
1984	1	0	1	19	23	Lost Divisional playoff to Chicago.

1986	3	2	1	46	37	Lost NFC Championship to Giants.
1987	3	3	0	80	37	**Won Super Bowl XXII.**
1990	2	1	1	30	34	Lost Conference Semifinal to San Francisco.
1991	3	3	0	102	41	**Won Super Bowl XXVI.**
1992	2	1	1	37	27	Lost Conference Semifinal to San Francisco.
1999	2	1	1	40	27	Lost Conference Semifinal to Tampa Bay.
2005	2	1	1	27	30	Lost Conference Semifinal to Seattle.
TOTAL:	38	23	15	799	651	
AVERAGE:	2	1	1	40	33	

Regular Season Individual Leaders

Season	Passing Yards		Receiving Yards		Rushing Yards	
1937	Sam Baugh	1127	Charley Malone	419	Cliff Battles	874
1938	Sam Baugh	853	Charley Malone	257	Andy Farkas	315
1939	Frank Filchock	1094	Andy Farkas	437	Andy Farkas	547
1940	Sam Baugh	1367	Dick Todd	402	Dick Todd	408
1941	Sam Baugh	1236	Wayne Millner	262	Frank Filchock	383
1942	Sam Baugh	1524	Dick Todd	328	Andy Farkas	468
1943	Sam Baugh	1754	Wilbur Moore	537	Andy Farkas	331
1944	Frank Filchock	1139	Wilbur Moore	424	Bob Seymour	315
1945	Sam Baugh	1669	Steve Bagarus	517	Frank Akins	797
1946	Sam Baugh	1163	Steve Bagarus	438	Dick Todd	266
1947	Sam Baugh	2938	Eddie Saenz	598	Jim Castiglia	426
1948	Sam Baugh	2599	Hal Crisler	599	Jim Castiglia	330
1949	Sam Baugh	1903	Hugh Taylor	781	Rob Goode	261
1950	Sam Baugh	1130	Hugh Taylor	833	Rob Goode	560
1951	Sam Baugh	1104	Hugh Taylor	444	Rob Goode	951
1952	Eddie LeBaron	1420	Hugh Taylor	961	Leon Heath	388
1953	Eddie LeBaron	874	Hugh Taylor	703	ChooChoo Justice	616
1954	Al Dorow	997	Hugh Taylor	659	Billy Wells	516
1955	Eddie LeBaron	1270	John Carson	443	Vic Janowicz	397
1956	Al Dorow	730	John Carson	504	Leo Elter	544
1957	Eddie LeBaron	1508	John Carson	583	Don Bosseler	673
1958	Eddie LeBaron	1365	Joe Walton	532	John Olszewski	505
1959	Eddie LeBaron	1077	Bill Anderson	734	Don Bosseler	644
1960	Ralph Guglielmi	1547	Bill Anderson	488	Don Bosseler	428
1961	Norm Snead	2337	Fred Dugan	817	Dick James	374
1962	Norm Snead	2926	Bobby Mitchell	1384	Bill Barnes	492
1963	Norm Snead	3043	Bobby Mitchell	1436	Dick James	384
1964	Sonny Jurgensen	2934	Bobby Mitchell	904	Charley Taylor	755
1965	Sonny Jurgensen	2367	Bobby Mitchell	867	Charley Taylor	402
1966	Sonny Jurgensen	3209	Charley Taylor	1119	A.D. Whitfield	472
1967	Sonny Jurgensen	3747	Charley Taylor	990	A.D. Whitfield	384
1968	Sonny Jurgensen	1980	Charley Taylor	650	Jerry Allen	399
1969	Sonny Jurgensen	3102	Charley Taylor	883	Larry Brown	888
1970	Sonny Jurgensen	2354	Charley Taylor	593	Larry Brown	1125
1971	Billy Kilmer	2221	Roy Jefferson	701	Larry Brown	948
1972	Billy Kilmer	1648	Charley Taylor	673	Larry Brown	1216
1973	Billy Kilmer	1656	Charley Taylor	801	Larry Brown	860
1974	Billy Kilmer	1632	Charley Taylor	738	Larry Brown	430
1975	Billy Kilmer	2440	Frank Grant	776	Mike Thomas	919
1976	Billy Kilmer	1252	Frank Grant	818	Mike Thomas	1101
1977	Billy Kilmer	1187	Jean Fugett	631	Mike Thomas	806
1978	Joe Theismann	2593	John McDaniel	577	John Riggins	1014

Season	Passing Yards		Receiving Yards		Rushing Yards	
1979	Joe Theismann	2797	Danny Buggs	631	John Riggins	1153
1980	Joe Theismann	2962	Art Monk	797	Wilbur Jackson	708
1981	Joe Theismann	3568	Art Monk	894	Joe Washington	916
1982	Joe Theismann	2033	Charlie Brown	690	John Riggins	553
1983	Joe Theismann	3714	Charlie Brown	1225	John Riggins	1347
1984	Joe Theismann	3391	Art Monk	1372	John Riggins	1239
1985	Joe Theismann	1774	Art Monk	1226	George Rogers	1093
1986	Jay Schroeder	4109	Gary Clark	1265	George Rogers	1203
1987	Jay Schroeder	1878	Gary Clark	1066	George Rogers	613
1988	Doug Williams	2609	Ricky Sanders	1148	Kelvin Bryant	498
1989	Mark Rypien	3768	Gary Clark	1229	Gerald Riggs	834
1990	Mark Rypien	2070	Gary Clark	1112	Earnest Byner	1219
1991	Mark Rypien	3564	Gary Clark	1340	Earnest Byner	1048
1992	Mark Rypien	3282	Gary Clark	912	Earnest Byner	998
1993	Mark Rypien	1514	Ricky Sanders	638	Reggie Brooks	1063
1994	Heath Shuler	1658	Henry Ellard	1397	Ricky Ervins	650
1995	Gus Frerotte	2751	Henry Ellard	1005	Terry Allen	1309
1996	Gus Frerotte	3453	Henry Ellard	1014	Terry Allen	1353
1997	Gus Frerotte	2682	M. Westbrook	559	Terry Allen	724
1998	Trent Green	3441	M. Westbrook	736	Terry Allen	700
1999	Brad Johnson	4005	M. Westbrook	1191	Stephen Davis	1405
2000	Brad Johnson	2505	Albert Connell	762	Stephen Davis	1318
2001	Tony Banks	2386	Rod Gardner	741	Stephen Davis	1432
2002	Patrick Ramsey	1539	Rod Gardner	1006	Stephen Davis	820
2003	Patrick Ramsey	2166	Laveranues Coles	1204	Trung Canidate	600
2004	Patrick Ramsey	1665	Laveranues Coles	950	Clinton Portis	1315
2005	Mark Brunell	3050	Santana Moss	1483	Clinton Portis	1516
2006	Mark Brunell	1789	Santana Moss	790	Ladell Betts	1154

COACHING HISTORY: 1937-1942 Ray Flaherty 47-16-3-.735; 1943 Dutch Bergman 6-3-1-.650; 1944-1945 Dud DeGroot 14-5-1-.725; 1946-1948 Turk Edwards 16-18-1-.471; 1949 John Whelchel 3-3-1-.500; 1949-1951 Herman Ball 4-16-0-.200; 1951 Dick Todd 5-4-0-.556; 1952-1953 Earl Lambeau 10-13-1-.438; 1954-1958 Joe Kuharich 26-32-2-.450; 1959-1960 Mike Nixon 4-18-2-.208; 1961-1965 Bill McPeak 21-46-3-.321; 1966-1968 Otto Graham 17-22-3-.440; 1969 Vince Lombardi 7-5-2-.571; 1971-1977 George Allen 67-30-1-.689; 1978-1980 Jack Pardee 24-24-0-.500; 1981-1992 Joe Gibbs 124-60-0-.674; 1993 Richie Petitbon 4-12-0-.250; 1994-2000 Norv Turner 49-59-1-.454; 2000-Terry Robiskie 1-2-0-.333; 2001 Marty Schottenheimer 8-8-0-.500; 2002-2003 Steve Spurrier 12-20-0-.375; 2004-present Joe Gibbs

WASHINGTON SENATORS

Home City: Washington, D.C.
Home Field: Capitol Park*   Capacity: 6,000
Origin of Name: The name was chosen because of Washington's position as the seat of the American government.

			Regular Season Record					
Season	League	GP	W	L	Pct	GB	R	OR
1886	NL	120	28	92	.233	60	445	791
1887	NL	122	46	76	.377	32	601	818
1888	NL	134	48	86	.358	37.5	482	731
1889	NL	124	41	83	.331	41	632	892

*-also known as Swampoodle Grounds

TOTAL:	4 years	500	163	337		170.5	2160	3232
AVERAGE:		125	41	84	.326	43	540	808

Regular Season Individual Leaders

Season	Home Runs		RBI's		Wins	
1886	Paul Hines	9	Paul Hines	56	Frederick Shaw	13
1887	Bill O'Brien	19	Bill O'Brien	73	Jim Whitney	24
1888	Bill O'Brien	9	Bill O'Brien	66	Jim Whitney	18
1889	Walt Wilmot	9	Sam Wise	62	Alex Ferson	17

COACHING HISTORY: 1886 Mike Scanlon 13-66-.165; 1886-1887 John Gaffney 61-102-.374; 1888 Walter Hewitt 12-29-.293; 1888 Ted Sullivan 36-57-.387; 1889 John Morrill 13-39-.250; 1889 Arthur Irwin 28-44-.389

WASHINGTON SENATORS

Home City: Washington, D.C.
Home Field: Griffith Stadium   Capacity: 6,500
Origin of Name: The team was named after the previous National League team.

Regular Season Record

Season	League	GP	W	L	Pct	GB	R	OR
1891	AA	135	43	92	.319	50	691	1067
1892	NL	151	58	93	.384	44.5	731	869
1893	NL	129	40	89	.310	46	722	1032
1894	NL	132	45	87	.341	46	882	1122
1895	NL	128	43	85	.336	43	837	1048
1896	NL	131	58	73	.443	33	818	920
1897	NL	132	61	71	.462	32	781	793
1898	NL	152	51	101	.336	52.5	704	939
1899	NL	152	54	98	.355	49	743	983
TOTAL:	9 years	1242	453	789		396	6909	8773
AVERAGE:		138	50	88	.365	44	768	975

Regular Season Individual Leaders

Season	Home Runs		RBI's		Wins	
1891	Frank Foreman	4	Deacon McGuire	66	Frank Foreman	18
1892	Henry Larkin	8	Henry Larkin	96	Frank Killen	29
1893	Sam Wise	5	Jim O'Rourke	95	Charles Esper	12
					Al Maul	12
1894	Bill Joyce	17	Ed Cartwright	106	George Mercer	17
1895	Bill Joyce	17	Deacon McGuire	97	George Mercer	13
1896	Bill Joyce	8	Albert Selbach	100	George Mercer	25
	G. DeMontreville	8				
1897	Tommy Tucker	5	G. DeMontreville	93	George Mercer	20
	Tom Brown	5				
	Albert Selbach	5				
1898	John Anderson	9	John Anderson	71	Gus Weyhing	15
1899	John Freeman	25	John Freeman	122	Gus Weyhing	17

COACHING HISTORY: 1891 Sam Trott 4-8-.333; 1891 Charles Snyder 23-46-.333; 1891 Dan Shannon 12-25-.324; 1891 Sandy Griffin 4-13-.235; 1892 Bill Barnie 13-21-.382; 1892 Arthur Irwin 34-46-.425; 1892 Danny Richardson 11-26-.297; 1893 Jim O'Rourke 40-89-.310; 1894-1897 Gus Schmelz 155-270-.365; 1897-1898 Tom Brown 55-59-.482; 1898 Jack Doyle 20-24-.455; 1898 James McGuire 19-49-.279; 1898-1899 Arthur Irwin 63-113-.358

WASHINGTON SENATORS
(became Minnesota Twins)

Home City: Washington, D.C.
Home Field: American League Park (1901-1902)
Griffith Stadium (1903-1960) Capacity: 27,410 [1961]
Origin of Name: Named after the previous National League team.

Regular Season Record

Season	League	GP	W	L	Pct	GB	R	OR
1901	AL	134	61	73	.455	21	683	771
1902	AL	136	61	75	.449	22	709	790
1903	AL	137	43	94	.314	47.5	438	691
1904	AL	151	38	113	.252	55.5	437	743
1905	AL	151	64	87	.424	29.5	560	613
1906	AL	150	55	95	.367	37.5	518	670
1907	AL	151	49	102	.325	43.5	505	690
1908	AL	152	67	85	.441	22.5	479	530
1909	AL	152	42	110	.276	56	382	655
1910	AL	151	66	85	.437	36.5	498	552
1911	AL	154	64	90	.416	38.5	624	760
1912	AL	152	91	61	.599	14	698	581
1913	AL	154	90	64	.584	6.5	596	566
1914	AL	154	81	73	.526	19	572	519
1915	AL	153	85	68	.556	17	571	492
1916	AL	153	76	77	.497	14.5	534	543
1917	AL	153	74	79	.484	25.5	543	566
1918	AL	128	72	56	.563	4	461	392
1919	AL	140	56	84	.400	32	533	570
1920	AL	152	68	84	.447	29	723	802
1921	AL	153	80	73	.523	18	704	738
1922	AL	154	69	85	.448	25	650	706
1923	AL	153	75	78	.490	23.5	720	747
1924	AL	154	92	62	.597	-	755	613
1925	AL	151	96	55	.636	-	829	669
1926	AL	150	81	69	.540	8	802	761
1927	AL	154	85	69	.552	25	782	730
1928	AL	154	75	79	.487	26	718	705
1929	AL	152	71	81	.467	34	730	776
1930	AL	154	94	60	.610	8	892	689
1931	AL	154	92	62	.597	16	843	691
1932	AL	154	93	61	.604	14	840	716
1933	AL	152	99	53	.651	-	850	665
1934	AL	152	66	86	.434	34	729	806
1935	AL	153	67	86	.438	27	823	903
1936	AL	153	82	71	.536	20	889	799
1937	AL	153	73	80	.477	28.5	757	841
1938	AL	151	75	76	.497	23.5	814	873
1939	AL	152	65	87	.428	41.5	702	797
1940	AL	154	64	90	.416	26	665	811
1941	AL	154	70	84	.455	31	728	798
1942	AL	151	62	89	.411	39.5	653	817
1943	AL	153	84	69	.549	13.5	666	595
1944	AL	154	64	90	.416	25	592	664

1945	AL	154	87	67	.565	1.5	622	562
1946	AL	154	76	78	.494	28	608	706
1947	AL	154	64	90	.416	33	496	675
1948	AL	153	56	97	.366	40	578	796
1949	AL	154	50	104	.325	47	584	868
1950	AL	154	67	87	.435	31	690	813
1951	AL	154	62	92	.403	36	672	764
1952	AL	154	78	76	.506	17	598	608
1953	AL	152	76	76	.500	23.5	687	614
1954	AL	154	66	88	.429	45	632	680
1955	AL	154	53	101	.344	43	598	789
1956	AL	154	59	95	.383	38	652	924
1957	AL	154	55	99	.357	43	603	808
1958	AL	154	61	93	.396	31	553	747
1959	AL	154	63	91	.409	31	619	701
1960	AL	154	73	81	.474	24	672	696
TOTAL:	60 years	9088	4223	4865		1590.5	39061	42157
AVERAGE:		151	70	81	.465	26.5	651	703

Playoff Record

Season	GP	W	L	R	OR	Result
1924	7	4	3	26	27	Won World Series.
1925	7	3	4	26	25	Lost World Series to Pittsburgh.
1933	5	1	4	11	16	Lost World Series to New York.
TOTAL:	19	8	11	63	68	
AVERAGE:	6	3	3	21	23	

Regular Season Individual Leaders

Season	Home Runs		RBI's		Wins	
1901	Mike Grady	9	Sam Dungan	72	Casey Patten	17
1902	Ed Delahanty	10	Ed Delahanty	93	Al Orth	19
1903	Jimmy Ryan	7	Albert Selbach	49	Al Orth	10
					Casey Patten	10
1904	Jake Stahl	3	Jake Stahl	50	Casey Patten	15
1905	Jake Stahl	5	Jake Stahl	66	Tom Hughes	16
					Casey Patten	16
1906	Charles Hickman	9	John Anderson	70	Casey Patten	19
1907	Jim Delahanty	2	Jim Delahanty	54	Casey Patten	12
	Dave Altizer	2				
1908	Oliver Pickering	2	Jerry Freeman	45	Tom Hughes	18
1909	Bob Unglaub	3	Bob Unglaub	41	Walter Johnson	13
1910	Norman Elberfeld	2	George McBride	55	Walter Johnson	25
	Harry Gessler	2				
1911	Harry Gessler	4	Harry Gessler	78	Walter Johnson	25
1912	Danny Moeller	6	Charles Gandil	81	Walter Johnson	32
1913	Danny Moeller	5	Charles Gandil	72	Walter Johnson	36
1914	Howard Shanks	4	Charles Gandil	75	Walter Johnson	28
1915	Charles Gandil	2	Clyde Milan	66	Walter Johnson	27
	Danny Moeller	2				
	Clyde Milan	2				
1916	Elmer Smith	2	Howard Shanks	48	Walter Johnson	25
1917	Joe Judge	2	Sam Rice	69	Walter Johnson	23

Season	Home Runs		RBI's		Wins	
1918	Joe Judge	1	Clyde Milan	56	Walter Johnson	23
	Howard Shanks	1	Howard Shanks	56		
	Walter Johnson	1				
	Val Picinish	1				
1919	Mike Menosky	6	Sam Rice	71	Walter Johnson	20
1920	Robert Roth	9	Robert Roth	92	Tom Zachary	15
1921	Bing Miller	9	Sam Rice	79	George Mogridge	18
					Tom Zachary	18
1922	Joe Judge	10	Joe Judge	81	George Mogridge	18
1923	Leon Goslin	9	Leon Goslin	99	Walter Johnson	17
1924	Leon Goslin	12	Leon Goslin	129	Walter Johnson	23
1925	Leon Goslin	18	Leon Goslin	113	Stan Coveleski	20
					Walter Johnson	20
1926	Leon Goslin	17	Leon Goslin	108	Walter Johnson	15
1927	Leon Goslin	13	Leon Goslin	120	Horace Lisenbee	18
1928	Leon Goslin	17	Leon Goslin	102	Sam Jones	17
1929	Leon Goslin	18	Leon Goslin	91	Firpo Marberry	19
1930	Joe Cronin	13	Joe Cronin	126	Lloyd Brown	16
1931	Joe Cronin	12	Joe Cronin	126	Alvin Crowder	18
1932	Henry Manush	14	Henry Manush	116	Alvin Crowder	26
			Joe Cronin	116		
1933	Joe Kuhel	11	Joe Cronin	118	Alvin Crowder	24
1934	Henry Manush	11	Joe Cronin	101	Earl Whitehill	14
1935	Jake Powell	6	Charles Myer	100	Earl Whitehill	14
1936	Joe Kuhel	16	Earl Kuhel	118	Jimmie DeShong	18
1937	John Lewis	10	Al Simmons	84	Jimmie DeShong	14
1938	Henry Bonura	22	Henry Bonura	114	Wes Ferrell	13
1939	John Lewis	10	Taffy Wright	93	Emil Leonard	20
1940	Gerald Walker	13	Gerald Walker	96	Sid Hudson	17
1941	Jake Early	10	Cecil Travis	101	Emil Leonard	18
1942	Mickey Vernon	9	Mickey Vernon	86	Bobo Newsom	11
1943	Stan Spence	12	Stan Spence	88	Early Wynn	18
1944	Stan Spence	18	Stan Spence	100	Emil Leonard	14
1945	Harlond Clift	8	George Binks	81	Roger Wolff	20
1946	Stan Spence	16	Stan Spence	87	Mickey Haefner	14
1947	Stan Spence	16	Mickey Vernon	85	Early Wynn	17
1948	Bud Stewart	7	Bud Stewart	69	Ray Scarborough	15
	Gil Coan	7				
1949	Eddie Robinson	18	Eddie Robinson	78	Ray Scarborough	13
1950	Irv Noren	14	Irv Noren	98	Sid Hudson	14
1951	Eddie Yost	12	Sam Mele	94	Connie Marrero	11
1952	Eddie Yost	12	Mickey Vernon	80	Bob Porterfield	13
			Jackie Jensen	80		
1953	Mickey Vernon	15	Mickey Vernon	115	Bob Porterfield	22
1954	Roy Sievers	24	Roy Sievers	102	Bob Porterfield	13
1955	Roy Sievers	25	Roy Sievers	106	Mickey McDermott	10
					Bob Porterfield	10
1956	Roy Sievers	29	Jim Lemon	96	Chuck Stobbs	15
1957	Roy Sievers	42	Roy Sievers	114	Pedro Ramos	12
1958	Roy Sievers	39	Roy Sievers	108	Pedro Ramos	14
1959	Harmon Killebrew	42	Harmon Killebrew	105	Camilo Pascual	17
1960	Jim Lemon	38	Jim Lemon	100	Chuck Stobbs	12
					Camilo Pascual	12

COACHING HISTORY: 1901 Jim Manning 61-73-.455; 1902-1903 Tom Loftus 104-169-.381; 1904 Malachi Kittredge 1-16-.059; 1904 Patrick Donovan 37-97-.276; 1905-1906 Jake Stahl 119-182-.395; 1907-1909 Joe Cantillon 158-297-.347; 1910-1911 Jim McAleer 130-175-.426; 1912-1920 Clark Griffith 693-646-.518; 1921 George McBride 80-73-.523; 1922 Clyde Milan 69-85-.448; 1923 Owen Bush 75-78-.490; 1924-1928 Stanley Harris 429-334-.562; 1929-1932 Walter Johnson 350-264-.570; 1933-1934 Joe Cronin 165-139-.543; 1935-1942 Stanley Harris 558-663-.457; 1943-1947 Oswald Bluege 375-394-.488; 1948-1949 Joe Kuhel 106-201-.345; 1950-1954 Stanley Harris 349-419-.454; 1955-1957 Chuck Dressen 117-212-.356; 1957-1960 Harry Lavagetto 247-348-.415

WASHINGTON SENATORS
(became Texas Rangers)

Home City: Washington, D.C.
Home Field: Griffith Stadium (1961)   Capacity: 27,410 [1961]
            RFK Stadium (1962-1971)   Capacity: 45,016 [1971]
Origin of Name: Named after the previous American League team.

Regular Season Record

Season	League	GP	W	L	Pct	GB	R	OR
1961	AL	161	61	100	.379	47.5	618	776
1962	AL	161	60	101	.373	35.5	599	716
1963	AL	162	56	106	.346	48.5	578	812
1964	AL	162	62	100	.383	37	578	733
1965	AL	162	70	92	.432	32	591	721
1966	AL	159	71	88	.447	25.5	557	659
1967	AL	161	76	85	.472	15.5	550	637
1968	AL	161	65	96	.404	37.5	524	665
1969	AL	162	86	76	.531	23	694	644
1970	AL	162	70	92	.432	38	626	689
1971	AL	159	63	96	.396	38.5	537	660
TOTAL:	11 years	1772	740	1032		378.5	6452	7712
AVERAGE:		161	67	94	.418	34.5	587	701

Regular Season Individual Leaders

Season	Home Runs		RBI's		Wins	
1961	Gene Green	18	Willie Tasby	63	Bennie Daniels	12
1962	Harry Bright	17	Chuck Hinton	75	Dave Stenhouse	11
	Chuck Hinton	17				
1963	Don Lock	27	Don Lock	82	Claude Osteen	9
1964	Don Lock	28	Don Lock	80	Claude Osteen	15
1965	Frank Howard	21	Frank Howard	84	Pete Richert	15
1966	Frank Howard	18	Frank Howard	71	Pete Richert	14
1967	Frank Howard	36	Frank Howard	89	Camilo Pascual	12
1968	Frank Howard	44	Frank Howard	106	Camilo Pascual	13
1969	Frank Howard	48	Frank Howard	111	Dick Bosman	14
1970	Frank Howard	44	Frank Howard	126	Dick Bosman	16
1971	Frank Howard	26	Frank Howard	83	Dick Bosman	12

COACHING HISTORY: 1961-1963 James Vernon 135-227-.373; 1963-1967 Gil Hodges 321-445-.419; 1968 Jim Lemon 65-96-.404; 1969-1971 Ted Williams 219-264-.453

WASHINGTON WHIPS

Home City: Washington, D.C.
Home Field: D.C. Stadium
Origin of Name: The name was chosen in a Name the Team Contest. The team was represented by the Aberdeen Club of Scotland.

Regular Season Record

Season	League	GP	W	L	T	GF	GA	BP	Pts	Pct
1967	USA	12	5	2	5	19	11	-	15	.625
1968	NASL	32	15	10	7	63	53	56	167	.580
TOTAL:	2 years	44	20	12	12	82	64	56	182	
AVERAGE:		22	10	6	6	41	32	28	91	.583

Playoff Record

Season	GP	W	L	GF	GA	Result
1967	1	0	1	5	6	Lost Championship game to Los Angeles.

Regular Season Individual Leaders

Season	Goals		Points		GAA (360 Min)	
1967	Jim Storrie	5	Jim Storrie	11	Robert Clark	0.92
1968	John Paletta	8	John Paletta	16		
			Jorge Siega	16		

COACHING HISTORY: 1967 Ed Turnbull 5-2-5-.625; 1968 Andre Nagy; 1968 Hicabi Emerkli

WASHINGTON WIZARDS
(were Washington Bullets)

Home City: Landover, Maryland
　　　　　Washington D.C.
Home Court: U.S. Air Arena (1973-present) *　　　Capacity: 18,756 [1997]
　　　　　　Baltimore Arena (1988-present)　　　Capacity: 12,289 [1995] (4 games a year)
　　　　　　MCI Center　　　　　　　　　　　　Capacity 20,674 [2006]
Origin of Name: The name was chosen in a Name the Team Contest which drew over 500,000 entries. Abe Pollin, the team's owner, decided on the name change due to the street-violence connotations of the name Bullets.

Regular Season Record

Season	League	GP	W	L	PPGF	PPGA	Pct	GB
1973-1974	NBA	82	47	35	101.9	100.4	.573	-
1974-1975	NBA	82	60	22	104.7	97.5	.732	-
1975-1976	NBA	82	48	34	102.8	100.4	.585	1
1976-1977	NBA	82	48	34	105.5	104.5	.585	1
1977-1978	NBA	82	44	38	110.3	109.4	.537	8
1978-1979	NBA	82	54	28	114.9	109.9	.659	-
1979-1980	NBA	82	39	43	107.0	109.5	.476	22
1980-1981	NBA	82	39	43	105.6	105.6	.476	23
1981-1982	NBA	82	43	39	103.5	102.6	.524	20
1982-1983	NBA	82	42	40	99.2	99.3	.512	23
1983-1984	NBA	82	35	47	102.7	105.6	.427	27
1984-1985	NBA	82	40	42	105.5	105.8	.488	23

*-known as Capital Center from 1974 to 1993

1985-1986	NBA	82	39	43	103.0	104.8	.476	28
1986-1987	NBA	82	42	40	106.0	107.3	.512	17
1987-1988	NBA	82	38	44	105.5	106.3	.463	19
1988-1989	NBA	82	40	42	108.3	110.4	.488	12
1989-1990	NBA	82	31	51	107.7	109.9	.378	22
1990-1991	NBA	82	30	52	101.4	106.4	.366	26
1991-1992	NBA	82	25	57	102.4	106.8	.305	26
1992-1993	NBA	82	22	60	101.9	108.9	.268	38
1993-1994	NBA	82	24	58	100.4	107.7	.293	33
1994-1995	NBA	82	21	61	100.5	106.1	.256	36
1995-1996	NBA	82	39	43	102.5	101.5	.476	21
1996-1997	NBA	82	44	38	99.4	97.7	.537	17
1997-1998	NBA	82	42	40	97.2	96.6	.512	13
1998-1999	NBA	50	18	32	91.2	93.4	.360	15
1999-2000	NBA	82	29	53	96.6	99.9	.354	23
2000-2001	NBA	82	19	63	93.2	99.9	.232	37
2001-2002	NBA	82	37	45	92.8	94.2	.451	15
2002-2003	NBA	82	37	45	91.5	92.5	.451	12
2003-2004	NBA	82	25	57	91.8	97.4	.305	22
2004-2005	NBA	82	45	37	100.5	100.8	.549	14
2005-2006	NBA	82	42	40	101.7	99.8	.512	10
TOTAL:	33 years	2674	1228	1446				604
AVERAGE:		81	37	44	101.9	103.1	.459	18

Playoff Record

Season	GP	W	L	PPGF	PPGA	Result
1973-1974	7	3	4	95.1	94.0	Lost Conference Semifinal to New York.
1974-1975	17	8	9	102.8	100.2	Lost Championship series to Golden State.
1975-1976	7	3	4	91.7	91.1	Lost Conference Semifinal to Cleveland.
1976-1977	9	4	5	104.3	104.7	Lost Conference Semifinal to Houston.
1977-1978	21	14	7	107.6	103.9	**Won NBA Championship.**
1978-1979	19	9	10	101.6	102.9	Lost Championship series to Seattle.
1979-1980	2	0	2	100.0	111.5	Lost 1st Round series to Philadelphia.
1981-1982	7	3	4	100.1	101.7	Lost Conference Semifinal to Boston.
1983-1984	4	1	3	93.8	96.5	Lost 1st Round series to Boston.
1984-1985	4	1	3	101.8	105.8	Lost 1st Round series to Philadelphia.
1985-1986	5	2	3	100.6	106.4	Lost 1st Round series to Philadelphia.
1986-1987	3	0	3	91.0	110.3	Lost 1st Round series to Detroit.
1987-1988	5	2	3	97.2	101.2	Lost 1st Round series to Detroit.
1996-1997	3	0	3	95.0	101.0	Lost 1st Round series to Chicago.
2004-2005	10	4	6	100.4	102.9	Lost Conference Semifinal to Miami.
2005-2006	6	2	4	101.7	101.5	Lost 1st Round series to Cleveland.
TOTAL:	129	56	73			
AVERAGE:	8	4	4	101.0	101.8	

Regular Season Individual Leaders

Season	Field Goal % (min. 70 games)		Points		Points per Game (min. 70 games)	
1973-74	Kevin Porter	.478	Elvin Hayes	1735	Phil Chenier	21.9
1974-75	Jimmy Jones	.518	Elvin Hayes	1887	Elvin Hayes	23.0
1975-76	Wes Unseld	.561	Phil Chenier	1590	Phil Chenier	19.9
1976-77	Mitch Kupchak	.572	Elvin Hayes	1942	Elvin Hayes	23.7
1977-78	Wes Unseld	.523	Elvin Hayes	1598	Elvin Hayes	19.7
1978-79	Wes Unseld	.577	Elvin Hayes	1789	Elvin Hayes	21.8

Season	Field Goal %		Points		Points per Game	
1979-80	Wes Unseld	.513	Elvin Hayes	1859	Elvin Hayes	23.0
1980-81	Mitch Kupchak	.525	Elvin Hayes	1439	Elvin Hayes	17.8
1981-82	Jeff Ruland	.561	Greg Ballard	1486	Greg Ballard	18.8
1982-83	Jeff Ruland	.552	Jeff Ruland	1536	Jeff Ruland	19.4
1983-84	Jeff Ruland	.579	Jeff Ruland	1665	Jeff Ruland	22.2
1984-85	Darren Daye	.512	Gus Williams	1578	Gus Williams	20.0
1985-86	Jeff Ruland	.554	Jeff Malone	1795	Jeff Malone	22.4
1986-87	Terry Catledge	.495	Moses Malone	1760	Moses Malone	24.1
1987-88	Terry Catledge	.506	Jeff Malone	1641	Jeff Malone	20.5
1988-89	Terry Catledge	.490	Bernard King	1674	Jeff Malone	21.7
1989-90	Charles Jones	.508	Bernard King	1837	Jeff Malone	24.3
1990-91	Pervis Ellison	.513	Bernard King	1817	Harvey Grant	18.2
1991-92	Larry Stewart	.514	Michael Adams	1408	Michael Adams	18.1
1992-93	Larry Stewart	.543	Harvey Grant	1339	Harvey Grant	18.6
1993-94	Don MacLean	.502	Don MacLean	1365	Don MacLean	18.2
1994-95	G. Muresan	.560	Calbert Cheaney	1293	Calbert Cheaney	16.6
1995-96	G. Muresan	.584	Juwan Howard	1789	Juwan Howard	22.1
1996-97	G. Muresan	.604	Juwan Howard	1570	Chris Webber	20.1
1997-98	Darvin Ham	.529	Chris Webber	1555	Chris Webber	21.9
1998-99*	Ben Wallace	.578	Mitch Richmond	983	Mitch Richmond	19.7
1999-00	Aaron Williams	.522	Mitch Richmond	1285	Mitch Richmond	17.4
2000-01	C. Laettner	.503	Richard Hamilton	1411	Richard Hamilton	18.1
2001-02	Jahidi White	.538	Michael Jordan	1375	Chirs Whitney	10.2
2002-03	B. Haywood	.510	Michael Jordan	1640	Jerry Stackhouse	21.5
2003-04	B. Haywood	.515	Larry Hughes	1148	Kwame Brown	10.9
2004-05	Jared Jeffries	.468	Gilbert Arenas	2038	Gilbert Arenas	25.5
2005-06	Etan Thomas	.533	Gilbert Arenas	2346	Gilbert Arenas	29.3

COACHING HISTORY: 1973-1976 K.C. Jones 155-91-.630; 1976-1980 Dick Motta 185-143-.564; 1980-1986 Gene Shue 231-248-.482; 1985-1988 Kevin Loughery 57-65-.467; 1987-1994 Wes Unseld 204-348-.370; 1994-1997 Jim Lynam 104-142-.423; 1996-1997 Bob Staak 0-1-.000; 1996-1999 Bernie Bickerstaff 82-85-.491; 1999-2000 Gar Heard 14-30-.318; 1999-2000 Darrell Walker 15-23-.395; 2000-2001 Leonard Hamilton 19-63-.232; 2001-2003 Doug Collins 74-90-.451; 2003-present Eddie Jordan

WATERLOO HAWKS

Home City: Waterloo, Iowa
Home Court: The Hippodrome
Origin of Name:

Regular Season Record

Season	League	GP	W	L	PPGF	PPGA	Pct	GB
1948-1949	NBL	62	30	32	58.9	59.2	.484	6
1949-1950	NBA	62	19	43	79.4	84.9	.306	19
TOTAL:	2 years	124	49	75				25
AVERAGE:		62	25	37	69.2	72.1	.395	13

Regular Season Individual Leaders

Season	Field Goals		Free Throws		Points	
1948-49	Dick Mehen	315	Dick Mehen	211	Dick Mehen	841
1949-50	Dick Mehen	347	Don Boven	240	Dick Mehen	892

*-minimum 40 games

COACHING HISTORY: 1948-1950 Charley Shipp 38-59-.392; 1949-1950 Jack Smiley 11-16-.407

WHITING CIESAR ALL-AMERICANS
(became Hammond Ciesar All-Americans)

Home City: Whiting, Indiana
Home Court: Whiting Community Center
Origin of Name: The team was owned by Eddie Ciesar.

Regular Season Record

Season	League	GP	W	L	PPGF	PPGA	Pct	GB
1937-1938	NBL	15	12	3	41.3	37.3	.800	.5

Playoff Record

Season	GP	W	L	PPGF	PPGA	Result
1937-1938	2	0	2	35.5	40.5	Lost 1st Round series to Oshkosh.

Regular Season Individual Leaders

Season	Field Goals		Free Throws		Points	
1937-38	Vince McGowan	57	John Wooden	39	Vince McGowan	144

COACHING HISTORY: Whitey Wickhorst 12-3-.800

WILMINGTON QUICKSTEPS

Home City: Wilmington, Delaware
Home Field: Union Association Park
Origin of Name: This was the minor league Eastern League team which won the Championship in 1884 before moving to the Union Association to replace the Philadelphia Keystones.

Regular Season Record

Season	League	GP	W	L	Pct	GB	R	OR
1884	UA	18	2	16	.111	44.5	35	114

Regular Season Individual Leaders

Season	Home Runs		RBI's		Wins	
1884	Charlie Bastian	2	Not Recorded		Edward Nolan	1

COACHING HISTORY: Joe Simmons 2-16-.111

WINNIPEG BLUE BOMBERS

Home City: Winnipeg, Manitoba
Home Stadium: Osborne Stadium (1950-1952)
                Canad Inns Stadium (1953-present)*   Capacity: 29,503 [2006]
Origin of Name: The name was coined by reporter Vince Leah who called the team the "Blue Bombers of Western Football" from a Grantland Rice description of Joe Louis a.k.a. The Brown Bomber.

Regular Season Record

Season	League	GP	W	L	T	OT	PF	PA	Pts	Pct
1950	CRU	14	10	4	0	NA	221	156	20	.714

*-known as Winnipeg Stadium 1953-2001

1951	CRU	14	8	6	0	NA	303	311	16	.571
1952	CRU	16	12	3	1	NA	394	211	25	.781
1953	CRU	16	8	8	0	NA	226	226	16	.500
1954	CRU	16	8	6	2	NA	202	190	18	.563
1955	CRU	16	7	9	0	NA	210	195	14	.438
1956	CFC	16	9	7	0	NA	315	228	18	.563
1957	CFC	16	12	4	0	NA	406	300	24	.750
1958	CFL	16	13	3	0	NA	361	182	26	.813
1959	CFL	16	12	4	0	NA	418	272	24	.750
1960	CFL	16	14	2	0	NA	453	239	28	.875
1961	CFL	16	13	3	0	NA	360	251	26	.813
1962	CFL	16	11	5	0	NA	385	291	22	.688
1963	CFL	16	7	9	0	NA	302	325	14	.438
1964	CFL	16	1	14	1	NA	270	397	3	.094
1965	CFL	16	11	5	0	NA	301	262	22	.688
1966	CFL	16	8	7	1	NA	264	230	17	.531
1967	CFL	16	4	12	0	NA	212	414	8	.250
1968	CFL	16	3	13	0	NA	210	374	6	.188
1969	CFL	16	3	12	1	NA	192	359	7	.219
1970	CFL	16	2	14	0	NA	184	332	4	.125
1971	CFL	16	7	8	1	NA	366	349	15	.469
1972	CFL	16	10	6	0	NA	401	300	20	.625
1973	CFL	16	4	11	1	NA	267	315	9	.281
1974	CFL	16	8	8	0	NA	258	350	16	.500
1975	CFL	16	6	8	2	NA	340	383	14	.438
1976	CFL	16	10	6	0	NA	384	316	20	.625
1977	CFL	16	10	6	0	NA	382	336	20	.625
1978	CFL	16	9	7	0	NA	371	351	18	.563
1979	CFL	16	4	12	0	NA	283	340	8	.250
1980	CFL	16	10	6	0	NA	394	387	20	.625
1981	CFL	16	11	5	0	NA	517	299	22	.688
1982	CFL	16	11	5	0	NA	444	352	22	.688
1983	CFL	16	9	7	0	NA	412	402	18	.563
1984	CFL	16	11	4	1	NA	523	309	23	.719
1985	CFL	16	12	4	0	NA	500	259	24	.750
1986	CFL	18	11	7	0	NA	545	387	22	.611
1987	CFL	18	12	6	0	NA	554	409	24	.667
1988	CFL	18	9	9	0	NA	407	458	18	.500
1989	CFL	18	7	11	0	NA	408	462	14	.438
1990	CFL	18	12	6	0	NA	472	398	24	.667
1991	CFL	18	9	9	0	NA	516	499	18	.500
1992	CFL	18	11	7	0	NA	507	499	22	.611
1993	CFL	18	14	4	0	NA	646	421	28	.778
1994	CFL	18	13	5	0	NA	651	572	26	.722
1995	CFL	18	7	11	0	NA	404	653	14	.389
1996	CFL	18	9	9	0	NA	421	499	18	.500
1997	CFL	18	4	14	0	NA	443	548	8	.222
1998	CFL	18	3	15	0	NA	396	588	6	.167
1999	CFL	18	6	12	0	NA	362	601	12	.333
2000	CFL	18	7	10	1	1	539	596	16	.444
2001	CFL	18	14	4	0	0	509	383	28	.778
2002	CFL	18	12	6	0	0	516	450	24	.667
2003	CFL	18	11	7	0	NA	514	485	22	.611
2004	CFL	18	7	11	0	NA	448	507	14	.389

2005	CFL	18	5	13	0	NA	474	558	10	.278
2006	CFL	18	9	9	0	NA	362	408	18	.500
TOTAL:	57 years	950	500	438	12	1	22125	21174	1013	
AVERAGE:		17	9	8	0	0	388	371	18	.533

Playoff Record

Season	GP	W	L	T	PF	PA	Result
1950	4	2	2	0	67	48	Lost Grey Cup Final to Toronto.
1951	1	0	1	0	1	4	Lost Division Semifinal to Edmonton.
1952	3	1	2	0	51	52	Lost Division Final to Edmonton.
1953	7	4	3	0	148	105	Lost Grey Cup Final to Hamilton.
1954	5	2	2	1	47	50	Lost Division Final to Edmonton.
1955	4	1	3	0	36	71	Lost Division Final to Edmonton.
1956	2	1	1	0	26	50	Lost Division Semifinal to Saskatchewan.
1957	6	3	2	1	75	62	Lost Grey Cup Final to Hamilton.
1958	4	3	1	0	95	72	**Won Grey Cup.**
1959	3	3	0	0	56	26	**Won Grey Cup.**
1960	3	1	2	0	29	30	Lost Division Final to Edmonton.
1961	3	3	0	0	78	29	**Won Grey Cup.**
1962	4	3	1	0	73	65	**Won Grey Cup.**
1965	5	3	2	0	74	81	Lost Grey Cup Final to Hamilton.
1966	3	1	2	0	42	43	Lost Division Final to Saskatchewan.
1971	1	0	1	0	23	34	Lost Division Semifinal to Saskatchewan.
1972	1	0	1	0	24	27	Lost Division Final to Saskatchewan.
1975	1	0	1	0	24	42	Lost Division Semifinal to Saskatchewan.
1976	1	0	1	0	12	14	Lost Division Semifinal to Edmonton.
1977	1	0	1	0	32	33	Lost Division Semifinal to B.C.
1978	1	0	1	0	4	38	Lost Division Semifinal to Calgary.
1980	2	1	1	0	56	48	Lost Division Final to Edmonton.
1981	1	0	1	0	11	15	Lost Division Semifinal to B.C.
1982	2	1	1	0	45	27	Lost Division Final to Edmonton.
1983	2	1	1	0	70	61	Lost Division Final to B.C.
1984	3	3	0	0	133	51	**Won Grey Cup.**
1985	2	1	1	0	44	57	Lost Division Final to B.C.
1986	1	0	1	0	14	21	Lost Division Semifinal to B.C.
1987	1	0	1	0	3	19	Lost Division Final to Toronto.
1988	3	3	0	0	84	60	**Won Grey Cup.**
1989	2	1	1	0	40	21	Lost Division Final to Hamilton.
1990	2	2	0	0	70	28	**Won Grey Cup.**
1991	2	1	1	0	29	50	Lost Division Final to Toronto.
1992	2	1	1	0	69	35	Lost Grey Cup Final to Calgary.
1993	2	1	1	0	43	52	Lost Grey Cup Final to Edmonton.
1994	2	1	1	0	38	30	Lost Division Final to Baltimore.
1995	1	0	1	0	21	36	Lost Division Semifinal to Baltimore.
1996	1	0	1	0	7	68	Lost Division Final to Edmonton.
2000	2	1	1	0	46	55	Lost Division Final to Montreal.
2001	2	1	1	0	47	40	Lost Grey Cup Final to Calgary.
2002	2	1	1	0	60	36	Lost Division Final to Edmonton.
2003	1	0	1	0	21	37	Lost Division Semifinal to Saskatchewan.
2006	1	0	1	0	27	31	Lost Division Semifinal to Toronto.
TOTAL:	102	51	49	2	1995	1854	
AVERAGE:	2	1	1	0	46	43	

Regular Season Individual Leaders

Season	Passing Yards		Receiving Yards		Rushing Yards	
1950	Jack Jacobs	1601			Tom Casey	637
1951			Neil Armstrong	1024		
1952	Jack Jacobs	3018			Lorne Benson	491
1953					Lorne Benson	563
1954	Jack Jacobs	1732			Gerry James	576
1955					Gerry James	1205
1956	Eagle Day	1814			Bob McNamara	1101
1957	Ken Ploen	1284			Gerry James	1192
1958	Jim Van Pelt	1445	Leo Lewis	679	Leo Lewis	1164
1959	Jim Van Pelt	2706	Ernie Pitts	1126	Charlie Shepard	1076
1960	Ken Ploen	1693	Ernie Pitts	659	Leo Lewis	923
1961	Hal Ledyard	1398	Farrell Funston	892	Leo Lewis	1036
1962	Ken Ploen	2097	Ernie Pitts	865	Leo Lewis	865
1963	Ken Ploen	2026	Farrell Funston	835	Roger Hagberg	695
1964	Ken Ploen	1878	Ernie Pitts	459	Leo Lewis	845
1965	Ken Ploen	1789	Farrell Funston	549	Dave Raimey	1052
1966	Ken Ploen	2323	Ken Nielsen	719	Dave Raimey	1223
1967	Ken Ploen	1382	Ken Nielsen	1121	Dave Raimey	772
1968	John Schneider	1949	Ken Nielsen	1031	Dave Raimey	781
1969	Wally Gabler	2288	Ken Nielsen	617	Bob Houmard	506
1970	Wally Gabler	1077	Rick Shaw	538	Bob Houmard	847
1971	Don Jonas	4036	Jim Thorpe	1436	Mack Herron	900
1972	Don Jonas	3583	Jim Thorpe	1260	Mack Herron	1527
1973	Don Jonas	3363	Bob LaRose	855	John Bledsoe	811
1974	Don Jonas	1309	Tom Scott	638	John Bledsoe	623
1975	Dieter Brock	1911	Bob LaRose	587	Jim Washington	665
1976	Dieter Brock	3101	Tom Scott	968	Jim Washington	1277
1977	Dieter Brock	3063	Tom Scott	1079	Jim Washington	1262
1978	Dieter Brock	3755	Joe Poplawski	998	Jim Washington	1032
1979	Dieter Brock	2383	Mike Holmes	1034	Jim Washington	918
1980	Dieter Brock	4252	Mike Holmes	1092	William Miller	1053
1981	Dieter Brock	4296	Eugene Goodlow	1494	William Miller	684
1982	Dieter Brock	4294	Rick House	1020	William Miller	1076
1983	Dieter Brock	1892	James Murphy	1126	Willard Reaves	898
1984	Tom Clements	3845	James Murphy	1220	Willard Reaves	1733
1985	Tom Clements	3697	Jeff Boyd	1372	Willard Reaves	1323
1986	John Hufnagel	3394	James Murphy	1746	Willard Reaves	498
1987	Tom Clements	4686	Perry Tuttle	1310	Willard Reaves	1471
1988	Tom Muecke	1892	James Murphy	1409	Tim Jessie	359
1989	Sean Salisbury	4056	James Murphy	1150	Tim Jessie	808
1990	Tom Burgess	3958	Rick House	883	Robert Mimbs	1341
1991	Tom Burgess	4212	Rob Crifo	775	Robert Mimbs	1769
1992	Matt Dunigan	2857	Larry Thompson	1192	Mike Richardson	1153
1993	Matt Dunigan	4682	Gerald Wilcox	1340	Mike Richardson	925
1994	Matt Dunigan	3965	Gerald Wilcox	1624	Blaise Bryant	1289
1995	Reggie Slack	2007	Gerald Wilcox	1024	Blaise Bryant	664
1996	Kent Austin	2135	Eric Guliford	758	Mike Richardson	378
1997	Chris Vargas	2618	Milt Stegall	1616	Ronald Williams	1120
1998	T.J. Rubley	1575	Chris Armstrong	1162	Eric Blount	544
1999	Kerwin Bell	4647	Milt Stegall	1193	D. McCullough	990
2000	Khari Jones	4142	Milt Stegall	1499	Cory Philpot	520
2001	Khari Jones	4545	Milt Stegall	1214	Charles Roberts	620

Season	Passing Yards		Receiving Yards		Rushing Yards	
2002	Khari Jones	5334	Milt Stegall	1896	Charles Roberts	1162
2003	Khari Jones	4016	Milt Stegall	1144	Charles Roberts	1554
2004	Kevin Glenn	2138	Milt Stegall	1121	Charles Roberts	1522
2005	Kevin Glenn	3571	Milt Stegall	1184	Charles Roberts	1624
2006	Kevin Glenn	3427	Milt Stegall	1269	Charles Roberts	1609

COACHING HISTORY: 1950 Frank Larson 10-4-0-.714; 1951-1953 George Trafton 28-17-1-.620; 1954-1956 Allie Sherman 24-22-2-.521; 1957-1966 Bud Grant 102-56-2-.644; 1967-1969 Joe Zaleski 10-37-1-.219; 1970-1973 Jim Spavital 23-39-2-.375; 1974-1977 Bud Riley 34-28-2-.547; 1978-1982 Ray Jauch 45-35-0-.563; 1983-1986 Cal Murphy 40-21-1-.653; 1985 Fred Glick 3-1-0-.750; 1987-1990 Mike Riley 40-32-0-.556; 1991 Darryl Rogers 9-9-0-.500; 1992 Urban Bowman 11-7-0-.611; 1993-1996 Cal Murphy 43-29-0-.597; 1997-1998 Jeff Reinebold 6-26-0-.188; 1998-Gary Hoffman 1-3-0-.250; 1999-2004 Dave Ritchie 52-44-1-1-.546; 2004-2005 Jim Daley 10-19-0-.345; 2006-present Doug Berry

WINNIPEG JETS
(became Phoenix Coyotes)

Home City: Winnipeg, Manitoba
Home Arena: Winnipeg Arena   Capacity: 15,393 [1995]
Origin of Name: Team owner Ben Hatskin was a friend of New York Jets owner Sonny Werblin and named the team in honor of them.

Regular Season Record

Season	League	GP	W	L	T	GF	GA	Pts	Pct
1972-1973	WHA	78	43	31	4	285	249	90	.577
1973-1974	WHA	78	34	39	5	264	296	73	.468
1974-1975	WHA	78	38	35	5	322	293	81	.519
1975-1976	WHA	81	52	27	2	345	254	106	.654
1976-1977	WHA	80	46	32	2	366	291	94	.588
1977-1978	WHA	80	50	28	2	381	270	102	.638
1978-1979	WHA	80	39	35	6	307	306	84	.525
1979-1980	NHL	80	20	49	11	214	314	51	.319
1980-1981	NHL	80	9	57	14	246	400	32	.200
1981-1982	NHL	80	33	33	14	319	332	80	.500
1982-1983	NHL	80	33	39	8	311	333	74	.463
1983-1984	NHL	80	31	38	11	340	374	73	.456
1984-1985	NHL	80	43	27	10	358	332	96	.600
1985-1986	NHL	80	26	47	7	295	372	59	.369
1986-1987	NHL	80	40	32	8	279	271	88	.550
1987-1988	NHL	80	33	36	11	292	310	77	.481
1988-1989	NHL	80	26	42	12	300	355	64	.400
1989-1990	NHL	80	37	32	11	298	290	85	.531
1990-1991	NHL	80	26	43	11	260	288	63	.394
1991-1992	NHL	80	33	32	15	251	244	81	.506
1992-1993	NHL	84	40	37	7	322	320	87	.518
1993-1994	NHL	84	24	51	9	245	344	57	.339
1994-1995	NHL	48	16	25	7	157	177	39	.406
1995-1996	NHL	82	36	40	6	275	291	78	.476
TOTAL:	24 years	1893	808	887	198	7032	7306	1814	
AVERAGE:		79	34	37	8	293	304	76	.479

Playoff Record

Season	GP	W	L	GF	GA	Result
1972-1973	14	9	5	55	49	Lost Championship series to New England.
1973-1974	4	0	4	9	23	Lost Quarterfinal series o Houston.
1975-1976	13	12	1	68	35	**Won WHA Championship.**
1976-1977	20	11	9	80	73	Lost Championship series to Quebec.
1977-1978	9	8	1	53	20	**Won WHA Championship.**
1978-1979	10	8	2	51	38	**Won WHA Championship.**
1981-1982	4	1	3	13	20	Lost Division Semifinal to St. Louis.
1982-1983	3	0	3	9	14	Lost Division Semifinal to Edmonton.
1983-1984	3	0	3	7	18	Lost Division Semifinal to Edmonton.
1984-1985	8	3	5	26	35	Lost Division Final to Chicago.
1985-1986	3	0	3	8	15	Lost Division Semifinal to Calgary.
1986-1987	10	4	6	31	32	Lost Division Final to Edmonton.
1987-1988	5	1	4	17	25	Lost Division Semifinal to Edmonton.
1989-1990	7	3	4	22	24	Lost Division Semifinal to Edmonton.
1991-1992	7	3	4	17	29	Lost Division Semifinal to Vancouver.
1992-1993	6	2	4	17	21	Lost Division Semifinal to Vancouver.
1995-1996	6	2	4	10	20	Lost Conference Quarterfinal to Detroit.
TOTAL:	132	67	65	493	491	
AVERAGE:	8	4	4	29	29	

Regular Season Individual Leaders

Season	Goals		Points		Penalty Minutes	
1972-1973	Bobby Hull	51	Bobby Hull	103	Steve Cuddie	119
			Norm Beaudin	103		
1973-1974	Bobby Hull	53	Bobby Hull	95	Duke Asmundson	85
1974-1975	Bobby Hull	77	Bobby Hull	142	Perry Miller	133
1975-1976	Bobby Hull	53	Bobby Hull	123	T. Bergman	111
1976-1977	Anders Hedberg	70	Anders Hedberg	131	Dave Dunn	129
1977-1978	Anders Hedberg	63	Ulf Nilsson	126	Kim Clackson	203
1978-1979	Morris Lukowich	65	Kent Nilsson	107	Scott Campbell	248
1979-1980	Morris Lukowich	35	Morris Lukowich	74	Jimmy Mann	287
1980-1981	Morris Lukowich	33	Dave Christian	71	Jimmy Mann	105
1981-1982	Dale Hawerchuk	45	Dale Hawerchuk	103	Bryan Maxwell	110
1982-1983	Dale Hawerchuk	40	Dale Hawerchuk	91	Bryan Maxwell	131
1983-1984	Paul MacLean	40	Dale Hawerchuk	102	Laurie Boschman	234
1984-1985	Dale Hawerchuk	53	Dale Hawerchuk	130	Laurie Boschman	180
1985-1986	Dale Hawerchuk	46	Dale Hawerchuk	105	Laurie Boschman	241
1986-1987	Dale Hawerchuk	47	Dale Hawerchuk	100	Jim Kyte	162
1987-1988	Dale Hawerchuk	44	Dale Hawerchuk	121	Laurie Boschman	227
1988-1989	Dale Hawerchuk	41	Dale Hawerchuk	96	Gord Donnelly	228
1989-1990	Pat Elynuik	32	Dale Hawerchuk	81	Shawn Cronin	243
	Paul Fenton	32				
1990-1991	Pat Elynuik	31	Phil Housley	76	Gord Donnelly	265
1991-1992	Ed Olczk	32	Phil Housley	86	Shawn Cronin	271
1992-1993	Teemu Selanne	76	Teemu Selanne	132	Tie Domi	249
1993-1994	Keith Tkachuk	41	Keith Tkachuk	81	Tie Domi	347
1994-1995	Alexei Zhamnov	30	Alexei Zhamnov	65	Keith Tkachuk	152
1995-1996	Keith Tkachuk	50	Keith Tkachuk	98	Dave Manson	205

COACHING HISTORY: 1972-1975 Bobby Hull 81-79-9-.506; 1974-1975 Rudy Pilous 34-26-5-.562; 1975-1977 Bobby Kromm 98-59-4-.621; 1977-1979 Larry Hillman 89-63-8-.581; 1979-1981 Tom McVie 21-69-18-.278; 1980-1981 Bill Sutherland 8-37-7-.221; 1981-1984 Tom

Watt 70-81-24-.469; 1983-1984 John Ferguson 2-3-0-.400; 1983-1986 Barry Long 87-94-25-.483; 1985-1986 John Ferguson 7-6-1-.536; 1986-1989 Dan Maloney 91-93-28-.495; 1988-1989 Rick Bowness 8-17-3-.339; 1989-1991 Bob Murdoch 63-75-22-.463; 1991-1995 John Paddock 106-138-37-.443; 1994-1996 Terry Simpson 43-47-7-.479

WORCESTER BROWN STOCKINGS

Home City: Worcester, Massachusetts
Home Field: Agricultural Grounds
Origin of Name: The players wore brown stockings.

Regular Season Record

Season	League	GP	W	L	Pct	GB	R	OR
1880	NL	83	40	43	.482	26.5	412	370
1881	NL	82	32	50	.390	23	410	492
1882	NL	84	18	66	.214	37	379	652
TOTAL:	3 years	249	90	159		86.5	1201	1514
AVERAGE:		83	30	53	.361	29	400	505

Regular Season Individual Leaders

Season	Home Runs		RBI's		Wins	
1880	Harry Stovey	6	Art Whitney	36	Lee Richmond	32
1881	Harry Stovey	2	Pete Hotaling	35	Lee Richmond	25
	Warren Carpenter	2				
1882	Harry Stovey	5	Jackie Hayes	54	Lee Richmond	14

COACHING HISTORY: 1880 Frank Bancroft 40-43-.482; 1881-1882 Freeman Brown 36-69-.343; 1882 Tommy Bond 5-22-.185; 1882 Jack Chapman 9-25-.265

YOUNGSTOWN BEARS
(were Pittsburgh Raiders)

Home City: Youngstown, Ohio
Home Court: South Field House
Origin of Name:

Regular Season Record

Season	League	GP	W	L	PPGF	PPGA	Pct	GB
1945-1946	NBL	33	13	20	46.6	50.5	.394	12.5
1946-1947	NBL	44	12	32	53.5	60.1	.273	19
TOTAL:	2 years	77	25	52				31.5
AVERAGE:		39	13	26	50.1	55.3	.325	16

Regular Season Individual Leaders

Season	Field Goals		Free Throws		Points	
1945-46	Moe Becker	115	Frank Baumholtz	76	Frank Baumholtz	274
1946-47	Milt Ticco	180	Charlie Joachim	102	Milt Ticco	406

COACHING HISTORY: 1945-1946 Paul Birch 13-20-.394; 1946-1947 Frank Shannon 12-32-.273

Appendix A: Team Nicknames

228th Battalion	Toronto (NHA 1916-17)
49ers	San Francisco (AAFC, NFL 1946 to present)
76ers	Philadelphia (NBA 1963-64 to present)
Aeros	Houston (WHA 1972-73 to 1977-78)
All Americans	Buffalo (NFL 1922 to 1923) Syracuse (ABL 1929-30)
All-Stars	Oshkosh (NBL 1937-38 to 1948-49)
Alleghenys	Pittsburgh (AA, NL 1882 to 1889)
Allmen Transfers	Cleveland (NBL 1944-45 to 1945-46)
Alouettes	Montreal (CRU, CFC, CFL 1950 to 1981, 1986) Montreal (CFL 1996 to present)
American Gears	Chicago (NBL 1944-45 to 1946-47)
Americans	New York (NHL 1925-26 to 1940-41) Brooklyn (NHL 1941-42) New Jersey (ABA 1967-68) Birmingham (WFL 1974)
Amigos	Anaheim (ABA 1967-68)
Angels	Los Angeles (AL 1961 to 1964) California (AL 1965 to 1996) Anaheim (AL 1997-2004) Los Angeles (AL 2005-present)
Apollos	Atlanta (NASL 1973)
Arcadians	Brooklyn (ABL 1925-26 to 1926-27)
Arenas	Toronto (NHL 1917-18 to 1918 19)
Argonauts	Toronto (CRU, CFC, CFL 1950 to present)
Aristocrats	Victoria (PCHA 1912-13 to 1915-16) Victoria (PCHA 1918-19 to 1919-20)
Astros	Houston (NL 1965 to present)
Athletic Supply	Columbus (NBL 1937-38)
Athletics	Philadelphia (NL 1876) Philadelphia (AA 1882 to 1891) Philadelphia (AL 1901 to 1954) Kansas City (AL 1955 to 1967) Oakland (AL 1968 to present)
Atoms	Philadelphia (NASL 1973 to 1976)
Avalanche	Colorado (NHL 1995-96 to present)
Aztecs	Los Angeles (NASL 1974 to 1981)
Badgers	Milwaukee (NFL 1922 to 1926)
Bandits	Tampa Bay (USFL 1983 to 1985)
Barons	Cleveland (NHL 1976-77 to 1977-78)
Barracudas	Birmingham (CFL 1995)
Bays	Baltimore (NPSL, NASL 1967 to 1969)
Beacons	Boston (NASL 1968)
Beaneaters	Boston (NL 1883 to 1906)
Bears	Chicago (NFL 1922 to present) Youngstown (NBL 1945-46 to 1946-47)
Beau Brummels	Rochester (AA 1890)
Bees	Boston (NL 1936 to 1940)
Bell	Philadelphia (WFL 1974 to 1975)
Bengals	Trenton (ABL 1928-29) Cincinnati (NFL 1968 to present)
Bicentennials	Hartford (NASL 1975 to 1976) Connecticut (NASL 1977)
Bills	Buffalo (NL 1879 to 1885) Buffalo (PL 1890) Buffalo (AAFC 1947 to 1949) Buffalo (AFL, NFL 1960 to present)
Bisons	Buffalo (NFL 1924 to 1927) Buffalo (NFL 1929)

	Buffalo (NBL 1937-38) Buffalo (NBL 1946-47)
	Buffalo (AAFC 1946)
Blackhawks	Chicago (NHL 1926-27 to present) Tri-Cities (NBL, NBA 1946-47 to 1950-51)
Blades	Baltimore (WHA 1974-75)
Blazers	Philadelphia (WHA 1972-73) Vancouver (WHA 1973-74 to 1974-75) FLorida (WFL 1974)
Blitz	Chicago (USFL 1983 to 1984)
Blizzard	Toronto (NASL 1979 to 1984)
Blue Bombers	Winnipeg (CRU, CFC, CFL 1950 to present)
Blue Jackets	Columbus (NHL 2000-present)
Blue Jays	Philadelphia (NL 1943 to 1944) Toronto (AL 1977 to present)
Blue Stockings	Toledo (AA 1884)
Blues	Hartford (NL 1876 to 1877) Cleveland (NL 1879 to 1884) Cleveland (AA 1887 to 1888) Kansas City (AA 1888 to 1889) Cleveland (AL 1902 to 1904) Buffalo (FL 1914 to 1915) Hartford (NFL 1926) St. Louis (NHL 1967-68 to present)
Blueshirts	Toronto (NHA 1912-13 to 1916-17)
Bobcats	Charlotte (NBA 2004-present)
Bombers	St. Louis (BAA, NBA 1946-47 to 1949-50)
Boomers	Calgary (NASL 1981)
Braves	Boston (NL 1912 to 1952) Boston (NFL 1932) Milwaukee (NL 1953 to 1965) Atlanta (NL 1966 to present) Buffalo (NBA 1970-71 to 1977-78)
Breakers	Boston (USFL 1983) New Orleans (USFL 1984) Portland (USFL 1985)
Brecks	Louisville (NFL 1922 to 1923)
Brewers	Milwaukee (AL 1901) Milwaukee (AL, NL 1970 to present)
Bridegrooms	Brooklyn (AA 1884 to 1889) Brooklyn (NL 1890 to 1898)
Bronchos	Cleveland (AL 1901)
Broncos	Denver (AFL, NFL 1960 to present)
Brown Stockings	Worcester (NL 1880 to 1882)
Browns	St. Louis (AA, NL 1882 to 1897) St. Louis (AL 1902 to 1953) St. Louis (NFL 1923) Cleveland (AAFC, NFL 1946 to 1995) Cleveland (NFL 1999 to present)
Bruins	Boston (NHL 1924-25 to present) Chicago (ABL 1925-26 to 1930-31) Chicago (NBL 1939-40 to 1941-42)
Buccaneers	Los Angeles (NFL 1926) New Orleans (ABA 1967-68 to 1969-70) Tampa Bay (NFL 1976 to present)
Bucks	Milwaukee (NBA 1968-69 to present)
Bulldogs	Quebec (ECHA 1908-09) Quebec (NHA 1910-11 to 1916-17) Quebec (NHL 1919-20) Canton (NFL 1922 to 1923) Cleveland (NFL 1924), Canton (NFL 1925 to 1926) Cleveland (NFL 1927) Boston (NFL 1929) New York (NFL 1949)
Bullets	Baltimore (BAA, NBA 1947-48 to 1953-54) Baltimore (NBA 1963-64 to 1972-73) Capital (NBA 1973-74), Washington (NBA 1974-75 to 1996-97)
Bulls	Chicago (NBA 1966-67 to present) Birmingham (WHA 1976-77 to 1978-79) Jacksonville (USFL 1984)
Burghers	Pittsburgh (PL 1890)
Burn	Dallas (MLS 1996-2004)
Calumet Buccaneers	Hammond (NBL 1948-49)

Canadiens	Montreal (NHA 1909-10) Montreal (NHA, NHL 1910-1911 to present)
Canaries	Spokane (PCHA 1916-17)
Canucks	Vancouver (NHL 1970-71 to present)
Capitals	Regina (WCHL 1921-22 to 1924-25) Washington (NHL 1974-75 to present)
Capitols	Washington (BAA, NBA 1946-47 to 1950-51) Washington (ABA 1969-70)
Cardinals	St. Louis (NL 1898 to present) Chicago (NFL 1922 to 1959) Detroit (ABL 1927-28) St. Louis (NFL 1960 to 1987) Phoenix (NFL 1988 to 1993) Arizona (NFL 1994 to present)
Caribous	Colorado (NASL 1978)
Caseys	Ft. Wayne (ABL 1925-26)
Cavaliers	Cleveland (NBA 1970-71 to present)
Celtics	New York (ABL 1927-28) Boston (BAA, NBA 1946-47 to present)
Centrals	Rochester (ABL 1925-26 to 1930-31)
CFLers	Baltimore (CFL 1994)
Chaparrals	Dallas (ABA 1967-68 to 1972-73) Texas (ABA 1970-71)
Chargers	Los Angeles (AFL 1960) San Diego (AFL, NFL 1961 to present)
Chase Brass	Cleveland (NBL 1943-44)
Chiefs	Kansas City (AFL, NFL 1963 to present) Atlanta (NPSL, NASL 1967 to 1972) Atlanta (NASL 1979 to 1981)
Chivas	Carson (MLS 2005-present)
Ciesar All-Americans	Whiting (NBL 1937-38) Hammond (NBL 1938-39 to 1940-41)
Civics	Ottawa (WHA 1975-76)
Clash	San Jose (MLS 1996-1999)
Clippers	Oakland (NPSL, NASL 1967 to 1968) San Diego (NBA 1978-79 to 1983-84), Los Angeles (NBA 1984-85 to present)
Colonels	Louisville (NL 1876 to 1877) Louisville (NL 1892 to 1899) Louisville (NFL 1926) Kentucky (ABA 1967-68 to 1975-76)
Colt 45s	Houston (NL 1962 to 1964)
Colts	Chicago (NL 1894 to 1897) Baltimore (AAFC, NFL 1947 to 1950) Baltimore (NFL 1953 to 1983) Indianapolis (NFL 1984 to present)
Comellos	Cincinnati (NBL 1937-38)
Comets	Haileybury (NHA 1909-10) Baltimore (NASL 1974 to 1975) Houston (WNBA 1997-present)
Concorde	Montreal (CFL 1982 to 1985)
Condors	Pittsburgh (ABA 1970-71 to 1971-72)
Conquistadors	San Diego (ABA 1972-73 to 1974-75)
Cosmos	New York (NASL 1971 to 1984)
Cougars	Victoria (PCHA, WCHL, WHL 1920-21 to 1925-26) Detroit (NHL 1926-27 to 1929-30) Detroit (USA, NASL 1967 to 1968) Carolina (ABA 1969-70 to 1973-74) Chicago (WHA 1972-73 to 1974-75)
Cowboys	Kansas City (NL 1886) Kansas City (NFL 1924 to 1926) Dallas (NFL 1960 to present) Calgary (WHA 1975-76 to 1976-77)
Coyotes	Phoenix (NHL 1996-97 to present)
Creamery Kings	Renfrew (NHA 1909-10 to 1910-11)

Crescents	Saskatoon (WCHL, WHL 1923-24 to 1925-26)
	Paterson (ABL 1930-31)
Crew	Columbus (MLS 1996-present)
Crimson Giants	Evansville (NFL 1922)
Crusaders	Cleveland (WHA 1972-73 to 1975-76)
Cubs	Chicago (NL 1899 to present)
Darts	Washington (NASL 1970 to 1971)
Devil Rays	Tampa Bay (AL 1998 to present)
Devils	New Jersey (NHL 1982-83 to present)
Diamondbacks	Arizona (NL 1998 to present)
Diplomats	Washington (NASL 1974 to 1981)
Discoverers	Columbus (AA 1883 to 1884) Columbus (AA 1889 to 1891)
Dodgers	Brooklyn (NL 1911 to 1957) Brooklyn (NFL 1930 to 943)
	Brooklyn (AAFC 1946 to 1948) Los Angeles (NL 1958 to present)
Dolphins	Miami (AFL, NFL 1966 to present)
Dons	Los Angeles (AAFC 1946 to 1949)
Doves	Boston (NL 1907 to 1908)
Dow A.C.S	FLint (NBL 1947-48)
Dragons	Barcelona (WLAF, WFL 1991 to 1992)
Drillers	Edmonton (NASL 1979 to 1982)
Ducks	Anaheim (NHL 2006-2007-present)
Duffey Packers	Anderson (NBL 1946-47 to 1949-50)
Dynamo	Houston (MLS 2006-present)
Dynamos	Denver (NASL 1974 to 1975)
Eagles	Philadelphia (NFL 1933 to present) St. Louis (NHL 1934-35)
	Detroit (NBL 1939-40 to 1940-41)
Earthquakes	San Jose (NASL 1974 to 1982) Golden Bay (NASL 1983 to 1984) San Jose (MLS 2000-2005)
Eclipse	Louisville (AA 1882 to 1891)
Eskimos	Edmonton (WCHL, WHL 1921-22 to 1925-26) Duluth (NFL 1923, 1926 to 1927) Edmonton (CRU, CFC, CFL 1950 to present)
Expos	Montreal (NL 1969 to 2004)
Express	Jacksonville (WFL 1975) Detroit (NASL 1978 to 1980) Los Angeles (USFL 1983 to 1985)
Falcons	Detroit (NHL 1930-31 to 1932-33) Detroit (BAA 1946-47) Atlanta (NFL 1966 to present) Toronto (NPSL, NASL 1967 to 1968)
FC	Dallas (MLS 2005-present)
Federal Hoosiers	Indianapolis (FL 1914)
Federals	Washington (USFL 1983 to 1984)
Fever	Indiana (WNBA 2000-present)
Fighting Saints	Minnesota (WHA 1972-73 to 1975-76) Minnesota (WHA 1976-77)
Fire	Chicago (WFL 1974) Birmingham (WLAF, WFL 1991 to 1992) Chicago (MLS 1998-present) Portland (WNBA 2000-present)
Firestone Non-Skids	Akron (NBL 1937-38 to 1940-41)
Flames	Atlanta (NHL 1972-73 to 1979-80) Calgary (NHL 1980-81 to present)
Floridians	Miami (ABA 1968-69 to 1969-70) (ABA 1970-71 to 1971-72)
Flyers	Philadelphia (NHL 1967-68 to present)
Fury	Philadelphia (NASL 1978 to 1980)

Fusion	Miami (MLS 1998-2001)
Galaxy	Frankfurt (WLAF, WFL 1991 to 1992), Los Angeles (MLS 1996-present)
Gallagher Trojans	Kankakee (NBL 1937-38)
Gamblers	Houston (USFL 1984 to 1985)
Gators	Miami (NASL 1972)
Gems	Detroit (NBL 1946-47)
Generals	New York (NPSL, NASL 1967 to 1968) New Jersey (USFL 1983 to 1985)
Germans	Buffalo (ABL 1926)
Giants	New York (NL 1886 to 1957) New York (PL 1890) New York (NFL 1925 to present) San Francisco (NL 1958 to present)
Glory	Ohio (WFL 1992)
Gold	Denver (USFL 1983 to 1985)
Gold Miners	Sacramento (CFL 1993 to 1994)
Golden Blades	New York (WHA 1973-74)
Golden Gate Gales	San Francisco (USA 1967)
Golden Seals	California (NHL 1970-71 to 1975-76)
Goodyear Wingfoots	Akron (NBL 1937-38 to 1941-42)
Gothams	New York (NL 1883 to 1885)
Grays	Milwaukee (NL 1878) Providence (NL 1878 to 1885)
Grizzlies	Vancouver (NBA 1995-96 to 2001), Memphis (NBA 2001 to present)
Gunners	St. Louis (NFL 1934)
Gunslingers	San Antonio (USFL 1984 to 1985)
Hakoahs	New York (ABL 1928-29)
Hawaiians	(WFL 1974 to 1975)
Hawks	Waterloo (NBL, NBA 1948-49 to 1949-1950) Milwaukee (NBA 1951-52 to 1954-55) St. Louis (NBA 1955-1956 to 1967-68) Atlanta (NBA 1968-69 to present)
Heat	Miami (NBA 1988-89 to present)
Highlanders	New York (AL 1903 to 1912)
Hoosiers	Indianapolis (NL 1878) Indianapolis (AA 1884) Indianapolis (NL 1887 to 1889) Ft. Wayne (ABL 1926-27 to 1930-31)
Hornets	Chicago (AAFC 1949) Charlotte (WFL 1975) Charlotte (NBA 1988-89 to 2001-2002) New Orleans (NBA 2002-2003 to present)
Hurricane	Houston (NASL 1978 to 1980)
Hurricanes	Carolina (NHL 1997-98 to present)
Huskies	Toronto (BAA 1946-46)
Independents	Rock Island (NFL 1922 to 1925)
Indians	Cleveland (AL 1915 to present) Oorang (NFL 1922 to 1923) Cleveland (NFL 1923) Akron (NFL 1926) Cleveland (NFL 1931)
Infants	Cleveland (PL 1890)
Innocents	Pittsburgh (NL 1890)
Invaders	Oakland (USFL 1983 to 1985)
Ironmen	Pittsburgh (BAA 1946-47)
Islanders	New York (NHL 1972-73 to present)
Jaguars	Jacksonville (NFL 1995 to present)
Jaws	San Diego (NASL 1976)
Jazz	New Orleans (NBA 1974-75 to 1978-79) Utah (NBA 1979-80 to present)

Jeeps	Toledo (NBL 1946-47 to 1947-48)
Jeffersons	Rochester (NFL 1922 to 1925)
Jets	Indianapolis (BAA 1948-49) New York (AFL, NFL 1963 to present) Winnipeg (WHA, NHL 1972-73 to 1995-96)
Jim White Chevrolets	Toledo (NBL 1941-42 to 1942-43)
Kautskys	Indianapolis (NBL 1937-38 to 1941-42) Indianapolis (NBL 1945-46 to 1947-48)
Kelleys	Duluth (NFL 1924 to 1925)
Kelly's Killers	Cincinnati (AA 1891)
Keystones	Philadelphia (UA 1884)
Kicks	Minnesota (NASL 1976 to 1981)
King Clothiers	Richmond (NBL 1937-38)
Kings	Los Angeles (NHL 1967-68 to present) Kansas City-Omaha (NBA 1972-73 to 1974-75) Kansas City (NBA 1975-76 to 1984-85) Sacramento (NBA 1985-86 to present)
Knickerbockers	New York (BAA, NBA 1946-47 to present)
Knights	New Jersey (WHA 1973-74) New York-New Jersey (WLAF, WFL 1991 to 1992)
Lakers	Minneapolis (NBL, BAA, NBA 1947-48 to 1959-60) Los Angeles (NBA 1960-61 to present)
Lancers	Rochester (NASL 1970 to 1980)
Legions	Racine (NFL 1922 to 1924)
Liberty	New York (WNBA 1997-present)
Lightning	Tampa Bay (NHL 1992-93 to present)
Lions	Brooklyn (NFL 1926) Detroit (NFL 1934 to present) British Columbia (CRU, CFC, CFL 1954 to present)
Lynx	Minnesota (WNBA 1999-present)
Machine	Montreal (WLAF, WFL 1991 to 1992)
Mad Dogs	Memphis (CFL 1995)
Magic	Orlando (NBA 1989-90 to present)
Manic	Montreal (NASL 1981 to 1983)
Maple Leafs	Toronto (NHL 1926-27 to present)
Mariners	San Diego (WHA 1974-75 to 1976-77) Seattle (AL 1977 to present)
Marines	Minneapolis (NFL 1922 to 1924)
Marlins	FLorida (NL 1993 to present)
Maroons	St. Louis (UA, NL 1884 to 1886) Toledo (NFL 1922 to 1923) Vancouver (PCHA, WCHL, WHL 1922-23 to 1925-26) Kenosha (NFL 1924) Montreal (NHL 1924-25 to 1937-1938) Pottsville (NFL 1925 to 1928)
Maulers	Pittsburgh (USFL 1984)
Maumees	Toledo (AA 1890)
Mavericks	Houston (ABA 1967-68 to 1968-69) Dallas (NBA 1980-81 to present)
Mercury	Phoenix (WNBA 1997-present)
Metro Croatia	Toronto (NASL 1975 to 1978)
Metropolitans	New York (AA 1883 to 1887) Seattle (PCHA 1915-16 to 1923-24)
Metros	Dayton (NBL 1937-38) Toronto (NASL 1971 to 1974)
Metrostars	New York/New Jersey (MLS 1996-2005)
Mets	New York (NL 1962 to present)
Mighty Ducks	Anaheim (NHL 1993-94 to 2005-2006)
Millionaires	Vancouver (PCHA 1911-12 to 1921-22)
Minutemen	Boston (NASL 1974 to 1976)

Miracle	Orlando (WNBA 1999-2002)
Molly Mcguires	Cleveland (AL 1912 to 1914)
Monarchs	London (WLAF, WFL 1991 to 1992), Sacramento (WNBA 1997-present)
Muskies	Minnesota (ABA 1967-68)
Mustangs	Chicago (USA, NASL 1967 to 1968)
Mutiny	Tampa Bay (MLS 1996-2001)
Mutuals	New York (NL 1876)
Mystics	Washington (WNBA 1998-present)
Naps	Cleveland (AL 1905 to 1911)
Nationals	Washington (UA 1884) Washington (AA 1884) Syracuse (NBL, NBA 1946-47 to 1962-63) Ottawa (WHA 1972-73) Washington (NL 2005 to present)
Nets	New York (ABA, NBA 1968-69 to 1976-77) New Jersey (NBA 1977-78 to present)
Nordiques	Quebec (WHA, NHL 1972-73 to 1994-95)
North Stars	Minnesota (NHL 1967-68 to 1992-93)
Nuggets	Denver (NBL, NBA 1948-49 to 1949-50) Denver (ABA, NBA 1974-75 to present)
Oaks	Oakland (ABA 1967-68 to 1968-69)
Oilers	Warren Penn (NBL 1937-38) Houston (AFL, NFL 1960 to 1996) ALberta (WHA 1972-73) Edmonton (WHA, NHL 1973-1974 to present) Tennessee (NFL 1997 to 1998)
Olympians	Indianapolis (NBA 1949-50 to 1952-53)
Olympiques	Montreal (NASL 1971 to 1973)
Ontarios	Toronto (NHA 1913-14 to 1914-15)
Orioles	Baltimore (AA, NL 1882 to 1899) Baltimore (AL 1901 to 1902) Baltimore (ABL 1926-27) Baltimore (AL 1954 to present)
Orphans	Chicago (NL 1898) Moose Jaw (WCHL 1921-22)
Outlaw Reds	Cincinnati (UA 1884)
Outlaws	Oklahoma (USFL 1984)
Pacers	Indiana (ABA, NBA 1967-68 to present)
Packers	Kansas City (FL 1914 to 1915) Green Bay (NFL 1922 to present) Chicago (NBA 1961-62)
Padres	San Diego (NL 1969 to present)
Palace Five	Washington (ABL 1925-26 to 1927-28)
Panhandles	Columbus (NFL 1922)
Panthers	Detroit (NFL 1925 to 1926) Michigan (USFL 1983 to 1984) FLorida (NHL 1993-94 to present) Carolina (NFL 1995 to present)
Patriots	Boston (AFL 1960 to 1970) New England (NFL 1971 to present)
Penguins	Pittsburgh (NHL 1967-68 to present)
Peppers	Newark (FL 1915)
Phantoms	Pittsburgh (NPSL 1967)
Phillies	Philadelphia (NL 1883 to present)
Pilgrims	Boston (NL 1909 to 1911)
Pilots	Seattle (AL 1969)
Pipers	Pittsburgh (ABA 1967-68, 1969-70) Minnesota (ABA 1968-69)
Pirates	Chicago (PL 1890) Pittsburgh (NL 1891 to present) Pittsburgh (NHL 1925-26 to 1929-30) Pittsburgh (NFL 1933 to 1938) Pittsburgh (NBL 1937-38 to 1938-39) Shreveport (CFL 1994 to 1995)

Pistons	Fort Wayne (NBA 1956-57) Detroit (NBA 1957-58 to present)
Posse	Las Vegas (CFL 1994)
Predators	Nashville (NHL 1998-99 to present)
Pride	Altoona (UA 1884)
Pros	Akron (NFL 1922 to 1925) Hammond (NFL 1922 to 1926) Memphis (ABA 1970-71 to 1971-72)
Pulaski Post Five	Detroit (ABL 1925-26)
Puritans	Boston (AL 1905 to 1906)
Quakers	Philadelphia (PL 1890) Philadelphia (NHL 1930-31)
Quicksilvers	Las Vegas (NASL 1977)
Quicksteps	Wilmington (UA 1884)
Racers	Indianapolis (WHA 1974-75 to 1978-79)
Raiders	Pittsburgh (NBL 1944-45) Oakland (AFL, NFL 1960 to 1981) New York (WHA 1972-1973) Los Angeles (NFL 1982 to 1994) Oakland (NFL 1995 to present)
Rams	Cleveland (NFL 1937 to 1945) Los Angeles (NFL 1946 to 1994) St. Louis (NFL 1995 to present)
Rangers	New York (NHL 1926-27 to present) Texas (AL 1972 to present)
Rapids	Colorado (MLS 1996-present)
Raptors	Toronto (NBA 1995-96 to present)
Ravens	Baltimore (NFL 1996 to present)
Real Salt Lake	Salt Lake City (MLS 2005-present)
Rebels	Pittsburgh (FL 1914-15) Cleveland (BAA 1946-47)
Red Bulls	New York (MLS 2006-present)
Red Caps	Boston (NL 1876 to 1882)
Red Legs	Cincinnati (NL 1944 to 1945)
Red Sox	Boston (AL 1907 to present)
Red Stockings	Cincinnati (AA 1882 to 1889)
Red Wings	Detroit (NHL 1933-34 to present)
Redjackets	Minneapolis (NFL 1929 to 1930)
Redman Tobaccos	Toledo (ABL 1930-31)
Reds	St. Louis (NL 1876 to 1877) Cincinnati (NL 1876 to 1880) Boston (PL, AA 1890 to 1891) Cincinnati (NL 1890 to present) Cincinnati (NFL 1933 to 1934)
Redskins	Boston (NFL 1933 to 1936) Washington (NFL 1937 to present) Sheboygan (NBL, NBA 1938-39 to 1949-50)
Renegades	Orlando (USFL 1985), Ottawa (CFL 2002 to 2005)
Rens	Dayton (NBL 1948-49)
Revolution	New England (MLS 1996-present)
Riders	San Antonio (WLAF, WFL 1991 to 1992)
Roadrunners	Phoenix (WHA 1974-75 to 1976-77)
Rockers	Cleveland (WNBA 1997 to 2003)
Rockets	Chicago (AAFC 1946 to 1948) Denver (ABA 1967-68 to 1973-74) San Diego (NBA 1967-68 to 1970-71) Houston (NBA 1971-72 to present)
Rockies	Colorado (NHL 1976-77 to 1981-82) Colorado (NL 1993 to present)
Rogues	Memphis (NASL 1978 to 1980)
Rosebuds	Portland (PCHA 1914-15 to 1917-18) Portland (WHL 1925-26)
Rosenblums	Cleveland (ABL 1925-26 to 1930-31)
Rough Riders	Ottawa (CRU, CFC, CFL 1950 to present)

Roughnecks	Tulsa (NASL 1978 to 1984)
Roughriders	Saskatchewan (CRU, CFC, CFL 1950 to present)
Rovers	Boston (USA 1967)
Rowdies	Tampa Bay (NASL 1975 to 1984)
Royals	New Westminster (PCHA 1911-12 to 1913-14) Rochester (NBL, BAA, NBA 1945-46 to 1956-57) Cincinnati (NBA 1957-58 to 1971-72) Vancouver (USA, NASL 1967 to 1968) Kansas City (AL 1969 to present)
Sabres	Buffalo (NHL 1970-71 to present)
Sails	San Diego (ABA 1975-76)
St. Patricks	Toronto (NHL 1919-20 to 1925-26)
Saints	St. Paul (UA 1884) New Orleans (NFL 1967 to present)
Scouts	Kansas City (NHL 1974-75 to 1975-76)
Seahawks	Miami (AAFC 1946) Seattle (NFL 1976 to present)
Seals	Oakland (NHL 1967-68 to 1969-70)
Senators	Washington (NL 1886 to 1889) Washington (AA, NL 1891 to 1899) Washington (AL 1901 to 1960) Ottawa (ECHA, NHA, NHL 1908-09 to 1933-34) Victoria (PCHA 1911-1912) Washington (AL 1961 to 1971) Ottawa (NHL 1992-93 to present)
Shamrocks	Montreal (ECHA, NHA 1908-09 to 1909-10) Toronto
Sharks	Los Angeles (WHA 1972-73 to 1973-74) Jacksonville (WFL 1974) San Jose (NHL 1991-92 to present)
Sheiks	Saskatoon (WCHL 1921-22 to 1922-23)
Shock	Detroit (WNBA 1998-present)
Showboats	Memphis (USFL 1984 to 1985)
Silver Kings	Cobalt (NHA 1909-10)
Silver Stars	San Antonio (WNBA 2003-present)
Sky	Chicago (WNBA 2006-present)
Skyhawks	Raleigh-Durham (WLAF 1991)
Skyliners	New York (USA 1967)
Sockers	San Diego (NASL 1978 to 1984)
Sol	Miami (WNBA 2000-present)
Somersets	Boston (AL 1901 to 1904)
Sounders	Seattle (NASL 1974 to 1983)
Sounds	Memphis (ABA 1974-75)
Southmen	Memphis (WFL 1974 to 1975)
Sparks	Los Angeles (WNBA 1997-present)
Spartans	Portsmouth (NFL 1930 to 1933) Philadelphia (NPSL 1967)
Spiders	Cleveland (NL 1889 to 1899)
Spirits	St. Louis (ABA 1974-75 to 1975-76)
Spurs	Chicago (NPSL 1967) Kansas City (NASL 1968 to 1970) San Antonio (ABA, NBA 1973-1974 to present) Denver (WHA 1975-76)
Squires	Virginia (ABA 1970-71 to 1975-76)
Stags	Chicago (BAA, NBA 1946-47 to 1949-50) Michigan (WHA 1974-75)
Stallions	Birmingham (USFL 1983 to 1985) Baltimore (CFL 1995)
Stampeders	Calgary (CRU, CFC, CFL 1950 to present)
Stapletons	Staten Island (NFL 1929 to 1932)
Stars	Syracuse (NL 1879) Syracuse (AA 1890) Houston (USA, NASL 1967 to 1968) St. Louis (NPSL, NASL 1967 to 1977) Los Angeles (ABA 1968-69 to 1969-70) Utah (ABA 1970-71 to 1975-1976) Charlotte (WFL 1974) New York (WFL 1974)

	Philadelphia (USFL 1983 to 1984) Baltimore (USFL 1985) Dallas (NHL 1993-94 to present)
Starzz	Utah (WNBA 1997-2002)
Steam Rollers	Providence (NFL 1925 to 1931)
Steamers	Shreveport (WFL 1974 to 1975)
Steamrollers	Providence (BAA 1846-47 to 1948-49)
Steelers	Pittsburgh (NFL 1939 to present)
Sting	Chicago (NASL 1975 to 1984) Charlotte (WNBA 1997 to present)
Stingers	Cincinnati (WHA 1975-76 to 1978-79)
Stokers	Cleveland (USA, NASL 1967 to 1968)
Stompers	Oakland (NASL 1978)
Storm	Portland (WFL 1974), Seattle (WNBA 2000-present)
Strikers	Ft. Lauderdale (NASL 1977 to 1983) Minnesota (NASL 1984)
Studebakers	Chicago (NBL 1942-43)
Sun	Southern California (WFL 1974 to 1975), Connecticut (WNBA 2003-present)
Suns	Phoenix (NBA 1968-69 to present)
Superbas	Brooklyn (NL 1899 to 1910)
Supersonics	Seattle (NBA 1967-68 to present)
Surf	California (NASL 1978 to 1981)
Surge	Sacramento (WLAF, WFL 1991 to 1992)
Tams	Memphis (ABA 1972-73 to 1973-74)
Team America	(NASL 1983)
Team Hawaii	(NASL 1977)
Teamen	New England (NASL 1978 to 1980) Jacksonville (NASL 1981 to 1982)
Tecumsehs	Toronto (NHA 1912-13)
Terrapins	Baltimore (FL 1914 to 1915)
Terriers	St. Louis (FL 1914-15)
Texans	Dallas (NFL 1952) Dallas (AFL 1960 to 1962) Houston (WFL 1974) San Antonio (CFL 1995) Houston (NFL 2002-present)
Thrashers	Atlanta (NHL 1999-2000)
Thunder	Portland (WFL 1975) San Antonio (NASL 1975 to 1976) Orlando (WLAF, WFL 1991 to 1992)
Tiger-Cats	Hamilton (CRU, CFC, CFL 1950 to present)
Tigers	Detroit (AL 1901 to present) Hamilton (NHL 1920-21 to 1924-25) Calgary (WCHL, WHL 1921-22 to 1925-26) Columbus (NFL 1923 to 1926) Brooklyn (NFL 1944)
Timbers	Portland (NASL 1975 to 1982)
Timberwolves	Minnesota (NBA 1989-90 to present)
Tip-Tops	Brooklyn (FL 1914 to 1915)
Titans	New York (AFL 1960 to 1962), Tennessee (NFL 1999-to present)
Tornado	Dallas (USA, NASL 1967 to 1981)
Tornadoes	Racine (NFL 1926) Orange (NFL 1929) Newark (NFL 1930)
Toronto City	Toronto (USA 1967)
Toros	Los Angeles (NPSL 1967) San Diego (NASL 1968) Miami (NASL 1973 to 1976) Toronto (WHA 1973-74 to 1975-1976)
Trail Blazers	Portland (NBA 1970-71 to present)
Triangles	Dayton (NFL 1922 to 1929)
Trojans	Troy (NL 1879 to 1882)

Twins	Minnesota (AL 1961 to present)
Unions	Baltimore (UA 1884) Boston (UA 1884) Kansas City (UA 1884) Milwaukee (UA 1884)
United	D.C. (Washington) (MLS 1996-present)
Vagabond Kings	Detroit (NBL 1948-49)
Vikings	Minnesota (NFL 1961 to present)
Virginias	Richmond (AA 1884)
Visitations	Brooklyn (ABL 1927-28 to 1930-31)
Vulcans	Birmingham (WFL 1975)
Wanderers	Montreal (ECHA, NHA, NHL 1908-09 to 1917-18)
Warriors	Philadelphia (ABL 1926-27 to 1927-28) Philadelphia (BAA, NBA 1946-47 to 1961-62) San Francisco (NBA 1962-63 to 1970-71) Golden State (NBA 1971-72 to present)
Whalers	New England (WHA 1972-73 to 1978-79) Hartford (NHL 1979-80 to 1996-97)
Whales	Chicago (FL 1914 to 1915)
Wheels	Detroit (WFL 1974)
Whips	Washington (USA 1967 to 1968)
Whirlwinds	Boston (ABL 1925-26) Paterson (ABL 1928-29 to 1929-1930)
White Horses	Cleveland (NBL 1938-39)
White Sox	Chicago (AL 1901 to present)
White Stockings	Chicago (NL 1876 to 1893)
Whitecaps	Vancouver (NASL 1974 to 1984)
Wild	Minnesota (NHL 2000-present)
Wind	Chicago (WFL 1975)
Wings	San Antonio (WFL 1975)
Wizards	Washington (NBA 1997-98 to present) Kansas City (MLS 1996-present)
Wolverines	Detroit (NL 1881 to 1888) Detroit (NFL 1928)
Wolves	Los Angeles (USA, NASL 1967 to 1968)
Wonders	Brooklyn (PL 1890)
Wranglers	Arizona (USFL 1983 to 1985)
Yankees	New York (AL 1913 to present) New York (NFL 1927 to 1928) New York (AAFC 1946 to 1949)
Yanks	Boston (NFL 1944 to 1948) New York (NFL 1950 to 1951)
Yellow Jackets	Frankford (NFL 1924 to 1931)
Zephyrs	Chicago (NBA 1962-63)
Zollner Pistons	Fort Wayne (NBL, NBA 1937-38 to 1955-56)

Appendix B: Stanley Cup Winners 1893–1907

Year	Team	Winning Coach
1892-1893	Montreal A.A.A.	
1893-1894	Montreal A.A.A.	
1894-1895	Montreal Victorias	Mike Grant
1895-1896	Winnipeg Victorias (February)	J.C.G. Armytage
1895-1896	Montreal Victorias (December)	Mike Grant
1896-1897	Montreal Victorias	Mike Grant
1897-1898	Montreal Victorias	Frank Richardson
1898-1899	Montreal Shamrocks	Harry Trihey
1899-1900	Montreal Shamrocks	Harry Trihey
1900-1901	Winnipeg Victorias	Dan Bain
1901-1902	Montreal A.A.A.	C. McKerrow
1902-1903	Ottawa Silver Seven	A.T. Smith
1903-1904	Ottawa Silver Seven	A.T. Smith
1904-1905	Ottawa Silver Seven	A.T. Smith
1905-1906	Montreal Wanderers	Cecil Blachford
1906-1907	Kenora Thistles (January)	Tommy Phillips
1906-1907	Montreal Wanderers (March)	Cecil Blachford

Appendix C: Grey Cup Winners Prior to 1950

Year	Winner	Opposition	Score	Winning Coach
1909	University of Toronto	Toronto Parkdale	26-6	Harry Griffith
1910	University of Toronto	Hamilton Tigers	16-7	Harry Griffith
1911	University of Toronto	Toronto Argonauts	14-7	A.B. Wright
1912	Hamilton ALerts	Toronto Argonauts	11-4	Liz Marriott
1913	Hamilton Tigers	Toronto Parkdale	44-2	Liz Marriott
1914	Toronto Argonauts	University of Toronto	14-2	Billy Foulds
1915	Hamilton Tigers	Toronto R.A.A.	13-7	Liz Marriott
1920	University of Toronto	Toronto Argonauts	16-3	Laddie Cassels
1921	Toronto Argonauts	Edmonton Eskimos	23-0	Sinc McEvenue
1922	Queen's University	Edmonton Elks	13-1	Billy Hughes
1923	Queen's University	Regina Roughriders	54-0	Billy Hughes
1924	Queen's University	Toronto Balmy Beach	11-3	Billy Hughes
1925	Ottawa Senators	Winnipeg Tammany Tigers	24-1	Dave McCann
1926	Ottawa Senators	Toronto University	10-7	Dave McCann
1927	Toronto Balmy Beach	Hamilton Tigers	9-6	H. Hobbs
1928	Hamilton Tigers	Regina Roughriders	30-0	Mike Rodden
1929	Hamilton Tigers	Regina Roughriders	14-3	Mike Rodden
1930	Toronto Balmy Beach	Regina Roughriders	11-6	ALex Ponton
1931	Montreal A.A.A.	Regina Roughriders	22-0	Clary Foran
1932	Hamilton Tigers	Regina Roughriders	25-6	Billy Hughes
1933	Toronto Argonauts	Sarnia Imperials	4-3	Lew Hayman
1934	Sarnia Imperials	Regina Roughriders	20-12	Art Massucci
1935	Winnipeg	Hamilton Tigers	18-12	Bib Fritz
1936	Sarnia Imperials	Ottawa Rough Riders	26-20	Art Massucci
1937	Toronto Argonauts	Winnipeg Blue Bombers	4-3	Lew Hayman
1938	Toronto Argonauts	Winnipeg Blue Bombers	30-7	Lew Hayman
1939	Winnipeg Blue Bombers	Ottawa Rough Riders	8-7	Reg Threlfall
1940	Ottawa Rough Riders	Toronto Balmy Beach	8-2	
	Ottawa Rough Riders	Toronto Balmy Beach	12-5	Ross Trimble
1941	Winnipeg Blue Bombers	Ottawa Rough Riders	18-16	Reg Threlfall
1942	Toronto R.C.A.F.	Winnipeg R.C.A.F.	8-5	Lew Hayman
1943	Hamilton FLying Wildcats	Winnipeg R.C.A.F.	23-14	Brian Timmis
1944	Montreal St.H-D. Navy	Hamilton FLying Wildcats	7-6	Glen Brown
1945	Toronto Argonauts	Winnipeg Blue Bombers	35-0	Ted Morris
1946	Toronto Argonauts	Winnipeg Blue Bombers	28-6	Ted Morris
1947	Toronto Argonauts	Winnipeg Blue Bombers	10-9	Ted Morris
1948	Calgary Stampeders	Ottawa Rough Riders	12-7	Les Lear
1949	Montreal ALouettes	Calgary Stampeders	28-15	Lew Hayman

Bibliography

BOOKS

Benson, Michael. *Ballparks of North America*. Jefferson, NC: McFarland, 1989.

Biesel, David B. *Can You Name That Team?* Metuchen, NJ: Scarecrow, 1991.

Bjarkman, Peter C. *Encyclopedia of Pro Basketball Team Histories*. New York: Carroll and Graf, 1994.

Brown, Gerry, and Michael Morrison, eds. *ESPN Sports Almanac*. New York: ESPN, annually.

Byrne, Jim. *$1 League (The Rise and Fall of the USFL)*. New York: Prentice Hall, 1986.

CFL Media/Public Relations Department. *Canadian Football League Guide*. Canadian Football League, annually.

Coleman, Charles L. *Trail of the Stanley Cup*. Dubuque, IA: Kendall/Hall, 1964.

Cosentino, Frank. *A Passing Game: A History of the CFL*. Winnipeg, Manitoba, Canada: Blizzard, 1995.

Creative Services Division of NFL Properties. *Official NFL Encyclopedia of Pro Football*. Scarborough, Ontario, Canada: NAL, 1982.

Currie, Gordon. *100 Years of Canadian Football*. Toronto: Pagurian, 1968

Devaney, John. *Story of Basketball*. New York: Random House, 1976.

Diamond, Dan, ed. *NHL 75th Anniversary Commemorative Book*. Toronto: McClelland & Stewart, 1991.

_____. *Total Hockey*, 2nd ed. New York: Total Sports, 2000.

Dobbs, Brian. *Ghosts of Haileybury.* Cobalt, Ontario, Canada: Highway Book Shop, 1997.

Donovan, Michael Leo. *The Name Game*. Whitby, Ontario, Canada: McGraw-Hill Ryerson, 1997.

Ferguson, Bob. *Who's Who in Canadian Sport*. Scarborough, Ontario, Canada: Prentice Hall, 1977.

Fischler, Stan, and Shirley Walton Fischler. *Hockey Encyclopedia (The Complete Record of Professional Hockey)*. New York: Macmillan, 1983.

Funk & Wagnalls New Encyclopedia. New York, 1975.

Hollander, Zander. *American Encyclopedia of Soccer*. Pickering, Ontario, Canada: Beaverbooks, 1980.

_____. *NBA's Official Encyclopedia of Pro Basketball*. New York: New American Library/NAL Books, 1981.

Hubbard, Jan, ed. *Official NBA Encyclopedia*, 3rd ed. New York: Doubleday, 2000.

Kane, Joseph Nathan. *Famous First Facts and Records*. New York: Ace, 1975.

Leblanc, Michael L., ed. *Professional Sports Team Histories*. Gale Research, 1994.

Lowry, Phillip J. *Green Cathedrals*. Addison Wesley, 1992.

Meserole, Mike. *Information Please Sports Almanac*. Houghton Mifflin, annually.

Mouton, Claude. *Montreal Canadiens, A Hockey Dynasty*. Toronto: Van Nostrand Reinhold, 1980.

Neft, David S., Bob Carroll, John Thorn and Michael Gershman. *Total Football*. New York: HarperCollins, 1997.

_____ and Richard M. Cohen. *Football Encyclopedia: The Complete History of Professional NFL Football from 1892 to the Present*. New York: St. Martin's Press, 1991.

_____ and _____. *Sports Encyclopedia Pro Baseball*. New York: St. Martin's, 1989.

Neft, David S., Roland T. Johnson, Richard M. Cohen and Jordan A. Deutsch. *Sports Encyclopedia Pro Basketball*. New York: Grosset & Dunlap, 1975.

_____,_____,_____ and _____. *Sports Encyclopedia Pro Football*. New York: Grosset & Dunlap, 1974.

Nemec, David. *Great Baseball Feats, Facts & Firsts.* Markham, Ontario, Canada: Penguin, 1989.
NFL Public Relations Department and Seymour Siwoff, Elias Sports Bureau. *Official National Football League 1989 Record & Fact Book.* New York: Workman, 1989.
NHL Communications Department and member clubs of the NHL. *National Hockey League Official Guide and Record Book.* Annually.
O'Reilly, Maurice. *Goodyear Story.* Elmsford, NY: Benjamin, 1983.
Pfeiffer, Gerald L. *Chicago Blackhawks: A Sixty Year History.* Park Ridge, IL: Windy City, 1986.
Proudfoot, Dan. *WHA Pro Hockey 76–77.* Markham, Ontario, Canada: Pocket, 1976.
Reichler, Joseph L., special editorial consultant. *Macmillan Baseball Encyclopedia.* 1976.
Rote, Kyle, Jr., and Basil Kane. *Kyle Rote Jr.'s Complete Book of Soccer.* New York: Simon & Schuster, 1978.
Sachare, Alex, ed. *Official NBA Basketball Encyclopedia,* 2nd ed. New York: Villard, 1994.
_____, and David Sloan. *Sporting News Official NBA Guide.* The Sporting News, 1989.
Sicinsk Larry. *1999 Hamilton Tiger Cats Almanac.* Burlington, Ontario, Canada: North Shore, 1999.
Surgent, Scott Adam. *Complete Historical and Statistical Reference to the World Hockey Association.* Tempe, AZ: Xaler, 1995.
Treat, Roger. *Encyclopedia of Football,* 16th rev. ed. Cranbury, NJ: A.S. Barnes.
Walter, Clair. *Book of Winners.* New York: Harcourt Brace Jovanovich, 1979.
Whitehead, Eric. *Cyclone Taylor: A Hockey Legend.* Markham, Ontario, Canada: Paper-Jacks, 1982.
_____. *The Patricks: Hockey's Royal Family.* Halifax, Nova Scotia, Canada: Formac, 1983.
World Almanac and Book of Facts. New York: Pharos, annually.
Zeman, Gary W. *Alberta on Ice.* Edmonton, Alberta, Canada: Westweb, 1985.

NEWSPAPERS AND PERIODICALS

Calgary Herald, Edmonton Journal, Edmonton Sun, Hockey Digest, Hockey News, Montreal Gazette, New York Times, Toronto Globe and Mail, Sporting News, Sports Illustrated.

CD-ROMS

Rosenberg, Jamie. *Microsoft Complete Baseball Guide.* Microsoft, 1995.
Thorn, John, and Pete Palmer. *Total Baseball.* Portland, OR: Creative Multimedia, 1994.

ONLINE SOURCES

Bradleyrd/apbr.html
geocities.com/Colosseum/5145/WFL
homepages.munich.netsurf.de/Thomas.Rymas
Lionbackers.com
majorleaguebaseball.com
mlb.com
mlsnet.com
nfl.com
pubweb.acns.nwu.edu
sover.net/~spectrum/nasl
sportingnews.com
wnba.com